P9-APR-987

RARY

FOURTH EDITION

ECONOMICS AND THE ENVIRONMENT

Eban S. Goodstein

Lewis & Clark College

www.wiley.com/college/goodstein

MONTGOMERY COLLEGE
GERMANTOWN CAMPUS LIBRARY
GERMANTOWN, MARYLAND

306956

MAY 2 7 2005

ACQUISITIONS EDITOR   Leslie Kraham

EDITORIAL ASSISTANT   Jessica Bartelt

MARKETING MANAGER   David Woodbury

ASSOCIATE PRODUCTION MANAGER   Kelly Tavares

PRODUCTION EDITOR   Sarah Wolfman-Robichaud

MANAGING EDITOR   Kevin Dodds

ILLUSTRATION EDITOR   Benjamin Reece

COVER DESIGN   Jennifer Wasson

PRODUCTION MANAGEMENT SERVICES   Leyh Publishing LLC

COVER IMAGE   Noah's Ark, by Edward Hicks 1846, © Philadelphia Museum of Art/COR

This book was set in Times Ten by Leyh Publishing LLC and printed and bound by Malloy Lithographers.
The cover was printed by The Lehigh Press, Inc.

This book is printed on acid-free paper. ∞

Copyright © 2005 John Wiley & Sons, Inc. All rights reserved.

No part of this publication may be reproduced, stored in a retrieval system or transmitted in any form or by any means, electronic, mechanical, photocopying, recording, scanning or otherwise, except as permitted under Sections 107 or 108 of the 1976 United States Copyright Act, without either the prior written permission of the Publisher, or authorization through payment of the appropriate per-copy fee to the Copyright Clearance Center, Inc. 222 Rosewood Drive, Danvers, MA 01923, (978)750-8400, fax (978)750-4470. Requests to the Publisher for permission should be addressed to the Permissions Department, John Wiley & Sons, Inc., 111 River Street, Hoboken, NJ 07030, (201)748-6011, fax (201)748-6008, E-Mail: PERMREQ@WILEY.COM.
To order books or for customer service please call 1-800-CALL WILEY (225-5945).

US ISBN: 0-471-47054-6
WIE ISBN: 0-471-65926-6

Printed in the United States of America

10 9 8 7 6 5 4 3 2 1

WITHDRAWN FROM LIBRARY

WITHDRAWN FROM LIBRARY

By this international commerce of geese, the waste corn of Illinois is carried through the clouds to the Arctic tundras, there to combine with the waste sunlight of a nightless June to grow goslings for all the land in between. And in this annual barter of food for light, and winter warmth for summer solitude, the whole continent receives as a net profit a wild poem dropped from the murky skies upon the muds of March.

—ALDO LEOPOLD

To Julian, Kristin, Roshan, Gene, Su-Yin, Matthias, Holly, Christi, John, Laura, Kerstin, Tara, Katie, Helen, Nick, Mike, Justin, Jules, and especially, Matthew. Thanks for teaching me some things.

Contents

PREFACE

This edition of *Economics and the Environment* retains the three interrelated advantages of its earlier incarnations: broad content; pedagogical clarity; and timely, well-integrated examples. There are a few significant additions, and examples and information have been updated throughout. For a chapter-by-chapter of suggestions for teaching out of this book, please see the *Instructor's Manual,* online at *www.wiley.com/college/goodstein.* Highlights include new material covering:

- Fisheries management, ITQs, and aquaculture
- Nonrenewable resource depletion in a Hotelling model
- A closer look at contingent valuation analysis
- The latest on L.A. Basin trading, the Genuine Progress Indicator, the Kyoto Protocol, NAFTA and "Chapter 11," and the "double-dividend" debate

In terms of content, the book provides a rigorous and comprehensive presentation of the "standard analysis," including the property-rights basis of environmental problems, efficient pollution control, benefit-estimation procedures, and incentive-based regulation. However, *Economics and the Environment* also incorporates broader topics as separate chapters, notably, the ethical foundations of environmental economics, an introduction to ecological economics, a safety-based approach to controlling pollution, the economic critique of growth, the potential for government failure, the promotion of "clean technology," and opportunities for sustainable development in poor countries.

The second major advantage of the book is clarity. *Economics and the Environment* is centered around four cleanly focused questions:

1. How much pollution is too much?
2. Is government up to the job?
3. How can we do better?
4. How can we resolve global issues?

These questions are introduced through a detailed case study of a "big" issue with which many students are familiar—global warming. The first section of *Economics and the Environment* then explicitly sets up the normative question, How much pollution is too much? It employs the tools of welfare economics and benefit–cost analysis to explore three possible answers.

The first is the efficient pollution level. The concept is explained, and students are introduced to the fundamentals of benefit and cost estimation. The book also features a detailed look at the use of benefit–cost analysis at the EPA. This edition includes an updated discussion of the static general equilibrium efficiency impacts of pollution taxes, and the implications for a "double-dividend."

The second pollution standard the book considers is a "safety" standard, which in fact continues to drive much environmental policy. The latter is placed solidly in the context of the economic growth debate, drawing on authors such as Hirsch, Daly, and Mishan.

The third standard is "ecological sustainability" as proposed by the ecological economics school. This standard is contrasted in an opposing chapter with "neoclassical sustainability"—dynamic efficiency presuming automatically rising social welfare. (The new Hotelling Model appendix appears here.) I shied away from doing this kind of comparison in the first edition because ecological economics was really just launching itself; by the second edition it had been around long enough for me to attempt a characterization. I have refined it a bit in this version, and I have added a game-theoretic interpretation of the Safe Minimum Standard.

Finally, tying together this first, normative section of the book, one also finds a vital discussion that is missing from other texts: the utilitarian ethical basis for the normative analysis, and its relation to an "environmental ethic." Most students come into an environmental economics course thinking that saving whales is very important, without knowing exactly why. The explicit welfare-based analysis in this chapter asks students to confront the assumptions underlying their own and others' world views.

The text fills a second major void in the second section, "Is Government up to the Job?" Most existing texts simply note that "government failure" is a potential problem when correcting for market externalities. In *Economics and the Environment,* the question of government's ability to effectively regulate pollution is carefully examined. The section begins with a discussion of the two primary obstacles to effective government action: imperfect information, and the opportunity for political influence over government policy. It then moves on to provide a succinct review of existing legislation and accomplishments on air, water, solid and hazardous waste, toxic pollution, and endangered species. Part II ends with a chapter on the often neglected subject of monitoring and enforcement.

The third section of the book, "How Can We Do Better?" tackles the (more) positive aspects of pollution regulation. Two chapters are devoted to the theory and practical application of incentive-based regulation—marketable permits and Pigouvian taxes. Appendices focus on instrument choice under uncertainty, and incentive-compatible regulation.

From here, the book examines an argument that attributes the root source of pollution to market failure in technological development, rather than in the arena of property rights. We consider the view that the market often fails to generate incentives for investment in "clean technology," as well as the feasibility of proposed solutions to this problem. In-depth discussion focuses on areas such as energy policy, pollution prevention, alternative agriculture, recycling, life-cycle analysis (including an appendix on input–output approaches), and "green" labeling.

Finally, *Economics and the Environment* devotes an entire section to the resolution of global pollution and resource issues. Part IV is centered around a definition and discussion of sustainable development, as put forward by the Bruntland Commission. Topics covered include the preservation of natural capital; population and per-capita consumption pressures; the relationship between poverty, sustainable development, and environmental protection in poor countries; international trade and the environment; and global pollution control agreements.

Economics and the Environment will appeal to three groups of instructors. The first are economists who are simply looking for a clear and concise presentation of the conventional approach to environmental and resource economics. The four-question format developed in the text provides a much simpler pedagogical handle than is available elsewhere. In addition, the book provides a wealth of examples from the current literature, as well as an explicit consideration of the government's role in environmental policy not available in competing works. Finally, the appendices cover advanced theoretical topics, ensuring that there is enough standard material to fill out a one-semester course.

The book will clearly appeal, however, to those with an interest in expanding the scope of environmental economics. *Economics and the Environment* moves beyond the standard analysis in five important areas. It provides a rigorous normative analysis of environmental goals; an in-depth evaluation of ecological economics; serious attention to the potential for government failure in pollution control; substantial discussion of dynamic issues of path dependence and technological change; and a sophisticated presentation of sustainable development in poor countries. The book seeks to incorporate into a well-developed economic analysis ideas that have emerged in the environmental and ecological sciences over the past few decades.

Given this orientation, instructors in environmental studies courses will also find this text to be unusually user friendly. Chapters on measuring the value of nonmarket goods, cost–benefit analysis, markets for pollution rights, incentives for investment in appropriate technology, the governmental role in pollution control, population and consumption pressures, global bargaining, and conservation in poor countries provide accessible material for environmental studies courses with a social-science focus.

Ultimately, the test of any textbook comes in the classroom. *Economics and the Environment* was written with students in mind. It addresses important questions raised in their lives and introduces them to the economist's view of some solutions.

Acknowledgments

First thanks go to Dallas Burtraw for our twice yearly conversations about what's hot, and especially to Peter Barnes and the Mesa Refuge for giving me the gift of two quiet, glorious weeks. Greg Tuke and Steve Clemmons helped make this, simultaneously, the most laid back and stimulating process one could imagine.

Laurie Johnson, Matt Kahn, Rich Howarth, Bob Berrens, Dennis Palmini, Nick Gomersall, Blair Sandler, Cynthia Browning, Rene Rosenbaum, Mariano Torras, Yeon-Su Kim, and Kurt Schwabe and several anonymous reviewers provided excellent comments on earlier revisions. Many of their suggestions have found their way into the final version of the book.

A synthetic work such as this depends on the contributions of the hundreds of economists and environmental scholars working in the field. Some of their names appear in the list of authors cited at the end of this book; undoubtedly many important contributors were omitted due to the scarce resource of space. Here, I would like to acknowledge helpful feedback and discussions with the following individuals:

Frank Ackerman	Tufts University
Dean Baker	Center for Economic and Policy Research
John Buell	College of the Atlantic
Steve Colt	University of Alaska–Anchorage
Peter Dorman	The Evergreen State College
Faye Duchin	Rensaleer Polytechnical Institute
Richard England	University of New Hampshire
Matthew Forstater	Gettysburg College
Sharman Haley	Merrit College
Darwin C. Hall	California State University–Long Beach
Jonathan Harris	Tufts University
Debra Holt	U.S. Department of Justice
David Goodman	University of California–Santa Cruz
Neva Goodwin	Tufts University
Robert Gottfried	University of the South
Douglas Greer	San Jose State University
Ann Ingerson	Sterling College
Kent Klitgaard	Wells College
Gunnar Knapp	University of Alaska–Anchorage
Michael Krasner	Queens College
Thea Lee	AFL-CIO
Rick Lostspeich	Indiana State University
William Moomaw	Tufts University
Janusz Mrozek	Georgia Tech
Carl Pasurka, Jr.	U.S. Environmental Protection Agency
Steve Polasky	University of Minnesota
Daniel Press	University of California–Santa Cruz
J. Barkley Rosser, Jr.	James Madison University
Peter Schwarz	University of North Carolina
Brett Snyder	U.S. Environmental Protection Agency
Eileen Van Ravensway	Michigan State University
Seid Zekavat	Loyola Marymount

Finally, thanks to my editor at John Wiley & Sons, Leslie Kraham, as well as Jessica Bartelt and Jenny Cardoza at Wiley, and Lari Bishop and Shoshanna Turek at Leyh Publishing, and to Kathy Anderson at Lewis & Clark.

INTRODUCTION

FOUR ECONOMIC QUESTIONS ABOUT GLOBAL WARMING

1.0 Introduction

Last weekend, I drove from my home in Portland, Oregon to Smith Rocks State Park to go rock climbing with a friend. We put about 300 miles on the car; less visibly, we pumped some 300 pounds of carbon dioxide (CO_2) into the air. This was our small daily share of the more than 25 billion pounds people around the world contribute annually from the burning of carbon fuels such as coal, oil, natural gas, and wood. Carbon dioxide is a **greenhouse gas**—a compound that traps reflected heat from the earth's surface and contributes to **global warming.** Other greenhouse gases include nitrous oxide from natural and human-made fertilizers; methane gas emitted from oil and gas production and transport, and from rice production and the digestive processes of cows and sheep; and chlorofluorocarbons (CFCs), once widely used for air-conditioning, refrigeration, and other industrial applications.[1]

As a result of industrialization and the ensuing rapid increase in greenhouse gases in our atmosphere, most scientists agree that the earth's surface temperature will rise over the next few decades. The extent of the warming is uncertain: Assuming no controls on greenhouse gas emissions, low-end estimates suggest an increase in the earth's average surface temperature of 2.5 degrees Fahrenheit by the year 2100. The official high-end prediction from the UN's International Panel on Climate Change is 11 degrees over this time period. To put that number in perspective, during the last ice age, the earth's average surface temperature was only 9 degrees Fahrenheit colder

---

[1]Chlorofluorocarbons also deplete the earth's protective ozone shield, a separate issue from global warming discussed in more detail in Chapter 23.

than it is today ("Shift in Stance" 2000). Over the course of 250 to 300 years, the outlook is obviously worse. A mid-range estimate over the long-term, assuming no efforts to curtail use of fossil fuels, is a warming of 18 degrees Fahrenheit (Cline 1991).

The potential consequences of this warming range from manageable to catastrophic. The first major impact will be on **agricultural output,** a direct effect of changing temperature and rainfall patterns. Rainfall has a dominant impact on agriculture. More northerly regions may actually experience an increase in precipitation and yields, but the current grainbelts of the United States and central Europe will become drier and agricultural output in these regions will probably fall. The net global effect through the mid-century is expected to be, on balance, negative, and will be particularly harsh in many Third World countries, which lack resources for irrigation and other adaptive measures. One study has estimated that an additional 30 million people worldwide will be at risk of hunger due to climate changes by 2050.[2]

Second, **natural ecosystems** will also suffer from climate change. The U.S. Environmental Protection Agency has estimated that, by the year 2050, the southern boundary of forest ecosystems could move northward by 600 kilometers, yet forests can migrate naturally at a much slower pace. Several major vegetation models predict large-scale forest die-backs in, among other places, the southern and eastern United States and the Amazon Basin. Massive disruption of the ecosystems and species extinction is thus likely; for example, many coral reefs across the planet will probably die. Diseases and pests are also likely to thrive in a warmer climate (Hadley Centre 1998; Bachelet 2001).

The third concern is the possibility of a **sea-level rise** as ice caps in northern latitudes and Antarctica begin to melt, and the warming ocean expands. An increase in sea level of three feet—well within the realm of possibility—would flood many parts of Florida, Louisiana, Boston, and New York City, as well as much of low-lying countries like Bangladesh and the Netherlands (unless they were protected by dikes). As many as 1 billion people live in areas that might be directly impacted.[3]

A warming of 2 to 3 degrees Fahrenheit over 100 years, a low-end estimate, would have far-reaching human and ecosystem effects, but would be a manageable event. A greater warming, however, would not only have a greater impact, but could also result in truly **catastrophic outcomes.** One of these would be the collapse and melting of the West Antarctic Ice Sheet, which would raise sea levels by about 20 to 30 feet. The ice sheet, the bottom of which lies below sea level, has collapsed and reformed several times over the last half-million years. Some scientists think that a warming of 4 degrees Fahrenheit or more would significantly raise the probability of this occurrence.[4]

---

[2]For an optimistic assessment of the impact on U.S. agriculture, see Mendelsohn (2001); for a critique, see Schlenker, Hanneman, and Fischer (2002); and for an overview of agricultural issues, see Hall (1997), and UK Meteorological Office (1998).

[3]The IPCC (1996) estimates suggest a sea-level rise of up to a meter by 2100 (but not stopping at that date!), with a best guess of 50 cm.

[4]O'Neil and Oppenheimer (2002) discuss this issue, as well as the possibility of a shutdown of the ocean's thermohaline circulation system in the North Atlantic. Ironically, if the Gulf Stream were to slow or stop, Northern Europe could be thrown into Ice Age conditions within a decade.

Global warming is an environmental reality that presents stark choices. On the one hand, substantial, short-term reductions in the human contribution to the greenhouse effect would require substantial changes in western lifestyles. In particular, our casual reliance on fossil fuels for transportation, heat, and power would have to be dramatically scaled back and new, clean energy sources developed. On the other hand, the consequences of inaction are potentially disastrous. By continuing to pollute the atmosphere, we may be condemning the next generation to even greater hardship.

This book focuses on the economic issues at stake in cases like global warming, where human actions substantially alter the natural environment. In the process, we will examine the following four questions.

1. **How much pollution is too much?** Many people are tempted to answer simply: Any amount of pollution is too much. However, a little reflection reveals that zero pollution is an unachievable and, in fact, undesirable goal. Pollution is a by-product of living; for example, each time you drive in a car, you emit a small amount of carbon dioxide to the air, exacerbating the greenhouse effect. The question really is "At what level are the benefits of pollution (cheap transportation in the case we started with) outweighed by its costs?"

   Different people will answer this question in different ways, depending upon their value systems: "Costs" of pollution may be defined narrowly, as strictly economic, or they may be broadened to include ethical considerations, such as fairness and the protection of rights. Costs may also be very difficult to measure. Nevertheless, it is clear that a rough weighing of benefits and costs is a critical first step for deciding "how much is too much."

2. **Is government up to the job?** After resolving the first question, we must then rely on government to develop and implement an economic plan to control pollution. But is our government able and willing to tackle the tough job of managing the environment? The costs and mistakes associated with bureaucratic decision making, as well as the likelihood of political influence in the process, will clearly have an impact on government's ability to respond effectively to the challenge.

   The first Earth Day was April 20, 1970. Also that year, the U.S. Congress passed the first major pollution control initiative, the National Environmental Policy Act, which, among other things, created the Environmental Protection Agency. Looking back over our thirty plus years of experience in regulating the environment, we have a record of both successes and failures to evaluate. Such an exploration can help us design policies to increase the effectiveness of the governmental response.

3. **How can we do better?** Suppose that as a society we decide on a particular target: for example, reduce carbon dioxide emissions to their 1990 level by 2010. Given the limitations that government might face, identified in the answer to the second question, how can we best achieve that goal? A long list of policies might be used: regulations, taxes, permit systems, technology subsidies (or their removal), research incentives, infrastructure investment, right-to-know laws, product labeling, legal liability, fines, and jail terms. Which policies will most successfully induce firms and consumers to meet the target?

4. **Can we resolve global issues?** Finally, regulating pollution within a single nation is a difficult task. Yet problems such as global warming transcend national boundaries. Brazilians say that they will stop cutting down and burning their rain forests to create crop and range land as soon as we stop driving gas-guzzling cars. (Although the United States has only 5% of the world's population, we account for over 21% of the greenhouse gases.) How can this kind of international coordination be achieved? Are economic development and environmental quality necessarily in conflict? And to what extent can the explosion in population growth and per capita resource use, which ultimately drive environmental problems, be managed?

Let us return to our discussion of global warming, and see what type of answers we might develop to these four questions. Global warming is a consequence of what is known as the **greenhouse effect.** Solar energy enters the earth's biosphere in the form of visible and ultraviolet light from the sun. The first law of thermodynamics—energy can be neither created nor destroyed—requires that this energy go somewhere, and much of it is radiated back into the biosphere as infrared radiation or heat. The greenhouse gases surrounding the earth let in the visible and ultraviolet light from the sun. Yet, like the glass surrounding a greenhouse, these gases trap the reflected infrared radiation (heat) close to the earth's surface.

Until the present time, the greenhouse effect has been primarily beneficial. Without the naturally occurring carbon dioxide shield, the average temperature on earth would be about 91 degrees Fahrenheit colder—well below the freezing point. The problem facing us today is the steady increase in human-made greenhouse gases, which began with the industrial revolution but dramatically accelerated after World War II. In less than two centuries, the concentration of greenhouse gases in the atmosphere has increased by more than 25%, and it is expected to double sometime in the next century if action is not taken to reduce emissions.

Is the greenhouse effect here yet? The earth's average temperature has risen a little more than 1 degree Fahrenheit over the last century. The 1990s have seen several of the hottest years on record; global temperature peaked in 1998, and the year 2002 was the second hottest. In 1995, the Intergovernmental Panel on Climate Change (IPCC), an organization of some 2,500 scientists operating under the auspices of the United Nations, made it official—the greenhouse effect is here. According to the IPCC, "the balance of evidence suggests that there is a discernible human influence on global climate." Since then, the evidence supporting human-induced warming has become even stronger (IPCC 1996; Hileman 2000).

Today, scientists are virtually unanimous in their belief that further warming will occur, but the magnitude of the warming is difficult to predict. After all, consider how often your local weather forecaster makes a bad call on the one-day forecast; with global warming, scientists are attempting to predict the weather fifty years into the future!

Uncertainty in predicting the degree of global warming is due primarily to the presence of **positive and negative feedback** effects. If it were only necessary to predict the impact of greenhouse gases on global temperature, the problem would be difficult enough. But changing temperatures will in turn affect many different parts of the earth and its surface, leading to either an acceleration of the warming (positive feedback) or a deceleration (negative feedback).

Two examples of the latter include the possibility that increasing cloud cover will reduce the amount of radiation entering the earth's atmosphere, or that higher rates of carbon dioxide will lead to higher rates of plant growth and thus more trapping of carbon dioxide in the air. Negative feedbacks would clearly be welcome, but unfortunately, positive feedbacks appear just as likely, if not more so, to occur. For example, higher temperatures may generate an increased rate of decay of organic material; lead to the emission of methane and CO_2 currently trapped in frozen bogs and peat fields at high latitudes; expose heat-absorbing darker earth under ice shields; or reduce the capacity of ocean organisms to fix carbon dioxide in their shells.

In the face of this uncertainty, what action should be taken to prevent or mitigate the consequences of global warming? Following the outline described, we can begin to tackle this daunting question piece by piece.

1.1 How Much Pollution Is Too Much?

First of all, where do we now stand on global warming emission targets? At the "Earth Summit" meeting in Rio de Janeiro in 1992, attended by the leaders of more than 140 countries, the industrialized nations signed a pledge to "try" to stabilize greenhouse gas emissions at 1990 levels by the year 2000. However, this promise was not kept. In the United States, low energy prices and strong economic growth boosted greenhouse gas emissions by 14% between 1990 and 2000.

Faced with the failure of this voluntary approach, at a meeting in Kyoto, Japan in 1997, the industrial countries of the world signed the **Kyoto global warming treaty.** The accord requires participating countries to reduce their emissions of greenhouse gases to around 5% below 1990 levels by about 2010. The treaty has been ratified by the European countries, Japan, and Canada, all of whom are beginning to take implementation measures. If and when Russia ratifies, the Kyoto accord will officially go into effect. However, in 2001 President Bush pulled the United States out of the Kyoto process, arguing that the country simply could not afford to tackle the global warming problem at this time. Instead, he has called for industry to take voluntary measures to reduce the rate of increase of emissions (not to reduce emissions themselves). Is Kyoto the right goal? Should emissions be reduced further? Or as Bush argues, not at all?

One way to answer this question is to use a benefit–cost framework. Quantifying the benefits and costs of reducing emissions is a difficult task, primarily because uncertainties loom very large in the case of climate change. On the benefits side, analysts are required to estimate the damages avoided, 100 years hence, by stabilizing CO_2 not only as it affects global agriculture and human health, but also species extinction and biodiversity. Moreover, across the planet, some regions will gain and others will lose; impacts will be proportionately larger in poor countries and smaller in rich countries. Developing countries will be hit the hardest because they tend already to be in warmer and drier parts of the planet, but more importantly, because they have fewer financial resources for adapting their agriculture or building sea walls.

Putting a monetary value on such benefits presents very difficult issues. Among them: How do we deal with uncertainty, and the possibility of cataclysmic change?

How do we value damage to future generations? Can we measure the value of intangible or "priceless" benefits such as human suffering and death averted or forests saved? How do we weigh the fact that certain countries will lose more than others in the warming process? These are issues we will explore in detail later in the book.

Nevertheless, and bearing in mind these very large uncertainties, economists have produced estimates of the total global benefits due to stabilizing emissions, and ultimately concentrations, of CO_2 and other greenhouse gases. Stabilizing CO_2 emissions at around 1990 levels might prevent losses of 2% of global gross domestic product (GDP). On the other hand, stabilization might actually lead to a reduction of 1% in global GDP, implying an overall net benefit from warming!

These figures do not take into account non-global warming benefits (**ancillary benefits**) of restrained greenhouse gas emissions. Energy conservation or fuel-switching away from coal and gasoline will help us reduce conventional air pollutants such as sulfur dioxide, nitrous oxide, and suspended particulates. For moderate reductions in greenhouse gas emissions, Burtraw et al. (2000) find that ancillary benefits alone actually outweigh the costs.[5]

What about the costs of stabilization? Here economists are divided into two camps. Some see relatively high costs to a policy of medium-term emission stabilization; a midrange estimate is about 1% of world GDP. Others, however, argue that energy efficiency and renewable energy technologies such as wind and solar electricity offer great promise for delinking economic growth from fossil fuel use relatively quickly, and thus achieving emission reductions at quite low cost. Koomey et al. (1998) argue that the Kyoto targets could actually be met at no net cost—initial investments in energy efficiency and renewable energy would be offset by fossil fuel savings.[6]

In the face of substantial uncertainty on both the benefit and cost sides, how do economists proceed? Often, they rely on the mid-range estimates. In the global warming case, based on such a mid-range approach, a prominent group of benefit–cost modelers have argued for modest reduction in greenhouse gas emissions—about 5–10% below a business-as-usual scenario in which carbon emissions wind up stabilizing at twice preindustrial levels. This target is well above the Kyoto goal of an emission freeze at 5% below 1990 levels. However, when benefit–cost analysts plug the low-cost scenarios into their models, or change other assumptions in a plausible fashion, benefit–cost models call for cuts in emissions greater than the Kyoto proposal, as much as 50% below a business-as-usual baseline (Cline 1998; Kolstad 1998; Weyant 1998).

Underlying the recommendations for only modest emission cutbacks is a belief that climate stability is important, but not critical to the well-being of humanity. The argument proceeds like this: People adapt to changing resource conditions. As emissions of greenhouse gases are regulated, the price of CO_2-based services will rise, and new low-CO_2 technologies will come on-line, ensuring that greenhouse gas concentrations eventually stabilize. Moreover, the development of new agricultural techniques

---

[5]Tol (1998) provides the range of cost estimates. Emission increases from 1990 to 2000 are from the Energy Information Administration (1999). Burtraw et al. (2000) argue that ancillary benefits appear to outweigh costs for reductions in the electricity sector resulting from a $10 per ton carbon tax, assuming that average costs are below marginal costs. All the benefits in this model are from nitrous oxide reduction.

[6]Weyant (1998) surveys the cost literature. See also Koomey et al. (1998) for a low-cost analysis.

will ensure that food supplies are maintained even in the face of a changing climate, and sea walls can be built to hold back rising sea levels. In addition, agriculture in some regions will gain from a warmer, wetter CO_2-enhanced climate, and cold-related deaths will decline. Some analysts even envision the winners from climate change assisting those (mostly in poor countries) who lose out from sea level rise and flooding. Clearly there will be significant losers from climate change, but on balance, the story goes, the quality of life for the average person in most countries can continue to rise even in the face of "moderate" climate change.

This mid-range benefit–cost perspective maintains that a policy of CO_2 stabilization at near 1990 levels is too costly. Investing resources and person-power in reducing greenhouse gas emissions will divert investment from schools or health care, lowering living standards for future generations. Benefit–cost analysis is needed to obtain the right balance of investment between climate protection and other goods and services that people value. However, when uncertainties dominate benefit–cost analysis, it is a very blunt, and sometimes misleading, tool. In the global warming case, a good number of economists argue that the future consequences of the current degradation of climate stability are simply too uncertain to justify making decisions about global warming based primarily on benefit–cost analysis (Jepma and Munasinghe 1998; Woodward and Bishop 1997).

Nevertheless, even though it is plagued by uncertainties, and even without considering ancillary benefits, it is important to recognize that narrow benefit–cost analysis does call for *some* action: a reduction of at least 5% to 10% below the business-as-usual baseline, stabilizing greenhouse gas concentrations a bit below twice preindustrial levels. And in 1997, 2,000 economists around the United States, including many prominent benefit–cost modelers, signed off on a public statement urging the U.S. government to take a more aggressive stance on reducing global warming. It read in part: "There are many potential policies to reduce green-house gas emissions for which the total benefits exceed the total costs" ("Economic Scene" 1997).

Note that these economists are prescribing an unstated ethical goal: Control pollution only if the measurable monetary benefits of doing so are greater than the measurable monetary costs. This is one answer to the question "How much is too much?" It is called an **efficiency standard** for pollution reduction.

However, there are ways of thinking about pollution standards other than through a comparison of economic costs and benefits. First there are issues of fairness: Inaction on our part—though it may provide for somewhat higher incomes today, particularly for citizens in affluent countries—may condemn future generations, in particular those in already poor countries, to even greater hardship. Can we justify actions today that, for example, will destroy entire island nations and their cultures? A second answer to the question "How much is too much?" emphasizes fairness. This is called a **safety standard.** Safety requires reducing pollution to (socially defined) "safe" levels, unless the costs of doing so are prohibitive.

Finally, there is the question of fundamental uncertainty regarding our impact on the planetary ecosystem. Benefit–cost analysts typically assume an intermediate case of predictable damages, but of course, a worst-case scenario might emerge. In a related vein, can we even begin to put benefit numbers on things we know nothing about? For example, what would be the value to future generations of the unique genetic code that will be lost as species extinction accelerates? In the face of this uncertainty, a third standard emerges—**ecological sustainability.** This standard requires protecting natural ecosystems from major changes, again, unless the costs of doing so are prohibitive.

The policies flowing from the safety and ecological sustainability standards are to meet the Kyoto greenhouse pollution reduction targets and then initiate a substantial reduction in emissions. Such a recommendation is strengthened by the argument that lost consumption from controlling CO_2 emissions in an affluent country like the United States really means very little over the long run. Because the happiness derived from consumption is in many ways a relative phenomenon, a general increase in income only accelerates the "rat race," leaving few better off in absolute terms. Efficiency proponents would respond that aggressive global warming actions will impose excessively high costs on the current generation and, by depressing current investment in capital, research, and education, on future generations as well.

As the public debate over global warming heats up in the United States, it will be conducted by those who maintain somewhat different **ethical** viewpoints. On one side, efficiency advocates will stress the measurable costs involved in reducing global warming and will advocate small reductions. On the other, proponents of safety and ecological sustainability will argue for major greenhouse gas cutbacks, focusing on uncertain but potentially devastating impacts on future generations.

The purpose of this book is not to sort out which answer is "correct," but rather to better understand the different positions. However, the first essential step in addressing any environmental problem is to decide, "How much pollution is too much?" Once this is resolved, it is then possible to move on to the second question.

1.2 Is Government Up to the Job?

For reasons we will explore further in this book, an unfettered free-market economy will produce too much pollution by almost anyone's standards. This suggests that government needs to step in and regulate market behavior in order to protect the environment. But government itself has its own limitations. Is government up to the job?

Two obstacles stand in the way of effective government action. The first is **imperfect information.** Regulators often have a hard time obtaining accurate information about the benefits and costs of pollution reduction. Benefits such as cancers reduced, visibility improved, and ecosystems salvaged are hard to measure and even harder to quantify. Costs are also hard to gauge accurately since they depend on the details of how an industry actually operates. Under these circumstances, even well-meaning bureaucrats may have a difficult time imposing regulations that achieve cost-effective control of pollution.

The second obstacle lies in the opportunity for **political influence.** Evaluating the importance of this problem requires a theory of governmental action. Economics, like all social sciences, is not a "value-free" pursuit. This is most apparent in political economy, where scholars of different political persuasions are in the business of analyzing government activity.

Traditional **conservatives** view governmental intervention as a necessary evil and argue for as limited a government role as is possible in all affairs, including environmental affairs. Conservatives argue that government legislators and regulators are self-interested individuals who desire to maximize their own well-being, rather than wholeheartedly pursue their stated public mission. Such officials, in theory, seldom act in the public interest but instead serve special interests. Special interests include, for example, coalitions of particular businesses, environmental groups, women's or civil rights groups, or labor unions.

In contrast to this conservative view, **progressives** view government as capable of promoting an activist agenda to serve the general interest of the public. Like conservatives, progressives acknowledge the possibility of government failure. Yet in contrast to the conservative position, progressives argue that the problem with government involvement in the economy is not primarily the existence of pluralistic special-interest groups, but is instead the dominance of big business and development interests in the legislative and regulatory process. For example, progressives point to well-financed lobbying by the fossil fuel industry as a major obstacle to the resolution of the global warming issue.

As the next section illustrates, these different perspectives on the potential for effective government action will determine views on the best policies for dealing with global warming.

1.3 How Can We Do Better?

As noted, at Kyoto, many of the industrial countries committed themselves in principle to reducing greenhouse gas emissions below 1990 levels. Carbon dioxide is the most important of the greenhouse gases, contributing about 60% of the total greenhouse effect. It is produced by the burning and decay of carbon-based materials: coal, oil, and plant matter. Given what we have just learned about the political economy of regulation, how do we set about controlling CO_2 emissions?

Government could take many possible actions to control carbon dioxide emissions. In a rough way, we can divide such measures into three categories. First is **command-and-control regulation,** the current, dominant approach to environmental protection. Under command and control, government would regulate CO_2 emissions by mandating the adoption of particular types of CO_2 abatement technology on, for example, coal-burning power plants. Other types of technology would be required for automobiles, still others for natural gas plants.

As we shall see, command-and-control regulation has been widely criticized as centralized and inflexible and, thus, much more costly than necessary. Many economists have advocated a switch to **incentive-based regulation.** Incentive-based approaches set emission targets and leave it up to industry to figure out the best way to comply. Incentive-based regulation gets its name from the fact that firms are provided with incentives to reduce emissions: A tax on pollution is one example.

Finally, government can intervene more directly to encourage the development and diffusion of new **clean technologies.** For example, government can force firms to meet energy-efficient design standards, such as building codes. Or government could promote clean technological change through its investment activities—for example, by favoring rail transport infrastructure over autos or providing research and development funding for solar energy. Which of these is the best method?

Of all the pollution control methods available, by and large, economists of all stripes agree that pollution taxes (and their kin, marketable permit systems, introduced next) can be a good policy. To deal with CO_2 emissions, for example, a tax based on the carbon content of fuels (a carbon tax) is one of the most effective policies we could impose. Under this kind of scheme, non-CO_2 fuels would be promoted over carbon-based fuels in the marketplace, and cleaner CO_2 fuels such as natural gas would be promoted over dirtier ones such as coal.

A narrow benefit–cost perspective suggests that the United States impose a modest carbon tax of approximately $10 per ton of emissions. Such a tax would first generate some reduction in CO_2 emissions as firms switched to existing technologies employing relatively cheaper fuel sources. Second, it would provide companies with the financial incentive to develop carbon-free technologies. The benefits of such a gradual approach would be to avoid serious disruption of economic affairs in countries like the United States, prevent an overcommitment of resources to global warming given the current uncertainty, and obviate the need for obtaining a complicated and difficult-to-enforce international agreement. The Kyoto targets could be met at a later date if evidence of substantial warming becomes more compelling. The Conservative American Enterprise Institute called for such a tax in 2002.[7]

Other economists have argued for an ecological sustainability standard: Given the irreversibility of global warming, aggressive action is warranted sooner rather than later.[8] Holders of this viewpoint press for a tax with substantial teeth. Estimates of between $50 and $100 per ton of greenhouse gas emissions seem to be consistent with the 1990-level target and may achieve some rollback. Such a tax would generate substantial revenues and could be made politically palatable were the funds rebated back to the public in the form of income tax cuts.

Such tax cuts should be targeted disproportionately to poorer citizens to reduce the impact of higher prices for necessities—gasoline, heat, and electricity. One study for the United States found that a $100 per ton tax would raise gasoline prices an estimated $.26 per gallon and electricity prices by $.02 per kWh ("White House Predicts Lower Costs" 1997).

In addition to the market-based approach represented by carbon taxes, progressive economists would argue for policies to promote energy efficiency and for a reorientation of government investment priorities. Koomey et al. (1998), for example, recommends that fuel, lighting, and power efficiency standards be strengthened or introduced. The authors also envision major government efforts to revamp our transportation infrastructure, including promotion of high-speed railways as a substitute for short plane flights, zoning laws to encourage denser patterns, greater investment in mass transit, and taxes to discourage auto transport.

Finally, government-funded research and development into new energy technologies, in particular those that utilize renewable, non–carbon-based sources, such as energy efficiency and solar, wind, and fuel cell power, might be promoted. Significant carbon taxes combined with substantial government-sponsored research and development into clean energy technologies and an aggressive approach to promoting efficient energy use is the "progressive" position on global warming.

---

[7]"Market Mechanism to Slow Global Warming," AEI-Brookings Joint Center for Regulatory Studies (www.aei.brookings.org).

[8]See Pearce (1991) or Goodland and El Serafy (1998) for example.

Conservative economists would be suspicious of government regulations mandating energy efficiency or government-funded research and development (R&D) of the alternative technologies recommended by the progressive program. The question they would ask about such an agenda would be: "Can the government do a better job developing appropriate technologies than the market already does?" First, conservatives would charge that the R&D pool is likely to become just another government pork barrel. Second, even granting efficient operation, some would maintain that government bureaucrats would have a hard time picking winners, determining which potential technologies are feasible, cost-effective, and environmentally benign.

Progressive economists would respond that existing government decisions such as energy tax breaks for fossil fuels, highway construction funds and other subsidies for auto transport, tax and zoning policies that encourage suburbanization, and high levels of poorly targeted R&D funding already constitute a defacto plan with major negative environmental and economic effects. The choice, therefore, is not between free markets and central planning, but rather between myopic and farsighted government policy.

Progressives maintain that on energy policy, our market system (which is *already* affected by substantial government involvement) has failed miserably to deliver appropriate technology. Because private investors do not take into account the tremendous costs to society of carbon-based fuels, incentives do not exist to develop appropriate technologies. In addition, a network of vested interests, inappropriate government subsidies already in existence, and substantial economies of scale all justify government involvement. Due to the massive nature of the market failure, the argument is that picking winners would not be hard: among the obvious candidates—energy efficiency technologies, photovoltaic solar cells, and wind power, to name a few.

How can we do better? Most economists would argue that a greater reliance on incentive-based approaches such as pollution taxes makes sense. Economists who hold a progressive viewpoint argue that, in addition, government should take a more active hand in promoting the development and diffusion of clean technology.

1.4 Can We Resolve Global Issues?

Whether the U.S. government relies primarily on traditional regulatory mechanisms to achieve its greenhouse gas reduction targets or also employs more incentive-based regulations and direct investment tools, our efforts will be in vain if other nations do not also comply with the treaty. Global warming requires a global solution. Many economists are pessimistic about the prospects for enforceable global agreements that substantially reduce carbon dioxide emissions in the near future.

CO_2 reduction is what is known as a **public good,** a good that is consumed in common. This means, for example, that if the United States cuts back CO_2 emissions by 20%, the whole world benefits. Thus, each country would prefer to see the other cut back and then "free ride" on its action. With every country being in this position, there is great incentive for signatories to a treaty to cheat on any agreement. One reason that nations are reluctant to commit to substantial carbon dioxide reductions is the fear that other countries will not comply, and thus their sacrifice will be meaningless in the long run.

However, economists are eager to be proven wrong. An ongoing experiment may shed some light on the potential for the success of the Rio agreement. In 1987, most countries of the world signed on to the Montreal Protocol, an agreement to drastically reduce the production of one of the greenhouse gases, CFCs, by 1996. In 1992, the treaty was strengthened and now calls for a complete ban. (The impetus to the agreement was actually *not* global warming, but rather destruction of the ozone layer—the primary problem with CFCs.) We will examine the success of the protocol and other international agreements in Chapter 23, where we also return for a final discussion of global warming. However, much hinges on whether poor countries such as India and China successfully adopt the CFC substitutes that have been developed to provide such basic goods as refrigeration.

This issue highlights another obstacle facing the Kyoto global warming treaty: the economic needs of Third World countries. Poor countries currently contribute about 30% of the world's CO_2 emissions. But high rates of population growth, increasing energy use per capita, and accelerated deforestation are expected to increase their contribution to 50% before the year 2025. Some would argue that it is both unrealistic and unfair to expect these countries to sacrifice economic growth by reducing CO_2 emissions in exchange for uncertain environmental gains.

Yet economic growth in many poor countries has its own environmental costs and may prove **unsustainable.** The economic growth process is often rooted in exploitative colonial relationships that have encouraged the establishment of lopsided, resource-dependent economies. In the modern context, debt has replaced colonial status as the mechanism by which wealth flows from the poor to the rich. Deforestation, overgrazing, and massive pollution from mineral and oil development persist, reinforced by a network of government policies favoring local elite and multinational corporate interests, all occurring in an environment where common property resources are available for exploitation. When economic growth fails to compensate for natural resources depleted in the process, the economic development process is unsustainable: That is, growth today comes at the expense of future generations. (For a more careful definition of sustainable development, see Chapter 21.)

It is clear that the economic needs of the world's poor nations must be placed at the forefront of an effort to reduce global warming. In this fashion, global agreements to control greenhouse gas pollution are most likely to succeed. But it is also true that developing countries have more to lose from global warming because they have fewer resources to finance adaptive measures, from resettlement to irrigation to dike building. It is possible that by adopting a combination of energy efficiency and conversion to renewable energy sources (biomass, wind, and solar) poor countries can substantially slow the rate of growth of CO_2 emissions while at the same time promoting sustainable development, which in turn will lower population growth rates. A commitment to the development and transfer of this kind of technology by wealthy nations would have to be part of a successful treaty to reduce greenhouse gas emissions.

Along these lines, an incentive-based pollution control approach pioneered by economists has been suggested for resolving equity issues between the First and Third Worlds: a **marketable permit system.** Such a system would work in the following way. First, a successor to the Kyoto treaty would determine a worldwide greenhouse gas emission target and then assign each country a quota, based for example on its total population. Thus, each person in the world might initially be permitted to make an equal contribution to global warming. But because the average Indian, for example, uses only 4% as much energy as the average American, Third World countries would have an excess supply of permits, while we in the First World would have an excess demand.

Because the permits are marketable, we would buy some from the poorer countries of the world to maintain our energy-intensive lifestyles. The funds generated could then be used to support the kind of investments in non-carbon fuels that poor countries will require to develop. Moreover, because we would now be paying directly for our global warming, we would have the incentive both to conserve energy and to seek out new clean energy technologies. (The Kyoto accord includes a prototype of this kind of emissions trading system, in the form of the "Clean Development Mechanism" discussed in Chapter 23.)

A marketable permit system could also be used to reduce emissions within a given country. One idea that has been put forward, called SkyTrust, would involve issuing one share of the total allowable U.S. carbon emission quota—set by the U.S. government—to each man, woman, and child in the country (Barnes 2001). A non-governmental organization would hold these shares in trust and each year auction them off to companies selling products that emit greenhouse gases (car manufacturers, oil companies, electric power producers, etc.). For each ton of carbon dioxide emitted annually, a company would have to buy a one-ton permit at auction. At the end of the year, each citizen would receive a check equal to the value of his or her share of permits in the annual auction; estimates put the likely dividend at more than $600 per person each year. This would be a terrific way to make controlling global warming pollution politically popular.

Tradeable permit systems of this kind put a price on pollution. Within a country, companies that can now emit carbon dioxide for free would find pollution becoming expensive. This would give companies an incentive to reduce emissions and, more importantly, would encourage the development of clean energy technologies, such as wind and solar power, and fuel cell vehicles. At the international level, selling carbon dioxide permits provides the financial means for poor countries to "leapfrog" the period of fossil-fuel intensive development and move straight to clean energy options.

Of course, nothing comes without a price. Although under the scheme outlined both poor countries and average Americans would reap financial benefits from the sale of permits, rich-country customers (those same average Americans) would pay much of the price of pollution reduction in the form of higher prices for energy, cars, and manufactured goods, at least in the short run. As usual, the essence of the economic debate boils down to a comparison of benefits (reducing global warming) versus costs (higher prices for goods and services). Do the benefits of aggressive action to reduce greenhouse gas emissions outweigh the costs? At this point, the case remains open. Some economists say reduce a little; others say reduce a lot. This book gives you the tools you need to better understand the debate and make up your own mind.

1.5 Summary

This chapter has provided an introduction to the scientific issues surrounding the buildup of greenhouse gases in our atmosphere and the resultant possibility of global warming. But global warming is only one of the myriad environmental challenges posed by human activity. From the siting of landfills at the local level, to regulations on chemical emissions from manufacturing plants that are issued by national governments, to international agreements designed to preserve species diversity, the need for a public that is informed of the underlying scientific issues is great.

Environmental economists must also rely on scientific assessment of the dangers posed by environmental degradation to ourselves and our descendants. However, this book is *not* focused on specific environmental concerns arising from our economic activity. Instead, the point is to *illustrate the framework* that economists use for approaching pollution problems. For any such concern, from landfill siting to chemical regulation to loss of species diversity, three general questions must be answered:

1. How much pollution is too much?
2. Is government up to the job?
3. How can we do better?

When, as is increasingly common, the issue is an international one, a fourth question must also be addressed:

4. Can we resolve global issues?

To this point, I have both outlined the questions raised and provided a sketch of the answers that arise when one grapples with the economics of environmental protection. As indicated, there is often lively debate among economists regarding the right answers. But what we do agree on is the centrality of these four questions. The rest of the book moves on to explain and explore a number of possible solutions. It is my hope that the reader will come away better equipped to address the local, national, and global environmental problems that we and our children have to overcome in the twenty-first century.

APPLICATION 1.0

Setting Goals for Greenhouse Gas Pollution, Take One

The Kyoto Protocol requires that greenhouse gases be stabilized at a level that prevents "dangerous anthropogenic interference" with the climate system. In an effort to help define what this means, O'Neil and Oppenheimer (2002) relate certain physical effects to rising temperature:

- At 2 degrees Fahrenheit, we can expect "large-scale eradication of coral reef systems" on a global basis.
- At 4 degrees Fahrenheit, an irreversible process leading to the collapse of the West Antarctic Ice Sheet and a sea-level rise of 25 feet becomes significantly more likely.
- At 6 degrees Fahrenheit, the shutdown of the Gulf Stream leading to a sudden, dramatic cooling in Northern Europe and accelerated warming in the South Atlantic becomes significantly more likely.

The authors conclude that it is impossible to prevent a 2 degree warming. Based on the relationships above, they call for holding global temperature increases to less than 4 degrees.

a. Is this an efficiency, ecological sustainability, or safety standard? Why?

APPLICATION 1.1

Setting Goals for Greenhouse Gas Pollution, Take Two

Estimating the economic costs of global warming is quite a difficult process. In a recent book examining the issue, Nordhaus and Boyer (2000) provided this disclaimer: "Attempts to estimate the impacts of climate change remain highly speculative. Outside of agriculture and sea-level rise the number of scholarly studies of the economic impacts of climate change remains small." Nevertheless, they undertook the process, as shown in Table 1.1.

Nordhaus and Boyer find small negative impacts for agriculture (–$4 billion) and sea-level rise (–$6 billion); argue that warming is likely to yield significant benefits for outdoor recreation (in crude terms, more golf days, +$17 billion); and maintain that the biggest negative impacts of climate change are likely to come from destroying parts of historically or culturally unique human settlements such as New Orleans or Olympia, Washington (–$6 billion), or from catastrophic climate change (–$28 billion). Overall they find a negative impact of only 0.5% of GDP. (Note this figure leaves out the costs of species extinction—no accounting for coral reefs here.) The analysis that underlies calls for "small" taxes on carbon dioxide ($10 per ton), leading to an ultimate rise in global temperature of close to 5 degrees Fahrenheit (compare to 4 degrees Fahrenheit in Application 1.0).

TABLE 1.1   Impacts of Global Warming in the United States: 2.5 degrees Celsius/5 degrees Fahrenheit (billions of 1990 dollars; year benefits are positive while damages are negative)

Market Impacts	
Agriculture	–$ 4
Energy	0
Sea level	–$ 6
Timber	0
Water	0
Total market	–$11

Nonmarket Impacts	
Health, water quality, and human life	–$ 1
Migration	na
Human amenity, recreation, and nonmarket time	$17
Species loss	na
Human settlements	–$ 6
Extreme and catastrophic events	–$25
Total nonmarket	–$17

Total (Market and Nonmarket Sectors)	
Billions of 1990 $	–$28
% of 1990 GDP	–0.5

Note: na = not available or not estimated.
Source: Nordhaus and Boyer (2000).

    a. Is this an efficiency, ecological sustainability, or safety standard? Why?

    b. One might question the value of basing environmental decisions on data that is "highly speculative." How do you think Nordhaus defends drawing conclusions based on numbers like those in Table 1.1?

KEY IDEAS IN EACH SECTION

1.0   **Global warming,** arising from the accumulation of **greenhouse gases** and the resulting **greenhouse effect,** poses a potentially severe threat to human welfare and natural ecosystems. Changing rainfall patterns that accompany warming may lead to reductions in **agricultural output,** particularly in poor countries, and major changes in **natural ecosystems,** including accelerated species extinction and higher rates of disease. **Sea level** will also rise. Although scientists largely agree that *global warming is already a reality,* the magnitude of the warming will ultimately depend on **positive and negative feedback** effects. Economists need to answer **four questions** to address a problem like global warming.

1.1   The first question is "**How much pollution is too much?**" The **Kyoto global warming treaty,** if implemented, would require reducing emissions to below 1990 levels. Is this the right target? Answering this question requires at least a rough weighing of costs and benefits; an **efficiency standard** relies solely on benefit–cost analysis; **safety** and **ecological sustainability standards** argue for reducing pollution to much lower levels. This is fundamentally an **ethical debate** over the proper way to weigh both costs and benefits. Initial attempts to define an efficient level of global warming have also provoked a technical debate over to what extent and how fast we can adopt energy efficiency and other cleaner energy technologies. **Ancillary benefits** of reducing greenhouse gas emissions must also be factored in.

1.2   Government action is necessary to reduce pollution in a market economy, but "**Is government up to the job?**" Two basic obstacles to effective government action are **imperfect information** and the **opportunity for political influence. Conservatives** view environmental regulation as a necessary evil best kept at the absolute minimum, believing that government action primarily serves special interests. By contrast, **progressives** see no way around an activist government role in environmental protection. From the progressive point of view, government failure results primarily from the influence of big business and development interests.

1.3   **Command-and-control regulation** is the dominant approach to pollution control today. In response to the question "**How can we do better?**" many economists have advocated adoption of **incentive-based** regulatory approaches, such as pollution taxes. Another option is the direct promotion of **clean technology** through actions such as R&D funding, infrastructure investment, zoning laws, and efficiency standards. Conservatives dispute the ability of government to achieve environmental goals by promoting clean technology.

1.4   **Resolving global issues** often requires international agreement. Such agreements, in turn, face two major obstacles. The first of these is the **public good** nature of environmental agreements. Once an agreement is signed, the incentives to free ride are great.

Second, poor countries often cannot afford to invest in environmental protection. At the same time, they cannot afford not to; economic growth may lead to **unsustainable development.** In practice, this means funds to resolve global pollution problems must come from rich countries. A **marketable permit system** for controlling global CO_2 emissions (1) provides a way to fund poor country efforts and (2) provides rich countries with the right incentives to seek out less polluting technology.

REFERENCES

Bachelet, Dominique, Ronald Neilson, James Lenihan, and Raymond Drapek. 2000. "Climate Change Effects on Vegetation Distribution and Carbon Budget in the United States." *Ecosystems* 4:164–185.

Barnes, Peter. 2001. *Who Owns the Sky?* Washington, DC: Island Press.

Burtraw, Dallas, Alan Krupnick, Karen Palmer, Anthony Paul, Michael Toman, and Cary Boyd. 2000. "Ancillary Benefit of Reduced Air Pollution in the U.S. from Moderate Greenhouse Gas Mitigation Policies in the Electricity Sector." *Discussion Paper 99-51.* Washington, DC: Resources for the Future.

Cline, William R. 1991. "Scientific Basis for the Greenhouse Effect." *The Economic Journal* 101, no. 407:904–919.

Cline, William R. 1998. "Comments on Climate Change Damages." *Economics and Policy Issues in Climate Change.* Edited by William Nordhaus. Washington, DC: Resources for the Future.

"Economic Scene." 1997. *The New York Times,* 13 February, C2.

Energy Information Administration. 1999. *Emissions of Greenhouse Gasses in the United States.* Washington, DC: EIA.

Goodland, R., and S. El Serafy. 1998. "The Urgent Need to Internalize CO_2 Emission Costs." *Ecological Economics* 27, no. 1:79–90.

Hadley Centre. 1998. *Climate Change and Its Impacts.* London: UK Meteorological Office.

Hileman, Bette. 2000. "Panel Reaffirms Human Influence on Global Warming." *Chemical and Engineering News* 78, no. 7:9.

IPCC. 1996. *Climate Change 1995: The Science of Climate Change.* Oxford: Cambridge University Press.

Jepma, Catrinus, and Mohan Munasinghe. 1998. *Climate Change Policy.* Cambridge: Cambridge University Press.

Kolstad, Charles. 1998. Integrated assessment modeling of climate change. In *Economic and Policy Issues in Climate Change,* Edited by William Nordhaus. Washington, DC: Resources for the Future.

Koomey, John, R. Cooper Richey, Skip Laitner, Alan Sanstad, Robert Markel, and Chris Murray. 1998. "Technology and Greenhouse Gas Emissions: An Integrated Scenario Analysis Using the LBNL-NEMS Model." Berkeley: Lawrence Berkeley National Laboratory.

Mendelsohn, Robert, ed. 2001. *Global Warming and the American Economy.* Cheltenham, UK: Edward Elgar.

Nordhaus, William, and Joseph Boyer. 2000. *Warming the World: Economic Models of Global Warming.* Cambridge, MA: MIT.

O'Neil, Brian, and Michael Oppenheimer. 2002. "Dangerous Climate Impacts and the Kyoto Protocol," *Science* 296:1792–1793.

Pearce, David. 1991. "The Role of Carbon Taxes in Adjusting to Global Warming." *The Economic Journal* 101, no. 407:938–948.

Schlenker, Wolfram, W. Michael Hanneman, and Anthony C. Fischer. 2002. The Impact of Global Warming on U.S. Agriculture: An Econometric Analysis. Paper presented at the World Congress of Environmental and Resource Economists, June, Monterey, CA.

"A Shift in Stance on Global Warming Theory." 2000. *The New York Times,* 26 October.

Tol, Richard. 1998. Comments on climate change damages. In *Economic and Policy Issues in Climate Changes,* edited by William Nordhaus. Washington, DC: Resources for the Future.

Weyant, John. 1998. The costs of carbon emission reductions. In *Economic and Policy Issues in Climate Change,* edited by William Nordhaus. Washington, DC: Resources for the Future.

"White House Predicts Lower Costs for Controlling Emissions." 1997. *The New York Times,* 16 July, A10.

Woodward, Richard, and Richard Bishop. 1997. "How to Decide When Experts Disagree: Uncertainty-Based Choice Rules in Environmental Policy." *Land Economics* 73, no. 4:492–507.

How Much Pollution Is Too Much?

The first step in protecting the environment is setting a goal: How clean do we want it to be? There is no "right" answer to this question, but whatever answer we choose, implicitly or explicitly, the costs of clean-up will be weighed against the benefits. Here we explore three different clean-up targets, each comparing costs and benefits in different ways: efficiency, safety, and sustainability. The focus is on both ethical and practical issues. We begin with a discussion of the utilitarian ethical framework that economists use, and then explore two fundamental reasons why unregulated markets tend to produce too much pollution from *any* perspective. We look carefully at the techniques economists have developed to measure the benefits and costs of environmental protection, the strengths and limitations of benefit–cost analysis, and the broader relationship between growth in material consumption and growth in well-being. How much is too much? This part of the book provides the tools to help you make up your mind.

CHAPTER 2

ETHICS AND ECONOMICS

2.0 Introduction

After reading the brief introduction to global warming, you are now more informed about the issue than 95% of the U.S. population. Suppose there were a presidential election tomorrow, and candidate A was supporting an efficiency standard. Based on the current benefit–cost analyses of reducing greenhouse gas emissions, he was advocating only a minimal carbon tax. Candidate B, by contrast, believed in an ecological sustainability standard and was pushing a much higher tax, combined with aggressive government action to promote clean technology. If you were a single-issue voter, for whom would you vote? Why?

If you voted for candidate A, you might have done so out of a concern for economic growth or jobs. You might even have reasoned that the economic slowdown brought on by increased regulation would actually penalize future generations more than the warming by reducing investment in education, capital, and new technology. If, on the other hand, you voted for candidate B, perhaps you did so because you thought it was unfair to punish our descendants for our wasteful consumption habits and that endowing them with an unpolluted environment was more important than providing them with a new, improved form of breakfast cereal. You might also have thought that we have a moral duty to preserve the species of the earth. Finally, you might have reasoned that new jobs would be created in the process of controlling carbon emissions.

The question "How much pollution is too much?" is what economists call a **normative** issue—it focuses our attention on what should be, rather than what is. Some are tempted to dismiss normative or ethical questions saying "it's just a matter of opinion." But in fact, in our society, opinion matters. The underlying ethical viewpoints held by lawmakers, regulatory and industry officials, and voters fundamentally influence the making of pollution policy. Like most countries, the United States already has a system of laws and regulatory agencies responsible for controlling the amount of pollutants emitted by factories, offices, farms, cars, and in the case of cigarettes, even people's lungs. Are the current laws too strict (as many in industry maintain) or do they need tightening up (as environmentalists argue)? Examining the ethical foundations of our own opinions will help us evaluate what is the "right" amount of pollution these laws ought to permit. Without a well-reasoned answer to this question, sensible environmental regulation becomes impossible.

In the first part of this book we will examine three different pollution standards: an **efficiency standard,** which carefully weighs benefits and costs; a **safety standard** emphasizing human health; and an **ecological sustainability standard,** which argues for the preservation of current ecosystems. Along the way we will explore the complex issues involved in measuring the costs and benefits of cleaning up our environment. Wrestling with this material probably will not change where you stand on the "growth versus environment" debate, but it should help you clarify why you think the way you do. This in turn will make you a more effective advocate of your position. And convincing others that your opinion is "better"—either more logical or more consistent with widely held social norms—is the basis for taking action to make our world a better place.

2.1 Utility and Utilitarianism

Economic analysts are concerned with *human* welfare or well-being. From the economic perspective, the environment should be protected for the material benefit of humanity and not for strictly moral or ethical reasons. To an economist, saving the blue whale from extinction is valuable only insofar as doing so yields happiness (or prevents tragedy) for present or future generations of people. The existence of the whale independent of people is of no importance. This human-centered (or anthropocentric) moral foundation underlying economic analysis is known as **utilitarianism.**

There are, of course, different perspectives. One such view is known as an **environmental ethic.** It can be put rather simply: *Independent of the utility of doing so,* people have a moral responsibility to treat the earth with respect. From the Native Americans, to Henry David Thoreau and John Muir, to Earth First! activism, this is an old and familiar idea in American culture. (Of course, a celebration of the unbridled exploitation of nature has also played a dominant role in American intellectual history.)[1] Aldo Leopold, considered by many to be the most influential environmental thinker of this century, stated it this way: "We abuse land because we regard it as a commodity belonging to us. When we see land as a community to which we belong, we may begin to use it with love and respect" (Leopold 1966).

As this quote suggests, many environmentalists are hostile to utilitarian arguments for protecting the environment. Indeed, an economic perspective on nature is often viewed as the primary problem, rather than part of the solution. The philosopher Mark Sagoff (1995) puts it this way:

> ... the destruction of biodiversity is the crime for which future generations are the least likely to forgive us. The crime would be as great or even greater if a computer could design or store all the genetic data we might ever use or need from the destroyed species. The reasons to protect nature are moral, religious and cultural far more often than they are economic. (618)

The focus on anthropocentric, utilitarian arguments in this book is not meant to discount the importance of other ethical views. Indeed, over the long run, nonutilitarian

---

[1]See Nash (1989) and Brown (1998).

moral considerations will largely determine the condition of the planet that we pass on to our children and theirs. But economic arguments invariably crop up in short-run debates over environmental protection, often playing pivotal roles.

Individual economists may in fact accept the environmental ethic as part of their personal moral code. However, in conducting their analysis, economists adopt a hands-off view toward the morality or immorality of eliminating species (or of pollution in general), because they are reluctant to impose a single set of values on the broader society. However, failing to make a judgment implies an ethical framework—and the moral philosophy underlying economics is utilitarianism.

Utilitarians have two hard questions to settle before they can apply their analysis to an issue like pollution. The first is, "What in fact makes people happy?" This is a very difficult question; the great religions of the world, for example, each offer their own spiritual answers. Economists respond at the material level by assuming that the consumption of goods brings happiness or utility. "Goods" are defined very broadly to include any and all things that people desire. These include both **market goods,** such as tomatoes, VCRs, and basketball shoes, and **nonmarket goods,** such as clean air, charitable deeds, or the view from a mountaintop. What makes something a good is a personal matter. Leon Walras, an economist who lived in the 1800s, put it in this rather provocative way:

> We need not concern ourselves with the morality or immorality of any desire which a useful thing answers or serves to satisfy. From other points of view the question of whether a drug is wanted by a doctor to cure a patient, or a murderer to kill his family is a very serious matter, but from our point of view, it is totally irrelevant. (Walras 1977, 65)

One can express the positive relationship between consumption of goods and utility in a mathematical relationship known as a **utility function.** We can write a utility function for a person named Aldo on a given day as

$$\text{Utility}_{Aldo} = U_{Aldo} (\overset{+}{\text{\# of tomatoes}}, \overset{+}{\text{\# of VCRs}}, \overset{+}{\text{\# of basketball shoes}},$$

$$\overset{+}{\text{lb of clean air}}, \overset{+}{\text{\# of charitable deeds}}, \overset{+}{\text{\# of mountaintop views}} \ldots)$$

where the . . . indicates all the other items Aldo consumes over the course of the day and the +s indicate that Aldo's utility rises as he consumes these goods. Another way to present Aldo's utility function is to compress all the goods he consumes into a consumption bundle, labeled X_A (the A is for Aldo), and write $\text{Utility}_A = U_A(X_A)$.

Now, the production of many of the market goods in his consumption bundle, X_A, also creates pollution, which Aldo doesn't like. So let us break out one element from Aldo's consumption bundle—P_A, the pollution to which Aldo is exposed. We can now write Aldo's utility function as $\text{Utility}_A = U_A(\overset{+}{X_A}, \overset{-}{P}_A)$, where the "–" above the pollution variable reminds us that Aldo's utility declines as his exposure to pollution increases.

This utility function illustrates a key assumption underlying most economic approaches to environmental issues: A fundamental trade-off for human happiness exists between increased material consumption (economic growth) and environmental quality. Whenever P_A goes down (the environment is cleaned up), X_A goes down too (other consumption falls), and vice versa. Put another way, the opportunity cost of environmental cleanup is assumed to be slower growth in the output of market goods.

One additional assumption about this utility–consumption relationship is often made: **More is better.** That is, Aldo is always happier when given more stuff. This may seem implausible. Why should Aldo want more than one ice cream cone if he is already full? The standard reply is, give it to a friend (which would make Aldo happy), or sell it and use the money to buy something he wants.

As we shall see, the "more is better" assumption is a crucial one. On the one hand, it provides substantial power to proponents of the efficiency standard. On the other hand, proponents of a safety standard argue that it incorrectly builds in a "bias" toward economic growth—ignoring the additional pollution it creates. Under the more is better assumption, growth *by definition* increases human happiness.

We will devote Chapter 11 of this book to a careful examination of this assumption. To the extent that more is *not* better, utilitarian arguments for protecting the environment at the expense of consumption growth become much stronger.

To summarize this section: In answer to the first question of what makes people happy, utilitarians argue consumption of market and nonmarket goods. The happiness trade-off between consumption and environmental quality can be conveniently expressed in the form of a utility function. A second and more controversial assumption often made is that, from the individual perspective, more of any such good always increases happiness. With this answer in hand, we can now move on to the second question facing utilitarians: "How does one add up individual happiness into social happiness?"

2.2 Social Welfare

If increases in consumption of both market and nonmarket goods make *individuals* happy, does this also mean that increases in individual consumption increase the overall welfare of a *society*? Answering this question involves incorporating issues of fairness and rights. How does one weigh a reduction in the happiness of one individual against an increase in the happiness of another? To make explicit their assumptions about fairness, economists often specify a **social welfare function,** which determines a "desirable" way of adding up individual utilities. In a society including Rachel (*R*), John (*J*), and many others (. . .), we can write:

$$SW = f(\overset{+}{U_R}(\overset{+}{X_R}, \overset{-}{P_R}), \overset{+}{U_J}(\overset{+}{X_J}, \overset{-}{P_J}), \ldots)$$

where again, the +s indicate that social welfare rises as each individual gets happier.

One commonly used social welfare function is just the sum of individual utilities:

$$SW = \overset{+}{U_R}(\overset{+}{X_R}, \overset{-}{P_R}) + \overset{+}{U_J}(\overset{+}{X_J}, \overset{-}{P_J}) + \ldots \qquad (1)$$

The original nineteenth-century utilitarians believed this to be the correct form, arguing that the "greatest good for the greatest number" should be the guiding principle for public policy. They thought that to implement such a policy would require measuring utility in a precise way, and they devised elaborate methods for comparing the relative happiness derived from consumption by different individuals.

Unlike classical utilitarians, modern economists do not rely on direct measurements of utility. However, to determine the "correct" level of pollution from a social welfare perspective, we do need to weigh one person's consumption against another's. One social judgment we might make is that *additions* to consumption are valued equally by individuals. This is called an assumption of **equal marginal utility of consumption,** and it allows us to weigh the welfare impact of changes in patterns of consumption directly. For example, under this assumption, if your income goes up by a dollar and mine goes down by a dollar, social welfare will remain unchanged.[2]

Given this assumption and the specification of the social welfare function in equation (1), *increases* in each person's happiness receive equal weight—social welfare goes up at the same rate when the utility of either a millionaire (John) or a street person (Rachel) rises. In fact, social welfare could potentially rise as millionaire John was made better off at street person Rachel's expense! When utility is simply added up, no allowance is made in the social welfare function for issues of fairness in the distribution of income among those alive today.

Social welfare function (1) also provides no special protection for the well-being of future generations; under the simple adding-up specification, social welfare might rise if the current generation went on a consumption binge at the expense of our descendants. This would be true, provided that the increase in consumption today more than offset the decrease in consumption tomorrow.

Finally, social welfare function (1) also assumes that pollution victims have no special rights. If, for example, Rachel lives downwind from John's steel factory and, as a result, suffers health damages of, let us say, $25 per day, this reduction in social welfare would be strictly offset by a gain in John's profits of $25. Equation (1) is thus "blind" to the distribution of the costs and benefits of economic events within the current generation, across generations, and between pollution victims and beneficiaries. All that matters for boosting social welfare is increasing net consumption of *both* market and nonmarket goods, regardless of who wins and who loses.

Equation (1) is in fact the "adding up" mechanism underlying an **efficiency standard** for pollution control. Under an efficiency standard, the idea is to maximize the **net benefits** (benefits minus costs) of economic growth, by carefully weighing the benefits (more consumption) against the costs (pollution and resource degradation). This is done without reference to who bears the costs or gains the benefits.

How can such a position be ethically defended? While pollution certainly imposes costs on certain individuals, efficiency advocates maintain that, over time, *most people will benefit* if the net consumption benefits from pollution control are maximized. Put in simple terms, lower prices of consumer goods for the vast majority (including necessities like food and energy) must be strictly balanced against protection of environmental quality and health.

---

[2]The assumption of equal marginal utilities of consumption within the relevant range is implicit behind the efficiency standard. See Kneese and Schulze (1985). The presentation through equation (2) follows Varian (1987). However, in the interests of clarity, I keep the "utility functions" constant across the equations and incorporate "weights" within the utility functions to illustrate changes in the underlying assumptions. One could also express the sustainability SW function as an unweighted sum subject to the constraint that the utility of the average future person is no less than that of the average current person.

The "blind" approach that efficiency supporters take toward the distribution of costs and benefits provides one extreme. By contrast, if Rachel is impoverished, we might assume that her marginal utility of income is *greater than* that of John; one dollar increases Rachel's happiness more than it increases John's. Then, in the interests of social well-being we might well want to weigh increases in Rachel's consumption more heavily than those of the affluent.[3]

In practice, the strict efficiency standard for pollution control is often modified to include "fairness weights" in the social welfare function. In particular, as we discuss further in Chapters 6 and 7, a concern for fairness to future generations is often incorporated. For example, we might wish to employ a **sustainability rule** that says social welfare does not rise if increases in consumption today come at the expense of the welfare of our children. Suppose that Rachel (now an "average" person) is not yet born, while John (also an "average" person) is alive today. Then our sustainable social welfare function would be written:

$$SW = w * \overset{+}{U_R}(\overset{+}{X_R}, \overset{-}{P_R}) + \overset{}{U_J}(\overset{+}{X_J}, \overset{-}{P_J}) + \ldots \tag{2}$$

where w is a weighting number big enough to insure that increases in John's consumption do not substantially penalize Rachel. Here, and unlike in equation (1), increases in happiness for the average individual today cannot come at the expense of future generations.

Finally, bring Rachel back to the present, living downwind from John's steel factory. She is now exposed to air pollution, P_R. She consumes this pollution, but recall that it is an economic "bad" and so enters her utility function with a negative sign. Proponents of a **safety standard** will argue that in the interests of personal liberty, Rachel has a *right* to protection from unsolicited damage to her health. As a result they will weight very heavily the negative effect of pollution in her utility function:[4]

$$SW = \overset{+}{U_R}(\overset{+}{X_R}, \overset{-}{w^*P_R}) + \overset{+}{U_J}(X_J) + \ldots \tag{3}$$

Now, social welfare rises substantially less with the production of steel than it does with less-polluting commodities. An extreme safety advocate, by choosing such a large value for the weighting number w, would essentially refuse to balance the benefits of the polluting steel process (cheaper steel, and all the products that steel contains) against the harmful impact of pollution.

The latter two specifications of the social welfare function—sustainability and safety—imply that a happy society is more than just the sum of its parts. Fairness criteria based on income distribution (both within and between generations) and personal liberty must be met as well. (When the more is better assumption is relaxed later

---

[3]This in fact is the classical utilitarian argument for income redistribution. Rawls (1971) provides a contractual argument in favor of weighting the consumption of the least well off.

[4]Equation (3) is a crude way of representing philosopher John Rawls' (1971, 61) lexicographic preference ordering that puts liberty of the person above material consumption. Kneese and Schulze (1985) specify the libertarian position as a decision rule requiring an actual Pareto improvement from any proposed social policy.

in the book, we will add yet another layer of complexity: Because my happiness from consumption depends on your level of consumption in a variety of ways, happiness will depend on *relative* rather than absolute levels of material welfare. As a result, in order to correctly specify social welfare, certain "noncompetitive" consumption items such as environmental health will also be weighted in the social welfare function.)

This section has illustrated three different forms for a social welfare function—efficiency, sustainability, and safety—each specifying how individual utility might be added up to equal social well-being. While these different social welfare functions may seem arbitrary, proponents of each will argue that, in fact, their vision reflects the "dominant viewpoint" in our society about the proper relationship between material consumption and social welfare.[5] Social welfare functions have the advantage of forcing advocates of utilitarian policies to precisely state and defend both their basic assumptions and the logic by which they reach their conclusions. As we proceed in this first part of the book, we shall see that the different pollution standards are defended ethically by making different assumptions about the proper form of both the utility and social welfare functions.

2.3 Summary

This chapter has provided an introductory discussion of the ethical foundations of economics. Economists maintain as a basic assumption that increases in material consumption of both market and nonmarket goods—including clean air and water—increase individual utility. Whether growth in material consumption, independent of fairness and rights, necessarily leads to an overall increase in *social* welfare depends on the form that is specified for the social welfare function. There is no "correct" social welfare function. But economists use social welfare functions to help clarify normative debates, including the one that concerns us: "How much pollution is too much?"

Three positions are often staked out in economic discussions regarding environmental protection. First, there are those who argue for a careful weighing of costs and benefits, with no attention paid to the distribution of those costs and benefits. This is an efficiency position. Second, there are safety standard supporters, who maintain that people have a right to have their health protected from environmental damage, regardless of the cost.

The third position is sustainability, which argues for protecting the welfare of future generations. While the sustainability criterion is easy to state, we will find that there is much debate about what sustainability means in practice. This is because future generations are affected by our current decisions in complex ways. For example, will our grandchildren be better off if we leave them oil in the ground, or if we exploit the oil deposits and invest the profits in developing new forms of energy? The answer to this question is not obvious.

---

[5]Arrow (1963) has analyzed the difficulties in democratically determining a social welfare function.

Insofar as the debate about resources and the environment focuses on the welfare of people, it remains a utilitarian one and in the realm of economics. Again, this is not to downplay the importance of noneconomic ethical views about the environment. However, the economic approach asks us to think clearly about the ways in which nature serves our social needs. By examining the ethical foundations of different views about the appropriate level of pollution, we can develop a better notion of why it is that we support either a modest or an aggressive position on slowing global warming.

APPLICATION 2.0

Social Welfare and Landfill Regulation

The U.S. Environmental Protection Agency issues regulations covering the design and construction of landfills for municipal solid waste. Landfills can represent a threat to environmental health if toxic chemicals leach from the waste into surrounding ground or surface waters.

The current regulations require certain design, construction, and maintenance standards extending beyond the post-closure period, including, in most cases, installation of impermeable liners and covers and groundwater monitoring. The purpose of the regulations is to insure safe containment of solid waste and to prevent future generations from having to bear cleanup costs from poorly disposed waste. (For more on the landfill issue, see Chapter 10.)

Even with the regulations, just under 10% of new landfills still pose what the EPA considers to be a "moderate" health risk for individuals who depend on contaminated groundwater: a greater than 1 in 1 million increase in the risk of contracting cancer. However, because so few people actually depend on groundwater within leaching distance of a landfill, the current regulations are predicted to reduce cancer by only two or three cases over the next 300 years. Potential benefits of the regulation not quantified by the EPA include increased ease of siting landfills, reduced damage to surface water, fairness to future generations, and an overall reduction in waste generation and related "upstream" pollution encouraged by higher disposal costs.

In aggregate, the regulations are expensive: about $5.8 billion, or around $2 billion per cancer case reduced. On a per household basis, this works out to an annual cost of $4.10 in increased garbage bills over the twenty-year life of a landfill.

1. Using the concept of social welfare represented respectively by equations (1) and (3), explain why the EPA's landfill regulation is (a) too strict and (b) not strict enough.

KEY IDEAS IN EACH SECTION

2.0 **Normative** questions ask what *should* be rather than what is. Economic analysis of normative issues proceeds by clearly stating underlying ethical assumptions.

2.1 The ethical foundation of economics is **utilitarianism,** a philosophy in which environmental cleanup is important solely for the happiness (utility) that it brings to people alive today and in the future. This philosophy is contrasted with an **environmental**

ethic, which values nature for its own sake. Economists assume that consumption of both **market goods** and **nonmarket goods** makes people happy. This relationship can be expressed in a **utility function,** with pollution entering as a negative consumption element. A utility function assumes a fundamental trade-off between growth in consumption and improvements in environmental quality. Economists often make one further key assumption about the consumption–utility relationship: **More is better.**

2.2 To add up individual utility, economists use a **social welfare function.** In such a function, one might assume **equal marginal utility of consumption** so that social welfare is just the sum of individual happiness, regardless of the distribution of benefits within a generation, across generations, or between victims and polluters. This SW function underlies the **efficiency standard,** which seeks to maximize the **net benefits** from steps taken to protect the environment. Alternatively, one might want to weight the consumption of poor people more heavily than rich people, victims more heavily than polluters (**safety standard**), or adopt a **sustainability rule** insuring that consumption today does not come at the expense of future generations. No social welfare function is "correct"; their use helps clarify underlying assumptions in normative debates over the right level of pollution.

REFERENCES

Arrow, Kenneth. 1963. *Social Choice and Individual Values.* New York: John Wiley.

Brown, Paul. 1998. "Towards an Economics of Stewardship, the Case of Climate," *Ecological Economics,* 26, no. 1:11–22.

Kneese, Alan V., and William D. Schulze. 1985. "Ethics and Environmental Economics." In *Handbook of Natural Resource Economics,* vol. 1, edited by A. V. Kneese and J. L. Sweeney. New York: Elsevier.

Leopold, Aldo. 1966. *A Sand County Almanac.* New York: Oxford University Press.

Nash, Roderick Frazier. 1989. *The Rights of Nature.* WI: University of Wisconsin Press.

Rawls, John. 1971. *A Theory of Justice.* Cambridge, MA: Harvard University Press.

Sagoff, Mark. 1995. "Carrying Capacity and Ecological Economics." *Bioscience* 45, no. 9, 610–619.

Varian, H. 1987. *Intermediate Microeconomics.* New York: W. W. Norton.

Walras, Leon. 1954. *Elements of Pure Economics.* Homewood, IL: Irwin.

3

POLLUTION AND
RESOURCE DEGRADATION
AS EXTERNALITIES

3.0 Introduction

Any economy depends on the ecological system in which it is embedded in two funda-mental ways, illustrated in Figure 3.1. First, human production and consumption processes rely on the environment as a **source** of raw materials; second, they also exploit the environment as a **sink** for waste materials. Both sources and sinks form what econo-mists call natural capital. **Natural capital** is the input that nature provides for our pro-duction and consumption processes. Pollution is the overuse of sinks; resource degradation is the overharvesting of sources. In this sense, pollution and resource degra-dation are flip sides of the same process, the excessive exploitation of natural capital.

What exactly do we mean by pollution? Consider three examples:

1. Tyler is eating in a smoky restaurant. Is he exposed to pollution?
2. Karen routinely comes in contact with low-level radioactive waste while working at a nuclear power plant. Is she exposed to pollution?
3. Marilyn is trying to get some sleep while his neighbor Tipper blares the sound system. Is he exposed to pollution?

For the purposes of this book, the correct answers are maybe, maybe, and yes. Econo-mists define "pollution" as a **negative externality:** a cost of a transaction not borne by the buyer or seller. Pollution is termed an externality because it imposes costs on peo-ple who are "external" to the producer and consumer of the polluting product.

In the first case, what if Tyler is the one smoking? While the smoke is undeniably doing damage to Tyler's lungs, he may be aware of the damage and yet, balancing plea-sure against risk, does not consider himself worse off. The second "maybe" is more dif-ficult. Exposure to radioactive waste increases Karen's risk of cancer and is clearly a by-product of human activity. However, if she fully understands the risk to her health of

FIGURE 3.1 Natural Capital: Sources and Sinks

performing the job, and yet shoulders it in exchange for a salary, then exposure to the waste is part of the bargain. That is, the exposure is not external to the transaction between her and her employer. Under these circumstances Karen would face a serious *occupational hazard,* which needs regulation on its own terms, but not a pollutant as we have defined it.[1] Finally, poor Marilyn is a clear-cut pollution victim. He is involuntarily being exposed to a negative by-product of Tipper's listening experience.

From an economist's point of view, market systems generate pollution because many natural inputs into the production of goods and services—such as air and water—are "underpriced." Because no one owns these resources, in the absence of government regulation or legal protection for pollution victims, businesses will use them up freely, neglecting the external costs imposed on others. For example, suppose the Stinky Paper Co. discharges polluted water into a stream, which kills the fish that people enjoy eating downstream. If Stinky were forced to compensate the fisher people for the damages it imposed (**internalize the externality**), the firm would in effect be paying for the water it used up. Water would no longer be "underpriced." As a result, Stinky would conserve on its use of water and would seek out ways to clean up its discharge. This, in turn, would raise the production costs of the firm.

Figure 3.2 provides a simple supply-and-demand analysis of the situation and yields an immediate prediction. If all firms are forced to pay their full social costs of production, the competitive supply curve will shift up. The market price for paper will be higher, and the quantity sold will be lower. The diagram indicates a general principle: It is difficult to reduce pollution without also reducing the supply of the polluting product.

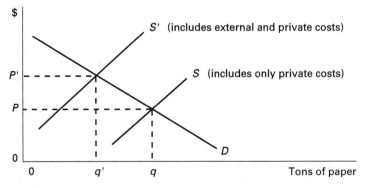

FIGURE 3.2 Social and Private Costs in the Paper Market

---

[1]These assertions require that Tyler and Karen *are indeed fully aware of the risks they face.*

Because the river water is commonly owned and is thus a "free" good, Stinky overexploits it, and the fisherfolk downstream are exposed to a negative externality of the paper production process. From an economic point of view, many pollution problems arise because environmental resources such as rivers are, by their nature, commonly owned. The rest of this chapter takes a closer look at the implications of this common ownership.

3.1 The Open Access Problem

Many forms of natural capital, both sources and sinks, are not (and cannot) be privately owned. Because of this, pure free-market systems will generate too much pollution (or resource degradation) by any of the standards considered in this book—efficiency, safety, or sustainability. There are two related reasons for this: The first is the **open access problem,** which often arises when natural capital is commonly held. The second, addressed in the next section, is the public goods problem. The open access problem can be stated simply: If people weigh private benefits against private (as opposed to social) costs, they will overexploit common resources when given open access.

This idea was popularized in the late 1960s by Garrett Hardin, who called it "The Tragedy of the Commons." He poses the problem facing a herder whose cattle forage on common land. Introducing one more cow onto the common grazing land would lead to a large private gain for this herder in the form of an additional animal available for sale or consumption. It would also lead to a small private loss, in that the degraded resource would provide less robust forage for the herder's existing animals. Of course the social cost would be much larger, given that most of the loss from the degraded rangeland is borne by other herders. But if the herder seeks to maximize his or her personal gain,

> the only sensible course for him to pursue is to add another animal to his herd. And another, and another. . . . Therein is the tragedy. Each man is *locked in* to a system that compels him to increase his herd without limit—in a world that is limited. Ruin is the destination toward which all men rush, each pursuing his own best interest in a society that believes in the freedom of the commons. (Hardin 1968, 1245)

Hardin suggests a stark and inescapable connection between common ownership of resources and their ultimate exhaustion. But, in fact, grazing and fishing grounds in most traditional societies have often been commonly held and managed quite sustainably for centuries. This was achieved by informal social constraints and traditions that prevented overexploitation. However, when such restraints break down as a result of "modernization" or population pressures, the open access problem emerges, and a tragedy of the commons is likely to result.[2]

The open access problem explains not only why sources of natural capital such as grazing land are degraded but also why environmental sinks like the air are polluted. For example, a factory owner might install a low-cost technology that generates substantial air pollution, in spite of the fact that he and his family live nearby and will be exposed to the toxic materials. The owner captures the full benefits of the pollution (the profit from "low-cost" production), while his family bears only a small portion of the total risk.

---

[2]See Bromley (1991) for a full discussion.

In combination with vastly more efficient technology, open access also explains the dramatic decline in populations of commercial fish species over the last few decades. Close to half of America's fisheries and more than 70% of global fisheries are over-fished; the North Atlantic is estimated to contain only one-third of the biomass of edible fish that were present in 1950. Modern technology in the form of bottom trawling is also damaging habitat, essentially clear-cutting, and not replanting, the ocean floor.

Fisheries off the New England coast have been particularly hard-hit. "The trawler catch in New England peaked in 1983 and has since fallen sharply. Stocks of flounder and haddock are at near record lows. The cod population is down. Bluefin tuna and swordfish have been depleted." But in spite of this situation, some fishers still oppose catch limits. "Straining to pay off mortgages on expensive boats, many fishermen say they don't have the luxury of *not* catching as much as they can as fast as they can."[3] Indeed, perversely, the incentive for any individual fisherperson is to employ more and more sophisticated technology to increase his or her share of a dwindling stock.

We can explore this overfishing issue further with the help of a hypothetical example. Suppose that fish cost a dollar a pound, and the marginal cost of running a vessel—including the fuel and salaries for crew and owner—is $250 per day. Then the rational response for fishing boats is to continue to fish as long as, on average, the catch exceeds 250 pounds. Suppose that the long-run relationship between the number of vessels and the total catch per day in a New England bay is illustrated in Figure 3.3. The catch level peaks at six boats, and after seven boats, drops off, reflecting fishing beyond a sustained yield level. If eight boats go out on a regular basis, then the breeding stock is harvested, and over time the population of fish declines.[4]

Given this information, consider the following Puzzle.

Number of vessels	Total catch (lb/day)
1	400
2	800
3	1200
4	1600
5	1900
6	2100
7	2100
8	2000

FIGURE 3.3 Vessels and Total Catch

[3]Quotes are from "Dead in the Water," *Wall Street Journal,* July 18, 1991. Data on global catch is from Helvarg (2003).

[4]This model is based on Gordon (1954). Professor Laurie Johnson at Denver University has developed a terrific in-class game to accompany this problem. To receive instructions, contact her at lauriejo@du.edu.

PUZZLE

Part 1. If there were open access to the bay and seven boats were already fishing, would you fish in the bay?

Part 2. If you ran the government fisheries board, how many boats would you allow out if you wanted to maximize total profits from the bay?

SOLUTION

Part 1. The revenue for the eighth boat is $1 times the average catch of 250 pounds, or $250. You'd earn a day's salary and cover costs if you went out, so it is worth it.

Part 2. Six is a common guess but it is incorrect. Six maximizes *revenue,* but profit is revenue minus cost. Table 3.1 puts together some additional information to help answer this part. Note that Table 3.1 changes the focus from total revenues and *total* costs, to *marginal* revenues and *marginal* costs—the addition to revenue and cost from sending out each additional boat.

To maximize the profit from the New England bay, additional boats should be sent out up to the point where the value of the addition to the total catch just exceeds the opportunity cost of sending out the boat. The fisheries board would stop at five boats, since the sixth would bring in only $200 in marginal revenue, less than enough to cover its costs of $250. The final column labeled marginal profit (the extra profit from each additional boat) makes this clear: After five boats, losses begin to accumulate.

TABLE 3.1 Calculating the Profit-Maximizing Harvest

Number of Vessels	Total Catch	Marginal Catch	Marginal Revenue	Average Catch	Average Revenue	Marginal Profit
1	400 lb	400 lb	$400	400 lb	$400	+$150
2	800	400	400	400	400	+150
3	1,200	400	400	400	400	+150
4	1,600	400	400	400	400	+150
5	1,900	300	300	380	380	+50
6	2,100	200	200	350	350	−50
7	2,100	0	000	300	300	−250
8	2,000	−100	−100	250	250	−350

Note that in addition to overfishing the resource, there is a second externality here. After four boats, some of the catch of the new entrants is *diverted from other boats.* When there is open access to the bay, however, individual fisherpeople don't recognize (but more importantly don't care) about these negative externalities imposed on the other boats; each bears only a small portion of the reduction in the total stock. Thus, boats continue to go out even when the total catch, and total revenue in the industry, declines. As a result of open access, in New England, a human and ecological tragedy is indeed unfolding.

Figure 3.4 develops a graphical analysis of the open access problem. Marginal revenue first stays constant and then falls, reflecting eventual declining marginal productivity as additional boats go out. Notice that the average and marginal revenue curves coincide up to four boats, but once declining marginal productivity kicks in, the marginal revenue curve lies below the average revenue curve. (This is due to the mathematical relationship between marginal and average values: As long as the addition to revenue equals the average revenue, the average stays constant and equal to the marginal value. However, when additions to revenue fall below the average, the average is pulled down.) Finally the constant marginal cost of sending out additional boats is represented by the straight line at $250.

Again, the figure tells us that private boats will go out as long as *average* revenue covers costs, even though the total profits earned in the industry are declining. Open access leads eight boats into the fishery. By contrast, the profit-maximizing catch level occurs where *marginal* revenue just exceeds marginal costs at five boats.

The profit earned in the industry is displayed visually as the sum total of the difference between marginal revenue and marginal cost for each boat that goes out—the light gray area in the diagram.[5] The dark gray area in the picture shows the *reduction in profit* for the industry as a result of overfishing. For the sixth through eighth boats, the marginal revenue is *less than* the marginal cost, leading to a drop in industry-wide profits. Clearly, the total industry-wide profit is largest at five boats.

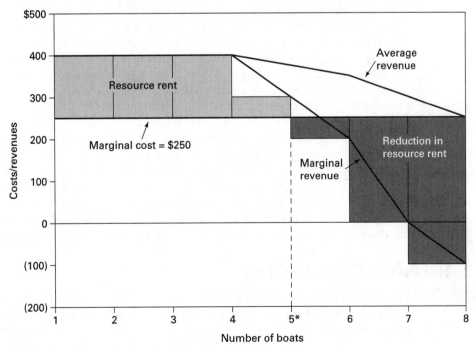

FIGURE 3.4 The Open Access Problem

---

[5]Technically, this is not profit but producer surplus, because the example ignores fixed costs. The language is chosen for ease of exposition.

In Chapter 2 we learned that an efficient outcome is one in which the net benefits produced by the economy are maximized. Here, the efficient number of boats is five. This is true since in this example, where the price of fish (and thus the consumer) is unaffected by the small changes in supply, net social benefits are just equal to profits.

The picture also illustrates a key feature of markets that rely on scarce natural capital either as sources or sinks. *When natural capital is used efficiently, long-run economic profits will be earned by those who retain access to the resource.* It is precisely those profits that attract entry into the market and lead to overexploitation of the source or the sink. These long-run profits, generated by restricted access to natural capital, are called **resource rents.** Comparable to rents earned by landlords at choice properties, these are rents due to ownership of (or limited access to) scarce natural resources.

In our example, open access into the fishery leads to an outcome in which profits in the industry are competed completely away. With eight boats, average revenue equals average cost, and all the boats just break even. But at the efficient level, where marginal revenue equals marginal cost, a substantial resource rent is earned. Adding up the difference between marginal revenue and marginal cost (marginal profit) for the first five boats, the resource rent turns out to be $650 per day.

In the New England case, economist Steven Edwards and biologist Steven Murawski estimated that fishing efforts off of the New England coast would have to be reduced by about 70% to eliminate overfishing and achieve an efficient harvest. This in turn would generate a resource rent in the industry of about $130 million (Tregarten 1992). The rent might go to the government in the form of fees for fishing rights or to the remaining fishermen and women in the form of profits. Edwards calculates that government revenues from a fee system would be sufficient to compensate those boats out of business due to restrictions, suggesting a politically feasible way out of this tough problem.

Fisherpeople in New England often resent governmental restrictions placed on access to fishing grounds; it is, after all, their livelihood and lifestyle at stake. However, without some kind of restraint on open access to common property resources, overuse to the point of exhaustion is the predictable consequence.

This section has illustrated three main points. First, when there is open access to common property, overexploitation will generally result since users will not take the externality costs of their actions into account. Second, government-imposed restraints on access to common property such as fisheries, clean air, and clean water will generate a resource rent, or long-run economic profit, for those who maintain access. Finally, this rent can sometimes be collected through taxes or fees and be used to reimburse those who lose out in the process of regulating and reducing access.

3.2 The Public Goods Problem

The open access problem may explain why there is a tendency for commonly held resources such as clean air and water or fisheries to be overexploited. But why does the government have to decide what to do about it? Instead, why don't the victims of negative externalities simply band together on their own to prevent pollution or overexploitation of resources? As we just noted, this was the response to environmental degradation of common grazing and fishing grounds in traditional societies. Informal social pressure and tradition were relied on to prevent overexploitation. The modern American equivalent would be to sue an offending company or individual for damages. Indeed, a few so-called

free-market environmentalists have advocated eliminating many environmental regulations, then relying on lawsuits by injured parties to "internalize" externalities.[6]

However, such private remedies to environmental degradation run into what economists call the **public goods problem.** Public goods are goods enjoyed in common; a classic example, though a little dated, is the warning service provided by a lighthouse. Technically, economists describe public goods as "non-excludable." Once in operation, it is impossible to exclude any passing boat from utilizing the warning beacon provided by the lighthouse.[7]

The provision of public goods is a problem for the free market due to the existence of two factors: transactions costs and free riding. To illustrate, consider a good that is enjoyed in common such as, for example, the noise level after 11 PM in Marilyn's neighborhood. Now suppose that neighbor Tipper cranks her sound system. Marilyn could go to the considerable trouble of obtaining signatures from all of his neighbors, getting money from them to hire a lawyer, filing a lawsuit, and possibly obtaining a legal injunction requiring Tipper to turn it down. The costs of undertaking this action are known as **transactions costs,** and they are particularly high because of the public nature of the injury.

If Marilyn does undertake the effort, he will benefit not only himself but also the entire neighborhood. Some of the neighbors might refuse to help out and instead **free ride** on Marilyn's provision of the public good. Instead, Marilyn decides it's not really worth organizing a lawsuit and tosses and turns in bed, hoping that someone else will make the effort. The result is that the demand for a quiet evening in the neighborhood, although it may be considerable, doesn't get expressed. It is not worth it to any one individual to overcome the transactions costs and the possibility of free riding to provide the public good of the lawsuit, although if Marilyn did, the social benefits might far outweigh the cost.

In most towns, the response to noise pollution is a government regulation called a nuisance law. With such a regulation in place, Marilyn can just call the cops, greatly reducing the costs associated with stopping the noise. The general principle is that without government intervention, public goods—in this case, a quiet evening—will be undersupplied. This is not to say that no public goods will be supplied. Some will, but less than the amount that society collectively is willing to pay for.

To see this, consider another example: private contributions to purchase and preserve wetlands and other valuable ecosystems in the United States. The organization, The Nature Conservancy, currently solicits funds to do this. Suppose such an organization sends a mailing to Mr. Peabody and Mr. Massey saying it needs $50 per foot to preserve the last 100 feet of a prime Appalachian trout stream. Now Peabody would be willing to pay $30 and Massey $40 toward the effort, for a total of $70 per foot. Thus, the monetary benefits of preservation exceed the costs by $20 per foot.

PUZZLE

Will The Nature Conservancy get enough in contributions to buy the land?

---

[6]See the introductory and concluding essays in Greve and Smith (1992).

[7]Pure public goods also have another characteristic: They are non-rival. This means that the one boat's use of the lighthouse service does not reduce the value of that service to others.

SOLUTION

Not necessarily. Peabody, figuring Massey will pay $40 per foot, may contribute only $10, while Massey, following the same logic, will contribute only $20, for a total of $30 per foot. As a result, each will try to free ride off the other's provision of the 100 feet of public good and sufficient funds will not be forthcoming.

We can approach this problem graphically, by examining the difference between the demand curve for a public good and a more conventional private good. In Figure 3.5A, let us assume that the trout stream is for sale to private individuals. Note that, for 100 feet of land, as above, Peabody would pay $30 per foot and Massey $40, but now they do not have to share it. As you may recall from a previous course, the demand curve for a private good is the horizontal sum of the individual demand curves. At a price of $30, Peabody demands 100 feet while Massey demands 120 feet, so total demand equals 100 + 120, or 220 feet. In a market for private goods, consumers face a single price, and each individual consumes as much as he or she wants to buy. Thus, total demand is met.

By contrast, when goods are public, all consumers face a given public quantity and must decide how much to pay. In Figure 3.5B, the trout stream has become a public good; Massey and Peabody must share whatever is purchased. For 100 feet of land, we know their collective value is $70 per foot; following this logic we can see that their total willingness to pay (or their demand) for any given amount of preservation is the *vertical* sum of the individual demand curves.

The true total demand for public goods is seldom expressed in the market for two reasons. First, unlike the case for private goods, some third party must organize the collection of funds to pay for the public good or to initiate a lawsuit against a polluter. Marilyn would have to drag himself out of bed and go collect signatures on a petition

A: Private Good

B: Public Good

FIGURE 3.5 Demand for Private and Public Goods

from the neighbors to convince a judge to tell Tipper to be quiet. More generally, there may be large costs associated with proving highly contestable environmental damages in a court of law. The need to support such efforts raises the *transactions costs*—the costs associated with making a market deal—for public goods.

Second, in the case of public goods, individuals have an incentive to *free ride* on the efforts of others. Though Massey and Peabody collectively value the land at more than its asking price, they may be unwilling to reveal their true preferences to a private agency or government collecting revenues to pay for the public good. Incentives to free ride are often dampened in small groups, where an individual can see his or her individual effort as "pivotal" to the success of the public effort, and/or a sense of group responsibility is carried by the members.[8] However, such conditions are unlikely to hold for most pollution control efforts, making free riding a serious obstacle for nongovernmental attempts to provide such goods.

To summarize this section, in contrast to private goods, public goods are consumed in common. The true demand for public goods will not be satisfied in pure market economies due to high transactions costs and free riding. Free-market environmentalists who advocate relying solely on the court system to internalize environmental externalities recognize these twin hurdles. Yet they believe these obstacles are not really that large, especially considering the costs associated with regulation. Most economists, however, argue that as a result of transactions costs and free riding, public goods such as clean air or water, rain forests, wilderness parks, and other environmental amenities, will be undersupplied in a laissez-faire market system.[9]

3.3 Summary

In this chapter we have analyzed two different aspects of communal property that contribute to the degradation of the environment. First, the open access problem explains why individuals would knowingly damage a resource upon which they depend. Second, the public goods problem explains, in part, why people cannot "buy" a clean environment, either by suing polluters or purchasing wilderness. Transactions costs are high, and there is a tendency for people to free ride on the efforts of others.

The point is that free-market forces do not provide the right incentives to insure that adequate care is taken to protect our environment. Given this, what should our response be? As we have noted, a few have argued that externalities can be adequately internalized by means of private lawsuits. A second, more common response, which we will examine in Chapters 18 through 20, is the call for development of more environmentally benign "clean" technologies that reduce pollution problems in the first place. However, the conventional response has been government regulation of pollution, which brings us back to our principal topic: How much is too much?

---

[8]See the review discussion in Mitchell and Carson (1989).

[9]Using the legal system to resolve externalities also involves very large administrative and transactions costs. For a general review of the economics of liability, see the symposium in the *Journal of Economic Perspectives,* 5, no. 3, Winter 1991, especially the article by Menell (1991).

APPLICATION 3.0

Getting Government Out of Pollution Control?

An article in the business magazine *Forbes* blasts the U.S. Environmental Protection Agency for implementing ineffectual, expensive, and corrupt policies: "U.S. environmental policy is out of control, costing jobs, depressing living standards and being run by politicians, scheming business people and social extremists" (Brimelow and Spencer 1992, 67). (I was actually not too surprised to find that politicians were running environmental policy, since that is, after all, part of the job they were elected to do.) Luckily, however, the article had a suggestion for eliminating our cumbersome pollution control bureaucracy:

> There is an environmental policy suited to the American Way: The development of property rights and the common law of tort. The threat of litigation will discourage pollution, with the details worked out between private parties. For example, neighbors could use "nuisance law" to sue a malodorous factory.
>
> Law students are taught in Environmental Law 101 that this approach didn't work, just as economics students are taught about "market failure"— the solution in both cases being government intervention. But modern scholarship suggests that the common law was indeed working until government intervened. (67)

The *Forbes* article went on to cite Greve and Smith (1992) as a source of this "modern scholarship" that advocates free-market environmentalism.

1. Although the term "market failure" was not used in this chapter, we did indeed identify such a beast in the form of the public goods problem. And most economists do maintain that resolving pollution problems privately through lawsuits will result in too much pollution. Explain the two reasons why.

APPLICATION 3.1

The Open Access Problem

Surrounding the Great Lake are four paper mills, each producing 100 tons of paper per year. The paper is sold on the national market for $2 per ton, and including all the costs of production, costs for each firm are $1 per ton. Thus each firm earns a pure economic profit of $1 per ton. These paper mills require fresh water to operate and also produce a pollutant called gunk, which the mills dump into the Great Lake.

New paper mills can also locate on the Great Lake and produce at a base cost of $1 per ton. However, for each new paper mill that arrives, the water will become more polluted with gunk, and each firm will have to install a water treatment facility to obtain freshwater. This externality associated with new plants will raise the costs of paper production at all facilities, including the new one, by $0.15 per ton for each new mill.

1. Assume there is open access to the Great Lake. If paper mills will continue to locate as long as there is any economic profit to be earned, how many new mills will be built? How many mills maximize total combined profits for the

paper producers? (Hint: Average revenue remains constant at $2. Create a table that compares average revenues with average and marginal costs as new firms locate around the lake.)

2. Draw a diagram of the marginal cost and marginal revenue curves with the number of mills on the horizontal axis. Assume that government regulation restricts lake access to the profit-maximizing number of firms. Show the resource rent earned by the mills that are allowed to operate.

3. Suppose that government regulation reduced the number of mills by one from the number that would have resulted given open access. Show that the increase in profits to the remaining firms (the resource rent) is sufficient to compensate the firm denied access for its lost profits.

KEY IDEAS IN EACH SECTION

3.0   **Natural capital** is the input that nature provides for our production and consumption processes. Pollution is the overuse of **sinks;** resource degradation is the overharvesting of **sources. A negative externality** is a cost of a transaction not borne by the buyer or seller. **Internalizing an externality** means forcing the source of the externality to bear the external costs imposed on others.

3.1   Negative externalities arise when there is **open access** to **common property** sources and sinks, such as air, water, or land. Traditional societies regulated access to common environmental resources using informal laws and restraints, but many of these have broken down. When access to natural capital is restricted, by either government action or private ownership, a **resource rent** is earned by those who retain access.

3.2   Is government regulation of the environment necessary to solve the open access problem? **Free-market environmentalists** believe polluters should be left unregulated and victims should sue to insure environmental quality. However, most economists argue that because a clean environment is a **public good,** the obstacles of high **transactions costs** and **free riding** mean that private negotiation in the courts would be inefficient (and also unsafe and unsustainable). Thus, government regulation is needed to internalize environmental externalities.

REFERENCES

Brimelow, Peter, and Leslie Spencer. 1992. "You Can't Get There from Here." *Forbes,* 6 July.

Bromley, Daniel. 1991. *Environment and Economy: Property Rights and Public Policy.* Cambridge, MA: Blackwell.

Gordon, H. 1954. "The Economic Theory of a Common Property Resource: The Fishery." *Journal of Political Economy* 62, no. 2:124–142.

Greve, Michael S., and Fred L. Smith. 1992. *Environmental Politics: Public Costs, Private Rewards.* Boulder, CO: Praeger.

Hardin, Garrett. 1968. "The Tragedy of the Commons." *Science* 168, 13 December.

Helvarg, David. 2003. "The Last Fish." *Earth Island Journal* 18, no. 1:26–30.

Menell, Peter S. 1991. "The Limitations of Legal Institutions for Addressing Environmental Risks." *Journal of Economic Perspectives* 5, no. 3:93–114.

Mitchell, Robert C., and Richard T. Carson. 1989. *Using Surveys to Value Public Goods.* Washington, DC: Resources for the Future.

Tregarten, Timothy. 1992. "Fishermen Find Fewer Fish." *The Margin* 7, Spring.

APPENDIX 3A

Overfishing, ITQs, and Aquaculture

3A.0 Modelling and Fishery

Fisheries are perhaps the most "tragic" of modern open access resources. Around the globe, common fishing grounds are being depleted at a dramatic pace. This appendix more closely examines the fishing model we developed in the chapter, policy tools to address overfishing, and the development of aquaculture (fish-farming) as a substitute for open-access harvesting.

First, the model. Figure 3A.1 is a generic diagram relating fishing effort to catch levels. The curve graphs the same relationship as the curve in Figure 3.3: average annual fishing effort (number of boats) versus the value of the average annual catch. The point at which the curve begins to bend downwards is considered the **maximum sustained yield.** If more than B^S boats head out in year 1, then the catch will be increased this year, but reduced next year, leading to a net decline in harvest. At the maximum sustained yield, the fishers will in fact be catching the equivalent of just the growth in the fish stock, leaving the breeding stock at its optimal size for the given resource base.

Figure 3A.1 also includes the total cost line. As in the chapter example, we assume that each additional boat adds a constant marginal cost to the total, so total costs increase at a constant rate. The efficient fishing level—the one that maximizes resource rent—occurs at B^*. Why? Because here, the total revenue (R^*) exceeds total costs (TC^*) by the greatest amount. Either a regulator or a private owner of the fishery would restrict access to the fishery to B^* boats. Note that B^* occurs

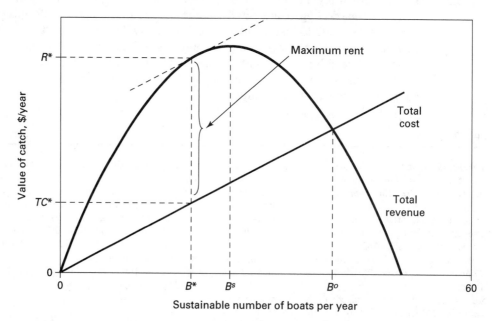

FIGURE 3A.1 Fishing Yields: Efficient, Sustainable, and Open Access

where the total revenue curve has the same slope as the total cost curve. To the left of B^*, the slope of the revenue curve is steeper than the total cost curve, indicating that the distance between the two (the resource rent) is growing. To the right of B^*, the slope of the revenue curve is flatter than the total cost curve, meaning that the gap between the two is shrinking. Thus resource rents are maximized where the slopes are equal.[1] And given the shape of the curves, one can see that, in this static model, an efficient outcome will never lead to over-fishing. Rents are always bigger on the left side of the maximum sustained yield point.

Note that at B^o, total revenue and total costs are equal—so all the resource rents have been competed away. This is the open access outcome we identified in the text, and it can easily occur beyond the point of a maximum sustained yield (although it does not have to, depending on the slope of the total cost curve—check this for yourself). This model thus illustrates that open access leads to overfishing.

At this point, we want to add in a dynamic wrinkle, one that we consider in much more detail in Chapter 6. It turns out that open access is not the only reason that fisheries might be overexploited from a biological point of view. The second has to do with the time value of money. Put simply, even a monopolist might choose to liquidate a private fishery if she could invest the resource rents generated from fish harvests more productively elsewhere.

Figure 3A.2 sets up this possibility for a privately owned fishing ground, and reproduces 3.A1 for a specific case: the maximum sustained yield is 1,250 pounds of fish for 25 days of effort. Fishing costs 10 extra dollars per day, so total costs rise at that constant rate. The efficient production level occurs at 21 fishing days, and at $1 a pound the resource rent is about $1,000. By contrast, Figure 3A.3 illustrates an alternative to sustainable harvesting. It shows the *maximum possible* harvest in year 1, a harvest which effectively destroys the resource for future use. Here, a maximum rent of close to $10,000 can be earned on 85 days of effort. (Note that the fish are not driven all the way to extinction: the productivity of the last days of effort drops due to the scarcity of fish, so it is not worth the extra costs of $10 per day to catch and sell the very last few pounds).

The fishery owner has a choice: a flow of $1,000 forever from the fishery, or $10,000 today. Which option yields the greatest profit? The answer to this question depends on the rate of interest the fisher could get on that $10,000. If it were, say 11%, then she could put the $10,000 in the bank and earn a flow of profits equal to $1,100 per year, forever. On the other hand, if the going interest rate were only 9%, then the fisher would earn only $900 per year after liquidating her fishery, and so maintaining the harvest at a sustainable yield level is a better investment. This example illustrates that the fishery is in fact a productive piece of natural capital, one that generates 1,000 pounds (and $1,000 dollars) of net value every year. Whether to invest instead in human-made capital depends on the relative productivity of that alternative asset.

---

[1]In contrast to the discussion in the text, Figure 3A.1 and the analysis in this appendix rely on discussions of *total* costs and benefits, instead of *marginal* costs and benefits. Rents are maximized when the difference between total costs and benefits are greatest, which is also where marginal costs and benefits are equal. When the slopes of the total cost and benefit curves are equal, marginal costs and benefits are equal. For more on the relationship between totals and marginals, see Chapter 4.

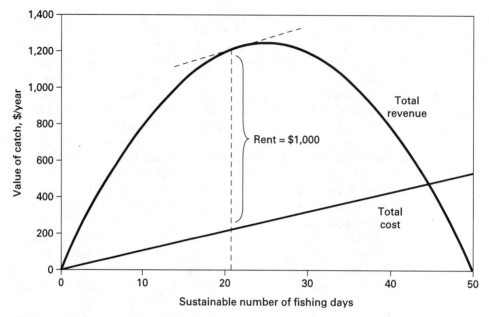

FIGURE 3A.2 Applying the Fisheries Model

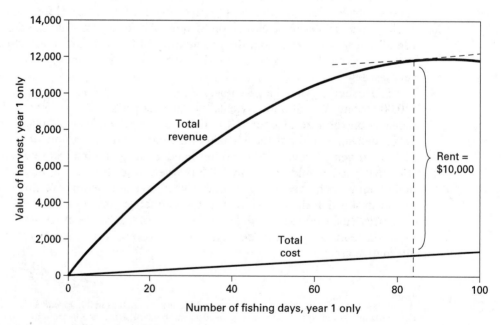

FIGURE 3A.3 The Liquidation Strategy

Referring to Figure 3A.2 we can also note an interesting relationship. This fishery contains about 12,500 pounds of fish, and its sustained yield is 1,250 pounds of fish. So the fishery is in fact growing at 10% per year. This suggests a profit-maximizing rule: If the interest rate is less than the rate of growth of the fishery, maintain the harvest below the sustained yield level. If, on the other hand, the fishery grows at a rate less than the going rate of interest, liquidate the fishery and invest the resource rent in human-made capital assets generating that higher level of return.

Higher interest rates thus make overexploitation of natural capital more likely. This reflects a greater time value of money. Higher interest rates mean that catching fish today yields a higher profit relative to catching fish tomorrow. And depending on the costs of fishing, in the presence of high profit opportunities elsewhere in the economy, the monopolist may now well "overfish"—that is, fish beyond the maximum sustained yield level. Would a monopoly owner actually drive a resource he owned to extinction? Yes, extinction is "efficient" (see chapter 4 for a precise definition) if the interest rate on alternate investments is high enough, the costs of fishing low enough, and the growth risk of the resource sufficiently low as well.

This discussion has suggested that there are two economic reasons for overfishing: open access to common property, and—even given private ownership—high interest or profit rates elsewhere in the economy. Both suggest a need for regulation to insure sustainability.

3A.1 Fisheries Policy

The standard regulatory recommendation for fisheries management from economists is a form of a cap-and-trade system called an individual transferable quota or ITQ. (For more on the generic pros and cons of marketable permits, see Chapter 16 and 17). The basic idea is that a fisheries board sets a total allowable catch or TAC, preferably at the efficient level, but definitely at or below the maximum sustained yield. Then each fisher receives a permit allowing a certain percentage of the TAC, equivalent to a specified tonnage of fish. These quotas can then be bought and sold, but at the end of the season, a fisher needs to be in possession of enough quotas to cover his or her total catch, or else face a stiff fine. How are ITQs distributed? They can be auctioned by the government, or they can be given away to existing fishers on a "grandfathered" basis; that is, fishers receive an allocation based on their catch history.

The advantage of ITQs over rigid allowances is the flexibility built into the system. If a boat is having a particularly good season, they can purchase or lease additional quota from vessels not having as much luck. And over the long run, more efficient fishers can buy out less efficient operators. Some have criticized ITQs for this kind of impact. ITQs systems encourage the departure of small operators, leaving more efficient boats (sometimes giant factory trawlers) a larger share of the market. While this may lead to a lower cost industry, it also leads to consolidation in an industry traditionally hosting small, independent producers.

A variety of practical problems is inherent to the implementation of any kind of fisheries regulation, including ITQs. Generic problems include political influence over fisheries boards, leading to excessive TAC levels, and difficulty monitoring mobile sources like fishing boats. So-called "by-catch"—fish accidentally caught for which boats don't have permits—is also a problem. By-catch is often dumped overboard to avoid fines, a wasteful process.

New Zealand has been our major laboratory for ITQs; most of the nation's fisheries have adopted the system. The results have been generally positive. While some small fishers have exited, they were the ones that were unhealthy to begin with. Sanchiro and Newell (2003) conclude that "the industry started out with a few big players (especially vertically integrated catch and food processing companies) and many small fishing enterprises, and it looks much the same today. The size of holdings of the larger companies, however, has increased" (10). In other words, small producers generally managed to survive, but big producers have gotten bigger. Fish populations have either stabilized or improved under the ITQ system, and fishers have altered their practices to avoid by-catch and stay below permitted levels. And finally, the total value produced by the fishery more than doubled between 1990 and 2000.

ITQ systems are one way to overcome the open access problem. A second way is to assign individual property rights in ocean resources to fish farmers. Aquaculture—the commercial raising and harvesting of fish in ocean environments over which fishers are granted exclusive rights—is an old industry with its roots in oyster farming. But in recent years the industry has expanded into freshwater species such as catfish and telapia and ocean raised salmon and shrimp. The U.S. industry more than doubled in size between 1985 and 2000.[2]

Aquaculture has the potential to both significantly decrease pressure on natural fisheries, and boost the productivity of the oceans. However, as currently practiced, aquaculture generates significant negative externalities, including the impact on the immediate ocean environment from fish waste, heavy metals, pesticides and antibiotics. In addition, fish feed for the carnivorous species such as salmon is often harvested unsustainably in the open ocean; approximately one third of the world's total annual ocean catch is currently used for fish food! And finally, aquaculture can destroy local habitats. For example, many of Thailand's mangrove swamps—shoreline stabilizers—have been cut down and converted to shrimp farms (Goldberg 2001; Nash 2001).

In a world likely to be inhabited by more than half again as many people by 2050, our ocean commons need to be maintained as an important source of both food and biodiversity. Effectively managing and restoring fisheries is a critical task. Some combination of ITQ management for open ocean fisheries (combined with regulations protecting habitat) and sustainable aquaculture must provide the answers.

REFERENCES

Goldberg, R.J., M.S. Elliot, and R.L. Taylor (2001). *Marine Aquaculture in the United States*. Arlington, VA: Pew Oceans Commission.

Nash, Colin, ed. 2001. *The Net-pen Salmon Farming Industry in the Pacific Northwest*. Seattle, WA: Northwest Fisheries Science Center.

Sanchero, James, and Richard Newell. 2003. "Catching Market Efficiencies," *Resources* 150:8–11.

---

[2]Fisheries Statistics and Economics Division, U.S. National Marine Fisheries Service (www.nmfs.gov).

THE EFFICIENCY STANDARD

4.0 Introduction

Some economists are fond of pointing out that achieving a goal of zero pollution not only would be prohibitively expensive but, indeed, might well be counterproductive. The view is that we should balance the costs and benefits of pollution reduction and seek, in general, to achieve an efficient amount of pollution. The idea that any level of pollution is "efficient" strikes many people as a bit odd. This chapter will thus begin by defining the efficient pollution level; then, illustrate how marginal analysis can be used, both in principle and in practice, to identify the efficient pollution level; and finally, discuss the utilitarian ethical defense of the efficiency standard.

4.1 Efficiency Defined

To understand what is meant by an efficient level of pollution, we need to look closer at the concept of efficiency. The term "efficient" in everyday parlance means a situation in which no resources are wasted. Economists use the term in a related but more specific way. The economic definition of efficiency was introduced by the Italian economist Vilfred Pareto in 1909 and is named in his honor.

> **Pareto efficient situation:** A situation in which it is impossible to make one person better off without making anyone else worse off.

When economists say an outcome is efficient, they almost always mean "Pareto efficient." I'll drop the Pareto most of the time as well, adding the modifier only when I want to remind the reader that we are using this specific definition.

The advantage of pursuing efficiency is that, conditional on the existing distribution of income, it makes the "economic pie" as big as possible. In fact, at the efficient outcome, the **net monetary benefits** produced by the economy will be maximized. This means that the total of all benefits that can be given a monetary value, both human-made and those generated by nature, minus all costs of production, both private and external, will be as large as possible at the efficient point. How do we know this? By applying the definition of efficiency. If it were possible to make someone better off without making someone else worse off (meaning that we are at an *inefficient* point), we could always make the "economic pie" of net benefits bigger by moving toward efficiency.

The first point to make about efficiency is that it need not be fair. This is illustrated clearly in Figure 4.1, showing two "economic pies." Pie 2 is more efficient than Pie 1 because it is bigger—it maximizes the benefits to society *as a whole.* Yet Pie 2 is clearly much less fair than Pie 1. Both in absolute and relative terms, B is worse off with Pie 2. Thus, on its own, efficiency may not be useful as a guide to good social outcomes. I recall first learning about Pareto efficiency in my microeconomics class and asking the teacher if it would be possible to have an efficient slave society. The answer was yes—freeing the slaves might not be "efficient" since, in monetary terms, the masters might lose more than the slaves would gain.

Yet whenever the economic pie is enlarged, it is *at least possible* for everyone to get a bigger slice in absolute terms. In Figure 4.1, a move from Pie 1 to Pie 2 could in *principle* provide both A and B bigger slices. Thus, any move towards efficiency can in theory be a "win-win" situation. We have already considered one such case: By restricting fishing in New England the government could generate enough resource rent to both compensate the fishers put out of business and allow the remaining boats to earn a decent living. Let us look at another such case involving the use of California's scarce water resources.

California is a semi-arid state with a vast agricultural industry and rapidly growing urban centers. Water is scarce, and an unlikely coalition of corporate farmers and environmentalists have supported moving to an open market in water rights to increase the efficiency with which existing supplies are used.[1] Farmers seek a profit from the sale of their water, while environmentalists are interested in forestalling the construction of ecologically disruptive new dams in the state.

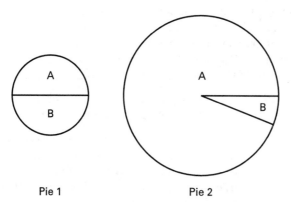

Pie 1   Pie 2

FIGURE 4.1 Pareto Efficiency versus Fairness

---

[1]This analysis is drawn from Gomez-Ibanez and Kalt (1990). For current policy initiatives, see www.calfed.ca.gov.

To simplify a complex story, farmland in California comes endowed with rights to a percentage of water from a given reservoir; currently farmers use about 85% of the state's water. The price for agricultural water charged by state and federal governments is much lower than that for metropolitan use: One study put the price of the former at $10 per acre foot, while the latter was priced at $100 per acre foot. This low price for agricultural water has resulted in such clearly inefficient but profitable uses as growing irrigated hay in Death Valley. This practice is inefficient because it shrinks the size of California's economic pie. The water could be used to produce output in other sectors of the economy with a higher monetary value—other less water-intensive crops, industrial products, or perhaps even green lawns (which raise the value of homes) in metropolitan areas. One study estimated that California's gross domestic product was about $5 billion lower than it would have been had water been allocated efficiently (cited in Gomez-Ibanez and Kalt 1990, 4).

We can analyze the situation by assuming the existence of two markets for water in California: agricultural and metropolitan, with no transfer in between. This situation is illustrated in Figure 4.2A. The state could move toward efficiency by combining the markets into one, as illustrated in Figure 4.2B, thus generating a single price of around $70.

One way to achieve this goal would be for the government bodies selling the water simply to raise the price to its market level, in this example, $70. One statewide initiative calling for a similar approach was defeated, not surprisingly, with heavy opposition from farm interests. Such an effort would clearly be efficient since the water not bought by farmers would be freed up for metropolitan use. However, it was thought to be unfair in the way it penalized farmers by changing the rules of the game mid-stream.

Yet, as is always the case when moving toward efficiency, a **Pareto-improving** alternative policy exists—one that actually does make everyone better off. In California, farmers could continue to purchase their old allotments at $10 but be allowed to resell them without restriction to the urban sector. In this case, the Death Valley farmer could continue to grow her hay but, by doing so, would be passing up substantial profit opportunities. By simply reselling her water she could make $90 per acre foot! Under this policy, farmers would gradually abandon inefficient farming practices and become "water tycoons." Reforms of this nature are now being sought in California.

Either policy—a single price or subsidized prices with water marketing—would put a lot of farmers out of the farming business, and the California economy would

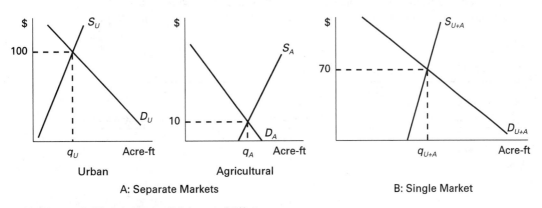

A: Separate Markets   B: Single Market

FIGURE 4.2 California Water Pricing and Efficiency

shift toward greater industrial and service-sector production. Overall, economists would predict that the monetary value of California production would rise as water flowed into higher-value uses. Thus, *both policies are efficient,* though the first one is unfair in many ways. (It is worth noting that both policies would also encourage urban growth in California, itself considered a problem by many people. Are green lawns in the suburban desert really an "efficient" use of water, that is, one that makes people happier overall? We will take a closer look at the complex relationship between growth and social welfare later in Chapter 11.)

One reason that economists like efficient outcomes is that, as in the California case, when moving from an inefficient outcome to an efficient outcome, it is at least possible to achieve a Pareto improvement, making everyone better off without making anyone else worse off. This means that equity need not, in theory, be sacrificed when moving from a less to a more efficient outcome. More often, however, there are almost always winners and losers from any change in economic policy, even those that increase economic efficiency. The point here is that efficiency and fairness are different notions. Efficient outcomes need not be equitable (or moral or fair), though they may be. At the same time, equitable outcomes need not be efficient, though they may be.

4.2 Efficient Pollution Levels

Now you may recall that we are supposed to be discussing the "right" amount of pollution. How does efficiency fit in here? Let's take the simplest example of pollution one can think of by following two workers, Brittany and Tyler, into their office in the morning.

They sit down at their desks, and Tyler pulls out a pack of smokes and proceeds to light up. Brittany hates cigarettes, but there's no rule against smoking in the office. Tyler's been smoking about five a day. Brittany is pretty desperate, so she considers a bribe. "How much would I have to pay you to smoke one less cigarette per day?" Tyler thinks it over. "One cigarette? I can put up with that for four dollars," he says. "Two per day?" she inquiries. "That'll be tougher. You'd have to pay me six more dollars for that one." The third cigarette, it turns out, could be eliminated for a bribe of an additional $8. They keep at it, developing Table 4.1.

The table reveals that, due to his addiction, Tyler is increasingly reluctant to give up each additional cigarette. Indeed, even after receiving a total of $28 for the first four, he would have to receive *an additional $12* to quit smoking altogether.

TABLE 4.1 Marginal and Total Costs of Cleanup

Number of Cigarettes Reduced	Additional Payment Required per Reduced Cigarette	Total Payment Required
1	$ 4.00	$ 4.00
2	$ 6.00	$10.00
3	$ 8.00	$18.00
4	$10.00	$28.00
5	$12.00	$40.00

Brittany has her own notion of the benefits of pollution reduction in the office. Getting rid of the first cigarette is essential to making the environment tolerable: She'd be willing to pay $10 to do so. Eliminating the next cigarette would make a big improvement but is not absolutely necessary. It's worth $8. Her private benefit schedule for cigarette reduction is illustrated in Table 4.2.

The benefits of additional pollution reduction decline for Brittany as the number of cigarettes smoked falls, because the health damage and discomfort she experiences also decline. Thus, she's only willing to pay $2 to get rid of the last cigarette, perhaps because she can take her daily coffee break (choose your poison) when Tyler chooses to light that one up.

Note here that we're focusing on reducing cigarettes (pollution) one at a time. Economists call this **marginal analysis.** The last unit of pollution reduced is called the **marginal unit;** the costs (to Tyler) of reducing that unit are called the **marginal costs,** and the benefits (to Brittany) from reducing that unit are called the **marginal benefits.** Comparison of marginal costs with marginal benefits will help us zero in on the efficient level of pollution.

To help us determine the efficient level of cigarette reduction, Figure 4.3 graphs the marginal costs and benefits of giving up cigarettes. On the horizontal axis we have the number of cigarettes reduced per day; on the vertical axis, dollars. Because marginals represent *changes* in total values as we move from one unit to the next, it is conventional to graph marginal values in between the units on the X axis. For example, the marginal cost of the fourth cigarette reduced is $10. Because this is the change in total cost as we move from 3 to 4 cigarettes reduced, you will notice that the $10 value is graphed halfway between 3 and 4.

The curve labeled "marginal costs of pollution reduction" illustrates the cost to Tyler of giving up additional cigarettes. It slopes upward, reflecting the fact that the first cigarette smoked can be given up at low cost by Tyler, although he would have to be mightily bribed to give up smoking altogether. The curve labeled "marginal benefits of pollution reduction" reflects the value to Brittany of a progressively less smoky environment. It slopes downward, because the health risk and discomfort from breathing secondary smoke decreases as the number of cigarettes is decreased.

You can probably guess where the efficient level of pollution reduction is going to be. (*X* marks the spot.) Indeed, two cigarettes reduced is the efficient number. Why? Because *at any other level of pollution, both parties can be made better off by trading.* To see this, consider the following Puzzle.

TABLE 4.2   Marginal and Total Benefits of Cleanup

Number of Cigarettes Reduced	Additional Willingness to Pay per Cigarette Reduced	Total Willingness to Pay
1	$10.00	$10.00
2	$ 8.00	$18.00
3	$ 6.00	$24.00
4	$ 4.00	$28.00
5	$ 2.00	$30.00

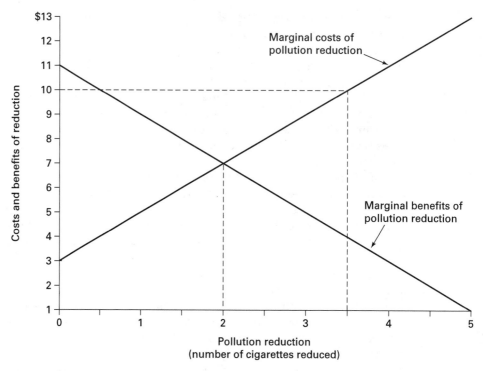

FIGURE 4.3 Marginal Costs and Benefits of Cleanup

PUZZLE

Tyler, who loves to smoke, would puff his way through five cigarettes a day if he were in the office by himself. Tyler is a selfish individual, and he has the right to smoke as much as he wants. Would he continue smoking five cigarettes if Brittany were around?

SOLUTION

The answer is no. Tyler is willing to give up one cigarette for $4, and Brittany is willing to pay him $10 to do so. Thus, he can make up to $6 in "profit" by accepting the initial bribe. Similarly, Tyler will accept $6 for the next cigarette, and Brittany would pay up to $8 to get him not to smoke it. Thus, he can earn an additional profit of up to $2 by reducing the second cigarette. Finally, Brittany would pay Tyler only $6 to reduce the third cigarette, and that would be less than the $8 necessary to get him to give it up. Thus, Brittany will pay Tyler to eliminate two cigarettes, and *both* will be better off than if Tyler smoked all five.

Clearly Tyler would not give up the second-to-last cigarette: Brittany would have to pay Tyler $10 to get him to give it up, and it is worth only $4 to her in increased comfort and safety. Only for those cigarettes where the marginal cost curve (Tyler's required compensation for reducing pollution) lies below the marginal benefit curve (Brittany's willingness to pay for pollution reduction), will Tyler be better off by striking a deal with Brittany than by smoking.

This example is worth close study (or, as I tell my students, this one will be on the test). To check to make sure you follow it, take a minute to explain to yourself why it is that, *at any level of pollution other than three cigarettes smoked (or two reduced), both parties can be made better off through a trade.* Three cigarettes smoked is the efficient level of pollution, because only at three cigarettes is it impossible to make one party better off without making the other worse off.

Here is an outcome that, while efficient, would strike many people as being unfair. Why should Brittany have to pay Tyler not to slowly poison her? This question is, as we will see, crucial in the discussion of a safety pollution standard. But efficiency defenders respond in two ways: First, they argue, the issue of whether polluters have a right to pollute or victims have a right to prevent pollution should not necessarily be settled in the victim's favor. While agreeing that fairness is an important issue, they feel ultimately that it is a matter of value judgment, thus lying outside the realm of economics.[2] But as we will see, the efficiency standard, in fact, has its own basis in "value judgments."

A more consistent defense of the efficiency standard is that, since efficient outcomes maximize the monetary size of the total pie, consistently pursuing efficient outcomes will, on balance, benefit most people over time. While Brittany might lose out from this level of cigarette pollution, she will benefit from efficient regulation elsewhere. For example, she may get lower-priced strawberries if pesticide use is regulated at an efficient, as opposed to a more stringent and costly safe, level.

In this section, we have employed marginal analysis to identify the efficient pollution level—where the marginal benefits and costs of pollution reduction are equal. At any other level of pollution, it is *possible* to make all parties better off by moving toward efficiency. This section has also illustrated that efficient outcomes need not accord with standard notions of fairness. We now move on to consider the relationship between a marginal analysis of pollution reduction and one based on total costs and benefits.

4.3 Marginals and Totals

As noted above, focusing on marginal costs and marginal benefits allowed us to isolate the efficient pollution level. This section digresses for a moment to illustrate the relationship between marginal and total cleanup costs and the marginal and total benefits of cleanup. The bottom panel of Figure 4.4 reproduces the marginal relationships in Figure 4.3 while the top panel graphs the total costs of cleanup (to Tyler) and the total benefits (to Brittany).

Both sets of curves illustrate the same information. The *total* costs of pollution reduction rise at an increasing rate, generating a curve that is bowed upward; another way of saying this is that the additional or *marginal* cost of each cigarette given up rises.

---

[2]In textbook neoclassical theory, of course, equity and efficiency are the two normative criteria that should drive policy. However, in practice, some environmental economists look only at efficiency. See Bromley (1990) for a discussion.

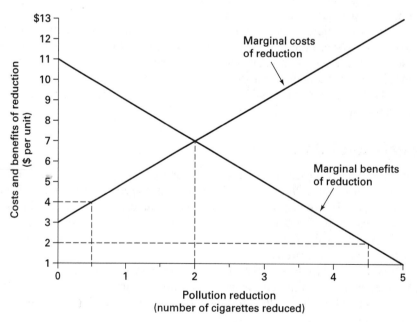

FIGURE 4.4 Marginals and Totals Compared: Costs and Benefits of Pollution Reduction

Similarly, the *total* benefits of cleanup rise at a decreasing rate, producing a downward bowed curve; thus, the *marginal* benefits of pollution reduction are falling.

How can we move from one set of curves to another? The marginal cost curve represents the change in total costs. Thus, as the figure illustrates, the marginal cost of the first cigarette reduced, $4, is just the change in the total cost curve between 0 and 1 cigarette reduced. Similarly, the marginal benefit of the fifth cigarette reduced, $2, is the change in the total benefits curve between 4 and 5 cigarettes reduced. The marginal curves graph the total change in *y* for a 1-unit change in *x*. But this is just the "rise" over the "run" of the total curve. Thus, the marginal curves graph the slopes of the total curves.[3]

Moreover, the area *under* the marginal cost curve equals the total cost. For example, the marginal cost of the first cigarette reduced, $4, plus the marginal cost of the second, $6, equals the total costs of two cigarettes reduced, $10. But $4 is just the area under the marginal curve between 0 and 1, while $6 is the area under the curve between 1 and 2. We will use this relationship often in the chapters ahead.

Finally, note that *the efficient pollution level does not occur where total costs equal total benefits* (at four cigarettes reduced). At this point, since total benefits and costs are equal, the net monetary benefits to "society" are zero. Instead, the efficient level occurs where the total benefit curve lies farthest above the total cost curve. Here, the net monetary benefits to Brittany and Tyler combined are maximized. At the point where total benefits and costs are equal, we know we have reduced pollution "too much" under an efficiency standard. At this point the *marginal* costs of reduction exceed the *marginal* benefits, given the conventional shapes of the benefit and cost curves.[4]

To summarize: The relationship between the marginal and total benefit and cost curves is a straightforward one. The marginal curves graph the change in the total curves or, equivalently, their slope. The upward slope of the marginal cost of reduction curve thus reflects total pollution control costs, which rise at an increasing rate. Similarly, the downward slope of the marginal benefit of reduction curve results from an assumption that the total benefits of reducing pollution increase at a decreasing rate. Controlling pollution to a level at which the total benefits of reduction equal the total costs results in too much control from an efficiency perspective.

4.4 The Coase Theorem Introduced

One interesting aspect of the efficiency perspective is that, under certain circumstances, whichever way initial rights over pollution are granted, the efficient level of pollution doesn't change! To see this, think for a minute about a situation in which Brittany is granted the right to ban smoking in the office. Will she do so?

Referring back to Figure 4.3, we can see that the answer is no. If Tyler were willing to give up his last cigarette for twelve dollars, he would enjoy smoking that cigarette more than, say, $11.99 in cash. Thus, he should be *willing to pay up to that amount* to be able to smoke it! Brittany, on the other hand, is now in the position of taking bribes, and her marginal benefit curve indicates she would rather have $2 than a smoke-free environment. So the two can strike a deal on the first cigarette.

---

[3]For those students with a calculus background, the marginal curve graphs the derivative of the total curve.

[4]In important cases, the curves may not be shaped this way. See Application 4.2 at the end of this chapter.

Similarly, because Tyler values the second at up to ten dollars, and Brittany will sell him a "smoking right" for anything over four dollars, there is room to deal. Finally, Tyler would pay eight dollars for the third cigarette, and Brittany would accept (though she would only be making $2 in profit, it is still profit!). Notice, they would not go on to four cigarettes though, because Tyler would pay only six dollars for it, and Brittany would demand eight dollars.

We have just shown that, for a simple case of pollution reduction uncomplicated by transactions costs and free riding (discussed in the last chapter), the efficient outcome is independent of whether pollution is legal or not. If polluter and victim can bargain easily and effectively, private negotiation should arrive at the efficient outcome regardless of who has the initial right to pollute or prevent pollution. This result is known as the **Coase theorem,** after Nobel prize–winning economist Ronald Coase.

Some have interpreted the Coase theorem to imply that from an efficiency perspective it does not matter who has to pay for pollution—victims or polluters. Either way, one arrives at an efficient solution. (Of course, on fairness grounds most would argue that polluters should have to pay for damages.) However, as Coase himself recognized, the theorem holds only under highly limited circumstances.

In fact, efficiency will in general be better served under a **polluter pays principle.** This is true for two reasons. The first of these is the public good nature of pollution cleanup discussed in the last chapter. In real-world settings, a single polluter typically affects a broad community. Requiring polluters to pay for the privilege of polluting is more likely to generate an efficient outcome than a policy that legalizes pollution and requires victims to pay. Having the polluter pay reduces the free riding and transactions costs associated with the latter policy.

More importantly, the assignment of liability has important long-run effects. If Brittany paid Tyler not to smoke, she would very likely soon find all the smokers in the office moving their desk close to hers! More generally, if firms are given the right to pollute (or are subsidized to reduce pollution), their costs will be lower. In the long run, this encourages entry into the market and creates more pollution (see Mohring and Boyd 1971). For example, when taxpayers at large pay for the construction of landfills, households and firms have little long-run incentive to minimize their production of garbage. On the other hand, if landfill construction costs are financed by "pay-by-the-bag" disposal fees, waste producers have an incentive to modify their long-run waste production strategies.

As we will see later, the Coase theorem is quite useful when analyzing the initial distribution of permits in a marketable permit system. For now, though, this example illustrates clearly the claim not only that zero pollution levels are very expensive (poor Tyler suffers severe nicotine withdrawals) but also that a solution more efficient than banning exists in which all parties are made better off.

To review this section, the Coase theorem demonstrates that in the absence of transactions costs and free riding, the efficient pollution control level can be achieved through negotiation regardless of who has the legal right to pollute or prevent pollution. In the real world, however, efficiency will generally best be served by following a polluter pays principle. This is true both because of transactions costs and free riding, and because long-run incentives for entry into the polluting industry are reduced when the polluter pays.

4.5 Air Pollution Control in Baltimore: Calculating the Efficient Standard

To give you a feel for how the efficiency standard might be applied in practice, let us look at a study that estimated the marginal benefits and marginal costs of reducing suspended particulate emissions in Baltimore under the current type of regulation (Oates, Portney, and McGarland 1989). Suspended particulates are small particles of ash or soot emitted as a by-product of burning fossil fuels for power or transport. They contribute to respiratory ailments, some of which are fatal, soil clothing and buildings, and reduce visibility. Figure 4.5 graphs the estimated marginal costs and benefits of different total suspended particulate (TSP) standards.

The marginal cost curve has the same shape as that in Figure 4.3; reducing particulate emissions becomes increasingly costly. To move from a standard of 110 to 109 parts per million would cost about $3 million, while tightening the standard from 95 to 94 parts per million would cost an additional $16 million. This is because under the regulations in Baltimore, source types with relatively low costs of reduction must trim their emissions first. To meet tougher standards, facilities facing higher control costs must also reduce emissions.

FIGURE 4.5 Particulate Standards in Baltimore: Identifying the Efficient Pollution Level
The marginal benefit curve is not shown in full for ease of presentation.
Source: Wallace E. Oates, Paul R. Portney, and Albert M. McGartland. 1989. "The Net Benefits of Incentive-Based Regulation: A Case Study of Environmental Standard Setting," Figure 2. *American Economic Review* 79, no. 5:1233–1242. Reprinted by permission.

The marginal benefit curve, on the other hand, is relatively flat. Unlike the cigarette case, the additional benefits of reduction do not decrease as the pollution level falls. Instead, the authors of the study assume that tightening the standard from 110 to 109 parts per million yields roughly the same benefits—reduced death, sickness, and soiling, and improved visibility—as moving from a standard of 100 to 99 parts per million. They estimate these benefits to be around $10 million for each one-unit decrease in the particulate standard.

To arrive at this monetary figure for benefits, the authors value each life saved at $2 million, each lost workday at $100, and each restricted activity day at $25. Monetary benefits were also estimated for soiling and visibility. Chapter 8 discusses the means by which environmental economists attempt to estimate dollar values for these "priceless" elements of our lives. But to preview briefly, as suggested by the smoking example, economists generally measure the benefits of pollution reduction based on society's willingness to pay for that reduction. The benefits of less smoke in the office were measured precisely by Brittany's willingness to pay for fewer cigarettes. Although this willingness-to-pay approach has problems we will explore in detail later, it captures the basic idea of trade-offs between a cleaner environment and all other goods.

The efficient standard occurs at about 98 parts per million. With a looser particulate standard, the additional benefits from reducing pollution up to 98 parts per million would be greater than the additional costs. However, moving to a standard tighter than 98 parts per million would entail additional costs exceeding the additional value of the benefits. Thus, net monetary benefits—the estimated value of clean air enjoyed by citizens of Baltimore minus the cleanup costs borne by Baltimore firms (and ultimately, to some extent, Baltimore consumers)—are maximized at the efficient standard.

4.6 The Ethical Basis of the Efficiency Standard

Let us look one last time at the cigarette example and use our utility and social welfare functions to clearly focus on the ethical assumptions underlying the efficiency standard. First, there are no "equity" weightings: Tyler and Brittany's utilities count equally in overall social welfare. Second, no distinction is made between the utilities of pollution victims and beneficiaries—Tyler's need for cigarettes holds just as much weight as Brittany's need for clean air. Together these conditions imply that the social welfare function underlying the efficiency standard looks like this:

$$SW = U_{Tyler} (\overset{+}{\#Cigs_T}, \overset{+}{\$_T}) + U_{Brit}(\overset{-}{\#Cigs_T}, \overset{+}{\$_B})$$

Note the negative sign over Tyler's cigarette consumption in Brittany's utility function. Cigarettes are a "bad," not a "good," for her and so lower her utility. The social welfare function clearly illustrates the value judgments underlying the efficiency standard. By *not* weighting income distribution, efficiency advocates by default maintain that the *status quo* is acceptable. By treating victims and beneficiaries equally, efficiency proponents do not acknowledge a "right" to protection from harmful pollutants.

Recall that, as we have stressed, the efficiency standard does not require that losers be compensated, even though this is possible. Suppose that company policy originally banned smoking in the office, but the office manager then decreed Tyler could smoke three cigarettes a day, offering Brittany no compensation in return. *This is still an efficient outcome,* since in dollar terms, the gain to Tyler is greater than the loss to Brittany.

It is worth stressing this point because many textbooks will refer to the efficient standard as "optimal" or "socially optimal." But unless, as economists, we are prepared to make judgments about who should win and who should lose in our society, efficient pollution control outcomes are not optimal for society. Rather, they simply balance the costs and benefits of pollution reduction at a level where net *monetary* benefits are maximized.[5]

Because a move to efficiency almost always creates losers as well as winners, such a move is not "socially optimal." Rather, the best defense of efficiency is that over time *most people* (NOT just polluters) will eventually reap net benefits from a move toward more efficient pollution standards. In concrete terms, most of us are *both* consumers of goods whose prices are raised by environmental regulation, and beneficiaries of cleaner air and water. Efficient regulation, according to its proponents, is the best way to balance these two concerns.

4.7   Summary

The efficiency approach puts the question of "How much pollution?" in a marginal cost, marginal benefit framework. In principle, we can replace "cigarettes reduced" with "pollution cleanup" in Figure 4.3, and the diagram will show us the efficient amount of nitrous oxide, sulfur dioxide, CFCs, dioxin, DDT, waste oil, particulates, heavy metals, litter, nuclear waste, or PCBs that "should" be in the environment. Of course, to make this approach operational, one needs to estimate a *dollar figure* for both the costs and benefits of reducing each unit of pollution. The benefit figure will include quantifiable savings such as those on medical care. But, as in the Baltimore case, it also must take into account less easily calculable benefits such as human lives saved and cancers avoided.

But why should any pollutant be in the environment? Society is willing to suffer pollution because it is an essential by-product of some good or service that people desire and because cleanup is not free. In Figure 4.6, the "supply curve" for pollution cleanup is just the marginal cost of reduction curve; it shows the increasing cost to society of eliminating additional units of pollution. This cost will be determined by the technology available for controlling the pollutant. The curve, for example, would shift down (toward the x axis) if cheaper ways of reducing pollution were discovered.

---

[5]If overall happiness or social welfare is somehow maximized by such a policy, it must be the case that *additions to income must generate equal increases in happiness for the two people,* or in economists' terms, the two must have the same **marginal utility of income.** This, in turn, would imply that since the dollar gain to Tyler exceeds the dollar loss to Brittany, the happiness gain to Tyler also exceeds the happiness loss to Brittany. Thus, there is an overall gain in total happiness by a move towards efficiency, regardless of whether Brittany is compensated. For the efficiency standard to maximize social welfare, the assumption of equal marginal utilities of income must be true in general: A dollar must yield equal happiness to a millionaire or to a street person. However, this is highly unlikely. Thus, we must conclude that, *on its own terms,* the ethical basis of the efficiency standard is a bit murky. This point is made in Kneese and Schulze (1985). Bromley (1990) also discusses the normative basis of the efficiency standard.

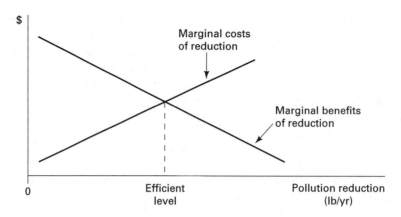

FIGURE 4.6 Marginal Costs and Benefits of Cleanup: The General Case

Society, on the other hand, clearly has a demand for pollution reduction. The "demand curve" for cleanup is the marginal benefits of reduction curve; it illustrates the increasing damages inflicted on people or the environment as the amount of cleanup decreases. The location of the curve depends on a variety of factors, such as the number of organisms (including people) affected, weather conditions, and defensive measures taken by those affected. In the Baltimore case, for example, the curve would shift up (away from the x axis) if more people moved into the city.

The efficient quantity of the pollution from the production of a desired product will occur just at the point where the additional costs of reduction are equal to the additional benefits of reduction. Any more reduction and the additional monetary costs borne by members of society exceed the additional monetary benefits; any less and there will be net social monetary benefits to be gained.

As our discussion of the open access and public good problems in the last chapter made clear, economists do not think that free markets generate the efficient amount of pollution. In the cigarette example, we saw that self-interested private parties, through their own negotiation, might arrive at the efficient level of pollution. But this was a rather special example, featuring perfect information about costs and damages, clearly defined property rights, zero transactions costs, and no free riding. In the real world, "markets for pollution" seldom develop naturally, and a more likely outcome in an actual office would be an inefficient one. Until recently the open access outcome would have meant complete pollution—five cigarettes per day; a safety-based regulation banning smoking completely would be more likely these days.

This chapter has employed the notion of marginal costs and marginal benefits associated with pollution reduction to illustrate how one might identify an efficient level of pollution. The problems involved in actually measuring benefits and costs will be explored in Chapters 8, 9, and 10. We have also seen that a move to more efficient pollution control almost always generates winners and losers, and since the losers are seldom compensated, such a move cannot be considered socially optimal. The best ethical defense of efficiency is thus that, since it maximizes the size of the measurable economic pie, over time "most" people will benefit from more efficient pollution control. We now turn to a very different perspective—a safety standard.

APPLICATION 4.0

More on Efficient Smoking[6]

These smoking problems are a little silly but are good at illustrating some basic lessons about efficiency. So, this time, Groucho and Harpo work together in the same office. Groucho smokes; Harpo hates smoke. Groucho currently smokes 12 cigars per day. He faces marginal costs of reducing smoking (withdrawal pains) equal to x, where x is the number of cigars reduced. In other words, the cost of giving up the first cigar is \$1, the second, \$2, and so forth. Harpo receives marginal benefits (reduced discomfort and risk of cancer) equal to $(12 - x)$ from Groucho reducing the number of cigars smoked.

It is possible to rent a Clean-Air Machine that reduces smoke in the air by 50% for \$10 per day. It is also possible to relocate Groucho in a different office so Harpo would not have to breathe any smoke at all for \$40 per day.

1. Draw a diagram showing the marginal costs and marginal benefits of pollution reduction, with the number of cigars reduced on the horizontal axis. Use this diagram to determine the efficient number of cigars reduced if machine rental or relocation are not allowed.
2. Suppose that the clean air machine is installed. What is the efficient number of cigars reduced now?
3. Recall that Groucho begins smoking twelve cigars a day. Is it more efficient to rent the machine or relocate Groucho to another room?
4. This problem has no transactions costs or free riding. The Coase theorem says that, in this kind of simple example, the efficient outcome should be achieved through negotiation even if Harpo has the power to banish Groucho to another office *at Groucho's expense.* Explain why.

APPLICATION 4.1

The Stray Cow Problem[7]

Rancher Roy has his ranch next to the farm of farmer Fern. Cattle tend to roam and sometimes stray onto Fern's land and damage her crops. Roy can choose the size of his herd. His revenues are \$6 for each cow he raises. The schedules of his marginal cost of production (MCP) and the damage each additional cow creates (marginal cow damage or MCD) are given below.

# of Cattle	MCP	MCD
1	\$3	\$1
2	3	2
3	4	3
4	5	4
5	6	5
6	7	6

[6]Thanks to Steve Polasky for the original version of this problem.
[7]Acknowledgments are due to the unknown author of the original version of this problem, which I borrowed from a University of Michigan problem set.

Farmer Fern can choose either to farm or not to farm. Her cost of production is $10, and her revenue is $12 when there are no cattle roaming loose. For each additional cow her revenue is reduced by the amount in the MCD column above.

To answer the following questions, you need to figure out four things: the profit-maximizing number of cows for Roy to own, his profits, whether or not Fern will farm, and what her profits will be. Remember that efficient outcomes maximize the net monetary benefits to both parties; in other words, total ranching plus farming profits. Finally, a diagram won't help for this problem.

1. What will be the outcome if there is no liability (Roy does not pay for any damages caused)?
2. What will be the outcome if Roy is liable for damages?
3. What is the efficient outcome (the outcome that maximizes total profits)?
4. Suppose it is possible to build a fence to enclose the ranch for a cost of $9. Is building the fence efficient?
5. Suppose the farmer can build a fence around her crops for a cost of $1. Is building this fence efficient?

APPLICATION 4.2

End-of-the-Pipe Control versus Pollution Prevention

The marginal cost of reduction curve illustrated in Figure 4.5 assumes a particular approach to reducing pollution, often called "end-of-the-pipe" control. In other words, when we draw that upward sloping MC curve, we assume that firms respond to regulation by maintaining the same basic production technology but adding on scrubbers or filters to clean up their emissions. Under these conditions, rising marginal costs of reduction are quite likely.

However, suppose that firms radically overhaul their production technology, so that they completely eliminate emissions. This is known as a "pollution prevention" strategy. An example might be a jeweler, who in the face of regulation adopts a closed loop production system. This is one in which all mineral waste products are recovered from recycled wastewater and then reused. What would the marginal cost of reduction diagram look like in this case?

1. Specifically, assume that reducing metal pollution by the first 1% required the installation of a $100,000 recycling system, but that the marginal cost of further reduction was zero. Draw the marginal cost of reduction curve.
2. Let the marginal benefit of reduction curve be equal to $(30,000 − 1/3 * x)$, where x is the percentage reduction in pollution (ranging from 0% to 100%). In this case, is installation of the recycling system efficient? What is the efficient cleanup level?

KEY IDEAS IN EACH SECTION

4.0   The efficiency standard argues for a careful balancing of the costs and benefits of pollution control.

4.1   Efficiency is defined as **Pareto efficient.** Pareto efficient outcomes maximize the measurable **net monetary benefits** available to a society. Thus, in any move toward efficiency, it is always *possible* for the winners to compensate the losers, a so-called **Pareto Improvement.** However, compensation is not required for efficiency, so efficient outcomes are not necessarily fair.

4.2   **Marginal analysis,** which compares the **marginal costs** of pollution reduction against its **marginal benefits,** is used to pinpoint the efficient pollution level. At any point other than the efficient level, both polluter and victim can *potentially* be made better off through negotiation.

4.3   The marginal curves graph the change in the total curves. The area under the marginal cost (benefit) curve equals the total costs (benefits). At the point where total costs and benefits are equal, net benefits are zero and pollution has been "overcontrolled" from an efficiency perspective.

4.4   The **Coase theorem** states that *in the absence of transactions costs and free riding,* private negotiation will arrive at the efficient pollution level, regardless of whether victims have the right to impose a ban or polluters have the right to pollute. In the real world, however, the **polluter pays principle** will lead to a more efficient outcome, since it generally reduces transactions costs and free riding, and does not distort the incentives for entry into the market.

4.5   The case of air pollution in Baltimore illustrates how the efficiency standard might be applied in practice.

4.6   The efficiency standard weights the utility of all individuals equally: rich and poor, current and future generations, and victims and polluters. Thus, outcomes are efficient even if the increased consumption by one group comes at the expense of another. This means that any individual move toward efficiency does not clearly increase social welfare. Nevertheless, efficiency can best be defended by arguing that, over time, most people will benefit in their role as consumers if efficiency is pursued at every turn.

REFERENCES

Bromley, Daniel. 1990. "The Ideology of Efficiency: Searching for a Theory of Policy Analysis." *Journal of Environmental Economics and Management* 19, no. 1:86–107.

Gomez-Ibanez, Jose A. and Joseph P. Kalt. 1990. *Cases in Microeconomics.* Englewood Cliffs, NJ: Prentice Hall.

Kneese, Alan V., and William D. Schulze. 1985. "Ethics and Environmental Economics." In *Handbook of Natural Resource Economics,* vol. 1, edited by A. V. Kneese and J. J. Sweeney. New York: Elsevier.

Mohring, Herbert, and J. Hayden Boyd. 1971. "Analyzing 'Externalities': 'Direct Interaction' versus 'Asset Utilization' Frameworks." *Economica* 38:347–361.

Oates, Wallace E., Paul R. Portney, and Albert M. McGartland. 1989. "The Net Benefits of Incentive-Based Regulation: A Case Study of Environmental Standard Setting." *American Economic Review* 79, no. 5:1233–1242.

CHAPTER 5

THE SAFETY STANDARD

5.0 Introduction

In the last chapter, we explored the logic of controlling pollution at an efficient level. The efficiency approach emphasizes trade-offs—pollution control has opportunity costs that must be weighed against the benefits of environmental protection. This is not, however, the kind of language one hears in everyday discussions of pollution control. Instead, pollution is more generally equated with immoral or even criminal behavior, a practice to be stamped out at all costs. In this chapter, we will explore the pros and cons of a safety standard, which, like much popular opinion, rejects a benefit–cost approach to decisions about the "correct" amount of pollution.

The **safety standard** springs fundamentally from fairness rather than efficiency concerns. Recall that the efficiency standard makes no distinction between victims and perpetrators of pollution. Instead, efficiency weighs the dollar impact of pollution on victims' health against the dollar impact on consumers' prices and polluters' profits. Each is considered to have equal say in the matter, based on the reasoning that in the long run most people will benefit as consumers from the larger pie made possible via efficient regulation. Advocates of a safety approach, on the other hand, contend that our society has developed a widespread consensus on the following position: People have a right to protection from unsolicited, significant harm to their immediate environment. Efficiency violates this right and is thus fundamentally unfair.

Curiously, there is also an efficiency argument to be made in favor of relying on safety standards. We know that the efficiency standard requires that the costs and benefits of environmental regulation be carefully measured and weighed. However, as we shall see in Chapters 8 and 10, many important benefits of protection are often left out of benefit–cost analyses because they cannot be measured. Moreover, as will be discussed in Chapter 11, material growth in our affluent society may primarily feed conspicuous consumption, fueling a rat race that leaves no one better off. If the measured costs of protection are overstated by this rat race effect, while the benefits are understated because they cannot be quantified, then safe regulation may in reality meet a benefit–cost test. Having said this, however, safety is more often defended in terms of basic rights, rather than on efficiency grounds.

5.1 Defining the Right to Safety

There is a saying that the freedom to wave your fist ends where my nose begins. In a similar vein, many Americans believe that the freedom to pollute the environment ends where a human body begins. Preventing positive harm to its citizens is the classic liberal (in modern parlance, libertarian) justification for governmental restraint on the liberties of others. At the extreme, permitting negative externalities that cause discomfort, sickness, or death might be looked upon as the equivalent of permitting the poisoning of the population for material gain.

The safety standard can thus be defended as necessary to protect **personal liberty.**[1] Viewed in this light, we require that pollution should be reduced to levels that inflict "minimal" harm on people. What constitutes minimal harm is of course open to debate. In practice, the U.S. Environmental Protection Agency (EPA) appears to consider risks below 1 in 1 million for large populations to be acceptable or "below regulatory concern." On the other hand, the EPA and other federal agencies tend to take action against risks greater than 4 in 1,000 for small populations, and 3 in 10,000 for large populations (Travis et al. 1987).[2] Risks that fall in between are regulated based on an informal balancing of costs against benefits and statutory requirements. One observer characterizes this back-and-forth process as permitting "an agency to take technological and economic factors into account, on a case-by-case basis, as long as it acts in good faith to make progress toward reducing and, we hope, eventually eliminating damage to the environment and risks to human health" (Sagoff 1988).

Based on this real-world experience, for the purposes of this book, we can define **safety** as a risk level of less than 1 in 1 million; risks greater than 1 in 10,000 are **unsafe;** and risks in between are up for grabs. (For comparison, police officers bear a risk of about 1 in 10,000 of being killed by a felon on the job.) Cancer risks are the most common health risks that are quantified this way.

Of course, many other health risks besides cancer are associated with pollution, such as impacts on the immune, nervous, and reproductive systems. However, the risks in these areas are much harder to quantify, and as yet there is no social consensus, as reflected in a judicial record, about exposure levels. Because noncancer health risks are not well understood, and because cancer risks can be estimated only with a substantial margin of error, the safety standard can be quite nebulous. As a result, the precise definition of safety must often be determined on a case-by-case basis through the give and take of politics. (As we will see in Chapter 10, pinning down the efficient pollution level can be quite difficult as well!)

In spite of this uncertainty, however, a safety standard in fact remains the stated goal of much environmental policy. As we explore further in Chapter 13, the basic antipollution laws covering air, water, and land pollution require cleanup to "safe" levels, period. There is no mention of a benefit–cost test in the legislation.

---

[1]For a more extended discussion, see Goodstein (1994). Shrader-Frechette (1991) presents a related defense of a safety (maximin) strategy against an efficiency (expected utility) standard.

[2]For a good discussion of the advantages and disadvantages of legislating health-based "bright-lines," see Rosenthal, Gray, and Graham (1992).

Ultimately, however, cost considerations *must* play a role in the political determination of safe pollution levels. Attainment of "objectively" safe standards in some areas would be prohibitively expensive. Indeed, while U.S. courts have thrown out regulatory standards for safety legislation based solely on benefit–cost analysis, at the same time they have allowed costs of attainment to be considered as one factor influencing the stringency of regulation. They also have interpreted safe to mean not the absence of any risk but the absence of "significant" risk. On the other hand, the courts have not allowed costs to be a factor in the determination of significant risk.

Accepting that some danger to human health is inevitable does not require abandoning the safety standard. For example, it is commonly accepted that we have a right to live free from violent behavior on the part of our neighbors. Now this right, like most others, is not enforced absolutely: We are willing to fund police departments, the court system, the construction of new jails, educational and job programs, and drug rehabilitation centers only to a certain level. Moreover, poor people receive much less protection than wealthy people do. Ultimately, the decision about how much violence to live with is a political one, influenced but not solely determined by willingness to pay.

One could characterize this approach as declaring the protection of all individuals from violent crime to be a societal right, then backing away from such a goal on a case-by-case basis in the face of rising cost. This results in a substantially different standard than would determining the police departments' homicide budget based on a benefit–cost analysis. In particular, the former will generally result in less violent crime. Returning to environmental concerns, a safety target of a maximum 1 in 1 million cancer risk may not always be economically feasible. But relaxing a safety standard that is too costly is quite different than adopting an efficiency standard.

In the real world, the safe level will certainly be influenced by the associated sacrifices in consumption. Nevertheless, safety advocates would argue that in the arena of environmental protection, costs are not and should not be a dominant factor in people's decision-making process.

Survey research seems to find widespread support for this claim. A majority of Americans consistently agree with the statement that "protecting the environment is so important that requirements and standards cannot be too high, and continuing improvements must be made regardless of the cost" (Blinder 1987). This is a very strong statement. Efficiency proponents suggest it represents softheaded thinking, and if the remark is taken literally, obviously it does. But a less harsh interpretation of this survey data is that people feel that, since *current levels* of pollution significantly affect human health and well-being, cleanup is justified regardless of the cost within the relevant range of possibilities.

To illustrate, one study asked residents of a Nevada community about their willingness to accept annual tax credits of $1,000, $3,000, and $5,000 per person in exchange for the siting of a potentially dangerous hazardous waste facility nearby. Contrary to the author's expectations, increases in the rebate had no measurable impact on approval of the facility. The results were "consistent with a threshold model of choice, whereby individuals refuse to consider compensation if the perceived risk falls in the inadmissible range. For those respondents where the risk was perceived to be too high, the rebates offered were not viewed as inadequate, but as inappropriate . . . most of the Nevada sample viewed the risks as inherently noncompensable . . ." (Kunreuther and Easterling 1990).

Behavior such as this suggests that one important benefit of environmental protection—the right not to be victimized—is unmeasurable. Casting this argument in terms of our social welfare function, in the interests of personal liberty, safety advocates put very strong weights on injuries to human health arising from pollution. To illustrate, let us return to our Chapter 4 example in which Brittany and Tyler were wrangling over smoking in the office. To a safety advocate, the social welfare function might look like this:

$$SW = U_{Tyler}(\overset{+}{\#Cigs_T}, \overset{+}{\$_T}) + U_{Brit}(\overset{-}{w * \#Cigs_T}, \overset{+}{\$_B})$$

where the weight w given to the negative impact of smoke on Brittany is a very big number, one that may well justify banning smoking altogether.[3]

Should smoking be banned in public places under a safety standard? This is a question for voters and courts to decide. One feature of the safety standard is its imprecision. No right is absolute, since rights often come in conflict with one another, and the political arena is where the issue is ultimately decided. What the safety standard maintains is that in the absence of a "compelling" argument to the contrary (which may included but is not limited to cost of attainment), damage to human health from pollution ought to be minimal. Individuals have a right to be free from the damage that secondary smoke inflicts.

5.2 The Safety Standard: Inefficient

The first objection to the safety standard is that it is, by definition, inefficient. Efficiency advocates make the following normative case against safety: Enshrining environmental health as a "right" involves committing "too many" of our overall social resources to environmental protection.

As a result of pursuing safe levels of pollution, regulators and voters have often chosen pollution control levels that may be "too high" based on a benefit–cost or efficiency standard. Consider, for example, the air toxics provision of the Clean Air Act Amendments of 1990, designed to control the emission of hazardous air pollutants. When the law was passed, the EPA estimated that at 149 industrial facilities nationwide, cancer risks to the most exposed local residents from airborne toxics were greater than 1 in 10,000; at 45 plants risks were greater than 1 in 1,000. The 1990 law required firms to impose control technology that, it was hoped, would reduce risks to below the 1 in 10,000 level.

While the costs and benefits of the legislation were difficult to pin down precisely, economist Paul Portney (1990) estimated that when the program is fully phased in, total costs will be $6 to $10 billion per year (about $60 to $100 per household). He also estimated that total benefits would be less than $4 billion per year ($40 per household).

---

[3]Kneese and Schulze (1985) formalize a libertarian social welfare function as one in which a Pareto improvement must actually take place for a policy to increase social welfare. The safety standard discussed here is not this restrictive.

Thus, "If these estimates are even close to correct, Congress and the President . . . [have shaken hands] on a landmark piece of legislation for which costs may exceed benefits by a substantial margin" (174). Why is this so?[4]

Portney argued that if people were better informed about the cost that they will bear as a result of the Clean Air Act, less stringent standards would have been imposed. And yet, the public debate over the Clean Air Act was clearly framed as "environment versus growth." The businesses that were most affected worked long and hard to get their message across. President Bush (senior) at one point spoke out against the measure as being too costly, though he ultimately signed on. In the midst of the debate, poll results indicated that 80% of the population felt that protecting the environment was more important than keeping prices down ("Americans" 1990). Thus it seems likely that the public was aware that the environmental benefits of the Act would not come without substantial sacrifice, though they may have been unaware of the exact magnitude. The alternative explanation would be that voters tend to view environmental health as a "rights" issue. One backs away from the defense of a right only when it becomes prohibitively expensive, not on the basis of a negative net-benefit analysis.

In other cases besides air toxics, pursuing safety undoubtedly generates a high degree of inefficiency. For example, consider the EPA's regulations for landfills mentioned in Application 2.0 (and discussed more fully in Chapter 10). In this case, even with the new regulations, just under 10% of landfills will still pose what the EPA considers to be a "moderate" health risk for individuals who depend on contaminated groundwater: a greater than 1 in 1,000,000 (but less than 1 in 10,000) increase in the risk of contracting cancer. However, because so few people actually depend on ground water within leaching distance of a landfill, the new regulations were predicted to reduce cancer by only two or three cases over the next 300 years. Potential benefits of the regulation not quantified by the EPA include increased ease of siting landfills, reduced damage to surface water, fairness to future generations, and an overall reduction in waste generation and related "upstream" pollution encouraged by higher disposal costs.

In aggregate, the regulations are expensive: about $5.8 billion, or approximately $2 billion per cancer case reduced. On a per household basis, this works out to an annual cost of $4.10 in increased garbage bills over the twenty year life of a landfill. An efficiency proponent would say that it is simply crazy (horribly inefficient) to spend so much money to reduce risk by so little. The $4.10 per year per household is an unjustified tax.

The landfill and air toxics cases both illustrate a more general point; regulations that protect small groups of people from risk will almost always be inefficient, since even relatively high risks will not generate many casualties. Here is a classic situation in which efficiency and fairness (measured as equal risk protection for small and large groups) conflict.

---

[4]The report is discussed in Greider (1992). For more detail on the air toxics law, see Chapter 13 and Rosenthal, Gray, and Graham (1992). In the same article, Portney (1990) argued that the acid rain provisions of the Clean Air Act would also be very inefficient. However, Burtraw et al. (1998) have since shown that the acid rain program is in fact easy to justify on efficiency grounds. Measurable benefits (mostly from reduced death and sickness, and improved visibility) will exceed the costs under virtually any set of assumptions. Indeed the estimated benefits for the acid rain program alone range from $23 to $26 billion—well above Portney's original speculation of $14 billion for the *entire* legislative package. But Portney's characterization of air toxics control as inefficient probably remains valid.

5.3 The Safety Standard: Not Cost-Effective

The second, and perhaps most telling criticism leveled at the safety standard is its lack of **cost-effectiveness.** A cost-effective solution achieves a desired goal at the lowest possible cost. In pollution control, this goal is often defined as "lives saved per dollar spent." The cost-effectiveness criticism is not that safety is a bad goal per se, but that it gives no guidance to insure that the maximum amount of safety is indeed purchased with the available resources. If safety is the only goal of pollution control, then extreme measures may be taken to attack "minimal" risk situations.

For example, the EPA, following its mandate from the Superfund legislation, has attempted to restore to drinking level purity the groundwater at toxic spill sites. Tens of millions of dollars have been spent at a few dozen sites on such efforts, yet cleanup to this level has proven quite difficult. According to one observer, cleaning up the aquifers is "like trying to get soap out of a sponge. You can wash it out ten or twelve times, but there's still some soap left." Critics have argued that rather than restoring the water to its original safe drinking quality, the goal should be simply to contain the contaminants. EPA's limited resources could then be redirected to preventing future spills. In 1990, the agency's entire groundwater protection program had an $11 million annual budget—less than the cost of many single Superfund cleanups ("Throwing Good Money" 1991).

More generally, economist Lester Lave points out that children have about a 5 in 1 million chance of contracting lung cancer from attending a school built with asbestos materials. This is dramatically less than the threat of death from other events in their lives, and Lave suggests that if our interest is in protecting lives, we would do better spending money to reduce other risks, such as cancer from exposure to secondary cigarette smoke, auto accidents, or inadequate prenatal nutrition and care (Lave 1987).[5]

A safety proponent might argue in response that devoting more resources to *each* of the first three problems would be a good idea, and in fact, the limits to dealing with them are not fundamentally limited resources, but rather a lack of political will. More generally, a safety advocate would respond that Lave's comparison is a false one, since funds freed up from "overcontrol" in the pollution arena are more likely to be devoted to increasing consumption of the relatively affluent than to saving children's lives. Taxpayers do put a limit on governmental resources for dealing with environmental, traffic safety, and children's welfare issues. Yet safety proponents ultimately have more faith in this political allocation of funds than in an allocation based on a benefit–cost test.

However, the politically determined nature of the safety standard can also set it up to fail from a cost-effectiveness perspective. Determining "significant harm" on a case-by-case basis through a political process is a far from perfect mechanism in which money and connections may play as large a part as the will of the electorate regarding environmental protection.

Chapter 12 of this book is devoted to a consideration of the government's role in environmental policy and will consider policies recommended to correct this kind of government failure. For now, safety proponents can respond only by saying that imperfect as

---

[5]Lave also points out that more people probably contract cancer from eating corn, which contains a natural carcinogen aflatoxin, than from asbestos-laden schools. To this, a safety proponent might respond that environmental protection is not about saving people from all hazards of life, but rather, in the interests of personal liberty, from hazards imposed upon them by others.

the political process is, voting remains the best mechanism for making decisions about enforcing rights. Moreover, as we will see, the benefit–cost alternative is certainly not "value-free" and is arguably as subject to influence as the political process itself.

Ultimately, however, given the limited resources available for controlling pollution, safety alone is clearly an inadequate standard for making decisions. Requiring regulatory authorities to insure a safe environment may lead them to concentrate on eradicating some risks while ignoring others. To deal with this problem, so-called **risk–benefit** studies can be used to compare the cost-effectiveness of different regulatory options. The common measure used in this approach is lives saved per dollar spent. This kind of cost-effectiveness analysis can be a useful guide to avoid an overcommitment of resources to an intractable problem. However, adopting a cost-effective approach does not mean backing away from safety as a goal. Rather, it implies buying as much safety as possible with the dollars allocated by the political process.

To summarize the last two sections, critics charge safety standards with two kinds of "irrationality": (1) inefficiency, or overcommitment of resources to environmental problems, and (2) lack of cost-effectiveness in addressing these problems. Criticism (1) is fundamentally normative and thus is a subject for public debate. In this debate, benefit–cost studies can be useful in pointing out just how inefficient the pursuit of safety might be. Criticism (2), however, does not question the goal of safety. Rather it suggests that blind pursuit of safety may in fact hinder efforts to achieve the highest possible level of environmental quality.

5.4 The Safety Standard: Regressive?

The final objection to a safety standard is based on income equity. Safety standards will generally be more restrictive than efficiency standards; as a result, they lead to greater sacrifice of other goods and services. Quoting efficiency advocate Alan Blinder: "Declaring that people have a 'right' to clean air and water sounds noble and high-minded. But how many people would want to exercise that right if the cost were sacrificing a decent level of nutrition or adequate medical care or proper housing?" (Blinder 1987, 138).

Blinder is worried that a fair number of people will in fact fall below a decent standard of living as a result of overregulation. While such dramatic effects are unlikely, given the level of hunger, poverty, and homelessness in our society, it is possible that stringent environmental standards are something poor people may simply not be able to afford. Currently, compliance with pollution regulations commits more than $200 billion of U.S. gross national product (GNP). Suppose that by moving from a safety standard to an efficiency-based standard we spent $30 billion less on environmental improvement. Would the poor be better off?

The first issue is: Who ultimately pays the hypothetical extra $30 billion for pollution control? It does appear that because much pollution is generated in the production of necessities—basic manufactured goods, garbage disposal, food, drinking water, electric power, and transport—the cost of environmental regulation is borne unevenly. In general, pollution control has a **regressive** impact on income distribution, meaning that the higher prices of consumer goods induced by regulation take a bigger percentage bite of the incomes of poor people than of wealthier individuals.

As one example, Walls and Hanson (1996) looked at the impact of some proposed automobile pollution taxes in California. They found that a tax on the annual emissions of each vehicle would cost poor folks (those in the bottom 20% of the income distribution) 2.35% of their annual income, while the average for all households was only 0.95% of annual income. Even if auto registration fees were lowered to compensate for the new tax, poor people would still pay substantially more relative to their annual incomes.

This regressive impact is fairly typical and extends to the economy-wide impact of pollution control measures. One analyst reports that overall costs as a fraction of income ranged from 0.76% to 1% for the poorest individuals to 0.16% to 1% for the wealthiest (Robison 1985).[6] This is in spite of the fact that wealthy individuals, through their consumption patterns, indirectly produce much more than their share of many common pollutants (Bingham, Anderson, and Cooley 1987).

On the other hand, poor and working-class people appear to benefit more from pollution control than the relatively wealthy. In the case of air pollution, for example, urban rather than suburban areas have been the primary beneficiaries of control policies. The effects are further magnified because those in the lower half of the income distribution have a harder time buying their own cleaner environment by way of air and water filters and conditioners, trips to spacious, well-maintained parks, or vacations in the country. Dramatic evidence of the exposure of low-income people comes from the autopsies of 100 youths from poor neighborhoods in Los Angeles. According to the pathologist, "Eighty percent of the youths had notable lung abnormalities . . . above and beyond what we've seen with smoking or even respiratory viruses. . . . It's much more severe, much more prevalent" (Mann 1991; see also Brajer and Hall 1992).

Hazardous waste facilities are situated primarily in poor communities and predominantly in minority communities. Table 5.1 shows the results from a groundbreaking study of hazardous waste landfills in the southeastern United States, where blacks make up one fifth of the total population. Three of the four facilities were in census areas where Blacks are in the majority; in all cases the total poverty rate was at least double the state average. Greater than 90% of the Black people in these areas were poor, compared to a 31% to 43% rural poverty rate for Blacks in the three states. Such high poverty rates in the affected areas suggest that Blacks in particular were benefiting little in economic terms from the presence of these major facilities.

This pattern of overrepresentation of minority populations in hazardous waste host communities has been borne out in studies in Atlanta and Los Angeles, where Hispanic communities are affected. Some evidence suggests the pattern holds for Native Americans as well. One of the worst PCB dumps in the country lies on the Mohawk Indian reservation along the St. Lawrence River ("Indian Tribes Contend" 1990).

Although some of the correlation between waste sites and minority communities is due to higher poverty rates, race appears to be an important independent factor. In

---

[6]See also the review of earlier literature in Cropper and Oates (1992).

TABLE 5.1   Race, Poverty, and Hazardous Waste Sites

Landfill (State)	Population (%)	Poverty Population (%)	
	Black	All Races	Black
Chemical Waste Management (Alabama)	90	42	100
SCA Services (South Carolina)	38	31	100
Industrial Chemical Co. (South Carolina)	52	26	92
Warren County PCB Landfill (North Carolina)	66	32	90

Source: U.S. GAO (1983). The data are based on subdivisions of political jurisdictions used by the Census Bureau for data gathering.

his summary of the evidence, Bullard (1991, 40) argues, "The facility siting controversy cannot be reduced solely to a class phenomenon . . . poor whites along with their more affluent counterparts have more options and leveraging mechanisms (formal and informal) at their disposal than do Blacks of equal status." More recent research confirms the independent link between race and exposure to environmental toxins.[7]

This type of inequity in siting of hazardous facilities has been dubbed **environmental racism** and has sparked a political movement among minority groups called the environmental justice movement. Indeed, some of the loudest calls for stricter enforcement of safety standards have come from poor and/or minority communities.

Because poor, working-class, and minority people, relative to their income, both pay more for and receive more from pollution control, it is difficult to evaluate its overall distributive impact. Thus, one cannot conclusively argue whether pollution control imposes net benefits or net costs on the lower half of the income distribution. Nevertheless, in important cases such as a carbon tax to slow global warming, which would raise the price of necessities, distributional issues need to be weighed carefully. Here, economists have recommended that much of the revenue raised from the tax be rebated back as income tax cuts disproportionately to those in the lower half of the income distribution.

Beyond the issue of distributional effects, efficiency critics of the safety standard point out correctly that the additional costs imposed on society are real. It is certainly possible that the money saved under an efficiency standard could, as Blinder implies it will, be used to fund basic human needs. However, safety proponents might argue in response that the funds would more likely be funneled into consumption among the middle and upper classes.

The last three sections have looked at criticisms of the safety standard—inefficiency, potential for cost-ineffectiveness, and the charge of regressive distributional impacts. All have some merit. And insofar as safe regulations are regressive in their net effect, safety advocates lose the moral high ground from the claim that their approach is "fairer" than efficiency. Yet, as we have seen, the alternative efficiency standard is open to its own criticisms. Perhaps no issue dramatizes the differences between these two standards better than the disposal of hazardous wastes.

---

[7]Brooks and Sethi (1997) provide both supporting data and a good literature review; see also Institute of Medicine (1999).

5.5 Siting Hazardous Waste Facilities: Safety versus Efficiency

In a 1992 internal memorandum to his staff, then chief economist at the World Bank, Lawrence Summers wrote: "Just between you and me, shouldn't the World Bank be encouraging more migration of the dirty industries to the [less developed countries]? . . . I think the economic logic behind dumping a load of toxic waste in the lowest-wage country is impeccable and we should face up to that." The memo, leaked to *The Economist* magazine, stirred considerable controversy. Brazil's environment minister responding to Summers' blunt analysis said, "It's perfectly logical but perfectly insane," and called for Summers' dismissal from the Bank.

Summers, in a letter to the magazine, maintained that his provocative statements were quoted out of context. "It is not my view, the World Bank's view, or that of any sane person that pollution should be encouraged anywhere, or that the dumping of untreated toxic wastes near the homes of poor people is morally or economically defensible. My memo tried to sharpen the debate on important issues by taking as narrow-minded an economic perspective as possible."[8] This "narrow-minded" view is what we have characterized as the efficiency perspective. However, we also know that the efficiency perspective—in this case, trade in waste—can be defended both morally and economically, since it provides *an opportunity* for making *all* parties better off. The morality of the trade depends upon the degree to which this promise is fulfilled.

Disposing of waste—hazardous, radioactive, or even simple nonhazardous municipal waste—has become an increasingly vexing and expensive problem. Such "locally unwanted land uses" (**LULUs**) impose negative externality costs on their immediate neighbors, ranging from the potential hazards of exposure to decreased land values, for the benefit of the broader society. This is true, even when very expensive protective measures are undertaken to reduce expected risk. For someone with a waste dump in his or her backyard, an "adequate" margin of safety means zero risk. By definition, communities do not want LULUs for neighbors, and the wealthier (and better organized) the community, the higher the level of safety the community will demand.

Because the benefits to the broader society of having toxic facilities are great, one possible solution to the problem of siting is to "compensate" communities with tax revenues generated by the facility, which would pay for schools, hospitals, libraries, or sewer systems. Poorer communities of course would accept lower compensation levels; thus, to reduce disposal costs some, including Summers have argued that government policy should promote this kind of "trade" in LULUs.[9] Should poor communities (or countries) be encouraged to accept dangerous facilities in exchange for dollars? The dumping controversy provides a classic example of the conflict between

---

[8]Summers' quotes are from "Let Them Eat Pollution," *The Economist,* 372, no. 7745, 8 February, 1992:66; and "Polluting the Poor," *The Economist,* 372, no. 7746, 15 February, 1992:6. Environment minister's quote is from *In These Times,* March 8, 1992.

[9]Kunreuther and Kleindorfer (1986) recommend that communities bid against one another to elicit their willingness to accept compensation in exchange for a LULU. Under such a procedure, the site would, in general, be located in the poorest community; however, the authors envision this process as a Pareto improving mechanism. In addition, the authors are not pure efficiency advocates, since they suggest government impose standards guaranteeing that "residents in all potential sites are convinced that they are sufficiently protected against adverse environmental effects. . . ." Shrader-Frechette (1991) marshalls several arguments against toxic trade.

the efficiency and safety positions on pollution control. Both sides maintain that their policy promotes overall social welfare.

First, let us consider the logic of the efficiency position. Summers defends his trade-in-toxics stance on two counts. First, if the physical damages to pollution rise as it increases, then pollution in cleaner parts of the world will do less physical damage than comparable discharges in dirty areas. In other words, Summers assumes the standard case of decreasing marginal benefits of cleanup. As he puts it: "I've always thought that under-populated countries in Africa are vastly under-polluted," relative to Mexico City or Los Angeles.

Summers' second point is that people "value" a clean environment less in poorer countries. In his words: "The concern over an agent that causes a one-in-a-million change in the odds of prostate cancer is obviously going to be much higher in a country where people survive to get prostate cancer than in a country where under-5 mortality is 200 per thousand." This difference in priorities shows up in the form of a much lower monetary value placed on all environmental amenities, including reduced risk of death. Thus, trading waste not only reduces the physical damage to the environment but also results in (much) lower dollar damages measured in terms of the fully informed willingness of the community to accept the waste. Firms will be able to dump their waste at a lower cost, *even including compensation costs,* thus freeing up resources to increase output and raise the gross global product.

Figure 5.1 presents a graphical analysis of Summers' position. Due to lower incomes (and lower population densities in some cases), the poor country has a marginal benefit of cleanup schedule lying below that of the rich country. In addition, because current pollution levels are relatively low in the poor country (PC_1 versus RC_1), the marginal benefits of cleanup are also low relative to the rich country. Transferring 10% of the waste from the rich country to the poor country reduces monetary damages (in the rich country) by the gray area and increases damages (in the poor country) by the hatched area. Overall, *monetary* damages from the pollution have been reduced by the trade.

Clearly there will be winners and losers in such a process. The winners include those in wealthy countries no longer exposed to the waste, those around the world who can buy products more cheaply if output is increased, firm managers and stockholders who reap higher profits (assuming imperfect competition), and those in the poor countries who obtain relatively high wage work at the dump sites or benefit from taxes levied against the dumping firms. The losers will be those poor country individuals, alive today and as of yet unborn, who contract cancer or suffer other diseases contracted from exposure, and those who rely on natural resources that may be damaged in the transport and disposal process.

Because dumping toxics is indeed efficient, we know the total monetary gains to the winners outweigh the total monetary loss to the losers. Thus, in theory, the winners could compensate the losers, and everyone would be made "better off." A higher risk of cancer in poor countries from exposure to waste might be offset by reduced risk of death from unsafe drinking water if, for example, revenues from accepting the waste were used to build a sewage treatment facility. In practice, however, complete compensation is unlikely. Thus, as we saw in Chapter 4, toxic dumping like any efficient strategy is not "socially optimal"; it can only be defended on utilitarian grounds if, over time, the great majority of the population benefits from the action. Summers

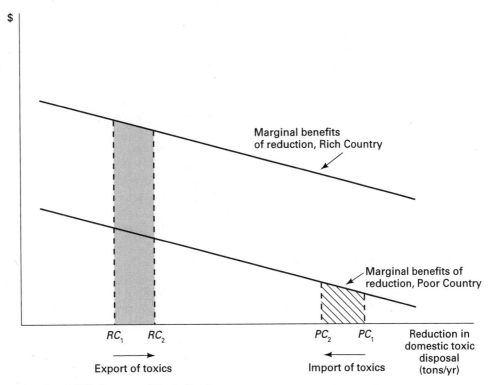

FIGURE 5.1 Efficiency and Toxic Trade

clearly believes it is in the interests of the people of poor countries themselves to accept toxic wastes.

The first response to this argument is, "What kind of world do we live in where poor people have to sell their health and the health of their children merely to get clean water to drink?" Shouldn't there be a redistribution of wealth to prevent people from having to make this kind of Faustian bargain? But an efficiency defender might note that socialist revolution is not a current policy option. Given that rich countries or individuals are not likely to give up their wealth to the poor, who are we to deny poor people an opportunity to improve their welfare through trade, if only marginally?

A more pragmatic response to the Summers argument is that, in fact, the majority of benefits from the dumping will flow to the relatively wealthy while the poor will bear the burden of costs. The postcolonial political structure in many developing countries is far from democratic. In addition, few poor countries have the resources for effective regulation. One could easily imagine waste firms compensating a few well-placed individuals handsomely for access, while paying very low taxes and ignoring any existing regulations.

In fact, a similar process may well explain the racial disparities in toxic site locations in the United States. Firms could historically deal with a predominantly white political power structure, disregarding the needs of disenfranchised black or Hispanic majorities. A survey of black neighbors of five toxic facilities reveals substantial majorities who felt that the siting process was unfair. In four of the five communities, a clear majority disagreed with a statement that the benefits clearly outweighed the costs of the facility; the community was split evenly in the fifth case (see the discussion in Bullard 1991, 86–95).

Even if poor country (or county) governments are genuinely motivated to regulate industry at the efficient level, have the resources or expertise to do so, and spread the benefits widely, they face an additional dilemma. Stiff regulation or high taxes will increase the rate of illegal dumping; unrestricted trade in waste may thus lower the welfare of the recipient country (Copeland 1991).

The basic criticism of the efficiency perspective is that the *potential* for a Pareto improvement is an insufficient condition to increase overall welfare. This is especially apparent in the case of international trade in toxics, where the benefits are likely to accrue to the wealthy in both rich and poor countries, while the costs are borne by poor residents of poor countries. In fact, we expect pollution policy to *actually increase* the welfare of most of those affected by the pollution itself.

On the other hand, safety proponents face a difficult issue in the siting of LULUs. A politically acceptable definition of "safety" cannot be worked out, since a small group bears the burden of any positive risk. Nobody wants a LULU in *his* or *her* backyard.

As a result, compensation will play an increasingly important role in the siting of hazardous facilities. And firms and governments will tend to seek out poorer communities where compensation packages will be lower. Yet there are at least two preconditions for insuring that the great majority of the affected population in fact benefit from the siting. The first of these is a government capable of providing effective regulation. The second is an open political process combined with well-informed, democratic decision making in the siting process.[10]

The siting of a LULU presents a case in which the important insight of efficiency proponents—that something close to a Pareto improvement is possible—can be implemented. But to do so requires that the enforceable pollution standard be quite close to safety. It also requires an informed and politically enfranchised population.

5.6 Summary

In the last two chapters we have wound our way through a complex forest of arguments to examine two different answers to the question, "How much pollution is too much?" Table 5.2 provides a summary of their features.

The first standard, efficiency, relies heavily on benefit–cost estimates. In theory, it requires precise calculation of *marginal* benefits and costs, and leads to maximization of the net monetary benefits to be gained from environmental protection. In practice, as we shall see later, benefit–cost analysts are able only to roughly balance benefits and costs. The efficiency standard requires a belief that intangible environmental benefits can be adequately measured and monetized. This in turn sanctions a "technocratic" approach to deciding how much pollution is too much.

---

[10]The Environmental Impact Statement procedure described in Chapter 7 has been credited with providing a forum for such efforts in the recent siting of incineration facilities in Utah (Clough and Wann 1990).

TABLE 5.2   Comparing Efficiency and Safety

1. SOCIAL GOAL

EFFICIENCY:	Marginal benefits equal marginal costs
SAFETY:	Danger to health/environment "minimized"

2. IMPLIED SOCIAL WELFARE FUNCTION

EFFICIENCY:
$$SW = U_A(\overset{+}{X_A}, \overset{-}{P_A}) + U_R(\overset{+}{X_R}, \overset{-}{P_R}) + U_T(\overset{+}{X_T}, \overset{-}{P_T}) + \ldots$$

SAFETY:
$$SW = U_A(\overset{+}{X_A}, w * \overset{-}{P_A}) + U_R(\overset{+}{X_R}, w * \overset{-}{P_R}) + U_T(\overset{+}{X_T}, w * \overset{-}{P_T}) + \ldots$$

Weights; $w > 1$

3. ADVANTAGES/DISADVANTAGES

EFFICIENCY:	Maximizes measurable net monetary benefits/ relies heavily on assumptions of benefit–cost analysis
SAFETY:	Seems to be consistent with public opinion/ often cost-ineffective and may be regressive

By contrast, the safety standard ignores formal benefit–cost comparisons to pursue a health-based target defined by an explicitly political process. In theory, under a safety standard, regulators are directed to get as close to a 1 in 1 million cancer risk as they can, while also pursuing more nebulous noncancer safety goals, all conditional on the funds allocated to them by the political system. In practice, regulators often back away from safety when faced with high compliance costs.

The social welfare function for the safety standard relies on a liberty argument, putting heavy weights on the welfare reduction from pollution. As a result, as is illustrated in Figure 5.2, a stricter pollution standard is called for than is implied by the efficiency standard. Efficiency proponents attack the "fairness" defense of safety with the charge that it is regressive—but this claim is hard to either verify or refute in general.

One point not highlighted in Table 5.2 is that the choice between the two standards does not affect the long-run employment picture. The more stringent safety standard may result in slightly more short-run structural job loss; yet it also creates more jobs in the environmental protection industry. (We will discuss this issue more fully in Chapter 9.) *The real trade-off is between increased material consumption and increased environmental quality.*

Beyond concerns of fairness, choice between the safety and efficiency standards also depends on two related factors. First, how fully do monetary estimates capture the benefits of environmental protection? Second, what real benefits would we gain from the increased consumption that is sacrificed by tighter environmental controls? If benefit estimates leave out much that is hard to quantify, or if increased material consumption just feeds a rat race that leaves no one any happier, then safety may be "more efficient" than efficiency! We will explore these two issues later in the first part of the book.

FIGURE 5.2 Costs, Benefits, Efficiency, and Safety

Before that, however, the next two chapters will consider a problem we have so far left off the table: sustainability. How should we deal the interests of future generations into environmental protection measures taken today?

APPLICATION 5.0

Controlling Air Toxics

As noted in the chapter, one of the Clean Air Act Amendments passed by the U.S. government in 1990 was designed to control the emission of hazardous air pollutants. The EPA released a publication that year that estimated that at 149 industrial facilities nation-wide, cancer risks to the most exposed local residents from airborne toxics were greater than 1 in 10,000; at 45 plants risks were greater than 1 in 1,000.

The new air toxics law required firms to impose control technology that, it was hoped, would reduce risks to below the 1 in 10,000 level. After the control technologies are installed, a follow-up risk analysis will be conducted to see if further control is necessary to further reduce any unsafe exposure. While the legislation does not require risk reduction to the 1 in 1 million level, that remains the long-run target.

1. Clearly, air toxics control is justified on safety grounds. Suppose that total benefits of the legislation just matched total costs, at $5 billion annually. Would air toxics control be justified on efficiency grounds?
2. Also as noted in the chapter, Portney (1990) has in fact criticized the legislation from an efficiency perspective. He puts estimated total costs at $6 to $10 billion per year, with total benefits at $0 to $4 billion per year. The air toxics legislation attacks some fairly significant risks. How can the estimated benefits be so low (as low as zero)?

3.   Suppose the air toxics regulations raised household expenditures on gasoline (due to extra controls on oil refineries) by an average of $20 per year. If millionaire Mary and janitor Jane each paid the extra $20, in what sense is the impact of the legislation regressive?

KEY IDEAS IN EACH SECTION

5.0   This chapter defines and then critically examines a **safety standard** for pollution control. Safety standards are defended primarily on fairness grounds. However, if unquantified benefits are large and/or the true costs of protection are overstated due to rat-race effects, then safe regulations may be more efficient than those passing a benefit–cost test.

5.1   Safety standards are defended on **personal liberty** grounds. A political consensus has developed that environmental cancer risks less than 1 in 1 million are considered **safe,** while risks greater than 1 in 10,000 are generally **unsafe.** There is no consensus on whether risks lying in between are safe. A precise safety standard cannot yet be defined for noncancer risks or ecosystem protection. In these areas, safe levels are determined politically on a case-by-case basis.

5.2   The first criticism of the safety standard is that it is often inefficiently strict. This is a normative criticism and is thus a proper subject for political debate.

5.3   The second criticism of the safety standard is that it fails to give sufficient guidance to insure **cost-effectiveness.** Cost-effectiveness is often measured in dollars spent per life saved. If regulators pursue safety at every turn, they may devote too many resources to eradicating small risks, while ignoring larger ones. This problem can be alleviated by using **risk–benefit analysis.** The cost-effectiveness criticism is not that too many resources are being devoted to environmental protection, but rather that these resources are not being wisely spent.

5.4   The final criticism of the safety standard is that it might have a **regressive** impact on income distribution. While poor people do pay a higher percentage of their income for pollution control than do rich people, poor, working class, and minority communities also benefit disproportionately. (The greater exposure borne by minorities is referred to as **environmental racism.**) Thus, the overall impact of environmental regulation on income distribution is uncertain. Moreover, it is not clear that freeing up resources from environmental control would in fact lead to increases in well-being among the poor.

5.5   The siting of a **LULU** is used to compare and contrast the efficiency and safety standards for pollution control. In such a case, efficiency is a very hard standard to implement because it ignores fairness issues. Thus, something like a safety standard is generally enforced. If a basic level of "safe" protection is afforded through effective regulation, however, Pareto improving compensation schemes can result in some movement toward efficient regulation.

REFERENCES

"Americans are Willing to Sacrifice to Reduce Pollution, They Say." 1990. *Wall Street Journal,* 20 April.

Bingham, Taylor H., Donald W. Anderson, and Phillip C. Cooley. 1987. "Distribution of the Generation of Air Pollution." *Journal of Environmental Economics and Management* 14:30–40.

Blinder, Alan. 1987. *Hard Heads, Soft Hearts.* New York: Addison-Wesley.

Brajer, Victor, and Jane V. Hall. 1992. "Recent Evidence on the Distribution of Air Pollution Effects." *Contemporary Policy Issues* 10:63–71.

Brooks, Nancy, and Rajiv Sethi. 1997. "The Distribution of Pollution: Community Characteristics and Exposure to Air Toxics." *Journal of Environmental Economics and Management* 32, no. 2:233–250.

Bullard, Robert D. 1991. *Dumping in Dixie: Race, Class and Environmental Quality.* Boulder, CO: Westview.

Burtraw, Dallas, Alan Krupnick, Erin Mansur, David Austin, and Deidre Farrell. 1998. "Reducing Air Pollution and Acid Rain." *Contemporary Economic Policy* 16, no. 4:379–400.

Clough, Kerrigan, and David Wann. 1990. "A Burning Issue." *The Bureaucrat,* Spring, 25–29.

Copeland, Brian R. 1991. "International Trade in Waste Products in the Presence of Illegal Disposal." *Journal of Environmental Economics and Management* 20:143–162.

Cropper, Maureen L., and Wallace Oates. 1992. "Environmental Economics: A Survey." *Journal of Economic Literature* 30, no. 2:675–740.

Goodstein, Eban. 1994. "In Defense of Health-based Standards." *Ecological Economics* 10, no. 3:189–195.

Greider, William. 1992. *Who Will Tell the People? The Betrayal of American Democracy.* New York: Simon & Schuster.

"Indian Tribes Contend with Some of Worst of America's Pollution." 1990. *Wall Street Journal,* 29 November.

Institute of Medicine. 1999. *Toward Environmental Justice: Research, Education and Health Policy Needs.* Washington, DC: National Academy Press.

Kneese, Alan V., and William D. Schulze. 1985. "Ethics and Environmental Economics." In *Handbook of Natural Resource Economics,* vol. 1, edited by A. V. Kneese and J. L. Sweeney. New York: Elsevier.

Kunreuther, Howard, and Douglas Easterling. 1990. "Are Risk Benefit Trade-offs Possible in Siting Hazardous Facilities?" *American Economic Review* 80, no. 2:252–256.

Kunreuther, Howard, and Paul Kleindorfer. 1986. "A Sealed-Bid Auction Mechanism for Siting Noxious Facilities." *American Economic Review* 76, no. 2:295–299.

Lave, Lester. 1987. "Health and Safety Risk Analyses: Information for Better Decisions." *Science* 236:297.

Mann, Eric. 1991. *LA's Lethal Air.* Los Angeles: Labor Community Strategy Center.

Portney, Paul. 1990. "Policy Watch: Economics and the Clean Air Act." *Journal of Economic Perspectives* 4, no. 4:173–182.

Robison, H. David. 1985. "Who Pays for Industrial Pollution Abatement?" *Review of Economics and Statistics* 67, no. 4:702–706.

Rosenthal, Alon, George M. Gray, and John D. Graham. 1992. "Legislating Acceptable Cancer Risk from Exposure to Toxic Chemicals." *Ecology Law Quarterly* 19, no. 2:269–362.

Sagoff, Mark. 1988. *The Economy of the Earth.* Cambridge, UK: Cambridge University Press.

Shrader-Frechette, K. S. 1991. *Risk and Rationality: Philosophical Foundations for Populist Reform.* Berkeley, CA: University of California Press.

"Throwing Good Money at Bad Water Yields Scant Improvement." 1991. *Wall Street Journal,* 15 May.

Travis, Curtis, S. A. Richter, E. A. Crouch, R. Wilson, and E. Klema. 1987. "Cancer Risk Management." *Environmental Science and Technology* 21, no. 5:415–420.

U.S. Government Accounting Office. 1983. *Siting of Hazardous Waste Landfills and Their Correlation with Racial and Economic Status of Surrounding Communities.* Washington, DC: GAO.

Walls, Margaret, and Jean Hanson. 1996. "Distributional Consequences of an Environmental Tax Shift: The Case of Motor Vehicle Emission Taxes." *RFF Discussion Paper 96–11.* Washington, DC: Resources for the Future.

SUSTAINABILITY: A NEOCLASSICAL VIEW

6.0 Introduction

The Iroquois Indians are said to have lived under a traditional directive to consider the impact of their decisions on the next seven generations. Due to the dramatic increase in the pace of technological change, it would be difficult for us today to even imagine with much precision the needs and wants of our descendants two hundred years hence. Yet, many decisions we make today have implications for the well-being of the seventh generation. In this chapter and the next, we will move beyond our efficiency versus safety debate over pollution control standards, and consider these long-run impacts. In the process, we will shift our focus from allowable standards for pollution to maximum targets for the exploitation of natural capital.

In fact, the two concepts are closely related. We can think of long-lived pollution as exhausting a natural resource called an **environmental sink**—the absorptive capacity of the environment. A critical feature of many of today's industrial pollutants is indeed their longevity. Each one of us carries in the fat cells of our bodies residues of the pesticide DDT even though it was banned from use in this country in the early 1970s. Chlorofluorocarbons released into the atmosphere today will continue to contribute to ozone depletion for decades. Certain types of high-level nuclear waste retain their toxicity for tens of thousands of years.

Pollutants such as these that accumulate in the environment are called **stock pollutants.** By contrast, pollutants that do their damage relatively quickly and are then either diluted to harmless levels or transformed into harmless substances are known as **flow pollutants.** Examples include acid rain, smog, and noise or heat pollution.

Stock pollutants use up the critical natural resource of environmental sinks. For example, our bodies are one sink that absorbs waste DDT to some level with minimal damage; we have already used up some, if not all, of that capacity. Stock pollutants that exhaust environmental sinks are one channel through which we of the current generation affect future generations. At the same time we also exploit scarce natural resources that are inputs into the economy—both renewable (water, wood, fish, and soil) and nonrenewable (minerals, oil, the genetic code in species). Economists refer to both these natural resource inputs and environmental waste sinks as **natural capital,** thereby stressing the notion that they are productive assets.

Most people accept that we have a responsibility to control our emission of stock pollutants and manage the planet's natural resources so as to provide future generations with a high quality of life. We can define this goal more precisely as **sustainability:** providing the typical person alive in the future with a standard of living, including both material *and* environmental welfare, at least as high as that enjoyed by the typical person today.[1] Achieving this goal may not be easy; as we have seen, material growth often comes at the expense of environmental quality and vice versa.

Discussions around sustainability have divided economists into two broad groups, **neoclassical** and **ecological.** (For purposes of argument, I'm going to draw very sharp distinctions between these two views; in reality many economists have one foot in both camps.)[2] The main bone of contention between these two groups is this: To what degree can **created capital,** or human-made capital, substitute for natural capital? In concrete terms, can we continue, for example, to replace natural topsoil with fertilizers, without substantially raising the cost of food production? Neoclassicals would say yes; ecologicals would say no.

Neoclassical economists view natural and created capital as substitutes in production. They are technological optimists, believing that as resources become scarce, prices will rise, and human innovation will yield high-quality substitutes, lowering prices once again. (For more on this point, see Appendix 6A.) More fundamentally, neoclassicals tend to view nature as highly resilient; pressure on ecosystems will lead to steady, predictable degradation, but no surprises. This view of small (marginal) changes and smooth substitution between inputs is at the heart of the broad neoclassical traditions in economics. (If you have taken intermediate microeconomics, let your mind drift back to a smooth, bow-shaped *isoquant;* now recall how two inputs such as capital and labor could be easily substituted for each other while keeping the total output level the same!)

From a broader perspective, neoclassicals generally believe that the global spread of market-based economies provide a powerful foundation for achieving a sustainable future. While still seeing a need for government regulations to control pollution and resource depletion, neoclassicals are generally optimistic and believe that as markets spread, living standards around the globe will continue to rise and population growth rates will fall, all within an acceptable range of environmental degradation. This is not to say that neoclassicals believe there are no trade-offs, only that sustainability is more or less assured in a well-functioning and properly regulated market system.

By contrast, **ecological economists** argue that natural and created capital are fundamentally **complements**—that is, they are used together in production and have low substitutability (L-shaped isoquants, for you micro fans). Technological pessimists, ecologicals

---

[1]This definition follows Pezzey (1992), who also discusses other possible interpretations of the term.

[2]The group I call "neoclassicals" is represented by the Association of Environmental and Resource Economists (AERE), founded in 1978. AERE is housed at a think tank in Washington, DC, called Resources for the Future (RFF). RFF's home page, including access to information on AERE, is www.rff.org.

The "ecologicals" group is the International Society for Ecological Economics, founded in 1988; browse ISEE at www.ecoeco.org.

believe that as the sinks and sources that make up our stock of natural capital are exhausted, human welfare will decline. Fundamentally, ecologists view natural systems as rather fragile. For example, if one component, say, of a fishery is disturbed, the productivity of the entire ecosystem may plummet. This vision of web-like linkages between nature and the economy has led this group to refer to itself as ecological economists.

In contrast to neoclassicals, ecological economists consider the globalizing world economy to be on a fundamentally unsustainable path, and that further ecological pressure in the form of population and consumption growth is likely to lead to real disaster. While not hostile to the spread of markets or to incentive-based approaches to resolving environmental problems, ecological economists see a largely expanded role for government in aggressively protecting our dwindling stock of natural capital.

Arguments between ecological and neoclassical economists can get rather heated—ecologicals refer to the latter disparagingly as "cornucopians" (look it up) while the charge of "doomsayers" flies back. But the debate is quite useful. Neoclassical views may be more helpful in some cases, ecological views in others. The issue ultimately boils down to the degree of substitution between natural and created capital, and this differs from case to case.

This chapter and the next provide two takes on sustainability, given these very different perspectives on the role of natural capital. We will start with the more optimistic neoclassical view.

6.1 Measuring Sustainability: Net National Welfare

Economists are hands-on types, and if we can't measure something, we find it hard to talk about it. In concrete terms, how do we know if we are achieving sustainability or not? Because neoclassical economists believe in a high degree of substitutability between natural and created capital, their approach to measuring sustainability is to weigh directly the material benefits of growth against its environmental costs, both measured in dollar terms.

The most widely used measure of the health of the economy is gross domestic product, or GDP. GDP is the government's measure of the final value of all goods and services produced and consumed in the market each year; it also equals the income earned and spent by consumers.

But GDP is a bad measure of sustainability: whether the typical person is better off or not in the long run. In short, GDP has at least four well-known problems.[3]

1. *GDP fails to include the value of nonmarket production.* Housework, child care, and volunteer work are the three biggies.
2. *GDP fails to subtract the costs of growth.* A true measure of welfare needs to account for the fact that raising GDP imposes costs on society. These include externalities: the direct health and productivity costs of pollution and congestion, borne by third parties. Sometimes these externality costs show up as what are called defensive expenditures—money spent to protect oneself from

[3]For a broader and accessible critique of GDP, see Cobb, Halstead, and Rowe (1995). Clifford Cobb compiled the ISEW, discussed in Section 6.6, for the book by his father, John Cobb, and Herman Daly (1989). Clifford Cobb and his colleagues have updated this measure, now calling it the Genuine Progress Indicator. The GPI is updated on the Web at Redefining Progress, www.redefiningprogress.org.

a deteriorating environment. Examples include increased doctor visits, water purifiers, and cell phones (to make traffic jams tolerable). Some analysts include as defensive expenditures measures to address crime and family breakdown, which they view as costs of economic growth (Cobb, Halstead, and Rowe 1995). When defensive expenditures boost final consumer demand, the GDP measure perversely counts them as increasing well-being!

The costs of growth also include increased spending on internalized externalities. These include the direct costs to industry and government of pollution control and cleanup (some $224 billion per year in the United States). Here again, GDP counts on the positive side of the ledger some expenditures on pollution abatement and cleanup. Thus, after the giant oil spill in Alaska by the Exxon *Valdez,* the cleanup money spent by the company translated into a big boost to Alaskan consumer spending, and thus GDP.

3. *GDP fails to account for the depreciation of the capital used up in production.* The U.S. government actually publishes an adjusted GDP measure, called net national product (NNP), which does take into account the depreciation of physical, human-made capital. However, our main concern here is the lack of accounting for the depreciation of natural capital—both sources and sinks—used up in the production of GDP.

4. *GDP reflects the experience of the "average" rather than the "typical" person.* GDP is reported on a per capita basis, showing the *mean* (average) value for a society. But for a measure of sustainability, we are interested in the welfare of the *median* (typical) person. If the income distribution in a country is getting more equal, median welfare will rise faster than if the typical worker finds him or herself being "downsized."

Given these four problems, we need a better measure of the welfare of the typical person—let us call such a measure of sustainability **net national welfare (NNW).** Currently, there is no universally agreed-upon approach to this kind of environmental/economic accounting. However, because such a measure would be quite valuable, economists have recently been focusing a lot of attention on calculating NNW.[4]

In principle, NNW can be defined as the total annual output of both market and nonmarket goods and services minus the total externality and cleanup costs associated with these products, minus the depreciation of capital, both natural and human-made, used up in production. Figure 6.1 shows the arithmetic.

The first step in calculating NNW is to augment GDP with nonmarket consumption—the value of leisure time, nonmarket work such as housecleaning and child care, and the value of capital services, such as owner-occupied housing. From augmented GDP, one then subtracts both market and externality costs associated with economic growth from GDP. These range from obvious pollution control expenses, to the increased congestion costs of commuting to work, to increased spending on health care due to environmental damage. Economists have developed a variety of

---

[4]See Nordhaus and Kokkelenberg (1999), and the special edition on green accounting of *Environment and Development Economics* 5, nos. 1 and 2, February/May 2000.

NNW = Total Output – Costs of Growth – Depreciation

    = GDP + nonmarket output
        – externality costs
        – pollution abatement and cleanup costs
        – depreciation of created capital
        – depreciation of natural capital

Note: This countrywide measure of NNW must be adjusted to reflect changes in income distribution, since sustainability requires that the *typical* person be no worse off.

FIGURE 6.1 Calculating Net National Welfare

techniques for estimating the costs of both pollution control and environmental damage. We will explore these methods in detail in Chapters 8 and 9.

As a last bit of arithmetic, one must subtract a depreciation fund—the amount of money necessary to replace the capital, both natural and created, used up in the production of GDP, and to provide for a growing population. Included in this fund would be depreciation of machines, plant, equipment and physical infrastructure, as well as much government investment in human capital, such as spending on education and health care.

The depreciation of human-made capital is relatively straightforward, but how does one value nonrenewable resources used up in production? Calculating the "right" depreciation rates for lost topsoil, species that become extinct, or exhausted petroleum reserves is difficult, controversial—and the subject of the next section.

The formula in Figure 6.1 gives a value for net national welfare on a countrywide basis. But a final adjustment for changes in income distribution is required—rather than look at the average (or per capita) NNW, we need to consider what is happening to the median individual.

Figure 6.1 gives us what we want, at least in principle—a way to measure sustainability. Our NNW figure incorporates both the (positive) material and (negative) environmental features of economic growth. Under the neoclassical assumption that reductions in environmental quality can be either remedied or substituted for by new technologies, subtracting the environmental costs of growth from the material benefits makes sense.

Recall that neoclassical economists are technological optimists. Essentially, they *assume* that NNW for the median individual has been rising over time and that we are thus, by definition, living in a sustainable economy. Is this a fair assumption? Let us defer that question until the end of the chapter and, until then, remain sustainability optimists.

Even as neoclassicals, however, we still recognize a variety of ways in which specific actions today can nevertheless lower the welfare of future generations below what it otherwise could be. Given that NNW is rising, neoclassicals argue for achieving *the maximum NNW over time,* a goal known as **dynamic efficiency.**

But maximizing NNW over time brings us back to the issue of measuring it. The next section turns to resource exploitation and its impact on the welfare of future generations. In the process, we'll tackle one of the thorny issues in sustainability accounting: measuring the depreciation of natural capital.

6.2 Natural Capital Depreciation

Any human-made capital good has a relatively fixed useful life before it wears out; a pizza delivery truck, for example, may last for five years. Each year, then, we say the truck has "depreciated" in value. Depreciation is a measure of how much of the truck is used up each year in the delivery process. How should we value the loss of natural capital—such as oil, timber, or species diversity—that we use up in production?

Let's begin answering this question with a

PUZZLE

Suppose that Mr. Bill has an oil field containing 100 barrels of oil on his property. He can hire a firm from a neighboring town to pump his oil at a total economic cost of $1 per barrel, but because it is scarce, the price of oil is $2 per barrel, well above cost.[5] Scarcity of the oil means that Mr. Bill can earn a **resource rent** of $1 per barrel from its production. Resource rents develop when, due to absolute scarcity of resources, prices get bid up above the total economic cost of production (see Chapter 3). They are thus a form of economic profit.

If all the oil is produced and sold today:

1. How much will Mr. Bill's *net* income (economic profits) rise for the year?
2. If Mr. Bill spends all the income on a new 80-inch color TV (which he keeps locked up in his bedroom), how much worse off are his children?
3. If Mr. Bill's family were the sole residents of the country of Billsville, how much would Billsville GDP rise?
4. How much would Billsville NNW rise?

The big question addressed by the Billsville situation is this: To what extent does GDP overstate true NNW due to the fact that the current generation is running down the stock of natural capital? We are seeking a way to measure the wealth that we of the current generation are taking away from future generations by using up scarce natural capital.

SOLUTION

Economic profits are equal to total income ($200) minus total economic costs ($100), or $100. This is just the resource rent. If Mr. Bill blows the money on a consumption binge, his children are also worse off by the value of the resource rent (not $200, since they too would have to pay $100 to get the oil out of the ground). Thus, *none* of this increased income can be devoted to Mr. Bill's consumption and still be sustainable. He needs to invest the entire $100 of resource rent in created capital to replace his natural capital and thus insure that his children are not being made worse off by his action.[6]

---

[5]Total economic costs include interest payments on borrowed capital and a "normal" profit for any equity financing. See any introductory microeconomic textbook for more on this concept.

[6]This is not strictly true if real interest rates exceed the real rate of growth of oil prices. In such a case, Bill could use a small portion of the profits to finance his own consumption and, utilizing the power of compound interest, not make his children any worse off.

Billsville GDP also rises by $100, the increase in net income. He now has the option of going on a shopping spree at the local Kmart. But, Mr. Bill *cannot* increase his consumption out of the oil profits (the resource rent) *without* penalizing his kids. Thus NNW does not rise at all!

Applying the Mr. Bill logic in the real world to the U.S. oil industry, government analysts estimated that U.S. GDP in 1987 overstated real NNW by between $23 billion and $84 billion (Nordhaus and Kokkelenberg 1999).[7]

Note in this example that Mr. Bill is not necessarily punishing his kids by draining the oil today. If he invests the resource rent productively, his kids may well be better off than if he were to leave them the untapped field. Investing resource rents will pay off, especially if, due to technological change, oil prices may actually fall in the future. Neoclassical economists, again reflecting an underlying technological optimism, often urge early exploitation of resources for precisely this reason. Ignoring the cost of extraction, if oil prices are rising in percentage terms at less than the going rate of interest (true over the last fifty years), Bill's family will clearly be better off if he develops the field today *and* banks the rents.

The oil-rich state of Alaska has actually pursued such an approach, diverting some of its oil tax revenues into the so-called Permanent Fund. Earnings from this giant investment fund (over and above the amount reinvested to keep the fund intact) are paid out annually to all Alaskans, totaling around $1,000 per person per year. Alaska has also invested in a lot of created capital—roads, telecommunications, a better-educated population. The fund and the greater stock of created capital may not fully compensate future generations of Alaskans for the depletion of the resource. Nevertheless, it does suggest how the current generation can directly substitute created wealth for natural wealth, making resource depletion sustainable in economic terms.

The Mr. Bill puzzle suggests a **depreciation rule** for natural capital: *Depreciation equals the measured value of the resource rent.*[8] The resource rent, not the full market value of the resource, is what future generations are losing by our exploitation of natural capital. It is also exactly the amount that needs to be saved and invested (for example, in a permanent fund, or in education, productive infrastructure, or research and development) if resource depletion is to be sustainable.

Figure 6.2 illustrates how one might calculate the resource rent from a supply-and-demand diagram for tropical hardwoods. The long-run supply curve (as you surely recall from an introductory course) reflects the full cost of production. Area *A*, between the supply curve and the price thus shows the resource rent earned by firms in the hardwood industry.[9]

---

[7]In addition to depreciation, these numbers include the value of the new discoveries as well as re-evaluation of existing reserves due to price changes.

[8]Solow (1992) develops this point and also provided the inspiration for the puzzle; see also Nordhaus and Kokkelenberg (1999).

[9]The area *A* is often considered to be Ricardian rent, not resource rent. However, a Ricardian rent can be thought of as a resource rent for a narrowly defined resource, for example, "low-cost timber." At any rate, all of the rent from the resource needs to be saved and invested to insure sustainability.

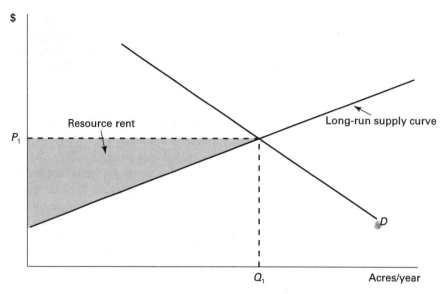

FIGURE 6.2 Measuring Resource Rent

A study by Repetto (1989) sought to estimate the NNW of Indonesia by calculating resource rents from the depletion of petroleum, timber, and topsoil, and then subtracting these figures from GDP. Repetto found that while GDP increased at a rate of 7.1% from 1971 to 1984, the adjusted measure of NNW grew by around 4%. Overall, Indonesia did make genuine economic progress across the decade but considerably less than was indicated by the growth in GDP. However, Repetto also notes that at least for a few years, Indonesian development was unsustainable. Between 1979 and 1981, according to our adjustment rule, natural capital was being depleted faster than investment was creating new capital.[10]

A PROBLEM WITH THE DEPRECIATION RULE

Our GDP adjustment requires that we subtract the estimated value of the resource rent to account for the depreciation of natural capital. In this way we do not count as income the reduction in wealth suffered by future generations. Unfortunately, the GDP adjustment rule is not perfect. There is a basic theoretical problem with the approach: The resource rent is measured using *today's* prices. And yet, prices today may not accurately reflect the fair value that future generations are liable to place on natural capital—whether it is oil, blue whales, wilderness, or medicinal products from the rain forest.

Market systems do not completely ignore the interests of the future when scarce resources are being consumed. For example, if rain-forest logging companies expect

---

[10]Repetto reports that gross investment was lower than resource depletion in those years. To maintain sustainability, net investment (which includes an adjustment for the depreciation of created capital) would have to exceed the drawdown of natural capital stocks. Repetto used the value-added in these industries as a measure of the resource rent, a rather crude approximation. World Bank (1992, 35) reports on similar efforts to adjust GDP in Mexico; see also Pearce and Atkinson (1993).

timber prices to rise at a rapid rate due to future shortages, they will hold off exploiting their holdings in order to reap greater profits. This mechanism, known as **profit-based conservation,** is illustrated in Figure 6.3 below, using a simple supply-and-demand analysis.

The supply curves S_1 and S_2 illustrate forest depletion in the *absence* of profit-based conservation. In period 1, all timber acreage that is profitable at the equilibrium price P_1 is brought onto the market. In period 2, the forest resource has shrunk dramatically, shifting the supply curve in and driving the price up to P_2.

However, firms are likely to recognize such an effect and therefore withhold some supply in the first period. This will shift the first-period supply curve in to S_1' and increase price to P_1'. Now more supply will be available in the second period, shifting the curve out to S_2' and reducing price to P_2'. Profit-based conservation thus tempers the current rate of depletion *and* drives up the current period price to reflect the resource scarcity. Thus, resource rents do take into account, in a limited way, the interests of future generations.

Profit-based conservation means that resource rents today do take into account future demand. However, this does not mean that the interests of future generations are being *fairly* represented. One reason for this is that property rights in developing countries are often uncertain, leading to "use it or lose it" behavior, increasing supply, and driving down prices and resource rents. This issue is explored further in Chapter 22. Uncertainty about future needs and preferences can also limit the effectiveness of profit-based conservation. A hundred years ago, it would have been virtually inconceivable to think that people would have actually wanted to have wolves and grizzly bears living close by. Thus, no private entrepreneurs contemplated establishing grizzly ranges in Montana in 1890.

Profit-based conservation insures that *some* resources will be conserved to satisfy the needs of the future and, thus, that prices and resource rents today will rise. But as we will see later in this chapter, a general feature of market psychology is that people

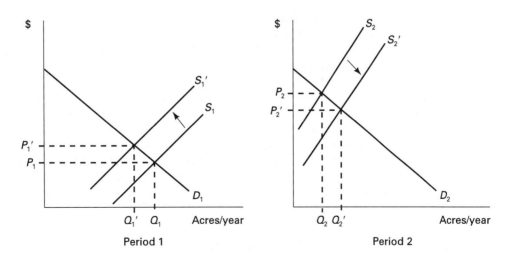

Tropical hardwood market

FIGURE 6.3 Profit-Based Conservation

prefer current over future consumption. This preference for current consumption will tend to generate unsustainably high levels of resource depletion and/or current consumption over investment. Thus, it is unlikely that today's resource rents reflect a fair accounting of the impact of resource depletion on future generations. Instead, adjusting GDP by the value of the resource rent probably reflects a *lower bound* of the true reduction in future wealth due to the drawdown in the stock of natural capital.

That being said, a rough approach to depreciating natural capital is to follow our depreciation rule. Let us end this section by returning to Mr. Bill's world to illustrate the two ways in which a measure of NNW that accounts for the depletion of natural capital can be useful.

1. **Indicator of progress.** If properly measured NNW rose over time, we could confidently say that society would be better off, since increases in material welfare would not be coming at the expense of future generations. In Mr. Bill's case, draining the oil field leads to no increase in NNW, but a $100 increase in GDP. Thus, the year the field is drained, the Bill family is not better off despite the increase in GDP.

2. **Sustainable resource use.** The difference between GDP and NNW that results from resource depletion must be "saved" in order to insure sustainability. This savings can take the form of investment in created capital (putting the money into a college fund). However, if the current generation is too consumption oriented and refuses to invest (Mr. Bill buys his TV), the savings gap would have to be made up by setting aside some natural capital for preservation, thus lowering GDP. Mr. Bill's children should cancel the development order rather than let him head off to the Kmart.

    More generally, suppose that GDP is $12,000 per capita, but we find that NNW is only $8,000 per capita. To ensure sustainability we must either (1) sock away $4,000 per capita in savings and investment in created capital or (2) begin preserving our natural capital.

This section has addressed an important technical issue: How can we measure progress toward sustainable development? From a neoclassical perspective, properly measured NNW subtracts resource rents from GDP. In addition, we have seen that it is possible to penalize future generations by consuming, rather than investing, resource rents. This is one case in which neoclassicals concede that individual resource development decisions may be unsustainable (while still assuming overall sustainability at the economy-wide level).

It is also possible to overexploit natural resources both because of the common property problem and because of the current generation's power over resource decisions. But why don't markets encourage investors to take a long view when it comes to protecting natural capital? We now move on to consider how the market in fact evaluates trade-offs between our needs and those of generations to come.

6.3 Future Benefits, Costs, and Discounting

In this section we will think about how to value benefits reaped by future generations that result from our actions today. Consider the following:

PUZZLE

Would you prefer to have $100 in real purchasing power this year or next year or are you indifferent? By "real purchasing power" I mean that if you opt to take the money next year, you will be compensated for any inflation. Assume you don't "need" the money any more this year than next.

SOLUTION

This one requires a little business acumen. It's better to take the money up-front, put it in the bank, and earn interest. As a result, you will have more "real purchasing power" next year than this year. For example, suppose the interest rate on a savings account were 3%, and there was no inflation. If you banked the $100, next year you would have $103 to spend.

Now, stop to think. Where exactly did that extra $3 come from? From the bank, obviously, but where did the bank get it? The bank had loaned out your money to a businessperson (or to the government) who in turn invested it in productive real assets: machines, buildings, roads, schools. A year later, thanks to your saving effort, and other people's ingenuity and labor, the economy as a whole was capable of producing 3 more dollars worth of stuff. At the national level, this year-to-year increase in productive capacity leads GDP to grow between 2% and 3% per year. This growth is the ultimate source of profits, interest, and wage increases.

This puzzle illustrates a crucial point: Investment is productive. As a result, at least from an individual's point of view, $100 today is worth more than $100 next year or $100 fifty years from now. From a social point of view, there is a major **opportunity cost to foregone investment.** Investment of $100 today is worth much more now than the same investment in the future.

How does this observation relate back to the environment? Let us return to a global warming example, suitably simplified. Suppose that, if unchecked, carbon dioxide emitted this year would generate global warming sufficient to raise sea levels, so in the year 2050 New Orleans would begin to flood. Let us also make the drastic simplifying assumption that this is the only damage the carbon dioxide emissions will ever do. Here are our options. First, for $15 billion spent today we could reduce our emissions enough to prevent this particular damage. Second, we could do nothing today. Then in the year 2050, for the cost of $15 billion (in today's dollar terms), a dike could be built to protect the city. Thus, our inaction would force our children to incur a $15 billion expense in fifty years (or evacuate the city). The issue on the table is this: Should we spend $15 billion this year to prevent $15 billion of damage to our descendants?

An efficiency advocate would argue no. To see why, consider the following response: We could compensate future generations for the damage we are doing to them by setting aside money today that would be available for dam construction in 2050. However, we wouldn't need to put aside $15 billion. We could put a smaller amount of money in the bank today, and by earning interest, it would grow over time to equal $15 billion. In fact, $15 billion in the year 2050 is equivalent to only $2.95 billion banked today at a 3% real (inflation-adjusted) rate of interest. Putting money aside into a bank account specifically to compensate future generations for depletion of natural capital is known as posting an **environmental bond.**

The Alaska Permanent Fund provides one example of an environmental bond. A second simple case is a bottle deposit. Currently, ten U.S. states require a refundable deposit of five to ten cents per can or bottle of soda or juice purchased. If you choose to throw your container out of the window of your car, the money is available for cleanup. (The deposit also provides an incentive for third parties to clean up the mess.)[11] On a larger scale, strip mine companies must post bonds sufficient to allow regulatory agencies to assure reclamation if the property is abandoned (Harvey 1978).

The potential for posting an environmental bond offers us a rationale for spending less on prevention today than the full value of the damage we inflict in future generations. When future benefits are not weighted as heavily as current benefits, we say that the future benefits have been **discounted.** The basic rationale behind discounting is that because investment is productive, resources on hand today are more valuable than resources available at a later date.

However, because in reality bonds are seldom posted, we have not yet settled the question of how much we "should" spend today to prevent New Orleans from drowning in fifty years. Before returning to this question, however, let us look a little more closely at the mechanics of discounting.

The figure of $2.95 billion mentioned above is known as the **present discounted value** (PDV) of $15 billion paid or received in the year 2050. Formally, the PDV of $$X$$ received in T years is the amount of money one would need to invest in the present to just receive $$X$$ in T years, at a specified rate of interest, or **discount rate,** r.

There is a simple formula for calculating the value of a future benefit in terms of today's dollars. If the discount rate is r, then the present discounted value of $$X$$ received in T years is

$$\text{PDV} = \$X/(1 + r)^T$$

Let us consider a real-world private investment decision to see how discounting works.

6.4 An Example of Discounting: Lightbulbs

A recent technological innovation has the potential to dramatically reduce electricity use throughout the world, leading to lessened reliance on fossil and nuclear fuels and, thus, substantial improvements in environmental quality. The product is the humble lighbulb. New compact fluorescent lightbulbs can replace standard incandescent bulbs, generate a similar quality light, use somewhere between one fifth and one tenth of the electricity, and last around ten times as long. So what's the catch? The up-front investment is substantially higher. Each compact fluorescent bulb costs about $15, compared with an initial cost for a standard incandescent of around $1.

Suppose you are the physical plant manager at a new hotel with 1,000 light fixtures and have to decide whether investing in these new bulbs is a good idea. How do

---

[11]Costanza and Perrings (1990) advocate a wider use of environmental bonding.

you proceed? The first step is to marshal the information that you have on the costs and benefits of the two options over their lifetimes. This is done in Table 6.1.

The numbers in Table 6.1 simplify the problem. In year 0 the investment is made: $15,000 for the compact fluorescents; $1,000 for the incandescents. The costs in subsequent years reflect the electricity bill and are $4,000 per year higher for the incandescents. We ignore the fact that the compact fluorescents last much longer than the incandescents and assume instead that they both burn out after four years. We also assume, as we will throughout the book, zero inflation (or, alternatively, that the figures are inflation-adjusted to reflect real purchasing power). Other than that, the numbers are realistic approximations.[12] The third line represents the net outlays from investing in option A, the compact fluorescents. On the face of it, buying the compact fluorescents appears to save $2,000 over the four years.

Unfortunately, choosing between the options is not this simple. The reason: The compact fluorescents require an extra $14,000 initial commitment. If, instead, you bought the incandescents, you could take that $14,000 (less electricity payments), put it in the bank, and earn interest on it. At a 10% interest rate, you would earn more than $1,000 during the first year alone.

Things have suddenly become quite complex. Fortunately, there is a simple way out: Calculate the PDV of the net savings from investing in compact fluorescents. The PDV will tell you how much, in today's dollars, investment in compact fluorescents saves over the alternative option. To calculate the PDV of the investment, simply apply the formula for each year and add up the values:

$$PDV = -14{,}000/(1+r)^0 + 4{,}000/(1+r)^1 + 4{,}000/(1+r)^2$$
$$+ 4{,}000/(1+r)^3 + 4{,}000/(1+r)^4$$

Table 6.2 provides the relevant calculations. How do we interpret the numbers in the table? Consider $2,732, the number in the fourth-year column and the 0.10 discount rate row. This is the PDV of $4,000 received in four years, if the interest rate is 10%. In other words, one would need to bank $2,732 today at a 10% interest rate to have $4,000 on hand in four years. If the interest rate were 0.00 (the first row), then one would have to have the full $4,000 on hand today to have $4,000 four years from now.

The last column of the table illustrates that if the interest rate is zero, the compact fluorescents do save $2,000. However, as the interest rate climbs to 5%, the investment looks less attractive, and at an interest rate of 10%, the compact fluorescents become

TABLE 6.1   Cash Outlays for Investing in Lighting

Option	Year					
	0	1	2	3	4	Total
A. Compact fluorescents	$15,000	$ 800	$ 800	$ 800	$ 800	$18,200
B. Incandescents	1,000	4,800	4,800	4,800	4,800	20,200
B – A. Savings from compact fluorescents	–14,000	4,000	4,000	4,000	4,000	2,000

---

[12]The example assumes the lights are on four hours per day, and that electricity costs $.08 per kWh.

TABLE 6.2   PDV of Savings from Compact Fluorescents Varies with the Discount Rate

Discount Rate	Year					
	0	1	2	3	4	Total
.00	–$14,000	$4,000	$4,000	$4,000	$4,000	+$2,000
.05	–14,000	3,810	3,628	3,455	3,290	+183
.10	–14,000	3,636	3,305	3,005	2,732	–1,320

the more expensive option. With this high interest rate, it is better to save the $14,000 on the initial investment and earn interest while paying out larger sums in electricity payments in later years. The main lessons to be learned here are that the higher the discount rate, (1) the less important are benefits earned down the road, and (2) the more important are initial expenses.

Private, for-profit decision makers, such as hotel managers, do not have to decide what discount rate to use when comparing future benefits with present costs. Businesses seeking to maximize profits should use the market rate of interest on investments of similar risk, that is, their opportunity cost of capital. A rate of 0%, 5%, or 10% will be determined in the financial marketplace. However, government policy makers must *choose* a discount rate for analyzing decisions about how much stock pollution to allow. What is the right discount rate for public choices, such as the level of legal carbon dioxide emissions?

6.5 Choosing the "Right" Discount Rate for Pollution Control

Let us return to our example of the New Orleans flood. Recall the essence of the case: We could spend $15 billion this year on carbon dioxide reduction to prevent widespread damage in fifty-some years. Should we do so?[13]

We have explored a more efficient alternative: an environmental bond. We know that if we set aside $2.95 billion this year, then at a 3% interest rate, we will have on hand the $15 billion in 2050. This option is more efficient since it leaves the current generation with an extra $12.05 billion to invest in other sectors of the economy. In the case of an environmental bond, all the externalities of the carbon dioxide pollution have been internalized, so the market rate of interest is the efficient discount rate.

In most cases, however, bonds are not posted. If future residents of New Orleans are not to be directly protected, should we then go ahead and spend $15 billion to prevent the flooding? Not necessarily. The argument goes this way: First, *assume* that due to technological improvements net national welfare "naturally" grows at, let us say for convenience, 3% per year. For simplicity, also assume that population growth is zero so that the growth rate of NNW for the typical person is also 3%.

Now, suppose we took action costing $15 billion today to stop global warming and the flooding of New Orleans in 2050. This would divert resources—engineers, scientists,

---

[13]Some would argue that we have a moral responsibility to prevent the sea-level rise, regardless of whether the impact on people can be eliminated by means of dike construction. There is nothing wrong with such an argument; however, it steps outside of the utilitarian framework we have established for this book.

production workers, bank loans—from investment in the production of other goods and services, lowering NNW this year by, let us assume, the full $15 billion. Now if NNW is $15 billion lower this year, next year, due to the cumulative nature of the growth process, it will be $15 * 1.03 = $15.45 billion less than it would have been, *even with no additional expenditure on pollution reduction.* The following year NNW will be depressed by $15.45 * 1.03 = $15.91 billion, and so on, until in the year 2050, NNW will be $76.2 billion less than it would have been had we not made that initial investment in pollution control! Figure 6.4 illustrates the way in which "diverting" $15 billion from investment throws the economy onto a lower-growth path, impoverishing those alive in 2050 by $76.2 billion, less the $15 billion necessary to build the dike.

Under this scenario, our children's generation as a whole would actually be $61.2 billion poorer as a result of our attempts to protect them from global warming. If we had not spent the $15 billion to reduce emissions and had instead invested it in the production of goods and services, they would have enough additional resources to encircle New Orleans by a dike and still have a large sum left over. If NNW grows at 3% per year, it is **dynamically efficient** to allow the sea level rise, even if no bond is established.

From a benefit–cost perspective, reducing carbon dioxide emissions today would make sense only if it cost less than $2.95 billion—the PDV of $15 billion in the year 2050 at a 3% discount rate. The moral: When comparing future benefits with present costs, *dynamic efficiency requires that future benefits be discounted at a rate of growth of NNW.*[14]

Now, this is a very simple story that requires at least one *caveat.* Expenditures on pollution control are unlikely to be wholly "wasteful," failing to contribute to NNW whatsoever. That is, $15 billion of pollution reduction expenditure is unlikely to reduce NNW by $15 billion, even in our simplified case where the direct benefits won't be realized for fifty years. This is true for two reasons. First, if there are unemployed resources present in the economy, these can be devoted toward pollution control and, in fact, boost GDP via a multiplier. Several such opportunities will be explored in the discussion of energy policy later in the book.

Second, if technological spillovers result from investment in pollution control, these, too, will contribute to the growth of NNW. One important benefit of investing in pollution control today is that it widens the technological menu available for future generations in this vital area. By initiating the development of pollution-reducing technology early, one can substantially decrease the cost to future generations of coping with similar problems.

---

[14]This is the efficient discount rate which guarantees dynamic efficiency, given that sustainability as defined here is assumed. Note that this discount rate is *not* chosen on intergenerational equity grounds; sustainability is assured by the assumption of positive growth in NNW.

See Dasgupta, Mäler, and Barrett (1999) for a similar view. Nordhaus (1991) also employs this discounting formulation, in addition to others. For an accessible presentation of discounting in the context of a growth model, see Gramlich (1982). Many neoclassical authors (e.g., Nordhaus) argue for discounting at a rate equal to the growth rate of the economy *plus* the rate of time preference. But including time preference builds in an inefficient bias toward current consumption. The true opportunity cost to future generations of today's foregone investment is the growth rate of NNW alone (see Cline 1999). Finally, Weitzman (1998) argues that the "far-distant" future should be discounted at the lowest possible rate likely to be realized, based on the rationale that the power of compound discounting renders other scenarios irrelevant.

For an extended discussion of discounting issues, see Portney and Weyant (1999).

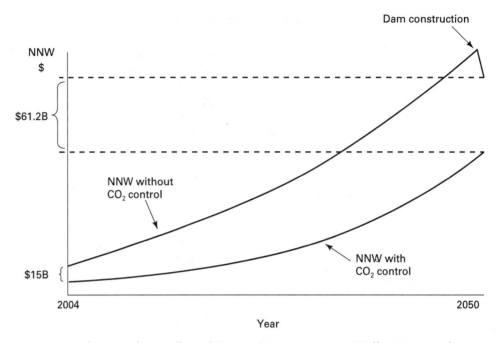

FIGURE 6.4 The Cumulative Effect of "Diverting" Resources into Pollution Control

In spite of these criticisms, dynamic efficiency requires that future benefits be discounted at a rate close to that of the growth of NNW. In the New Orleans example, discounting future benefits in this way would mean inaction on the pollution front today. We know such inaction is efficient; that is, it maximizes the size of the economic pie for our children as a whole. Is it also a good idea?

Consider this possibility: We choose not to reduce CO_2 emissions and NNW as a result is $76.2 billion higher in 2050 than it otherwise would have been. However, due to the winds of economic fortune, most of this wealth accumulates in Kansas, and the residents there are unwilling to pay for a dike to protect New Orleans. As a result, New Orleans residents lose their beloved city and all their property and (immobile) possessions. If in turn the total damage to New Orleans is less than $15 billion, we have the now familiar case in which an outcome is efficient but in many ways unfair. Discounting at the rate of growth of NNW is efficient; as a result, it generates the *potential* for a Pareto improvement. In the case of stock pollutants, however, an environmental bond is necessary to insure that such a Pareto improvement actually occurs.

The choice of the "right" discount rate is controversial and also quite important. In one benefit–cost study of global warming discussed in the introductory chapter, an efficient policy response varies dramatically depending upon the choice of the discount rate. Under the "maximum damage" scenario, a discount rate of 4% implies that an efficient tax on greenhouse gases would be $2.44 per ton of carbon, leading to reductions in greenhouse gases of less than 5% from uncontrolled levels. On the other hand, a zero discount rate reflecting a "low- or no-growth economy" implies an efficient carbon tax of $65.94 per ton, which would lead to an estimated 33% reduction in greenhouse gas emissions.

6.6 Social Discounting versus Market Discounting

How fast, if at all, is NNW actually growing? Knowing the answer to this question would be useful for at least two reasons. First, we just learned that this rate of growth of NNW, if positive, is the dynamically efficient discount rate when a bond is not posted. More significantly, the critical debate between neoclassical and ecological economists in large measure rides on this question—if NNW is growing, economic growth is sustainable and neoclassicals are right (at least for now). If NNW is falling, the ecological vision is more persuasive.

Unfortunately, there is no agreed-upon methodology for estimating NNW, although economists have been working hard in this area. As suggested in the earlier part of this chapter, the basic problem is that there are many judgment calls that go into the construction of such an index of NNW. This lack of consensus means that we cannot sort out in a "scientific way" whether or not our economy is sustainable in neoclassical terms; that is, whether NNW is rising or falling.

In some ways, this should be obvious. People have very differing opinions about whether the typical person is getting better off or worse off with economic growth. These differing opinions reflect an underlying complexity that makes NNW very difficult to measure.

However, the available studies do shed light onto the dynamically efficient discount rate. Moreover, some measure of "progress" is necessary; by default, many politicians and much of the general population view GDP as a measure of social welfare. Perhaps the main value in calculating NNW is to see whether growth in GDP serves as a good proxy for growth in real social welfare.

Two early attempts by neoclassical researchers, Nordhaus and Tobin (1972) and Zolatas (1981), estimated growth rates for NNW of 0.5% to 1% for periods ranging from 1929 to 1977. The studies showed no clear correlation between growth in GDP and growth in NNW in the United States.[15] For example, Nordhaus and Tobin find that the rate of growth of NNW dropped by more than 50% after 1947; at the same time, growth of GDP accelerated. From this we can conclude that the popular perception of GDP as a measure of economic welfare may well be misguided.

The most ambitious recent attempt to calculate NNW has been undertaken by a California think tank called Redefining Progress. Table 6.3 illustrates how their measure, called the Genuine Progress Indicator or GPI, was developed for the year 2000. It follows, more or less, the formula identified earlier in the chapter:

$$NNW = GDP + \text{non-market output}$$
$$- \text{externality and clean-up costs}$$
$$- \text{depreciation of natural capital}$$
$$- \text{depreciation of created capital}$$

The GPI subtracts $1.6 trillion from GDP for pollution and clean-up costs, with the largest amount coming from "long-term environmental damage": climate change and loss of biodiversity. Costs arising from short-term environmental impacts (air, water, and noise pollution, and household abatement expenditures) total approximately $100 billion. How do the researchers arrive at these numbers? Read on! Estimating

---

[15]Both studies in fact looked at GNP, a closely related measure to GDP.

**TABLE 6.3 The 2000 Genuine Progress Indicator
(Billions of 1996 Dollars)**

GDP*	**$6,258**
NON-MARKET OUTPUT	
Housework and parenting	2,079
Volunteer work	97
Other	840
EXTERNALITY AND CLEAN-UP COSTS	
Household abatement	−14
Water pollution	−53
Air pollution	−39
Noise pollution	−16
Ozone depletion	−313
Long-term environmental damage	−1,179
DEPRECIATION OF NATURAL CAPITAL	
Wetlands	−412
Farmlands	−171
Nonrenewable resources	−1,497
Old-growth forests	−90
DEPRECIATION OF CREATED CAPITAL	476
OTHER COSTS OF GROWTH	
Commuting and auto accidents	−613
Unequal income distribution	−959
Underemployment	−115
Net foreign borrowing	−324
Loss of leisure time	−336
Other	−989
GPI	**$2,630**

*The GPI actually starts with the Personal Consumption category of GDP (omitting government spending, business spending, and net exports). But for ease of exposition, and to keep the relationship consistent with the presentation in the chapter, I label personal consumption as GDP. In fact, GDP in 2000 was $9.2 trillion.
Source: Cobb, Glickman, and Cheslog (2001).

environmental damage costs as well as the costs of pollution abatement are the subjects of Chapters 8 and 9 of this text.

From earlier in this chapter, however, you should have an idea of the right way to estimate the value of the natural capital depreciated: the lost wetlands and used up renewable and non-renewable resources. In principal, researchers at Redefining Progress should use as a measure the resource rent yielded through the development of these resources.[16] The researchers estimate that over $2 trillion of natural capital was used up in 2000, including $412 billion in loss of services from wetlands, $90 billion from old growth forests, and $1,497 billion in nonrenewable resources.

---

[16]For wetlands, one would need to recognize that much of the in situ value (or rent) takes the form of non-market services.

Finally, the GPI also subtracts a category of "Other Social Costs," including the use of "equity weights" that adjust the social welfare function for increased inequality, and the costs of underemployment and lost leisure time. In 2000, GPI researchers concluded that while GDP equaled $6.2 trillion (in 1996 dollars), the GPI was only $2.6 trillion. It is worth stressing that this is only one estimate of an adjusted GDP; many controversial assumptions go into constructing such an index, but the GPI does illustrate in principal how researchers go about trying to calculate Net National Welfare.

Beyond just the simple magnitude of the GPI, Figure 6.5 shows how the growth rate in per capita GDP compared with that of the estimated GPI. During the 1950s and 1960s the two grew at roughly the same rates. During the 1970s GPI growth slowed dramatically, turning negative in the 1980s, and recovering a bit during the 1990s. The downturn in GPI in the 1970s and 1980s was due primarily to stagnating median family incomes, growing income inequality, nonrenewable resource exhaustion, and long-term environmental damage. The 1990s recovery reflected a rise in real wages for the median household, a slowdown in the growth of inequality, and a drop in the rate of loss of natural capital—farmlands, wetlands, old-growth forests, and mineral resources (Cobb, Glickman, and Cheslog 2001).[17]

Consistent with the findings of Nordhaus and Zolatas, Figure 6.5 illustrates that there is no clear correlation between growth in GDP and growth in GPI. GDP growth therefore appears to tell us little about trends in overall welfare. Finally, the average rate of growth of per capita GPI over the entire period was 1.1%; since 1970 it has been 0.1%. To conclude, from the limited evidence available, even according to more neoclassical studies, the average historical rate of growth of NNW in the United States appears to be 1% or less over the long-term. This suggests that for evaluating social decisions, a discount rate in a range of 0% to 1% is dynamically efficient.

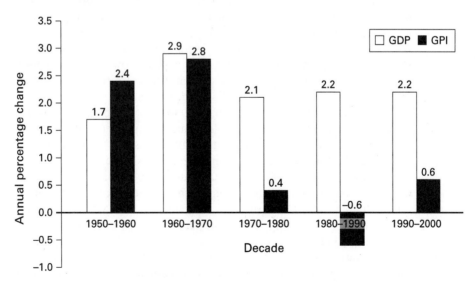

FIGURE 6.5 Growth in per Capita GDP versus per Capita GPI
Source: Cobb, Glickman, and Cheslog (2001).

---

[17]The GPI can be accessed on the Web at www.redefiningprogress.org.

What discount rates are in fact used by the government and the private sector? One important branch of the federal government, the Office of Management and Budget, requires a uniform 5% discount rate for most of the benefit–cost studies it reviews. Although uniformity across governmental departments is certainly desirable, a discount rate of 5% is clearly inefficient. At such a rate, future benefits weigh in with very little force. For example, $100 received in ten years would be discounted to $62; the PDV of a $100 benefit received in twenty-five years falls to less than $30! Such shortsightedness cannot be justified on economic grounds. The Environmental Protection Agency typically uses a slightly lower 3% discount rate (Office of Management and Budget).[18]

Decision makers in the private sector have shorter time horizons than government agencies. Companies often require profit rates on the order of 15% or more to initiate an investment. Private profit rates are higher than the growth of NNW for two reasons. First, they reflect only the private benefits of investment and fail to account for the external costs of growth.

Second, such high returns are required to induce people to save and invest their income, rather than consume it today. This in turn reflects what economists refer to as **positive time preference**—a widespread desire to consume today rather than save for tomorrow. The famous environmental economist A. C. Pigou called this our "faulty telescopic facility." Positive time preference leading to high market discount rates is one way in which the market penalizes investments with long-term payoffs.

It is worth noting, however, that low discount rates are not always "pro-environment." Any undertaking with high up-front costs and a long stream of future benefits will look better with a low discount rate. Huge dams may thus be favored by low discount rates, since people will enjoy the cheap electricity and recreational opportunities for decades. The point here is that using market discount rates of 5% or 10% or 15% dramatically undercounts the benefits that future generations reap from current investment—whether those benefits are low-cost energy from hydro-plants or a cleaner environment.

This is a very important point. Along with open access to common property (Chapter 3), high market discount rates explain how our actions today penalize the welfare of future generations. Due to high discount rates, we fail to make many long-lived investments that could benefit our descendants.

Neoclassicals assume, however, that we are still making *enough* investments to insure sustainability. They argue that, due to rapid technological progress, NNW is nevertheless still rising (though not as fast as possible). As a result, our descendants will still be better off than we are, in spite of our shortsightedness.

Ecologists, by contrast, argue that these two fundamental economic problems—open access to common property and high market discount rates—have already led to unsustainable exploitation of natural capital. In other words, they maintain, our failure to invest in protecting natural capital has already begun to impoverish our descendants in very literal terms.

To summarize: This section has argued that, in terms of real welfare improvements for society as measured by neoclassicals, $1 "diverted" to environmental protection has an opportunity cost that grows between 0% and 1% per year. That

---

[18]Criticisms of the OMB policy among environmental economists are widespread. See Howe (1990). For a dissenting view, based on a project selection criteria, see Quirk and Terasawa (1991).

is, investing $1 elsewhere in the economy will lead, on average, to increases in well-being of the typical person that grow in a slow but compounding fashion over time. From a neoclassical perspective, ignoring this opportunity cost in environmental decisions by government will lead to lower welfare for future generations.

While future benefits must be discounted somewhat, private decision makers use much higher discount rates than the efficient rate—the growth rate of NNW. This leads market actors to neglect investments with long-term benefits, thereby depressing future living standards below their maximum achievable levels.

6.7 Summary

Like the Iroquois Indians, we can recognize our ability to alter the welfare of our descendants dramatically, both for good and for bad. In the material sphere, we clearly have a responsibility to endow future generations with the productive capital—both natural and created—sufficient to generate a quality of life at least comparable to our own. However, the means of achieving this goal of sustainable development remain subject to intense debate.

This chapter examines the neoclassical view of sustainability. Neoclassical economists share two underlying assumptions: (1) created capital can generally substitute for natural capital in production, and (2) technological progress will uncover these substitutes as natural capital becomes scarce. These two assumptions imply that we are not "running out of resources."

When analyzing sustainability, the first task for an economist of any stripe is measurement. Neoclassicals have worked on an index of net national welfare, which includes data on economic growth and its associated environmental costs to chart the progress of "quality of life" for the typical individual. Calculating NNW requires subtracting from (adjusted) GDP both the externality costs of growth and the attendant depreciation of natural capital.

Neoclassicals do recognize that future generations can be made worse off by today's "overexploitation" of resources. More precisely, if the resource rent from an exploited resource is consumed, rather than productively invested, then the resource depletion is unsustainable. Moreover, the value of the resource rent is also our (imperfect) measure of the depreciation of natural capital that has to be subtracted from GDP to arrive at NNW. The measure is imperfect, since it is calibrated in prices that reflect the current generation's dictatorial power over resource decisions.

While neoclassicals do concede that individual resource exploitation decisions may be unsustainable, they believe generally that net national welfare rises with economic growth and that sustainability is thus assured. Implicit in this assumption is a faith that technological progress will allow us to replace the services of natural capital with those of created capital.

Under these circumstances, development decisions made with future benefits and costs discounted at the rate of growth of NNW are both dynamically efficient and sustainable. If NNW is growing, investment "diverted" to environmental protection carries with it an opportunity cost of foregone investment that also grows over time at a compound rate. This means that maximizing the overall size of the economic pie for future and current generations, *if the pie is growing,* should be done using the tools of benefit–cost analysis and discounting.

And yet, even within the neoclassical framework, discounting remains controversial. First, while discounting is efficient, it may not be fair. We saw this when our friends from Kansas, for example, failed to fund the New Orleans dike. Second, expenditures on pollution control need not "crowd out" investment in NNW, thus shifting the economy onto a lower-growth path.

Our look at discounting also revealed that, due to a positive time preference, market actors discount the future at a much higher rate than is dynamically efficient. This reduces investments in projects with long-term benefits and lowers the welfare of future generations below the maximum level that could be achieved. In spite of this, neoclassicals argue, we still currently invest enough to insure sustainability.

Finally, we have assumed in this discussion that increases in material consumption (and thus, NNW) actually increase human welfare. In other words, we have uncritically accepted the "more is better" assumption to justify some level of environmental degradation. Chapter 11 will look more closely at this issue.

Peering 200 years into the future, the neoclassical vision is fairly optimistic. Market systems, given the proper government regulation of environmental sinks and sources, will induce the technological innovation necessary to overcome any widespread shortages of natural capital. We now turn to a more challenging view of the prospects for the seventh generation.

APPLICATION 6.0

Thinking Sustainability

From an economic point of view, sustainability is about maintaining a high quality of life for future generations. To see how difficult this problem is to address, try and answer the following questions: From a quality-of-life point of view, would you rather have been born in 1920, 1950, or 1980? Assume that you would have been born in the same country and region, but that you don't know your parents' income, or your gender or race ahead of time. If you prefer 1980, this may suggest we have been on a sustainable track until now. Does it also imply that we are currently on a sustainable track? If you prefer an earlier year, what unsustainable decisions did your parents' or grandparents' generations make?

APPLICATION 6.1

Dynamic Efficiency, Equality, and Sustainability

Suppose Pandora is deciding how to dispose of some hazardous waste. She can contain it safely at a cost of $175 or bury it in the local landfill. If she chooses the second option, in ten years' time the stuff will have seeped out enough to permanently ruin the vineyard of Bacchus, who lives next-door to the landfill. The vineyard has a value to him in ten years of $450 (i.e., he'd sell it then for $450). This is the only damage the hazardous waste will ever do. Assume there is no inflation.

1. What is the present value of $450 in ten years at a discount rate of 10%?
2. In the absence of regulation, Pandora is likely to bury the stuff and save $175. If the interest rate is 10%, is it *efficient* for Pandora to bury her waste in the landfill? To answer this, discuss how Bacchus could maximize his utility if he had

the legal right to prevent the dumping (and was not an ardent environmentalist). What does this say about the relative size of the total net monetary benefits
under the two alternatives? How do total net benefits relate to efficiency?

3. Is burying the waste equitable? Why or why not? Could the use of an environmental bond satisfy a fairness problem if it exists?

4. Is burying the waste sustainable from a neoclassical point of view? From an
ecological point of view? Why or why not?

APPLICATION 6.2

Mining and Economic Development

One economic development paradox receiving recent research attention has been the
"dismal" economic performance of many mineral-dependent countries in the Third
World. On average, they have fared very poorly: Per capita GDP has actually fallen in
three quarters of the sample of fifteen countries studied, and they have accumulated
some of the highest relative debt levels in the world.

This poor performance is in many ways surprising: In principle, economic rent
from mineral production can be used for investment in other sectors of the economy,
spurring economic growth. Tilton (1992) explains this apparent contradiction partially
as a result of unproductive investment of the economic rent. "Rent lost through waste
and needlessly high production costs contribute nothing to economic growth. The
same holds true for rents spent on current consumption or rents captured and expatri-
ated by foreign interests. Even those rents that are invested can retard economic
growth if they are used unwisely" (23).[19]

1. If per capita GDP had risen in these mineral-dependent countries, would they
necessarily have achieved "sustainable development"? Why or why not?

2. Does the evidence presented suggest that countries are better off not developing their mineral wealth?

KEY IDEAS IN EACH SECTION

6.0 We reduce the stock of natural capital available for future generations in two ways:
first, the emission of **stock pollutants,** which exhaust **environmental sinks;** and second,
the exploitation of natural resources. (**Flow pollutants** have no long-term impact.)
Although both **neoclassical** and **ecological economists** agree on the definition of **sustainability,** they disagree on the best means of achieving it. The former believe that
created capital can **substitute** for **natural capital** on a widespread basis; the latter
believe that the two are **complements.**

6.1 **Net national welfare (NNW)** is the measure proposed by neoclassical economists to
try and indicate whether quality of life (material *and* environmental welfare) has, in
fact, been rising or falling. Measuring NNW requires correcting four major problems

[19]Tilton also identifies two other factors: "distortions" such as wage inflation and currency appreciation
induced by mineral booms, and the slow pace of mineral development arising from investor insecurity. From
a sustainability perspective, however, and given the potential for waste and distortions, a slow pace of mineral development may ultimately turn out to be a plus. This will be less true if mineral prices fall in relative
terms. See also Sachs and Warner (1999). For a strong defense of early development, see Radetzki (1992).

with GDP. If NNW is rising, then the goal of maximizing NNW over time is called **dynamic efficiency.**

6.2   This section develops a **depreciation rule** to account for the depletion of natural capital when measuring NNW: Depreciation can be approximated by the **resource rent.** Resource rents reflect the interests of future generations, *albeit* in a weak form, through **profit-based conservation.** However, the current generation's dictatorial power over resource use means that current resource prices are arguably still too low from a fairness point of view. Finally, a measure of NNW is important both as an **indicator of progress** and as a measure of **sustainable resource use.**

6.3   Because resources invested today are productive, there is a major **opportunity cost to foregone investment.** Therefore, future costs and benefits from today's actions must be **discounted.** For example, as illustrated by the New Orleans case, an **environmental bond** posted and invested this year will pay for much larger damages incurred in the future. The current value of benefits (costs) received (borne) at a given future date is called the **present discounted value** and can be calculated via a simple formula.

6.4   The use of discounting is illustrated in the light bulb example. A higher **discount rate,** in this case, the interest rate, means a lower present discounted value. High discount rates thus mean that current costs and benefits are weighed much more heavily than those occurring in the future. Private decision makers use the market interest rate for making decisions. But when sustainability is the goal, a different, lower discount rate must be chosen.

6.5   If NNW is growing, a discount rate equal to the rate of growth of NNW is **dynamically efficient.** Dynamic efficiency means that NNW for future generations is as large as possible. However, just as for the simple efficiency concept discussed in Chapter 4, dynamic efficiency need not be fair.

6.6   Several attempts to estimate NNW in the United States have found little correlation between changes in NNW and changes in the conventional progress measure, GNP. They also suggest that NNW has been growing at a rate of between 0% and 1%. One recent study argues that NNW actually declined during the 1980s. Market discount rates (profit rates) are much higher than this, since they do not include the social costs of growth and do reflect a **positive time preference** on the part of consumers. Along with open access to common property, high market discount rates explain why we fail to invest at a fully efficient rate in natural capital.

REFERENCES

Cline, William. 1999. "Discounting for the Very Long Term." In *Discounting and Intergenerational Equity,* edited by Paul Portney and John Weyant. Washington, DC: Resources for the Future.

Cobb, Clifford, Mark Glickman, and Craig Cheslog. 2001. "The Genuine Progress Indicator 2001 Update," *Redefining Progress Issue Brief.* San Francisco: Redefining Progress.

Cobb, Clifford, Ted Halstead, and Jonathan Rowe. 1995. "If the GDP Is Up, Why Is America Down?" *The Atlantic Monthly,* October, 59–78.

Costanza, Robert, and Charles Perrings. 1990. "A Flexible Assurance Bonding System for Improved Environmental Management." *Ecological Economics* 2:57–75.

Daly, Herman, and John Cobb. 1989. *For the Common Good.* Boston: Beacon Press.

Dasgupta, Partha, Karl-Goran Maler, and Scott Barrett. 1999. "Intergenerational Equity, Social Discount Rates, and Global Warming." In *Discounting and Intergenerational Equity,* edited by Paul Portney and John Weyant. Washington, DC: Resources for the Future.

Gramlich, Edward M. 1982. *Benefit–cost Analysis of Government Programs.* Englewood Cliffs, NJ: Prentice-Hall.

Harvey, Michael D. 1978. "Paradise Reclaimed? Surface Mining Control and Reclamation Act of 1977." *Houston Law Review* 15:1147–1174.

Howe, Charles. 1990. "The Social Discount Rate." *Journal of Environmental Economics and Management* 18, no. 2:1–2.

Krautkremer, Jeffrey. 1998. "Nonrenewable Resource Scarcity," *Journal of Economic Literature* 36, no. 4:2065–2107.

Nordhaus, William D. 1991. "To Slow or Not to Slow: The Economics of the Greenhouse Effect." *The Economic Journal* 101, no. 407:920–937.

Nordhaus, William, and Edward Kokkelenberg, eds. 1999. *Nature's Numbers: Expanding the National Economic Accounts to Include the Environment.* Washington, DC: National Academy Press.

Nordhaus, William, and James Tobin. 1972. *Economic Growth.* New York: Columbia University.

Office of Management and Budget. 1999. *OMB Circular No. A-94, Appendix C.* Washington, DC: The White House OMB.

Pearce, David, and Giles D. Atkinson. 1993. "Capital Theory and the Measurement of Sustainable Development: An Indicator of 'Weak' Sustainability." *Ecological Economics* 8, no. 2:103–108.

Pezzey, John. 1992. "Sustainability: An Interdisciplinary Guide." *Environmental Values* 1, no. 4:321–362.

Portney, Paul, and John Weyant. 1999. *Discounting and Intergenerational Equity.* Washington, DC: Resources for the Future.

Quirk, James, and Katsuaki Terasawa. 1991. "Choosing a Government Discount Rate: An Alternative Approach." *Journal of Environmental Economics and Management* 20, no. 1:16–28.

Radetzki, Marian. 1992. "Economic Development and the Timing of Mineral Exploitation." In *Mineral Wealth and Economic Development,* edited by John E. Tilton. Washington, DC: Resources for the Future.

Repetto, Robert. 1989. "Nature's Resources as Productive Assets." *Challenge* 32, no. 5:16–27.

Sachs, Jeffrey, and Andrew Warner. 1999. "The Big Push, Natural Resource Booms, and Growth." *Journal of Development Economics* 59, no. 1:43–76.

Solow, Robert. 1992. *An Almost Practical Step Toward Sustainability.* Washington, DC: Resources for the Future.

Tilton, John E. 1992. "Mineral Wealth and Economic Development: An Overview." In *Mineral Wealth and Economic Development,* edited by John Tilton. Washington, DC: Resources for the Future.

Weitzman, Martin. 1998. "Why the Far Distant Future Should Be Discounted at Its Lowest Possible Rate." *Journal of Environmental Economics and Management* 36, no. 3:201–208.

World Bank. 1992. *World Development Report 1992: Development and the Environment.* New York: Oxford University Press.

Zolatas, Xenophon. 1981. *Economic Growth and Declining Social Welfare.* New York: New York University Press.

APPENDIX 6A

Nonrenewable Resource Economics 101

6A.0 The Hotelling Model

Earlier in the chapter, I made the argument that resource owners would respond to perceived future shortages of their commodity via "profit-based conservation." Economists use a simple model, originally credited to Harold Hotelling (1931) to derive this kind of predicted relationship between resource stocks and prices over time. Here is one version.

Suppose 100 tons of a brand new mineral is discovered only in the country of Billsville. The President, Mr. Bill, modestly names this new resource Billite. Billite is a useful substitute for gold in dental applications. Billite entrepreneurs intend to sell all their Billite either this year or next year.[1] In this case, what happens to the price of Billite over time?

---

[1]We are assuming a two-period model; the basic result easily extends to a large number of periods. The model can also be extended to the case of rising marginal costs, and to monopolistic markets (Hanley 1997). The same qualitative results described here still hold.

Some assumptions: Billite is produced at a constant marginal cost of $10, up to the supply limit of 100 tons. The Billite industry is competitive (100 small producers, each with one ton each), so that Billite prices are also driven down to the point at which demand and marginal cost are equal. Investors can earn a 10% interest (or "discount") rate elsewhere in the economy. And the inverse demand curve for Billite is the same in both periods: $P = \$80 - q$, where P is the price and q is the total quantity demanded. Figure 6A.1 illustrates this situation, assuming a decision has initially been made to split the supply evenly between the two periods.

Note the strange, L-shaped supply curves, reflecting the absolute scarcity of Billite. As a result of the scarcity, the price is $30 per ton, so the producers each earn $20 per ton in resource rent, even though the industry is competitive. Is this equal division of product across the two periods an equilibrium?

No. Suppose that a producer decided to shift her ton of Billite sales from period 2 to period 1. In that case, the period 1 price would fall a little bit (from $80 - 50 = \$30$ to $80 - 51 = \$29$), and the period 2 price would rise a little bit, (to $80 - 49 = \$31$). But even with the lower first period price, the producer would be able to invest her now $19 in first period profits at 10% interest, thus earning a total by the end of the second period of $19 + \$1.90 = \$20.90$. So her choice is between having $20 in the second period, or $20.90, and she chooses the latter.

Is this 51/49 division of Billite an equilibrium? If one more producer shifts, he sacrifices $21 in rent in the second period and drives down the price in the first period by another $1; if he invested his (now) $18 in first period profits he would have $18 + 1.80 = \$19.80$. Not enough to justify the switch. So, the equilibrium outcome would be:

	Quantity	Price
Period 1	51	$31
Period 2	49	$29

So far, we have illustrated how "profit-based conservation" works. Clearly, the Billite producers will not sell their whole stock this year, but will instead conserve

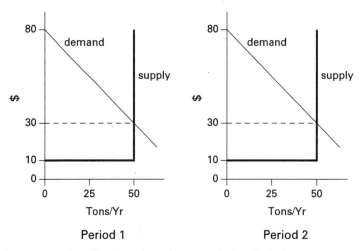

FIGURE 6A.1   Billite Supply and Demand, Two Periods

close to half to sell next year. If additional periods are added to the model, some stock will also be saved for future periods. Given a positive discount rate, however, the stock will eventually all be sold, and as the supply diminishes, the price will rise to the **choke price** of $80—just high enough to eliminate all demand.

Even in this two-period model, more is indeed sold today than tomorrow, and consequently, the price of Billite rises over time. This reflects the opportunity cost of holding Billite stocks in the ground. The higher the discount rate, the more attractive are the foregone alternative investments, and the faster the stock will be depleted.

Not surprisingly, given that the market is competitive and producers have perfect information, the competitive outcome is **dynamically efficient.** The 51/49 split maximizes the present value of the net benefits to producers and consumers. (See if you can prove this to yourself.)[2]

Note also an interesting fact: In equilibrium, the resource rent rises between the two periods by a figure very close to the discount rate. The increase is $2 over an initial value of $19—approximately 10%. (An exact match would have been achieved if we could have changed the quantities in the Billite example by fractions of tons). Thus, the equilibrium condition for the Hotelling model is:

$$RR_2 = (1 + r)RR_1$$

The resource rent in period 2 must equal the period 1 resource rent multiplied by one plus the discount rate.[3]

The intuition here is simple. If the marginal resource rent rises at less than the discount rate, people will not hold on to the resource, and by selling more today, current prices will be driven down while future prices rise. Conversely, if the resource rent is rising at a rate faster than the interest rate, people will want to hold their resource stocks, raising today's prices and lowering future prices, and thus the rate of growth of the value of the resource.

In this way, the Hotelling Model provides a precise forecast of the growth path of resource rent and thus nonrenewable resource prices. Since the price of the resource equals the marginal production costs plus the resource rent, $P = MC + RR$, the percentage increase in P is $\Delta P / P = (\Delta MC + \Delta RR) / (MC + RR)$. Given that MC is constant ($\Delta MC = 0$), this means that $\Delta P / P = \Delta RR / (MC + RR)$. Finally, since $\Delta RR / RR$ equals the discount rate, then prices should rise at a rate somewhat less than the discount rate, depending on the magnitude of marginal production costs. (If for example, $MC = 0$, then resource price increases would be predicted to exactly equal the discount rate).

6A.1 Testing the Model

In point of fact, however, over the last 40 years, non-renewable resource prices have shown no signs of rising at all. Krautkremer (1998) tracked prices for aluminum, lead, copper, magnesium, nickel, iron, tin, zinc and silver from 1967 to 1994 and found that,

---

[2]The net benefits are the area above the marginal cost curve and below the demand curve (the difference between willingness to pay by consumers and willingness to supply by producers). Show that, with a 10% discount rate, the sum of the two period net benefits are maximized at 51,49 by exploring the value of net benefits at nearby options (50,50 and 52,48).

[3]This condition is sometimes stated in terms of "marginal user cost," which is the present discounted value of the net benefits of a resource decision made today.

while prices jumped around quite a bit, no upward trends were observed. Two possible explanations account for this. First, looking forwards at available supply and demand conditions, market actors see no long term shortfalls of these basic commodities within a relevant time frame—say 20 years. In other words, the L-shaped up-turns in supply in Figure 6A.1 in fact, lie well outside market demand for the foreseeable future.

The second explanation relates to cost reductions. As mining and processing technology steadily advances, lower and lower grade ores can be mined cost-effectively. This shifts the supply curve down and out, further reducing any imminent scarcity.

Questions remain about oil: though oil prices have yet to show any long term increase, as is discussed further in Chapter 7, some observers believe that global oil production will peak in the next 30 years, and possibly as soon as the next decade. If this is so, then the reason that oil prices have yet to rise lies in the fact that producers do not have perfect information; there remains significant disagreement about the size of economically recoverable oil reserves. (Cambell and Laherrere 1998).

Resource economics provides another reason besides poor information why current oil or other nonrenewable resource prices may be "too low" from a sustainability perspective. The wealth represented by natural resources is not equally distributed across time. We of the current generation are endowed with 100% of this wealth. This gives us **dictatorial power** over resource decisions. If we were short-sighted enough, our descendants could not stop us from squandering it all in the next few years, because it is ours by default. Another way to say this is that although current prices may reflect the scarcity of natural capital, the prices do not reflect a fair distribution of natural capital between those of us alive today and those who will follow.

How does dictatorial control over resource use affect prices? Since we today own all of the tropical timber, this increases our perceived wealth. Higher perceived wealth increases demand, and leads to greater levels of exploitation.

Imagine instead that we gave the forests to future generations by setting them aside in preserves. We allow harvesting, but only if we put the full value of the resource rent into a savings account on behalf of our grandchildren—similar to the Alaska Permanent Fund. This increase in cost for current harvesting would shift the supply curve back and drive timber prices up, a process illustrated in Figure 6A.2. Note that (assuming inelastic demand) the *resource rent itself now rises* by the value of the grey area minus the triangle marked *x*, plus the hatched area.

This example illustrates that the "intergenerational distribution of wealth" itself affects prices, and thus resource rents. Under profit-based conservation, future generations have to indirectly buy from us the privilege of using tropical timber; if instead, we bought from them the right to use it up, the current price would be higher.[4]

Why does this matter? From a practical point of view, we learned in Chapter 6 that to calculate NNW, we subtract from GDP our measure of the depreciation of natural capital, which was the resource rent. Dictatorial power means that today's resource prices are too low, and thus measured rents are unlikely to reflect a fair accounting of the impact of resource depletion on future generations. Instead, adjusting GDP by the

---

[4]Howarth and Noorgard (1990) explore this point formally in an overlapping generations, general equilibrium model. They show that all prices (and thus resource rents) are contingent on the intertemporal distribution of the stock of natural capital.

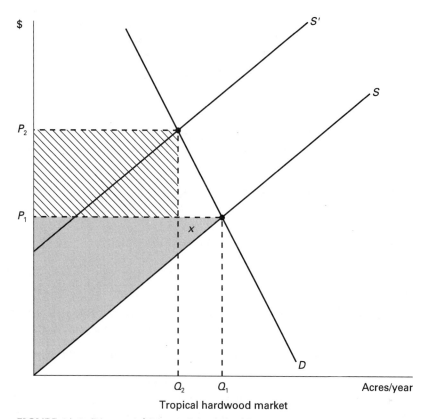

FIGURE 6A.2 Dictatorial Power, Prices, and Resource Rent

value of the resource rent probably reflects a lower bound of the true reduction in future wealth due to the drawdown in the stock of natural capital.

To summarize this Appendix, the Hotelling Model concludes that in a world of perfect foresight, competitive firms should allocate stocks of nonrenewable natural resources in such a fashion that prices rise sufficiently to insure that the resource rent increases at the rate of interest. The observed failure of resource prices to rise over the last forty years may reflect either no imminent shortage, or in the case of oil, imperfect information about the size of stocks.

Resource prices may also be too low from a sustainability perspective due to the dictatorial power over resource use enjoyed by current generations. The fact that we, and not our grandchildren, effectively own the planet's stocks of minerals, forests, and biodiversity raises our perceived wealth and thus our inclination to spend it down.

REFERENCES

Cambell, C. J., and Laherrere, J. H. 1998. The end of cheap oil. *Scientific American* 278, no. 3:78–83.

Hanley, Nick, Jason Shogren, and Ben White. 1997. *Environmental Economics in Theory and Practice*. Oxford, UK: Oxford University Press.

Hotelling, Harold. 1931. "The Economics of Exhaustible Resources," *Journal of Political Economy* 39:137–175.

Howarth, Richard B., and Richard B. Noorgard. 1990. "Intergenerational Resource Rights, Efficiency and Social Optimality." *Land Economics* 66, no. 1:1–11.

CHAPTER 7

SUSTAINABILITY: AN ECOLOGICAL VIEW

7.0 Introduction

Back in 1971, the well-known biologist Paul Ehrlich presented a way of thinking about environmental problems now called the **IPAT equation:**

environmental **I**mpact = **P**opulation * **A**ffluence * **T**echnology

The IPAT relation suggests that we think about three main causal factors underlying environmental problems: population growth, growth in consumption per person (affluence), and the damage per unit of consumption inflicted by the available technology. The IPAT equation also points broadly toward solutions: addressing both overpopulation and overconsumption and cleaning up dirty technologies (Ehrlich and Holdren 1971). To make the equation more concrete, consider the global emissions of carbon dioxide from cars at the beginning of the twenty-first century[1]:

$$
\begin{array}{cccc}
\boldsymbol{I} & = & \boldsymbol{P} & \boldsymbol{A} & \boldsymbol{T}
\end{array}
$$

$$
\frac{CO_2 \text{ emissions}}{\text{per year}} = \{6 \text{ billion people}\} * \frac{\{0.1 \text{ cars}\}}{\{\text{person}\}} * \frac{\{5.4 \text{ tons } CO_2\}}{\{\text{car per year}\}}
$$

$$
= 3.45 \text{ billion tons } CO_2/\text{yr}
$$

Now, get set for some depressing mathematics. By the year 2050, global population could rise to approximately 10 billion people. Affluence (the number of cars per person) is likely to more than quadruple. The IPAT equation tells us that, holding technology constant, CO_2 emissions from autos would thus rise by eightfold; alternatively, to keep CO_2 emissions constant, technology would have to advance so that each auto could reduce emissions by a factor of 8.

---

[1]Estimates courtesy of the American Council for an Energy Efficient Economy.

This, in fact, is not so hard to imagine. We could, for example, develop fuel cell–powered cars that run on hydrogen gas derived from solar power, which would emit very low levels of CO_2. But IPAT has much broader implications. Consider, for example, the environmental impacts of the eightfold increase in mining, oil drilling, lumbering, and manufacturing needed to support construction of even solar powered vehicles for the larger and more affluent population; or consider the impacts on the natural environment if road construction expands along with auto use.

Ecological economists are technological pessimists—fundamentally they believe that rapid increases in population, and even faster increases in consumption, are putting unsustainable pressure on our natural resource base. In individual cases such as fuel cell–powered cars, created capital may substitute for natural capital. But at a general level, created and natural capital are complements in production. That is to say, ecologicals believe that we are "running out" of the natural capital that forms the base of our economic well-being: both natural resources, such as freshwater and top-soil, and the environmental sinks that absorb our wastes.

What is meant by "unsustainable" pressure? First, there is the gradual reduction in human welfare as the environment is degraded and natural resources become scarce and expensive. (This is in contrast to the neoclassical view, which purports that the degraded environment can be either repaired or substituted for, and technological improvements can overcome resource scarcity and rising prices.)

More radically, ecological economists view the global ecosystem in which our economy is embedded as fragile, in the sense that accumulating stresses may lead to catastrophic changes in the system itself. For example, climate change from unchecked global warming or increased radioactive exposure from unchecked ozone depletion could radically alter the natural environment. Of course, ecosystems are subject to catastrophe all the time—for example, when lightning causes fire in a forest. Catastrophe, when severe enough, in fact forms grist for the mill of evolution, by favoring individuals within species better adapted to new conditions. So nature itself is not threatened. "Saving the planet" is not the issue.

However, individual species (or human cultures) do not always survive environmental catastrophe. Ecologicals believe that our economy depends in countless, often subtle ways on the natural environment *as it exists today.* If this is true, major environmental changes brought on by the stress of the doubling and then redoubling of population and consumption levels could lead to very large and sudden declines in human welfare.

The ecological economics view implies that, for the sake of future generations, governments need to engage in a much more aggressive program to rein in the twin pressures of population and consumption growth on the deteriorating stock of natural capital. In addition, although ecologicals see distinct limits to technological solutions, government needs to promote clean technology as a short-run strategy for dealing with the inexorable mathematics of IPAT. Later in this book, Chapter 21 will explore solutions to the problem; Chapter 11 addresses overconsumption; and Chapters 18 through 20 focus on clean technology promotion. This chapter will flesh out the ecological view and consider its implication for government resource policy.

7.1 Malthus and Ecological Economics

In 1798, the Reverend Thomas Malthus wrote a book that has given the economics profession a bad name ever since. Called *An Essay on the Principle of Population,* Malthus laid out a simple proposition with a dire and seemingly inescapable outcome. Assuming (1) that the food supply grows only *arithmetically* (increasing at a constant rate of, say, 10 million tons of grain per year), and (2) that a healthy population grows *geometrically* (doubling every thirty to fifty years), the prospects for long-run human progress are dim. Eventually, Malthus argued, population growth would outstrip the food supply, leading to increasing human misery, famine, disease, or war. This in turn would provide a "natural" check on further population growth.

This **Malthusian population trap** is illustrated in Figure 7.1. As population grows geometrically, and the food supply increases only arithmetically, available food per person declines. Eventually, some form of natural check halts or even reverses population growth. Malthus was one of the first modern economists, and this, his most famous work, led to economics being labeled "the dismal science."

Malthus's theory should sound familiar. Ecological economists in fact trace their lineage back to Malthus and are sometimes called **neomalthusians.** Malthus' theory clearly reflects technological pessimism, viewing land as an irreplaceable source of natural capital. But surely, wasn't Malthus wrong?

Certainly, his gloomy prediction has yet to come true on a global scale; population growth continues even in the face of substantial poverty worldwide. To date, we have indeed avoided a Malthusian fate because of impressive technological developments in the fields of agriculture, health care, and birth control.

These technological advances have challenged Malthus' basic assumptions. First, it need not be the case that agricultural output grows only arithmetically. From about 1950

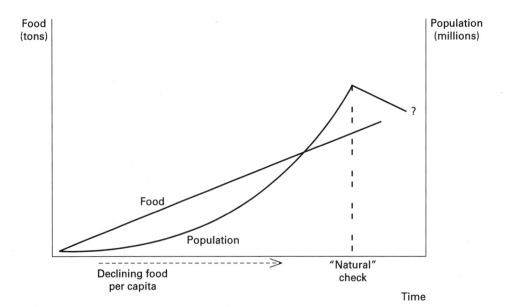

FIGURE 7.1 The Malthusian Population Trap

through the 1980s, world agriculture underwent a so-called **Green Revolution.** The Green Revolution centered around new, hybrid forms of wheat, rice, and corn seeds that produced much higher yields per acre than did conventional seeds. The results were dramatic. From 1950 to 1984, world grain output increased by a factor of 2.6. Over the same period, world population roughly doubled. Thus, from 1950 to the mid-1980s, history did not validate Malthus' first assumption. Both agricultural output and population increased geometrically, with food supply actually outstripping population growth (Brown and Young 1990).

Malthus' second assumption, that population growth increases geometrically, also does not always hold. Not including immigration, wealthy countries have very low population growth rates, often *below* zero. The availability of effective birth control, not foreseen by Malthus, has meant that families are able to control their "natural" reproductive tendencies if they so desire. As we shall see in Chapter 21, as countries develop economically, most people in fact do limit their fertility.

But, in recent years classic Malthusian conditions have again begun to prevail at the global level. Between 1984 and 2000, grain output per acre improved little, and population growth began to move ahead of growth in food production. Over the period, world grain output per person fell 11% (Brown 2002).

What is the explanation for this reversal in trends? Partly, the Green Revolution has exhausted its potential. By 1985, for example, 80% of India's wheatlands had already been converted to the high-yielding seed varieties, and much of the developed world had reached the limits of additional crop gains from fertilizer use.

In addition, the productivity gains of the Green Revolution were not evenly shared. In many cases, the shift to large-scale agriculture displaced and impoverished small farmers, leading to greater poverty and hunger. Moreover, a substantial portion of the increased grain production went to feed cattle, pigs, and chickens, not to feed people directly. This increased meat output serviced First World markets and those of the relatively affluent urban middle class in poor countries. Finally, influenced by western consumption habits and advertising, poor people in poor countries began to abandon traditional, balanced diets (beans and corn, lentils and rice) for processed western foods—white bread and soft drinks in particular. Thus, it is not clear that a higher percentage of the world's population was actually eating any better at the end of the Green Revolution than at its beginning.[2]

In spite of dramatic productivity gains, the Green Revolution was not able to reduce poverty and malnutrition substantially in many poor countries. Thus, as the technological revolution winds down, and its environmental and social consequences take hold, neomalthusian views are again gaining adherents. There is concern that a cycle of poverty → population growth → poverty, and so on, will overwhelm the positive effects of economic growth on population in poor countries. And unless effective population control measures are taken, global population would continue to increase well above the 9 billion level until some natural check—famine, war, or disease—emerges.

Malthus was truly the forerunner of ecological economists, because he captured both senses in which fundamental limits on natural capital lead to unsustainable development.

---

[2]Goodman and Redclift (1991) make this case for Latin America.

First, there is a steady decline in available food per capita, leading to rising prices and gradual impoverishment. Second, he predicted an eventual catastrophic change in the ecosystem-economy relationship: fatally weakened immune systems in the human species; famine arising in years of bad harvest; peaceful economies suddenly giving way to economies based on theft and plunder.

Ecological economists are, however, more than reborn Malthusians. First, the sources of stress on the environment have shifted from population to both population and consumption. More significantly, ecological economists have, as we shall see in the next section, turned to ecologists for guidance in measuring sustainability. The definition of sustainability remains the same as for neoclassicals: insuring a non-declining standard of living for the typical member of a future generation. However, the means have changed. In the ecological view, because economic functions are embedded in nature, **sustainability requires handing down to future generations local and global ecosystems that largely resemble our own.**[3]

More specifically, the ecosystems we pass on must be resilient. In resilient ecosystems, external stresses do not lead to catastrophic change. **Ecosystem resilience** is in turn a function of the number and complexity of the underlying interspecies interactions. A quick example: Salmon fisheries in the Pacific Northwest have collapsed, and many are on the verge of extinction. The reasons for this are complex, but clear-cut logging has played an important role. In an old-growth forest, fallen conifers create dams, which in turn develop spawning pools; different types of hardwood trees—maple and later alder—provide food for insects upon which young salmon smolts feed. Large trees throughout the watershed protect streams from devastating debris flows during heavy rains. Slowly these trees have been removed and replaced by a much less diverse second-growth forest, destroying the resilience of the ecosystem. Now, catastrophic events like mud flows, once a part of stream rejuvenation, scour and destroy the salmon habitat.[4]

Ecological economists claim, essentially, that we are doing to ourselves what we have done to the salmon; in complex and perhaps unknowable ways, we are dismantling the delicate physical and biological structure that underlies the resilience of the ecosystems on which we depend. This in turn dramatically increases our economic vulnerability to any large-scale ecosystem shifts that we may induce. This, in a nutshell, is basic ecological economic theory. But what does it mean in practice?

7.2 Measuring Sustainability

Because ecological economists do not believe that natural and created capital are substitutes, they reject the NNW approach to measuring sustainability developed in the

---

[3]Common and Perrings (1992) put it this way: "An ecological economics approach requires that resources be allocated in such a way that they do not threaten the stability either of the system as a whole or key components of the system," (31). The authors define system stability as "Hollings-resilience": the "propensity of a system to retain its organizational structure following perturbation," (16–17). Arrow et al. (1995) provide a declaration by prominent ecological economists defending ecosystem resilience as the appropriate measure of sustainability.

[4]A neoclassical economist would point out here that farmed salmon has largely replaced wild salmon in stores; in spite of the collapse of the traditional salmon ecosystems, salmon are not scarce. How would an ecological economist respond to this critique?

last chapter. If environmental quality and natural resources are not, in general, capable of restoration or substitution, it does not make sense to subtract the reductions in natural capital from the increases in created capital to arrive at a measure of welfare.[5]

Instead, ecologicals use **physical measures of ecosystem resilience and resource stocks weighed against population and consumption pressure** as their measure of sustainability. Recall that from an ecological point of view, the only way to insure that future generations are not penalized by our actions is to hand down a stock of natural capital that largely resembles our own. This means, for example, on the global warming and ozone depletion fronts, our current impacts are not sustainable. This follows since everybody agrees that, unchecked, they will lead to large-scale changes in the global environment. (Of course, neoclassicals argue that we could adapt to, and therefore do not *necessarily* need to stop, these changes.)

Ecological economists have looked to ecological studies to find other signs of "limits" to growth. For example, Vitousek et al. (1986) calculated that humans now appropriate directly or indirectly 40% of what they called the "net primary production" of organic material on land. In other words, humans are currently consuming close to half of the vegetable matter growing on earth. From the ecological point of view (no substitute for photosynthesis!): "If we take this percentage as an index of the human carrying capacity of the earth; and assume that a growing economy could come to appropriate 80% of photosynthetic production before destroying the functional integrity of the ecosphere, the earth will effectively go from half to completely full during the next . . . 35 years" (Rees and Wackernagel 1994, 383).

Let's pause for a

PUZZLE

The authors of the previous quote are applying the IPAT equation and assuming that the combined effect of increasing population and consumption will lead to a doubling of the human appropriation of biomass in thirty-five years. What are they "forgetting" and why are they "forgetting" it? Another way to phrase the question is this: How would a neoclassical economist respond to this dire prediction, and how would the ecologically minded author reply?

SOLUTION

The neoclassical response is that the ecologicals are forgetting technology: Innovations in biotechnology and plant breeding will boost yields per acre to compensate for the growth in P (population) and A (affluence). History provides some comfort here: In spite of massive increases in food production, New England now has a much heavier forest cover than it did in the mid-1800s. Massachusetts, Connecticut, Rhode Island, and Vermont all have close to or more than double the forested acreage found in the previous century (Sedjo 1991).

---

[5]Ecological economists refer to the last chapter's neoclassical definition of sustainable resource use, in which resource rents are fully invested in created capital, as "weak" sustainability. They refer to the ecological formulation—an intact stock of natural capital—as "strong" sustainability. See Daly (1996, 79).

The ecological comeback is that history provides little guidance for assessing the impact of geometric economic growth. While technology may have been able to accommodate the last 100 years of increase on an initially "empty" planet to 6 billion people and their consumption needs, we are now facing a 35-year doubling of combined population-consumption impacts on an already crowded planet. Yes, technology will improve, but ecologists argue that available land poses a fundamental, relatively short-term constraint. Therefore, "forgetting" technology is justified. We will return to this core area of disagreement again at the end of the chapter.

One last example of an ecological accounting of sustainability relates to freshwater use. Postel, Daly, and Ehrlich (1996) find that humans now use about 54% of the surface water runoff that is geographically accessible. The authors do consider one technology option, calculating that new dam construction could increase accessible runoff by 10% over the next thirty years, but note that population is expected to increase by 45% over the same period. Of course, other technological possibilities exist, chief among them are increases in the efficiency of water use. However, ecological economists would argue that freshwater prices are likely to increase substantially over the next few decades and that adequate substitutes are unlikely to be forthcoming.

More fundamentally, however, ecologicals following the IPAT logic would have us consider the broader ecological impacts of significant increases in the demand for water. Dam construction in remote areas, for example, often has high ecological externality costs. Water conflicts throughout the world are already driving many freshwater creatures to the brink of extinction and beyond, destroying industries and livelihoods in the process. Some have argued that water wars between nations will soon follow (Postel 1996). Beyond the "simple" question of access to cheap water, ecological economists believe that resource scarcity will lead us to fundamentally damage many of the ecosystems on which our economic and cultural lives depend.

In this section, we have seen that ecological economists rely on physical measures of either resource stocks or the absorption capacity of environmental sinks, to judge whether or not our use of natural capital is sustainable. If natural resources have no good substitutes on the horizon, and demand is a large portion of current supply (water or primary vegetation, ecologicals argue) then our use is unsustainable. If the absorptive capacity of environmental sinks is exceeded, leading to long-term alterations in the environment from stock pollutants (ozone-depleting CFCs, carbon dioxide), then our use of those sinks is unsustainable.

Since ecologicals reject the notion that, in general, created capital can substitute for natural capital, they reject as well the neoclassical idea that protecting natural capital carries with it a large opportunity cost in terms of foregone investment. If future generations need local and global ecosystems very much like our own for their economy to function at a reasonable level, then the best thing we can do for them is to "protect natural capital." But if ecological economists argue that much of our current activity is unsustainable, how do we know in any particular case? And more importantly, if we are supposed to protect natural capital, which pieces do we protect first?

7.3 The Precautionary Principle

The underlying question from the ecological perspective is this: To what extent, if any, can we afford to further run down the existing stock of natural capital? The concept of "sustainability" was originally used in the context of a specific resource. For example, a "sustained yield" of timber can be generated when the harvest rate does not exceed the growth rate of new forest. One of the founders of ecological economics, Herman Daly, has raised this idea to the economy-wide level by proposing the following:

> **PRECAUTIONARY PRINCIPLE**[6]
> Never reduce the stock of natural capital below a level that generates a sustained yield unless good substitutes are currently available for the services generated.

The first thing to note about the Precautionary Principle is that it is like a commandment—it says, "Thou shalt protect natural capital without good substitutes," *regardless of the cost* of doing so. In other words, under the presumption that future generations will benefit from preserving resources, the Precautionary Principle requires that the current generation make potentially large sacrifices on their behalf. While this is fine in theory, in practice the rule must be modified. At some point, the costs of preserving natural capital might simply become so high that political support for the Precautionary Principle would disappear.

Given this caveat, we first need to address what we mean by the "yield" of a resource. The important aspect of natural capital from our utilitarian perspective is not the capital itself: that is, the oil, the old-growth forest, or the clean air. Rather the important feature is the flow of services from that capital: inexpensive transportation, biodiversity resources and wilderness experiences, environmental health.

To determine the availability of substitutes requires focusing on two factors: **uniqueness** and **uncertainty combined with irreversibility.** First of all, do the services provided by the natural capital in question currently *have* substitutes? Each day, for example, more than a hundred species of plants or animals are destroyed as a consequence of tropical deforestation. The primary use value from this natural capital is its medicinal and genetic properties; currently, an average of one in four pharmacy purchases contains rain forest–derived compounds. Suppose that of the millions of species alive in the forest, one and only one contains a chemical compound effective in curing many types of cancer. In that case, clearly that species and the rain forest that harbors it are unique natural capital.

A question closely related to uniqueness is the *technological potential* for substitution. Each species, for example, represents a unique DNA blueprint that has evolved over millions of years. While we may be able to imagine substitutes for rain-forest products generated by advanced technology, are such options feasible within the relevant

---

[6]I am not aware of the genesis of the term "precautionary principle." It was popularized in 1998 via the "Wingspread Statement on the Precautionary Principle." See *Rachel's Environment & Health Weekly*, #586, February 19, 1998. This formulation follows Daly (1996) who puts it this way for renewables: "Keeping the annual offtake equal to the annual growth increment (sustainable yield) is equivalent to maintenance investment," and then adds, "The general rule would be to deplete non-renewables at a rate equal to the development of renewable substitutes," (81–82). The way I reformulate it, the rule applies to both renewables and nonrenewables.

time frame? In cases of unique natural capital—where good substitutes do not now, or will not soon, exist for the services flowing from the natural capital being destroyed—the stock should be protected, according to the Precautionary Principle.

It is possible, of course, that species extinction can proceed for some time at the current rate with no loss of unique medicinal or genetic value for humans. The remaining (millions) of species may provide an adequate resource base for developing medicines and biotechnologies on a sustained-yield basis. But they may not.

This example highlights another issue that arises in attempting to apply our sustainability criterion: the **uncertainty** of benefits flowing from natural capital. The genetic resources of the rain forest may yield tremendous improvements in health care and agricultural productivity, or they may prove relatively fruitless. (It is estimated, with substantial uncertainty, that approximately 1,400 rain forest species contain anti-cancer properties [Collins 1990, 32].)[7] In the case of the rain forest, beyond the major loss of pharmaceutical material, the ultimate consequences of destroying so vast an ecosystem are essentially unknowable. Similarly, as we saw in the introductory chapter, the atmosphere may be able to absorb current emissions of greenhouse gases with minor changes in global temperature, but alternatively the real possibility exists of major catastrophe.

While there is substantial uncertainty about the potential yield of some natural capital, decisions to degrade capital stocks such as rain forests or the atmosphere are often **irreversible.** Once these resources are depleted, they can be restored only at great cost, if at all. Uncertainty combined with irreversibility provide what is known as an option value to natural capital (discussed further in Chapter 8). That is, preservation of the stock is valuable merely to keep our options open. The greater the uncertainty and the more severe the irreversibility, the more caution should be exercised in the exploitation of natural capital.

RENEWABLE RESOURCES AND THE SAFE MINIMUM STANDARD

One point worth stressing is that if the future benefits from preserving our options are truly unknown, then it is not just hard but *impossible* to make decisions about preservation on a benefit–cost basis. If we do not know, even within a large range what the benefits of preservation may be, then benefits cannot be usefully compared to costs. This fact has led some economists to advocate what is called a **safe minimum standard** (SMS) for resources with highly uncertain future value (Ciriacy-Wantrup 1968; Bishop 1978). Safe minimum standard advocates argue that unique resources should be preserved at levels that prevent their irreversible depletion, unless the costs of doing so are "unacceptably" high, with this limit determined by political support for preservation.[8] (For a game-theoretic exposition of the SMS, see Appendix 7A.)

Figure 7.2 illustrates the basic idea behind the SMS. The horizontal axis shows the current stock of a renewable resource, in this case, mating pairs of spotted owls in a forested area. The S-shaped line relates the stock of owls alive today to the stock of

---

[7]The author also provides the 25% estimate for pharmaceutical content. For more detailed discussions of the economics of tropical deforestation, see Chapters 22 and 23.

[8]Bishop (1978) introduced the "unreasonable cost" constraint. Both he and Ciriacy-Wantrup (1968) argue as well that the costs of preservation are, on a society-wide basis, likely to be low.

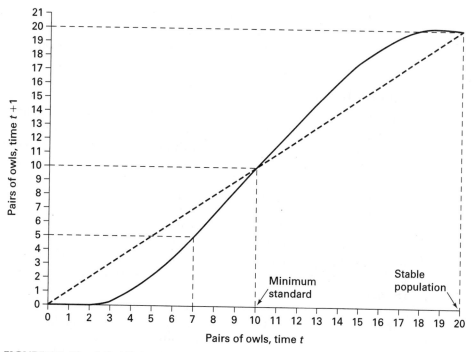

FIGURE 7.2 The Safe Minimum Standard

owls around next year, graphed on the vertical axis. So, for example, if there are 7 pairs alive this year, there will be 5 pairs alive next year, implying that the natural death rate exceeds the birth rate. Carrying this logic further, if there are 5 pairs next year, there will be only 2.5 pairs the year after that, and so on, to extinction. Points on the 45-degree line reflect stable populations, because the number of owls in period $t + 1$ is the same as in period t.

The point where the S curve first crosses the 45-degree line (10 pairs) is called the minimum standard (MS); any fewer owl pairs than the MS, and the species begins to decline in numbers, eventually slipping into extinction. With more pairs than the MS, however, the species will recover, since a given stock this period produces a larger stock next period, and so on. Eventually, the population size will stabilize at 20 pairs. (Extra credit question: Why does the S curve bend back down, and not keep rising?) The safe minimum standard lies a bit to the right of the MS—say 12 pairs—at the point where the resource can be guaranteed to recover on its own.

The safe minimum standard argument is often applied to endangered species. Each species has highly unique biological properties, with uncertain future genetic value; and *Jurassic Park* aside, species extinction is irreversible. Moreover, endangered species often serve as **indicator species** for threatened ecosystems. Thus, saving the spotted owl in the Pacific Northwest means saving a complex and biodiverse old-growth forest ecosystem. Especially considering their role as indicators, endangered species clearly merit protection under a Precautionary Principle approach.

In fact, as we shall see in more detail in Chapter 13, endangered species legislation is the one major national law currently on the books that reflects ecological sustainability as an underlying goal. The law states that natural capital in the form of species be protected from extinction regardless of the cost.

NONRENEWABLE RESOURCES

But what about resources less unique than species, which also may have fairly certain future value—oil, for example? In the last chapter, we considered a neoclassical approach to the sustainable use of petroleum—Mr. Bill was acting sustainably so long as he invested and did not consume the resource rent from oil production. How do ecologicals approach this issue?

Currently, world petroleum consumption is about 20 billion barrels per year. Oil is a finite (nonrenewable) resource; while predictions are uncertain, oil supplies are sufficiently limited so that within the next fifty years, the price should rise to greatly curtail its use as a fuel for everyday transportation or electricity generation. Shell Oil predicts production to peak in 2030; the World Resources Institute sees a production peak between 2007 and 2014, all against a backdrop of much higher world demand (Romm and Curtis 1996; MacKenzie 1997).

Ignoring the (major) environmental impact of oil consumption, are we penalizing our children's generation by depriving them of a more abundant oil supply? In fact, doesn't the use of any nonrenewable resource violate our sustainability criterion?

The answer is no if we as a society can somehow offset the reduction in natural capital through the use of created capital. In that case, oil is not really a unique resource. For example, solar, wind, and biomass technologies may power hydrogen fuel-cell vehicles and provide cheap heat and electricity as oil stocks are depleted. Markets can act as one powerful social mechanism for replacing natural capital with created capital. As oil becomes increasingly scarce, its price will rise, inducing firms to search out and develop new technologies that serve similar functions or that use the existing oil with much greater efficiency. However, there is little evidence that oil prices today reflect any long-run scarcity. Figure 7.3 charts the inflation adjusted price of oil imported into the United States over the last fifty years. As one can see, real prices today remain low.

The figure does reveal several big jumps in oil prices resulting from political-economic events. In 1974, 1978, and 2000, the OPEC oil cartel used its monopoly power to increase price, and in 1990, the Gulf War created great uncertainty about short-run oil supplies. The early OPEC price increases did have their predicted impact on energy use. Overall oil consumption in developed nations declined dramatically during the early eighties as firms and consumers adopted efficiency measures, but after 1985 consumption rose again and during the nineties stabilized at mid-seventies levels.

Because there has been no long-run upswing in prices, private investors in the Unites States have not yet been involved on a large scale in developing or marketing alternative energy technologies, with the exception of government-subsidized nuclear power and, increasingly, wind power. However, in many other countries where, due to taxes, oil and gasoline prices are much higher, market forces are working more successfully to promote the development of substitute technologies. For example, in Denmark, high electricity prices and an aggressive government tax credit program

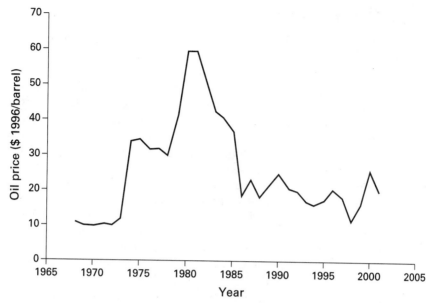

FIGURE 7.3 Inflation-Adjusted Oil Prices, 1968–2001
Source: U.S. Energy Information Administration.

have led to the explosive growth of wind power production, now serving more than 10% of the country's total needs (Flavin and Dunn 1998).

From an ecological perspective, energy use in the United States is not following the Precautionary Principle. It is unsustainable, since both prices and government R&D funding levels are too low to encourage sufficiently rapid deployment of substitutes. Given this, the ecological argument goes, future generations will be penalized in the form of higher prices for transportation and petrochemical products such as plastics. (More significantly, fossil fuel combustion poses long-term threats to the resilience of the regional and global ecosystems in the form of urban air and water pollution and global warming.)

Following the Danish approach, Daly (1996, 83) argues that for oil use to be sustainable, taxes should be high enough so that gas prices are equal to those of the *currently available* substitute (e.g., ethanol fuel derived from biomass such as corn).

We will take a much closer look at U.S. energy policy in Chapter 20. For now, let us summarize: This section has explored the logic of managing our global stock of natural capital via the Precautionary Principle. The basic point is that depleting the natural capital stock is consistent with a broadened definition of sustainable yield, if and only if substitute services of comparable quality *will be* provided for future users from created capital. How should this rule figure into development decisions? We have looked at two cases. Endangered species are unique renewable resources with uncertain future value, whose exploitation is also irreversible. Here, ecologicals advocate a safe minimum standard. For nonrenewable resources, such as oil, the pace of technological change must be weighed against the rate of resource depletion.

7.4 Markets, Governments, and the EIS

As a society, how could we implement the Precautionary Principle? Since many economic decisions are market-based, the first issue we need to explore is the degree to which unregulated market behavior promotes sustainability. Markets do provide incentives for sustainable use of privately owned natural capital. In this case, the owner has a strong economic interest in protecting the sustainability of the resource, either for her own profit or to maintain resale value. This will be true even if the resource currently has little value (say a stand of young timber), provided that the services it yields in the future will be sufficiently profitable. This phenomenon, which we discussed in the last chapter, is known as **profit-based conservation.**

Moreover, well-functioning markets have a built-in mechanism for promoting sustainability: As currently valued resources become scarce, their prices rise, encouraging efficient use and the development of substitute products. Whether the price increases occur early enough to allow for the development of substitutes is the issue highlighted in our previous discussion of the oil market.

But even when markets are working well, sustainability is not guaranteed. In the agricultural sector, for example, in spite of private ownership, current rates of soil erosion and depletion of nonrenewable irrigation sources are not sustainable over the longer term, even ignoring population growth.[9] Here we again run into the "faulty telescopic faculty" of the current generation, which we expressed in the last chapter in the language of discounting.

As we saw in the hotel lighting example, individuals interested in maximizing their profits from an investment should discount future benefits at the market rate of interest. However, because market interest rates are substantially higher than the rate of growth of NNW (5% to 10% versus 0% to 1%), rational private individuals will discount future benefits well above what we identified as the rate consistent with sustainability. Furthermore, there is mounting evidence that consumers, homeowners, and businesspeople implicitly discount at even higher rates for many investment decisions. For example, a payback period as short as four months, equivalent to a discount rate of 300%, has in the past not been sufficient to induce consumers to invest in energy-efficient appliances.[10]

Thus, even where property rights are well-defined and resources are currently profitable, **high market discount rates** work against sustainable use. In many cases, however, natural capital is a common property resource with free access: Here the public goods problem exacerbates overexploitation. As a result of these factors, market systems do tend to diminish the stock of natural capital, both renewable and nonrenewable.

Ecological economists believe that markets, in the face of growing population and affluence, are not doing an adequate job of guaranteeing sustainability due to excessive discounting, open access to common property, uniqueness of resources, uncertainty combined with irreversibility, or too slow a pace of technological change. As a result, they argue for greater government involvement to promote sustainability by protecting natural capital. Governments can rise to this challenge in many different

---

[9]See the discussion in Section 7.5.

[10]This example is from Gately (1980); see also Ruderman, Levine, and McMahon (1987).

ways; Parts II to IV of this book explore issues ranging from pollution regulation to population control. The remainder of this section will consider direct regulation of development as one response.

In 1970, the U.S. Congress passed the National Environmental Policy Act (NEPA), mandating a modern version of the Iroquois "seventh-generation" approach to development decisions. One section of the act required that government agencies prepare an **Environmental Impact Statement (EIS)** for "legislation or other major federal actions significantly affecting the quality of the human environment." The statement must include:

(i)   Any adverse environmental effects that cannot be avoided should the proposal be implemented;

(ii)   Alternatives to the proposed action;

(iii) The relationship between local short-term uses of man's environment and the maintenance and enhancement of long-term productivity; and

(iv)   Any irreversible and irretrievable commitments of resources that would be involved in the proposed action should it be implemented (Section 102 of Title I, NEPA; cited in Bear 1987a).

The law also requires that public comments be solicited in the drafting of the impact statement. More than half the states have subsequently adopted their own versions of the EIS to assist them in their decision making.

The EIS has forced every arm of the federal government to at least take notice of environmental considerations in its decision-making process. As one observer notes:

> The . . . process is applied, albeit unevenly, to the broadest range of federal activities of any environmental statute: highways and dams to be sure, but also to the formulation of programs, promulgation of regulations, development of new weapons systems, recommendations for Senate approval and consent to treaties, biotechnology experiments, even the abandonment of railroad tracks—the list extends as far as the federal government's reach. Major projects have been delayed, or in rare instances, cancelled, because of the information revealed through the analysis of environmental impact statements. (Taylor 1984, 17)

The basic philosophy behind the EIS is that the government should identify potential adverse environmental impacts of its actions and recommend superior alternatives. Further, by opening up the process to public comment, much broader perspectives on the likely effects can be incorporated into the decision-making process.

As a planning tool, the EIS has had its share of success stories. When it works well, it encourages agency officials to respond to the environmental concerns of the public—environmentalists, developers, workers, and citizens—and hammer out an ecologically sound compromise on development issues.[11]

However, even on its own terms, the process has its faults. The rather nebulous charge to identify adverse negative effects has lead to a situation in which "the usefulness of the NEPA process to decision makers often is weakened by a persistent tendency to overload NEPA documents with a voluminous amount of irrelevant or

---

[11]Taylor (1984) provides a good overview of the EIS process.

highly technical data. No one wants to read such documents: not public citizens, not members of public interest groups, not judges, and certainly not decision-makers," (Bear 1987b, 74). More importantly, there is no process by which post-project compliance with the recommended mitigation measures is assured.[12]

Finally, the EIS process imposes costs on both government and the private sector. From an industry perspective, the EIS provides an opportunity for environmentalists to drag out the permitting process, engaging in what is known as **paralysis by analysis.** Consider an extreme example. In October 1980, Occidental Petroleum filed an application to drill for oil in the Pacific Palisades area of Los Angeles. The project was highly controversial; the primary environmental concern centered around an unstable slope on an adjacent property. After (1) 20 public hearings, (2) a 788-page final Environmental Impact Review (California's EIS), (3) initial disapproval by the city, and (4) the preparation of a subsequent supplemental EIR incorporating recommended changes, the project was approved by a 10–4 vote of the city council in January 1985. However, a citizen's group then filed and won a suit challenging, among other points, the adequacy of the EIR. Occidental then appealed this decision. Finally, in 1989, a ballot initiative prohibiting drilling in the area was introduced and passed (Waterhouse 1987).

On the one hand, this example illustrates the positive aspects of the EIS process. Substantial input by the affected public went into an important development decision, and final appeal to the courts insured that the process itself was fair. The initiative vote prohibiting drilling might be seen as ultimately validating the effort. On the other hand, the case highlights the potential pitfalls. Out of a ten-year EIS process, what appeared to be a politically acceptable compromise emerged. Ultimately, however, the entire effort became entangled in a legal snare, focusing less on issues of substance than of procedure. Government regulatory efforts to promote sustainability such as the EIS will invariably entail these types of costs and delays associated with bureaucratic decision making.

The EIS is one direct government regulation that seeks to implement the Precautionary Principle. In the past, the neoclassical assumption has often held sway: generally, the exploitation of natural capital would lead to increases in human welfare over time, with conservationists being forced to prove the reverse in order to slow the rate of resource depletion. The EIS has shifted some of that burden of proof to developers.

More radical governmental measures than the EIS have been proposed to protect natural capital. In the 1970s Herman Daly was arguing that the government should set **resource depletion quotas** (Daly 1991). These would determine the maximum quantity of key resources that the country as a whole would be legally allowed to consume in a given year.

While this may sound utopian, Friends of the Earth International (1995) in the Netherlands is pushing just such an approach, and the Danish government has accepted the idea of these kinds of resource consumption limits in principle. Table 7.1 lists some of the targets that Friends of the Earth is proposing. Closer to home, some of our environmental laws are beginning to look like resource depletion quotas—the 1990 Clean Air Act limits total emissions of SO_2 by power plants to 8.95 million tons per

---

[12]The quote is from Bear (1987b). For successes, see Sanderson (1987). On post-EIS monitoring, see Culhane (1987).

TABLE 7.1   Proposed Resource Depletion Quotas for Europe

Resource	Present Annual Use per Capita	Optimum Annual Use per Capita	Optimum Change Needed (%)	Interim Target 2010 (%)
Energy CO_2 emissions	7.3 tonnes	1.7 tonnes	−77	−26
Nonrenewable raw materials				
Cement	536 kg	80 kg	−85	−21
Pig iron	273 kg	36 kg	−87	−22
Aluminum	12 kg	1.2 kg	−90	−23
Chlorine	23 kg	0 kg	−100	−25
Wood	0.66 m^3	0.56 m^3	−15	−15

Source: Friends of the Earth International, *Sustainable Europe Campaign Newsletter,* no. 2, August 1995.

year. This in effect is a depletion quota for an environmental sink—the air. A national ceiling on carbon dioxide emissions would be another resource depletion quota.

Clearly, applying the Precautionary Principle means augmenting market decisions. These can be rather tame governmental regulations, such as the EIS, or much more aggressive measures, which from a conservative perspective begin to look like dreaded "ecosocialism." The ecological economics view undoubtedly requires much stronger government intervention to promote sustainability than we are currently seeing.

Yet government involvement has its own limitations. As we will discuss further in Chapter 12, it is not clear to what extent government has the ability or the interest to promote sustainability. Beyond an increasingly short time horizon, the direction of technological progress is very hard to foresee. Thus, judgments made by government agencies or private researchers about the sustainability of any particular action, oil depletion, for example, will be just that—judgments subject to uncertain science and political influence.

On the one hand, detailed governmental involvement in *most* economic development decisions is undesirable on liberty grounds and would, in any case, likely be ineffective. Nevertheless, it is clear that, in a good many cases, unbridled exploitation of our natural capital will lead to a degradation of the quality of life for future generations. Regulations to promote sustainability will have the most impact on the welfare of future generations if they are concentrated on instances where (1) natural capital delivers a unique flow of valuable resources, with no technological substitutes on the near horizon, or (2) future benefits are uncertain and depletion of the resource is irreversible.

7.5 The Ecological-Neoclassical Debate in Context

In many respects, the debate between ecologicals and neoclassicals over sustainability reflects the same underlying issues as the differences between the safety and efficiency camps. Both ecologicals and safety proponents view environmental protection as a special commodity that should not be traded off for more of "everything else."

Safety proponents privilege a clean environment on the grounds of individual liberty and the right to be free of assaults on the body; ecologicals argue that, in general, natural capital has no good substitutes for which it can be traded. Both groups reject benefit–cost analysis, arguing that the benefits of protection cannot be adequately captured, and both groups therefore rely on physical, not monetary, measures of their underlying goals: safety and sustainability.

Note that in advocating for strict standards, both safety proponents and ecologicals make utilitarian arguments: Environmental protection is *good for people* because the society-wide opportunity cost of protection is relatively low. Moreover, we have not to this point questioned the underlying assumption that more is better. If increasing material affluence in fact does not lead to greater well-being, a hypothesis we will explore in Chapter 11, then the "low opportunity cost" case for the safety and ecological positions is strengthened.

Efficiency advocates and neoclassicals respond that the safety and ecological positions are too extreme. They insist that there are trade-offs and that we can pay too much for a pristine environment. Resources and person power invested in reducing small cancer risks or preserving salmon streams, for example, are resources and people that then cannot be invested in schools or health care. Benefit–cost analysis is needed to obtain the right balance of investment between environmental protection and other goods and services. Moreover, in the sustainability debate, neoclassicals argue that history is on their side: Malthusian predictions have been discredited time and time again.

Indeed, in recent years, prominent natural scientists (though not economists) in the ecological economics community have made stunningly bad forecasts. Paul Ehrlich, who introduced the IPAT equation, also predicted in the 1960s that "the world is rapidly running out of food" (Ehrlich 1974, 12). Ehrlich also bet neoclassical economist Julian Simon that the prices of half a dozen key minerals would rise during the 1980s: Ehrlich lost (Tierney 1990). Finally, a well-known mid-1970s report called *Limits to Growth* (Meadows et al. 1972) predicted (incorrectly) that many natural resource supplies would begin to decline sharply in the mid-1980s.

The problem with all of these early predictions, as with Malthus' original one, was that they dramatically underestimated the impacts of changing technologies. Looking just at the *P* and the *A* and essentially ignoring the *T* (technology) in the IPAT relation has not, in the past, proven to be justified. Neoclassicals point to these failed predictions to support their basic assumption that natural and created capital are indeed good substitutes—we are not "running out" of natural resources or waste sinks.

Ecologicals respond that history is not a good guide for the future. One hundred and fifty years after the beginning of the industrial revolution, the argument is that accumulating stresses have begun to fundamentally erode the resilience of local and global ecosystems upon which the economy ultimately depends. Indeed, ecologicals have largely shifted their 1970s concerns about running out of nonrenewable minerals and oil to other resources: biodiversity, fresh water, environmental waste sinks, productive agricultural land. While ecologicals stretching back to Malthus have indeed done their share of crying wolf, this does not, of course, mean the wolf won't yet come.

Let us end this chapter with an examination of an ongoing debate between ecological and neoclassical economists over the scarcity of one specific form of natural capital: topsoil. David Pimentel is an ecologist and prominent member of the Ecological Economists society. Along with several co-authors, he published an article in the journal *Science* in 1995 claiming that topsoil losses cost the United States some $27 billion per year in reduced agricultural productivity. This is a big number—about a quarter of total U.S. farm output.

In a stinging response, neoclassical economist Pierre Crosson (1995) accused Pimentel et al. (1995) of ignoring evidence contrary to their position. Crosson himself had earlier published an estimate of agricultural losses due to erosion at closer to $500 million per year, smaller than Pimentel's by a factor of 50. Two other studies ignored by the Pimentel et al. article backed Crosson's position.

So, are we running out of topsoil? Not being a soil scientist or even an agricultural economist, I am not going to settle this debate for you here. (A great term paper topic!) But one point to take away is this: The I in the IPAT equation—productivity declines from topsoil loss—arising from a given level of population, a given level of demand (affluence), and a given type of technology can be quite hard to pin down. A second point. We do know that *unless* more environmentally friendly agricultural techniques are developed, this impact will quickly grow in the face of a doubling of P, and at least a doubling of A.

And indeed, this point is one that Crosson himself makes explicit. His position is that productivity declines due to topsoil erosion, while real, will be dwarfed by the expected three- to fourfold increase in world food demand over the next fifty years (Toman and Crosson 1991, 19–25). And in the area of world food supply, while there are some optimists, even many neoclassical economists are worried about the ability of the food system to cope, especially with problems of chronic undernourishment (see Chapter 10 in World Resources Institute 1997). Even if we are not destroying our stock of topsoil as rapidly as Pimentel argues, the logic of IPAT and the ghost of the Reverend Malthus nevertheless still hang over our shoulders as we consider the world's food prospects.

7.6 Summary

This chapter examines the ecological economic view of sustainability. The basic theory resembles Malthus: geometric population growth bumping up against limited agricultural potential. But ecologicals stress problems arising from both population and consumption pressures on a much broader spectrum of natural capital—from fresh water, to planetary temperature, to biodiversity.

Ecological economists may have resurrected the dismal science, but the perspective is not without hope. Ecologicals challenge us to think about fundamentally redesigning our economy so that it restores rather than degrades natural systems, accrues rather than depletes natural capital. Can it be done?

Paul Hawken, a businessman and author of a book called the *Ecology of Commerce* (1995), offers a vision of a transformed economy in which business practices mimic natural systems. His idea is that, like nature, businesses need to develop technologies that run on "solar income" (direct sunlight, wind power and biomass) as opposed to "solar wealth" (fossil fuels), and for which "all waste is food." This means that wastes from one production process become inputs into another, so that ultimately, pollution as we know it disappears. One of the most interesting examples of ecological design is the so-called "living machine"—a series of pools supporting a complex artificial wetland which digests human waste, turning raw sewage into fresh drinking water. The ecological perspective seeks to expand this metaphor of the closed loop—where waste from one sector is food for another—to the macro-economy at large.

But an economy that conforms to an ecological design will not emerge without major changes in government policy. Ecologicals see the need for widescale, far-reaching social initiatives to control population and consumption growth, and to promote clean technology. We will turn to the details of policy for achieving these goals in Parts II to IV of the book.

In addition to the ecological perspective, in the last four chapters, we have laid out three other possible standards for environmental protection. The four are illustrated in Table 7.2: efficiency, safety, neoclassical sustainability, and ecological sustainability. We now want to ask, "What tools does economics offer to help us identify real-world target levels of pollution cleanup or resource protection?"

As indicated in Table 7.2, implementing the efficiency and neoclassical sustainability standards requires a full accounting of the costs and benefits of environmental protection. And so, for these standards, clearly we need to know how to measure benefits and costs. But this is not true for the goals of safety and ecological sustainability. Safety is measured via a health-based standard, and sustainability by ecological measures of ecosystem resilience. If safety proponents and ecologicals reject benefit–cost analysis, what more can economics contribute toward defining their goal?

Advocates of the safety and ecological standards need to learn about benefit and cost estimation techniques, if only for defensive purposes. To paraphrase the famous economist Joan Robinson: The purpose of studying economics is not to learn ready-made answers to economic questions. Rather, it is to learn how to avoid being fooled by (second-rate) economists. Learning the right way to measure costs and benefits is crucial for understanding neoclassical claims about how big the trade-offs between consumption and the environment really are.

Given this context, the next three chapters will explore the methods economists have developed for measuring the benefits of environmental protection and its costs, and for weighing one against the other.

APPLICATION 7.0

A Growth Parable[13]

Suppose that a bacterium lives in a test tube and the bacteria population doubles every minute, so that at the end of one minute there are two, at the end of two

TABLE 7.2 Four Normative Standards for Environmental Quality

Standard	Rule	Implementation
1. EFFICIENCY	MB of reduction = MC of reduction	Benefit–cost analysis
2. SAFETY	Health risk < 1 in 1 million	Risk assessment
3. NEOCLASSICAL SUSTAINABILITY	Discount future at rate of growth of NNW; invest all resource rents	Benefit–cost analysis
4. ECOLOGICAL SUSTAINABILITY	Protect natural capital	Weigh resource stock against population and consumption growth

---

[13]Thanks to Dennis Palmini for suggesting this problem, which he adopted from Perry (1994).

minutes there are four, and so on. Suppose also that at the end of fifteen minutes, the food supply runs out.

1. How many bacteria will be around at the end of fifteen minutes?
2. How many bacteria will be around at the end of fourteen minutes?
3. When will half of the food be used up?
4. What percentage of the food will be left at the end of thirteen minutes? Do you think that, after thirteen minutes, "Joe Average" bacterium would be easily persuaded that a food crisis was at hand?
5. Suppose, in spite of your answer to question 4, that at the beginning of the thirteenth minute the bacteria do get a wake-up call. They begin a crash scientific program, putting the best bacteria minds to work on growing more food. Success! By the beginning of the fourteenth minute, the bacteria manage to quadruple the remaining food supply. How much time do they buy themselves?
6. Is there a difference between these bacteria and people that might give us some hope for our long-run survival? If so, is it likely to work through *P, A,* or *T?*

KEY IDEAS IN EACH SECTION

7.0   Beginning with the **IPAT equation,** ecological economists argue that sustainability is threatened by geometric growth in both population and consumption per person (affluence). Ecologicals are dubious that technology can solve these problems because of two underlying assumptions. First, they argue that created capital cannot generally substitute for natural capital in production. Second, because the economy is embedded in what they believe is a rather "fragile" set of ecosystem relationships, accumulating stresses on natural ecosystems may lead to sudden large declines in human well-being.

7.1   Ecologicals' intellectual lineage can be traced back to Malthus and his **population trap;** ecologicals are sometimes called **neomalthusians.** Through the mid-1980s, Malthus was "wrong," thanks in large measure to the Green Revolution in agriculture. However, gains from the Green Revolution have tapered off. Ecologicals share the Malthusian view that population (and consumption) pressures lead initially to steady and eventually to catastrophic declines in human welfare. Ecologicals differ from Malthus in that they rely on an ecological definition of sustainability: **ecosystem resilience.**

7.2   As with neoclassicals, the first task for an ecological economist is measurement. Ecologicals employ **physical measures of ecosystem resilience and resource stocks weighed against population and consumption pressure** as their measure of sustainability. If demand for resources without good substitutes is a large portion of current supply, then our use is unsustainable. If the absorptive capacity of environmental sinks is exceeded, leading to changes in ecosystems from stock pollutants, then our use of those sinks is unsustainable.

7.3   To achieve sustainability, ecologicals have proposed the **Precautionary Principle** for development decisions. In this framework, any reduction in the stock of natural capital must be compensated for by created capital capable of generating a comparable flow of services. Applying the rule to **unique** resources that also have **uncertain** future value and whose destruction is **irreversible** requires protection up to a **safe minimum standard.** Endangered species fit this bill, especially given their role as **indicator species.** For less unique resources, such as oil, exploitation must be weighed against the pace of technological change.

7.4   Some features of well-functioning markets promote sustainability: Ownership rights encourage **profit-based conservation,** and rising prices in the face of resource scarcity encourage the increasingly efficient use and the development of substitute products. However, **high market discount rates** and the dominance of common property resources work against market achievement of sustainability. Given these problems, ecologicals see a much more aggressive role for government in protecting natural capital. As the **Environmental Impact Statement (EIS)** process illustrates, government efforts to promote sustainability have their own drawbacks, such as **paralysis by analysis,** and yet are essential in key areas. **Resource depletion quotas** are a more restrictive means of protecting natural capital.

7.5   Finally, the safety-efficiency debate over pollution standards is similar in nature to the ecological-neoclassical debate over natural resource exploitation. Both safety proponents and ecologicals argue that human society as a whole is best off protecting environmental quality at a high level *regardless of the trade-offs.* Ecologicals make this case by arguing that natural and created capital are not good substitutes in production. Neoclassicals counter that trade-offs are real, because perceived resource limits can be overcome via technology. The topsoil debate illustrates that these issues are not easy to resolve.

REFERENCES

Arrow, Kenneth, Bert Bolin, Robert Costanza, Partha Dasgupta, Carl Folke, C. S. Holling, Bengt-Owe Jansson, Simon Levin, Karl-Goran Mäler, Charles Perrings, and David Pimentel. 1995. "Economic Growth, Carrying Capacity and the Environment." *Science* 268, 28 April:520–521.

Bear, Dinah. 1987a. "The National Environmental Policy Act and the Council on Environmental Quality." In *Environmental Impact Assessment,* edited by Nicholas A. Robinson. Albany, NY: NYS Bar Association.

Bear, Dinah. 1987b. "Does NEPA Make a Difference?" In *Environmental Impact Assessment,* edited by Nicholas A. Robinson. Albany, NY: NYS Bar Association.

Bishop, Richard C. 1978. "Endangered Species, Irreversibility, and Uncertainty: The Economics of a Safe Minimum Standard." *American Journal of Agricultural Economics* 60, no. 1:10–18.

Brown, Lester R. 2002. *Eco-Economy.* New York: Norton.

Brown, Lester R., and John E. Young. 1990. "Feeding the World in the Nineties." In *State of the World, 1990,* edited by Lester R. Brown. New York: Norton.

Ciriacy-Wantrup, S. V. 1968. *Resource Conservation: Economics and Policies,* 3rd ed. Berkeley, CA: University of California Press.

Collins, Mark. 1990. *The Last Rainforests.* New York: Oxford University Press.

Common, Mick, and Charles Perrings. 1992. "Towards an Ecological Economics of Sustainability." *Ecological Economics* 6, no. 1:7–34.

Crosson, Pierre. 1995. "Soil Erosion and Its On-Farm, Productivity Consequences: What Do We Know?" *RFF Discussion Paper 95–29.* Washington, DC: Resources for the Future.

Culhane, Paul G. 1987. "Environmental Impact Statements and Post Decision Management: Theory and Practice." *Environmental Impact Assessment,* edited by Nicholas A. Robinson. Albany, NY: NYS Bar Association.

Daly, Herman. 1996. *Beyond Growth: The Economics of Sustainable Development.* Boston: Beacon Press.

Daly, Herman. 1991. *Steady State Economics,* 2nd ed. Washington, DC: Island Press.

Ehrlich, Paul R. 1974. *The Population Bomb.* Washington, DC: Sierra Club.

Ehrlich, Paul R., and John Holdren. 1971. "Impact of Population Growth." *Science* 171, no. 3977:1212–1219.

Flavin, Christopher, and Seth Dunn. 1998. "Responding to the Threat of Climate Change," *State of the World 1998,* edited by Lester Brown, Christopher Flavin, and Hillary French. New York: Norton.

Friends of the Earth International. 1995. *Sustainable Europe Campaign Newsletter,* no. 2, August.

Gately, Dermot. 1980. "Individual Discount Rates and the Purchase and Utilization of Energy-Using Durables: Comment," *Bell Journal of Economics* 11, no. 1:373–374.

Hawken, Paul. 1995. *The Ecology of Commerce.* New York: Harper.

MacKenzie, James. 1997. *Oil as a Finite Resource: When Is Global Production Likely to Peak?* Washington, DC: World Resources Institute.

Meadows, Donella, Dennis Meadows, Jorgen Randers, and William Behrens. 1972. *Limits to Growth.* New York: Universe Books.

Perry, David. 1994. *Forest Ecosystems.* Washington, DC: John Hopkins University Press.

Pimentel, D., C. Harvery, P. Resosudarmo, K. Sinclair, D. Kurz, M. McNair, S. Crist, L. Shpritz, L. Fitton, R. Saffourri, and R. Blair. 1995. "Environmental and Economic Costs of Soil Erosion and Conservation Benefits." *Science* 267, no. 24:1117–1123.

Postel, Sandra L. 1996. "Forging a Sustainable Water Strategy." In *State of the World, 1996,* edited by Lester Brown. New York: Norton.

Postel, Sandra L., Gretchen C. Daly, and Paul R. Ehrlich. 1996. "Human Appropriation of Renewable Fresh Water." *Science* 271, 9 February:785–788.

Rees, W. E., and M. Wackernagel. 1994. "Ecological Footprints and Appropriated Carrying Capacity: Measuring the Natural Capital Requirement of the Human Economy." In *Investing in Natural Capital: The Ecological Approach to Sustainability,* edited by A. Jansson, M. Hammer, C. Folke, and R. Costanza. Washington, DC: Island Press.

Romm, Joseph, and Charles B. Curtis. 1996. "Mideast Oil Forever?" *The Atlantic Monthly* 277, no. 4:April, 57.

Ruderman, H., M. D. Levine, and J. E. McMahon. 1987. "The Behavior of the Market for Energy Efficiency in Residential Appliances Including Heating and Cooling Equipment," *The Energy Journal* 8:101–124.

Sanderson, Richard. 1987. "EPA and NEPA: Cases in Point." In *Environmental Impact Assessment,* edited by Nicholas A. Robinson. Albany, NY: NYS Bar Association.

Sedjo, Roger A. 1991. "Forest Resources: Resilient and Serviceable." In *America's Renewable Resources,* edited by Kenneth D. Frederick and Roger A. Sedjo. Washington, DC: Resources for the Future.

Taylor, Serge. 1984. *Making Bureaucracies Think: The EIS Strategy of Environmental Reform.* Palo Alto, CA: Stanford University Press.

Tierney, John. 1990. "Betting the Planet." *New York Times Magazine,* 2 December, 52.

Toman, Michael, and Pierce Crosson. 1991. "Economics and Sustainability: Balancing Trade-offs and Imperatives." *Discussion Paper ENR-91-05.* Washington, DC: Resources for the Future.

Vitousek, P. M., P. R. Ehrlich, A. H. Ehrlich, and P. Matson. 1986. "Human Appropriation of the Products of Photosynthesis." *BioScience* 36:328–373.

Waterhouse, William. 1987. "California's Experience in Permitting Project Applicants to Prepare Environmental Impact Reports." In *Environmental Impact Assessment,* edited by Nicholas A. Robinson. Albany, NY: NYS Bar Association.

World Resources Institute. 1997. *World Resources 1996–97.* Washington, DC: WRI.

APPENDIX 7A

Game Theory and the Safe Minimum Standard

Applying a safe minimum standard (SMS) is recommended when fundamental uncertainty about the value of natural capital means that benefit–cost analysis simply cannot be undertaken. The SMS requires that natural capital be preserved unless the costs of doing so are "prohibitively high." This appendix, following Palmini (1999), illustrates that the SMS is generally equivalent to a social decision rule that delivers **minimum regrets.**[1] This means that under an SMS, the worst possible outcome will usually be avoided. Unless the costs of preservation are quite high, the SMS will insure minimum regrets in a world where future outcomes are highly uncertain.

Figure 7A.1 captures the essence of the problem. Society is faced with a decision to develop a dam on a river. If the development decision is made, this will drive to extinction species of plants or animals which may or may not provide a cure for a nasty disease, a disease, which in turn, may or may not materialize. The branches of the figure illustrate all these possible outcomes. At the end of each branch is the payoff to society from choosing to develop or preserve the river and its inhabitants, under different states of the world. Note that we cannot attach probabilities to any of these outcomes. We have no way of knowing which outcome is more or less likely.

Starting from the top, if the river is developed and no disease emerges, society gains net benefits of B_{dev}. Development with a disease yields B_{dev}, minus the costs of the disease, C_{dis}. Preservation with no disease generates net benefits of B_{pres}. If there is a disease, a cure may or may not be found.[2] If a cure is found, net benefits will still be B_{pres}. If no cure is found, net benefits will be $B_{pres} - C_{dis}$.

Got that? If not, go over it again.

Now put a little content to the game, and assume the following:

  1. $B_{dev} > B_{pres}$
  2. $C_{dis} \gg B_{dev}$ (>> means "is much greater than")

Assumption 1 says that, ignoring the disease potential, development yields more net benefits than preservation. Without this assumption, we simply preserve the resource and go home. Assumption 2 tells us that this is a bad disease, which will generate large costs.

Now with this setup, which option "should" society choose? If we are interested in minimizing the cost of being wrong, then preservation is generally the right answer. Table 7A.1 helps show this. It illustrates the "regrets" matrix of payoffs: Each cell shows, on balance, how society fares under different states of nature, *including the opportunity cost of the foregone option.* For example, if the decision is made to develop, and no disease emerges—the first entry in the table—society has few regrets. The development benefits exceed the foregone preservation benefits. However, in the event that the disease strikes, the development decision generates serious regrets, in the form of net costs instead of net benefits.

---

[1]Technically Palmini (1999) evaluates a "mini-max regrets" game solution, in which society chooses the policy delivering the minimum of maximum possible regrets under each strategy choice. But for the purposes of pedagogy, it seems simpler to refer to it as a minimum regrets solution.

[2]Palmini (1999) includes R&D costs for the cure in his model. They are omitted here for ease of exposition.

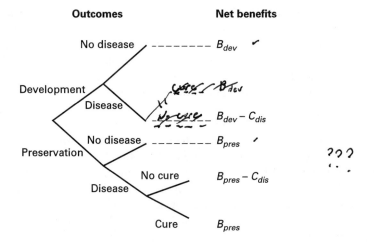

B_{pres}: Net benefits of preservation
B_{dev}: Net benefits of development
C_{dis}: Costs of disease

FIGURE 7A.1 The SMS Game
Source: Adapted from Palmini (1999).

TABLE 7A.1   The Regrets Matrix

	No Disease	Disease/Cure	Disease/No Cure
Development	$B_{dev} - B_{pres}$	$(B_{dev} - C_{dis}) - (B_{pres})$	$(B_{dev} - C_{dis}) - (B_{pres} - C_{dis})$
Preservation	$B_{pres} - B_{dev}$	$(B_{pres}) - (B_{dev} - C_{dis})$	$(B_{pres} - C_{dis}) - (B_{dev} - C_{dis})$

(Cells in gray are the maximum in absolute values.)
Source: Adapted from Palmini (1999).

The two gray cells are the *maximum* regret outcomes: Development generates the highest social costs in the event that a disease emerges and a cure would have been found. On the other hand, preservation is the most costly if a disease emerges but no cure is found, since development benefits are sacrificed and people still suffer from the disease.

When society seeks to minimize its regrets, it will choose to preserve the resource if:

The maximum development regret > The maximum preservation regret

or

$$|(B_{dev} - C_{dis}) - (B_{pres})| > |(B_{pres} - C_{dis}) - (B_{dev} - C_{dis})| \qquad (1)$$

which simplifies to

$$C_{dis} > 2 * (B_{dev} - B_{pres}) \qquad (2)$$

Equation (2) tells us to preserve the river as long as the costs of the disease are larger than twice the net benefits of development minus the benefits of preservation. Now recall from our assumptions above that the costs of the disease are assumed to be *much bigger* than (more than twice as big as) the development benefits. This means that equation (2) holds true as long as our underlying assumptions remain reasonable. This result thus proves the point: The SMS is a strategy that usually minimizes the costs of being wrong.

Equation (2) also tells us that even under complete uncertainty, preservation is not *always* the best strategy. If contrary to our assumptions, the foregone development benefits get large relative to both the costs of the disease and the other benefits of preservation, a conservation decision will no longer generate minimum regrets. This intuition is captured less formally in the SMS rule that natural capital should be protected unless the costs of doing so are "prohibitively" high. And as we shall see in Chapter 13, the Endangered Species Act does include the "God Squad" provision, in which species protection can be overruled if the foregone development benefits of preserving the species can be shown to be quite large.

REFERENCES

Palmini, Dennis. 1999. "Uncertainty, Risk Aversion and the Game Theoretic Foundations of the Safe Minimum Standard: A Reassessment." *Ecological Economics* 29, no. 4:463–472.

MEASURING THE BENEFITS OF ENVIRONMENTAL PROTECTION

8.0 Introduction

The efficiency and neoclassical sustainability frameworks we have discussed in the last few chapters appear to give us a very precise answer to the question: "Are we polluting too much?" Yes, if the marginal benefits of reduced pollution (both today and in the future) exceed the marginal costs of reduction. However, determining the efficient pollution level requires that we first devise accurate measures of both the benefits and costs of decreased pollution.

The benefits of pollution control can be divided into two categories: **market benefits** and **nonmarket benefits.** For example, cleaning up a river may lead to increases in commercial fish harvests, greater use of tourist services, and fewer medical expenses and days lost at work due to waterborne diseases. Measuring these market benefits in dollar terms is a natural approach.

However, economists have also devised methods for measuring nonmarket benefits. In our example these would include increased recreational use of the river (boating, swimming, fishing), the enjoyment of greater species diversity in the river, and a reduction in premature death due to diseases contracted from bad water. Nonmarket benefits are measured by inferring how much money people *would be willing to pay* (or accept) for these benefits if a market for them did exist.

Complicating the measurement of nonmarket benefits is the need to estimate the *risk* associated with industrial pollutants. For example, consider the case of poly-chlorinated biphenyls (PCBs), industrial chemicals widely used until the late 1970s as lubricants, fluids in electric transformers, paints, inks, and paper coatings. PCB-contaminated waste dumps remain fairly widespread throughout the country today. PCB exposure is related to developmental abnormalities in people and causes cancer in laboratory animals. However, the risk to humans from exposure to low levels of PCBs is not precisely known and can only be determined to lie within a probable range. The need to estimate, rather than directly measure, both nonmarket benefits and risk means that benefit measures for pollution reduction are necessarily fairly rough.

By a similar token, the direct costs of reducing pollution can be measured in terms of the increased expense associated with new pollution control measures and additional regulatory personnel required to insure compliance. However, indirect costs resulting from impacts on productivity and employment can only be inferred.

The next three chapters will take a close look at methods of measuring and comparing the benefits and costs of environmental cleanup. The principal conclusion is that benefit–cost analysis is far from a precise science. As a result, pinpointing the "efficient" pollution level can be achieved only within broad boundaries, if at all.

8.1 Use, Option, and Existence Value: Types of Nonmarket Benefits

The nonmarket benefits of environmental protection fall into three categories: use, option, and existence values. **Use value** is just that—value in use. Returning to our river example, if people use a clean river more effectively for swimming, boating, drinking, or washing without paying for the services, then these are nonmarket use values.

We discussed the concept of **option value** in the previous chapter in connection with rain-forest preservation. An environmental resource will have option value if the future benefits it might yield are uncertain and depletion of the resource is effectively irreversible. In this case, one would be willing to pay something merely to preserve the option that the resource might prove valuable in the future. In certain cases option value may actually be negative; that is, people may value a resource today less than its expected future use value. However, in many important environmental applications, option value will be positive.[1]

Finally, economists have indirectly included moral concerns about environmental degradation, including empathy for other species, in their utilitarian framework under the heading **existence value.** For example, if a person believed that all creatures had a "right" to prosper on the planet, then they would obtain satisfaction from the protection of endangered species, such as the spotted owl or the right whale, even if these species had no use or option value. The desire to leave an unspoiled planet to one's descendants (a bequest motive) will also endow species or ecosystems with an existence value.

As an example of the potential importance of existence value, a survey-based study by Boyle and Bishop (1987) estimated that Wisconsin taxpayers were willing to pay $12 million annually to preserve the striped shiner, an endangered species of tiny minnow with virtually no use or option value. As we will see, the results of this type

---

[1]I focus here on option value arising from supply uncertainty, as in the rainforest case, which seems most applicable to resource issues. Freeman (1985) shows that supply-side option value will be positive if supply is assured. If a project delivers supply only with a positive probability, a positive sign for option value will be more likely the greater the uniqueness of the resource. But option value is usually brought up only in the context of unique resources. To illustrate a case in which supply-side option value will actually be negative, consider a resource with perfect substitutes, such as a dollar bill. A risk-averse individual would have to be paid to accept a fair lottery to preserve a dollar bill for possible future use.

of study must be interpreted with care. However, the Boyle and Bishop results do seem to indicate a substantial demand for the preservation of species for the sake of pure existence.

The **total value** of an environmental resource is the sum of these three components:

$$\text{Total Value} = \text{Use Value} + \text{Option Value} + \text{Existence Value}$$

8.2   Consumer Surplus, WTP, and WTA: Measuring Benefits

Having defined the types of benefits that nonmarket goods generate, the next step is measurement. The benefit measure for pollution reduction that economists employ is the increase in **consumer surplus** due to such a reduction. Consumer surplus is the difference between what one is willing to pay and what one actually has to pay for a service or product. A simple illustration: Suppose that it is a very hot day and you are thirsty. You walk into the nearest store perfectly willing to plunk down $1.50 for a small soft drink. However, you are pleasantly surprised to discover the price is only $.50. Your consumer surplus in this case is $1.00.

To illustrate how one would apply the consumer surplus concept to an environmental good, let us return to the example we employed in Chapter 3, in which Mr. Peabody has a private demand for the preservation of a trout stream in Appalachia. This demand may be based on his expected use, option, or existence value or a combination of all three. His demand curve is illustrated in Figure 8.1.

Initially, ten acres of stream have been preserved. Assume Mr. Peabody did not pay for this public good. Nevertheless, he still benefits from it. His consumer surplus from the first acre preserved is his willingness to pay ($60), less the price ($0), or $60. We can portray this consumer surplus graphically as the area *A*, lying below the demand curve and above the price (zero) for the first unit. Similarly, for the second acre he is willing to pay about $59, which is also his consumer surplus since the good

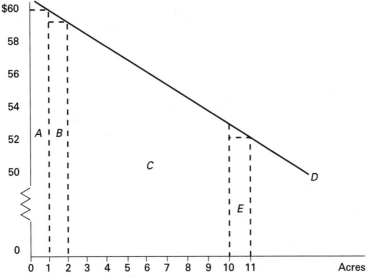

FIGURE 8.1 Consumer Surplus from Preservation

has a zero price. Consumer surplus from this unit is represented graphically as area *B*. Peabody's *total* consumer surplus from the initial ten acres is represented graphically by the entire area *A + B + C*.

Now suppose that a nature preservation society buys an extra acre of stream land. The benefits of this action for Peabody will be his increase in consumer surplus, area *E*. But this is just the price he is willing to pay for a one-acre increase! For small increases in the stock of a public good enjoyed at no charge by consumers—such as trout streams, or clean air or water—*the price that people are willing to pay is a close approximation to the increase in consumer surplus that they enjoy.*

This analysis suggests that one can measure the benefits of environmental improvement simply by determining people's **willingness to pay** (WTP) for such improvement and adding up the results. However, WTP is not the only way to measure consumer surplus. An alternate approach would be to ask an individual his or her minimum **willingness-to-accept** (WTA) compensation in exchange for a degradation in environmental quality. In our example, Peabody could be persuaded to give up the eleventh acre of stream in exchange for a little more than $52.[2]

In theory, WTP and WTA measures are both good approximations to the change in consumer surplus from a small change in a public good such as environmental quality. Economists predict that WTA will be a bit higher than consumer surplus, because individuals are actually made a bit richer when they are compensated for damage. On the other hand, WTP should be a bit lower than consumer surplus, since people will be made poorer if they actually have to pay for environmental improvement. However, the differences should not, in theory, be large since the income changes involved are not big.

To date, however, the evidence does not support this prediction. As can be seen in Table 8.1, reported WTA values are typically found to be from two to seven times as high as WTP. This discrepancy has persisted, even in studies such as Brookshire and Coursey (1987), where the researchers specifically attempted to control for factors that might lead to inflated WTA figures.[3]

How can we explain the divergence between WTP and WTA benefit measures? One possibility is that, for psychological reasons, people are more willing to sacrifice to maintain the existing quality of the environment than they are to improve environmental quality beyond what is already experienced. People may adopt the *status quo* as their reference point and demand higher compensation to allow environmental degradation than they are willing to pay for making improvements. If this hypothesis, known as **prospect theory,** is correct, it would reshape our marginal benefit curve for pollution reduction as illustrated in Figure 8.2 (see Kahneman and Tversky 1979). Here, the marginal benefits of reduction rise dramatically just inside current levels of pollution.

A second explanation for the divergence between WTP and WTA is based on the degree of substitutability between environmental quality and other consumption goods.

---

[2]In this example, I use WTP for improvement from the status quo and WTA for degradation to the status quo, where the status quo is ten acres. These are, respectively, compensating and equivalent variation measures. One can also use WTP for improvement to the status quo and WTA for degradation from the status quo. For a further discussion, see Freeman (1979).

[3]See the discussion in Knetsch (1990) and Mitchell and Carson (1989). The mean results from Brookshire and Coursey are presented in Table 8.1 for consistency with the other studies. However, their median WTA values also tended to exceed WTP by a substantial margin.

TABLE 8.1   Disparities between WTP and WTA, selected studies

Study	Year of Study ($)	
	WTP	WTA
Brookshire and Coursey (1987)	$ 12.92	$ 95.52
Kahneman et al. (1990)	2.21	5.78
Kachelmeier and Shehata (1992)	6.00	11.00
Adamowicz et al. (1993)	4.76	9.30
Boyce and McCollum (1993)	215.00	12,233.00
MacDonald and Bowker (1994)	105.00	735.00
Shogren et al. (1994)	0.90	3.50
Morrison (1997)	0.99	2.20

Source: Brown and Gregory (1999). Brookshire and Coursey (1987).

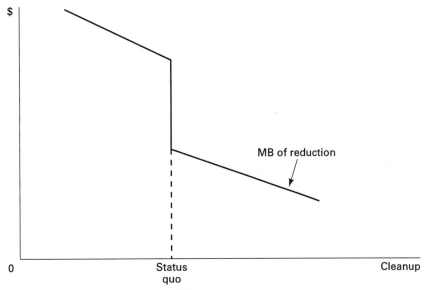

FIGURE 8.2 Prospect Theory and Marginal Benefits of Cleanup

Consider, for example, a case where people are asked their WTP and WTA to reduce the risk of cancer death for members of a community from air pollution. A substantial reduction in the risk of death is something that, for many people, has very few good substitutes. Nevertheless, a person whose income is limited will be able to pay only a certain amount for such a guarantee. On the other hand, because good substitutes for a reduced risk of death cannot be purchased, the compensation necessary for accepting such a risk might well be very large, even greater than the individual's entire income.

Some have argued that this "no good substitutes" argument is of limited value in explaining the measured discrepancy between WTP and WTA. Can it really be true, for example, that a stand of trees in a local park (the good in the Brookshire and Coursey study in Table 8.1) has no adequate substitute for people in the community? Appendix 8A and Chapter 11 both take up in more detail the degree to which environmental goods and more common consumption items might actually substitute for one another in the provision of utility.

Regardless of the explanation, the WTA/WTP disparity is clearly important as economists try to place a value on improved or degraded environmental quality. The standard practice in contingent valuation research is to use WTP, on the basis that WTA measures are too hard to estimate reliably (Arrow et al. 1993). But the right measure to use probably depends on the underlying property rights. If we think of common property resources such as clean air and water as belonging to "the people," then WTA compensation for their degradation would appear to be the more correct measure of pollution damages. Bromley (1995) notes that both hazardous waste and oil spill legislation explicitly vest the public with rights to a clean environment by giving them the right to compensation for damages. Under this kind of property rights regime, WTP is clearly the wrong measure and will generate underestimates of the underlying resource value.

Using WTP or WTA as benefit measures generates one additional concern. Rich people, by the simple virtue of their higher incomes, will be willing to pay more for environmental improvement and will require more to accept environmental degradation. In other words, using WTP or WTA to assess the benefits of identical pollution control steps in rich and poor areas will lead to a higher benefit value for the wealthy community. As we will see, the ethical dilemma posed by this measurement approach shows up strongest when comparing WTP and WTA for reduction in the risk of death or illnesses between rich and poor countries.

8.3 Risk: Assessment and Perception

The first step in actually measuring the benefits of pollution reduction is to assess the risks associated with the pollution. As noted in the introduction, this can be a difficult process. Information on health risks comes from two sources: epidemiological and animal studies. Epidemiological studies attempt to evaluate risk by examining past cases of human exposure to the pollutant in question. For example, in the case of PCBs, developmental abnormalities such as lower birth weights, smaller head circumference, and less developed cognitive and motor skills have been found in three separate communities of children whose mothers suffered substantial exposure. There is also limited evidence of a link between occupational exposure to PCBs and several types of cancer.

In animal studies, rats and mice are subjected to relatively high exposures of the pollutants and examined for carcinogenic effect. PCBs have been found to generate cancers in animal studies. The combined epidemiological and animal evidence has led the U.S. Environmental Protection Agency to label PCBs as probable human carcinogens (this discussion of PCBs is drawn from Glenn, Foran, and Putten 1989).

Due to concern about PCB (and other industrial pollutant) contamination of the Great Lakes, Glenn et al. (1989) undertook an evaluation of the risk of eating Lake Michigan sport fish. In this case, as in any risk assessment, it is necessary to estimate the number of cancers likely to happen from different levels of exposure. From animal studies, the number of extra tumors generated as a result of high exposure to PCBs is known. Translating this information to a human population requires two steps: First, the cancer incidence from high levels of exposure among animals must be used to predict the incidence from low levels; and, second, the cancer rate among animals must be used to predict the rate among people.

The assumptions made in moving from high-dose animal studies to low-dose human exposure constitute a **dose-response model.** A typical model might assume a linear relationship between exposure and the number of tumors, use a surface-area scaling factor to move from the test species to humans, and assume constant exposure for seventy years. Such a model would generate a much higher estimated risk of cancer for humans than if a different model were used: for example, if a safe threshold exposure to PCBs were assumed, if a scaling factor based on body weight were employed, or if exposure were assumed to be intermittent and short-lived.

The point here is that risk assessments, even those based on large numbers of animal studies, are far from precise. Because of this imprecision, researchers will often adopt a **conservative modeling** stance, meaning that every assumption made in the modeling process is likely to overstate the true risk. If all the model assumptions are conservative ones, then the final estimate represents the upper limit of the true risk of exposure to *the individual pollutant.* Even here, however, the health risk may be understated due to synergy effects. Certain pollutants are thought to do more damage when exposure to multiple toxic substances occurs.

Bearing this uncertainty in mind, the study by Glenn et al. (1989) estimated that, due to high levels of four industrial pollutants in the Great Lakes (PCBs, DDT, dieldrin, and chlordane), eating one meal per week of Lake Michigan brown trout would generate a conservative risk of cancer equal to almost 1 in 100. That is, for every 100 people consuming one meal per week of the fish, at most, one person would contract cancer from exposure to one of these four chemicals. The study concluded as well that high-consumption levels would likely lead to reproductive damage. There are, of course, hundreds of other potentially toxic pollutants in Lake Michigan waters. However, the risks from these other substances are not well-known. For comparison with the Glenn et al. study, Table 8.2 lists the assessed mortality risk associated with some other common pollutants and hazards, as well as the associated uncertainty.

The risk figures in Table 8.2 are the estimated number of annual deaths due to the activity, divided by the exposed population. Thus, at most, 2 out of every 10,000 people exposed to air pollution in the eastern United States will die from it each year. This is a

TABLE 8.2 Annual Mortality Risks with Associated Uncertainty

Action	Annual Risk of Death	Uncertainty
Drinking water (EPA limit, chloroform)	6×10^{-7}	Factor of 10
Drinking water (EPA limit, trichloroethylene)	2×10^{-9}	Factor of 10
Air pollution (eastern United States)	2×10^{-4}	Factor of 20, downward only
Peanut butter (four tablespoons per day)	8×10^{-6}	Factor of 3
Cigarette smoking (one pack per day)	3.6×10^{-3}	Factor of 3
Motor vehicle accidents	2.4×10^{-4}	10%
Police killed on duty (by felons)	1.3×10^{-4}	10%

Source: Wilson and Crouch (1987).

conservative estimate, since the uncertainty, as much as twenty times, is primarily downward. Avid peanut butter fans will be disappointed to learn that it contains a naturally occurring carcinogen, aflatoxin. However, one would have to eat four tablespoons of peanut butter each day of one's life to raise the cancer risk by 8 in 1 million. This figure could be three times higher (24 out of 1 million) or three times lower (2 out of 1 million).

The Scientific Advisory Committee of the Environmental Protection Agency has ranked environmental hazards in terms of the overall risk they present for the U.S. population. The committee's results are presented in Table 8.3.

The overall risk from a particular pollutant or environmental problem is equal to the product of the actual risk to exposed individuals multiplied by the number of people exposed. Thus, topping the EPA's list are environmental problems likely to affect the entire U.S. population—global warming, ozone depletion, and loss of biodiversity. The relatively low-risk problems are often highly toxic—radionuclides, oil spills, and groundwater pollutants—but they affect a much more localized area.

Risks of equal magnitude do not necessarily evoke similar levels of concern. For example, although risks from exposure to air pollution in the eastern United States are somewhat smaller than risks from cigarette smoking, as a society we spend tens of billions of dollars each year controlling the former, devoting much less attention to the latter. As another example, airline safety is heavily monitored by the government and the press, even though air travel is much safer than car travel.

The acceptability of risk is influenced by the degree of control an individual feels he or she has over a situation. Air pollution and air safety are examples of situations in which risk is imposed upon an individual by others; by contrast, cigarette smoking and auto safety risks are accepted "voluntarily."

TABLE 8.3   Relative Risks as Viewed by the EPA

Relatively High Risk
  Habitat alteration and destruction
  Species extinction and loss of biodiversity
  Stratospheric ozone depletion
  Global climate change
Relatively Medium Risk
  Herbicides/pesticides
  Toxics, nutrients, biochemical oxygen demand, and turbidity in surface waters
  Acid deposition
  Airborne toxics
Relatively Low Risk
  Oil spills
  Groundwater pollution
  Radionuclides
  Acid runoff to surface waters
  Thermal pollution

Source: U.S. Environmental Protection Agency (1990).

Other reasons that the public perception of risk may differ substantially from the actual assessed risk include lack of knowledge or distrust of experts. Given the uncertainty surrounding many estimates, the latter would not be surprising. Either of these factors may explain why the public demands extensive government action to clean up hazardous waste dumps (1,000 cancer cases per year) while little is done to reduce naturally occurring radon exposure in the home (5,000 to 20,000 cancer deaths per year) (Gough 1989). The issue of imposed risk may also factor in here. However, to the extent that lack of knowledge drives public priorities for pollution control, education about risks is clearly an important component of environmental policy.[4]

Finally, economists do know that people in general are **risk averse;** that is, they dislike risky situations. Risk aversion explains, for example, why people buy auto theft insurance even though, on average, they will pay the insurance company more than the expected risk-adjusted replacement value of their vehicle. By purchasing insurance, people are paying a premium for the certain knowledge that they will not face an unexpected loss in the future. Risk aversion also partially underlies the option value placed on a natural resource.

If people are risk averse, then we should expect them to give extra weight to measures that avoid environmental disasters. Much of the concern over issues such as global warming and nuclear power probably arises from risk aversion. It seems sensible to many people to take measures today to avoid the possibility of a catastrophe in the future, even if the worst-case scenario has a relatively low probability.

Indeed, if people are quite risk averse, this becomes another reason for choosing a safer rather than a more efficient standard for pollution cleanup, or an ecological rather than a neoclassical standard for protecting natural capital.[5]

8.4 Measuring Benefits I: Contingent Valuation

With the risk of additional pollution established, the final step in estimating the benefits of changes in environmental quality is to obtain actual value measures. One might think that the most straightforward way of assessing benefits would be simply to ask people their WTP or WTA. Economists do use survey approaches for measuring the benefits of environmental protection, called **contingent valuations** (CVs), because the survey responses are "contingent" upon the questions asked. However, interpreting the results from CV studies is far from a straightforward process.

An example: Johnson (1999, 2003) looked at the WTP of residents of Washington State to accelerate cleanup of leaking underground storage tanks at gasoline stations. Doing so would protect groundwater from contamination. Phone surveyors obtained basic background information about the respondents, including their estimated monthly expenditures on gasoline, their levels of concern about environmental risk, and their general positions on environmental issues. After providing some details about the benefits of the proposed cleanup policy, surveyors asked:

---

[4]For extended discussions of these issues, see Bromley and Segerson (1992) and Shrader-Frechette (1991).
[5]See Appendix 7A for an elaboration on this point.

> "If you had the opportunity, would you vote to require oil companies to begin tank overhaul immediately if it were on the ballot right now?" (Johnson 2003)

After obtaining a "yes," "no," or "don't know" response, the surveyor then introduced a "price" for the cleanup policy:

> "When deciding whether to support the measure, people are usually concerned not just about the environmental issue at hand, but also with how much it will cost them. … Suppose [that to pay for the cleanup], you had to spend $X [amount varied randomly among respondents] more per month over the next 18 months on gas, over and above $Y, your previously reported monthly household gasoline expenditures that you currently spend? In this situation, do you think the measure would be worth the groundwater reserves that would be protected?"

Note that the surveyors reminded people how much they were spending on gas per month (Y) when they asked the respondents for their additional WTP for the cleanup, so that the respondents would think hard about opportunity cost. And as one would expect, the introduction of a personal cost to the cleanup policy significantly reduced the number of yes votes—with higher costs leading to more and more no votes. By varying the amount that people were required to pay in the survey (and also by statistically controlling for factors such as income differences between respondents and pre-existing proenvironment sentiment), Johnson was able to construct a "demand curve" for the cleanup that looked something like Figure 8.3.[6]

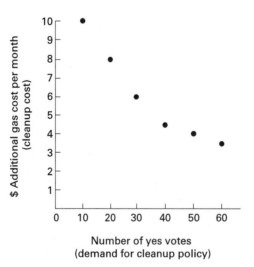

FIGURE 8.3 The CV Method of Measuring Consumer Surplus

---

[6]This figure is not based on data from Johnson.

Here is a quick

PUZZLE

What is approximate consumer surplus to the individuals in the sample if the cleanup in fact occurs and costs $4 per person?

SOLUTION

The first 10 folks get approximately $10 − $4 = $6; the next 10 get about $8 − $4 = $4; the folks from 20 to 30 get $6 − $4 = $2 each; from 30 to 40, the respondents get $4.50 − $4 = $.50; the next batch, from 40 to 50, have a WTP equal to the cost, so they neither gain nor lose; and the final batch of folks—from 50 to 60— are made a little worse off by the policy since their WTP is less than the cost: $3.50 − $4 = −$.50. Multiplying through by 10 for each group, gives a net gain in consumer surplus from cleanup equal to $60 + $40 + $20 + $5 + $0 − $5 = $120.

The contingent valuation survey approach to eliciting WTP and consumer surplus is easy to understand in principle. However, interpreting the results from a CV study is anything but straightforward. As with any survey, the answers given depend heavily on the way the questions are presented. This is especially true of surveys attempting to elicit true WTP (or WTA) for changes in environmental quality, since the respondents must be made to recognize the actual dollar costs associated with their answers. Contingent valuation researchers have identified at least four sources of possible error in their survey estimates: hypothetical bias, free-riding, strategic bias, and embedding bias.

The first possibility that emerges in interpreting CV results is the possibility of a **hypothetical bias.** Since the questions are posed as mere possibilities, respondents may provide equally hypothetical answers—poorly thought out or even meaningless. Second, as we discussed in Chapter 3, the potential for **free-riding** always exists when people are asked to pay for a public good. In Johnson's survey, if a respondent thought a yes vote would in effect require a personal contribution towards the leaking tank cleanup, he might vote no while still hoping that others would vote yes—and that others would pick up the bill. In that case, the public good of groundwater protection would be provided to the free-rider without cost. In this case, Johnson's respondent would have an incentive to understate his true WTP to CV researchers.[7]

In contrast, **strategic bias** arises if people believe they really do not have to pay their stated WTPs (or forgo their WTAs) for the good in question, say groundwater cleanup. Suppose, for example, the respondent thought that a big oil company would ultimately pick up the tab, and gas prices wouldn't rise as much as the stated hypothetical price. Under these circumstances, why not inflate one's stated WTP? This would be a particularly good strategy if the respondent thought that larger WTP values in the survey results (as expressed through a higher percentage of yes votes) would lead to a higher likelihood of mandated protection for the groundwater.

---

[7]In small group experiments free-riding is less prevalent than most economists would have predicted. See Mitchell and Carson (1989).

Finally, the most serious problem with CV surveys is revealed by an observed **embedding bias.** Answers will be strongly affected by the context provided about the issue at stake. This is particularly evident when valuation questions are "embedded" in a broader picture. In the case of the striped shiner mentioned in the introduction to this chapter, Wisconsin residents may well have felt differently about the shiner if they had first been asked their WTP to protect the Higgins-eye pearly mussel, another endangered species. In this case preservation of the one species is probably a good substitute for preservation of the other. That is, by stating, on average, a WTP of $4 to protect the shiner, Wisconsin residents, in fact, may have been willing to commit those resources to preserving a species of "small water creatures."[8]

On the other hand, might Wisconsinites, via their commitment to the shiner, be expressing a desire to preserve the broader environment or even to obtain the "warm glow" of giving to a worthy cause? Knetsch and Kahnemann (1992) maintain that the interpretation of CV responses is quite difficult in the face of this embedding bias. In one experiment they found that median WTP to improve rescue equipment decreased from $25 to $16 when respondents were first asked their WTPs to improve disaster preparedness. When respondents were first asked their WTPs for environmental services, then their WTPs for disaster preparedness, then their WTPs for improving rescue equipment and personnel, estimates fell to $1. Which of these estimates is the "true" WTP for rescue equipment?

Johnson's groundwater study was in fact designed to tease out the degree to which the context in which CV studies are presented can influence WTP answers. In the version you read above, respondents were asked their WTPs if "oil companies" were forced to do the cleanup. A different version substituted "gas stations," and added the following caveat: "Most gas stations are independently owned, and have small profit margins because they are very competitive. Even though they *advertise* well-known brands of gas made by the major oil producers, most gas stations are not owned by the oil companies themselves."[9] Johnson also randomly varied the percentage of the total cleanup costs that respondents were told these businesses (either big oil companies or small gas stations) could pass on to consumers in the form of higher prices.

Johnson found that people were more willing to vote to pay higher gas prices for the tank repair policy if they thought businesses were also paying their fair share. And this effect was much stronger if big oil companies were paying for the cleanup than if the regulation was going to be imposed on small independent gas stations. Her conclusion was that the perceived fairness of the policy strongly influenced individual WTP. This reinforces the point that, depending upon the context in which CV studies are presented, answers can vary widely.

The embedding problem in particular has generated a tremendous amount of research attention. Based on this research, CV advocates argue that in most studies, respondents in fact vary their answers in a predictable fashion to changes in the scope or sequence of questions posed. This means that a well-designed survey—one focusing on the particular policy proposal at hand—can provide solid, replicable information, at least for WTP. But such high-quality studies can be expensive. CV analyses of the damages caused by the *Exxon Valdez* oil spill, for example, cost a reported 3 million dollars.

---

[8]Bishop and Welsh (1992) make this point.

[9]At the time the study was conducted.

In addition, such ambitious efforts are relatively rare. In their generally favorable review of CV analyses, Mitchell and Carson (1989) conclude that "it is still quite difficult to obtain data from CV surveys which are sufficiently reliable and valid to use for policy purposes, and that the dangers of attempting to draw conclusions from poorly conceived or executed studies are great" (15). Most CV results must therefore be carefully reviewed for potential biases before they are accepted as reasonable estimates of true WTP or WTA.[10]

In spite of these criticisms, the CV approach is increasingly being used by economists, policy makers, and courts. This is because it provides the *only available means* for estimating nonmarket benefits based primarily on **existence value,** such as the benefits of preserving the striped shiner. These existence benefits are potentially quite large. In the case of the Exxon *Valdez* oil spill in Alaska in 1988, CV estimates of damages were on the order of $30 per household, for a total of $3 billion. This is roughly three times what Exxon actually paid out in damages ("Value of Intangible Losses" 1991).

CV is called a "stated preference" approach to eliciting nonmarket values, since people are asked to state their preferences in surveys. We now turn to two other methods that rely instead on the "revealed preference" of consumers. These approaches impute a price-tag for the nonmarket value of a resource from the demand or "revealed preference" of consumers for closely related market goods. As we will see, because revealed preference methods depend on the actual use of the nonmarket good by consumers, they can pick up use and option value, but not existence value.

8.5 Measuring Benefits II: Travel Cost

The first of these market-based approaches to estimating nonmarket values is known as the **travel-cost method.** This approach is used to measure the benefits associated with recreational resources, such as parks, rivers, or beaches. The basic idea is to measure the amount of money that people expend to use the resource (their "travel cost"). By relating differences in travel cost to differences in consumption, a demand curve for the resource can be derived and consumer surplus estimated.

A simple case is illustrated in Figure 8.4. Assume that 1,000 people live in each of three concentric rings, areas A, B, and C, surrounding a national forest. All these people are identical in terms of their income and preferences. People in area C live furthest from the forest, and face travel costs of $50 to use the resource for a day; they take only one trip per year. Folks in area B must pay $25 to visit the forest; they take 6 trips per year. Finally, area A people can wander in for free, and they do so 15 times per year.

We can use this information to derive the demand curve shown in Figure 8.4, which plots the relation between travel cost and visits. With this demand curve in hand, total consumer surplus can be determined from the following formula:

---

[10]Carson, Flores, and Hanneman (1998), Rollins and Lyke (1998), and Randall and Hoehn (1996) defend CV from the embedding critique. Harrison and Lesley (1996) discuss CV costs. Mitchell and Carson (1989) and Arrow et al. (1993) provide best-practice standards. Mitchell (2002) and Whittington (2002) discuss the state of the art.

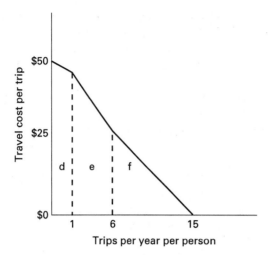

FIGURE 8.4 Demand Curve Derived from Travel-Cost Data

Total Consumer Surplus = Area A surplus + Area B surplus + Area C surplus =
1,000 people * (d + e + f)
+ 1,000 people * [(d + e) – 6 * 25]
+ 1,000 people * (d – 50)

The 1,000 people living in area A get a huge amount of surplus—the entire area under the demand curve, or d + e + f in surplus from their 15 trips, and they have no travel costs. Area B residents receive d + e, but have to pay $25 in travel costs for each of their six trips. Finally, note that the folks from area C get very little net surplus (d – 50). They take only one trip, and are almost indifferent between going and not going.

Of course, in the real world, people are not identical—they have different incomes, tastes, and opportunity costs for travel. How do economists deal with these complications when applying the travel-cost method?

A study on the recreational benefits of Florida beaches for tourists provides a good example. Bell and Leeworthy (1990) surveyed 826 tourists leaving Florida by plane or car and obtained information on days spent at the beach and expenses incurred to use the beach, including hotel/motel or campground fees, meals, travel to and from the beach, and access fees and other beach expenses. They also gathered data on initial travel costs in and out of the state, length of stay, age, income, and perception of the crowds and parking conditions at the beaches. Their basic hypothesis was that, holding all the other factors constant, lower beach expenses would lead tourists to spend a greater number of days at the beach.

Using a statistical technique called multiple regression analysis, the authors were able to control for all other factors and isolate the impact of beach expenses on consumption. They found that demand was price inelastic, with a 10% increase in "price" leading to only a 1.5% decrease in time on the beach, *ceteris paribus*. The average tourist spent 4.7 days on the beach, incurring an estimated daily expense of $85. With this information, Bell and Leeworthy estimated consumer surplus for all 4.7 days to be $179, for an average per day of $38. With 70 million tourist days per year, the authors calculated that Florida's beaches yield a flow of value to tourists equal to $2.37 billion annually.

Evaluating the reliability of a travel-cost study boils down to determining how good a job the authors have done controlling for "other factors" that might affect recreation demand. For example, the beach study has been criticized because Bell and Leeworthy did not control for the opportunity cost of the tourists' time. An extreme example shows why this might effect their result: Suppose an idle playboy and a heart surgeon, in all other respects identical, were two of the tourists surveyed. Suppose further that hotel prices were lower in the area visited by the playboy, and he was observed to stay longer in the area and visit the beach more frequently. The incorrect inference would be that the lower prices caused the higher number of visits when, in fact, the surgeon simply could not afford to stay away from work (see Shaw 1991).[11]

Another very important external factor for travel-cost analysis is the presence of alternative recreational opportunities. In Figure 8.3, for example, suppose that some folks who lived in area C had access to a second, equally close forest. In that case, they might choose to travel to the original forest only every other year, shifting the observed demand curve in and reducing the measured surplus for all groups, C, B, and A. But the existence of this second, more distant forest, would in fact have little impact on the actual surplus gained by folks in area A from visits to the original forest. The travel-cost method has been extended to address this type of issue as well.[12]

8.6 Measuring Benefits III: Hedonic Regression

Like the travel-cost approach, the final method used for valuing nonmarket resources estimates benefits from observed market behavior. This method, **hedonic regression,** uses the change in prices of related (complementary) goods to infer a willingness to pay for a healthier environment. The word "hedonic" means "pertaining to pleasure"; a hedonic regression estimates the pleasure or utility associated with an improved environment. As in the travel-cost method, regression techniques are used to hold constant factors that might be causing prices to change other than a degradation in environmental quality.

A good application of the hedonic regression method evaluates the damages arising from PCB contamination of sediments in the harbor of New Bedford, Massachusetts. The presence of PCBs was first made public in 1976; by 1983, about one-half the residents were aware of the pollution. Mendelsohn et al. (1992) attempt to measure the damage suffered in the community by examining the decline in real estate prices associated with the presence of this hazardous waste.

Their first step was to gather data on 780 single-family homes that had been sold more than once between 1969 and 1988. The authors' approach was to examine the relative decline in prices for those homes whose repeat sales spanned the pollution period, using regression techniques to control for home improvements, interest rates, the length of time between adjacent sales for the same property, property tax changes, and per capita income in New Bedford. Assuming that knowledge of the pollution

---

[11]Hof and King (1992) point out that the Bell and Leeworthy's model is not a "travel-cost study" but rather an "on-site cost study." They evaluate the relative merits of these two approaches.

[12]This is accomplished using Random Utility Models. See the discussion in Freeman (1993).

was widespread by 1982, houses located closest to the most hazardous area, where lobstering, fishing, and swimming were prohibited, had their prices depressed by about $9,000 (1989 dollars), *ceteris paribus*. Homes in an area of secondary pollution, where bottom fishing and lobstering were restricted, experienced a relative decline in value of close to $7,000.

Multiplying these average damage figures by the number of homes affected, the authors conclude that total damages experienced by single-family homeowners were close to $36 million. This estimate does not include the impact on renters or on home-owners in rental neighborhoods. Based on the results from this and other studies, firms responsible for the pollution have since paid at least $20 million in natural resource damage claims.

As with the travel-cost method, the key challenge in a hedonic regression study lies in controlling for other factors that may affect the change in the price of the related good. The following section illustrates this difficulty when hedonic regression is used in its most controversial application: valuing human life.

8.7 The Value of Human Life

The most ethically charged aspect of benefit–cost analysis is its requirement that we put a **monetary value on human life.** I recall being shocked by the notion when I first learned of it in a college economics class. And yet, when we analyze the value of environmental improvement, we clearly must include as one of the most important benefits reduction in human mortality. If we seek to apply benefit–cost analysis to determine the efficient pollution level, we have no choice but to place a monetary value on life. Alternatively, if we adopt a safety standard, we can merely note the number of lives an action saves (or costs) and avoid the direct problem of valuing life in monetary terms.

And yet, because regulatory resources are limited, even the safety standard places an implicit value on human life. In the past, the U.S. Department of Transportation has generally initiated regulatory actions only in cases where the implicit value of life was $1 million or more, the Occupational Safety and Health Administration employed a cutoff of between $2 million and $5 million, while the Environmental Protection Agency used values ranging from $475,000 to $8.3 million ("Putting a Price Tag on Life" 1988). Courts also are in the business of valuing life when they award damages in the case of wrongful death. In the past, courts have often used the discounted future earnings that an individual expected to earn over her lifetime. This approach has some obvious flaws: It places a zero value on the life of a retired person, for example.

Efficiency proponents argue that the best value to put on life is the one people themselves choose in the marketplace. Hedonic regression can be used to estimate this value. By isolating the wage premium people are paid to accept especially risky jobs—police officer, firefighter, coal miner—it is possible to estimate a willingness to accept a reduction in the risk of death, and implicitly, the value of a life.

For example, we know from Table 8.2 that police officers face about a 1 in 10,000 higher risk of being killed by felons than the general population. Suppose that, holding factors such as age, work experience, education, race, and gender constant by means of regression analysis, it is found that police officers receive on average $500 more per year in salary than otherwise comparable individuals. Then we might infer that, collectively, police officers are willing to trade $5 million (10,000 police times $500 per officer) for one of their lives. We might then adopt this $5 million per life figure for use in estimating the environmental benefits of reducing risk and thus saving lives.

Note that this is not the value of a specific life. Most individuals would pay their entire income to save their own life or that of a loved one. Rather, the regression attempts to measure the amount of money the "average" individual in a society requires to accept a higher risk of death from, in our case, environmental degradation.[13] Yet, an overall increase in mortality risk *does* mean that human lives are in fact being exchanged for a higher level of material consumption.

Even on its own terms we can identify at least three problems with this measure. The first is the question of *accurate information:* Do police recruits really know the increased odds of death? They might underestimate the dangers, assuming irrationally that it "won't happen to me." Or, given the prevalence of violent death on cop shows, they might actually overestimate the mortality risk. The second problem with this approach is *sample selection bias.* Individuals who become police officers are probably not representative of the "average" person regarding their preference toward risk. People attracted to police work are presumably more risk seeking than most.

A third problem with applying this measure to environmental pollution is the *involuntary nature of risk* that is generated. In labor markets, people may agree to shoulder a higher risk of death in exchange for wages; however, people may require higher compensation to accept the same risk imposed upon them without their implicit consent. Polluting the water we drink or the air we breathe is often discussed in terms of violating "rights"; rights are typically not for sale, while labor power is. We have explored the issue of a "right" to a clean environment already when we evaluated the safety standard in Chapter 5.

Hedonic regression researchers have attempted to control for these factors as best they can. In a comprehensive review of wage-risk studies Viscusi (1993) concludes that a value of between $3.6 million and $8.4 million (1998 dollars) is an appropriate estimate for the value of a statistical life for the United States and other wealthy countries. By contrast, studies conducted in Bangladesh put the value there at only $150,000 (Khanna and Chapman 1996).

Using hedonic measures to value life thus raises a basic question: To what extent are labor market choices to accept higher risk really "choices"? Consider the following recent description of twelve-year-old Vicente Guerrero's typical day at work in a modern athletic shoe factory in Mexico City:

> He spends most of his time on dirtier work: smearing glue onto the soles
> of shoes with his hands. The can of glue he dips his fingers into is marked
> "toxic substances . . . prolonged or repeated inhalation causes grave
> health damage; do not leave in the reach of minors." All the boys ignore
> the warning. ("Underage Workers" 1991)

Vicente works at his father's urging to supplement the family income with his wages of about $6 per day.

---

[13]For this reason, some economists prefer to call the measure the "value of a statistical life" instead of the "value of a life." I use the latter term since the lives at stake are indeed quite real, even if they are selected from the population somewhat randomly.

From one perspective, Vicente does choose to work in the factory. By doing so, he respects his father's wishes and raises the family standard of living. However, his alternatives are grim. Vicente's choices are between dying young from toxic poisoning or dying young from malnutrition. In important respects, Vicente's choices were made for him by the high levels of poverty and unemployment into which he was born.

Similarly, the "choice" that a worker in a First World country makes to accept higher risks will also be conditioned by general income levels and a whole variety of politically determined factors such as the unemployment rate and benefit levels, access to court or regulatory compensation for damages, the progressivity of the tax structure, social security, disability payments, food stamps and welfare payments, and access to public education and health-care services. All these social factors influence the workers' alternatives to accepting risky work. By utilizing a hedonic regression measure for the value of life, the analyst implicitly is either endorsing the existing political determinants of the income distribution or assuming that changes in these social factors will not affect the measure very much.

Valuing life by the "acceptance" of risk in exchange for higher wages reflects the income bias built into any market-based measure of environmental benefits. The hedonic regression method values Vicente's life much less than that of an American worker of any age simply because Vicente's family has a vastly lower income. Proponents of this approach would argue that it is appropriate, since it reflects the real differences in trade-offs faced by poor and rich people. We have already come across this issue when we discussed the siting of hazardous waste facilities in Chapter 5. The point here is to recognize this core ethical dilemma posed by using hedonic regression to determine a value of life.

8.8 Summary

This chapter has discussed the methods that economists use for valuing the nonmarket benefits of environmental quality. The focus has been on problems with such measures. Consider the questions an analyst has to answer in the process of estimating, for example, the benefits of PCB cleanup:

1. Is consumer surplus a good measure of benefits, especially when valuing life?
2. Which measure should be used: WTP or WTA?
3. How reliable is the risk assessment?
4. How good are the benefit measures?
5. What discount rate is used to value future benefits?

There simply are no generally accepted answers to any of these questions. A good benefit analyst can only state clearly the assumptions made at every turn and invite the reader to judge how sensitive the estimates might be to alternative assumptions.

In spite of their many uncertainties, however, nonmarket estimates of environmental benefits are increasingly in demand by courts and policy makers. As environmental awareness has spread, claims for natural resource damages are finding their way into courts more and more frequently. One important court decision confirmed the right to sue for nonuse-value damage to natural resources and explicitly endorsed the contingent valuation methodology as an appropriate tool for determining existence or option value (Kopp, Portney, and Smith 1990). In addition, policy makers require benefit estimates for various forms of benefit–cost analysis. As we will discuss further in Chapter 10, all new major federal regulations have been required to pass a benefit–cost test when such tests are not prohibited by law.

In a very ambitious article in the journal *Nature,* an interdisciplinary group of scientists attempted to put a value on the sum total of global ecosystem services—ranging from waste treatment, to gas regulation, to nutrient cycling (Costanza et al. 1997). They concluded, stressing the huge uncertainties involved, that ecosystems provide a flow of market and nonmarket use value greater than $33 trillion per year, as against planetary product (world GDP) of $18 trillion.

The authors use many of the tools described in this chapter. In justifying their effort, they state: "although ecosystem valuation is certainly difficult and fraught with uncertainties, one choice we do not have is whether or not to do it. Rather, the decisions we make as a society about ecosystems imply valuations (although not necessarily in monetary terms). We can choose to make these valuations explicit or not . . . but as long as we are forced to make choices, we are going through the process of valuation" (Costanza et al. 1997, 258).

Ultimately, economists defend benefit measures on pragmatic grounds. With all their flaws, the argument goes, they remain the best means for quantifying the immense advantages associated with a high-quality environment. The alternative, an impact statement like the EIS discussed in the previous chapter, identifies the physical benefits of preservation in great detail but fails to summarize the information in a consistent or usable form.

At this point, benefit analysis is a social science in its relative infancy, which, nevertheless, is being asked to tackle very difficult issues and has already had major impacts on public policy. Thousands of environmental damage studies have been completed in the last two decades. Perhaps the wealth of research currently underway will lead to greater consensus on acceptable resolutions to the problems identified in this chapter.

APPLICATION 8.0

A Travel-Cost Example

Now it is time for your first consulting job as an environmental economist. The Forest Service would like to know whether they should set aside some national forest land, previously slated to be logged, for hiking. You are helping with a travel-cost analysis to estimate the benefits of setting aside the land.

Survey data has been gathered from 500 hikers who visited a forest in a neighboring state. Using a statistical technique called regression analysis, you have controlled for differences in income, employment status, age, and other important factors that might affect the number of hiking trips taken. Taking these factors into account, you have developed the following relationship:

Cost to Get to Hiking Areas	Hiking Trips per Person per Year
$20	8
40	6
80	2

1. Graph the demand curve for hiking trips as a function of the "price"—the travel cost.
2. Based on demographic information about the people living in the vicinity of the proposed park, you have estimated that 50,000 people will take an average of four hiking trips per year. For the average person, calculate: (1) the consumer surplus for a single visit to the new park; (2) the total consumer surplus for an average visitor (*hint:* the area of a triangle is 1/2 [*B* * *H*]); and (3) the total expected consumer surplus per year from the proposed park.

APPLICATION 8.1

Calculating the Value of Life

In your second consulting job, you have been trying to estimate the willingness-to-accept risk on the part of workers. You have gathered data on a variety of blue-collar occupations, ranging from clerical work to truck driving to coal mining. Controlling for age, gender, education, work experience, and race, you have uncovered the following relationship:

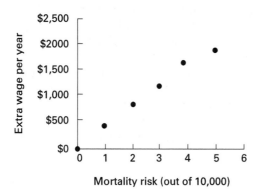

1. What is your estimate of the "value of a statistical life"? What does this mean?
2. Why might this value be a poor estimate of the value placed on lives saved from pollution reduction (three reasons)?

APPLICATION 8.2

Moving from Mouse to Person

This problem is designed to illustrate some of the difficulties raised in doing scientific risk assessments. As a public health specialist for the Environmental Protection Agency, it is now your job to figure out the risk to the public of contracting cancer from exposure to ET-2, a chemical compound used in printing shops. You know from animal studies that mice, when exposed to airborne ET-2 at levels of 1 part per 10,000 for 8 hours a day, contract cancer at an elevated rate. In particular, 10 additional mice per 1,000 develop tumors when exposed to ET-2.

1. The mice have been exposed to ET-2 at a level of 1 part per 10,000. But since people are bigger than mice, exposure generating an equivalent effect in humans would have to be much larger. You can pick one of two "reasonable" approaches for adjusting the exposure to account for size differences:

   a. Body-weight scaling factor:

$$\text{exposure per human} = \text{exposure per mouse} * (50 \text{ kg per human}/.015 \text{ kg per mouse})$$

   b. Surface-area scaling factor:

$$\text{exposure per human} = \text{exposure per mouse} * (1.50 \text{ m}^2 \text{ per human}/.01 \text{ m}^2 \text{ per mouse})$$

   Use the formulas to produce two different estimates of the exposure per human, measured in parts per thousand, required to generate 10 extra cancers per 1,000 people exposed for 8 hours per day.

2. Now you need to estimate the number of tumors likely to develop as a result of *real-world* exposure to ET-2. Engineers at your agency have estimated that, if ET-2 is unregulated, the typical airborne exposure will be 1 part per 100,000. Once again you have a choice of models.

   a. If you choose a *linear* dose-response model, the number of tumors is strictly proportional to the actual exposure. That is, a 1% increase in the exposure level will lead to a 1% increase in the number of tumors. The formula is:

$$\# \text{ of tumors per } 1,000 = 10 * (\text{actual exposure}/\text{exposure required to generate 10 tumors per 1,000})$$

   b. If you choose a *threshold* model, you are assuming that exposure below some limit, say 1 part per 10,000, is "safe"—that is, not likely to cause any additional cancer.

   Use the linear dose-response formula in part (2a) to produce *two different* estimates of the number of additional cancers per 1,000 people exposed to ET-2 if it is unregulated. You will get two different estimates, depending on which scaling factor from part 1 you use. Under the threshold model, how many additional cancers are to be expected? Does it matter which scaling factor you use?

3. Which is the most *conservative* risk assessment? Why?

KEY IDEAS IN EACH SECTION

8.0   There are both **market and nonmarket benefits** to environmental protection. Market benefits are measured at their dollar value; a value for nonmarket benefits must be estimated using economic tools.

8.1   The **total value** of an environmental benefit can be broken down into three parts: **use, option,** and **existence values.**

8.2   Economists consider the benefits of environmental protection to be equal to the **consumer surplus** gained by individuals through such environmental measures. For a freely provided public good, like clean air or water, a consumer's **willingness to pay (WTP)** for a small increase in the good or **willingness to accept (WTA)** a small decrease should be a good approximation to consumer surplus gained or lost. In actuality however, measured WTA is almost always substantially greater than measured WTP. **Prospect theory** provides one explanation for the difference; a second depends on the closeness of substitutes for the good in question.

8.3   Environmental risks must be estimated by means of epidemiological or animal studies. The estimated risk to humans will vary depending upon such factors as the assumed **dose-response model.** The risk to the population at large from an environmental hazard depends upon both the toxicity of the pollutant and the number of people or animals exposed. Public perceptions of relative risk often differ from those based on scientific risk assessment. Among other factors, this may be due to a distrust of scientists, as well as **risk aversion.**

8.4   The first approach used for estimating nonmarket benefits is based on survey responses and is known as **contingent valuation (CV).** CV studies are controversial due to the possibility of **free riding,** and **strategic, hypothetical,** and **embedding biases.** However, CV is the only available approach for estimating benefits of environmental protection based primarily on **existence value.**

8.5   Another approach for estimating nonmarket benefits is the **travel-cost method,** used principally for valuing parks, lakes, and beaches. Researchers construct a demand curve for the resource by relating information about travel cost to the intensity of the resource use, holding all other factors constant.

8.6   The final method of measuring the nonmarket benefits of environmental protection is known as **hedonic regression.** This approach estimates the benefits of an increase in environmental quality by examining the change in the price of related goods, holding all other factors constant.

8.7   Hedonic regressions, which rely on the wage premium for risky jobs, are used to place a **value on human life.** This is often necessary if benefit–cost analysis is to be used for deciding the right amount of pollution. This is a gruesome task; yet, even if regulators do not explicitly put a dollar value on life, some value of life is implicitly chosen whenever a regulatory decision is made. As a market-based measure, hedonic regression will assign a higher value of life to wealthier people, since their WTP to avoid risks is higher. This poses an obvious **moral dilemma.**

REFERENCES

Arrow, Kenneth, Robert Solow, Edward Leamer, R. Radner, and H. Schuman. 1993. "Report of the NOAA Panel on Contingent Valuation." *Federal Register* 58, no. 10:4201–4614.

Bell, Frederick, and Vernon Leeworthy. 1990. "Recreational Demand by Tourists for Saltwater Beach Days." *Journal of Environmental Economics and Management* 18, no. 3:189–205.

Bishop, Richard C., and Michael P. Welsh. 1992. "Existence Value and Resource Evaluation." Unpublished paper.

Boyle, Kevin J., and Richard C. Bishop. 1987. "Valuing Wildlife in Benefit-Cost Analysis: A Case Study Involving Endangered Species." *Water Resources Research* 23:942–950.

Bromley, Daniel W., and Kathleen Segerson, eds. 1992. *The Social Response to Environmental Risk.* Boston: Kluwer.

Bromley, Daniel. 1995. "Property Rights and Natural Resource Damage Assessments." *Ecological Economics* 14, no. 3:129–135.

Brookshire, David S., and Don L. Coursey. 1987. "Measuring the Value of a Public Good: An Empirical Comparison of Elicitation Procedures." *American Economic Review* 77, no. 4:554–566.

Brown, Thomas C., and Robin Gregory. 1999. "Why the WTA-WTP Disparity Matters." *Ecological Economics* 28:323–335.

Carson, Richard, Nicholas Flores, and W. Michael Hanneman. 1998. "Sequencing and Valuing Public Goods." *Journal of Environmental Economics and Management* 36, no. 3:314–323.

Costanza, R., R. d'Arge, R. de Groot, S. Farber, M. Grasso, B. Hannon, K. Limburg, S. Naeem, R. V. O'Neill, J. Paruelo, R. G. Rakin, P. Sutton, and M. van den Belt. 1997. "The Value of the World's Ecosystem Services and Natural Capital." *Nature* 387, no. 6630:253–259.

Freeman, A. Myrick, III. 1979. *The Benefits of Environmental Improvement.* Washington, DC: Johns Hopkins.

Freeman, A. Myrick, III. 1985. "Supply Uncertainty, Option Price, and Option Value." *Land Economics* 61, no. 2:176–181.

Freeman, A. Myrick, III. 1993. *The Measurement of Environmental and Resource Values: Theory and Methods.* Washington, DC: Resources for the Future.

Glenn, Barbara S., J. A. Foran, and Mark Van Putten. 1989. *Summary of Quantitative Health Assessments for PCBs, DDT, Dieldrin and Chlordane.* Ann Arbor, MI: National Wildlife Federation.

Gough, Michael. 1989. "Estimating Cancer Mortality." *Environmental Science and Technology* 8, no. 23:925–930.

Harrison, Glenn, and James Lesley. 1996. "Must Contingent Valuation Studies Cost So Much?" *Journal of Environmental Economics and Management* 31, no. 1:79–95.

Hof, John G., and David A. King. 1992. "Recreational Demand by Tourists for Saltwater Beach Days: Comment." *Journal of Environmental Economics and Management* 22:281–291.

Johnson, Laurie. 1999. "Cost Perceptions and Voter Demand for Environmental Risk Regulation: The Double Effect of Hidden Costs." *Journal of Risk and Uncertainty* 18, no. 3:295–320.

Johnson, Laurie. 2003. "Consumer Versus Citizen Preferences: Can They Be Disentangled?" Working paper, University of Denver.

Kahneman, Daniel, and Amos Tversky. 1979. "Prospect Theory: An Analysis of Decisions Under Risk." *Econometrica* 47, no. 2:263–291.

Khanna, Neha, and Duane Chapman. 1996. "Time Preference, Abatement Costs and International Climate Change Policy: An Appraisal of IPCC 1995." *Contemporary Economic Policy* 13, no. 2:56–66.

Knetsch, Jack. 1990. "Environmental Policy Implications of Disparities Between Willingness to Pay and Compensation Demanded Measures of Values." *Journal of Environmental Economics and Management* 18, no. 3:227–237.

Kopp, Raymond J., Paul R. Portney, and V. Kerry Smith. 1990. "Natural Resource Damages: the Economics Have Shifted After *Ohio v. United States Department of the Interior.*" *Environmental Law Reporter* 20:10127–10131.

Mendelsohn, Robert, Daniel Hellerstein, Michael Huguenin, Robert Unsworth, and Richard Brazee. 1992. "Measuring Hazardous Waste Damages with Panel Models." *Journal of Environmental Economics and Management* 22, no. 3:259–271.

Mitchell, Robert C. 2002. "On Designing Constructed Markets in Valuation Surveys." *Environmental and Resource Economics* 22, no. 1, 2:297–321.

Mitchell, Robert Cameron, and Richard T. Carson. 1989. *Using Surveys to Value Public Goods: The Contingent Valuation Method.* Washington, DC: Resources for the Future.

"Putting a Price Tag on Life." 1988. *Newsweek,* 11 January, 40.

Randall, Alan, and John Hoehn. 1996. "Embedding in Market Demand Systems." *Journal of Environmental Economics and Management* 30, no. 3:369–380.

Rollins, Kimberly, and Audrey Lyke. 1998. "The Case for Diminishing Marginal Existence Values." *Journal of Environmental Economics and Management* 36, no. 3:324–344.

Shaw, W. Douglas. 1991. "Recreational Demand by Tourists for Saltwater Beach Days: Comment." *Journal of Environmental Economics and Management* 20:284–289.

Shogren, Jason, Seung Y. Shin, Dermot Hayes, and James Kliebenstein. 1994. "Resolving Differences in Willingness to Pay and Willingness to Accept." *The American Economic Review* 84, no. 1:255–270.

Shrader-Frechette, K. S. 1991. *Risk and Rationality: Philosophical Foundations for Populist Reform.* Berkeley, CA: University of California Press.

"Underage Workers Fill Mexican Factories, Stir U.S. Trade Debate." 1991. *Wall Street Journal,* 8 April.

U.S. Environmental Protection Agency. 1990. *Reducing Risk: Setting Priorities and Strategies for Environmental Protection.* Washington, DC: U.S. EPA.

"Value of Intangible Losses from Exxon *Valdez* Spill Put at $3 Billion." 1991. *The Washington Post,* 20 March.

Viscusi, Kip. 1993. "The Value of Risks to Life and Health." *Journal of Economic Literature* 31, no. 4:1912–1946.

Wilson, Richard, and E. A. C. Crouch. 1987. "Risk Assessment and Comparisons: An Introduction." *Science* 236:267–270.

Whittington, D. 2002. "Improving the Performance of Contingent Valuation Studies in Developing Countries." *Environmental and Resource Economics* 22, no. 1, 2:323–367.

APPENDIX 8A

WTA and WTP Redux

In the previous chapter, I noted that there is a large and persistent gap between people's estimated WTP for environmental cleanup, and their WTA compensation in exchange for environmental degradation. Two explanations have been offered for this. The first is prospect theory: People form an attachment to the status quo, and thus feel less strongly about cleanup than they do about degradation. A second explanation flows from conventional economic theory. It turns out, as this appendix shows, that when goods have few substitutes, WTA *should* be higher than WTP. We will also review here the results of an interesting experiment that tried to sort out whether observed WTA/WTP disparities are best explained by this "no good substitutes" argument, or prospect theory, and think a little more about why it matters.

8A.1 An Indifference Curve Analysis[1]

Since this appendix is optional, I am going to assume that you recall perfectly how indifference curve analysis works from a previous course and jump right into the diagrams. Figure 8A.1 shows my indifference curve map for standard quarters and one of the state quarter series, the one with Wyoming on the tails side. The curves are drawn in a straight line, implying that, to me, the goods are perfect substitutes, with a (marginal) rate of substitution of 1:1. I am not a coin collector, I just like money. So I am equally as happy with 4 standard quarters and 1 Wyoming quarter as with 1 standard and 4 Wyomings.

Now suppose I am at point A (2,2). What is my *maximum* WTP to get one more Wyoming and move to point B (3,2)? The answer is illustrated by the distance marked WTP in the diagram; if I paid $.25 to get to B, I would be just as well off as I was at A—paying anything less makes me better off. Therefore, $.25 is my *maximum* WTP.

Let's change the rules. Suppose I am still at point A (2,2). What is my *minimum* WTA to give up a chance to move to B (3,2)? To be equally happy as I would

---

[1]This presentation follows Hanneman (1991) and Shogren et al. (1994).

have been at B, I need to be given income until I am on the same indifference curve as B. But that is the distance marked WTA on the diagram—again one standard quarter or $.25. When goods are perfect substitutes, WTA and WTP should be identical.[2]

In Figure 8A.2 the trading gets more serious. I am now confronted with a choice of spending money to reduce my risk of death: Let's say I can do this by laying out additional dollars each month on pesticide free, organic vegetables. On the horizontal axis, the risk of death gets more severe as we move toward the origin. For the

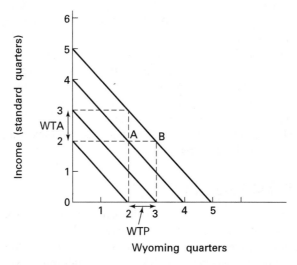

FIGURE 8A.1 WTA/WTP: Perfect Substitutes

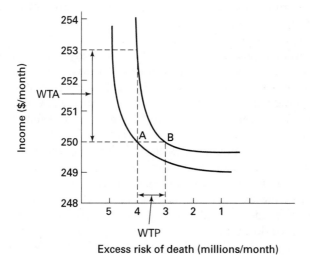

FIGURE 8A.2 WTA/WTP: Poor Substitutes

---

[2]Ignoring small income effects.

purposes of illustration, let us also say that each additional $1 per month spent on pesticide-free veggies reduces my extra risk of dying by 1 out of a million.

Note that these indifference curves are not straight lines; instead they have the conventional bowed-in shape. The slope of the indifference curves decreases as risk levels decrease, reflecting a decreasing rate of marginal substitution. At high levels of risk I am willing to trade a lot of income to reduce risk a little. But as my risk level decreases, I am less willing to accept cash in exchange for further safety. Put another way, at high risk levels, cash is not a good substitute for risk reduction.

As the diagram shows, when goods are not perfect substitutes, WTA will tend to be higher than WTP—a lot higher when the indifference curves are more steep, indicating poor substitutability. If I start at point A (with $250 per month and a 4 out of a million increased risk of death by pesticide consumption), then my *maximum* willingness to pay to move to an excess risk of 3 out of a million is the line segment labeled WTP—equivalent to $1. By contrast, my *minimum* WTA compensation to stay at an excess risk level of 4 out of a million is illustrated on the income axis. To be equally content as I would have been at point B, I would have to be given cash sufficient to get me out to the higher indifference curve, or $3. It is apparent from this diagram that WTA will generally be bigger than WTP, and the difference will increase as one moves along the horizontal axis toward the origin and higher risk levels.

8A.2 Prospect Theory or Substitutability?

Shogren et al. (1994) had fun trying to sort out the explanation—prospect theory or poor substitutes—for the observed differences between WTA and WTP by doing experiments with a panel of college students. In the first experiment, the panel members were given an initial endowment of $3 and a small piece of candy. The researchers then conducted a series of trials to find out how much students would be WTP to upgrade to a brand name candy bar. In an alternate series of experiment, different students were given the cash and the candy bar, and asked their WTA cash to downgrade to the small piece of candy.

The second experiment raised the ante: Students were given $15 and a food product like a conventional deli sandwich, which of course bears a low risk of a possible infection from pathogens such as salmonella. Students were then asked how much they would pay to upgrade to a stringently screened food product, with a very low risk of infection. In addition to hearing a bit about the symptoms of salmonella infection, they were also provided with the following sort of information: "The chance of infection of salmonellosis is 1 in 125 annually. Of those individuals who get sick, 1 individual out of 1,000 will die annually. The average cost for medical expenses and productivity losses from a mild case of salmonella is $220."

In the last stage of the experiment, the researchers flipped the property rights. This time, they gave the students the screened food product and the $15, and then asked their WTA cash to downgrade to the conventional product. (In both cases, of course, the students had to actually eat the sandwiches!) Each subject participated in either both WTP experiments or both WTA experiments, but no individual was involved in WTP *and* WTA sessions. Finally, each of the 142 participants sat through several trials to allow them to gain experience with the experimental procedure.

In the candy bar experiment, WTA and WTP quickly converged very close to the market price of $.50. However, for risk reduction, WTA remained well above WTP, even after 20 repeated trials. For exposure to salmonella, the mean WTA was $1.23, twice the WTP of $.56. The authors concluded that this experiment, along with subsequent work, provides support for a "no-good-substitutes" explanation of the WTA/WTP discrepancy, as opposed to one based on prospect theory. Do you agree?

Advocates of prospect theory might respond that candy bars or other low value items do not provide a good test of the two theories: people are not likely to become attached to a candy bar or a coffee mug in the same way that they might become attached to a grove of trees in a local park. In this sense, the two explanations begin to converge. People are attached to the status quo because there are no good substitutes for environmental degradation from the status quo!

Regardless of the explanation, this experiment also illustrates that the choice of WTP or WTA in some sense flows naturally from the assignment of property rights. If people own the conventional sandwich, then it makes sense to ask their WTP to upgrade; if they own the superior sandwich, then it is natural to ask their WTA to downgrade.

REFERENCES

Hanneman, Michael. 1991. "Willingness to Pay and Willingness to Accept: How Much Can They Differ?" *American Economic Review* 81, no. 3:635–647.

Shogren, Jason, Seung Y. Shin, Dermot Hayes, and James Kliebenstein. 1994. "Resolving Differences in Willingness to Pay and Willingness to Accept." *The American Economic Review* 84, no. 1:255–270.

MEASURING THE COSTS OF ENVIRONMENTAL PROTECTION

9.0 Introduction

In the summer of 1997, the Environmental Protection Agency tightened the national air quality standard for smog—ground-level ozone. The agency developed official cost estimates for this regulation ranging from $600 million to $2.5 billion per year. Yet, some opponents of the regulation came up with much higher numbers: The U.S. Department of Defense, for example, put compliance costs for that agency alone at $1.36 billion annually ("EPA Plans" 1997).

On the face of it, measuring the costs associated with environmental cleanup appears to be a substantially easier task than measuring benefits. One can simply add up all the expected expenditures by firms on pollution control equipment and personnel, plus local state and federal government expenditures on regulatory efforts, including the drafting, monitoring, and enforcing of regulations. This **engineering approach** to measuring cost is, by far, the most widespread method in use.

However, because engineering cost estimates are often *predicted* costs, they require making assumptions about future behavior. For example, cost estimates may assume full compliance with pollution laws or assume that firms will adopt a particular type of pollution control technology to meet the standards. To the extent that these assumptions fail to foresee the future accurately, engineering cost estimates may be misleading on their own terms. Indeed, in the early 1990s, the EPA overestimated the costs of sulfur dioxide control by a factor of 2 to 4; "credible" industry estimates were eight times too high (Burtraw 1996; Harrington, Morgenstern, and Nelson 1999).

Moreover, from the economic point of view, there are additional problems with the engineering approach. Economists employ a measure of cost known as **opportunity cost:** the value of resources in their next best available use. Suppose the new smog laws lead to engineering costs of $2 billion per year. If as a society we were not devoting this $2 billion to pollution control, would we be able to afford just $2 billion in other goods and services? More? Less? The answer to this question provides the true measure of the cost of environmental protection.

Engineering cost estimates will overstate true social costs to the extent that government involvement (1) increases productivity by increasing the efficiency with which available resources are used, forcing technological change, or improving worker health or ecosystem services; and/or (2) reduces structural unemployment.

On the other hand, engineering cost estimates will underestimate true social costs to the extent that government involvement (1) lowers productivity growth by diverting investment, and/or (2) induces structural unemployment, and/or (3) increases monopoly power in the economy. Finally, so-called "general equilibrium" effects of environmental regulation can either raise or lower the costs of regulation. This chapter will first examine EPA estimates of engineering costs and will then consider the degree to which these estimates overstate or understate the "true" costs of environmental protection.

9.1 Engineering Costs

Engineering cost estimates require the use of accounting conventions to "annualize" capital investments; in other words, to spread out the cost of investments in plant and equipment over their expected lifetimes. Table 9.1 provides EPA estimates of the current and historical "annualized" engineering costs of pollution control in the United States since the major federal programs were initiated in the early 1970s.

The figures in Table 9.1 for 1990 to 2000 are estimated and assume full compliance with pollution control regulations. Fixed capital costs for each year are determined by depreciating on a straight-line basis and assuming firms pay a 7% interest rate on funds borrowed to finance the investment.

The table shows historical and current annual pollution control expenditures for four categories of pollutant—air, water, land, and chemicals—as well as an "other" category including unassigned EPA administrative and research expenses. The costs listed cover all direct compliance and regulatory expenses for pollution control, including investments in pollution control equipment and personnel, the construction of municipal water treatment plants, and the bill your family pays to your local garbage collector. (Note that these costs are not identical to the costs of environmental regulation: Even without regulations, the private sector would undertake some amount of sewage treatment and garbage disposal!)

As a nation, we have indeed been devoting increasing attention to pollution control. Over a period of twenty-five years, total spending has risen from $37 billion to more than $224 billion, measured in 1998 dollars. Perhaps more significantly, pollution control as a percentage of GNP had been predicted to rise from less than 1% in 1972, to 2.1% in 1990, to more than 2.8% by 2000, more than doubling its claim on the nation's resources. By comparison, in 1998 about 10.5% of GNP was spent on health care, while close to 0.8% was spent on the category of "sporting goods."

Chapter 12 is devoted to an overview of the current regulatory framework. At this point however it is useful to note some trends in the projected pollution control costs

TABLE 9.1 U.S. Annualized Pollution Control Costs (1998 $ billion)

Type of Pollutant	Year						
	1972	1975	1980	1985	1990	1995	2000
AIR							
Air	$11.1	$15.3	$24.8	$ 32.9	$ 38.9	$ 51.4	$ 61.6
Radiation	$ 0.0	$ 0.2	$ 0.2	$ 0.2	$ 0.6	$ 1.0	$ 1.3
WATER							
Quality	$12.8	$19.7	$32.1	$ 42.9	$ 54.7	$ 67.8	$ 80.5
Drinking	$ 1.1	$ 1.6	$ 2.8	$ 4.0	$ 4.8	$ 7.5	$ 9.2
LAND							
Waste Disp.	$11.8	$13.1	$19.1	$ 21.9	$ 34.9	$ 45.8	$ 53.3
Superfund	$ 0.0	$ 0.0	$ 0.0	$ 0.5	$ 2.4	$ 6.6	$ 11.3
CHEMICALS							
Toxics	$ 0.0	$ 0.0	$ 0.6	$ 0.5	$ 0.8	$ 1.6	$ 1.7
Pesticides	$ 0.1	$ 0.2	$ 0.7	$ 0.7	$ 1.4	$ 1.9	$ 2.4
OTHER	$ 0.1	$ 0.7	$ 1.3	$ 1.0	$ 2.3	$ 3.0	$ 3.2
TOTAL	$37.3	$51.9	$81.5	$104.3	$141.0	$194.1	$224.3
% of GNP	0.9	1.2	1.6	1.8	2.1	2.6	2.8

Note: Both the costs and GNP shares from 1990 to 2000 are estimated.

Source: Alan Carlin, 1990. *Environmental Investments: The Cost of a Clean Environment, Summary.* Washington, DC: U.S. EPA.

revealed by Table 9.1. The EPA predicted that air pollution expenses would rise by about $9 billion per year through the mid-1990s, primarily due to the passage of the 1990 Clean Air Act Amendments. Table 9.1 also suggests that water costs would continue to rise as local governments spent more on wastewater treatment facilities and the private sector continued to invest in the control of industrial and agricultural discharges. Finally, of all categories, the cost of land disposal was projected to grow the fastest; it was expected to more than triple from $22 billion to $64 billion between 1985 and 2000. Much of this increase is due to more stringent requirements mandated during the 1980s for the disposal of solid and hazardous waste and the design of underground storage tanks, as well as the very rapid recent growth in the Superfund program. Superfund is the common name for the legislation requiring cleanup of old hazardous waste sites.

Table 9.1 provides some idea of the direct expenses associated with pollution control in the United States. The question we seek to answer in the rest of this chapter is: Do these engineering estimates understate or overstate the true social costs of environmental protection?

9.2 Productivity Impacts of Regulation

Undoubtedly, the biggest unknown when it comes to estimating the costs of environmental protection is its impact on *productivity*. Productivity, or output per worker, is a critical economic measure. Rising productivity means the economic pie per worker is growing. A growing pie, in turn, makes it easier for society to accommodate both the needs of a growing population and the desire for a higher material standard of living.

Between 1974 and 1995, productivity growth in the Unites States averaged only 1%, well below the 3% rate the American economy experienced in the 1950s and 1960s. Because growth is a cumulative process, such small changes in productivity can have dramatic long-run effects. Figure 9.1 illustrates the impact that the productivity slowdown has had on economic output.

If, rather than declining after 1974, productivity growth had continued at its 1950 to 1970 rate of 3%, GDP in 2002 would have been more than $6 trillion greater than it actually was! The productivity slowdown has been attributed to a variety of causes. Oil price shocks in the 1970s, the transition to a low-productivity service economy, increasingly shortsighted American managers, poorly educated or motivated American workers, a resource drain into defense spending, lack of government spending on infrastructure, and a legal system that encourages excessive litigation and government regulation have all been labeled as suspects.[1]

Some have charged that environmental regulations specifically have been a major contributor to the productivity slowdown. By contrast, others have argued that pollution control efforts can *spur* productivity growth by forcing firms to become more efficient in their use of resources and adopt new and cheaper production techniques. As we will see, this debate is far from settled. But because productivity growth compounds over time, the impact of regulations on productivity—whether positive or negative—is a critical factor in determining the "true" costs of environmental protection.

First, let us evaluate the pro-regulation arguments. Theoretically, regulation can improve productivity in three ways: (1) by improving the short-run efficiency of

FIGURE 9.1 The Impact of Slow Productivity Growth on GDP

---

[1]See Baily and Chakrabarti (1988); Melman (1987); Bowles, Gordon, and Weisskopf (1991); and Aschauer (1990) for differing perspectives on this issue.

resource use; (2) by encouraging firms to invest more, or invest "smarter" for the long run; (3) by reducing health-care or firm level cleanup costs, which then frees up capital for long-run investment.

We ran into the short-run efficiency argument in our Chapter 1 discussion of global warming. Some economists think tremendous cost savings are to be gained immediately if firms would only adopt already existing, energy-efficient technologies—more efficient lighting, cooling, heating, and mechanical systems.

However, other economists are suspicious that these so-called "free lunches" are actually widespread, arguing on theoretical grounds that "there ain't no such thing." Why would competitive firms ignore these huge cost-saving opportunities if they really existed? Chapter 20 is devoted to a discussion of energy policy and the free lunch argument. For now, recognize that should regulation force firms to use energy more cost-effectively, greater output from fewer inputs, and thus an increase in productivity, will result.

The second avenue by which regulation may increase productivity is by speeding up, or otherwise improving, the capital investment process. The so-called **Porter hypothesis,** named after Harvard Business School Professor Michael Porter, argues that regulation, while imposing short-run costs on firms, often enhances their long-run competitiveness (Porter and van der Linde 1995; Goodstein 1997). This can happen if regulation favors forward-looking firms, anticipates trends, speeds investment in modern production processes, encourages R&D, or promotes "outside-the-box," nonconventional thinking.

For example, rather than installing "end-of-the pipe" equipment to treat their emissions, some firms have developed new production methods to aggressively reduce waste, cutting both costs and pollution simultaneously (see Barbera and McConnell 1990, and "Some Companies Cut Pollution" 1990). In this case, regulation has played a **technology-forcing role,** encouraging firms to develop more productive manufacturing methods by setting standards they must achieve.

Finally, the third positive impact of regulation on productivity flows from the health and ecosystem benefits that arise from environmental protection. In the absence of pollution control measures, the U.S. population would have experienced considerably higher rates of sickness and premature mortality. In addition, firms that rely on clean water or air for production processes would have faced their own internal cleanup costs. These factors would have reduced productivity directly and also indirectly, as expenditures on health care and private cleanup would have risen dramatically. This spending, in turn, would have represented a drain on productive investment resources quite comparable to mandated expenditures on pollution control.

Productivity may also be dampened in a variety of ways. First, regulation imposes direct costs on regulated firms; these costs may crowd out investment in conventional capital. Second, a further slowdown in new investment may occur when regulation is more stringent for new sources of pollution, as it often is. Third, regulation will cause higher prices for important economy-wide inputs such as energy and waste disposal. These cost increases, in turn, will lead to reductions in capital investment in secondary industries directly unaffected by regulation, for example, the health and financial sectors of the economy.

Finally, regulation may frustrate entrepreneurial activity. Businesspeople complain frequently of the "regulatory burden" and "red tape" associated with regulation, including environmental regulation. Filling out forms, obtaining permits, and holding public hearings all add an additional "hassle" to business that may discourage some investment.

However, in spite of the chorus of voices attacking regulation as one of the main culprits in explaining low levels of recent American productivity growth, evidence for this position is not strong. An examination of five heavily regulated industries by Barbera and McConnell (1990) concluded that only 10% to 30% of the productivity decline in these industries could be accounted for by environmental regulation. Since most industries experienced substantially less regulation than the five examined in the study, the economy-wide effect would presumably be smaller.[2]

Nevertheless, because of the cumulative nature of economic growth, even productivity declines well under 1% have major effects over the long run. For example, Barbera and McConnell suggest that, on an economy-wide basis, less than 10% of the 2% productivity slowdown after 1970 can likely be attributed to environmental regulation. Assume for the purposes of illustration that federal environmental regulations depressed labor productivity growth from 1.1% to 1% beginning in 1974 (thus, accounting for 5% of the total slowdown). Then, in the absence of any federal pollution regulation, *GDP ceteris paribus* would have been more than $90 billion larger in 1990.[3]

Hazilla and Kopp (1991) and Jorgenson and Wilcoxen (1990) undertake much more sophisticated counterfactual exercises and arrive at aggregate productivity impacts of $125 billion and $143 billion, respectively, for federal air and water pollution control efforts undertaken since 1970. These figures suggest that the indirect costs of existing pollution control efforts, measured roughly in foregone GNP, may be even larger than the direct engineering estimates.[4]

However, these figures are of only limited usefulness, since the *ceteris paribus* assumption does not hold. As the studies themselves acknowledge, they ignore all the important *positive* influences that regulation may have had on productivity growth. Repetto (1990) examined the positive effects (avoided costs) resulting from environmental expenditures on productivity in the electric utility industry, the sector most heavily impacted by regulation. He found that rough adjustments for reductions in emissions due to environmental regulation were large enough to offset the productivity declines found in earlier studies.

In summary, federal environmental regulations primarily put in place in the 1970s and 1980s have reduced measured productivity in heavily regulated industries

---

[2]These results are consistent with a number of other industry-level studies finding small productivity effects. See the review in Goodstein (1994) as well as Boyd and McClelland (1999), Xepapadeas and de Zeeuw (1999), and Morgenstern, Pizer, and Shih (1997).

[3]GNP per civilian worker was $41,353 in 1974. Productivity growth of 1% would have raised that figure to $48,489 by 1990; growth of 1.1% would have increased productivity to $49,263. Given the civilian labor force in 1990, this translates into a GNP differential of $91 billion.

[4]Jorgenson and Wilcoxen estimate that regulations depress long-run GNP by 2.59%. This was $143 billion in 1990. The Hazilla and Kopp figure is from Table 3, "social cost" minus "EPA compliance cost" in 1990. Hazilla and Kopp attempt to measure cost as foregone consumer surplus. Because consumers and firms substitute away from higher priced goods, foregone GNP is not an accurate measure of lost welfare. They find that GNP is depressed by 5.85% in 1990, almost double the Jorgenson and Wilcoxen estimate. Both sets of authors use quite complex general equilibrium models to arrive at their conclusions. For a rather critical discussion of the Jorgenson-Wilcoxen model, see Joskow (1992). See also the review in Goodstein (1994).

somewhat; yet, such effects account for only a small portion of the total productivity slowdown. In addition, in the absence of regulation, productivity would have fallen anyway due to increased illness and the subsequent diversion of investment resources into the health-care field. Finally, there is scattered evidence for productivity improvements arising from regulation, following both the Porter hypothesis and the energy-efficiency lines of argument. Rolling back environmental laws to their 1970 status, even if this were possible, would, at best, make a small dent in the problem of reduced U.S. productivity and might easily make things worse.

Nevertheless, due to the large cumulative effects on output of even small reductions in productivity growth, minimizing potential negative productivity impacts is one of the most important aspects of sensibly designed regulatory policy. As we shall see in Chapters 16 and 17, regulations can be structured to better encourage the introduction of more productive, and lower-cost, pollution control technologies.

9.3 Employment Impacts of Regulation

The second potential "hidden cost" of environmental protection is jobs. Here, however, political rhetoric has generated far more heat than light. An example: In 1990, the Clean Air Act Amendments were being considered by the U.S. Congress. Businesses opposed to the legislation hired economists to forecast possible job losses. Here are two of my favorite predictions:

- This study leaves little doubt that a *minimum* of two hundred thousand (plus) jobs will be quickly lost, with plants closing in dozens of states. This number could easily exceed one million jobs—and even two million jobs—at the more extreme assumptions about residual risk.
- Initiatives such as the acid rain legislation would, in this respect, achieve only the dubious distinction of moving the United States towards the status of a second-class industrial power by the end of the century.

Now in spite of forecasts like this, the law did pass in 1990. And here we are in the new century.

Did jobs drop as much as predicted—or even anywhere close? Between 1990 and 1997—a period in which substantial reductions in SO_2 emissions were achieved—an average 1000 workers per year were laid off nationwide as a direct result of the Clean Air Act Amendments, for a total of 5,000 jobs lost nationwide. This is a very small number.[5] But thanks to an overheated political dialogue, American concerns about job losses from environmental protection run deep. In one *Wall Street Journal* poll, an astounding one third of the respondents thought it somewhat or very likely that their own jobs were threatened by environmental regulation ("Americans Are Willing to Sacrifice" 1990).

Over the last thirty years, economists have looked closely at the employment impacts of environmental regulation. Three lessons stand out clearly. First, at the economy-wide level there is simply no trade-off between jobs and the environment.

---

[5]The first prediction is from Hahn and Steger (1990); the second is from National Association of Manufacturers/Data Resources Incorporated (1987). The actual layoff figures are form Goodstein (1999).

As we shift spending into environmental cleanup, jobs follow. Second, as illustrated in the previous example, actual layoffs from environmental protection have been small. On average, about 2,000 jobs per year are lost nationwide as a consequence of regulation. And finally, in spite of widespread belief to the contrary, pollution intensive firms are not fleeing rich countries such as the United States to escape environmental regulation.

Widespread fears of job loss from environmental protection, however, need to understood in the context of a "deindustrialization and downsizing" process that became increasingly apparent to U.S. citizens during the 1980s and 1990s. Over the last couple of decades, the United States lost millions of manufacturing jobs, due primarily to increased import competition both from First World nations and the newly industrializing countries of Korea, China, and Brazil. At the same time, U.S. manufacturers increasingly began to "offshore" production, investing in manufacturing facilities in low-wage countries rather than at home. High-paying manufacturing jobs have traditionally been the backbone of the blue-collar middle class in the United States. Has environmental regulation contributed to this dramatic shift away from manufacturing and over to service employment? The surprising answer is no.

On the one hand, stringent pollution regulations might be expected to discourage investment in certain industries, mining and "dirty" manufacturing, in particular. This will contribute to **structural unemployment,** most of which will disappear in the long run as displaced workers find new jobs elsewhere in the economy. In essence, regulation cannot "create" long-run unemployment; instead, it will contribute to a shift in the types of jobs that the economy creates. Indeed, the best comprehensive estimate available suggests that, in 1991, just less than 2 million jobs were directly or indirectly related to pollution abatement in the United States.[6]

This notion of job shifting should be familiar to you from the first week of your Econ 100 class, in which you undoubtedly saw a diagram that looked something like Figure 9.2. This production possibilities frontier (or transformation curve) shows how the economy has shifted from 1970 to 2004. If regulation were to have caused widespread unemployment, the economy would have moved from point A to point C.

However, again referring back to your Econ 100 class, you know that during the late-1990s the U.S. economy was operating very close to full employment: at point B. Indeed, the Federal Reserve Board raised interest rates several times during this period to try to cool down the economy, by *raising* the unemployment rate. Clearly, the constraint on economy-wide job growth in recent years has been the inflationary fears of the Fed, not an economy devoting 2.8% of output to environmental protection.

What kinds of jobs are generated by environmental spending? In fact, environmental protection provides employment heavily weighted to the traditional blue-collar manufacturing and construction sectors. Figure 9.3 illustrates this point, providing an estimated breakdown of the composition of nonagricultural jobs directly

---

[6]By "directly and indirectly," I include multiplier effects. For example, a complete accounting of jobs in the aluminum recycling industry needs to include workers in the steel industry who make the machines to recycle aluminum, as well as workers who make the equipment to make the steel to make the aluminum recycling machines, and so on. Economists use input-output models (see Appendix 19A) to capture all these indirect effects. The 2 million figure is from U.S. Environmental Protection Agency (1995).

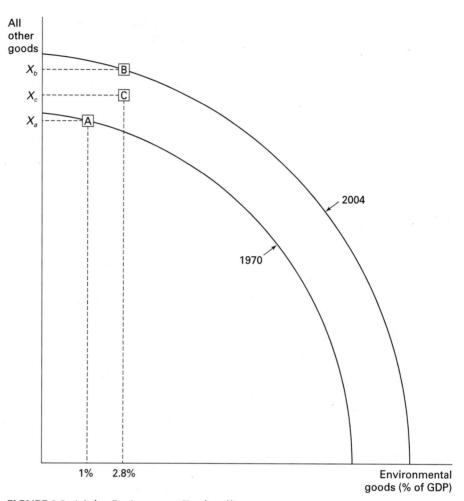

FIGURE 9.2 A Jobs–Environment Trade-off?

and indirectly dependent on environmental spending in 1991 (the latest year for which data are available), with comparative figures for the economy as a whole.

While only 20% of all nonfarm jobs were in the manufacturing and construction sectors in 1991, 31% of employment generated by environmental spending fell in one of these categories. By contrast, only 12% of environment-dependent jobs were in wholesale and retail trade, finance, insurance or real estate, compared to 29% for the economy as a whole. And in spite of criticisms that environmental regulation creates jobs only for pencil-pushing regulators, less than 12% of environmental employment was governmental, as compared to an economy-wide government employment rate of 17%.

How can we account for these results? Environmental protection is an industrial business. In 1991, the private sector spent $22 billion on pollution control plants and equipment and $43 billion on pollution control operations, ranging from sewage and solid waste disposal to the purchase and maintenance of air pollution control devices on

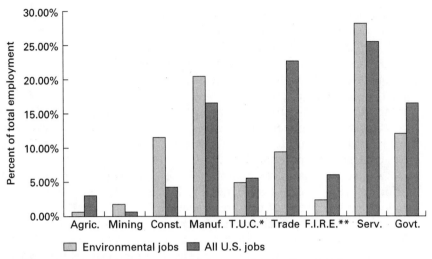

FIGURE 9.3 Jobs Dependent on Environmental Spending (1991)
*Transportation, utilities, and communication
**Finance, insurance, and real estate
Source: Author's calculations from U.S. Environmental Protection Agency (1995) and *Employment and Earnings,* Washington, DC: U.S. Department of Labor.

smokestacks and in vehicles. Federal, state, and local governments spent about $12 billion on the construction of municipal sewage facilities. In addition, only 2% of all environmental spending went to support the government's direct regulation and monitoring establishment. The EPA's total budget was less than 4% of all spending (Rutledge and Leonard 1992; monetary values are in 1990 dollars). The bulk of environmental spending thus remains in the private sector, generating a demand for workers disproportionately weighted to manufacturing and construction and away from services. This is not to say that environmental spending creates only high-quality, high-paying jobs. But it does support jobs in traditional blue-collar industries.

Of course, the 2 million jobs in the environmental industry in 1991 were not net jobs created. If the money had not been spent on environmental protection, it would have been spent elsewhere—perhaps on health care, travel, imported goods, or investment in new plant and equipment. This spending, too, would have created jobs. In the long run, the level of economy-wide employment is determined by the interaction of business cycles and government fiscal and monetary policy. However, in the short run, and locally, where we spend our dollars does matter for employment. If, instead of spending $224 billion on the environment in 2000, we had spent only $200 billion, would there have been more or fewer jobs in the U.S. economy *that year* (in the short run)?

Clearly fewer if we had spent the $24 billion saved importing foreign-made goods. Perhaps more if we had spent the money on labor-intensive products made at home. As a rule, money spent on sectors that are both more labor-intensive (directly and indirectly) and have a higher domestic content (directly and indirectly) will generate more American jobs in the short run. Environmental spending is often either labor-intensive or has a high domestic content.

To illustrate, a study done for the Department of Sanitation in New York City found that boosting the percentage of waste that was recycled from 3% to 25%, while reducing the percentage incinerated from 76% to 57%, would result in a permanent net increase in local employment of around 400 jobs per year. This was true, even accounting for the higher taxes necessary to pay for the somewhat higher cost per ton for the recycling option. The increase in jobs arose first because recycling is labor—rather than capital—intensive, leading to a higher local payroll generating bigger indirect employment effects in the city. Second, New York City produces little of the equipment necessary to manufacture incinerators, so incineration had a low "domestic" content (Breslow et al. 1992).[7]

At the national level, analyses of the employment impact of pollution control efforts have revealed a similar story. For example, Wendling and Bezdek (1989) found that some 95% of the direct expenditure on acid rain pollution control equipment products and processes would accrue to U.S. firms. As a result, a net increase in jobs was foreseen from the acid rain control policies they analyzed. Job losses in high-sulfur coal mining, electric utility, and electricity-intensive sectors would be more than balanced by pollution control jobs created from the expenditure of several billion dollars per year. Overall, Wendling and Bezdek predicted a net employment gain from acid rain control. The majority of macro-level studies of environmental protection have generated similar conclusions (see Goodstein 1999).[8]

Most of the time, if you hear a sentence that begins with "All economists agree," you should head for the door. But in this case, there is agreement that at the economy-wide level *there is simply no such thing* as a **jobs–environment trade-off.**

Of course, this knowledge will not be comforting to the manufacturing or mining worker who *has* lost his or her job due to regulation. Short-run, structural unemployment impacts from environmental regulation (or any other cause) should not be minimized. **Plant shutdowns** cause considerable suffering for workers and communities, particularly for older workers who find it difficult to retool. Moreover, the disappearance of high-wage manufacturing jobs is indeed cause for concern. Yet, fears of such effects from pollution control efforts are liable to be greatly overblown since industry officials can gain politically by blaming plant shutdowns due to normal business causes on environmental regulations. Keeping this in mind, based on employer responses, the U.S. Department of Labor has collected information on the causes of mass layoffs (greater than 50 workers). Table 9.2 presents this data, covering 75% of all layoffs at large employers and 57% of all manufacturing plants.

On average, according to employers' own estimates, environmental regulation accounted for less than one tenth of one percent of all mass layoffs nationwide. In the survey, *seven plants per year* closed primarily as a result of environmental problems. If we double the figures to account for the remainder of manufacturing jobs, on average, 2,000 lost positions per year could be partially attributed to environmental regulation.

---

[7]Because recycling also requires capital spending on "imported" equipment, the two options did not differ greatly in either their labor intensity or their "domestic" content. However, the differences were large enough to translate into an employment advantage for recycling.

[8]Environmental regulation can also boost net job growth somewhat because it provides an ongoing, recession-proof stimulus to aggregate demand.

TABLE 9.2   Mass Layoffs, 1995–1997

Reason for Layoff	Layoff Events			People Laid off		
	1995	*1996*	*1997*	*1995*	*1996*	*1997*
Total, all reasons	4,422	5,692	5,605	926,775	1,158,199	1,103,146
Environment related*	**9**	**7**	**5**	**2,816**	**1,098**	**541**
Automation	6	14	9	4,284	5,522	2,117
Bankruptcy	78	103	80	20,144	21,247	21,637
Business ownership change	120	167	121	28,482	46,425	25,141
Contract cancellation	103	87	61	18,700	19,269	11,813
Contract completion	459	557	759	100,289	124,506	175,572
Domestic relocation	63	76	76	11,059	11,323	15,241
Financial difficulty	249	263	153	58,473	56,749	39,634
Import competition	51	72	66	8,527	13,684	12,493
Labor–management dispute	20	32	32	3,370	14,119	16,149
Material shortages	19	21	14	2,666	2,821	1,705
Model change-over	17	18	18	7,589	6,799	5,716
Natural disaster	7	16	5	2,117	3,599	892
Overseas relocation	14	26	38	3,713	4,326	10,435
Plant or machine repairs	31	23	19	3,867	5,169	2,362
Product line discontinued	20	35	45	4,392	6,037	9,505
Reorganization within company	384	578	482	86,331	115,669	78,324
Seasonal work	1,688	2,173	2,434	385,886	488,398	499,331
Slack work	515	831	656	78,514	112,313	90,382
Vacation period	66	69	92	14,221	11,844	13,499
Weather-related curtailment	87	97	63	10,619	9,802	8,652
Other	253	266	211	42,153	55,265	39,821
Not reported	163	161	166	28,563	22,215	22,184

*Includes environmental- and safety-related shutdowns.
Source: U.S. Bureau of Labor Statistics, Local Area Unemployment Statistics Division.

The number of actual layoffs due to environmental regulation is clearly much smaller than is generally believed. As noted above, one third of the entire U.S. workforce perceived a threat to their jobs from environmental protection measures! In reality, forty times more layoffs resulted from ownership changes than from environmental measures.[9] However, rather than shutdowns, one might expect *new* investment to occur in poorer countries with less strict pollution regulations. How serious is this problem of flight to so-called **pollution havens?**

In their survey of twenty-five years of research on this issue, Jaffe et al. (1995, 133) conclude: "Studies attempting to measure the effect of environmental regulation on net exports, overall trade-flows, and plant location decisions have produced estimates that are either small, statistically insignificant, or not robust to tests of

---

[9]The Department of Labor figures presented here are consistent with a variety of other surveys covering the 1970s and early 1980s, including one that incorporated small businesses. See the discussion in Goodstein (1999).

model specification." In other words, in spite of looking hard, economists have found precious little evidence to suggest that the competitiveness of U.S. manufacturing firms has been hurt by environmental regulation.

Why have the effects not been greater? First, pollution control costs are a small portion of total business costs, and second, costs are only one factor influencing business location decisions.[10] In addition to costs, factors as diverse as access to markets and the quality of life are important components of business location decisions. A study by Koechlin (1992) identified, in order of importance, market size, wages, tax rates, political stability, access to the European market, and distance to the United States as the primary determinants of U.S. investment abroad. Finally, much pollution control technology is embedded in modern plant designs. This means that a chemical factory built by a multinational corporation in South China will in fact look a lot like one built in West Virginia. Given these factors, most U.S. direct foreign investment continues to be in developed countries with environmental regulations comparable to our own.

A recent exception to this rule may perhaps be found in Mexico. Plants within one hundred kilometers of the U.S. border, known as *maquiladoras,* have for more than a decade been able to import and export products freely. While these plants are required, in theory, to meet U.S. federal environmental standards, in practice, the underfunded Mexican government has not vigorously enforced the law. Due to its close proximity, low wages, and lax environmental enforcement, Mexico may attract investment that would otherwise occur in the United States ("Border Boom's Dirty Residue" 1991).

The most dramatic instance of plants moving South occurred in the wood furniture industry in the Los Angeles area. Based on rather sketchy evidence, it is estimated that four to five plants per year moved to the maquiladora region over the three-year period from 1988 to 1990, *partially* as a result of environmental regulations. This accounted for a loss of about 350 jobs per year.[11] The L.A. basin has the worst air pollution in the United States and some of the toughest emission control standards. Solvent-based coatings for wood furniture evaporate easily, contributing to smog; 1988 regulations in the Los Angeles area mandated the phase-in of expensive collection chambers to contain the solvent emissions. As of 1990, there were *no* regulations in the maquiladora region pertaining to emissions from solvents.

An added, if not primary, inducement for these firms to relocate was lower wages and benefits. The average hourly wage in L.A. was $8.92; across the border it was $0.77. In addition, as U.S. employers, the firms were required to pay $1.75 per hour in worker's compensation. The equivalent Mexican tax was only $0.13. For furniture makers, labor *and* environmental costs were clearly significant factors in the decision to locate in Mexico. More generally, a 1988 survey of 76 maquiladora plants found that 10% listed environmental factors as *among* the main reasons for locating in Mexico (see U.S. GAO 1991, and "A Warmer Climate" 1990).[12]

---

[10]On the relative importance of pollution control costs, see Dean (1992). For an interesting dissenting view, see Chapman (1991).

[11]These mid-range estimates are from U.S. GAO (1991), based on 78% of employers reporting stringent air pollution controls as one reason for moving.

[12]The survey results are discussed in Sanchez (1990).

However, a more comprehensive look at investment in the maquiladora region by Grossman and Krueger (1991) confirms that environmental factors are, in general, relatively unimportant. Industries with higher pollution abatement costs are not overrepresented in the maquiladora area, although those with higher labor costs are. At this point, we can conclude that the direct costs associated with pollution control have not been a major factor in influencing plant location decisions. Highly polluting industries are relocating to poor countries; the reason, however, is low wages. Yet, as the furniture making industry illustrates, in certain cases environmental control costs can rise sufficiently to become a dominant concern. Moreover, as the Mexican case demonstrates, once having relocated, firms certainly take advantage of looser pollution standards.

As a final note on a possible jobs–environment trade-off in southern California, Berman and Bui (1997) conducted a detailed study comparing heavily regulated plants (of all types) in the region with similar plants in the rest of the country. They found no decrease in employment at existing California plants, and no effect on California jobs from increased bankruptcies or decreased investment. Indeed, the authors conclude: "In contrast to the widespread belief that environmental regulations cost jobs, the most severe episode of air quality regulation in the United States probably created a few jobs."

This section has established that, first, economy-wide, net job loss has not resulted from environmental protection. As many, if not more, new jobs have been created than have been lost. At the national level, debates that assume a **job versus the environment** trade-off are, thus, based on pure myth. Second, gross job loss due to environmental protection has been surprisingly small. Approximately 2,000 workers per year have been laid off in recent years, partially as a result of regulation. Finally, the flight of U.S. manufacturing capital overseas appears to be driven much more by wage differentials than stringent environmental rules. In spite of these facts, the fear of job loss remains widespread, as indicated by the poll results cited above. Much of the political resistance to environmental protection remains motivated by such fears.

Such concerns are understandable in a nation experiencing a dramatic and painful economic restructuring and where occasional plant shutdowns due to environmental regulation are highly publicized. In individual cases, such as the recent restrictions imposed on the timber industry to protect the old-growth forest in the Pacific Northwest or clean air requirements faced by the Appalachian high-sulfur coal industry, local unemployment has undoubtedly been exacerbated by environmental regulation.

Even in these two worst-case scenarios, however, job losses have been in the low thousands. Beyond numbers, of course, many of the jobs lost have been relatively "good" unionized, high-paying ones, and reemployment opportunities for some workers are quite limited. These negative effects should not be ignored and can be partially alleviated through job-retraining programs, conversion efforts, notification requirements for plant closing, and moving allowances for individuals displaced from pollution-intensive industries. Both the 1990 Clean Air Act and President Clinton's spotted owl initiative included substantial funding for worker retraining. A small portion of the funds spent in the Northwest was targeted at retraining timber workers in forest restoration work.[13]

---

[13]For a closer look at the employment impact of protecting spotted owl habitat, as well as a more extended discussion of worker adjustment programs, see Goodstein (1999).

9.4 Monopoly Costs

To this point, we have focused on two factors that might cause the social costs of regulation to be different than engineering cost estimates: impacts on productivity and employment. A third area of concern is the impact that regulation might have on the growth of monopoly power.

Complying with environmental regulations can impose substantial fixed costs on firms, such as purchasing control equipment, paying for permits, and hiring environmental lawyers, engineers, and scientists. Higher fixed costs in turn generate economies of scale, which can cause smaller firms to be squeezed out of business. Thus, one potential cost of environmental regulation is an increase in monopoly power in the economy (see "Small Businesses Complain" 1992, and "Small Companies See Growth" 1992).[14]

The best example of such a trend can perhaps be found in the solid and hazardous waste disposal industries. From a highly competitive market structure in the early 1970s, the industry has been transformed by regulation: Big firms such as Waste Management and Browning Ferris now control about 50% of the market share. This increased concentration, along with a number of landfill closings in the late 1980s, lead to a period of very high prices and profits (see "Economics of Trash" 1992, and "Recycling" 1990). Indeed, according to an acquaintance of mine who works in the solid waste business in Washington State, many small town officials are convinced that the strict landfill regulations were masterminded by the big waste haulers in order to reduce competition!

Monopoly power has two drawbacks: the first relates to efficiency and the second to fairness. Because of lack of competition, monopolies may not produce efficiently (X-inefficiency); in addition, monopolies tend to sell goods at a price above production cost, thereby "artificially" restricting demand (allocative inefficiency). These inefficient practices both represent a real opportunity cost to society measured in terms of foregone goods and services.

Most public concern about monopoly, however, focuses on fairness issues: the ability of firms with market power to "rip off" consumers. In the waste management field, for example, one New York township discovered it was being overcharged some 50% by a major firm ("Economics of Trash" 1992).[15]

Might monopoly profits actually be a good thing? Some economic observers have defended monopolists' ability to earn high profits, *if* they are funneled back into investment in new plants and equipment or research and development. The *Wall Street Journal*, for example, credits Japan's impressive strides toward energy efficiency to an informal agreement between the nation's big firms and the government. Energy companies are allowed to keep prices high, "provided the windfalls are channeled into energy research" ("How Japan Became So Energy Efficient" 1990).[16] And Tawil (1999) argues that cities captured some of waste-hauler's monopoly profits, allowing them to fund household hazardous waste collection and curbside recycling programs.

---

[14]For more systematic economic evidence of the impact of regulation on optimal scale, market power, and profitability, see Evans (1986), Pashigian (1984), Hughes, Magat, and Ricks (1986), and Tawil (1999).

[15]From an economist's point of view, however, such overcharging is not a true cost. Rather, high monopoly prices produce a (generally) unfair redistribution of wealth, from consumers to stockholders.

[16]The original theory is due to Schumpeter.

To sum up: An increase in market share for large firms is a likely consequence of environmental regulation. If this increase in market share also leads to increased monopoly power, the opportunity cost of environmental protection will probably exceed engineering cost estimates. How significant the costs arising from enhanced monopoly power really are is not known.

9.5 General Equilibrium Effects

The last important area in which there may be "hidden" costs (or benefits) of regulation lies in what economists call **general equilibrium (GE) effects.** These effects of regulation are felt throughout the economy, as opposed to effects felt in the specific regulated sector (partial equilibrium effects).

For example, if regulation raises the cost of waste disposal, and this raises the cost of hospital services, then the higher cost of hospitals will be one general equilibrium effect of regulation. On the other hand, when the price of hospital services rise, people tend to opt for more in-home care, thus mitigating the impact of the rise in hospital costs.

To make this issue concrete, suppose you were working at the EPA and trying to figure out the cost of a new air-quality regulation on coal-burning power plants. To simplify matters, first assume that there are 100 coal plants nationwide and each would install scrubbers, costing $100 million apiece. In that case, the estimated cost of the regulation would be $10 billion (100 plants * $100 million). Yet, even ignoring other compliance options (like switching to low-sulfur coal), this would be only a partial equilibrium estimate.

In fact, the higher cost for electricity would reduce electricity demand, as people conserved more. Hence, utilities would probably retire rather than retrofit some of the coal plants, leading to lower overall costs. Taking into account the general equilibrium effects in the electricity market, the real costs of the regulation would be lower than your partial equilibrium estimate. Of course, you would also want to calculate impacts throughout the economy of higher electricity prices.

Hazilla and Kopp (1991) undertook just such a study that broke the U.S. economy down into thirty-five sectors, finding that in the short run, engineering cost estimates tended to *overstate* economy-wide costs significantly—by as much as 50%. This is because engineering costs ignore the substitution opportunities (like energy efficiency) available to consumers as the price of regulated commodities rise.

While short-run substitution leads to lower than expected costs, general equilibrium effects can also raise costs indirectly by reducing labor supply. This impact has loomed large in a recent theoretical debate among economists over the so-called **double-dividend hypothesis.** In the early 1990s some economists (including myself, in the first edition of this book) were arguing that a shift to pollution taxes might be a good thing, and not just because it would reduce pollution. In addition, we claimed, if the revenues were used to cut taxes on labor or capital, pollution taxes might make the whole economy operate more efficiently, thus generating a "double dividend." The notion was that we should shift from taxing "goods" (work effort and investment) to taxing "bads" (pollution), leading to both less pollution and more output.

Unfortunately, this appealing idea of increased efficiency may not be true. (It does, however, remain the case that lower payroll taxes would promote low-skill job growth.) To see this, we need to delve a little more deeply into how economists measure costs. We saw in the previous chapter that environmental benefits were measured as the increase in consumer surplus when cleanup, a public good, was provided. Costs can be measured similarly, as the *decrease* in total surplus: consumer surplus plus producer surplus. Producer surplus is the difference between what a seller gets for a product and the minimum she would be willing to sell it for.[17] We add in producer surplus here because regulations typically reduce private profits, and this reduction in profits is a cost to society.

Figure 9.4 illustrates a supply-and-demand diagram for corn; at price *P*, consumer surplus is equal to area *a*, while producer surplus is shown as area *b*—the difference between market price and the supply curve. (Recall from economics principles that the supply curve in a competitive market reflects the marginal costs of production. Thus, it illustrates the producer's minimum willingness to accept payment in exchange for its product.)

Now let us set up a simple general equilibrium economy in which there are three goods: corn (a private good), police protection (a public good), and water (a nonmarket good—people get it free from the stream). To provide the public good, there is a payroll tax per hour on labor, paid by employers. Finally, to round out our little economy, the production of corn leads to erosion, which pollutes the water.

We can illustrate the corn market in Figure 9.5. This figure looks just like the previous figure, except there are now two supply curves. *S* is the supply curve showing only private costs, while *S'* is the "true" supply curve, including both private and external social costs. Thus *C'* is the efficient level of corn production—where the true supply and demand curves intersect.

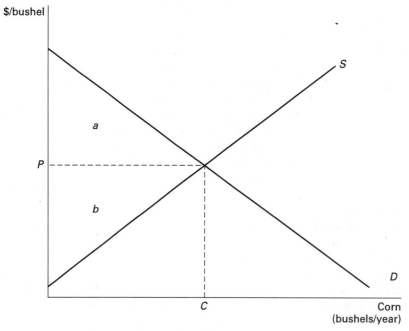

FIGURE 9.4 Producer and Consumer Surplus

---

[17]Long-run producer surplus is another name for resource rent.

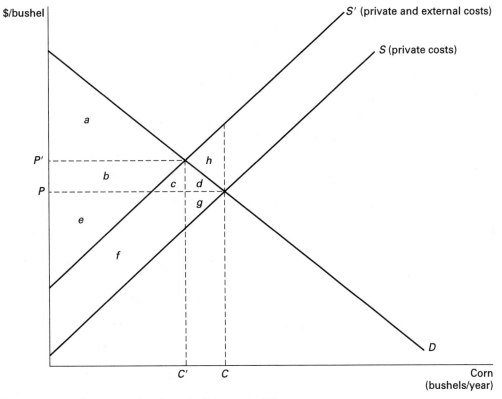

FIGURE 9.5 Efficiency Gains from Environmental Taxes

How do we know this? If the corn price is at P, instead of P', then people from C' to C are getting corn who are not willing to pay the full cost of production, including the externalities. The triangle h represents the costs to society of this overproduction and is known as the **deadweight loss** in total surplus from the unregulated pollution.

The way to see this social loss is to add up the total surplus at C and compare it to the surplus at C'. At C, total surplus is consumer surplus $(a + b + c + d)$ plus producer surplus $(e + f + g)$ *minus externality costs* $(f + c + d + g + h)$, for a total of $(a + b + e - h)$. At C', with the externalities internalized, total surplus is just consumer plus producer surplus: $(a + b + e)$. Thus, the size of the pie—total surplus—is greater at C' than C, by exactly the deadweight loss, area h.

So, the first point here is that taxing corn leads to efficiency gains of h, since it internalizes the pollution externality and eliminates the deadweight loss. Now, suppose we use the income from the pollution tax (area $f + c$) to reduce labor taxes? Won't this yield even more efficiency gains—a double dividend?

Figure 9.6A illustrates the labor market, with the nominal (money) wage on the vertical axis and the supply of hours (by workers) and the demand for hours (by firms) on the horizontal axis. This time there are two demand curves: D shows the labor demand without the tax; D' shows the lower demand with the tax. Note that the tax itself generates a deadweight loss equal to the hatched area. From L' to L, there

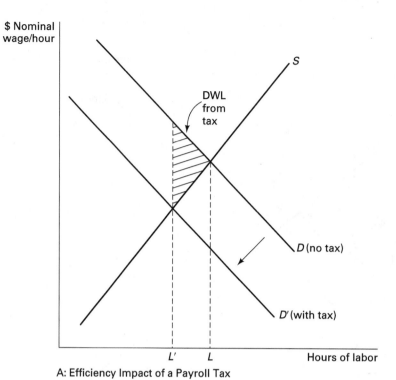

A: Efficiency Impact of a Payroll Tax

B: Efficiency Impact of Pollution Taxes

FIGURE 9.6 A Double Dividend in the Labor Market?

are firms willing to pay the true (untaxed) cost of labor, but they are unable to do so because of the tax.

Why have the tax in the first place, then, if it creates deadweight loss? Because the efficiency gains from providing the public good of police protection—not shown here in a diagram—are greater than the losses from the tax.

To summarize: To this point we know that taxing pollution improves efficiency directly; we also have learned that the existing labor tax generates inefficiency in the labor market, but that this is the price we must pay to obtain a needed public good. Here is the question we still need to answer: What are the implications of reducing the payroll tax by using revenues from the pollution tax?

Figure 9.6B shows that there are two offsetting effects. On the one hand, the demand for labor shifts up to D'' as the payroll tax is cut. This effect led to initial optimism about a double dividend. On the other hand, and this is the hidden general equilibrium effect, the supply of labor also shifts up to S'. Why? Because as the price of corn rises due to the tax, an hour of work buys less corn. In other words, the real wage falls. As a result, people substitute labor for leisure, and work less.[18]

As I have drawn it, the reduction in supply outweighs the increase in demand, and the net effect is to increase, not decrease, inefficiency in the labor market—by the gray area. Of course, it could go the other way. The overall jury is still out on the double-dividend hypothesis, but some research suggests that environmental taxes may have on balance negative general equilibrium effects—in some cases the indirect costs may even be large enough to offset the direct benefits![19]

Let's stop to summarize this rather complicated section: A first general equilibrium effect—substitution away from higher-priced products—leads engineering cost estimates to be too high. By contrast, when regulation raises prices and if this in turn reduces labor supply, costs will be higher than engineering estimates. This means that the efficiency promise of the double-dividend hypothesis cannot always be realized.

Unless you have taken intermediate microeconomic theory (and even then), upon your first reading of this section I suspect that you have only a vague idea what I have been talking about. General equilibrium effects are hard to comprehend because the interactions are quite complicated. And from a policy perspective, precisely because these general equilibrium costs (and benefits) are so deeply hidden, no one besides (a few) economists currently care much about them. Nevertheless, these indirect costs are just as real as the more obvious direct ones. The take-home message of this section is, again, that a careful reckoning of environmental protection costs can be as difficult as developing good benefit measures.

---

[18]Only the substitution effect on labor supply is operable here, because the tax shift is revenue neutral. Goodstein (2001) shows, however, that for families, increased prices may well induce increased rather than decreased labor supply, recovering the double dividend.

[19]The most accessible introduction to this topic is Goulder and Parry (2000). For a skeptical view, see Goodstein (2003). Bovenberg and Goulder (1996) argue that in a GE framework, optimal carbon taxes may actually be negative—that is, an efficient policy would require subsidizing global warming! Fullerton and Metcalf (1996) maintain that regulations that create rents, and thus raise product prices, have big distorting effects on labor and/or capital markets; this leads to the ironic conclusion that CAC regulation may be much more efficient (in the short run) then IB regulation (see Chapter 16). Finally, Jaeger (2000) argues against the anti-double dividend view, maintaining that a proper specification of the pollution problem within a GE model reclaims the double-dividend.

9.6 Summary

This chapter has explored different ways to evaluate the costs of environmental protection. Engineering cost data are much easier to obtain than nonmarket benefit information; as a result, the EPA has been able to put a 2000 price tag of $224 billion on our federal, state, and local pollution control efforts.

However, even on their own terms, engineering cost estimates are only as good as their predictions regarding, for example, compliance and control technologies. More significantly, engineering estimates do not generally incorporate indirect effects, such as negative or positive productivity impacts, negative or positive impacts on structural unemployment, monopoly costs, or general equilibrium effects.

A number of economic studies have found a small, negative impact on productivity growth from environmental regulation. However, none of these studies incorporates the positive effect (reduced costs) on productivity resulting from improved health and lower medical expenses, increased short-run efficiency of resource use, or long-run Porter hypothesis effects. Thus, the net impact on the productivity growth slowdown remains uncertain but is undoubtedly small. Nevertheless, small declines in productivity growth have big long-run effects and should be a primary concern in regulatory design.

On the employment front, environmental regulation has not lead to any net job loss in the economy; there is simply no evidence of a long-run "jobs versus the environment" trade-off. Instead, regulation has led to a shift in the types of jobs. Rather surprisingly, regulation-induced employment is heavily weighted to manufacturing and away from services. Gross job losses partially due to environmental protection in the 1990s were on the order of 1,500 to 2,000 per year. Finally, there is little evidence to support widespread capital flight to "pollution havens."

Regarding monopoly power, an increase has likely resulted from regulation. However, the magnitude of this effect is not known. Finally, economists are only beginning to evaluate and quantify the general equilibrium impacts of regulation.

Due to these four different indirect effects, the "true" social cost of regulation (its opportunity cost) may vary widely from engineering cost estimates. This point again highlights the relative imprecision of benefit–cost analysis for determining the "efficient" pollution level. As noted in the introduction to this chapter, the official range of cost estimates for new ozone reduction regulations introduced in 1997 varied from $600 million to $2.5 billion—a factor of 4. (In the heat of the political debate surrounding the regulatory proposal, some of President Clinton's business advisers were claiming that costs might reach $60 billion per year!) However, an imprecise tool can still be better than no tool at all. In the next chapter we will examine several recent applications of cost estimates for environmental regulation in benefit–cost analysis.

In this chapter we have learned that spending on improved water quality rose by an estimated $30 billion between 1990 and 2000. The meaning of a figure this large is very hard to comprehend. Considering the opportunity cost may make it a bit clearer. With $30 billion, we as a society could do one of the following: fully insure one third of the 37 million Americans who currently have no health insurance at all. Or, we could purchase for the richest one half of one percent of families in the country a new, fully loaded Cadillac STS sedan every year.

These two extreme examples suggest what could be done with the resources we are currently devoting to new efforts in air pollution control. They raise an interesting question: What are we really sacrificing to clean the environment? Basic necessities? Or luxury goods? As we noted, from an efficiency perspective, this issue is not important: Utility derived from luxury cars is equivalent to utility derived from better health or superior air quality. However, from the safety or ecological standpoint, spending money on environmental quality raises human welfare more than an equivalent sum spent on increased material consumption. From these perspectives, the opportunity cost of environmental quality is not adequately measured in dollars alone.

APPLICATION 9.0

The Importance of Productivity

Two well-known economists, William Baumol and Alan Blinder, have stated that, in the long run, "nothing contributes more to reduction of poverty, to increases in leisure, and to the country's ability to finance education, public health, environmental improvement and the arts" (1991, 356) than the rate of growth of productivity.

1. Define productivity.
2. See if you can verify Baumol and Blinder's very strong claim ("*nothing* contributes more . . .") through the following exercise. Assume GNP in the United States is $5 trillion and that the labor force remains constant in size and fully employed. Estimate the value in GNP in one year's time if productivity growth is 3%. What if it were only 2%? How much will GNP fall in two years' time if productivity growth remains at 2% rather than 3%? In three years?
3. Why might environmental regulation reduce productivity growth?
4. Why might it increase productivity growth?
5. Even if, on balance, environmental regulation has not reduced productivity growth, are negative productivity impacts from regulations something we should still worry about?

APPLICATION 9.1

Jobs and the Environment

In 1992, the United States was the odd country out at the Rio Earth Summit. President Bush chose not to sign an otherwise universally approved treaty on biodiversity, and his administration successfully weakened an agreement designed to curb carbon dioxide emissions thought likely to cause global warming. In both cases the President maintained he was, in the *Wall Street Journal's* paraphrase, "protecting American jobs from environmental extremists." Since then, the jobs versus the environment rhetoric has escalated, with several industry-sponsored studies forecasting job losses in the millions if the United States were to achieve the greenhouse gas reduction targets specified in the Kyoto global warming treaty ("President's Clumsy Handling" 1992, and Goodstein 1999).

1. Based on the information presented in this chapter, would signing the environmental treaties originally under consideration be likely to generate an economy-wide net decrease in the number of U.S. jobs? Why or why not?

2. Is it likely that U.S. workers in particular industries might lose their jobs partially as a result of the treaties? If the impact of the treaties were comparable to current environmental regulations, how many workers per year might face layoffs? How might the blow to these workers be cushioned?

3. Suppose that people around the country felt it was unfair for workers to lose their jobs due to greenhouse gas regulation. Based on what you learned in the previous chapter on benefit estimation (Chapter 8), how could we measure this moral concern, and include it as a cost of the regulation?

KEY IDEAS IN EACH SECTION

9.0   The standard method of estimating the costs of environmental protection, simply adding up direct compliance and regulatory expenses, is called an **engineering approach.** Economists, however, would like to measure the **opportunity cost:** the value of goods and services foregone by investing in environmental protection. Opportunity costs include four indirect effects: productivity impacts, employment impacts, the growth of monopoly power, and general equilibrium effects.

9.1   In 2000, the United States spent about $220 billion per year on pollution control measures, measured in engineering terms. Between 1970 and 2000, environmental protection expenditures jumped from less than 1% to more than 2.8% of GNP, more than doubling their claim on the nation's resources.

9.2   The productivity slowdown of the 1970s has been partially blamed on environmental regulation. The main argument is that regulatory expanses divert investment from new plant and equipment. Several economic studies indicate that a small portion of the slowdown (less than 10%) may be due to environmental protection measures. However, this does not take into account possible positive impacts on productivity growth from more efficient resource use, **Porter hypothesis** effects, or a healthier population and resource base. One study that attempted to incorporate environmental benefits found no overall drop in productivity growth due to regulation. Nevertheless, even small negative effects on productivity growth can impose large costs in the long run.

9.3   This section reviews the employment impact of environmental regulation and makes three main points. First, at the economy-wide level, environmental protection has *not* generated a **jobs–environment trade-off.** If anything, environmental protection appears to have boosted aggregate employment slightly. Second, extrapolating data from a large sample of employer responses, gross job loss from **plant shutdowns** due to environmental regulation was about 1,500 to 2,000 workers per year during the nineties. Therefore, little **structural unemployment** can be attributed to regulation. Finally, it appears that in only a few cases have U.S. firms invested in **pollution havens** to avoid environmental regulations.

9.4   Regulation can increase **monopoly power** by imposing high fixed costs on firms, which are more easily met by larger companies. Increases in monopoly power can generate costs in the form of inefficient production and pricing, and monopoly pricing is generally perceived to be unfair. Neither the extent nor the cost of a regulation-induced increase in market power is known.

9.5   **General equilibrium (GE) effects** work in two directions. Because people substitute away from products when regulation raises their price, engineering estimates tend to overstate the short-run costs of regulation. On the other hand, environmental taxes and marketable permit systems may be more costly than previously thought, because by raising product prices, they lower real wages and may discourage work effort creating **deadweight loss.** Some studies have found this effect may be big, and this has cast doubt on the general validity of the **double-dividend hypothesis.**

REFERENCES

"A Warmer Climate for Furniture Makers," 1990. *Los Angeles Times,* 14 May.

"Americans Are Willing to Sacrifice to Reduce Pollution, They Say." 1990. *Wall Street Journal,* 20 April.

Aschauer, David Alan. 1990. *Public Investment and Private Sector Growth.* Washington, DC: Economic Policy Institute.

Baily, Martin N., and Alok K. Chakrabarti. 1988. *Innovation and the Productivity Crisis.* Washington, DC: Brookings.

Barbera, Anthony J., and Virginia D. McConnell. 1990. "The Impact of Environmental Regulations on Industry Productivity: Direct and Indirect Effects." *Journal of Environmental Economics and Management* 18:50–65.

Baumol, William, and Alan Blinder. 1991. *Macroeconomics: Principles and Policy.* New York: Harcourt Brace Jovanovich.

Berman, Eli, and Linda Bui. 1997. *Clearing the Air: The Impact of Air Quality on Jobs,* Washington, DC: Economic Policy Institute.

Berman, Eli, and Linda T. M. Bui. 1997. *Clearing the Air: Implication of Environmental Regulation for the Economy and the Environment in the South Coast Air Basin.* Washington, DC: Economic Policy Institute.

"Border Boom's Dirty Residue Imperils U.S. Mexico Trade." 1991. *New York Times,* 31 March.

Bovenberg, A. Lans, and Lawrence Goulder. 1996. "Optimal Environmental Taxation in the Presence of other Taxes: General Equilibrium Analyses." *American Economic Review* 86, no. 4:985–999.

Bowles, Samuel, David Gordon, and Thomas Weisskopf. 1991. *After the Wasteland.* Armonk, NY: Sharpe.

Boyd, Gale, and John McClelland. 1999. "The Impact of Environmental Constraints on Productivity Improvement in Integrated Paper Plants." *Journal of Environmental Economics and Management* 38, no. 2:121–142.

Breslow, Marc, John Stutz, Paul Lignon, Frank Ackerman, Nancy Ilgenfritz, and Peter Murad. 1992. *Socioeconomic Impacts of Solid Waste Scenarios for New York City: A Report to the New York City Department of Sanitation.* Boston: Tellus Institute.

Burtraw, Dallas. 1996. "Trading Emissions to Clean the Air: Exchanges Few but Savings Many." *Resources,* winter, no. 122:3–6.

Carlin, Alan. 1990. *Environmental Investments: The Cost of a Clean Environment, Summary.* Washington, DC: U.S. EPA.

Chapman, Duane. 1991. "Environmental Standards and International Trade in Automobiles and Copper: The Case for a Social Tariff." *Natural Resources Journal* 31, no. 3:449–462.

Dean, Judith. 1992. "Trade and the Environment: A Survey of the Literature." *Policy Research Working Paper WPS966.* Washington, DC: World Bank.

"Economics of Trash Shift as Cities Learn Dumps Aren't So Full," 1992. *Wall Street Journal,* 2 June.

"EPA Plans to Tighten Pollution Rules." 1997. *Wall Street Journal,* 6 June, A16.

Evans, David B. 1986. "The Differential Effect of Regulation Across Plant Size: Comment on Pashigian." *The Journal of Law and Economics* 29:187–200.

Fullerton, Don, and Gilbert Metcalf. 1996. "Environmental Controls, Scarcity Rents and Pre-existing Distortions." Paper presented at the American Economic Association Meetings, January 1997.

Goodstein, Eban. 1994. *Jobs and the Environment: The Myth of a National Trade-off.* Washington, DC: Economic Policy Institute.

Goodstein, Eban. 1997. *A New Look at Environmental Regulation and U.S. Competitiveness.* Washington, DC: Economic Policy Institute.

Goodstein, Eban. 1999. *The Trade-off Myth: Fact and Fiction about Jobs and the Environment.* Washington, DC: Island Press.

Goodstein, Eban. 2001. "Labor Supply and the Double Dividend." *Ecological Economics* 42, no. 2:101–106.

Goodstein, Eban. 2003. "The Death of the Pigovain Tax? Policy Implications of the Double Dividend Debate." *Land Economics* 79, no. 3:402–414.

Goulder, Lawrence, and Ian Perry. 2000. "Green Tax Reform and the Double Dividend." *AERE Newsletter* 20, no. 1:9–13.

Grossman, Gene M., and Alan B. Krueger. 1991. "Environmental Impacts of a North American Free Trade Agreement." *Working Paper 3914.* Cambridge, MA: National Bureau of Economic Research.

Hahn, Robert, and Wilbur Steger. 1990. *An Analysis of Jobs at Risk and Job Losses from the Proposed Clean Air Act Amendments.* Pittsburgh, PA: CONSAD Research Corporation.

Harrington, Winston, Richard Morgenstern, and Peter Nelson. 1999. "Predicting the Costs of Environmental Regulation." *Environment* 41, no. 7:10–14.

Hazilla, Michael, and Raymond J. Kopp. 1991. "Social Cost of Environmental Regulations: A General Equilibrium Analysis." *Journal of Political Economy* 98:4.

"How Japan became So Energy Efficient: It Leaned on Industry," 1990. *Wall Street Journal,* 10 September.

Hughes, John S., Wesley Magat, and William A. Ricks. 1986. "The Economic Consequences of the OSHA Cotton Dust Standards: An Analysis of Stock Price Behavior." *The Journal of Law and Economics* 29:29–59.

Jaeger, William. 2000. "Optimal Environmental Taxation." *Working Paper.* Williamstown, MA: Williams College.

Jaffe, Adam B., Steven R. Peterson, Paul R. Portney, and Robert N. Stavins. 1995. "Environmental Regulation and the Competitiveness of U.S. Manufacturing: What Does the Evidence Tell Us?" *Journal of Economic Literature* 33, no. 1:132–163.

Jorgenson, Dale W., and Peter J. Wilcoxen. 1990. "Environmental Regulation and U.S. Economic Growth." *Rand Journal of Economics* 21, no. 2:314–340.

Joskow, Paul. 1992. "Carbon Taxes and Economic Welfare: Comment." *Brookings Papers on Economic Activity: Microeconomics 1992.* Washington, DC: Brookings.

Koechlin, Timothy. 1992. "Determinants of the Location of U.S.A. Foreign Investment." *International Review of Applied Economics* 6, no. 2:203–216.

Melman, Seymour. 1987. *Profits Without Production.* Philadelphia, PA: University of Pennsylvania Press.

Morgenstern, Richard, William Pizer, and Jhih-Shyang Shih. 1997. "Are We Overstating the Real Costs of Environmental Protection?" *Discussion for 97-36-REV.* Washington, DC: Resources for the Future.

National Association of Manufacturers/Data Resources Incorporated. 1987. *Acid Rain Legislation and the Economy: Executive Summary.* Washington, DC: NAM.

Pashigian, Peter B. 1984. "The Effects of Environmental Regulation on Optimal Plant Size and Factor Shares." *The Journal of Law and Economics* 28:1–28.

Porter, Michael, and Claas van der Linde. 1995. "Toward a New Conception of the Environment-Competitiveness Relationship." *Journal of Economic Perspectives* 9, no. 4:97–118.

"President's Clumsy Handling of Earth Summit Results in a Public-Relations Disaster for Him," 1992. *Wall Street Journal,* 15 June.

"Recycling: The Newest Wrinkle in Waste Management's Bag," 1990. *Business Week,* 5 March.

Repetto, Robert. 1990. "Environmental Productivity and Why It Is So Important." *Challenge* 33, no. 5.

Rutledge, Gary L., and Mary L. Leonard. 1992. "Pollution Abatement and Control Expenditures, 1972–1990." *Survey of Current Business* 72, no. 6:25–41.

Sanchez, Roberto A. 1990. "Health and Environmental Risks of the Maquiladora in Mexicali." *Natural Resources Journal* 30, no. 1:163–186.

"Small Businesses Complain that Jungle of Regulations Jeopardize Their Futures." 1992. *Wall Street Journal,* 11 June.

"Small Companies See Growth Potential in Preventing Environmental Problems." 1992. *Wall Street Journal,* 1 June.

"Some Companies Cut Pollution by Altering Production Methods." 1990. *Wall Street Journal,* 24 December.

Tawil, Natalie. 1999. "Flow Control and Rent Capture in Solid Waste Management." *Journal of Environmental Economics and Management* 37, no. 2:163–201.

U.S. Environmental Protection Agency. 1995. *The U.S. Environmental Protection Industry: A Proposed Framework for Assessment.* Washington, DC: U.S. EPA, Office of Policy Planning and Evaluation.

U.S. GAO. 1991. "Some U.S. Wood Furniture Firms Relocated from Los Angeles Area to Mexico," *GAO/NSIAD-91-191.* Washington, DC: U.S. Government Accounting Office.

Wendling, Robert M., and Roger H. Bezdek. 1989. "Acid Rain Abatement Legislation: Costs and Benefits." *OMEGA International Journal of Management Science* 17, no. 3:251–261.

Xepapadeas, Anastosios, and Aart de Zeeuw. 1999. "Environmental Policy and Competitiveness: The Porter Hypothesis and the Composition of Capital." *Journal of Environmental Economics and Management* 37, no. 2:165–182.

BENEFIT–COST
IN PRACTICE:
IMPLEMENTING THE
EFFICIENCY STANDARD

10.0 Introduction

Our goal in this first part of the book has been to answer the normative question: "How much pollution is too much?" The first answer we considered was to reduce pollution to "the efficient level." From the efficiency perspective, pollution should be controlled until the additional costs of control just outweigh the additional benefits. Determining the efficient level first requires methods for calculating *all* the benefits and costs of environmental protection in dollar terms. Having spent the last two chapters developing tools to accomplish this, *albeit* imprecisely, we are now in a position to put the two sides together and attempt to pinpoint the efficient pollution level. This process is known as benefit–cost analysis.

Benefit–cost studies currently play an important, but not dominant, role in federal environmental regulation. Air, water, and hazardous waste are primarily regulated under a safety standard, with cost considerations playing a relatively minor role. For example, the Clean Air Act requires air standards that protect human health, while the Clean Water Act sets as its final goal zero discharge into navigable waters, with an intermediate target of "fishable and swimmable waters." In neither case are compliance costs mentioned.

And so, for example, in 1997 the EPA passed a regulation to tighten smog standards for which its own estimated costs ($600 million to $2.5 billion) exceeded the measurable benefits ($100 million to $1.5 billion). Why did it do this? On safety grounds. In spite of the negative benefit–cost picture, the regulations were expected to save lives and allow more people to exercise safely outside ("Clintonites Debate" 1997). In fact, the courts have ruled that the air and water protection statutes, along with national hazardous waste legislation, explicitly prohibit benefit–cost tests for new regulations.

On the other hand, pesticides, insecticides, and other toxic substances are regulated under an efficiency standard. Chemicals and pesticides cannot be banned unless the benefits of doing so are (roughly) shown to exceed the costs.

Even for the safety statutes, though, since 1981, the EPA has been required to conduct formal benefit–cost analyses of any new regulation expected to cost more than $100 million. These benefit–cost studies, known as **regulatory impact analyses (RIAs),** are prepared for new safety standard regulations, such as the ozone tightening done in 1997, even though their results cannot legally determine the regulatory decision. Why do them then? Under a safety standard, the agency is still directed to select "the regulatory alternative maximizing net benefits from those alternatives within the scope of the law." In our terminology, the EPA is supposed to examine several different options and, among all the options that achieve a safety goal, pick the most efficient.[1]

Given that conservatives often push hardest for the use of benefit–cost tests, many environmentalists view benefit–cost analysis as merely a political tool for rolling back environmental gains, in part by burying the regulatory process under a mound of paperwork.[2] And at its worst, benefit–cost analysis is indeed used as an excuse to gloss over hard moral choices and provide a rubber stamp for preconceived notions about the right course of action. One EPA employee privately characterized the results of a RIA he had worked on as follows: "I wouldn't bet a week's salary on the results, but it justified the rule."

However, at its best, a benefit–cost study will clarify the decision-making process. As we will see in this chapter, a "good" benefit–cost study can highlight the trade-offs that regulators face when setting standards. What is meant by a **good benefit–cost study?** It will follow accepted procedures for estimating benefits and costs, provide a clear statement of all assumptions, point out uncertainties where they exist, and suggest realistic margins of error.

In this chapter, we will review two benefit–cost studies conducted by the EPA. The first focuses on a very detailed problem—exposure to the leachate from lead solder in water pipes (solder is the material used to fuse pipes together). In addition to the specificity of the problem, the benefits of reduced exposure to lead are fairly well-known. Nevertheless, even here, there is substantial uncertainty surrounding the benefit and cost estimates, casting some doubt over the usefulness of the final results.

---

[1]For an extensive evaluation, see Morgenstern (1997). The quote from the executive order is cited in Fraas (1984). Presidents Reagan and Bush directed the EPA to simply maximize net benefits. President Clinton's executive order directed the EPA to conduct a benefit–cost analysis for significant regulatory actions and select options that "maximize net benefits" to the extent permissible by law. But "net benefits" are now parenthetically qualified to include "potential economic, environmental, public health and safety, and other advantages; distributive impacts; and equity" (see Goodstein 1995).

[2]Even some supporters of efficiency standards opposed the 1995 efficiency-based legislation, arguing that it was in fact a thinly disguised attempt to paralyze the regulatory process (Portney 1995).

The second RIA had a much broader mandate: to evaluate the benefits and costs of establishing design standards and performance regulations for the nation's 6,000 plus municipal solid waste landfills. Aside from the obvious difficulties associated with tackling such a vast problem, and in contrast to the lead case, the health and environmental benefits of stricter regulation for landfills are both highly uncertain and hard to quantify.

These two studies illustrate both the potential and limitations of benefit–cost analysis from a technical point of view. We will also evaluate the degree to which political interests can affect the benefit–cost process. Finally, we will consider the charge that, given its limitations, benefit–cost analysis is simply not up to the task of specifying the "right" level of pollution.

10.1 Doing Benefit–Cost: Lead Standards

Under the Safe Drinking Water Act, the EPA is required to establish action standards for lead in drinking water. Lead concentrations from leachate higher than the action level would require remedial action—installation of pH control devices and inhibitors to reduce corrosion and/or public education campaigns to inform people how to reduce risks of lead in drinking water. Table 10.1 illustrates the three options the agency considered for lead leached from solder.

Option A is the most stringent, with action levels for both small (<50,000 people) and large (>50,000 people) systems occurring at 5 micrograms per liter. Option B loosens the standard for small systems to 15 μg/l. The rationale for this option is based on the increased per user expense associated with corrosion control in smaller systems. The high fixed costs of retrofitting such a system would be spread out over fewer users. Thus, they would have to pay higher water bills than large system users if option A, where the same protection level is afforded all users, was chosen. Option C relaxes both standards to 15 μg/l.

To estimate costs, the EPA first had to determine which of the more than 63,000 systems nationwide would require remedial action, and at what level, to achieve the three different targets.[3] With this difficult feat accomplished, the next step was to establish engineering cost estimates for the different steps to be taken: monitoring

TABLE 10.1   Proposed Action Levels for Lead Leached from Solder

Option	System Type	Action Level
A	Small	5 μg/l
	Large	5 μg/l
B	Small	15 μg/l
	Large	5 μg/l
C	Small	15 μg/l
	Large	15 μg/l

Source: U.S. Environmental Protection Agency (1991a).

---

[3]Some systems were expected not to be able to achieve the targets with the available control technology. These were expected to achieve reductions to 10 μg/l and to continue their public education campaigns.

water, conducting corrosion control studies, installing lime contractors to control pH, installing inhibitors, and mounting public education campaigns. After undertaking these two tasks, the study gives a plus or minus 50% range for uncertainty in its cost estimates, due to factors such as "the effectiveness of treatment, current corrosion control practices, nationwide contaminant occurrence levels, as well as uncertainty regarding what specific actions will be required by the states in the implementation of this rule" (U.S. Environmental Protection Agency 1991a, 1-6).

On the benefits side, the agency had the luxury of dealing with a compound that is a well-established "bad actor." Lead drinking pipes, after all, have been given credit for the fall of the Roman Empire! Considerable research has been done documenting the negative effects of lead exposure. Table 10.2 lists the health costs associated with lead in drinking water. Items that the EPA was able to consider directly are marked with an *.

Of this long list, the EPA was able to quantify benefits only for hypertension, chronic heart disease, stroke, and death in adult males and reduced intelligence in children. (Feminists might speculate on the reasons for the lack of data on women!) Most of the other health effects of lead exposure fall into the category of suspected but not confirmed. As the RIA states: "Many categories of health effects from lead exposure cannot be quantified—credible dose-response functions are not yet available" (U.S. Environmental Protection Agency 1991a, 5-1). Finally, other nonwater benefits the RIA notes it does not consider are reduced lead content in sewage sludge, and longer pipe life and reduced water leakage from corrosion control.

TABLE 10.2   Health Costs of Lead Exposure

MEN (age group)
*   a. Hypertension (adult)
*   b. Heart disease, stroke, and death (ages 40–59)
      c. Possible item b. (ages 20–40; >59)
      d. Cancer

WOMEN
      e. Possible hypertension, heart disease, stroke, and death
      f. Fetal effects from maternal exposure, including diminished childhood IQ, decreased gestational age, and reduced birth weight
      g. Possible increases in infant mortality
      h. Cancer

CHILDREN
      i. Interference with growth
*   j. Reduced intelligence
      k. Impaired hearing, behavioral changes
      l. Interference with PNS development
      m. Metabolic effects, impaired heme synthesis, anemia
      n. Cancer

*Items that the EPA was able to consider directly.
Source: U.S. Environmental Protection Agency (1991a).

The EPA tried to get at *some* of the benefits of lead reduction for children indirectly by estimating the reduction in screening and subsequent mitigation costs due to the regulation. About 20% of American children are routinely screened for lead content in their blood; depending upon the lead level found, further screening and treatment are recommended. The agency estimated the savings from such testing and treatment resulting from tighter regulation. The EPA included not only the direct costs but also the opportunity cost of the parents' time. (Stress and suffering costs were not included.) Ultimately, however, as we shall see, these benefits proved to be very small.

The EPA also included as a benefit a reduction in the number of severely impacted children, those with an IQ of 70 or less. As a measure of the benefits, the agency used the expected reduction in compensatory education expenses. The authors of the study recognized this to be "a clear underestimate." Their preferred measure would have been parents' willingness to pay to avoid (or willingness to accept) a mentally handicapped child.

The direct effects of lead exposure to children were measured via a reduction in earnings resulting from lowered "intelligence." EPA again used the controversial IQ measure to measure general cognitive ability. It then used studies linking lead exposure to lower IQ, and lower IQ to lower earnings, to estimate the benefits of reduced exposure. The agency took into account three effects of lowered IQ on earnings: first, lowered innate "ability"; second, lowered educational attainment; and third, lowered labor force participation rates.

For adult males, the EPA was able to quantify benefits associated with reduced hypertension, heart disease, stroke, and premature death. For hypertension, benefits included direct outlays for medical care and the value of lost workdays. Again, no estimates were included for pain and suffering. For heart disease and stroke, the agency relied on a more theoretically correct approach—willingness to pay to avoid risk of disease. However, the most closely related study available looked at chronic bronchitis, arriving at a figure of about $1 million per case. The EPA used this number, reasoning that the symptoms of the two former diseases are at least as severe as the latter. Finally, the EPA placed a value on deaths avoided of $2.5 million. Recall that this is at the low end of the range discussed in Chapter 8.

Given all the assumptions and uncertainties associated with these estimates, the authors of the study "assume," based on "professional judgment," that the "true" benefit measure could be as much as two times as high, or 70% below, the actual value the estimation procedure generates. This "two-times" upper bound *does not* include all of the benefit categories identified in the discussion above that the EPA could not quantify. The authors, sensibly, could provide uncertainty ranges only for the estimates they did undertake.

Bearing in mind both the uncertainty and incomplete coverage, Table 10.3 provides the annual benefit estimates for the different categories of health effects. Option A, the strictest alternative, yields the highest total benefits; option C the lowest.

Table 10.3 illustrates in its boldest form the accounting procedure necessary for using benefit–cost analysis to determine the "right" amount of pollution. If you find it morally disturbing to see in print, "Number of deaths reduced: 672, Value: $1,680 million," rest assured that most people do and that this is a healthy sign. Whether you ultimately reject or accept the benefit–cost logic, it is important to keep in mind that people's lives and well-being, not dollars, are at stake in decisions about pollution levels. The dollars are placeholders for consumption items—ranging from better health

TABLE 10.3   Annual Estimated Benefits of Reducing Lead in Drinking Water (1988 $million)

	Option		
	A	**B**	**C**
ADULT MALES			
Hypertension			
Cases reduced/yr	685,302	635,199	246,479
Value	$ 430	$ 399	$ 155
Heart Attack			
Cases reduced/yr	884	818	315
Value	$ 884	$ 818	$ 315
Stroke			
Cases reduced/yr	657	609	235
Value	$ 657	$ 609	$ 235
Death (Heart Disease)			
Cases reduced/yr	672	622	240
Value	$1,680	$1,555	$ 599
CHILDREN			
Treatment cost reduced	*	*	*
Additional education reduced	$ 2	$ 2	$ 2
Lowered IQ			
Children no longer affected	205,221	188,313	68,133
Value	$ 942	$ 864	$ 313
IQ <70			
Children no longer affected	784	738	325
Value	$ 40	$ 38	$ 17
TOTAL	$4,635	$4,286	$1,635

*Less than $1 million.
Source: U.S. Environmental Protection Agency (1991a).

care to luxury cars—that may make people happier and must be given up to reduce the risk of death from lead in drinking water.

The final step in the benefit–cost analysis is to compare the total costs and benefits of the different standards over the assumed twenty-year life of the existing lead solder–based water delivery system. In this case, a discount rate of 3% was used. Table 10.4 displays the guts of the benefit–cost study as it appears in the RIA: the total present discounted values of costs and benefits over the life of the project.

Now, having made it through many long and tedious chapters of this text to finally get to the point where you, as an informed economist, can read a benefit–cost analysis, use the information in Table 10.4 to see if you can answer the $64,000

PUZZLE

Which option is the most efficient?

TABLE 10.4   Summary Benefit–Cost Results, Lead Solder (1998 $ million)

	Option		
	A	**B**	**C**
Total Benefits	$68,957	$63,757	$24,325
Total Costs	$ 6,272	$ 4,156	$ 3,655
B/C Ratio	11.0	15.3	6.7
Marginal Benefits	$ 5,192	$39,400	$24,325
Marginal Costs	$ 2,117	$ 500	$ 3,655
Marginal B/C Ratio	2.5	78.8	6.67

Note: Figures are based on 20-year life, 3% discount rate.
Source: U.S. Environmental Protection Agency (1991a).

SOLUTION

Let's see, this is multiple choice, so why not pick the one in the middle, right? Wrong. The correct answer is option

A

Why? The efficient option will maximize the size of the economic pie or the **net monetary benefits** to society. But this is just total benefits minus total costs. Unfortunately, there is no line in Table 10.4 illustrating net monetary benefits, so we must do the math ourselves. Subtracting total costs from total benefits, we find net benefits for option A are estimated to be $62,685 million, for option B $59,601 million, and for option C $20,670 million.

Another way to see that option A is the most efficient is to use marginal analysis: C is clearly a good buy, since marginal benefits ($24,325 million) exceed marginal costs ($3,655 million). Should we move from C to B? Yes, here the additional benefits ($39,400 million) are *much* larger than the additional costs ($500 million). Finally, should we move from B to A? Again the answer is yes. Marginal benefits ($5,192 million) still exceed marginal costs ($2,117 million), though not by as much as in the move from C to B. Figure 10.1 illustrates this using our familiar marginal benefit/marginal cost of cleanup diagram. Because the marginal benefits curve lies above the marginal cost curve, option A is more efficient than option B.

The summary in Table 10.4 (and Figure 10.1) gives us a very neat story. The numbers "speak for themselves." Option A is clearly the most efficient. The regulator can glance at the table, make the efficient decision, and go home. However, is the information in Table 10.4 the whole story? Well, of course not. We just spent a whole section stressing the uncertainty of both the cost and benefit estimates.

Figure 10.2 provides a somewhat more realistic and less neat way of looking at the data. The graph shows benefits, measured in billions of dollars, on the vertical axis and costs, also measured in billions, on the horizontal axis.

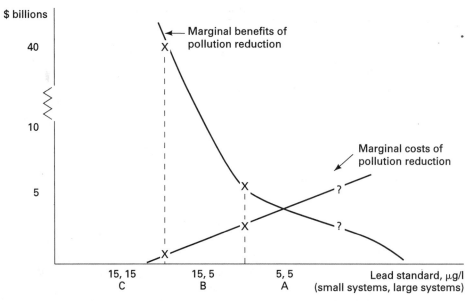

FIGURE 10.1 Estimated Benefits and Costs of Reducing Lead ($billion)

First note that the estimates for options A, B, and C all lie above the line labeled "B/C Ratio = 1." The **benefit–cost ratio** is just the value of the benefits of the option divided by the costs. A B/C ratio greater than one means total benefits exceed total costs, while a B/C ratio that is a fraction means that total benefits are less than total costs. Because all three options have a ratio greater than one, all three options clearly pass a simple total-benefits-greater-than-total-costs test.

The circles reflect the uncertainty bounds around the estimates discussed previously. The fact that the circles for A and B overlap so substantially suggests that the differences between these options reported in Table 10.4 are essentially meaningless. For example, the $6 billion benefit difference between the two is swamped by an uncertainty of roughly $60 billion up to the top of each circle and $30 billion down to the bottom. Similarly, the costs of the two programs could, in reality, vary much more than the $2 billion difference between points A and B.

At the same time, however, option C can be clearly distinguished from options A and B. There is no overlap with A and only a bit with B. Even including the uncertainty, options A and B are more efficient than C.

Which option did the EPA recommend? Interestingly, the EPA did not choose option A, the one its "best guess" identified as most efficient and which, in this case, is clearly the safest. In fact, the report *never acknowledged* that A is estimated to be the most efficient. Instead, the agency fell back on the uncertainty in the benefit estimates and opted for the less expensive option B. In the report's words: "The diagram [Figure 10.2] indicates that, when all uncertainties are weighed, the net benefits of corrosion control under alternative A may not be meaningfully different than those associated with alternative B" (U.S. Environmental Protection Agency 1991a).

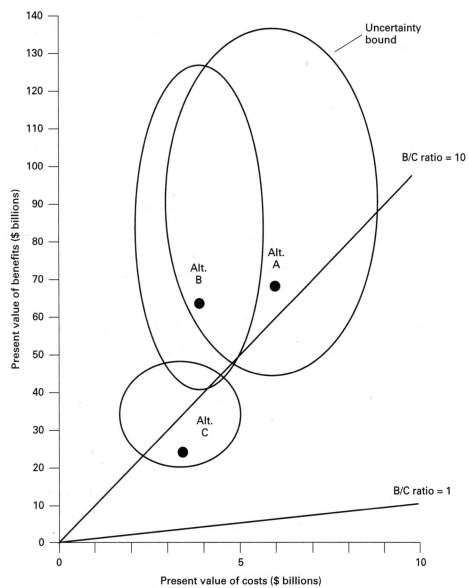

FIGURE 10.2 Uncertainty of Benefit–Cost Estimates for Corrosion Control

Source: U.S. Environmental Protection Agency (1991a).

On the other hand, they may well be different; they may be dramatically larger! Figure 10.2 is rather deceptive. While appearing to be an example of "good" benefit–cost analysis by including "all" uncertainty, the diagram in fact, does not reflect *most of the uncertainty*. As was noted, many potential health and nonhealth benefits were ignored since it could not be monetized.

Nevertheless, given the uncertainty illustrated in the graph, and the much larger uncertainty arising from omitted benefits, it is clear that the choice between A and B could not be made on benefit–cost grounds. Given also the general conservative, anti-regulation philosophy of the Bush administration in power at the time, the choice of the less costly option B was perhaps not surprising.

This case illustrates that, due to substantial uncertainty surrounding health effects and benefit measures for reducing even a well-studied compound such as lead, benefit–cost analysis cannot discriminate between "relatively" close options. Ultimately, the choice between A and B could not be and was not made on efficiency grounds. On the other hand, benefit–cost analysis is capable of discerning "big differences" between policies. C is clearly inefficient relative to A or B. A critic would respond, of course, that we could save the time and money devoted to a benefit–cost study: A simple look at the lives saved in Table 10.3 makes it clear that C is an inferior policy.

As a final technical point, the major table in the EPA document, Table 10.4, relies on the B/C ratio to summarize the options. But note that B/C ratios have nothing to do with efficiency. Option A has a lower ratio (11) than option B (15.3), yet is more efficient. B/C ratios alone do not tell us very much. From an economist's point of view, Table 10.4 is missing the most important line: total net benefits. The option with the **maximum net benefits** is the most efficient, and it should be clearly identified in a summary table such as Table 10.4.

10.2 Doing Benefit–Cost: Landfill Regulation

If the lead case illustrates the pitfalls that emerge when working with a relatively well-defined problem, the second RIA highlights more common difficulties in benefit–cost analysis—poor data, long-time horizons, and hard-to-quantify benefits. The EPA, under the Resource Conservation and Recovery Act (RCRA), was directed to draft regulations for the siting, construction, and maintenance of municipal solid waste landfills. Originally, the agency evaluated five alternatives but ultimately focused on two. The first was a "pollute and cleanup" approach that imposed no design standards on landfills, requiring only groundwater monitoring and corrective action for any pollutants detected above the legal level defined in the Safe Drinking Water Act. This option reflected the minimal regulatory approach consistent with the RCRA law.

The second option took a preventive approach, requiring landfills designed to forestall any groundwater contamination. Depending upon site conditions, these designs might require soil compaction, clay or synthetic liners, leachate collection systems, and relatively impermeable covers. Both regulations imposed some location restrictions and required monitoring for a postclosure period of ten to forty years.

EPA engineers and economists faced a difficult problem in assessing the comparative costs and benefits associated with these options at more than 6,000 landfill sites around the country. As a result, many simplifying assumptions went into the study. Of course, assumptions are necessary in any social scientific work; the question that an outside observer would ask is, will the results change substantially if other, equally plausible assumptions are used?

In this case, we have one indication of how important assumptions can be to the final results. The agency's approach was to compare the additional costs and benefits of each option to a "baseline" scenario, or continuation of current practice. The RIA was initiated in 1985; at the time, a reasonable baseline assumption was that most current landfills were unlined with vegetative covers. This assumption meant that achieving the EPA's preferred rule, which required liners and impermeable covers in many cases, would be quite costly. In 1990, the agency completed a two-volume RIA under this assumption.

Over the 1985 to 1990 time period, however, many states began requiring higher design standards, including liners and covers. After determining that these changes might substantially affect the results of the RIA, the agency obtained better information about state practices. The EPA then issued a revised benefit–cost analysis assuming a baseline with more stringent existing regulations. While the benefits of both options were reduced under this assumption, the additional costs fell by a much larger margin—in the case of the "prevent" option, from \$14.8 billion to \$5.7 billion. Clearly, the EPA's original assumption was outdated by the time the study was completed. Yet, benefit–cost analysts, without access to unlimited information and charged with producing numbers, are forced to make such assumptions. One can only speculate about the possibility of other sensitive assumptions buried in the two-volume study.

The EPA's cost estimates, based on the engineering approach, include expenses associated with "land clearing, excavation, equipment, labor, liner materials and groundwater monitoring wells." Not surprisingly, the bulk of added costs over the baseline (70%) for the "pollute and cleanup" option were for corrective action, while 50% of the added costs for the prevention option went for liners.

In the benefit category, the EPA attempted two quantitative estimates: reduction in cancer risk and avoided cost of replacing damaged groundwater. Note that these are different measures of the same benefit—access to healthy drinking water—and thus cannot be added together. The health risk from solid waste landfills arises primarily from the presence of small quantities of hazardous household and industrial waste such as paints, oils, solvents, insecticides, and pesticides. These carcinogenic substances can be leached out of a landfill by rainfall and find their way into surrounding groundwaters.

On the cancer side, the EPA baseline estimate is low. Under the baseline regulatory framework, over the next 300 years the agency predicts 5.7 cancers nationwide would result from drinking contaminated groundwater. This estimate suffers from the well-known uncertainties associated with assessing the cancer risk from hazardous waste, mentioned in Chapter 8 and detailed in National Research Council (1991). In this case, the uncertainty is compounded by the need to model the highly uncertain process by which toxics leach out of the landfill and into groundwater, all over a very lengthy period.

The reason the risk estimate is so low is not because unregulated landfills are "safe." The EPA estimated that 55% of existing landfills posed cancer risks from groundwater on the order of 10^{-4} to 10^{-5} for surrounding residents—greater than our 1 in 1,000,000 safety threshold. New, unregulated landfills were assumed by the agency to expose individuals to this risk level at about 6% of the sites (Office of Technology Assessment 1989; U.S. Environmental Protection Agency 1990). (For comparison, police officers face a risk of about 10^{-4} of being killed by a felon while on duty.) Instead, cancer case estimates are low because the number of people who actually depend on groundwater from wells within one mile of a landfill, the agencies assumed cut off from contamination, is quite small. For example, more than 50% of new landfills were assumed to have no wells at all within one mile, so the cancer risk was estimated to be zero. If the demand for groundwater increases as population grows, the estimated cancer figure would be higher.

Both regulatory options—pollute and cleanup and prevent—reduced expected cancers by 2.4 over the 300-year period. These two estimates are identical, in part because the EPA (unrealistically) assumes full compliance with groundwater monitoring laws and reporting and correction of all violations. However, the maximum estimated number of cancers reduced under either option would be only 5.7.

As an alternative measure to cancers avoided, the EPA estimated the cost of replacing damaged groundwater (dangerous or bad-tasting or foul-smelling) with an alternative supply. This approach probably overstates benefits: In effect, the estimate assumes society is willing to pay enough to insure 100% safety for affected residents nearby. Here, discounting plays a big role, due to the long time horizon considered. A $1 million water supply built 250 years into the future and discounted at 3% (the rate used in the RIA) has a present discounted value of only $617! Table 10.5 reproduces the final net–benefit analysis.

Under the assumptions that (1) *all* benefits are captured by mitigating the effects on groundwater, and (2) the study's complex modeling process generates "precise" benefit and cost predictions, then by an efficiency standard, both policies are losers. Simply requiring landfills to monitor their discharges on an annual basis and comply with *existing* water laws costs $2.5 billion more than would simply supplying groundwater users with an uncontaminated supply. Moving to a pollution prevention strategy makes matters even worse.

Other benefits the EPA study mentions, but does not quantify, include reduced surface water contamination, avoidance of failures in groundwater monitoring and cleanup, existence value of groundwater, and increased public confidence in landfill siting. The latter could be quite important in the face of "Not in My Backyard" (NIMBY) movements opposing new landfill sites. The EPA study suggests an upper limit of $84 million per year in potential savings from expediting the site selection process (U.S. Environmental Protection Agency 1991b).

In addition to these unquantified benefits, the EPA further suggests that stricter regulation will have favorable equity implications. The EPA study is implicitly saying that *if* we set aside $270 million in the bank today as an **environmental bond,** we would have enough money to provide alternate water supplies for all those relying on water that becomes contaminated in the future. However, only this *potential* is revealed by the benefit–cost analysis. In actuality, no such payments are being proposed. Under these circumstances, a prevention strategy first avoids imposing high cleanup costs on future generations and second reduces the potential that a landfill

TABLE 10.5 Marginal Analysis of Landfill Regulation (1988 $million)

Regulatory Scenario	Total Cost over Baseline	Groundwater Benefits over Baseline	Net Benefits
1. Pollute and Cleanup	$2,670	$120	−$2,550
2. Prevent Pollution	$5,770	$270	−$5,500

Note figures are based on one set of new landfills, 300-year period, 3% discount rate.
Source: U.S. Environmental Protection Agency (1991b).

will become a federal (taxpayers') burden. The authors, in effect, are suggesting that we weight the utility of (1) future victims and (2) taxpayers-at-large more heavily than the utility of local garbage producers alive today.

Of course, as in all moves toward efficiency, an alternative policy exists that could satisfy both equity and efficiency concerns: an environmental bond. One could tax solid waste disposal and set aside a fund equivalent to $270 million for building new water supplies. In this way, there would be no future victims, and federal dollars would not be committed to a cleanup. Additional money would still have to be spent for groundwater monitoring but none for cleanup.

As a final point, the EPA study also makes a common double-counting error by suggesting the existence of another possible uncounted benefit of a stricter standard: limiting the impact on property values surrounding the landfill. Yet, property values fall due to perceived health concerns; this is the identical damage being measured by the cost of supplying an area with fresh water.

The two studies reviewed here are examples of "good" benefit–cost analysis. The authors work hard to clearly state and justify all assumptions; they also state what they view to be reasonable upper and lower bounds for their benefit and cost estimates. Nevertheless, in part because the EPA works with a limited budget, and in part because of the nature of benefit–cost analysis, it is still relatively easy to criticize the studies on their own terms.

Common pitfalls, even in sophisticated benefit–cost studies such as these, include double counting of either costs or benefits and reliance on benefit–cost ratios rather than maximum net benefits for project selection. More significantly, it is apparent that the precision presented by best-guess estimates such as those presented in Tables 10.4 and 10.5 is illusory. Given the unquantified benefits and the uncertainty associated with measuring both benefits and costs, dollar figures placed on net benefits or even the ranking of similar alternatives in terms of net benefits, are simply not reliable.

Most efficiency advocates accept this charge but still argue that efficiency as a goal makes sense and that benefit–cost analysis brings a useful light to bear on the policy decision-making process. Ultimately, what are the numbers in the lead and landfill studies telling us? In the case of lead, the EPA has identified many tangible benefits associated with restricting leachate from solder. A standard at least as stringent as option B is clearly justified following the efficiency logic. Sorting out A versus B is not really possible, but B relative to C is a good buy.

On the other hand, the EPA's recommended landfill rule or, indeed, requiring compliance with existing water laws, does not appear to be wise public policy *from an efficiency perspective.* The EPA analysts presumably thought hard about potential benefits of stricter landfill regulation. Clearly, some important benefits could not be quantified, but even if their benefit estimates were twenty times as large, the policy of relatively strict regulation would still be inefficient. When benefits outweigh costs by a margin large enough to subsume reasonable uncertainty, or *vice versa,* good benefit–cost studies can help us select the more efficient option, if that indeed is our goal.

10.3 Political Influence in Benefit–Cost

One of the advantages of benefit–cost analysis, according to its advocates, is that it substantially reduces political influence in the policy arena. A naive claim in its favor is that benefit–cost analysis "allows the numbers to speak for themselves." In reality, as we have seen, if one tortures the numbers sufficiently, they will often confess to the analyst's viewpoint. The real advantage of benefit–cost analysis is that it places limits on the type of data torturing that can go on. For example, an economist may set out to prove that more stringent regulations of landfills are desirable on efficiency grounds. Within admittedly broad limits, however, her benefit and cost estimates are constrained by the methodology we have outlined in the last three chapters. It may well be that the numbers simply cannot credibly support her case.

How elastic are the bounds within which good benefit–cost studies must stay? This section will explore four ways in which political influence affects the benefit–cost process: through regulatory politics, agenda control, the hard numbers problem, and paralysis by analysis.

We can use the landfill RIA to examine how **regulatory politics** might influence the drafting of a benefit–cost study. The EPA's benefit–cost studies are reviewed by the Office of Management and Budget (OMB), which had an obvious deregulatory bias under the Reagan and first Bush administrations. EPA administrators who were political appointees probably shared this general antiregulation conservative philosophy. Nevertheless, they presumably had no desire to forward regulatory proposals to OMB only to have them shot down. Therefore, the EPA benefit–cost analysts who actually prepared the report certainly faced some pressure, stated or unstated, from their superiors to generate numbers in support of their preferred rule. Yet such activities could not be done flagrantly since the OMB, industry, and possibly environmental watchdog groups had their own economists reviewing the documents.

One might speculate on a political scenario underlying the landfill study. In the face of dramatic local public resistance to landfill siting, EPA officials probably felt originally that prevention-based regulation made sense. In its benefits analysis, The EPA took the traditional cancers-reduced approach to measuring benefits; however, the results came out shockingly low. In the landfill report, the analysts chose *not* to monetize these benefits as they did for lead. The discounted benefits for the few lives saved by either policy option would have probably been less than $10 million and would have looked downright silly against costs in the billions.

In what one might read as an attempt to boost the benefits, EPA took the somewhat unconventional step of measuring groundwater benefits in terms of replacement cost, in effect, assuming that society was interested in 100% safety. Still, the benefit numbers came out low. The final step was to (dramatically) reduce the cost estimates by revising the baseline assumptions (and reducing the regulatory requirements somewhat). Even here, as Table 10.5 shows, the numbers did not look good. After taking two not-unreasonable measures that improved the health-based net benefits measure, the EPA still could not defend its preferred rule on a benefit–cost basis. Ultimately, the agency argued for the preferred rule based on the reasoning, not easily quantifiable, that a strict standard would lead to increased public confidence and facilitate the siting process and would be more equitable than a pollute and cleanup standard.

This purely speculative scenario suggests how regulatory politics might have influenced a benefit–cost process in subtle fashions. Another way that political decisions can affect a benefit–cost study is in its timing. The study may simply be put off until the important decisions have already been made. Thus, in spite of clear language direct from the U.S. President, that required the EPA to choose the most efficient option as identified by the RIA, it seems peculiar that in neither the lead nor the land-fill case was this actually done. From an efficiency perspective, the lead decision generated "underregulation," in the landfill case "overregulation." In both cases, the estimated efficiency loss was about $3 billion.

According to one EPA source, the efficient outcome was not chosen in part because the benefit–cost process was not initiated until very late in the policy process. In other words, the timing of the benefit–cost studies insured that they did not have a major impact on the policy outcome (Brett Snyder, personal communication, March, 1992).

Regulatory politics can clearly have an impact either on the underlying assumptions and presentation of a RIA or in the timing of the study. It is naive to believe that economists and engineers who work in regulatory agencies practice their craft in isolation from broader political forces. On the other hand, both the lead and landfill examples also make it clear that benefit–cost analysis is not wholly arbitrary. It is hard to justify the loose lead standard (option C) or *either* of the landfill options on efficiency grounds.

Given the fact that the "accepted methodology" puts some constraints on benefit–cost analysis, political influence shows up subtly in its impact on natural and social scientific debates. Corporate interests have used their resources to try and **control the scientific agenda** by funding conferences and targeting research in certain areas. For example, the American Paper Institute and the Chlorine Institute have aggressively promoted research downplaying the health effects of dioxin, a chemical used in these industries, while ignoring accumulating evidence to the contrary. The Chlorine Institute hosted a conference on dioxin, the discussions of which it "then interpreted to suit its purposes," according to the *Wall Street Journal* ("How Two Industries" 1991). Exxon sponsored a similar effort that many observers felt was aimed at discrediting the contingent valuation method of estimating existence value discussed in Chapter 8. CV studies were being used to assess oil spill damages in the wake of the Exxon *Valdez* oil spill in 1989. And the Formaldehyde Institute has sponsored substantial research questioning the link between cancer in laboratory animals and in people.

The difference between the perspectives of industry, government, and academic scientists is reflected in a poll showing that 80% of the first group, 63% of the second group, and only 40% of the last group believed that a threshold existed below which exposure to cancer-causing agents was risk-free (Greider 1992). Even academic scientists, however, must often obtain research funding from industry. In agriculture, for example, Curtis (1991) argues that industry funding sources dominate. Perhaps for this reason, Cropper et al. (1991) report that academic scientists who commented on EPA pesticide benefit–cost studies generally supported the position of pesticide manufacturers.

In addition to regulatory politics and agenda control, benefit–cost studies have also been criticized for providing a false sense of precision to decision makers. This is known as the **hard numbers problem.** The apparently "hard" numbers in the summary tables for the two benefit–cost studies are really soft when uncertainty and incomplete benefit coverage are factored in. Yet, decision makers are often not interested in "uncertainty" and incompleteness; they want an answer and often one that supports their particular political agenda. Appropriately crafted tables such as 10.4 or 10.5 fit this bill perfectly.

One EPA analyst revealed the kind of political pressure to produce hard numbers he faced when doing benefit–cost: "Recently, estimates of benefits and costs of alternative lead regulations were developed in order to promote one specific alternative. Discussions of the enormous uncertainties inherent in those estimates had no discernible impact [on decision makers] until a graphical presentation was provided. While the presentation involved a degree of bureaucratic risk to the analyst, the significance of the uncertainty [was made apparent to decision makers]. . . . In passing, I note the risk to the analyst was realized [he was punished], but he slept better" (Schnare 1990, 151).

Of course, plenty of "bad" benefit–cost studies step outside the accepted methodology. Washington, DC, is full of think tanks representing a variety of political viewpoints, all cranking out benefit–cost studies in support of their policy viewpoint. Many of these reports are poorly done, and yet, these hard numbers are widely reported and have an impact on policy decisions.

Finally, in the two cases we have considered here, regulators were not *required* to choose the option identified as most efficient by the benefit–cost analysis. In fact, in neither case did they do so. However, when an efficiency test is enshrined as law, opponents of regulation can resort to the legal system and exploit the uncertainty in the process to delay or block the implementation of regulations. This is known as **paralysis by analysis** (Andrews 1984, 79). Two major environmental statutes require regulations to pass an efficiency test—the Toxic Substances Control Act (TSCA) and the Federal Insecticide, Fungicide and Rodenticide Act (FIFRA).

Under TSCA, the EPA tried for over ten years to phase out the remaining uses of asbestos, a mineral product well-known to cause lung cancer. The two big users left were in cement pipe and automobile brakes. In the early 1990s, an appeals court rejected the EPA's proposed phase-out of these products on several grounds. Although the EPA had in hand what it thought was a good benefit–cost study showing a substantial surplus of benefits over costs, the court ruled that the EPA (1) had not adequately considered less costly alternatives, (2) had not adequately evaluated the environmental dangers of substitute products (non-asbestos brakes and piping), and (3) had not followed proper procedures for public comment on the dangers of asbestos.

Without dwelling on the merits of the case, it should be evident from this chapter that trying to "prove" in a court of law that any regulatory decision not only has positive net benefits but also is the *most* efficient option is a virtual impossibility. As a result of this decision, some have concluded that the provision for banning existing substances under TSCA is essentially unworkable.

In summary, politics clearly influences the benefit–cost process, just as they would any alternative decision-making tool. In spite of this, however, the benefit–cost analysis methodology does provide a "consensus" framework for helping to judge the balance between measurable benefits and costs. There is such a thing as good benefit–cost. However, the only way to assure that the good benefit–cost is carried out is to assure adequate review of the study and opportunities for appeal by the affected parties. Given the technical nature of benefit–cost methodology, Campen (1986) has suggested that the government provide funds to community groups and others who seek to challenge government studies. Finally, legal standards that mandate efficiency are a poor idea on their own terms. Benefit–cost is just not capable of identifying efficient outcomes with a precision that can stand up in court.

10.4 Is Benefit–Cost Up to the Job?

In practice, benefit–cost analysis of pollution regulations should be evaluated on two grounds. First, given all its uncertainties and measurement problems, is it capable of identifying the efficient pollution level? Second, is efficiency (static or dynamic) in pollution control the right standard, or are generally more stringent safety or ecological standards preferred? This section addresses the first question. We have already talked at length about the second.

Comparing costs and benefits when intangible factors such as human life and health dominate has been compared to the problem of "appraising the quality of a horse-and-rabbit stew, the [tiny] rabbit being cast as the consequences that can be measured and evaluated numerically, and the [gigantic] horse as the amalgam of external effects, social, emotional and psychological impacts and historical and aesthetic considerations that can be adjudged only roughly and subjectively. Since the horse [is] bound to dominate the flavor of the stew, meticulous evaluation of the rabbit would hardly seem worthwhile" (cited in Dorfman 1978).

One could argue that in the lead case analyzed previously, where human life and health were indeed at stake, the RIA told us little that we did not already know. Given the well-known adverse health impacts of lead alone, option C was not a realistic regulatory alternative. At the same time, promoting B over A was not a "scientific" decision, even within the logic of benefit–cost. The large "horse" of uncertainty in comparing these options was much bigger than the very small "rabbit" that could be assessed with any measure of scientific consensus.

On the other hand, the landfill RIA identified surprisingly small health effects. As a result, a comparison of damaged groundwater with compliance costs appears to identify prevention-based or even pollute and cleanup regulation as inefficient. Even here, however, the study was unable to include a big part of the horse: difficult to measure benefits such as expedited landfill siting.

Clearly, benefit–cost analysis cannot pinpoint the efficient pollution level with the accuracy suggested by the diagrams in this book. Indeed, a recent report critical of benefit-cost analysis concluded: "Cost-benefit analysis cannot overcome its fatal flaw: it is completely reliant on the impossible attempt to price the priceless values of life, health, nature and the future . . . Cost benefit analysis has not enriched the public dialogue; it has impoverished it, covering the topic with poorly understood numbers rather than clarifying the underlying clashes of values" (Heinzerling and Ackerman 2002, 20, 33). Proponents of benefit-cost, respond however that it can provide a useful framework for a general "balancing" of benefits against costs. In addition, and in particular, when the horse of intangible benefits does not become so large as to dominate the flavor of the benefit stew, benefit–cost analysis can be used to rank dissimilar proposals in terms of efficiency.

10.5 Summary

Lurking behind any benefit–cost study is the central question of this part of the book: Is the efficiency standard a good idea in environmental protection? We will return to this issue one more time in the next chapter. Let us here summarize the two cases just illustrated, focusing on a narrower question: Is benefit–cost a useful tool for identifying efficient outcomes?

In the lead case, option A was both the most efficient and safest of those considered. Here, a move in the direction of efficiency as identified by the benefit–cost study would also have been a move in the direction of safety and would thus have been good policy by both pollution standards considered in this book.

But the lead case also illustrates a serious bias that can arise in benefit–cost analysis: the tendency to ignore environmental benefits that cannot be monetized. In the lead RIA, the analysts themselves fell into the trap of believing that they had captured and were weighing "all" of the uncertainty in their summary diagram. In fact, most of the potential environmental benefits were not even considered in the final decision to choose option B. Ultimately, easy-to-measure costs weighed in more heavily than difficult-to-measure benefits.

Moving now to the landfill case, the practical effect of the RIA was to force the EPA to think hard about the wisdom of requiring expensive preventive measures to attack very low risk levels. In the initial stages of the RIA, more expensive options than the final rule were considered but rejected. Ultimately, the impact was to reduce the cost of the regulation for little, if any, sacrifice in benefits. In this case, the RIA generated movement from an extreme safety position in the direction of efficiency. However, due to uncertainty, unquantifiable benefits, and equity concerns, the final option selected was much safer than efficiency. Paradoxically, in spite of the vastly greater complexity of the landfill problem, the RIA procedure was more useful in promoting a "balancing" of benefits and costs than in the narrowly defined lead case.

Is benefit–cost up to the job? Benefit–cost studies can identify more or less efficient options in a rough way, provided the differences in the net benefit figures are "big enough" to overcome all the associated uncertainty and incomplete coverage in the measurements.

APPLICATION 10.0

What's Wrong with This Picture?

As an aid to Governor Blabla, you are given the task of recommending whether or not the state should locate a low-level nuclear waste facility in a rural county. The nuclear industry provides you with a cost–benefit study it has conducted that gives you the following information:

COST–BENEFIT SUMMARY FOR PROPOSED WASTE FACILITY

Prepared by the Center for the Objective Study of Nuclear Issues.

Conclusion: The project will result in net benefits of $3 billion, with a benefit–cost ratio of 13. While these figures, of course, depend on the assumptions of the study, the very large net benefit figure, along with the extraordinarily high benefit–cost ratio, both indicate that the project will remain attractive under most plausible assumptions. We therefore strongly recommend initiating the proposal.

Assumptions:

1. Discount rate of 10%
2. Principal costs:
   a. Worker exposure
   b. Risk of accidental exposure during transport
   c. Reduction to zero of the land value at the storage site
   d. Construction and maintenance
3. Principal benefits:
   a. Reduced exposure at current temporary storage sites
   b. Job creation—1,000 temporary, 200 permanent jobs
   c. Extends life of existing nuclear power plants by ten years
      i. Lower electricity costs for consumers
      ii. Saves 7,000 jobs
   d. Increased profits for local service industries

   Note: Benefits under points b. and c.ii. are given double weight due to high unemployment in the county.

4. Risk assessment:
   a. Exposure/fatality assumptions from the U.S. Department of Energy
   b. Probability of fatal exposure due to transport accident: 1/100,000,000 miles; Source: U.S. Department of Energy
   c. Value of a statistical life: $1 million

1. Do you believe the report?
2. See if you can find six separate problems with the study.
3. What further information would you like to have prior to making a recommendation to the governor?

APPLICATION 10.1

Benefit–Cost Controversy

When taken to its extreme, the logic of benefit–cost analysis can generate some strange conclusions. In one case, researchers wanted to determine the value that mothers placed on their children's lives. In Indiana in 1985, parents were not fined for failure to have car seats for infants and toddlers, though they were legally required. Also, some parent's would not take the time to fasten car-seats correctly. Carlin and Sandy (1991) reckoned that this behavior (failure to purchase or correctly use car seats) on the part of the mothers raised the risk of death to their children by 0.0004, or four out of ten thousand, from birth to age four. They collected data on

190 people (all women) leaving a shopping mall with their kids; only 33% either had a car seat or were using it correctly.

Carlin and Sandy calculated that properly hooking the kids in would take about 69 hours over four years. They hypothesized that the opportunity cost of women's time would be an important determinant of whether or not car seats were installed or properly used. And using a statistical model, they in fact concluded that controlling for (some) other factors, moms with a higher opportunity cost to their time (generally, a higher foregone wage) were statistically less likely (though not at a high level of confidence) to install or properly use a car seat.

From this, they calculated that a wage increase equal in value to about $2.40 per hour would, all other things equal, induce a mom to forgo installing or properly using a car seat—all this leading finally to an estimated value of a child's life of:

$2.40 per hour saved * 69 hours saved per mom / 0.0004 lives lost per mom = $418,597 per life lost

Note this number is well below the $6 million figure used by the EPA for adults, even accounting for inflation since the time of the study.

1.   Does this conclusion make sense to you? If not, why not?

KEY IDEAS IN EACH SECTION

10.0   To have a chance of identifying the efficient level of pollution, a **good benefit–cost study** is required. For major regulations, the EPA is required to do a benefit–cost study called a **regulatory impact analyses (RIA),** though the results are not legally binding.

10.1   In the regulation of lead solder, many important potential health benefits of the regulation could not be quantified. In spite of this, **benefit–cost ratios** for all options were greater than one. However, the final choice of options could not be made on efficiency grounds, due to uncertainty. The lead case also illustrates that the most efficient option in a benefit–cost study will be the one maximizing **net monetary benefits.**

10.2   The landfill RIA highlights common difficulties in benefit–cost—**poor data, long-time horizons,** and **hard-to-quantify benefits.** In spite of this, because so few people are likely to be affected by contaminated groundwater in the vicinity of landfills, the measurable benefits of strict regulation are likely to be small. Nevertheless, the EPA chose to balance fairness to those likely to be affected, as well as to future taxpayers, against efficiency, and chose an inefficient, prevention-oriented strategy. Note that an **environmental bond** policy could have satisfied both fairness and efficiency concerns.

10.3   Benefit–cost is not immune from political influence. This section examined the impact of **regulatory politics, agenda control, the hard numbers problem,** and **paralysis by analysis.** However, any decision-making tool will be subject to political influence. The advantage of benefit–cost is that it sets up rules that define, in a more-or-less objective way, a good study.

10.4   Benefit–cost is most useful for identifying efficient options when hard-to-quantify benefits, such as lives lost or ecosystems destroyed, do not dominate the horse-and-rabbit stew of benefits. One example would be the landfill case. Under these circumstances, clear differences between options, based on net monetary gain, are most likely to emerge.

REFERENCES

Andrews, Richard N. L. 1984. "Environmental Decisions, Past and Present." In *Environmental Policy Under Reagan's Executive Order,* edited by V. Kerry Smith. Chapel Hill, NC: University of North Carolina Press.

Campen, James. 1986. *Benefit–cost and Beyond.* Cambridge, MA: Ballinger.

Carlin, Paul S., and Robert Sandy. 1991. "Estimating the Implicit Value of a Young Child's Life." *Southern Economic Journal* 58:186–202.

"Clintonites Debate Cost of a Bad Air Day." 1997. *Wall Street Journal,* 9 June, p. A1.

Cropper, Maureen L., William N. Evans, Stephen J. Berardi, Maria M. Ducla-Soares, and Paul R. Portney. 1991. "The Determinants of Pesticide Regulation: A Statistical Analysis of EPA Decisionmaking." *Discussion Paper CRM 91–01.* Washington, DC: Resources for the Future.

Curtis, Jennifer. 1991. *Harvest of Hope: The Potential of Alternative Agriculture to Reduce Pesticide Use.* San Francisco, CA: Natural Resources Defense Council.

Dorfman, Robert, ed. 1978. *Measuring Benefits of Government Investments.* Washington, DC: Brookings.

Fraas, Arthur G. 1984. "Benefit–cost Analysis for Environmental Regulation." In *Environmental Policy Under Reagan's Executive Order,* edited by V. Kerry Smith. Chapel Hill, NC: University of North Carolina Press.

Goodstein, Eban. 1995. "Benefit-Cost at the EPA." *Journal of Social Economics* 24, no. 2:375–389.

Greider, William. 1992. *Who Will Tell the People?* New York: Simon & Schuster.

Heinzerling, Lisa, and Frank Ackerman. 2002. *Pricing the Priceless: Cost-Benefit Analysis of Environmental Protection.* Washington, DC: Georgetown Environmental Law and Policy.

"How Two Industries Created a Fresh Spin on the Dioxin Debate." 1991. *Wall Street Journal,* 8 August.

Morgenstern, Richard, ed. 1997. *Economic Analyses at EPA: Assessing Regulatory Impact.* Washington, DC: Resources for the Future.

National Research Council. 1991. *Environmental Epidemiology: Public Health and Hazardous Wastes.* Washington, DC: National Academy Press.

Office of Technology Assessment. 1989. *Facing America's Trash: What Next for Municipal Solid Waste?* Washington, DC: U.S. GPO.

Portney, Paul. 1995. "Chain Saw Surgery." *The Washington Post,* 15 January, p. C3.

Schnare, David W. 1990. "Raid on Sanity: Policy and Economic Analysis of Radionucleide Removal From Drinking Water." In *Radon, Radium and Uranium in Drinking Water,* edited by C. Richard Cothern and Paul Rebers. Chelsea, MI: Lewis Publishers.

U.S. Environmental Protection Agency. 1991a. *Final Regulatory Impact Analysis of National Primary Drinking Water Regulations for Lead and Copper.* Washington, DC: U.S. EPA, Office of Drinking Water.

U.S. Environmental Protection Agency. 1991b. *Addendum to the Regulatory Impact Analysis for the Final Criteria for Municipal Solid Waste Landfills.* Washington, DC: U.S. EPA, Regulatory Analysis Branch, Office of Solid Waste.

U.S. Environmental Protection Agency. 1990. *Regulatory Impact Analysis for the Final Criteria for Municipal Solid Waste Landfills.* Washington, DC: U.S. EPA, Regulatory Analysis Branch, Office of Solid Waste.

IS MORE REALLY BETTER? CONSUMPTION AND WELFARE

11.0 Introduction

The typical American family owns "twice as many cars, drives two-and-a-half times as far, uses 21 times as much plastic, and travels 25 times as far by air as did their parents in 1950" (Durning 1991, 156–158).

Progress, or overconsumption?

Within the benefit–cost efficiency framework, there is simply no room for the concept of "overconsumption." The whole point of doing a benefit–cost study, after all, is to insure that we do not sacrifice too much consumption in pursuit of environmental quality. From an efficiency perspective, our generation's increase in consumption over what our parents enjoyed clearly reflects progress.

How then can overconsumption be viewed as an environmental problem? First, consumption (or affluence) crops up in the IPAT equation from Chapter 7:

$$\text{environmental } \mathbf{I}\text{mpact} = \mathbf{P}\text{opulation} * \mathbf{A}\text{ffluence} * \mathbf{T}\text{echnology}$$

IPAT suggests that one of the three main causes of environmental decline is the growth in the consumption of material goods. Why? From an ecological perspective, pessimism is in order about the possibility for technological progress to keep up with the pace of consumption (and population) growth. Thus, for ecologists, the fact that consumption levels are high and growing gets translated into overconsumption as a serious environmental problem. Efficiency advocates, by contrast, are technological optimists and so do not view consumption itself as a serious issue.

If, as ecologicals believe, technological progress cannot offset the environmental impact of a quadrupling of consumption over the next fifty years, then this is one sense in which overconsumption is indeed a major environmental issue. But this chapter focuses on a second argument against high consumption. It does so by questioning a key assumption of the efficiency standard and benefit–cost analysis: "More is better."

Recall that our target of an efficient outcome was defined as one in which it is impossible to make one person better off without making someone else worse off. In practice, "better off" means "having more goods." We should remember that goods can include environmental amenities, such as hikes in the mountains, nice views, or clean air, but these are considered by benefit–cost economists to simply be goods that are literally exchangeable for hair conditioners, air conditioners, or video games. They are exchangeable because having more of one of these goods means having less of another. This in turn means they can ultimately be valued in monetary terms, if only indirectly, along the lines spelled out in Chapter 8.

But what if more isn't really better? If material gain in fact does not lead to greater happiness, then efficient outcomes do not really increase welfare. If more isn't better, then the trade-off identified by benefit–cost analysis—more environmental protection means less of all other stuff—loses much of its force, and safety or ecological sustainability goals make more sense. Finally, if more isn't better, then it is certainly fair to say that society is "overconsuming" resources.

11.1 Money and Happiness

One crude but accurate way to state the more is better assumption underlying benefit–cost analysis is that "Money buys happiness." Does it? According to Jesus, Buddha, Poor Richard, and a recent fortune cookie, the answer is no. However, let's take a look at the more scientific findings of survey researchers on this issue.

For more than two decades, researchers have been asking groups of people about the relationship between income and happiness in their lives. The results of many studies in America and western Europe reveal a strikingly similar conclusion: Money buys very little happiness, and it does so at a decreasing rate. Table 11.1 shows the results from a ten-nation European survey, including more than 15,000 people. These figures are typical of those found in most other studies and illustrate what has been called the **Easterlin paradox.**[1]

Rising income is clearly correlated with increased life satisfaction only up to around the median income, and the poorest people in a nation are only a bit less happy than the richest. About one in five poor people consider themselves very happy; this figure rises only to about one in four for the wealthiest 25% of the population. Living amongst riches rather than rags is by no means a guaranteed road to happiness.

Moreover, among western countries, people in wealthier nations often report being less happy than those in poorer ones. Ireland, for example, with one third of the per capita income of the United States, ranks consistently higher on the life satisfaction scale.[2] And the percentage of the U.S. population reporting themselves to be

---

[1]After his seminal article (1974).

[2]There are substantial intercountry differences. The French, for example, claim to be much less happy than the Belgians. Researchers conclude that this in part reflects social norms about reporting life satisfaction.

TABLE 11.1   Income and Reported Happiness

Income Quartile	Percent "Satisfied" or "Very Satisfied" with Life as a Whole	Percent "Very Happy"
Lowest quartile	70%	19%
Second quartile	78	22
Third quartile	82	25
Highest quartile	85	28
Income refused or don't know	83	27

Source: Ingelhart and Rabier (1986, 23).

"very happy" has remained roughly constant since 1957, despite personal consumption expenditures per capita having roughly doubled (Durning 1991, 156–158).

Why is it that money doesn't buy much happiness, and only does so up to a point? We will consider two answers to this question, the first rooted in the psychology of consumption, the second in the material realities of modern life.

11.2 Social Norms and the Rat Race

Here is Adam Smith (1966), writing in the year 1759:

> From whence, then, arises that emulation which runs through all the different ranks of men, and what are the advantages which we propose by that great purpose of human life which we call bettering our condition? To be observed, to be attended to, to be taken notice of with sympathy, complacency, and approbation are all the advantages which we can propose to derive from it. It is the vanity, not the ease or the pleasure which interests us. (70)

I have an eleven-year-old friend, who recently reported to his mother that he wanted a pair of brightly colored, baggy pants manufactured by a company called Skidz. These pants were retailing for $54, and so his mother was a bit reluctant to buy him the pants. She offered to make him a pair that looked and felt identical, figuring she could do that for as little as $10. "No way," said her son. The homemade pair would not have the Skidz label on the back and that was really what made them *cool*. She asked him if he really wanted her to spend $44 for a label, and he said without hesitation, "Yes."

In our affluent society, access to food and shelter sufficient for *basic* survival is widely, though not universally, available.[3] Under these circumstances, much consumption of goods and services takes on a profoundly "social" character. The utilitarian value of the Skidz pants—their warmth, comfort, and cheerfulness—was much less important to my friend than the fact that they were "way cool." Along the same lines, the pleasure felt by the owner of an expensive sports car lies not only in the excitement of fast driving, but also, and perhaps more importantly, in the image of a fast-driving man the car provides to both the owner and others.

---

[3]The growth in demand at homeless shelters and soup kitchens in our country reminds us of the severity of this problem.

The social norms that we satisfy through our consumption are established in the communities in which we seek membership and recognition. The type of community may range from a romantic community of two, to the nuclear or extended family, to a circle of friends, to a neighborhood, to a religious or ethnic group, to a union or professional organization, but the need to belong to at least one of these groups is a powerful motivating force. Critics of growth argue that much of our consumption—from the clothes we wear, to the food we eat, to the cars we drive—is geared not only or even primarily to attain physical warmth, nourishment, comfort, or transportation, but rather to attain membership and recognition in one of these communities.

The point here is *not* to pass a value judgment on this process in which we all participate. Rather, the idea of consumption norms simply explains the observation that money fails to buy much happiness. On the one hand, greater income increases access to intrinsically useful goods and services. On the other, as people grow wealthier the expectations of the community rise, and keeping up with social consumption norms becomes more costly.

One can divide the social motives for consumption into three rough categories: bandwagon, snob, and Veblen effects (Leibenstein 1950).[4] **Bandwagon effects** refer to a desire to consume something because others are as well, in order to conform to a social norm. Television commercials frequently play on the bandwagon effect. McDonald's recently ran a campaign advertising "Food, Folks and Fun." The message was clear: Come on down and join the party, and incidentally, you can eat here too.

At the same time, Burger King was trying to set itself off from the crowd with its slogan: "Sometimes, You Gotta Break the Rules." The appeal here was to the **snob effect**—the desire to do or consume something because others aren't. The snob effect is usually attributed to those buying expensive products to differentiate themselves from the common herd. But the sentiment may also be exploited, as in the Burger King case, to sell the humble hamburger. Or to take another example, it can be seen in the college professor who takes pride in driving a beat-up car to show that he, unlike the rest of the world, does not care about material goods. The desire for Skidz pants expressed by my friend's son showed both bandwagon and snob influences—they were cool both because cool people were wearing them and because uncool people were not.

The words "bandwagon" and "snob" are perhaps poorly chosen, because they have rather negative connotations. But the desire to join in and the desire to be different in fact reflect quite normal, universal, and important social drives. For example, the desire to "get ahead" in any pursuit—sport, music, science—reflects both the snob effect (get ahead of one's peer group) and the bandwagon effect (become like those who are already ahead).

The final social motive underlying consumption is named for Thorstein Veblen, an economist who argued that status could often be achieved in our society through the open display of wealth, what he termed "conspicuous consumption."[5] The **Veblen effect** is the purchase of expensive goods in order to illustrate to the community that the owner is a person of "substance"—that is, someone with money and the power that money brings. Its purpose is to elicit envious statements such as "He wears a

---

[4]Bagwell and Bernheim (1996) explore the microfoundations of Veblen-type consumption decisions in a signaling context.

[5]For a recent reformulation, see Bagwell and Bernheim (1996).

Rolex" or "She drives a BMW" or "He belongs to the High Society Country Club." Part of the "coolness" of Skidz pants was certainly their high price—wearing them said to the rest of the kids in the class: "My parents have got the power to get me what I want, even if it costs a lot of money." While the Veblen effect is related to the snob effect, the two are not identical. Veblen goods hold appeal primarily because their expense denotes membership in a certain social class; as noted, the definition of a snob good varies from consumer to consumer and need not involve expensive goods.

To the extent that material consumption is not geared to utilitarian functions but is rather a means to an end of satisfying social needs for membership and status in a community, it is not surprising that attaining more material goods fails to increase happiness to any significant degree. Among both poor and rich, bandwagon and snob effects will greatly influence the degree of satisfaction obtained from consumption. Whether it is the right sound system to impress your friends, the right bike for joining a motorcycle gang, the right T-shirt to wear to a party, the right beer to serve at a cookout, the right restaurant to please your sweetheart, the right suit to keep your job, the right school for your children, or the right street address to get into a particular golf foursome, membership and recognition in the community is an important by-product of consumption. As people get wealthier, "basic" needs multiply; in other words, it costs more to satisfy social norms.

Having said that, it is clear that many people do *want* more material things. Indeed, survey research reveals that "getting ahead" in terms of income is clearly correlated with increases in reported life satisfaction. While rich people are on average only a bit happier than poor people, people who have *recently* gotten richer are much more satisfied with their lives than people who have *recently* gotten poorer. Social satisfaction from consumption apparently requires not just keeping up but getting ahead of "the Joneses." *Exceeding* the consumption norms established by one's peer group, family, and personal expectations appears to be the material route to happiness.[6]

However, while "getting ahead" may make sense from the individual perspective, competitive consumption is a strategy that yields much smaller benefits to individuals when pursued at society-wide level. If everyone is racing for entry into the next highest social group, it becomes much harder to get there; and for every winner in the race, there will be losers. Moreover, everyone now needs to run harder just to stay in the same place.

The common name for this kind of situation is a **rat race.** The two distinguishing features of a rat race are that (1) everyone would be better off if the race was canceled, and (2) given that everyone else is racing, each individual is better off trying to win.

This situation can be analyzed through the so-called **prisoner's dilemma** model. (Suggestion: Stall your class by asking your professor to explain the name "prisoner's dilemma.") Figure 11.1 illustrates the situation facing two students, Arnold and Maria, who have been asked to bring soft drinks to a party. Each student can choose to bring either Coca-Cola or budget cola. For the purposes of argument, assume that the quality of the products are identical—blindfolded, people on average don't prefer one to the other. (Suggestion: Stall your class by bringing in supplies for a demonstration taste test.) But Coke, given its large advertising budget, has developed some name recognition.

Suppose that the initial social norm among the students is to drink the budget brand. If both parties then go for the budget brand, nobody is embarrassed by bringing

---

[6]These ideas are developed further in Mishan (1968), Scitovsky (1986), Daly (1987), and Schor (1991).

Maria

		Coke	Budget
Arnold	Coke	$U_M = 8$ $U_A = 8$	$U_M = 7$ $U_A = 12$
	Budget	$U_M = 12$ $U_A = 7$	$U_M = 10$ $U_A = 10$

U_M = Maria's utility
U_A = Arnold's utility

FIGURE 11.1 The Rat Race as a Prisoner's Dilemma

a product perceived to be cheap. As a result, the utility of both students is 10. This is clearly preferred to an outcome in which the social norm is to buy Coca-Cola—since the quality is the same, and the cost is higher. As a result, the Coke–Coke outcome yields utility of only 8 to each student.

But in this setup, it will be hard to maintain budget–budget choices as the social norm. Consider what happens if Arnold goes budget while Maria shells out for Coke. Maria receives (subtle) praise for exceeding the social norm, so her utility rises to 12, while Arnold is (quietly) shamed and finds his utility falling to 7. The same holds true in reverse if Maria buys budget while Arnold goes with Coke.

While both parties would prefer the budget–budget outcome, both have strong incentives to "cheat" on any informal agreement to maintain the budget-brand social norm. If on the one hand, Maria chooses budget, Arnold can gain at Maria's expense by exceeding the social norm and going for Coke. If on the other hand, Maria exceeds the norm, Arnold is better off defending himself by doing the same. Regardless of what choice Maria makes, Arnold is better off choosing Coca-Cola, and vice versa.

Landers, Rebitzer, and Taylor (1996) identify a real-world prisoner's dilemma operating in professional organizations. They find in a survey of legal firms that attorneys are "overworked" in the sense that they would like to trade increases in income for time off. But publicly, lawyers are afraid to admit their desire for shorter hours, fearing that this will signal to partners that they are unproductive (even if they are not). As a result, the social norm for hours worked is too high—everyone would be made better off if a lower-standard workweek could be agreed on and enforced. This change in norms would scale back the rat race, lowering both incomes and material consumption, while raising leisure time.[7]

By framing the rat race as a prisoner's dilemma, we can see how social consumption norms get ratcheted upward. A rat race will often emerge whenever people send social signals through their consumption or workplace behavior, and especially when bandwagon, snob, or Veblen effects dominate the motives underlying the desire for more material goods. And, if the social satisfaction obtained from material gain is indeed

---

[7]The authors frame their argument in a signaling context. The key assumptions are that the pool of professionals reap spillover benefits from having more productive team members, and that long hours are a signal for high productivity. For more on overwork, see Schor (1991) and Application 11.1.

dependent on surpassing one's neighbors, economic growth simply cannot quench the social desires that people attempt to satisfy through increased consumption.

11.3 Positional Goods and Consumption Externalities

One reason that money does not seem to buy much happiness is because of the social psychology of consumption. However, another reason is rooted in the realities of modern-day growth. One of the paradoxes of our affluent society is that, even as we grow wealthier, access to certain goods becomes more and more difficult. Consider the widespread shortage of "affordable housing" in the United States. In the 1970s, when median family income was about the same in real terms as it is today, the average mortgage payment on a house was about 18% of family income. Now it is 30% or higher, effectively putting home ownership out of the reach of an increasing number of Americans.

Paradoxically, the housing shortage is occurring at the same time that many cities face massive vacancy rates: Boarded-up buildings are a common sight in many of our cities. The shortage is clearly not one of housing units but rather of units in "desirable" neighborhoods: ones that are prosperous and safe, and have good schools. However, housing in desirable neighborhoods is a good for which there is either a fixed or at least very inelastic long-run supply. Thus, one effect of the massive "suburbanization of America" that has been occurring over the last forty years has been an increase in the price of housing within the commuting shadow of all major cities. At the same time, these areas developed many of the urban problems that people were attempting to leave behind: increasing congestion, traffic jams, longer commuting time, higher crime rates, and in general a lower quality of life for residents. Simultaneously, citizens left behind in the inner city have seen their communities deteriorate drastically as members of the middle class fled to the suburbs, shrinking the tax base of the cities.

Driving this process has been increased private demand for "better housing." While many individuals did get such housing, the social outcome was less positive. The limited supply of this good in the suburbs was rationed through both higher prices and increased congestion. Concurrently, property values in the cities plummeted, and the quality of life for many residents there has become increasingly desperate. Two economic concepts help explain this phenomenon: positional competition and consumption externalities.

Goods with a fixed or inelastic long-run supply, such as uncrowded suburbs within an easy commute to the city, are referred to as **positional goods. Positional competition** is the competition for these goods. Some simple examples of positional goods are fifty-yard-line Super Bowl tickets, Rembrandt paintings, or spacious seaside vacation homes. Less obvious examples include commuter highways, slots in prestigious four-year colleges, creative work, jobs with status and authority, green space in the city, accessible wilderness, and clean air and water.

As people grow wealthier, the demand for these positional goods increases. In the face of this growing demand, some rationing scheme is necessary. For privately owned goods, say football tickets, the price rises to eliminate the excess demand and clear the market. For many **public goods,** however, the price mechanism is ineffective. Here the rationing takes place through congestion, for example, as seen in traffic jams.

Higher relative prices for positional goods combined with increasing congestion in their consumption has generated a degradation in the quality of life for many people, at the same time that the per capita consumption of TVs, dishwashers, camcorders, fast-food outlets, computers, pain relievers, and a million other commodities has increased. To obtain access to many of the goods that people took for granted only a generation ago, we must either pay a higher proportion of our income or accept a degradation in quality. This is not to say that economic growth has been on the balance negative. The point is that increased positional competition generates an important and often unrecognized cost of economic growth.

Hirsch (1976) likens positional competition to a concert hall, where the individuals in the front row stand up to get a better view, and then everyone in the entire arena has to stand. Eventually, everyone is uncomfortably up on their tiptoes, but no one can see any better than they could while sitting down! Once again, getting ahead makes sense from an individual perspective, but the social result is to leave everyone worse off.

Positional competition often generates **consumption externalities.** These are benefits and costs of consumption not borne by the consumer—in Hirsch's example, blocking a neighbor's view. Or consider the private decision to commute by car. Although it may save twenty minutes of the driver's time, it also reduces the speed at which others can get to work by contributing to traffic jams. More generally, the cumulative effect of thousands of private decisions to move to the suburbs is to introduce many of the problems of the city: increasingly depersonalized communities, deteriorating schools, rising crime rates, and environmental degradation.

Positive consumption externalities, on the other hand, play an important role in creating a livable neighborhood. For example, if a neighbor keeps up his house and yard in an attractive fashion, it increases the value of the surrounding property. Sociologist William Julius Wilson has argued that many of the problems facing inner-city minority teenagers, from unemployment to drug abuse, stem from the lack of a vital positive externality—middle-class role models among their neighbors (Wilson 1987).

Consumption externalities are important in other markets beside housing. An individual's decision regarding educational attainment has important externalities, both positive and negative. On the one hand, there is such a clear social benefit to having a populace able to read and write that all agree the government must subsidize and indeed mandate a basic education. On the other hand, advanced education is in many respects a type of positional competition. One's decision to obtain a master's degree in business administration increases one's chance of getting a scarce "prestige" job, but at the same time decreases the chances of those without the degree. "Credentials inflation"—the competitive process by which degree requirements for entry into a given career are ratcheted upward—is a negative consumption externality.

Pure positional competition is what economists call a **zero-sum game.** For every person who gains access to a positional good, someone else must give it up. As positional goods become more important in our economy, increases in income channeled into this competition fail to be translated into overall increases in human welfare. This holds doubly true when consumption decisions bear important negative externalities, as in the case of housing and advanced education.[8] These two factors help explain the paradox that although individuals act rationally to increase their wealth, collectively we fail to grow much happier.

---

[8]Of course, advanced education can have positive consumption externalities as well. Improvements in technology resulting from advanced training is the most obvious example.

11.4 Welfare with Social Consumption

It is useful to recast the arguments of the preceding section into our utility/social welfare function framework. To do so requires that we divide up each individual's consumption bundle into **competitive** and **noncompetitive** elements, X^c, X^{nc}. The former contains (1) rat race items—those that bring utility primarily because their consumption involves exceeding social norms; (2) positional goods; and (3) goods with significant negative consumption externalities. The noncompetitive bundle includes everything else: goods consumed primarily for their intrinsic utility (taste, warmth, relaxation); leisure time spent with family and friends; physically or intellectually challenging activities; and many environmental goods such as clean air, water, and health.

In practice, this competitive/noncompetitive distinction may be a difficult one to make. Under which category does bike riding fit? The biking experience itself is very noncompetitive, and yet some of the pleasure serious enthusiasts feel for the sport is driven by competitive social norms—wearing the latest clothing or owning the most up-to-date machine. Yet in principle it is possible to sort out the consumption components that are fashion- or status-driven from the consumption components of the sport itself.

By doing so, we can rewrite Aldo's utility function as:

$$U_A = U(\overset{+}{X_A^{nc}}, \overset{+}{X_A^{c}}, \overset{-}{X_{NA}^{c}})$$

The last term, X_{NA}^c, stands for the competitive consumption bundle of all people who are Not Aldo *(NA);* the negative sign above X_{NA}^c indicates that Aldo's happiness *decreases* as the social consumption of others goes up. Aldo still gets happier by increasing his consumption of both noncompetitive (X_A^{nc}) and competitive goods (X_A^c); more remains better for Aldo as an individual. But his overall happiness now depends on the consumption levels of his peer group.

There are two lessons to be learned from this form of the utility function. The first is that economic growth that increases the supply of competitive consumption goods need not increase happiness (though it may). Every time one person gets ahead, a new standard is set for the community. Indeed, competitive consumption goods are often sold by making people who don't buy the product feel worse off! (Consider, for example, the typical deodorant campaign that exploits insecurities about being left out and unhappy.)

The second lesson is that, under this form of the utility function, increases in the stock of noncompetitive consumption goods unambiguously raise social welfare. Many if not most environmental "goods"—human health, appreciation of natural beauty, respect for both human and nonhuman life—are primarily noncompetitive. One person's enjoyment of his health does not "raise the standard" to which others must aspire. Similarly, land set aside for parks is land not available for private development as part of status-enhancing positional competition. Thus a case can be made for weighting these items more heavily than material consumption in a social welfare function.

What are the economic implications of all this? Brekke and Howarth (2002) show that, when relative consumption becomes important, three conclusions emerge. First, taxes on the consumption of status goods become efficient; they increase overall well-being by discouraging excessive work effort and increasing leisure. They also reduce unnecessary production and thus pollution. Second, people tend to overvalue increases in private consumption (given the negative externalities imposed on others), and undervalue noncompetitive public goods and improved environmental quality. Thus willingness-to-pay measures need to be adjusted upwards to reflect the true increase in well-being generated by a cleaner environment. In the case of global warming, for example, they estimate that the efficient tax on carbon dioxide is 50% higher than that yielded by conventional benefit–cost analysis.

Finally, in economies where status goods are important, GDP growth fails to capture real increases in social welfare on yet one more ground. As discussed in Chapter 6, economists have in fact made several attempts to construct a social welfare index that reflects some of the disamenities of economic growth. The idea is to adjust our basic measure of economic growth—GDP—to better capture the "true" trend in social welfare over the last few decades. If you turn back to Table 6.3, you will find a description of the Genuine Progress Indicator, or GPI.

GPI claim proponents to have uncovered a dramatic slowdown in improvements in the average quality of life over the last few decades, while GDP continued to rise at a steady pace. The GPI does this in part by accounting for the negative consumption externalities arising from positional goods discussed in this chapter. For example, in addition to the conventional externality costs, Daly and Cobb deduct from augmented GDP the costs of urbanization, increased commuting time, and auto accidents. They also subtract the rising price of land.

Yet for purposes of the index, the GPI researchers accept the conventional assumption that "More is Better." According to the GPI authors: "Our calculus of economic well-being has failed to take into account that happiness is apparently correlated with relative rather than absolute levels of wealth or consumption. Having more is less important than having more than the 'Joneses.' Yet in the absence of any way to quantify this sense of relative well-being, we have ignored this important finding in our index, just as others have" (Daly and Cobb 1989, 415). If they had devised such a measure, it seems likely that net national welfare would have increased even less than they estimate over the past thirty years, despite the tremendous growth in GDP.

To summarize: If social norms drive much material consumption, and positional goods and consumption externalities are relatively important in the economy, a strong utilitarian argument can be made for environmental protection. The happiness trade-off between environmental protection and economic growth is not as great as it seems.

11.5 Controlling the Impact of Consumption

A society in which consumption becomes the primary means of achieving social status is known as a **consumer culture.** The reasons for the advance of the consumer culture in rich countries are complex, including factors as diverse as the increasing mobility of both workers and jobs and the subsequent breakdown in community, increasing exposure to television and advertising, and a decline in the moral influence of religion, which traditionally preached an antimaterialistic message.

Some people have argued that as environmental awareness spreads, people in wealthy countries can be persuaded to abandon their affluent lifestyles, and begin, for example, riding bikes to work. Yet, the advance of the consumer culture appears to be pervasive and very deep-seated. I see it best through a comparison of generational attitudes. I admit to being a bit shocked when I asked my six-year-old niece why she wouldn't let me cut the huge L.A. Gear tag off her new tennis shoes. "That's what makes them cool," she said. My young niece's strong brand identification—the shoes made her happy *because* of the label—was the result of a shift in marketing strategy by clothing firms. When I was small, firms marketed children's clothes to their parents, and the emphasis was on rugged and practical. Now Saturday morning cartoons are filled with clothing ads targeted directly at children, with the emphasis on beauty and status. My parents, of course, had much less exposure to marketing and find my attachment to many of our family gadgets a bit puzzling.

Thus, even if you believe that high levels of consumption in affluent countries are a major environmental threat, it is hard to imagine making much headway against the consumer culture via moral arguments alone. This section discusses two potential *economic* instruments for reducing consumption: **consumption taxes** and the **regulation of advertising.**

From the IPAT equation we know that the environmental impact of consumption can be reduced either by reducing consumption directly or by cleaning up the technology associated with producing and delivering consumption goods. The second strategy appears more attractive, both because it seems to entail less sacrifice and because it can accommodate the increasing demands of poor countries for a higher material standard of living. But in fact, as we shall see in this section, developing cleaner technologies also requires reducing consumption today in order to finance investment in research and development.

Many economists have argued for nonenvironmental reasons that the U.S. consumption rate is too high, or equivalently, that the national savings and investment rate is too low. During the 1980s, national savings declined from around 8% to 2.4% of net national product and by 2000 had actually gone negative, while the foreign debt skyrocketed. The argument is made that for the last two decades, we have been financing current consumption at the expense of investment in created capital, which in the words of economist William Nordhaus portends a "decline in living standards for the future" (Nordhaus 1989).[9] Nordhaus makes, in effect, a nonenvironmental sustainability argument for reducing current consumption.

Nordhaus and others have called for an increase in taxes (income or sales) to reduce consumption and increase savings and investment. The ultimate purpose, however, is to *boost* consumption in the future. This is clearly not the policy goal proposed here. Yet, if the revenues from such a tax were invested in the generation of new, clean technologies, such as those discussed in Chapters 18 and 19, this kind of policy could achieve the goal of reducing the environmental *impact* of consumption. This would be true despite the fact that consumption levels themselves had only temporarily declined.

Alternatively, taxes could be used to divert resources away from consumption in rich countries to sustainable development efforts in poor countries. Funds could be

---

[9]The existence of the savings rate decline has been challenged by, among others, Blecker (1990), who is nevertheless still worried about inadequate investment.

used for a variety of purposes, from debt relief, to family planning, to land reform or resource protection efforts, to transferring clean energy and manufacturing technologies to poor countries.

It is sometimes argued that high levels of consumption are necessary for a modern economy to operate, and that a reduction in consumption would lead to high levels of long-run unemployment. Does such a consumption–employment link exist? Not in the long run. For example, assume the government raises $100 million in taxes to pay for condoms for use in the developing world. In this case, the $100 million fall in consumption is made up for by an increase in spending in the birth control industry. Intuitively, as jobs are lost in the tourism industry (consumption), they are added in the manufacturing of new birth control devices. While short-run unemployment may increase, in the long-run workers will be able to find new jobs.[10]

The point here is that *consumption reductions* in rich countries need not imply *output or employment reductions*. Rather, the drop in consumption can be matched by an increase in consumption in poor countries, which can provide jobs in rich countries. (Such an increase in consumption in poor countries is desirable on environmental grounds for reasons discussed in the last part of this book.) Or consumption reductions may be matched by an increase in savings and investment in rich countries, which also provide employment. If this investment is focused in the direction of developing clean technologies, then the goal of reducing the environmental impact of consumption will have been achieved, despite the fact that overall consumption in the affluent country declines only temporarily.

As a final point, in rich countries, social consumption theory has a rather startling implication: Beyond an initial adjustment period, in which people lowered their expected consumption levels, a shift of resources from current consumption to investment or development assistance would not reduce overall social happiness or welfare.

Put in more practical terms, suppose that income taxes in the United States were raised gradually in a progressive fashion, so that ultimately the highest group faced a marginal tax rate of 50%, while poor Americans maintained the same tax rate. Suppose as well that the additional money raised was diverted to investment in environmental technology: to the training of scientists and engineers, and to research and development. Social consumption theory says that in the long run, on average, people would be just as content. (Incidentally, wealthy Americans did pay a 70% marginal tax rate or higher throughout the 1950s, 1960s, and 1970s.) The problem with this theory, of course, is that there is an initial adjustment period in which people are dissatisfied. Given this, the political prospects for new taxes to promote sustainability—either environmental or economic—are not favorable. For example, President Clinton's energy tax proposal of 1993, which targeted deficit reduction, was watered down to a small increase in the gasoline tax. Even then, it passed by a very narrow margin.

Beyond taxes, a second possible strategy for controlling consumption is to regulate advertising. For such a strategy to make sense, one must first make the case that advertising in fact raises aggregate consumption levels. It is possible that advertising merely causes people to switch brands, leading to no overall increase in consumption.

---

[10]For a more involved discussion of the business-cycle macroeconomic impacts of consumption-reducing tax increases, see Nordhaus (1989) and Moore (1990). The former concurs with this analysis; the latter presents a less optimistic, post-Keynesian rejoinder.

On the other hand, in the United States, we receive massive exposure to advertising. Indeed, TV might be thought of as the church of the late twentieth century. By the time the typical American reaches college, he or she will have spent three to four hours a week watching TV ads, about 100,000 of them in all (Durning 1991). These advertisements all preach a variation of the same underlying social message: satisfaction through purchase. Such a constant propaganda barrage may well induce us to consume more than we otherwise would.

Assuming that advertising does have a major positive impact on overall consumption, effective regulation of advertising remains a difficult task. From an economic point of view, advertising plays a very important function—fostering competition by providing consumers information about the availability, quality, or price of a product.[11] Advertising can be thought of as a useful product itself, the production of which generates a negative externality, in the same way that paper production generates water pollution. Regulation should focus on controlling the negative externality—the promotion of consumer culture—rather than the product itself.

One way this has been traditionally accomplished is through the regulation of advertising on children's television. The government sets limits on the number of minutes per hour that can be devoted to advertising and has in the past prohibited the mixing of advertisements and entertainment. These regulations were dramatically loosened in the early 1980s under the banner of deregulation by the conservative Reagan administration but were tightened up somewhat in the early 1990s (Durning 1991).

Another way to try and sort out "good" commercials from "bad" ones is by medium. Ads in the print and radio media have a harder time exploiting emotional weaknesses to develop brand identification than do television ads. They thus tend to provide much more useful information about price, quality, and availability. Local and trade-specific advertising also tend to be more information intensive than national advertising does. Perhaps reflecting the limited economic usefulness of national television advertising, many European countries have commercial-free television. (They finance the production of TV programs with tax dollars.)

In the United States, one possible policy measure would be to institute a "pollution tax" on national TV advertising. As with any tax, such a measure would cause firms to shift resources away from television to other media, or out of advertising altogether.

In the long run, any successful attempt to rein in the growth of per capita consumption in rich countries will require a broad social movement that challenges the consumer culture and its values head on, a discussion well beyond the scope of this book.[12] Economic analysis does provide us with some useful insights, however. First, policies of shared sacrifice may in fact lead to little reduction in overall welfare, if the happiness derived from consumption is relative. If this view is widely held, it suggests people will more likely accept a tax increase to reduce their consumption for a "good cause," such as their children's welfare. Second, reducing consumption in rich countries need not

---

[11]For a discussion of the economic costs and benefits of advertising, see Scherer (1980).
[12]See for example, Durning (1991), Daly and Cobb (1989), Wachtel (1983), or Schor (1991).

lead to an increase in unemployment. Rather, labor and other resources can shift into production of goods for consumption in poor countries or into investment in clean technologies. Finally, a common proposal to restrict the advance of consumer culture, regulation of advertising, must be approached carefully because of the economic benefit—information—that advertising can generate.

11.6 Summary

The central metaphor behind benefit–cost analysis and the efficiency standard is a perceived environment–growth trade-off. More environmental protection in the form of regulations, bans, and red tape means higher costs and ultimately fewer "goods" for consumers. Princeton economist Alan Blinder asks, "Why should everyone be required to have a Cadillac environment, 'regardless of the cost'?" (Blinder 1987)

Overconsumption critics respond in two ways. First, ecological economists argue that technology is increasingly less capable of providing substitutes for natural capital, and that the long-run costs of "business as usual consumerism" are much higher than efficiency advocates envision. Second, some economists have questioned the fundamental assumption that more is better, which underlies Blinder's defense of efficiency. Because much of the satisfaction derived from consumption is social rather than intrinsic in nature, and because of the negative externalities in the competition for positional goods that growth engenders, the benefits of economic growth are much smaller than conventionally measured.

If the more is better assumption underlying efficiency analysis is often simply wrong, then the case for pursuing safety or ecological sustainability instead is strengthened. When more isn't better, "efficient" outcomes aren't really efficient, that is, welfare enhancing. As a result, stricter safety or ecological sustainability standards *may actually be more efficient* than an approach grounded in conventional benefit–cost analysis.

The global impact of consumption growth is becoming larger as more and more people look to material consumption to satisfy social needs for membership and status in a community—the advance of consumer culture. Two policies were explored for controlling the growth of consumption. The first was a tax, with the proceeds going to finance either investment in clean technology or increased consumption in poor countries. An important point is that declines in consumption in rich countries need not reduce overall employment; instead, they can represent a shift of resources including labor into other productive sectors. However, as social consumption theory predicts, tax policies lower utility in the short run, and are thus very difficult to sell politically.

The second policy involved regulating advertising, on the grounds that it promotes the growth of an unsustainable consumer culture. The danger here is that advertising can play a useful economic function, providing information and promoting competition. One possibility would be a "pollution tax" on national television advertising, which tends to be heavy on emotional appeal and low on information content.

This chapter concludes the first part of the book, and our discussion of "How much pollution is too much?" At one end of the spectrum we have considered efficiency as a target. In learning about the efficiency standard, we explored the tools that economists have developed to measure environmental protection benefits and costs, and the use of benefit–cost analysis. We have also examined the logic of promoting efficiency over time (dynamic efficiency) through discounting, granting the neoclassical assumption that technological progress will offset all resource shortages and that, as a consequence, human welfare will continue to rise.

At the other end of the spectrum, we have considered two stricter standards: safety and ecological sustainability. Both these approaches reject benefit–cost analyses and argue for protecting the environment "regardless of the cost." But in evaluating these approaches we learned that there really is no such thing as a free lunch; ultimately trade-offs do emerge, even if they are not as severe as neoclassicals believe.

So, how much is too much? This ultimately is a values question and cannot be resolved by economics alone, but the goal of the last eleven chapters has been to provide information and analytical tools you need to better resolve the question in your own mind. In the next presidential election, global warming is likely to be an important issue. Whether you support a candidate speaking for an efficiency, a safety, or an ecological sustainability standard for carbon dioxide emissions, you now have a better understanding of the issues at stake in your decision.

APPLICATION 11.0

Overworked Americans

In the United States, the flip side of increasing consumption over the last thirty years has been increasing hours of work. Schor (1991) calculates that on the average, full-time employees worked an additional 163 hours per year more in 1987 than they did in 1969. For men, the increase was about 98 hours, for women, 305. The increase arose because of both longer hours per week and more weeks worked.

The increase in hours of work is surprising first because it goes against historical trends: Until 1940, the length of the workday fell continuously, and workers gained additional vacation time. This forward progress has continued in most European countries, which have strong unions. U.S. manufacturing employees work almost two months per year longer than their German or French counterparts.

The increase in work hours is also surprising because economists assume that leisure is a normal good: As people get richer they should consume more of it. Instead, leisure appears to be an inferior good. Since 1948 U.S. output per worker has more than doubled: In other words, we could consume at the level of our parents in early adulthood, and *take every other year off.* Instead, we work a little harder and consume more than twice as much.

1. Schor identifies two chief culprits behind the increased workweek: hiring incentives and the lack of a strong union movement to push for shorter hours. As far as incentives go, in spite of the fact that employers must, by law, pay time and a half for overtime, they seem to prefer this to hiring new employees. Why do you think this might be?

2.   Among salaried and professional employees, Schor argues that increased competition has led to a natural upward progression in hours spent at the office. The monster workweek experienced by young doctors is becoming common for corporate lawyers, accountants, architects, and other professionals. In an increasingly competitive environment, " 'enough' is defined not by some pre-existing standard like the length of the workday, but by the limits of human endurance" (Kanter, as cited in Schor 1991, 70). Some economists respond: There is nothing wrong with this lengthening of the workweek. If people didn't like it, they could just quit and choose less demanding jobs, with more leisure and less consumption. Do you agree?

KEY IDEAS IN EACH SECTION

11.1   This chapter considers arguments that economic growth in affluent countries fails to deliver increases in welfare. **The Easterlin paradox** refers to survey data showing that increases in income boost reported happiness only slightly, and only to about the median income level.

11.2   One way to explain the Easterlin paradox is that satisfaction from consumption depends on one's consumption relative to social norms. Social consumption patterns are influenced by **bandwagon, snob,** and **Veblen effects.** When people attempt to obtain happiness by competing in consumption levels, the process often degenerates into a self-defeating **rat race,** which can be modeled as a **prisoner's dilemma.**

11.3   **Positional competition** is competition over goods with a limited long-run supply, or **positional goods.** Private positional goods are rationed by their increasingly high price; **public goods** are rationed by congestion. Competition over pure positional goods is a **zero-sum game.** Negative **consumption externalities** are often generated through positional competition.

11.4   This section illustrates how the utility function changes in the presence of social consumption and positional goods. Goods must be divided up into **competitive and non-competitive consumption** bundles. While more of everything is still better at the individual level, externalities generated by other's consumption now depress each individual's utility. It is thus no longer true that increases in society-wide consumption must increase happiness.

11.5   A **consumer culture** is one in which the primary means of achieving social status is via material consumption. Two economic policies for reducing the spread of consumer culture are **consumer-reducing taxes** and the **regulation of advertising.** However, economic tools can change attitudes only if they are part of a much broader cultural movement.

REFERENCES

Bagwell, Laurie Simon, and Douglas Bernheim. 1996. "Veblen Effects in a Theory of Conspicuous Consumption." *American Economic Review* 86, no. 3:329–348.

Blecker, Robert A. 1990. "The Consumption Binge Is a Myth." *Challenge* 33, no. 3:22–30.

Blinder, Alan. 1987. *Hard Heads, Soft Hearts.* New York: Addison-Wesley.

Brekke, Kjell Arne, and Richard B. Howarth. 2002. *Status, Growth and the Environment: Goods as Symbols in Applied Welfare Economics.* Northampton, MA: Edward Elgar.

Daly, Herman E. 1987. "The Economic Growth Debate: What Some Economists Have Learned but Many Have Not." *Journal of Environmental Economics and Management* 14, no. 4:323–336.

Daly, Herman E., and John J. Cobb, Jr. 1989. *For the Common Good.* Boston: Beacon Press.

Durning, Alan. 1991. "Asking How Much Is Enough." In *State of the World,* 1991, edited by Lester R. Brown. New York: W. W. Norton.

Easterlin, Richard. 1974. "Does Economic Growth Improve the Human Lot: Some Empirical Evidence." In *Nations and Households in Economic Growth.* New York: Academic Press.

Hirsch, Fred. 1976. *Social Limits to Growth.* Cambridge, MA: Harvard University Press.

Ingelhart, Ronald, and Jacques-Rene Rabier. 1986. "Aspirations Adapt to Situations—But Why Are the Belgians So Much Happier than the French?" In *Research on the Quality of Life.* Ann Arbor: University of Michigan Press.

Landers, Renee, James B. Rebitzer, and Lowell J. Taylor. 1996. "Rat Race Redux: Adverse Selection in the Determination of Work Hours in Law Firms." *American Economic Review* 86, no. 3:349–372.

Leibenstein, Harvey. 1950. "Bandwagon, Snob and Veblen Effects in the Theory of Consumers' Demand." *Quarterly Journal of Economics* 64:183–207.

Mishan, E. J. 1968. *The Costs of Economic Growth.* London: Staples Press.

Moore, Basil J. 1990. "Why Investment Determines Savings." *Challenge* 33, no. 3:54.

Nordhaus, William. 1989. "What's Wrong with a Declining National Savings Rate?" *Challenge* 32, no. 4:22–26.

Schor, Juliet B. 1991. *The Overworked American.* New York: Basic Books.

Scitovsky, Tibor. 1986. *Human Desire and Economic Satisfaction.* New York: York University Press.

Smith, Adam. 1966. *The Theory of Moral Sentiments.* New York: Augustus M. Kelly.

Wachtel, Paul. 1983. *The Poverty of Affluence.* London: Free Press.

Wilson, William Julius. 1987. *The Truly Disadvantaged.* Chicago: University of Chicago.

PART

II

IS GOVERNMENT
UP TO THE JOB?

The first part of this book focused on an explicitly normative question: How much pollution is too much? We analyzed several possible answers to that question—efficiency, safety, and ecological sustainability—from both ethical and practical points of view. Having set a goal, at least in our own minds, we can now consider how to get there. As it turns out, we have one primary vehicle: government. From Chapter 3, we know that private markets generate too much pollution from *both* efficiency and safety perspectives. Thus, it is up to government to devise policies that modify market behavior and reduce pollution.

Government has a variety of tools at its command to attack the pollution problem, ranging from regulations and bans, to pollution taxes and marketable permit systems, to subsidy policies and infrastructure and R&D investments. But, before discussing policy details, we first need to consider a more central question: Is government up to the job?

In recent years, many people have become skeptical of government's ability to accomplish positive goals. This increased distrust may well have been fueled by the rising number and severity of problems we now expect government to resolve: shoring up disintegrating families, tackling increasingly violent crime and drug abuse, reducing unemployment, poverty, homelessness and hunger, controlling inflation, providing worker training and retraining, insuring the safety of consumers and workers, *and* protecting the environment. As we have demanded more from government, we have perhaps become more aware of its limitations.

This part of the book provides an overview of governmental efforts to control pollution. Chapter 12 begins by developing a theory of government action that highlights two primary issues: the information-intensive nature of environmental regulation and the potential for political influence in the regulatory process. In light of this theory, Chapter 13 reviews the major environmental legislation and Chapter 14 evaluates regulatory accomplishments and constraints. Finally, Chapter 15 deals with a vital, yet often overlooked, component of environmental regulation: enforcement and compliance.

The conclusions reached in this part of the book may seem harsh. At their best, regulators marshal the available information about environmental impacts and control costs and lurch in a steady, yet cumbersome, fashion to define and achieve an environmental goal: "efficiency," "safety," or "sustainability." At their worst, regulators become partners in a corrupt process where back-door deals are struck with disregard for environmental consequences. More generally, legislating, drafting, and enforcing regulations is a complex, tedious affair the outcome of which bears the stamp of the various organized interests likely to be affected. In general, interests with more resources have more influence.

Just as markets fail to deliver many desirable social goals, including a clean environment, so too does government have its own failings. It would be naive to think otherwise. The point of this section is to isolate and identify these problems so that government policies to promote a cleaner planet can become more successful. Is government up to the job of protecting the environment? This is really a rhetorical question. If it is not, we had better make it so. It is the principal tool we have.

THE POLITICAL ECONOMY OF ENVIRONMENTAL REGULATION

12.0 Introduction

In 1970, the U.S. Congress passed the Clean-Air Act, declaring it the law of the land that the air breathed by Americans should provide "an adequate margin of safety . . . requisite to protect the public health." Yet early in the twenty-first century, some tens of millions of people were still exposed on occasion to ground-level ozone (smog) concentrations considered dangerous; air toxic emissions at some industrial facilities still remained high enough to impose cancer risks greater than 1 in 1,000 to surrounding residents.

Is this evidence of government failure? Some would turn these figures around, saying instead, look how far we have come. Many cities now meet the ozone standard that didn't in 1970; more significantly, consider how many *would* be failing today if we had not taken the measures we have. We shall look in more detail at the overall impact of regulation, which can be viewed as a glass half-empty of half-full, in the next few chapters. However, many would still argue that thirty years is a long time to wait for a law to be enforced.

What lay behind this slow progress? Scientific uncertainty as to an "adequate margin of safety"? High compliance costs? Other priority areas at the Environmental Protection Agency (EPA)? Insufficient funds allocated to the EPA by Congress? Industry influence over legislators and regulators? All of these factors have played a role. The point here, however, is simply to illustrate that passing a law is only the first step in the long process of changing market behavior.

Economists have identified two main obstacles that stand in the way of effective government action to control pollution. The first is the highly **imperfect information** that regulators possess. To begin with, regulators are never given a clear-cut goal. For most pollutants, it is difficult, if not impossible, to define "safe" emission levels in purely scientific terms. Thus, a political definition of safety, based on technical information, must be worked out. More generally, the available risk assessments give only rough, if any, indications of health risks, while cost estimates can be equally unreliable. Moreover, regulators must often turn for information to the very sources they seek to regulate. Thus, as we shall see, many economists have focused on improving regulators' access to information as a crucial strategy for improving regulation.

However, ultimate uncertainty about the "facts" means that any decision to promote safety or efficiency, while informed by the technical merits of the case, will also leave substantial room for bureaucratic discretion. With the opportunity for discretion comes the opportunity for **political influence.** Government officials clearly have motivations other than fulfilling the letter of the law: career building or satisfying ideological preferences, for example. Given the existence of bureaucratic discretion, industry and environmental groups deploy substantial resources to affect elections, government legislation, and regulatory decisions.

This chapter will begin by detailing the generic process of environmental regulation and then go on to explore, in some detail, the obstacles presented by poor information and political influence. Finally, we consider briefly what lessons the disastrous environmental policies followed by the former Soviet Union hold for western market-oriented democracies. Chapter 13 will then provide a more detailed overview of the major environmental laws now in effect.

12.1 The Process of Environmental Regulation

Today, the level of ozone concentration in the air (known as the ambient pollution level) officially designated by the government as providing an "adequate margin of safety" is 0.08 parts per million (ppm). Where did this particular environmental regulation, and thousands of others like it, come from? The history of a regulation such as ozone control is a three-step process.

STEP 1. U.S. CONGRESS PASSES BILL

Of course, step 1 doesn't come out of nowhere. First, there must be a generally perceived environmental problem. Next, some enterprising congressperson or congressional aide decides to make the problem a top issue. Then legislation is drafted, and industry and environmental lobbyists line up support for and against and try to insert friendly amendments. Finally, legislation is passed, and the President signs on.

Even though this first step takes several years, the legislation is usually not very specific. Because of compromises struck between various parties, the language of the bill is often purposefully vague or even contradictory. All this leads to:

STEP 2. EPA DRAFTS REGULATIONS

Congress usually delegates to the EPA the hard work of figuring out the exact meanings of terms such as "safety," "prudent," and "reasonable balance." The EPA tries to translate the bill's language into actual regulations, specifying either allowable levels of emissions or of ambient pollution.

As we saw in Chapter 10, the process of creating a major new regulation requires the EPA to generate a regulatory impact analysis, a technical document that includes extensive documentation of both the scientific basis for its decision and its likely economic impact, including compliance costs. Yet the EPA most often has only limited information about the environmental impacts of pollutants and the technologies available for their control. Thus, during the process of drafting regulations, the agency will ask for comments from industry and environmental groups. Before the regulations can become law, they must also officially go through several rounds of public comment, to which the agency is legally required to respond. Thus, interest groups are formally incorporated into the decision-making process.

Part of this is self-defense on the EPA's part—many decisions the agency makes will be appealed or one side or the other will sue. Former EPA administrator William Ruckelshaus estimated that 80% of the EPA's rules were subsequently challenged in court (Bryner 1987, 117). For example, in the late 1970s the ozone standard mentioned previously was revised upward from 0.08 ppm to 0.12 ppm under the threat of industry lawsuits, and this revision itself was challenged in court by both industry and environmentalists. In 1997, after again being sued by environmentalists and in the light of new scientific evidence, the EPA tightened the standard back to the original 0.08 ppm.

This information-gathering and public-comment phase can take a couple of years when it proceeds smoothly. Generally, however, Congress fails to appropriate enough money for the EPA to do all its tasks, and certain regulations get put on the back burner. Finally, the President's staff in the Office of Management and Budget reviews the new regulation and may send it back to the EPA with recommended revisions.

Typically, the EPA regulations will provide general guidelines for industries and municipalities to follow. However, the implementation details are left to:

STEP 3. STATE GOVERNMENTS IMPLEMENT AND ENFORCE REGULATIONS

The EPA often requires state governments to submit plans detailing how they intend to achieve the agency's goals. In the ozone case, for example, the state agency would need to tell the EPA what measures it intended to take to control emissions from vehicle tailpipes and stationary sources such as petroleum refineries in order to come into compliance with the 0.08 ppm ambient air standard. Failure to do so would, theoretically, result in the EPA mandating certain measures, although it might just result in more delay. Thus, the hard economic choices are often left to state officials. Enforcement, too, is primarily a state function, although the EPA does have its own enforcement division to supplement state efforts.

There are three major points to be taken from this brief review of the legal process. First, even when it operates on schedule, drafting regulations is a cumbersome and time-consuming process. Because information about benefits and costs is highly imperfect and not widely available, legislators and regulators have provided many opportunities for affected parties to explain their positions.

In this process, the United States has adopted a **judicial model of regulation.** The EPA is expected to adhere to strict procedural guidelines for accepting and addressing comments and must build a quasi-legal case for each major regulation it issues. Even under ideal circumstances, regulators gather their information in a forum where both sides are doing their best to obscure, rather than clarify, the underlying issues. This process tends to exaggerate differences over scientific and economic issues rather than generate a consensus position the agency can accept as the "truth."

Moreover, those interested in stalling regulations have ample opportunity to do so merely by flooding regulators with extraneous information. For example, about seven feet of shelf space was required to hold more than 4,000 comments, all of which required responses, that the EPA received on a single proposal (Bryner 1987, 115). "Paralysis by analysis" is a frequent outcome.

Finally, the regulatory process can be influenced at dozens of points. The following provides only a partial list of opportunities for interested parties to shape the final outcome: drafting of initial laws or insertion of amendments; discussions with high EPA officials or mid-level technicians involved in the agency's day-to-day work; formal and informal public comments; limiting or enlarging the budget that Congress and state legislators provide for regulatory agencies to do their work; meeting with the President's oversight agency in the Office of Management and Budget; influencing state implementation plans and state enforcement mechanisms; suing in court for changes once regulations have finally been put into place; and, finally, bargaining with enforcement officials over compliance.

Given the complex nature of the regulatory task, regulators *must* turn to industry and private groups for information about the potential benefits and costs of regulation. Moreover, since Congress itself has no way of knowing whether the EPA is making wise decisions, following our familiar system of checks and balances, the regulatory process itself has been consciously opened up to all interested parties. A complex, legally binding, decision-making process (the judicial model) has been put in place to prevent abuse of power by regulatory bureaucrats. Yet, the politics of information gathering itself has often yielded regulatory gridlock.

12.2 Regulation under Imperfect Information

The Environmental Protection Agency was founded in 1970 as an independent agency within the executive branch of government. It now employs more than 16,000 people in 10 regional offices and Washington, DC, with an annual budget of more than $6 billion. The agency is required to develop, implement, and enforce regulations under dozens of different laws. In addition, the EPA has many other ongoing projects and responsibilities, including the regulation of tens of thousands of water pollution sources and hazardous waste dumps, hundreds of thousands of stationary air pollution sources, millions of automobiles, and hundreds of new chemicals and pesticides introduced each year (Bryner 1987, 94).

To accomplish these tasks, the EPA is obviously provided only limited resources. Thus, the agency has to determine priorities—not all of its regulatory functions can be performed adequately without spreading personnel too thin. As a result, in virtually all of its decisions, the agency gathers or generates less than full information about the problem before acting.

The extent of this information gap was revealed by a joint EPA-Amoco study of benzene air pollution at an Amoco oil refinery in Virginia. In 1990, the agency issued regulations to control benzene emissions from wastewater ponds at refineries. These regulations, based on research done in 1959, proved dramatically far off base. When the joint study project was completed in 1993, ponds were discovered to be polluting at a level twenty times lower than predicted, while the real benzene pollution problem arose on the loading docks where fuel was pumped into barges.

Amoco eventually constructed a $41 million treatment system to deal with pollution from the ponds, while much more extensive pollution from the loading docks, which could have been controlled for $6 million, went unregulated and unabated.[1] How could such a situation develop? In general, prior to writing a regulation, the EPA has neither the staff nor the legal right to conduct the kind of intensive examination of an industrial facility as it eventually did in the Amoco case. Usually, the agency can sponsor only limited research of its own; as a result it must turn to industry, environmental groups, or university researchers for much of its data.

In addition to relying on outdated or poor information, the EPA must also contend with a **reporting bias** when it turns to industry for information about compliance costs. To illustrate the problem, suppose the EPA seeks to regulate a pesticide thought to contaminate groundwater. The agency is considering a ban on the use of a pesticide in high-risk counties. As is discussed in the next chapter, pesticides are regulated under an efficiency standard—Congress has directed the EPA to weigh benefits against costs in this case. Figure 12.1 illustrates our efficiency standard diagram.

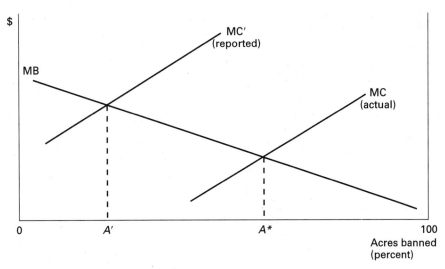

FIGURE 12.1 Regulation with Imperfect Information

[1]The EPA refused to grant Amoco a waiver based on the study's results. The agency said that loading dock regulations will be forthcoming in the mid-1990s. See "What Really Pollutes?" 1993.

The true marginal benefits and costs of the ban are reflected by the curves labeled MB and MC. If the EPA had access to this information, efficiency would require a ban applying to A^* acres. However, suppose the EPA must rely on agrichemical company sources for information about how much it will cost farmers to switch over to alternative pest control methods. Industry has a clear incentive to lie and overstate the cost (MC′). If the industry does so and the EPA uses the industry estimates, the agency will ban A' acres, an inefficiently low number.

There are two responses to this reporting bias problem. The first is to improve the **in-house analytic capability** of the agency. While the EPA will never have the resources to fund all the research it needs, concentrating on training and retaining technical personnel is a basic aspect of improved regulation. However, political developments can work against this goal. For example, following the general trend toward privatization of services, much of the EPA's technical work over the last two decades has been contracted out to private consulting firms. The ostensible motive was to save money (a goal that, in fact, proved elusive), but the net result was to reduce the agency's technical capabilities. Reliance on contractors reached the point, according to some critics, that the agency could not even evaluate whether contract work was being performed well.[2] Moreover, many of the consulting firms also depend for their livelihoods on contracts from industries regulated by the EPA. Reducing outside contracting would help build up the EPA's technical expertise and reduce conflicts of interest.

The second approach to the information problem is to rely on so-called **incentive-compatible regulation.** Regulation designed to elicit truthful information is called incentive-compatible because the *incentive* for the regulated party is *compatible* with the regulatory goal. Using the mix of tools at their command, regulators can, in fact, do better than is illustrated in Figure 12.1 As we will discuss more fully in Appendix 16B, it turns out that if regulators were to control pesticide use by taxing rather than banning it, then firms wold have an incentive to *understate* rather than overstate their control costs. In Appendix 16B we also find that an appropriate mix of taxes and marketable permit systems (discussed more fully in Chapters 16 and 17) can help provide just the right incentives for truth telling.

12.3   Bureaucratic Discretion and Political Influence

Regardless of the degree to which the EPA is able to hone its information-gathering and evaluation abilities, regulatory issues will never be resolved in a clear-cut fashion. The ambiguous and often contradictory goals provided by Congress, as well as the underlying uncertainty in scientific and economic analyses, insure that bureaucrats will retain substantial **discretion** in regulatory decision making. Because regulatory decisions impose substantial costs on affected industries, businesses will devote resources to influence the discretion that regulators exercise (in ethical, questionably ethical, and unethical manners) just as they devote resources to minimizing labor or energy costs.

In addition, simply because a business lobbies for regulatory relief does not mean that the relief is unjustified. It remains true that industry has the best knowledge

---

[2]See the congressional testimony of Joel S. Hirschorn, quoted in "Cleaning Up" 1990, and "U.S. Says Lack of Supervision" 1992.

about the likely impact of regulation and that bureaucrats have the power to arbitrarily impose substantial burdens on firms for reasons that are not obvious. Thus, the ability of industry (and environmental groups) to lobby regulators is not necessarily a bad thing. The problem is that legitimate access can become transformed into undue influence. This section will consider factors that motivate bureaucrats to stray from "doing their job."

Environmental regulators are expected by the public to pursue their congressionally mandated goals: efficiency or safety in pollution control. However, like all other people, they have personal interests to consider. To the extent that they are able, bureaucrats are likely to use their positions to satisfy three types of goals: agency building, external career building, and job satisfaction.

Many observers of bureaucracy (both governmental and corporate) have argued that a primary goal of managers is **agency growth.** Protecting and enlarging the agency budget, of course, can make the agency more effective in doing its primary job, but it also provides more perquisites (new computers, travel, opportunities for promotion, etc.) and prestige for agency personnel. A bias toward unwarranted growth may lead to "over-regulation" (especially from an efficiency point of view) as the agency personnel engage in new activities to justify greater funding. On the other hand, it may just lead to wasted money.

The second factor that regulators keep in mind is **external career building.** A few years ago I interviewed for a job in the Antitrust Division of the U.S. Justice Department. The typical career track, I was told, involved working at Justice for five years, at which point one's salary topped out. Most people then went on to work for law firms or economic consulting firms that *defended* companies from antitrust suits. This so-called **revolving door** between industry and its regulators is widespread. EPA employees need to keep in mind future career options when making tough regulatory decisions.

While there are some jobs in environmental organizations or academic institutions, most private-sector jobs for people with experience in the EPA, and virtually all the high-paying ones, are in private industry. Table 12.1 provides a partial listing of some EPA top administrators who have subsequently worked for industries in the field of hazardous waste management *only.* (The administrator is the EPA chief.)

Table 12.1 provides only a partial view through the revolving door, since it focuses on a single industry and only on top administrators. Indeed, one could point to a few top EPA administrators with environmental credentials.[3] The fact that the individuals listed in Table 12.1 went on to work for industries that they previously regulated does not necessarily mean that they were unable to set aside private interests to serve their public mission. However, the potential for conflict of interest clearly exists. More significantly, in the struggle to define exactly what the public interest really is, top policy makers are clearly aware of the industry position since they are on intimate terms with many from that side of the aisle. They may be less aware of what it is like to live next to a hazardous waste dump.

This leads us to the third bureaucratic motivation that might influence regulatory policy: **job satisfaction.** Are bureaucrats likely to use their discretion to draft and

---

[3]David Gardner, an assistant administrator under President Clinton, was a Sierra Club employee. William Reilly, Bush's EPA administrator, served as head of the (conservative) environmental group the Conservation Foundation.

TABLE 12.1 The Revolving Door: EPA and the Hazardous Waste Industry

Name	Government Position	Industry Position
William Ruckelshaus	Administrator, EPA	Director of Weyerhauser[a], Monsanto[a], CEO of Browning Ferris[b]
Douglas Costle	Administrator, EPA	Chairman, Metcalf and Eddy[c]
Lee Thomas	Administrator, EPA	CEO, Law Environmental[c]
Walt Barber	Acting Administrator, EPA	VP, Chemical Waste Management[b]
Al Alm	Deputy Administrator, EPA	VP, SAIC[c]
Joan Bernstein	General Counsel, EPA	VP, Chemical Waste Management[b]
Chris Beck	Assistant Administrator, EPA	CEO, Air & Water Technologies[c]
Rita Lavelle	Assistant Administrator, EPA	Consultant to waste industry
Jack Ravan	Regional Administrator, EPA	Pres., Rollins Env. Services[b]
Jack Schram	Regional Administrator, EPA	Dir., Govt. Affairs, Waste Management[b]
Marcia Williams	Director, EPA Office of Solid Waste	Washington Rep., Browning Ferris[b]
James Sanderson	Policy Advisor, EPA	Attorney, Chemical Waste Management[b]
Gary Dietrich	Director, EPA Office of Solid Waste	VP, Consulting Firm doing work for Waste Management[b]
Brian Malloy	Enforcement Attorney, EPA	Attorney, Chemical Waste Management[b]
Jeff Miller	Enforcement Task Force, EPA	Attorney, Chemical Waste Management[b]
Susan Vogt	Deputy Asst. Administrator, EPA	Washington Rep., Law Environmental[c]

[a]Resource or chemical corporations regulated by the EPA.
[b]Hazardous waste firms.
[c]Superfund (waste cleanup) contractors or consultants.
Source: William Sanjour (1992, Appendix B). Used with permission.

enforce aggressive or meek laws? Three factors come to play here: **ideology, power, and the quiet life.** First, regulators with either an environmental or free-market ideological bent may satisfy their own personal preferences for more or less regulation. Second, regulators may impose harsh restrictions on industry because it provides them with power and authority. Conservatives have often charged that the EPA is staffed by power-hungry, environmental zealots. And on the face of it, it seems more likely that persons attracted to a job in the EPA would be sympathetic to environmental concerns.

While this claim is hard to evaluate in general, one can point to counterexamples. For example, Landy, Roberts, and Thomas (1990, 181) note that the EPA's Office of Pesticide Programs was transferred intact from the Department of Agriculture, where it had favored "expeditiously licensing new pesticides."

One factor that would mitigate environmental activism within the agency is the contrasting desire for "a quiet life." The road to advancement within a bureaucracy is often to avoid antagonizing outside interests and to proceed with caution when doing so. The outcome is an emphasis on procedure over substance. Stalon (1990) argues that this generates a substantial bias towards the *status quo.*

One of the most outspoken environmental critics of the EPA is William Sanjour, an agency employee whose job has been protected by the U.S. Congress under a whistle-blower provision. (Between 1989 and 1992, Sanjour, while still officially employed, was given no assignments in the agency.) Sanjour (1992) argues that EPA employees are more interested in keeping their heads low than in sticking their necks out. Because industry is highly concerned with the process of drafting the details of regulations, mid-level bureaucrats often find themselves in day-to-day contact with industry officials. Here, "in addition to real and hinted at job opportunities," EPA officials become aware that "people who cooperate with the lobbyists find that the lobbyist will lobby for their advancement with upper management. Those who don't cooperate will find the lobbyists lobbying for their heads" (9).

This section has identified three potential goals beyond their legislative mandate that bureaucrats might pursue: agency growth, external career building, and job satisfaction. Growth suggests, if anything, a tendency toward overregulation; career building would lead to underregulation; and job satisfaction might generate either. As a result, it is not possible to identify an *a priori* bureaucratic bias. However, it is worth keeping in mind that bureaucrats are people too. Like anyone else, they take pride in a job well-done—serving the public interest as they see it.

12.4 Who Wins the Influence Game?

The answer to this question, of course, depends upon whom you ask. Environmentalists would point to twenty or thirty years of delay in enforcing the Clean Air Act; industry would respond that the laws themselves make unrealistic demands. Rather than answer this question outright, we can identify the resources available to the two sides and the arenas in which the parties tend to prevail.[4]

The two types of resources in the political world are **votes** and **dollars.** In general, environmentalists are better at martialing voting support, while industry has greater monetary resources at its command. Tough environmental laws command broad public support in the polls, even when the opportunity cost of higher prices is explicitly factored in. Thus, environmentalists have a large natural political constituency. Moreover, environmentalists are a more trusted source of information about environmental issues among the public than either industry or government officials (McCallum and Covello 1989).

This advantage is translated into influence in the crafting of national environmental protection legislation. Ten major national environmental organizations (Sierra Club, National Wildlife Federation, National Audubon Society, Environmental Defense Fund, Natural Resources Defense Council, Wilderness Society, Nature Conservancy, Greenpeace, Ducks Unlimited, and World Wildlife Fund) represent about 12 million members. These groups hire experts to analyze the benefits and costs of new policies, lobbyists to spread this information and promote environmental legislation, and lawyers to sue government agencies. The combined annual policy analysis, lobbying, and legal budgets of these groups runs well into the millions of dollars, a substantial sum, but much less than the resources that industry can bring to bear. However, environmental dollars often have greater leverage among many legislators due to the votes they represent, as well as a higher perceived level of credibility.

---

[4]For a more formal approach based on information asymmetry, see Selden and Terrones (1993). Consistent with the observations below, their model predicts strong laws and weak enforcement.

It is probably fair to say that environmentalists have won substantial gains in drafting and passing national environmental protection laws. This is reflected in the general tendency of environmental law to set safety rather than efficiency standards for pollution control, as well as the passage of substantial environmental legislation under conservative Presidents Bush (senior) and Reagan.

Due to their ability to mobilize voters, grassroots environmental movements have also done well at the local level, particularly in blocking the siting of new facilities (power plants, landfills, incinerators) and, in some cases, promoting alternatives such as recycling. Environmentalists have also had some success leveraging their voting power at the state level (California, Wisconsin, New York) but have also faced severe challenges in states traditionally dominated by particular industries (Louisiana, oil, gas, and chemicals; and Kentucky, coal).

If environmentalists have the edge in votes, industry has a clear-cut dollar advantage. The Chemical Manufacturers Association (CMA), for example, has a $48 million annual budget. The Sierra Club, by contrast, has a budget of about $20 million, but at least a fifth of that goes to fund raising. The Sierra Club, in addition, focuses on a wide variety of environmental issues ranging from wilderness protection, to natural resource management, to pollution control. The CMA by contrast is more focused on the environmental regulatory process. Moreover, the CMA borrows most of its scientific expertise (toxicologists, epidemeologists, economists) from its member companies, while the Sierra Club must keep them on staff.

A few of the dozens of other major industry trade groups with a strong lobbying presence in Washington include the American Petroleum Institute, the Fertilizer Institute, the American Paper Institute, and the Chlorine Institute. In addition, most of the large chemical, petroleum, and manufacturing firms maintain their own Washington staffs, and/or hire DC law firms to lobby on their behalf (see "Doing More with Less" 1992, and "Earth Day" 1992).

Dollars can be used to buy a number of things useful for influencing the regulatory debate: technical studies, lobbying staff, the promise of future jobs, access to legislators and regulators and votes (through advertising).

As I have stressed, control over information is a crucial aspect of regulation. Thus, the ability to hire "experts" to conduct **technical studies** of benefits and costs is an important channel of influence. Grieder (1990) describes a "full court press" launched by industry against the EPA's proposed technological standard for injection of hazardous wastes into deep wells. The Chemical Manufacturers Association, along with many of its members—Monsanto, CYRO Industries, Dow, Dupont, BP Chemicals, Celanese, Cynamid, and ARCO—met repeatedly with mid-level EPA officials in 1989, providing them with data about the cost of the new proposals as well as warnings of plant shutdowns. Some of the lobbyists threatened political repercussions if the agency did not respond. According to one EPA official: "We were attacked on a technical basis—the kind of case they felt they could make in a lawsuit if we didn't yield. Industry argued there would be huge costs if we went forward with the proposed rule. Depending on who you listened to, it was the end of the world" (Greider 1990, 138).

The EPA's final rule was ultimately watered down substantially. The point here is not were the company's claims correct, which they may have been. Rather, in the information war surrounding the impact of the regulation, environmentalists did not have the resources to bring much expert testimony to bear. Moreover, even if they had access to information about costs, environmental groups did not have the **staff** capacity of the chemical companies. Dozens of industry lobbyists repeatedly delivered the same message to mid-level EPA officials, as well as to President Bush's staff. In this particular case, Greider (1990) provides some evidence that pressure from a close Bush adviser influenced the final EPA decision (Greider 1990, 140).

Money buys information, lobbying and legal staff, and **access** to politicians and regulators. Out-and-out bribery—I'll contribute $5,000 to your campaign if you vote against bill X—is not common in the United States, though it is not unknown. Instead, the more money one contributes to a political campaign (or party), the more often one gets to meet with the politician or his or her appointees at the EPA to make one's case known. In an information war, where all sides can make a "reasonable" case on the surface, access is easily translated into influence. For example, an EPA official would be unlikely to refuse to meet with the representatives of the Sunshine Chemical company if they had contributed several thousand dollars to his boss's political party. He would, however, be more likely to shunt off a meeting with a grassroots environmental group from Sunshine's hometown to someone lower down in the agency hierarchy. The more often he hears Sunshine's case, the more reasonable it is likely to seem.

Finally, dollars can buy votes through advertising. Good examples are found in California, where many laws are passed directly by the voters through ballot initiatives. An ambitious proposal put forward by environmentalists, dubbed "Big Green," was defeated after industry spent $16.5 million in opposition, more than four times what supporters could muster ("Environmental Initiative" 1990). However, buying votes is not easy. A nuclear industry TV campaign in Nevada actually increased opposition to the siting of a waste facility in the state ("Nevadans Dump" 1992). And just before writing this chapter, I witnessed an election in Washington State in which a former timber industry lobbyist raised almost $600,000, outspending her environmental opponent by 3–1, in a race for commissioner of public lands. The industry candidate blanketed the airwaves with what I thought were quite effective commercials, but ultimately still lost.

Industry has not been able to translate its dollar advantage into many clear-cut victories at the legislative level. Tough environmental laws remain on the books. However, industry is much more effective in using its resources to dilute the impact of these laws. Through the revolving door, domination of information generation and delivery, large legal staffs, and superior access to politicians and political appointees, industry probably wins more often than it loses in all of the steps subsequent to the passage of laws. From the public comment phase in the drafting of regulations by the EPA, through the implementation and enforcement of these laws by state officials, through the budgeting of resources to these agencies, through the opportunity for court challenges, through bargaining over compliance, industry has many opportunities to influence how the ultimate regulatory process will work.

Washington lawyer Lloyd Cutler, whose firm has represented many corporate clients, put it this way: "It would be wrong to think that corporations are on top or ahead. They feel very put upon or defeated. It's true that they manage to survive and deal and push things off—they feel the added costs of regulation exceed the benefits [editor's note: an efficiency perspective!]—but they would say the notion that they now control or dominate the health and safety agencies is just crazy." Still, Cutler explained, "It's harder to pass a law than to stop one. On the whole, I would say the professional lobbyists and lawyers prefer to live in this world where there are so many buttons to push, so many other places to go if you lose your fight" (Greider 1990, 134).

Given this balance of power—environmentalists with the edge in the national legislative arena, business dominant in the regulatory sphere—an unfortunate dynamic develops. Environmentalists, anticipating that laws will be weakened upon implementation, try to push through Congress very stringent, sometimes unachievable goals. Industry, galvanized by this threat, pours more resources into mitigating the regulatory impact.

One of the big losers in this regulatory bazaar is public respect for the law. Americans increasingly believe that government has been captured by "a few big interests" who are able to mold the law as they see fit. While in fact neither side fully dominates the entire process, the mere fact that so many aspects of regulation are open to negotiation invites scandal and public suspicion. If public belief in the ability of government to solve problems further diminishes, this in itself will pose a difficult challenge to resolving environmental problems.

There are many potential solutions to the problem of bureaucratic discretion and political influence; several will be explored later in this book. At this point we shall focus on the potential for political reform of the regulatory process itself.

12.5 Political Reform of Regulation

Efforts at gaining political influence are often a form of the positional competition discussed in the last chapter. In such a zero-sum game, the gains of one party can only come at the expense of another. Under these circumstances, a natural tendency is to overinvest resources in unproductive competition. This situation can be analyzed through the prisoner's dilemma model, last seen in our Chapter 11 discussion of the rat race. Figure 12.2 illustrates the situation in a hypothetical regulatory decision about an emissions standard.

Each side must decide how many lobbyists to deploy. If neither group lobbies, then a standard of 4 parts per million (ppm) will be set. Note that an identical result will occur if both sides send a lobbyist—the extra efforts cancel one another out. If environmentalists don't lobby and industry does, then a loose standard of 6 ppm will result. If, on the other hand, industry doesn't lobby and environmentalists do, a strict standard of 2 ppm will emerge.

What will be the likely outcome of this kind of setup? If there is no agreement to restrict lobbying, environmentalists must assume that industry will lobby (and vice versa for industry). Thus, each side will choose a lobbying strategy for defensive purposes, even though the same outcome could be achieved at lower cost. Moreover, the process is likely to escalate into a full-blown "lobby race" as each side tries to forestall the other from gaining an advantage.

An agreement to limit lobbying seems in the interests of both parties. If cheating on such an agreement were easily observable, the agreement would be self-enforcing: If industry observed environmentalists cheating, it could simply retaliate by sending in

		Environmentalists	
		Don't lobby	Lobby
Industry	Don't lobby	4 ppm	2 ppm
	Lobby	6 ppm	4 ppm

FIGURE 12.2 A Zero-Sum Lobbying Competition

its own lobbyist. However, if cheating is not easily detectable, as is the case in lobbying, the agreement will break down as each side cheats to protect itself from the possibility that the other will cheat!

The prisoner's dilemma model implies that cooperation rather than competition might be in everyone's best interest. How might this insight actually be applied in the regulatory arena? One approach is to adopt a **corporatist model of regulation.** Here, regulations would be explicitly decided in a bargaining context between representatives of "corporate" groups—the EPA, private firms, and environmental organizations.[5] In exchange for being included at the table, all the groups would have to agree to abide by and support the final outcome. The EPA would, thus, be given much more flexibility in determining policy and be insulated from subsequent lawsuits. In essence, the corporatist model accepts that "a few big interests" determine the details of government environmental policy and provides a more efficient forum for them to do so.

European countries have adopted a more corporatist approach to regulation than we have in the United States. The fruits of corporatism can be seen in efforts by the Netherlands; since 1989 the Dutch government has instituted a series of "environmental covenants" with different industries. These covenants are voluntary agreements among government regulators and industry to reduce specific pollutants by specified amounts, which once signed have the force of a contract under civil law (see Bryner 1987, and Ministry of VROM 1994).

However, it is not clear how well corporatist regulation really works, nor whether it can be successfully translated to the United States.[6] Corporatism requires trimming back general public access to decision makers and is often perceived as a restriction of democracy. Who, for example, gets a seat at the table? Indeed, some believe that the environmental movement has already been split between the "conservative" DC-based national groups and more "radical" grassroots organizations, with the latter accusing the former of selling out to industrial interests (see "War Among the Greens" 1992). Moreover, the national groups have few members from working-class or minority communities, which have their own environmental interests.

Unlike European countries (and Canada), the United States does not have a strong labor or social-democratic political party to counterbalance the political

---

[5]Bryner (1987) presents the conventional arguments for corporatist regulation. Landy et al. (1990) attack corporatism as "managed pluralism" but defend a stronger leadership role for the EPA.

[6]For a harsh critique of Finnish corporatism, see Hukinnen (1995).

influence of business. Partly for this reason, Americans have been much more distrustful of placing discretionary decision-making power in the hands of government bureaucrats than have Europeans. In the United States, it is not clear that the national environmental groups—unaccountable to the voters—or indeed the EPA, have the power to represent and enforce the public's general interest in environmental protection. Thus, many people would oppose trading in the restrictions imposed on bureaucratic discretion under the current judicial regulatory model for a more goal-oriented, but less open, corporatist model.

If excess resources are indeed being devoted to influencing the political process, a straightforward economic response would be tax lobbying. A more feasible proposal would perhaps be to eliminate the status that lobbying now holds as a **tax-deductible business expense.** More generally, **campaign finance reform** could serve to reduce efforts by all sides to gain advantage. Unfortunately, given the benefits to incumbent politicians of the existing system, genuine campaign finance reform has proven quite difficult to achieve.

Finally, moving more responsibility for regulation to the state level, known as **environmental federalism,** would both bring issues closer to those affected and reduce the influence of Washington-based interests. Ironically, business ascendancy over the national environmental agenda during the Reagan years probably prompted the renewal of activism at the state level observed in the late 1980s and early 1990s.[7] The case against such environmental federalism is that competition between states for business will lead to lower overall levels of environmental protection. The seriousness of this latter problem remains unclear.[8]

Political reform of the regulatory process might occur through a move away from a judicial to a corporatist model; by reducing the role of money in politics through a tax on lobbying or campaign finance reform; or through decentralization. However, while potentially helpful, none of these reforms would fundamentally challenge the underlying problems of imperfect information and political influence in the regulatory process. Indeed, these two issues have led some to despair of government's ability to stem the process of environmental decline. As an extreme example of government failure, we turn briefly to the experience in the former Communist nations.

12.6 Lessons from Communism

Since the fall of the Berlin Wall in 1989, an increasingly frightening portrait of environmental conditions in the former Communist regimes has begun to emerge. Driven to industrialize at all costs and in spite of official laws mandating strict environmental protection, officials in the state-owned industries proceeded to raise the level of poison in the land, water, and air to fatal degrees. Commenting on the widespread use of highly toxic pesticides such as DDT; the contamination and exhaustion of agricultural water resources; urban centers with air pollutants typically five times above legal levels; rivers and seas filled with untreated agricultural, industrial, and human waste; and death and disease from the Chernobyl nuclear accident and military nuclear wastes, one set of authors concluded: "When historians finally conduct an autopsy on the

---

[7]Portney et al. (1991) suggest this line of argument.
[8]See the discussion in Cropper and Oates (1992).

Soviet Union and Soviet Communism, they may reach the verdict of death by eco-cide" (Feshbach and Friendly 1992, 1).

What lessons can we learn from this story? Traditional conservatives have argued that the lesson is a simple one: "free-market economics, good; government involvement in the economy, bad." Yet, with the Soviet model of a centrally planned economy discredited, the environmental problems the globe faces are now generated primarily by market economies and market-driven growth. Thus, the traditional conservative lesson provides us with only limited guidance. Clearly, governments can create environmental disasters that rival, if not exceed, those generated by private economic actors. Yet, in capitalist countries, government *is not* the primary source of environmental problems.

Instead, with both world population and economic activity continuing to grow, the Soviet story is best viewed as a cautionary tale: Without an *effective* governmental process forcing economic actors to pay for the externalities they impose on others, ecocide is a future that may await many countries, if not the entire globe.

Most economic comparisons between communism and capitalism have focused on the market versus private ownership distinction. Yet, in capitalist countries, environmental degradation is the result of factors *external* to market transactions. A **demand for environmental protection** can be expressed only through government action. Thus, the key issue is the responsiveness of the political system to this kind of demand.

Given this, the political distinction between western countries and the former USSR—democracy versus totalitarianism—is probably more relevant to environmental concerns than the market/state ownership distinction. When scientists or environmentalists in the Soviet Union attempted to bring information forward, they did so only at personal risk and generally found themselves cut off from any effective means of communication. Whenever economic decision makers can insulate themselves from those exposed to pollution—either through control over information or suppression of dissent—externalities are unlikely to be accounted for by the political system.

For example, one need not look to the Soviet Union to find governmental abuses of the environment. Many of the worst hazardous waste sites in our country resulted from U.S. military programs, shrouded in cold war secrecy. At the Hanford nuclear site in eastern Washington, for example, the U.S. Department of Energy has created a gargantuan waste problem, the extent of which is only now becoming clear after fifty years of tight information control.[9] The cleanup at Hanford, if indeed it goes through, is expected to cost at least $60 billion—more than the entire Superfund program directed at civilian dumps. In the United States, however, the potential for this kind of environmental abuse by the government has been largely reigned in by mandated public scrutiny of major decisions: the environmental impact statement process described in Chapter 7.

Consider another example. Agricultural workers in many poor market-oriented countries employ the same environmentally destructive agricultural techniques so decried in the Soviet Union. These include the widespread use of pesticides such as DDT that have been banned in developed countries.[10] Farmworkers and their families

---

[9]One obstacle the Department of Energy faces in its cleanup efforts is a widely acknowledged "credibility" problem, due to its history of providing inaccurate or misleading statements to the public regarding the extent of the health and environmental hazards at weapons facilities. See Office of Technology Assessment (1991).

[10]See, for example, Murray and Hoppin (1992).

who bear the brunt of the environmental costs in these countries have neither access to information about alternatives nor sufficient political power to challenge the marketing efforts of the firms who profit from the sale of these chemicals. (Indeed, farmworkers in our own country have much less influence over environmental policy than suburban professionals who provide the core support for major environmental groups.)

Both **access to information** and the practice of **effective and widespread democracy** are thus necessary ingredients for successful environmental policy. Without them, citizens will be unable to translate their demand for environmental protection into a reality. Absent substantial pressure from those affected, government will have neither the power nor the inclination to force economic decision makers—whether state bureaucrats, managers of private corporations, or ordinary citizens—to internalize the external environmental costs generated by their actions.

Part IV of this book will explore how this prescription of knowledge and power might be applied in poor countries, to address problems ranging from population growth to conservation. Here in the United States a general trend toward accountability has been embodied in environmental law, ranging from the EIS, to requirements for public hearings in the regulatory process, to more recent innovations such as the **Toxics Release Inventory.** In 1986, after a chemical factory in Bhopal, India, exploded, killing and maiming thousands, the U.S. Congress passed the Emergency Planning and Right-to-Know Act. The act required companies to publicly report on their releases of 450 chemicals suspected or known to be toxic, many of them unregulated.

The Toxics Release Inventory provides self-reported data on chemical releases on a plant-by-plant basis across the country. This information is now on the Web at www.epa.gov/tri; you can go there and check out emissions from a plant in your neighborhood! The TRI has a variety of goals, but an important one has been to make industry decision makers more accountable to the communities in which they operate. The TRI has spawned a variety of community-based, nonregulatory efforts to reduce chemical emissions. It provides a good example of how expanded information and effective democracy can serve to internalize externalities associated with economic production (Sarokin and Schulkin 1991, and Hadden 1989). (For more on the TRI, see Chapters 13 and 14. The impact of the TRI on emissions is discussed in detail in Chapter 19.)

What, then, are the environmental lessons from communism? Given that government action is needed to force market actors to account for external costs, the experience of the former USSR teaches that "*unaccountable* government intervention is bad." When government uses its authority to silence its critics or distort and control information flows, or when those on the receiving end of environmental externalities have little real power, government failure in the environmental arena is likely. Strict environmental laws, without a vigilant, informed citizenry, are hollow laws.

12.7 Summary

This chapter has provided an introduction to the political economy of regulation. The regulatory process begins with national legislation. The EPA then translates the law into specific regulations. Finally, state governments implement and enforce the guidelines developed by the EPA. The United States has adopted a judicial model of regulation in which the EPA is required to go through a formal and elaborate process of information gathering and public hearings and must establish a quasi-legal basis for its major regulatory actions. The judicial model is designed to limit abuse of authority by regulatory bureaucrats but can be easily exploited to generate regulatory gridlock.

From an economic point of view, the primary obstacle to effective regulation is imperfect information. Regulators have only limited resources with which to gather information on the costs and benefits of a proposed rule, and so must often turn to the very sources they regulate for information about the problem. This sets up a reporting bias problem: How can regulators be sure the information they receive is correct? One way is to train and retain qualified technical personnel within the regulatory agency. Another way is to design regulatory policy to minimize incentives for distortion.

Regardless of how much good information the agency collects, however, bureaucrats will still be left with substantial discretion in interpreting how environmental laws are to be implemented. Consideration of bureaucratic interests—agency building, personal career building, and job satisfaction—reveal no necessary bias toward over- or underregulation. Yet discretion raises the problem of political influence.

Who wins and who loses in the influence game? I argue that due to their superior ability to mobilize votes, environmentalists sometimes make substantial gains in the legislative arena, while given their monetary advantage, industry tends to come out ahead in the regulatory process. The big loser from this adversarial structure is public faith in the rule of law. Public disenchantment with the EPA is a serious problem since an effective and respected regulatory agency is the principal tool we now have for controlling market externalities.

The prisoner's dilemma model suggests that competition between environmentalists and industry to influence bureaucrats leads to an inefficiently high level of lobbying and lawsuits. One suggested response to this problem has been to replace the judicial model of regulation, which imposes many legal restrictions on the EPA's behavior, with a corporatist model, giving the EPA much more discretion. Corporatism could potentially foster a more cooperative spirit between industry and environmentalists and is more widespread in Europe. Critics of corporatism argue, however, that in the U.S. context, where the government bureaucracy is relatively weak, corporatism amounts to a sellout to industry interests.

More straightforward ways of reducing lobbying include eliminating its tax-exempt status and instituting campaign finance reform. Environmental federalism would also help reduce the influence of Washington, DC–based interests but might lead to interstate competition to weaken standards.

Many have argued that the collapse of the Soviet Union demonstrates the ecological superiority of market-based economic systems over centrally planned systems. Environmental disaster in the former USSR certainly confirms that state socialism is not the answer to environmental problems. But the problem remains: Market-based economic systems have the potential to ultimately generate ecocide on a level comparable to that of communism.

The relevant lesson from the former USSR is that a lack of effective democracy will doom well-meaning government environmental initiatives to failure. Economic decision makers—whether state planners or private managers—will only take external environmental costs into account (internalize them) if those who bear the costs have the political power to force internalization. Nurturing effective democracy, in turn, requires both empowering citizens and providing access to information. The Toxics Release Inventory provides a good example of this in the United States.

This chapter has focused on the obstacles that the information-intensive regulatory process has encountered in attempts to achieve its legislative target—efficiency, safety, or sustainability in pollution control. The potential solutions discussed here have focused on procedural or political reforms such as better information gathering, a move to corporatism, campaign finance reform, and right-to-know laws.

By contrast, Part III of this book will focus on economic reforms of the pollution control process. Chapters 16 and 17 explore one option: a system of regulation that relies on *economic incentives,* requiring less information and fewer bureaucratic decisions. A second possibility is discussed in Chapters 18 through 20. Rather than reform the regulatory process itself, instead refocus government pollution control policy on the promotion of clean technology, which reduces pollution in the first place. A final, and more optimistic view is that, in spite of the many problems with the regulatory process, overall it has worked surprisingly well. We will take up this line of argument in the next two chapters.

APPLICATION 12.0

Corporatist Solutions?[11]

To implement portions of the 1990 Clean Air Act, the EPA adopted a distinctly corporatist approach—negotiating the regulatory details with representatives from industry, the states, and big environmental groups. Agreement was reached by representatives of these generally hostile groups on regulations designed to encourage the use of so-called "clean" fuels. Industry benefited by having gasoline content standards set on an average basis rather than for every gallon of fuel. This provision reduced costs substantially. Environmentalists won a favorable resolution of an ambiguity that Congress had left in the law about the maximum allowable vapor pressure for fuels.

1. As the price for participation, all of the parties to the agreement pledged not to sue the EPA over its final clean fuel regulations. Assume the agreement to sue is not legally binding. What incentives do the parties at the table have to abide by their promise not to sue?

2. The *New York Times* reports that all parties involved were happy with the clean fuels decision, calling it a "win–win" solution. Relabel the prisoner's dilemma diagram in Section 12.5, using the strategies "negotiate" and "negotiate and sue," and the payoffs "average gas content" or "per gallon gas content" (for industry) and "strict vapor emissions" or "lax vapor emissions" (for environmentalists). Does the diagram illustrate, in principle, that all parties can be made better off by making an enforceable pledge not to sue?

---

[11]This problem is drawn from information reported in "U.S. Agencies Use Negotiations" (1991).

3. In spite of the apparent success of the clean fuels negotiations, the EPA has made little headway in encouraging other corporatist endeavors. At the time of this particular deal, the Consensus and Dispute Resolution Staff at the agency had succeeded in getting agreements in only 12 out of 600 cases. Why might corporatist strategies be hard to implement in the United States?

4. In fact, not everyone was happy with the agreement. One critic of the corporatist approach, Stephen Viederman, put it this way: "'Where you stand,' according to Miles Law, 'depends on where you sit.' Who comes to the table is undeniably central to what is decided at the table. . . . The good news [about the clean fuels decision] was a broader participation in rule-making, with the views of business and industry balanced by other groups" ("Who Comes to the Table" 1991). Based on the criticisms of corporatism discussed in Section 12.5, what do you think Viederman's bad news might be?

APPLICATION 12.1

The Power of Information

Head to www.epa.gov/tri, read the *TRI Overview,* and then find out about the toxic releases for several plants in your zip code, or one nearby. Do you find that the information is reported in an understandable form? Do you get any sense of the relative risk of exposure from the toxic releases reported? What has been happening to the reported releases over time? This data is self-reported by the companies. Do you trust its accuracy? If you were concerned about the health risk posed by the toxic releases in your neighborhood, what would you do about it?

KEY IDEAS IN EACH SECTION

12.0 This chapter discusses two primary obstacles to effective government regulation of pollution: **imperfect information** and the opportunity for **political influence.**

12.1 The "generic" regulatory process has three steps: (1) passage of a law by Congress and the President, (2) drafting of regulations by the EPA, and (3) implementation and enforcement by state officials. The United States currently relies on a **judicial model of regulation,** which reduces bureaucratic discretion but also can lead to regulatory gridlock.

12.2 The first obstacle facing regulators is highly imperfect information. Because the agency has so many tasks, it often drafts rules based on inadequate or poor data. In addition, the agency must deal with a **reporting bias** when it turns to outside groups for information. Two ways to address this problem are to improve **in-house analysis** and rely on **incentive-compatible regulation.**

12.3 Imperfect information gives rise to **bureaucratic discretion** in drafting and enforcing regulations. Bureaucratic motivations include **agency building, external career building** (influenced by the **revolving door**), and **job satisfaction.** Job satisfaction, in turn, can depend on **ideology,** the exercise of **power,** and the maintenance of a **quiet life.**

12.4   Where there is bureaucratic discretion, there is the opportunity for political influence. Political resources wielded by environmental groups and industry include **votes** and **dollars.** Dollars are useful for buying (1) **technical studies,** (2) lobbying **staff,** (3) **access** to decision makers, and (4) votes. This book argues that environmentalists win more often at the legislative stage of the regulatory process, while industry wins more often at all subsequent stages.

12.5   The prisoner's dilemma model suggests that competition for political influence is a zero-sum game, leading to an overinvestment in lobbying. Political reforms that might reduce this wasted effort include adopting a **corporatist model of regulation,** moving toward more **environmental federalism, campaign finance reform,** and eliminating the **tax-deductible status** of lobbying. The first two policies, however, are not without costs, while the latter two have proven politically quite difficult.

12.6   The Communist experience illustrates the potential for massive government failure in the regulatory process. Such failure is most likely when citizens are unable to express their political **demand for environmental regulation.** Doing so requires both **access to information** and **effective and widespread democracy.** The **Toxics Release Inventory** provides a good example of government action to encourage such trends in the United States.

REFERENCES

Bryner, Gary C. 1987. *Bureaucratic Discretion.* New York: Pergammon.

"Cleaning Up." 1990. *The Atlantic,* October.

Cropper, Maureen, and Wallace Oates. 1992. "Environmental Economics: A Survey." *The Journal of Economic Literature* 30, no. 2:675–740.

"Doing More with Less: Trade Groups Feel Recession's Pinch." 1992. *Chemical Week,* 10 June.

"Earth Day Plus 20 and Counting." 1992. *Smithsonian* 21, no. 1:46.

"Environmental Initiative Rejected in California." 1990. *Wall Street Journal,* 4 November.

Feshbach, Murray, and Alfred Friendly, Jr. 1992. *Ecocide in the USSR.* New York: Basic Books.

Greider, William. 1990. *Who Will Tell the People? The Betrayal of American Democracy.* New York: Simon & Schuster.

Hadden, Susan. 1989. "Right-To-Know: What It Can Mean for Citizens." *The EPA Journal,* May–June.

Hukinnen, J. 1995. "Corporatism as an Impediment to Ecological Sustenance: The Case of Finnish Waste Management." *Ecological Economics* 15, no. 1:59–76.

Landy, Marc, Marc Roberts, and Stephen R. Thomas. 1990. *The Environmental Protection Agency: Asking the Wrong Questions.* New York: Oxford University Press.

McCallum, David B., and Vincent T. Covello. 1989. "What the Public Thinks About Environmental Data." *EPA Journal,* May/June.

Ministry of VROM. 1994. *Towards a Sustainable Netherlands.* The Hague: VROM.

Murray, D. L., and P. Hoppin. 1992. "Recurring Contradictions in Agrarian Development: Pesticide Problems in Caribbean Basin Non-Traditional Agriculture." *World Development* 20, no. 4:597–606.

"Nevadans Dump Dump Ads." 1992. *Bulletin of Atomic Scientists,* 48, no. 4.

Office of Technology Assessment. 1991. *Complex Clean-up: The Environmental Legacy of Nuclear Weapons Production.* Washington, DC: U.S. GPO.

Portney, Paul, Katherine Probst, and Adam Finkel. 1991. "The EPA at Thirtysomething." *Discussion Paper CRM 91–03.* Washington, DC: Resources for the Future.

Sanjour, William. 1992. *What EPA Is Like and What Can Be Done About It.* Washington, DC: Environmental Research Foundation.

Sarokin, David, and Jay Schulkin. 1991. "Environmentalism and the Right-To-Know: Expanding the Practice of Democracy." *Ecological Economics* 4:175–189.

Selden, Thomas M., and Marcoe E. Terrones. 1993. "Environmental Legislation and Enforcement: A Voting Model with Asymmetric Information." *Journal of Environmental Economics and Management* 24, no. 3:212–228.

Stalon, George. 1990. "Is Regulation What Regulators Do?" *Discussion Paper ENR90-05.* Washington, DC: Resources for the Future.

"U.S. Agencies Use Negotiations to Pre-empt Lawsuits Over Rules." 1991. *New York Times,* 23 September.

"U.S. Says Lack of Supervision Encouraged Waste and Fraud in Contracts: Billions Misspent in Last Decade Auditor Finds." 1992. *New York Times,* 2 December.

"War Among the Greens." 1992. *Newsweek,* 4 May.

"What Really Pollutes? Study of a Refinery Proves an Eye-Opener." 1993. *Wall Street Journal,* 29 March.

"Who Comes to the Table?" 1991. New York: Jessie Smith Noyes Foundation.

AN OVERVIEW
OF ENVIRONMENTAL
LEGISLATION

13.0 Introduction

Perhaps the most striking aspect of the U.S. national environmental regulation is its brief history. As recently as thirty-five years ago, the United States had *no* major federal legislation controlling the discharge of pollutants into the air and water, *no* national regulations covering the disposal of hazardous waste onto land, *no* process for reviewing new chemicals, only a limited procedure for registering new pesticides, and *no* protection for endangered species.

Prior to 1970, the states had sole responsibility for pollution control activities, but even at the state level, serious efforts at environmental protection have only a short history. Oregon initiated the first statewide air pollution control effort in 1952; only California had mandated tailpipe emission standards for cars by 1970. In the late 1950s and 1960s, as national attention began focusing on environmental problems, the federal government passed a variety of laws encouraging such decentralized efforts to regulate air and water pollution. These laws sponsored research on the health effects of pollution, provided resources for technical assistance and mechanisms for resolving cross-boundary disputes, and put informal pressure on U.S. automakers to reduce vehicle emissions.

On April 20, 1970, Americans celebrated Earth Day for the first time. Also that year, motivated by increasing public awareness, dissatisfaction with slow state regulatory efforts, and little improvement in the pollution performance of U.S. cars, the U.S. Congress struck out on a different, centralized environmental road. The Clean Air Act amendments of 1970 embraced a new philosophy in which minimum standards for air pollution control for the entire nation would be set in Washington. During the remainder of the decade, a similar approach was adopted for water pollution, solid and hazardous waste disposal, and chemical and pesticide registration.

By historical standards, environmental protection efforts are still in their childhood. Nevertheless, environmental protection is growing up fast. As is detailed in Chapter 9, the share of national output devoted to the environment has increased from about 1% to more than 2.5% over the last thirty years. This chapter provides an overview of national legislation in five areas: air pollution, water pollution, hazardous waste, toxic substances, and endangered species.

With this background laid, in the next chapter we will then move on to consider the actual accomplishments of this legislation, criticisms of regulation, and an evaluation of the prospects for future regulatory success.

13.1 Cleaning the Air

The original **Clean Air Act** (CAA), passed in 1963, focused on federal assistance to the states. Major amendments to the CAA occurred in 1970, 1977, and 1990 and have shaped the national regulatory framework.[1] The CAA (as amended) mandates a safety standard. Standards are to be set to "provide an **adequate margin of safety** ... to protect the public ... from any known or anticipated adverse effects associated with such air pollutants in the ambient air." Congress explicitly ruled out a consideration of costs and benefits in the attainment of this goal. Yet, as we saw in Chapter 5, completely safe levels of many pollutants, short of zero discharge, do not exist. One of the difficulties the EPA has had in implementing the CAA has been in hammering out a politically acceptable definition of safety.

The CAA distinguishes two types of air pollutants. First are the so-called **criteria (or common) air pollutants:** particulates, sulfur dioxide, carbon monoxide, nitrogen oxide, ground-level ozone (smog), and lead. All these pollutants generate a variety of respiratory and heart-related problems, some contribute to cancer, and lead also causes neurological diseases. Ground-level ozone, better known as smog, should not be confused with ozone in the upper atmosphere. Ground-level ozone is a harmful pollutant, while the ozone layer surrounding the earth provides a shield protecting us from dangerous ultraviolet rays. Similarly, carbon monoxide (CO)—the fatal gas that accumulates in a closed garage when the car is running—should not be confused with carbon dioxide (CO_2). Carbon dioxide, which is the major contributor to global warming, is also emitted from cars but is not now regulated by the federal government.

In addition to the criteria pollutants, Congress was also concerned about other less common air pollutants, which are also carcinogenic or interfere with reproductive, immune, or neurological systems. These pollutants, now called **hazardous air pollutants** or **air toxics,** are also regulated under a safety standard, but in a different fashion than the criteria pollutants.

For the criteria pollutants, Congress directed the EPA to develop **National Ambient Air Quality Standards (NAAQS). Ambient air quality** refers to the average quality of air in a particular region. Each criteria pollutant was to be given a primary

---

[1]Portney (1990) provides a good detailed discussion of air pollution policy. For details on the 1990 Clean Air Act amendments, I relied on Robinson and Pease (1991) and Milkanovich (1992).

standard designed to protect human health, and a secondary standard that focused on protecting wildlife, visibility, and ecological systems. Table 13.1 lists the primary NAAQS for the six criteria pollutants.[2]

The NAAQS are minimum standards, uniform around the country. In other words, regardless of the variation in compliance costs, all regions are expected to meet the NAAQ levels of air quality. If they desire, states are allowed to impose stricter standards.

What about areas already cleaner than the NAAQS? The 1977 CAA amendments set up a three-tiered system designed to prevent the significant deterioration of air quality. National parks and other scenic areas were designated Class I, in which air quality was to be maintained at the current level. Most areas were put into Class II, in which some deterioration was allowed. In the remaining areas, Class III, air quality was allowed to fall to the level of the NAAQS, but not below.

Once the NAAQS were set, each state was required to develop a **state implementation plan** detailing how emissions from both **stationary sources** (factories, power plants) and **mobile sources** (cars, trucks, airplanes) would be controlled in order to meet the ambient standards. To do this, state environmental officials first had to divide up their territory into so-called **air quality control regions,** geographic areas sharing similar air pollution problems. The plan would then provide an implementation strategy for each region.

For stationary sources, the EPA requires states to use what is known as **technology-based regulation.** For all new sources, the states must mandate the type of pollution technology required for new plants. These New Source Performance Standards (NSPS)

TABLE 13.1   Primary NAAQS for Criteria Air Pollutants, 1997

Pollutant	Averaging Time	Concentration Level	
		ppm	$\mu g/m^3$
Particulate matter (PM10)	Annual	—	50.0
	24-Hour	—	150.0
Particulate matter (PM2.5)	Annual	—	15.0
	24-Hour	—	65.0
Sulfur dioxide	Annual	0.030	80.0
	24-Hour	0.140	365.0
Carbon monoxide	8-Hour	9.000	10.0
	1-Hour	35.000	40.0
Nitrogen oxide	Annual	0.053	100.0
Ozone	8-Hour	0.008	—
Lead	Max quarterly	—	1.5

Source: Portney (1990, Table 3-2), who cites as his source The Office of Planning and Standards (1987), *National Air Quality and Emissions Trend Report,* Research Triangle Park, NC: U.S. EPA. The particulate standards for PM2.5 were introduced in 1997 (but will not be binding for several years), at the same time that the ozone standard was tightened; see "Clinton Sharply Tightens Air Pollution Regulations," *New York Times,* June 26, 1997, p. A1.

[2]Only sulfur dioxide has a secondary standard tighter than the primary standards. Carbon monoxide has no secondary standard; for particulates, nitrogen oxide, ozone, and lead, the secondary standard is identical to the primary standard. See Portney (1990, 35).

require firms to install the "best technological system of emissions reduction" commercially available at the time the standards are set. Note that NSPS technology may not be sufficient to achieve the NAAQ standard; it is simply supposed to represent a serious effort to get there.

State regulators are also supposed to define even more stringent technology-based regulation for sources wishing to locate in areas that have not achieved the NAAQ standards (**non-attainment areas**). Such firms must use the lowest achievable emission rate (LAER) technology. Those wishing to locate in Class I (pristine) areas are theoretically required to achieve yet another standard, the best available control technology (BACT). In practice, there is often little difference between NSPS, LAER, and BACT.

Until 1990, states were not required to impose technology-based regulations on existing sources. However, the 1990 Clean Air Act amendments require the states to define and impose RACT, reasonably available control technology, on existing sources in non-attainment areas. RACT, BACT, LAER, NSPS—these acronyms seem bewildering upon introduction, and in fact, the actual regulatory process is quite tortured. The legal struggle to define what these different terms mean for individual industries has been one of the primary battlegrounds in the information war discussed in the last chapter.

There are two major, ongoing exceptions to the technology-based regulation of stationary sources common under the CAA. Authorities in the Los Angeles area are experimenting with an incentive-based program designed to provide firms with substantial flexibility in achieving targets for emissions of criteria pollutants. The 1990 CAA amendments also provided for a similar flexible system to control acid rain. This alternative incentive-based approach will be explored in detail in Chapters 16 and 17.

To control emissions of criteria pollutants from mobile sources, the CAA has put most of the burden on auto manufacturers, requiring several rounds of reductions in vehicle emissions for new cars. This policy, however, has been criticized as a cost-ineffective strategy for achieving the NAAQS, because it builds in equally high costs for auto consumers in both clean and dirty areas. In other words, rural residents wind up paying for cleanup they may not need in the form of higher-priced cars. The EPA has also required non-attainment areas to use more closely targeted programs, including vehicle inspection programs and since 1990 the sale of reformulated (lower-polluting) fuels. In addition, as we will discuss further in Chapter 20, California has implemented a zero-emission vehicles program in an attempt to meet the NAAQ standard.

To summarize: For the criteria pollutants the regulatory process is now well advanced and progress has been made on several fronts, though problems remain. By contrast, the air toxics case illustrates regulatory gridlock at its extreme. Under the 1970 CAA statute, the EPA was instructed to identify and regulate hazardous air pollutants, defined as substances "which may reasonably be anticipated to result in an increase in mortality or an increase in serious, irreversible, or incapacitating reversible illness."[3] As with the criteria pollutants, the CAA established "an ample margin of safety" as the regulatory target.

Over the next twenty years, the process went into a deep stall. The EPA argued that a literal interpretation of the CAA's safety mandate would require a

[3]This discussion of the air toxics program draws from Robinson and Pease (1991), who also provide the quote from the 1970 CAA.

zero-discharge standard, effectively banning dozens of valuable industrial chemicals. Unwilling to take such a severe step, the agency chose to ignore the problem, regulating only a couple of air toxics during the 1970s. Environmentalists sued the agency, arguing that bans were not necessary; instead, high levels of (expensive) controls should be imposed on products without substitutes. A compromise along these lines was developing in the late 1970s but collapsed with the election of President Reagan in 1980, who had campaigned on a deregulatory agenda.

During the first half of the decade, the EPA chose to "study the problem." However, by the late 1980s, pressure was building for action: The 1984 explosion of a chemical plant in Bhopal, India, and the congressionally mandated release of plant-by-plant chemical emissions (the TRI discussed in the last chapter) prodded the EPA into a study revealing that cancer risks from air toxics in 205 communities around the country exceeded 1 in 1,000.

The impasse was finally addressed in the 1990 Clean Air Act. The 1990 amendments adopt technology-based regulation, requiring the EPA to specify MACT (maximum achievable control technology) for different sources emitting 189 air pollutants presumed to be hazardous. The EPA can add or delete substances from this list. MACT was not supposed to achieve an "ample margin of safety" immediately, since Congress mandated that it be selected with some consideration of attainment cost. However, once MACT had been put in place (theoretically in 1996), additional control measures would be required to reduce any residual cancer risk down to a level of at least 1 in 10,000 for the most exposed population, with an ultimate risk target of 1 in 1 million for the population at large.

Thus, after twenty years of stalled progress and contentious litigation, policy makers finally took the bull by the horns and defined more clearly what was meant by an "ample margin of safety." The process of regulating air toxics is now underway. The 1990 CAA amendments, however, address only stationary sources of hazardous air pollutants. Portney (1990) reports that only 20% of air toxics are in fact emitted by stationary sources that fall under the purview of the amendments. Thus, air toxic emissions from small and mobile sources remain uncontrolled under current legislation.

Figure 13.1 provides a general outline of the Clean Air Act amendments. To summarize: The CAA sets a general goal of "safety" for the two categories of criteria and hazardous pollutants. Emissions of the criteria pollutants are regulated with the intent to achieve an ambient air quality standard within each air quality control region. By contrast, hazardous pollutants must meet emission standards ultimately designed to reduce cancer risks to the most exposed to *at least* 1 in 10,000. Finally, both programs are technology-based. With a few exceptions, regulators decide on particular pollution control technologies that firms are then required to adopt.

13.2 Fishable and Swimmable Waters

The first national water pollution law was passed in 1899. Its simple intent was to prevent industries from disrupting navigation by literally clogging rivers and streams with sludge, sawdust, or fiber. There was little national activity beyond this until the 1950s and 1960s when the federal government began assisting and encouraging states to develop their own pollution standards. In 1972, however, Congress opted for a centralized strategy with the passage of the **Federal Water Pollution Control Act**

Clean Air Act

Criteria pollutants   *Hazardous pollutants*

Stationary sources → EPA sets NAAQS (primary, secondary) → EPA sets ambient standards for class I, II areas

Mobile sources → Congress, EPA set vehicle emission standards

States develop implementation plans

Stationary sources → EPA sets emission standards (MACT) → EPA conducts risk analysis → Further control measures required

Stationary sources
• Technology-based regulation (NSPS, LAER, BACT, RACT)
• L.A. Basin Trading Program

Mobile sources
• Inspection programs
• Clean fuels
• Low emission vehicles

FIGURE 13.1 Outline of the Clean Air Act as Amended

(FWPCA). In combination with the **Clean Water Act** of 1977, this legislation provides our basic water pollution framework.[4]

FWPCA laid out an ambitious safety-based goal: the achievement of **fishable and swimmable waters** by 1983. However, the legislation set its sight beyond this charge, which we might consider a reasonable safety standard as defined in Chapter 10 (the elimination of "significant" risk). FWPCA, in fact, called for the elimination of all risk—zero discharge of pollutants into navigable waters by 1985. Needless to say, this last goal has not been met. Finally, the act prohibits the discharge of "toxic materials in toxic amounts," another ambiguous phrase that has provided grist for the regulatory lawyers' mill.

Individual states are left to draft their own water quality emissions guidelines. For consistency with the FWPCA, they must be sufficiently strict to allow swimming and some types of fishing. However, states are free to draft stricter regulation, for example, to protect water habitat or undeveloped rivers.

The approach used to achieve state water quality targets is in many ways similar to the regulation of air toxics described in the previous section. In 1972, Congress envisioned two initial rounds of technology-based controls. The EPA was directed to determine the best practical technology (BPT) and a more stringent best available

---

[4]The next few paragraphs are based on the more detailed discussion in Freeman (2000).

technology (BAT) so that all industrial dischargers could have the technologies installed by 1977 and 1983, respectively. The timetable proved too stringent, however, and was amended in 1977.[5] It took until 1988 for the EPA to issue all (save one) of its BAT regulations. Once BAT is in place, the EPA has the authority to impose a third round of even more stringent (better than the best!) technology-based controls on sources contributing to the pollution of lakes or streams that have yet to achieve state ambient quality standards.

In addition to installing BPT and then BAT (or BAT alone for newcomers), each discharger must hold a permit that specifies his or her legal pollution emission level. State agencies are by and large responsible for the permitting process and for enforcing compliance. The process does not always run smoothly. In the mid-1990s, the states of Alaska and Idaho together had a backlog of more than 1000 permit applications (see "The EPA" 1998).

One of the major sources of water pollution is improperly treated sewage. As a result, a principal component of federal clean water legislation has been the provision of **grants to municipalities** for the construction of sewage facilities. From 1965 to 1991, close to $100 billion in federal dollars were committed for this purpose. While the increased federal spending displaced spending by state and local authorities, overall federal aid did *accelerate* the pace of sewage treatment. In addition, financing sewer projects with federal tax dollars proved less regressive than local financing. However, because the federal aid came in the form of large grants, local incentives to carefully monitor construction costs were reduced and costs inflated.

Finally, federal clean water legislation has focused primarily on stationary point sources of pollution (factories and sewage plants). However, **non-point water pollution** (runoff from storm sewers in urban areas, and from farms and construction sites) has always been an important source of water pollution. Today, siltation and nutrient loading from agricultural runoff are the primary pollution sources affecting the nation's streams, rivers, and lakes (Griffin 1991).[6] The rapid destruction of the nation's wetlands from pollution and drainage has also become a major environmental concern.

The federal clean water legislation puts responsibility for regulating non-point pollution on the states; the 1987 Water Quality Act requires states to develop so-called "best-management practices" to control runoff from industrial and agricultural sites. Progress in this area has been slow because the diverse nature of the non-point problem makes centralized, technology-based regulation infeasible.

Two ways to control non-point water pollution are to (1) reduce runoff and (2) reduce the volume of pollutants available to be mobilized, a "pollution-prevention" strategy. As an example of the latter, farmers have begun adopting so-called conservation-tillage practices, which leave stubble in fields to reduce runoff. In addition, a variety of measures have been introduced that reduce overall pesticide use. We will look more closely at some of these steps in Chapter 19. Finally, the EPA has also begun experimenting with permit trading between point and non-point

---

[5]An additional technology category, best conventional technology, was also added here (Freeman 2000).
[6]The primary problem for estuaries is still a point source: municipal water treatment facilities.

sources. Under these experimental schemes, point sources can pay non-point sources to reduce pollution as an alternative to installing point source technology controls.[7]

13.3 Hazardous Waste Disposal on Land

The 1970s was the decade of air and water pollution legislation. In the 1980s, concern shifted to land disposal of hazardous waste. Although the initial law covering hazardous waste disposal, the **Resource Conservation and Recovery Act** (RCRA, pronounced *ricra*), was passed in 1976, actual regulation did not get underway until 1980 and accelerated when the law was amended by Congress in 1984.[8] RCRA is concerned with current disposal practices. The second major piece of hazardous waste legislation deals with abandoned dump sites. The Comprehensive Environmental Response, Compensation and Liability Act (CERCLA, better known as **Superfund**) was passed in 1980 and amended in 1986.

What exactly is hazardous waste? One inclusive definition is any substance that poses a potential, substantial threat to human health or the environment. However, resolving what this means has proved a thorny problem. The EPA has developed a **RCRA list** of several hundred substances and waste flows deemed to be hazardous, based on criteria such as ignitability, corrosivity, reactivity, and toxicity. However, certain materials—oil-drilling muds and mine tailings—were granted immunity from hazardous waste regulation under RCRA. Some states, such as California and Washington, have instituted more stringent definitions that effectively double the volume of substances regulated as hazardous (Office of Technology Assessment 1992).

A typical hazardous waste dump will include many substances known or suspected to either be carcinogenic or to have adverse effects on reproductive, immune, or neurological systems. While hazardous waste thus clearly poses a potential threat to human health and the environment, what are the actual risks? This is a very contentious topic. Most exposure to waste occurs when chemicals leach out of dumps in rainwater or into the air in vaporous form. However, because the numbers of people living in close proximity to the dumps is small, and because residents come and go, it is difficult to establish whether elevated levels of disease sometimes found by such dumps occur by chance or as a result of exposure to water. Moreover, because many wastes are quite long-lived, long-term effects that are difficult to predict must be factored in.

Love Canal, a one-time suburb of Niagara Falls, New York, is the best-known example of a hazardous waste dump. From 1942 to 1953, the Hooker Chemical and Plastics Corporation (now Occidental Chemical) buried millions of pounds of chemical wastes encased in metal drums in the abandoned canal. Hooker then sold the site to the city for $1 as a possible location for an elementary school. A suburban housing development soon grew up around the area. However, the drums rusted, and liquid waste began to pool on the surface and seep into people's basements. In 1978, after growing concern by residents over reported health effects—ranging from the loss of

---

[7]Details on the pilot programs can be found at www.epa.gov/owow/watershed/trading/tradingpolicy.html.

[8]RCRA also authorizes the EPA to regulate a variety of nonhazardous wastes. These include wastes at municipal landfills (discussed in Chapter 10), as well as hazardous industrial wastes exempted from official designation as "RCRA hazardous wastes," for example, oil-drilling muds or incinerator ash.

fur on pets to birth defects and breast cancer—and the detection of high levels of chemicals in some homes, the state of New York ordered the area immediately around the dump evacuated.

Love Canal is probably the most extensively studied hazardous waste site in the world, yet many questions remain about possible health effects. Two early studies of elevated cancer rates and chromosomal defects among Love Canal residents—which sparked a second round of evacuations—have since been discredited. However, the New York State Department of Health did find roughly double the expected rate of low birth-weight babies in a low-lying area adjacent to the dump during the period of active dumping, as well as a statistically significant increase in babies born with birth defects after the chemicals were dumped (see Vianna and Polan 1984, and Brown 1989). Paigen et al. (1987) found that children who had lived in the canal area were shorter and weighed less than a control group.

The Love Canal case illustrates first that improperly handled hazardous waste can pose a real health threat. Second, establishing the full extent of adverse health effects is quite difficult. A recent government-sponsored scientific review panel, charged with assessing public concern that hazardous waste poses a serious threat to public health, concluded only that such concern could be neither confirmed nor refuted (National Research Council 1991, 1).

Nevertheless, because of the limited routes of exposure, and the small numbers of people living in the close vicinity of dumps, many have argued that hazardous waste is unlikely to pose a national health threat comparable to that of air and water pollution.[9] Following this line of reasoning, the EPA's Science Advisory Panel did not list hazardous waste as a primary concern for ecological, welfare, or health risks (see Table 8.3). At Love Canal, after the dump had been capped with a layer of clay, the streams cleaned up, and other remedial action taken, the New York State Department of Health Commissioner concluded in 1989 that some homes in the area could be safely reoccupied (Brown 1989).

However, in spite of official assessments that downplay the overall risk from hazardous waste, the public remains quite concerned. Partly, this has to do with a disagreement over the normative goal of environmental policy. Under a safety standard, the fact that the numbers at risk of exposure are small does not lessen concern. Concern over hazardous waste also has to do with the visibility of victims. While tracing a birth defect directly to a neighboring waste dump is difficult, it is easier than linking it to smokestack emissions a hundred miles away. Finally, the public remains wary of scientific risk assessment; given the current state of knowledge about possible effects of hazardous waste, such skepticism might be warranted.

The volume of hazardous waste is significant. Each year, American industry and households generate about 40 million tons that fall under RCRA regulation; much of the remainder is disposed of through liquid discharges regulated by the Clean Water Act (Sigman 2000). Household hazardous waste takes the form of used motor oil, house paint, pesticides, and batteries. The bulk of waste is produced by industry.

[9]Four million people live within one mile, and 40 million within four miles, of a Superfund site (National Research Council 1991).

Shapiro (1990) reports that, although there were more than 650,000 generators of hazardous waste, about 2% of these produce 95% of the total.

What happens to all this waste? Common disposal methods include surface impoundment, landfilling, injection into deep underground wells, direct or indirect discharge into surface waters, incineration, and treatment. However, under the presumption that disposal on land posed the greatest long-term environmental threat from hazardous waste (and given that discharge into water and air was already regulated), the 1984 RCRA amendments built in a strong **bias against land disposal.** The legislation essentially puts the burden of proof on firms to demonstrate that the disposal method is indeed safe (Wagner 1991). Deep well injection, incineration, recycling, and water discharge are thus likely to become the most common disposal methods in the future.

The regulatory framework for hazardous waste disposal under RCRA has a three-part focus. First, as noted, the EPA has been required to designate which substances are to be deemed hazardous. RCRA then requires cradle-to-grave tracking of such wastes. When hazardous waste is shipped it must be accompanied by a manifest, stating its origin and intermediate stops. This manifest system was designed to discourage illegal dumping, though its effect on this process is unclear.[10]

Finally, RCRA requires that facilities that treat, store, or dispose of hazardous wastes are to be regulated under a safety standard. To accomplish this goal, RCRA imposes location restrictions and requires personnel training, groundwater monitoring, closure and post-closure plans, and adequate insurance coverage. Under RCRA, facilities can also be forced to clean up old dump sites under their jurisdiction in order to receive a permit (Wagner 1991). However, the stringency of regulations vary from program to program. As we saw in Chapter 12, the EPA's final regulatory standards for deep-well injection of wastes (finalized in 1989) were successfully challenged as too onerous by the chemical industry.

RCRA governs the current disposal of wastes. By contrast, CERCLA, or Superfund, provides a mechanism for cleaning up abandoned dump sites. Superfund takes its name from a $8.5 billion pool of money collected by the government in the form of taxes on the chemical and petroleum industries, a general corporate environmental tax, and personal income tax revenues to finance dump cleanups.

However, Superfund also provides a more controversial funding mechanism. Any party that disposed of waste in a particular dump, legally or not, can be sued by the government to finance the entire cost of the cleanup. This system, known as **strict, joint, and several liability,** was put in place as a way to fund cleanups without spending additional government dollars. If the government could find one responsible party, the theory went, that party would then have the incentive to uncover other dumpers. However, the system has developed into a legal morass. Rather than bear what are potentially tremendous cleanup costs, firms have devoted resources to suing one another and the government over who will pay what share. Detroit automakers, for example, sued more than 200 parties, including the Girl Scouts, to contribute to one Michigan cleanup ("The Toxics Mess" 1992).

---

[10]Shapiro (1990) notes that most waste (95%) never officially leaves the site at which it is generated; moreover, incentives for illegal dumping, bypassing the manifest system altogether, still exist.

Given this situation, the legal costs of Superfund have begun to mount. As a percentage of cleanup costs, legal fees and other transaction expenses range from 23% to 31% (Sigman 2000). Probst and Portney (1992) estimated that about $8 billion could be saved from currently designated Superfund sites if retroactive liability provisions were eliminated and cleanup was financed solely out of the trust fund.

The liability system under Superfund does have one attractive efficiency feature: The fact that waste *generators,* not just disposal facility operators, are held strictly responsible for the ultimate fate of their waste clearly provides a powerful incentive for careful management practices today. **Fear of future liability** under Superfund has spurred manufacturers both to seek methods for reducing their use of hazardous chemicals and to take greater care in their disposal practices. (For more on this point, see Chapter 19.) Moreover, Superfund liability applies to a broader spectrum of potentially hazardous materials than does RCRA regulation.

In addition, some fear that weakening the retroactive liability provisions under Superfund in order to reduce legal costs may send the wrong signal to industry about government's future intent to force polluters to pay. Retroactive liability also encourages private parties to initiate cleanups of non-Superfund sites.[11]

Beyond high legal costs, Superfund has been bedeviled by other problems, including site selection, costly cleanup efforts and resolving the "How clean is clean?" issue. By 2000, from a universe of some 40,000 dump sites nationwide, the EPA had designated 1,402 as high-priority Superfund sites. Figure 13.2 shows the status of these sites: A total of 757 sites had been cleaned up to varying degrees. Average per site cleanup cost estimates range from $27 million to $50 million (Probst and Portney 1992). Total cleanup costs for the currently designated sites alone are estimated to run to at least $51 billion. Given these problems, Congress has long considered major changes to the Superfund program; as of 2004, however, no revision had been undertaken.

Superfund also authorizes the EPA to conduct emergency action at sites where immediate risks to the public or the environment are present. From 1980 to 2000, the agency had undertaken remedial emergency action at more than 3,200 sites. More than 40,000 people were evacuated from their homes, with close to 90% eventually returning. Alternative water supplies had been supplied to 200,000 people (Superfund Emergency Response Web site, www.epa.gov/superfund/health/er/; Sigman 2000).

13.4 Chemicals and Pesticides

So far, this chapter has given a brief review of the legislation governing the disposal of wastes into the air and water, and onto the land. The government has also passed two laws that share the ostensible goal of restricting the use of environmentally dangerous products in the first place. The Federal Insecticide, Fungicide and Rodenticide Act (**FIFRA**) and the Toxic Substances Control Act (**TSCA,** pronounced tosca) provide a mechanism for the EPA to review both new and currently marketed pesticides and

---

[11]For an extensive discussion, see Probst and Portney (1992). The authors point out that, on the surface, prospective rather than retroactive liability is all that is necessary to affect current management practices. However, Superfund's retroactive structure has clearly underscored to firms what strict liability will mean.

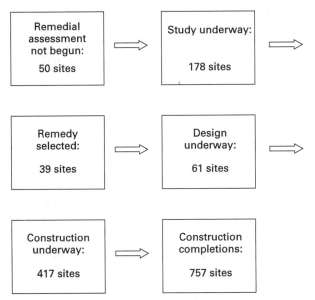

FIGURE 13.2 Status of Superfund Sites on the National Priorities List, End of FY 2000

chemicals, respectively, for their environmental impact. The agency can then recommend restrictions on such products, *if* they can be justified on a benefit–cost basis. Thus, unlike the other major pollution statutes just described, FIFRA and TSCA direct the EPA to pursue an explicit balancing of costs and benefits in the regulatory process. **Efficiency** rather than safety is the intended goal.

FIFRA was originally passed by Congress in 1947 to protect farmers from fraudulent claims by pesticide manufacturers. Amendments in 1964, 1972, 1978, and 1988 have provided the legislation with an environmental mandate. Under FIFRA, all new pesticides must be registered with the EPA; to obtain approval for major new ingredients, manufacturers must conduct and submit scientific studies of an agent's toxicity. This can be an expensive and time-consuming process. According to an industry source, registering a major new ingredient will cost between $5 million and $7 million in scientific studies, and take as long as five years (R. Sherref, as quoted in Shapiro 1990). The EPA is then expected to weigh the benefits of approving the new pesticide (lower costs to farmers and, ultimately, food prices for consumers) against the environmental costs.

If evidence accumulates that an *existing* pesticide is harmful, the EPA can institute a benefit–cost analysis of the product and, depending upon the findings, limit or restrict its use. This so-called **special review** process entails a lengthy, trial-like procedure. Finally, under the 1972 amendments, the EPA was required to reregister hundreds of existing pesticides that had already been registered without environmental analysis. However, until 1988, when it was forced to do so by Congress, the EPA took no action on this front.

The EPA's cost–benefit analyses under FIFRA have been subject to criticism, primarily on the benefits side. In theory, pesticide benefits should be measured as the

net increase in consumer surplus from lower food prices, plus any change in growers'
and manufacturers' profits. Ironically, if pesticides boost yields, farmers as a group
may be worse off since crop prices fall and demand is unresponsive to price decreases
(inelastic). In the agricultural case, one also needs to subtract additional subsidy payments to farmers resulting from an increase in yields. To do this properly, one would
need good estimates of the pesticide's effectiveness relative to the next best alternative, as well as the price responsiveness of demand (elasticity) for different crops in
question, and good input and output price data.[12]

This information is generally hard to get. In fact, for pesticide registration, the
EPA has often done no benefits estimation at all. Instead the agency relies on the
manufacturer's willingness to expend money on the registration process as evidence
that the project will yield some benefit. The EPA in fact does not even require any
evidence that the pesticide is effective; thus it cannot even begin a formal benefit
analysis. As a result, the process for new pesticides looks only at risks and is essentially a "loose" safety standard.[13]

Under the special review process for existing pesticides, the agency does engage
in benefits analysis, but there are no formal guidelines for conducting such an assessment. In addition, available information is often poor. Thus the quality of the benefits
assessment will vary from study to study. Cropper et al. (1991) find that numerical
benefit estimates were available for only 167 of the 245 food use decisions they studied in the special review process.

In an interesting look at the political economy of the special review process,
Cropper et al. found that regulators did in fact respond to the information presented
in the benefit–cost analyses. Pesticide uses were more likely to be canceled the greater
the associated health and environmental risks. At the same time, higher estimated
costs of cancellation reduced the likelihood that such an action would be taken.

Cropper et al. (1991) also find substantial evidence for political influence. Comments by environmentalists (often concerned about protecting marine life) dramatically increased the likelihood of restriction, while comments by growers and
academics (primarily representing industry) had the opposite effect. Environmentalists commented on 49% of the decisions, while growers and academics commented on
38% of the decisions. On any particular decision, the combined influence of the latter
group outweighed that of the former. Of course the influence of the pesticide manufacturer, involved throughout the process, was also very important but could not be
independently identified. In addition, during the early years of the deregulatory Reagan administration, environmentalists did not participate at all in the public comment
process, although the influence of growers increased.

This brief discussion of the benefit–cost process under FIFRA highlights several of
the points made in Chapter 12. First, information about the benefits and costs of regulation is not easy to obtain. Second, regulators must often turn to regulated firms to

---

[12]For a discussion of the issues involved in pesticide benefit estimation, see Gianessi, Kopp, and Puffer (1989).
[13]See Shistar, Cooper, and Feldman (1992) for a fuller discussion. Cropper et al. (1991) report maximum
accepted risks in the special review process of 1.1 in 100 for applicators, 3.1 in 100,000 for mixers, and 1.7 in
10,000 for mixers.

obtain access to the information that is available. Third, lobbying resources and political orientations matter; special review decisions were clearly affected by the presence of industry and environmental advocates. Finally, lobbying is not the only thing that matters. Controlling for the presence of industry and environmental advocates, regulators did respond to their legislative mandate of weighing costs against benefits.

The legislation governing toxic chemicals, TSCA, was passed in 1976. In a fashion similar to FIFRA, TSCA requires the EPA to review all new chemicals and provides the agency with the authority to restrict the use of existing chemicals. However, TSCA gives the government much less leverage than does FIFRA. Under TSCA, the EPA must be notified ninety days before the manufacture of a new chemical. However, no scientific data need be included with the notification. The agency then uses the pre-manufacture period to review the chemical. Since most of the new chemicals will not be accompanied by substantial test data, the EPA must rely on toxicity comparisons with similar compounds. Even here, however, information is quite slim. One study that examined a subsample of the 65,000 plus chemicals regulated by the EPA estimated that, for 78% of chemicals with production in excess of 1 million pounds, no toxicity data existed.[14]

As a pointed example of how little we know about chemical toxicity, in 1996 Theo Colborn, a scientist at the World Wildlife Fund, published a book called *Our Stolen Future*. She linked evidence of declining sperm counts and a rising reported incidence of breast cancer to so-called "endocrine disruptors"—fairly common synthetic chemicals the structure of which mimics that of natural hormones. At this writing Colborn's thesis about human health impacts remains controversial—for example, human sperm count declines appear to be geographically isolated. But there is clear evidence that wildlife populations have been damaged by exposure to these chemicals.

If the EPA does determine that the new product may pose an unreasonable health risk, the agency can prohibit manufacture of the chemical until the manufacturer provides sufficient data to make a final decision on the product. Otherwise, the product is presumed safe. The EPA currently reviews 1,000 to 2,000 new chemicals each year.

For existing chemicals, the EPA must go through a formal legal procedure, which can easily take more than two years, merely to require testing. A similar legal process is then necessary to justify, on a benefit–cost basis, any proposed restrictions on the chemical. As of 2000, the EPA had requested tests on more than 540 chemicals and had issued final regulations for only nine chemicals. However, the EPA has used the threat of regulation to reach agreements with manufacturers, such as restrictions on occupational exposure, for several hundred chemicals. As discussed in Chapter 10, the EPA's ten-year effort to restrict asbestos use under TSCA was thrown out by the courts in 1991 for failing to meet a rigorous efficiency standard. Because TSCA places a much higher legal burden of proof on the EPA than does FIFRA, there has been substantially less regulatory activity under the former statute.

While TSCA regulates the *use* of chemicals, an information-based law appears to have had a much bigger impact on U.S. chemical *emissions*. In 1986, after a chemical factory in Bhopal, India, exploded, killing and maiming thousands, the U.S. Congress passed the Emergency Planning and Right-to-Know Act. The act required companies

---

[14]This result is from a National Academy of Sciences study, reviewed in Shapiro (1990).

to report on their releases of 450 chemicals suspected or known to be toxic, many of them unregulated at the time. The so-called **Toxics Release Inventory (TRI),** mentioned briefly at the end of Chapter 12, provides self-reported data on chemical releases on a plant-by-plant basis across the country.

The TRI data first went public in 1989 and proved to be startling: Industry was emitting nearly 5 billion pounds of chemicals of various toxicities, mostly substances that were either unregulated or under legal limits. In the face of public relations pressures generated by the TRI list, many big chemical firms adopted pollution prevention programs.

The TRI numbers provide evidence of success. Overall, releases of the seventeen most toxic chemicals fell by 51% from 1988 to 1994 (Davies and Mazurek 1997; Videras and Alberini 2000). Arora and Cason (1996) provide evidence that firms with more public exposure reduced emissions the most. Unlike all the other laws discussed in this chapter, the TRI did not mandate emission reductions or indeed have any particular goal other than informing the public about emissions. Its success suggests that preventing pollution at industrial plants, either through recycling or source reduction—discussed further in Chapter 19—is relatively inexpensive.

13.5   Endangered Species Protection

The **Endangered Species Act (ESA)** is our one piece of ecologically motivated environmental legislation. The law, passed in 1973, requires protection of a certain type of natural capital—species—regardless of the cost. The rationale for the law is strictly anthropocentric: "these species ... are of aesthetic, ecological, educational, historical, recreational and scientific value to the Nation and its people" (as cited in Jost 1996).

The strict implications of the law became apparent in the mid-1970s, when a University of Tennessee law school student filed suit and successfully halted the construction of a nearly completed $110 million dam. The reason? A new species of fish called the snail darter had been discovered downriver. Upset by the successful lawsuit, Congress created the so-called "God Squad"—an appointed committee with the authority to overrule ESA decisions on efficiency grounds.

Ironically, the God Squad concluded that the dam in fact didn't make sense even on benefit–cost terms. Finally, Congress overrode the God Squad and authorized construction by a special act of legislation. A new population of snail darters, meanwhile, had been discovered elsewhere, and in 1984 the status of the fish was upgraded from "endangered" to "threatened."

Under the ESA, federal agencies are required to list animals and plant species considered to be **endangered** or **threatened** (likely to become endangered). Recovery plans for these organisms must be developed and then **critical habitat** designated. Once this had been done, both public and private actors must refrain from damaging this habitat. (Technically, the act prohibits "taking" of a listed species, and the Supreme Court has ruled that this includes damaging their habitat.) Both the listing and habitat designation decisions are supposed to be purely scientific, with no consideration of economic costs or benefits.

In 2000, there were 1,238 listed species, 960 endangered and 268 threatened. Some 4,000 other species are potential candidates for listing (Jost 1996; Easter-Pilcher 1996). The scientific basis for deciding which critters and plants to list is far from precise; Metrick and Weitzman (1996) find that both larger and perceived "higher" life forms are more liable to get listed, while Easter-Pilcher (1996) finds little consistency in the scientific justifications across listings. In 1990, ten feathered or fuzzy species (eight birds, one bear, one panther) accounted for more than half of all federal expenditures on recovery.

These expenditures are not large: In 1995 the government spent about $80 million in total on listing and recovery, about the cost of a few miles of interstate highway (Jost 1996). However, the ESA has been embroiled in controversy because, its critics allege, it imposes large economic costs on private landholders. Recall that the statute prohibits all actors—public and private—from disturbing the critical habitat of a listed species. This means, in practice, that should an endangered animal be discovered on your property, then you might not be able to develop it—no matter how much you paid for it.

Now, from an economic perspective, markets should be able to adapt readily to this kind of situation. If such surprise discoveries happened often, then people would begin to pay attention to them. One might even expect potential property buyers to demand "ESA surveys" before they buy land. Indeed, such surveys are routine now for uncovering the presence of hazardous waste. The fact that we don't see a market for ESA surveys suggests the problem is fairly isolated. And the data bear this out. From 1987 to 1991, the U.S. Fish and Wildlife Service engaged in 2,000 formal consultations on development proposals under the ESA; 18, less than 1% were blocked (Schlickeisen 1996). And in an analysis of two recent endangered species actions involving fish protection on the Colorado and Virgin rivers, Berrens et al. (1998) found very small impacts on employment and income; for some areas the impacts were positive, for others negative. In no case did impacts rise above $\frac{3}{10}$ of 1% change from the baseline forecasts.

Nevertheless, the ESA, like all regulations, imposes costs on the private sector, and in certain cases, these have been large and dramatic. Perhaps the best-known case involves protection of the spotted owl in the old-growth forests of the Pacific Northwest. While a far cry from the disaster predicted by critics, owl protection beginning in 1994 has meant that a few thousand timber jobs lost in the 1990 recession have not reappeared. (As noted in Chapter 9, this case, along with high-sulfur coal mining, represent by far the most severe local jobs–environment trade-offs found in the United States.)

However, the overall Pacific Northwest economy performed quite well in the late 1990s, with very low unemployment rates. Many area economists (Power 1996) attributed the robust growth of the non-timber economy to largely the high quality of life—including protected forests—found there. Finally one benefit–cost study found that the nationwide WTP for owl preservation exceeded the costs, implying that owl preservation met the standard not only of ecological sustainability but also of efficiency (Haigne, Vincent, and Welle 1992).

Beyond high and/or unfairly distributed compliance costs, the ESA has received two other types of criticism. The first is economic. The ESA is all stick and no carrot; in its current format it gives landowners no incentive to go beyond the letter of the law. (Indeed, some have argued that it provides an opposite, very perverse incentive. Upon discovering an endangered critter, landowners might be tempted to "shoot, shovel, and shut up." True, but the penalties if caught are very high!)

The second criticism is biological. The ESA's focus on species rather than ecosystems distracts attention from the primary task—preserving biodiversity. Too much energy can be devoted to saving a single species while a rich ecosystem goes down the tubes. (This is similar to the criticism that the safety standard provides no guide to cost-effectiveness.) As a result, interest has turned to the identification and preservation of so-called "hot spots"—ecosystems rich in threatened or endangered biodiversity. In spite of these criticisms, however, a 1995 National Academy of Sciences review of the ESA was generally favorable (National Research Council 1995).

13.6 Summary

This chapter has provided a brief look at the existing structure of national environmental protection legislation. Table 13.2 provides a summary. The three statutes governing disposal on land and in the air and water have as their goal the achievement of a safe and clean environment, irrespective of the cost. In fact, costs do enter through the back door, in decisions about the resources the EPA can devote to each area and in the specific regulations that emerge to implement the laws. However, the clear intent of the legislation is to target environmental cleanup at a level much higher than efficiency would dictate.

By contrast, the two statutes governing the introduction of new pesticides and chemicals seek explicitly to balance the costs and benefits of environmental protection, in an attempt to achieve something like efficient regulation. (Chemical *emissions* have also been affected by the public relations pressure generated from the TRI.) Finally, the Endangered Species Act is our only major statute that explicitly seeks ecological sustainability as a goal.

Given this background, we turn now to an evaluation of the successes and failures of this impressive, if young, regulatory structure.

TABLE 13.2 **Principal Resource Protection Laws**

Resource or Pollutant	Major Legislation	Standard
Air	Clean Air Act (Amended, 1990)	safety
Water	FWPCA; Clean Water Act	safety
Land	RCRA: new sites, CERCLA (Superfund): old sites	safety
Pesticides	FIFRA	efficiency
Chemicals	TSCA	efficiency
Species	ESA	ecological sustainability

APPLICATION 13.0

Time to Regurgitate

1. Give some examples of technology-based regulation.
2. Give some examples to show how safety-based legislation can be inefficient. Give some examples to show how efficiency-based legislation can be unsafe. Give an example in which ecological sustainability-based legislation also happens to lead to an efficient outcome.

KEY IDEAS IN EACH SECTION

13.0   This chapter reviews the major federal environmental laws and their accomplishments in five areas: waste disposal (1) in the air, (2) in the water, and (3) on land; (4) the regulation of new and existing pesticides and chemicals; and (5) protection of endangered species.

13.1   The **Clean Air Act** and its amendments require regulation to achieve an **adequate margin of safety.** Two types of pollutants, **criteria (common)** and **hazardous air pollutants (air toxics),** are regulated differently. The EPA sets **National Ambient Air Quality Standards (NAAQS)** for criteria pollutants and a health-based standard for air toxics. States must develop **implementation plans** to bring both **stationary** and **mobile sources** into compliance with standards. **Non-attainment areas** face special requirements. In all cases, the EPA relies on **technology-based regulation,** specifying particular types of technology firms must use; for example, NSPS, LAER, BACT, RACT, and MACT.

13.2   Water quality regulation, under the **Federal Water Pollution Control Act** and the **Clean Water Act,** also has safety as its target, mandating **fishable and swimmable waters.** Technology-based regulation (BPT, BAT) is employed. The government has invested directly through **grants to municipalities,** for sewage treatment plants. Difficult to regulate **non-point sources** are now the major contributors to water pollution.

13.3   Two statutes deal with hazardous waste disposal on land, both requiring a **safety standard.** The **Resource Conservation and Recovery Act (RCRA)** has created the **RCRA list:** a variety of substances that must be disposed of in a controlled fashion. RCRA has a built-in **bias against land disposal** of hazardous waste. Assessing the actual health risks from hazardous waste dumps such as the one at **Love Canal** is difficult. Nevertheless, in contrast to popular opinion, the EPA's science advisory board views hazardous waste as a **relatively low priority** environmental problem. **Superfund** is the second hazardous waste statute, dealing with existing dumps. Cleanups are financed through a trust fund and by means of **strict, joint, and several liability.** While the latter has led to high legal costs, **fear of future liability** may have had a positive effect on current disposal practices. Superfund has been bedeviled by **high costs, uncertain benefits,** and **slow progress.**

13.4   The statutes regulating new and existing pesticides (**FIFRA**) and chemicals (**TSCA**) are based on an **efficiency standard.** Both laws have a registration and screening process for new substances, and both provide for **special review** of existing substances. Benefit–cost analysis to support efficient regulation under these laws is often sketchy to nonexistent. Many more regulatory actions have been taken under FIFRA than TSCA because the burden of proof under the former lies more with industry and less with the EPA. The **Toxic Release Inventory (TRI),** taking an information-based approach, has proved an effective weapon to promote the reduction of chemical emissions.

13.5   The **Endangered Species Act (ESA)** seeks ecological sustainability—the protection of natural capital—as its goal. The act requires listing of **endangered** and **threatened** species on a scientific basis and prevents activities that disturb **critical habitats.** The ESA has been criticized because of the costs it imposes on a small number of landholders and rural workers, lack of incentives for participation, and a focus on species instead of ecosystems.

REFERENCES

Arora, Seema, and Timothy N. Carson. 1996. "Why Do Firms Volunteer to Exceed Environmental Regulations? Understanding Participation in the EPA's 33/50 Program." *Land Economics* 72, no. 4:413–432.

Berrens, Robert, David Brookshire, Michael McKee, and Christian Schmidt. 1998. "Implementing the Safe Minimum Standard Approach: Two Case Studies from the U.S. Endangered Species Act," *Land Economics* 74, no. 2:147–161.

Brown, Michael H. 1989. "A Toxic Ghost Town." *Atlantic,* July.

Colborn, Theo, Diane Dumanaski, and John Peterson Myers. 1996. *Our Stolen Future.* New York: Penguin.

Council on Environmental Quality. 1991. *Environmental Quality.* Washington, DC: U.S. GPO.

Cropper, Maureen L., William N. Evans, Stephen J. Berardi, Marie M. Ducla-Soares, and Paul R. Portney. 1991. "The Determinants of Pesticide Regulation: A Statistical Analysis of EPA Decisionmaking." *Discussion Paper CRM 91–01.* Washington, DC: Resources for the Future.

Davies, Terry, and Jan Mazurek. 1997. *Industry Incentives for Environmental Improvement: Evaluation of U.S. Federal Initiatives.* Washington, DC: Global Environmental Management Initiative.

Dower, Roger C. 1990. "Hazardous Wastes." In *Public Policies for Environmental Protection,* edited by Paul Portney. Washington, DC: Resources for the Future.

Easter-Pilcher, Andrea. 1996. "Implementing the Endangered Species Act." *Bio-Science* 46, no. 5:355–362.

"The EPA and States Found to be Lax on Pollution Law." 1998. *New York Times,* 7 June, p. A1.

Freeman, A. Myrick. 2000. "Water Pollution Policy." In *Public Policies for Environmental Protection,* edited by Paul Portney and Robert Stavins. Washington, DC: Resources for the Future.

Gianessi, Leonard P., Raymond J. Kopp, and Cynthia A. Puffer. 1989. "Regulating Pesticide Use: Social Costs, Policy Targeting and Economic Incentives." *Discussion Paper QE89–21.* Washington, DC: Resources for the Future.

Griffin, Robert Jr. 1991. "Introducing NPS Water Pollution." *EPA Journal,* December, 6–9.

Haigne, Daniel A., James W. Vincent, and Patrick G. Welle. 1992. "Benefits of Preserving Old-Growth Forests and the Spotted Owl." *Contemporary Policy Issues* 10, no. 1:13–26.

Jost, Kenneth. 1996. "Protecting Endangered Species." *CQ Researcher* 6, no. 15:339–357.

Metrick, Andrew, and Martin L. Weitzman. 1996. "Patterns of Behavior in Endangered Species Preservation." *Land Economics* 72, no. 1:1–16.

Milkanovich, Valerie. 1992. "Clean Air Act Amendments." *Memorandum.* Albany, NY: New York State Energy Office.

National Research Council. 1991. *Environmental Epidemiology: Public Health and Hazardous Wastes.* Washington, DC: National Academy Press.

National Research Council. 1995. *Science and the Endangered Species Act.* Washington DC: National Academy Press.

Office of Technology Assessment. 1992. *Managing Industrial Solid Wastes.* Washington, DC: U.S. GPO.

Paigen, Beverly, Lynn R. Goldmann, Mary M. Magnant, Joseph Highland, and A. T. Steegman, Jr. 1987. "Growth of Children Living Near the Hazardous Waste Site, Love Canal." *Human Biology* 59, no. 3:489–508.

Portney, Paul R. 1990. "Air Pollution Policy." In *Public Policies for Environmental Protection,* edited by Paul Portney. Washington, DC: Resources for the Future.

Power, Thomas M., ed. 1996. *Economic Well-Being and Environmental Protection in the Pacific Northwest.* Missoula, MT: University of Montana.

Probst, Katherine N., and Paul R. Portney. 1992. *Assigning Liability for Superfund Cleanups.* Washington, DC: Resources for the Future.

Robinson, James C., and William S. Pease. 1991. "From Health-Based to Technology-Based Standards for Hazardous Air Pollutants." *American Journal of Public Health* 81, no. 11:1518–1522.

Schlickeisen, Roger. 1996. "Should the Endangered Species Act Be Re-enacted Without Major Changes? Yes." *CQ Researcher* 6, no. 15:339–357.

Shapiro, Michael. 1990. "Toxic Substances Policy." In *Public Policies for Environmental Protection,* edited by Paul Portney. Washington, DC: Resources for the Future.

Shistar, Terry, Susan Cooper, and Jay Feldman. 1992. *Unnecessary Risks: The Benefit Side of the Pesticide Risk-Benefit Equation.* Washington, DC: National Coalition Against the Misuse of Pesticides.

Sigman, Hillary. 2000. "Hazardous Waste and Toxic Substances Policy." In *Public Policies for Environmental Protection,* edited by Paul Portney and Robert Stavins. Washington, DC: Resources for the Future.

"The Toxics Mess Called Superfund." 1992. *Business Week,* 11 May.

Vianna, Nicholas J., and Adele K. Polan. 1984. "Incidence of Low Birth Weight Among Love Canal Residents." *Science* 226, no. 4679:1217–1219.

Videras, Julio, and Anna Alberini. 2000. "The Appeal of Voluntary Environmental Programs: Which Firms Participate and Why?" *Contemporary Economic Policy* 18, no. 4:449–460.

Wagner, Travis. 1991. *The Complete Guide to Hazardous Waste Regulations.* New York: Van Nostrand Reinhold.

CHAPTER 14

THE REGULATORY RECORD: ACHIEVEMENTS AND OBSTACLES

14.0 Introduction

The last chapter provided an overview of the major environmental legislation in the United States. What has twenty-five years of regulation actually accomplished? Beyond that, how can the regulatory process be improved?

Two lines of criticism have been leveled at the current regulatory approach. First, from a normative perspective, efficiency advocates have charged that current legislation often buys relatively small environmental benefits at a substantial cost. Second, regardless of whether the pollution control target chosen is efficiency, safety, or ecological sustainability, the existing regulatory system is more expensive than it need be. By building in greater flexibility and harnessing economic incentives, many economists argue that we could buy our current level of environmental quality at a substantially lower cost.

However, assuming we can improve the regulatory process in this way, a final question remains. By their very nature, regulatory approaches are limited to control of narrowly defined pollutants, and work best for stationary and "point" sources; moreover regulatory gains may be swamped by economic growth. In order to achieve sustainability, does government need to move beyond internalizing externalities through regulation, and directly promote the development of clean technology?

14.1 Accomplishments of Environmental Regulation

After more than two full decades of extensive environmental regulation and the expenditure of hundreds of billions of dollars on pollution control, where do we now stand? The record is clearest for air pollution. As Table 14.1 reveals, in absolute terms, ambient concentrations of all of the criteria air pollutants declined over the period from 1982 to 2001. Declines were largest for lead (94%), due largely to a

TABLE 14.1   Progress in Reducing Air Pollution
(Average Nationwide Ambient Concentrations)

	Percentage Reduction in Average Ambient Concentrations	
	1982–2001	1992–2001
Particulates	24	14
Sulfur dioxide	52	35
Nitrogen oxides	24	11
Carbon monoxide	62	38
Lead	94	25
Ozone	18	3

Source: National Air Quality 2001 Status and Trends
(U.S. EPA, www.epa.gov).

phase-out of leaded gasoline beginning in 1984. Over the period, sulfur dioxide concentrations dropped by 52%, carbon monoxide by 62%, and particulates by 24%. Comparable progress has been made in reducing concentrations of nitrogen oxides (down 24%) and ground-level ozone (down 18%). [Recall that ground-level ozone, or smog, is created from a mixture of nitrogen oxides (NOx), volatile organic compounds (VOCs), and sunlight.] The big drops in SO_2 and CO in the 1990s reflect new regulatory standards put in place by the Clean Air Act Amendments of 1990.

However, for nitrogen oxides and ozone, much of the total reduction in pollution concentrations was already achieved by 1992, as seen in the second column of Table 14.1. Forward momentum in these areas has slowed substantially, virtually stalling out for ozone. Further progress on NOx (an ozone component) will also be tough: unlike all the other criteria pollutants—which showed reductions in emissions over the period from 1970 to 1994, paralleling the Table 14.1 improvements in air quality—nitrogen oxide emissions actually increased by approximately 14% (*The Statistical Abstract of the United States, 1996,* Table 374). At the same time, NOx air quality did improve somewhat, indicating that new source growth—mostly autos—was occurring in less polluted areas.

With the exception of ozone, impressive headway towards reducing absolute concentrations of the criteria air pollutants has been made; for lead the gains have been quite spectacular. For most Americans, the air we breathe today is substantially cleaner than it was for our parents' generation. And this is in spite of economic output in the country more than doubling over the last thirty years.

In many areas, however, some of the NAAQS are still violated, at least during parts of the year, with the biggest offender being ozone. As Figure 14.1 illustrates, in 2001, 131 million people lived in counties where at least one NAAQS was violated at some time over the course of the year. Ozone is likely to remain a stubborn and serious air pollution problem, affecting roughly one-third of the population to varying degrees, as long as cities remain dependent upon private gasoline powered autos for

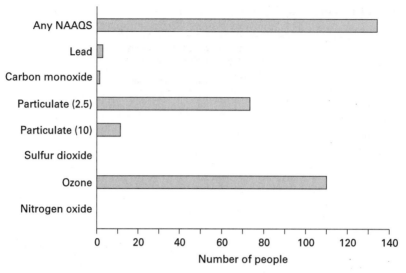

FIGURE 14.1 People Living in Non-attainment Counties, 2001
Source: National Air Quality 2001 Status and Trends (U.S. EPA, www.epa.gov).

transportation. (Indeed, after the tightening of the ozone standard in 1997, many more areas will begin failing to meet the new, more stringent NAAQS.)

Air toxic regulation mandated in the 1990 CAA amendments got underway only in the mid-1990s. However, as noted in the last chapter, since 1986 companies have had to report their chemical emissions in the Toxics Release Inventory publicly, and public pressure has led to substantial *voluntary* progress in the reduction of chemical emissions—on the order of 50% for seventeen chemicals targeted by the EPA. Most of these reductions were of airborne emissions; the firms would have been required to make these particular reductions by the late 1990s under the CAA amendments (Davies and Mazurek 1997). It appears that the twin hammers of public pressure along with a looming regulatory deadline, have had a significant impact on air toxic emissions.

Turning now to water quality, forward progress has been less dramatic. Table 14.2 illustrates some good news: On average, fewer U.S. rivers and streams were in violation of water quality standards in the 1990s than in the 1970s. There is also some bad news: fish consumption advisories rose during the last decade for most toxins. At the end of the 1990s, the U.S. EPA (2000) reported that about 40% of U.S. streams, lakes, and estuaries were still too polluted to support fishing and swimming. Reviewing this and other data, Freeman (2000) concludes that, overall, small gains in water quality have been achieved over the last thirty years.

Buried within these averages though are some clear-cut success stories. Rivers in many urban areas, for example, are dramatically cleaner than they were during the 1970s. This has facilitated urban waterfront redevelopment in cities across the country. But while some streams and rivers have shown significant improvement, others have deteriorated. A study of trends in stream water quality from 1978 to 1987 at close to 400 locations nationwide found that overall, average water quality had

TABLE 14.2   Trends in U.S. Water Quality

	Percentage of Streams in Violation of Standards				
	Fecal Coliform	Dissolved Oxygen	Total Phosphorus	Total Cadmium	Total Lead
1975–1980	33.7	6.0	4.5	2.5	9.0
1990–1995	27.2	1.7	2.5	<1.0	<1.0
	Number of Fish Consumption Advisories, Selected Toxins				
	Mercury	PCBs	Chlordane	Dioxins	DDT
1993–1994	995	355	103	59	40
1997–1998	1,857	634	111	62	34

Source: U.S. Geological Survey and U.S. EPA, Office of Water, as reported on the Council of Environmental Quality Web site: *www.ceq.doe.gov.*

improved at about 14%, deteriorated at 9%, and remained the same at 76% of the measuring stations (Council on Environmental Quality 1991, 261).[1]

According to the EPA, absolute levels of water quality have failed to improve much in large measure because increases in non-point water pollution, particularly agricultural runoff, have offset regulatory gains (Carlin 1990). Of course, as in the case of air pollution, the achievements of the regulatory program would look better compared to where we would have been in the absence of federal controls.

Regulation *has* had a major effect on point sources of water pollution. Industrial discharges of two conventional water pollutants (suspended solids and dissolved oxygen) declined by more than 90% from 1982 to 1987. This improvement resulted from the installation of BPT and BAT technologies, as well as the diversion of substantial industrial effluent to municipal waste facilities for treatment. In part because of this latter phenomenon and in part due to population growth, the substantial government investment in sewage treatment over the last three decades has merely held the line on water pollution. For example, in 1988, municipal discharges of suspended solids and dissolved oxygen were comparable to mid-1960 levels, though below the peak discharges recorded in 1973 (Carlin 1990).

There is little available data on trends in toxic emissions into surface water, yet toxic pollutants pose a serious obstacle to achieving a goal of "fishable and swimmable" waters. A 1992 EPA report identified 46 sites nationwide where estimated cancer risks from occasional fish consumption (one or two meals per month) were significant—on the order of 1 in 10,000. People who depend more heavily on fish from inland waters—including some Native American and rural populations—face substantial additional risk. In the mid-1990s, about 4,000 health bans or advisories were in effect across the country (Environmental Defense Fund 1992). Finally, groundwater pollution from pesticides and hazardous waste dumps, a topic addressed in Chapter 19, has begun to emerge as an increasing environmental problem.

[1]The composite quality figures reported here average trends in fifteen different pollutants. See also Carlin (1990).

Evaluating the impact of hazardous waste legislation is difficult. The ostensible goal of RCRA (and Superfund liability) has been to prevent future Love Canals. Relatively strict regulations governing land disposal appear to have reduced the flow of hazardous waste into landfills by more than 50% between 1986 and 1995. However, rising disposal costs have also probably raised the rate of illegal dumping. On net, the volume of toxic waste generated by companies also declined by about 50% from 1986 to 1995, though the overall toxic content of the waste appears to have stayed constant—implying that the concentration of hazardous chemicals in the waste that is disposed has increased (Sigman 2000).

The cleanup of old dump sites has proceeded at a slow pace; as noted, about 700 sites have been cleaned up. However, as Probst and Portney (1992) detail, it is not clear how much of the limited progress is due to the nature of the beast (the need for careful evaluation and consideration of options) and how much is due to excessive litigation or bureaucratic foot-dragging.

Unlike air, water, and land disposal laws, pesticides and chemicals are regulated under a benefit–cost standard, and so should be evaluated in these terms. Cropper et al. (1991) found that the estimated value of a life saved under the pesticide review process has been $35 million—well above the $5 to $10 million value used in benefit–cost analysis. They argue that pesticide regulation has thus been inefficiently strict: marginal costs outweigh marginal benefits. A second source of serious inefficiency in pesticide regulation has been the "grandfathering" of old, more dangerous pesticides that were already on the market at the time the laws were passed. Recent reforms have begun to attack this problem: As one example, as I began writing the revision to this chapter, the EPA banned a common household pesticide called Durban. (For more on pesticides, see Chapter 19.)

Less progress has been made on evaluating the toxicity of new chemicals. Given the limited information on these compounds, whether the EPA's screen for new chemicals successfully achieves its stated goal of efficient regulation is difficult to assess. However, many chemicals known to be toxic at high doses have accumulated at low levels in the body fat of the American population (Commoner 1990; Sigman 2000).

Finally, of the species listed in the late 1990s as either threatened or endangered, 41% are stable or improving, 35% are declining, 23% face an uncertain future, and 1%—seven species—have become extinct. Only five species have been delisted after a successful recovery, and eleven upgraded from endangered to threatened.

What are we to make of this record? Let us for the moment take an optimistic view. In spite of the fact that economic activity more than doubled from 1970 to 2004, the general criteria air pollution picture has actually improved somewhat, dramatically for lead. In addition, large reductions in air toxics have been recorded over the last 15 years. Industrial emissions of some waterborne pollutants have dropped dramatically and, overall, water quality has probably improved a bit beyond 1970 levels. Regulation of hazardous waste *is* likely to prevent the development of future "Love Canals." And the rising cost of disposal, along with the "right-to-know" TRI regulation and the potential for Superfund liability, is beginning to focus corporate attention on reducing waste through pollution prevention. Particularly nasty new pesticides are not likely to make it through the EPA's initial screen, and under prodding from Congress the agency will restrict the use of the worst of the existing pesticides by the beginning of the century. Finally, only a few listed species have slipped into extinction.

The fact that regulation has managed to hold the line against economic growth is in itself an impressive accomplishment. Can this success continue? At the end of the chapter, we will turn to a somewhat darker view of the prospects for continued regulatory accomplishment. First, however, we will look at more specific criticisms of the current regulatory structure.

14.2 Normative Criticisms of Regulation

The national laws covering pollution into the air and water and onto land are governed by a safety standard. We have seen that defining safety has posed a difficult problem. In practice, pursuing a safety standard generally involves buying the highest level of protection possible given the political constraints on regulatory authority and the available dollars allocated by the political process. On the other hand, laws governing the use of toxic substances require regulatory actions to meet an efficiency standard. Here, the government weighs costs and benefits in a more or less crude fashion, depending upon the information available.

Not surprisingly, efficiency advocates attack the pursuit of safety as inefficient; safety advocates counter that efficiency standards provide the public with an inadequate level of environmental protection. Economists, perhaps due to their professional training, tend to be efficiency advocates, so one will often find economists leveling normative criticisms at safety-based environmental protection laws. For example, Portney (1990) is critical both of the uniformity of standards and the high level of protection afforded to remote areas under the Clean Air Act. Uniformity fails to account for the fact that the benefits and costs of control may vary between sites, and Portney finds it "hard to see why the allowable degradation should be the same in all [Class I] areas, since they are not equally endowed with resources or amenities." Similarly, Freeman (2000) suggests that some water quality standards be relaxed on a case-by-case basis. Sigman (2000) also argues that most, but not all, RCRA regulations and Superfund cleanups are inefficient; that is, benefits measured using a lives-saved metric of $5 to $10 million per life do not justify costs. For land disposal, again, this is because typically, very few people are exposed to toxic contaminants from landfills and Superfund sites.

Economists are not wrong to level efficiency criticisms at safety standard environmental legislation; in some cases, particularly when marginal benefits are very close to zero, the argument may be quite convincing. It is, however, important to remember that economists have no special authority when it comes to proscribing what the appropriate target of pollution control *should be*.[2]

As usual, efficiency criticisms are most persuasive when they suggest that an *actual* improvement in environmental quality will result from a move from safety to efficiency. Cropper et al. (1991), for example, argue: "Since there are a variety of public

---

[2]Bromley (1990) makes an argument along these lines.

policy measures, both environmental and otherwise, which are capable of preventing cancer at much lower costs [than the $35 million per life saved from pesticide regulation], we might be able to reduce the cancer rate through a reallocation of resources."

The problem with this line of reasoning is that the resources freed up from less stringent pesticide regulation, to the extent they are properly estimated, would reemerge as higher profits for pesticide manufacturers and lower food prices for consumers. They would not likely be channeled into other "public policy measures" to improve environmental health.[3] Thus, only a potential and not an actual Pareto improvement would emerge by relaxing pesticide regulations to achieve efficiency gains.

14.3 Cost-Effectiveness Criticisms of Regulation

In contrast to normative questions of goal setting, an area that economists do have special authority in is cost-effectiveness analysis. **Cost-effectiveness** in environmental protection means achieving a desired goal—whether it is safety or efficiency—at the lowest possible cost. Part III of this book will be devoted to an extended discussion of cost-effectiveness; at this point, it is useful to outline the basic criticisms of existing policy.

As you probably learned when you were about three years old, one of the best ways to discredit someone is to call them a name. Economists have coined a not-very-flattering label for the current regulatory approach: **command-and-control (CAC)** regulation. CAC involves two parts. The first is the **uniform emission standards** typically mandated under the Clean Air and Water acts, and under RCRA. All similar sources are "commanded" to meet identical emission levels. The problem with uniform emission standards (from a cost-effectiveness point of view) is that they fail to take advantage of differences in costs between firms.

To use a simple illustration, consider two neighboring oil refineries. Refinery A, which has the ability to reduce emissions of, say, nitrogen oxides at very low cost, is expected to meet the same standard as next-door refinery B, a firm with very high costs of reduction. The reason this is not cost-effective is simple: The same overall emission reduction (and local air quality) could be achieved at lower cost by having the low-cost firm meet a tighter emission standard, while relaxing the standard for the neighboring high-cost firm. Chapters 16 and 17 will review a variety of mechanisms—collectively known as *incentive-based regulation*—that harness market incentives to achieve this kind of **cost-saving, pollution-neutral** result.

However, there is one area in which current legislation does not require uniform standards: New sources and old sources are generally treated much differently. The Clean Air Act requires more stringent control technologies for new sources (the New Source Performance Standards); RCRA allows for regulations to differ between existing and new hazardous waste facilities; FIFRA and TSCA regulate the introduction of new pesticides and chemicals on a preemptive basis but challenge existing substances only on case-by-case review.

The reason for this type of "grandfathering" (providing special protection for existing sources) is not hard to understand. It is politically much easier to pass pollution control laws that have their largest impact on firms not currently around to object.

---

[3]Only if the EPA shifted its internal resources away from pesticide regulation toward other priority areas would a very small portion of these net benefits serve other "public policy measures."

However, regulating new sources more stringently introduces a **new source bias.** Because higher costs are now attached to new investment, firm managers and consumers will hold on to their old, polluting technologies longer than they otherwise would. For example, rather than build new, cleaner electricity generating facilities, firms may stretch out the lives of older, dirtier ones. Similar effects have been observed for new cars (Maloney and Brady 1988; Gruenspecht and Stavins 2002).[4] Or, to consider another case, some new pesticides that have been denied registration are actually safer than substitutes already approved for use on the market.

A new source bias reduces the cost-effectiveness of a given policy in both the short and long run. In the *short run,* regulators impose tougher standards on new sources that are likely to be cleaner already, ignoring existing and potentially more severe problems. For example, in some places, one cost-effective way of reducing urban air pollution may be buying up and junking old, highly polluting cars.[5] The *long-run* cost effect, however, is probably more severe. By slowing down investment in new technology, the pace of technological change itself slows down. With less technological progress, long-run pollution control costs fall slower than they otherwise would.

To review, the first aspect of CAC regulation is the emission standards which the government "commands": uniform for all similar areas and sources, with the often perverse exception that new sources are more stringently regulated than old ones. Both uniformity and the new source bias serve to reduce the cost-effectiveness of regulation.

The second, "control" part of the name refers to the **technology-based regulatory approach** employed by much current regulation. NSPS, BACT, RACT, MACT, LAER, BPT, BAT: Defining all these acronyms involves regulators in a highly detailed process of specifying precisely which technologies firms will employ. There are two cost-effectiveness problems here. First, in the short run, a uniform technological mandate is unlikely to provide the cheapest pollution control solution for different firms all over the country. This lack of flexibility inherent in centralized, technology-based regulations raises costs.

Again, however, long-run cost effects are probably more important. Technology-based regulation works against technological improvements in several ways. First, once a firm has installed BACT (Best Available Control Technology), for example, it has no incentive to do better. Second, the firm actually has a positive incentive *not* to do better. If, for example, it discovered a better technique for pollution reduction, and the EPA then decided to deem this new technology BACT, the firm might legally be required to upgrade its pollution control technology at other new facilities. Firms have a distinct incentive to keep the agency from upgrading the state-of-the-art technological standard. Finally, if in spite of these obstacles, firms do seek an innovative, non-BACT approach, they must first obtain regulatory clearance to do so.

What would be an alternative to technology-based regulation? Again, we will explore this issue further in Chapters 16 and 17, but in essence, the regulator might simply specify a pollution goal for each firm and then let each firm achieve its goal

---

[4]Greene and Duleep (1992) provide estimates of elasticities of scrappage with respect to price of around −1 for automobiles.

[5]Old cars are very polluting. Whether a purchase program is cost-effective depends upon (1) whether the cars purchased are heavily driven *and* are not likely to be soon retired anyway, and (2) the purchase price. Economists are currently studying these issues. See, for example, Alberini, Harrington, and McConnell (1993).

as it sees fit. Provided that *monitoring and enforcement resources were adequate* to ensure that firms were complying, such a flexible system could result in the same emission levels at much lower cost in the short run, and provide substantially better incentives for cost-reducing technological progress in pollution control in the long run.

To summarize: Many economists would argue that the current command-and-control regulatory strategy is cost-ineffective. That is, we could achieve the same goals—whether safety, efficiency, or ecological sustainability—at much lower cost, by shifting to more flexible, incentive-based approaches.

Incentive-based regulation, however, is still regulation. Firms must be punished for exceeding allowable emissions of pollutants. Some have argued that this kind of "stick" strategy of forcing firms and consumers to internalize externalities—no matter how flexibly it is designed—will face an increasingly difficult task holding the line on environmental quality.

14.4 Beyond Regulation? Promoting Clean Technology

As documented above, regulation has scored substantial successes. First, there has been some real improvement, most noticeably in air quality for millions of people. Second, environmental quality elsewhere is being held roughly constant in the face of increasing economic growth.

However, some hold a darker view of the prospects for future regulatory success. This pessimistic outlook rests on three assumptions. First, economic growth can eventually swamp the regulatory process. As noted, relatively little recent progress has been made in reducing smog and nitrogen oxide emissions. In spite of tremendous investment in sewage treatment facilities, emissions from these sources have improved only marginally, if at all. And while regulation may forestall particularly egregious insults such as Love Canal, the fact remains that as the economy grows, industry continues to generate more and more hazardous wastes and toxic chemicals, and *these must go somewhere.* Even if stored according to best practice, it is argued that general exposure levels must ultimately increase.

Second, regulation has already picked off the "easy" targets—stationary air pollution sources and point water pollution sources. In fact, urban smog is due largely to automobiles, while non-point pollution has become the dominant water quality problem. Regulating these diffuse sources will prove much more difficult. In economic terms, the marginal costs of a regulatory approach to controlling pollution are likely to rise significantly for the next generation of problems.

We can see how these two issues interact using the IPAT equation from Chapter 7. Increases in economic growth (A) increase environmental impacts, unless offset by improvements in technology (T). The argument is that if the marginal costs of pollution control are rising, then this will undercut the ability of new technology to counterbalance an ever-growing increase in material affluence.

As a final point, even if regulation is successful in one media, say improved air quality, the "reduced" pollution is likely to squeeze out somewhere else. For example, coal power plants reduce sulfur dioxide by "scrubbing" the sulfur out of the gaseous emissions. However, this process produces a hazardous sulfur sludge, which must be disposed of on land. Or, limits on industrial discharge of water pollutants have caused an increase in discharge through municipal sewage facilities. Or, RCRA's tough regulations for land disposal, focused on a handful of sites, are likely to increase the rate of on-site incineration of hazardous waste. This will occur at thousands of points across the country, spawning an additional regulatory headache.

Economists call this the **piecemeal problem.** Regulating the environment a piece at a time will lead firms to seek out substitute media for disposal. Under these circumstances, regulation ultimately boils down to channeling dangerous substances into areas where they do the least environmental harm.

However, by focusing on improvements in air quality or water quality or land disposal practices, one loses sight of the bigger picture: Is overall environmental quality being affected by regulation? Reviewing much of the evidence presented in this chapter, the noted ecologist Barry Commoner (1990, 40) concludes: "there is inescapable evidence that the massive national effort to restore the quality of the environment has failed."

Nevertheless, our thirty-year experience with regulation has not been futile. While we may not have achieved our ambitious target of creating a safe and clean environment, and in spite of the many political-economic obstacles faced, regulation has made a major difference in the environmental quality experienced by Americans. The real question is, Can regulation continue to at least hold the line against continued economic growth and even begin to improve the state of the environment?

Economic growth clearly requires increasingly strict emission standards in order to maintain the same level of environmental quality. If (1) tightening regulation leads to ever-rising marginal costs of reduction, or if (2) the pollution "reduced" squeezes out elsewhere, regulatory strategies will clearly fail over the long run.

Is there a way out of this trap? Yes. Our standard assumption is that firms reduce pollution using an **end-of-the-pipe** strategy. That is, faced with a regulation requiring lowered emissions, firms make small adjustments to their production process: say, adding on a scrubber to the "end of the pipe" or switching to a cleaner and more expensive fuel.

Consider an example of a firm trying to reduce particulate emissions, measured in parts per million (ppm). Under these circumstances, the marginal cost of reduction curve takes on the familiar look of Figure 14.2A: That is, it becomes increasingly difficult (expensive) to clean up emissions as the standard tightens from 100 ppm to 0 ppm.

However, one effect of regulation might be to induce firms to seek out whole new technologies that avoid emitting the pollutant of concern in the first place—a **pollution prevention** strategy. In this case, the marginal cost curve takes on the shape of Figure 14.2B. Here, if the firm bears an initial expense to significantly alter its production process (z), the marginal costs of reduction, and consequently pollution emissions, go to zero. Because the firm no longer emits the pollutant in question, there are no marginal costs of reduction below a level of 90 ppm. Note that *once the new technology is in place,* both the piecemeal problem and the problem of rising marginal cost disappear.

Which technology will the firm adopt? That depends on a comparison of the total costs of the two options. In this simple example, the firm will go with an end-of-the-pipe solution if the area under the marginal cost curve is smaller for Figure 14.2A, as

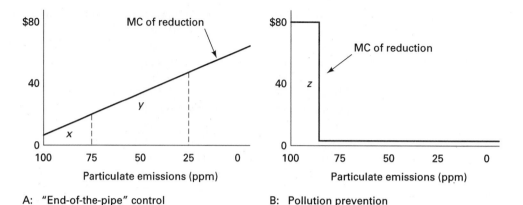

A: "End-of-the-pipe" control

B: Pollution prevention

FIGURE 14.2 Two Technologies for Particulate Control

opposed to Figure 14.2B. This is true for a standard of 75 parts per million ($x < z$), but as the required cleanup increases to 25 parts per million, the pollution prevention technology becomes the cheaper approach ($x + y > z$).

Unfortunately, the story is not this simple. The real-world problem is that firms have little incentive to invest in developing the pollution prevention technology in the first place until regulatory costs become very high, especially because regulations are easier to fight politically as they become more stringent and costly. Investment in the cleaner technology, of course, would have led to reductions in cost—through research and development, "learning by doing," and economies of scale.

But a lack of investment means that the cleaner technology seldom exists as an easy, reliable, or low-cost alternative. A chicken-and-egg problem thus emerges: Stricter emission standards are too costly (not politically feasible) using end-of-the-pipe approaches, but new pollution prevention technologies will not be developed by industry until stricter emission standards are required. This in turn implies that the "stick" of regulation—no matter how flexible—may never be strong enough to prod firms into investing in pollution prevention strategies.

In Chapter 18 we will explore further why normal market processes tend not to generate clean technologies of this type—which involve major rather than marginal changes in production processes. But as a preview: To achieve sustainability it may be necessary to supplement the stick of regulation with the carrot of direct government investment in, and promotion of, clean technologies.

The take-home message of this section is that, unless regulation induces major technological change, we cannot escape the logic of IPAT. That is, if the marginal costs of control continue to rise, then technology simply cannot offset the impact of increased growth. This means that the quality of the environment must deteriorate over time. The key issue then becomes: Can regulation alone drive technological innovation, or must the government take a more active role investing in clean technology?

14.5 Summary

This chapter has looked back at our thirty-five–year pollution control record. In summary, it is probably fair to say that regulation has managed to hold the line against economic growth. It is of course possible to view this accomplishment either as a cup that is half full or half empty.

Normative criticisms of the existing laws have been directed both at safety standards (too costly) and efficiency standards (insufficiently safe). These criticisms are important and were dealt with at length in the first part of this book. However, we now want to leave our discussion of the goals of environmental policy behind and begin to consider more effective implementation. The question we will move on to address in Part III of the book is: How can we improve the cost-effectiveness of environmental protection?

Whether our goal is safety, efficiency, or ecological sustainability, this chapter has identified three features of the current command-and-control regulatory system that tend to work against cost-effectiveness: uniform emission standards, a new source bias, and a technology-based approach. By contrast, we will argue in Chapters 16 and 17 that much more flexibility could be built into the regulatory process and incentives harnessed to improve overall cost-effectiveness. However, for a more flexible approach to succeed, careful emissions monitoring will be required, and adequate enforcement resources must be available. The next chapter will explore the monitoring and enforcement record to date and provide some suggestions for doing better.

Finally, while a switch to more flexible regulation is in many cases a good idea, more flexible regulation is still regulation, facing three obstacles to continued success. First, economic growth is a real challenge to effective regulation. As the volume of activity increases, so does the volume of harmful externalities. Second, non-point, mobile, and other widely dispersed sources, difficult to regulate by traditional methods, have all become more important players in the pollution story. Finally, the piecemeal problem—in which pollution regulated in one media squeezes out into another—places a limit on the level of overall environmental cleanup that regulation can ultimately provide. These factors imply that beyond regulation, the direct promotion of clean technology is another important role for government. How to do this wisely will be addressed in Chapters 18 to 20.

APPLICATION 14.0

Regulating Nukes

In an interesting article, England and Mitchell (1990) report on the progress of regulation in the nuclear power industry.

1. The first civilian nuclear reactor began operation in 1957. Yet the agency in charge of overseeing the nuclear industry "had fewer than a dozen active regulations in 1970." One explanation for fairly lax safety regulation was the (mistaken) belief that a threshold existed below which exposure to radiation was safe. Why did this belief persist? One reason was that "centralized [government] funding of radiation research ... encouraged a methodological inbreeding which underestimated the scope of nuclear hazards."

Use the concepts of the *revolving door* and *agenda control,* both explained in Chapter 12, to explain how the regulatory establishment could persistently underestimate health risks from exposure to radiation.

2. In the 1970s, the laissez-faire regulatory attitude shifted. From a hands-off approach in 1970, to "several dozen [active regulations] by 1972, and several hundred by 1977." Is this burst of regulatory activity in the 1970s consistent with the pattern we saw in other areas? What do you think explains it?

3. In the nuclear area, it is possible to view regulatory achievements in either a positive or gloomy light. From 1974 to 1984, reported emissions of four out of the six radioactive elements studied by England and Mitchell either declined or remained stable, in spite of a tripling of electrical output from the nuclear industry over the period. However, in spite of constant or declining emission levels, the *total amount* of these four radioactive materials in the environment was substantially higher in the mid-1980s than the mid-1970s. How can you explain this?

KEY IDEAS IN EACH SECTION

14.1 This section provides a progress report. There has been success in reducing criteria air pollutants, though forward movement in several areas has stalled out. However, tighter regulation for particulates and ozone may lead to more improvement over the next decade. On the air toxic front, large emission reductions have been driven by a combination of regulation and bad publicity from the TRI. Gains in water quality from point-source regulation have been balanced by increases in non-point pollution. The impact of regulation on land disposal of waste and chemical safety is hard to evaluate. One study indicates that pesticide regulation is inefficiently strict, though not strict enough to be safe. Finally the ESA has also had mixed success—generally preventing extinction, but failing to promote recovery.

14.2 Efficiency advocates, some of whom are economists, often criticize the current safety-based laws from a normative perspective. They argue that the air, water, and land disposal statutes often have marginal benefits well below marginal costs and *should* thus be weakened. Safety proponents respond that many of the statutes are insufficiently strict. Economists, of course, have no special authority to decide what the right level of pollution ought to be.

14.3 The current regulatory approach, dubbed **command-and-control (CAC),** is not **cost-effective. Uniform emission standards** and a **new source bias** (the "command" aspects) along with **technology-based regulation** (the "control" aspect), mean that the regulatory system has little flexibility to adapt to local conditions. Provided that monitoring and enforcement are adequate, increased flexibility can allow firms to pursue **cost-saving, pollution-neutral** measures. In addition, the CAC system discourages technological innovation in pollution control technology.

14.4 Is regulation alone sufficient? Obstacles to further regulatory progress include economic growth, the increasing importance of non-point and mobile pollution sources, and the **piecemeal problem.** These three factors imply that the marginal cost of **end-of-the-pipe** regulation will rise; unless regulation induces rapid techno-logical change, leading to **pollution prevention,** the quality of the environment must deteriorate. But the "chicken-and-egg" relationship between regulation and new technology development suggests a critical role for the direct government pro-motion of clean technology.

REFERENCES

Alberini, Anna, Winston Harrington, and Virginia Mc-Connell. 1993. "Determinants of Participation in Acceler-ated Vehicle Retirement Programs." Paper presented at the Eastern Economic Association Meetings.

Bromley, Daniel. 1990. "The Ideology of Efficiency: Search-ing for a Theory of Policy Analysis." *Journal of Environ-mental Economies and Management* 19, no. 1.

Carlin, Alan. 1990. *Environmental Investments: The Cost of a Clean Environment, Summary.* Washington, DC: U.S. EPA.

Commoner, Barry. 1990. *Making Peace with the Planet.* New York: Pantheon.

Council on Environmental Quality. 1991. *Environmental Quality.* Washington, DC: U.S. GPO.

Cropper, Maureen L., William N. Evans, Stephen J. Berardi, Maria M. Ducla-Soares, and Paul R. Portney. 1991. "The Determinants of Pesticide Regulation: A Statistical Analysis of EPA Decisionmaking." *Discussion Paper CRM 91-01.* Washington, DC: Resources for the Future.

Davies, Terry, and Jan Mazurek. 1997. *Industry Incentives for Environmental Improvement: Evaluation of U.S. Fed-eral Initiatives.* Washington, DC: Global Environmental Management Initiative.

England, Richard, and Eric P. Mitchell. 1990. "Federal Regu-lation and Environmental Impact of the U.S. Nuclear In-dustry." *Natural Resources Journal* 30:537–559.

Environmental Defense Fund. 1992. *The Contamination of Our Natural Waters: A Report on State Fish Advisories and Bans in the United States.* Washington, DC: EDF.

Freeman, A. Myrick. 2000. "Water Pollution Policy." In *Public Policies for Environmental Protection,* edited by Paul Portney and Robert Stavins. Washington, DC: Resources for the Future.

Greene, David, and Kili Duleep. 1992. "Costs and Benefits of Automotive Fuel Economy Improvement: A Partial Analysis." *ORNL-6704.* Oak Ridge, TN: Oak Ridge National Laboratory.

Gruenspecht, Howard, and Robert Stavins. 2002. "New Source Review Under the Clean Air Act: Ripe for Reform." *Resources* 147:19.

Maloney, Michael T., and Gordon L. Brady. 1988. "Capital Turnover and Marketable Pollution Rights." *Journal of Law and Economics* 31, no. 1:203–226.

Office of Technology Assessment. 1992. *Managing Indus-trial Solid Wastes.* Washington, DC: U.S. GPO.

Portney, Paul R. 1990. "Air Pollution Policy." In *Public Policies for Environmental Protection,* edited by Paul Portney. Washington, DC: Resources for the Future.

Probst, Katherine N., and Paul R. Portney. 1992. *Assigning Liability for Superfund Cleanups.* Washington, DC: Resources for the Future.

Sigman, Hillary. 2000. "Hazardous Waste and Toxic Sub-stances Policy." In *Public Policies for Environmental Pro-tection,* edited by Paul Portney and Robert Stavins. Washington, DC: Resources for the Future.

U.S. Environmental Protection Agency. 2000. *Water Quality Conditions in the United States: A Profile from the 1988 National Water Quality Inventory Report to Congress.* Washington, DC: U.S. EPA, Office of Water.

U.S. Environmental Protection Agency. 1991. *Superfund: Environmental Progress.* Washington, DC: U.S. EPA.

MONITORING AND ENFORCEMENT

15.0 Introduction

OK: so the law is on the books, the EPA has written its regulations, states have developed their implementation plans and permitting processes. Now one last step remains. Monitoring for violations and enforcing the law is, as they say, a dirty job, but one that is essential to the entire regulatory process. Tough environmental regulations mean little if society does not have the resources or willpower to back them up. Monitoring and enforcement are particularly important, as we shall see in Chapters 16 and 17, when firms are allowed to have greater flexibility in pursuing innovative—and cost-saving—pollution reduction options.

This chapter begins with a look at the economics of crime and punishment. With this background, we move on to examine the degree to which firms appear to comply with environmental laws. We then consider some of the political-economic pressures faced by enforcement officials; private enforcement of environmental law through citizen suits; and ways in which the EPA might restructure the enforcement process to achieve more cost-effective compliance. The bottom line is that monitoring and enforcement is much less effective than it could and should be.

15.1 The Economics of Crime

Economists tend to view the decision by an individual to comply with an environmental law in terms of economic motivations. While good citizenship—obeying the law simply because it is the law—certainly plays a role in affecting behavior, it is also useful to analyze compliance decisions in terms of benefits and costs.

The benefits that come from complying with environmental laws are essentially the avoided costs of punishment: monetary costs (fines and penalties), a damaged reputation (both for corporations and individuals), and the fear of jail terms. The expected benefits depend upon two factors: the magnitude of the punishment if imposed and the likelihood of getting caught and convicted. The costs of compliance, on the other hand, are simply the additional outlays needed to install, service, and maintain pollution control equipment, and complete the relevant paperwork.

Figure 15.1 illustrates a hypothetical marginal cost–marginal benefit analysis for a manager in a coal-fired power plant who has to decide what percentage of the time she plans to be in compliance with the sulfur dioxide emission standards on her state permit. The marginal benefits of compliance start out high, because with a low compliance rate the probability of a detectable air quality violation—and subsequent punishment—rises. However, at higher compliance levels, the probability of getting caught declines, and so the marginal benefits (MB) of compliance also fall.

What are some of the costs of compliance? Let us assume that the major cost is maintaining the scrubbers that remove sulfur dioxide from the plant's gaseous emissions. The marginal costs of maintenance are initially low because the manager can divert engineers from other tasks to work on the scrubbers at relatively low cost. However, as engineers spend more time inspecting and repairing scrubbers, the other tasks they neglect become more and more important. Thus the costs of additional maintenance time begin to rise. As usual, X marks the spot: The manager will choose a C^* compliance level. At higher levels, the additional costs of compliance outweigh the additional benefits, and vice versa for lower levels.

The basic insight of this model is that compliance with the law will increase as the marginal benefits of compliance rise or the marginal costs fall. There are two basic ways to increase the marginal benefits of compliance. First, increase the severity of punishment. Increasing fines or prison terms or the public exposure of offenders will tend to improve environmental performance by shifting the MB curve up and to the right.

However, the benefits of compliance depend not only on the magnitude of the punishment but also on the probability of getting caught and convicted. Increased monitoring activity by enforcement officials will have an effect similar to increased punishment levels. In a study of water pollution enforcement, for example, Magat and

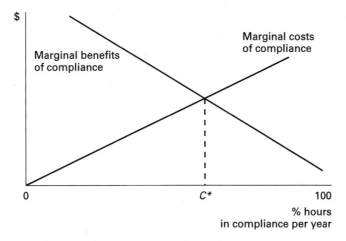

FIGURE 15.1 The Private Compliance Decision

Viscusi (1990) found that pulp and paper firms were much more likely to be in compliance with their discharge permits after an inspection by state or EPA officials.

The ability of punishment levels and detection and conviction probability to substitute for one another—known as the **punishment–detection trade-off**—can be useful to regulators. In theory, higher penalties can always substitute for lowered enforcement efforts. In the extreme, if the EPA could enforce the death penalty for any violation of sulfur dioxide emission standards, the agency could probably get by with one inspector for the entire country, saving taxpayers a lot of money! In reality, the law (and common norms of justice) place limits on total fines that can be levied, as well as the severity of criminal sanctions. In addition, firms cannot pay unlimited fines. Bankruptcy always looms in the background as a constraint on overly high monetary penalties. Given these limitations on penalties, increased detection becomes an attractive strategy.

A cost-effective way to increase monitoring is to focus regulatory attention on **repeat offenders.** Thus, if enforcement officials could commit to a policy of increased inspections for any firm found in violation, firms would have substantially greater incentive to obey the regulations. Russel (1990) recommends that the EPA "sentence" firms who have violated the law twice in a row to frequent audits for an extended period.

Alternatively, a greater use of electronic **continuous emissions monitors,** instead of physical on-site inspections, would have a similar effect. In the 1990s, only 11% of the 10,000 air pollution sources for which they were technically and economically feasible had such automatic monitoring devices. EPA officials estimate that such electronic monitors are about ten times as likely to detect a violation as will an on-site inspection (U.S. Government Accounting Office 1990). The EPA's new acid rain program requires continuous monitoring, and regulators have no discretion: fines are imposed for all violations. The consequence has been very high rates of compliance.

Raising the marginal benefits of compliance through more certain or more severe punishment will thus lead to fewer violations. Lowering the marginal costs of compliance will have a similar effect. If regulators can force polluters to install a pollution control technology with very low *marginal costs* of operation (regardless of the upfront fixed cost), then once that technology is in place, the polluter has little incentive not to comply with the law. In the extreme, if a control technology automatically insures compliance, then the marginal cost line in Figure 15.1 shifts down to become a straight line at zero dollars, and the manager chooses full compliance. In this case (zero marginal costs), the EPA need only check that the equipment has been properly installed.

Indeed, this argument provides some of the rationale behind the command-and-control regulatory approach, discussed in the last chapter, that dominates current legislation. The notion was that, once a firm had installed BAT or NSPS or BPT, the marginal costs of meeting the regulations would be sufficiently low to insure high compliance rates. As we will see, however, this theory has not proven correct, and the need for ongoing monitoring to insure compliance remains.[1]

A principal reason that technology-based regulation has not provided automatic compliance is that the performance of control equipment tends to deteriorate over

---

[1]Tietenberg (1985) points out that the high initial cost of technology-based regulation raised incentives for not installing pollution control technology in the first place. However, as we shall see, so-called initial compliance rates have been fairly good.

time. For example, catalytic converters on cars are automatic pollution control devices with zero marginal costs of operation. Unfortunately, over time they lose their effectiveness.[2] As a result, the EPA has mandated emission control inspection and maintenance programs for automobiles in many areas.

However, current inspection procedures themselves, mostly done at auto repair shops, are highly imperfect. One EPA study found that 69% of facilities passed vehicles that were intentionally designed to fail the test. As a result, the agency is considering requiring testers to use more expensive, more reliable equipment. This technology—with high up-front costs but lower marginal costs for a proper test—presumably will increase compliance among private-sector inspectors who are supposed to be increasing compliance by auto owners! For this strategy to succeed, however, the new testing equipment must remain reliable over time (Harrington and McConnell 1993).

15.2 The Economics of Punishment

In addition to developing a marginal benefit–marginal cost framework for analyzing decisions to commit crimes, economists have also focused attention on punishment issues. On an economic basis, which punishments are preferred, **jail terms** or **fines?** Table 15.1 provides a listing of the costs and benefits associated with each option.

Fines have two principal benefits over incarceration. First, they have much lower administrative and other social costs. Jail terms entail not only prisons and guards but also the lost tax revenues and output from the jailed individual. Second, to impose jail terms prosecutors must prove guilt "beyond a reasonable doubt"; fines can be levied under a much lower standard of evidence (Segerson and Tietenberg 1992).

On the other hand, fines also have drawbacks. Principal among these is the ability to **shift fines:** Typically, a corporation will pay only a portion of the monetary penalty it is assessed. Other parties will pick up some of the tab, including insurance companies; taxpayers (firms can write off cleanup efforts or damage payments but not actual fines); and/or consumers, as firms pass on fines in the form of higher prices. For example, Exxon's total bill for the 1987 *Valdez* oil spill in Alaska's Prince William Sound was more than $3 billion—$2 billion in cleanup costs and just more than $1 billion in penalties and fines. Of this total, however, insurers paid about $400 million (Goodstein 1992)[3]; assuming a 30% corporate income tax, Exxon benefited by paying at

TABLE 15.1   Fines versus Jail Terms

	Fines	Jail Terms
Benefits	Low social costs; lower level of proof	Cannot be shifted; large reputation effect
Costs	Can be shifted; often too small for deterrence	High social costs; high level of proof

---

[2]One study revealed that up to 25,000 miles of use, 45% of the cars meet the carbon dioxide standard; with more than 50,000 miles, only 10% of vehicles do so. Council on Environmental Quality (1984, 71).

[3]The author also discusses the degree to which insurance companies can shift some of these costs back to the insured firm by increasing their premiums; this will depend upon their ability to monitor the behavior of the insured firm.

least $500 million in reduced income taxes; finally, oil companies capitalized on the accident by boosting gas prices substantially ("Gasoline Prices" 1989).[4]

The penalties assessed in the *Valdez* case were truly spectacular. More commonly, however, the magnitude of fines are limited by statute and often bargained down by corporate attorneys. Fines are often criticized as only a **slap on the wrist,** that is, providing no real deterrent. From 1985 to 1992, Weyerhaeuser—a major international paper company—racked up 122 penalized violations at its three Washington State plants, paying $721,000 in fines, bargained down from an initial $1 million. "In many cases, Weyerhaeuser continued over the years to illegally discharge the same pollutant into the same waterway . . . paying the fine with little protest" ("Penalties" 1992). The fines in this case were not trivial—averaging about $6,000 per incident and $100,000 per year—but at the same time they had little immediate deterrent effect.

The Weyerhaeuser fines were about double the state average of $3,220 for violations that were actually penalized. However, many other violations were detected but not punished, and still others went undetected.[5] The EPA's inspector general was posed the following question by a U.S. senator: "Is it your testimony that the EPA's enforcement policies are so weak that it frequently pays polluters to keep polluting and pay the EPA's small fines rather than clean up their act?" "Absolutely," was the official response. ". . . We have found that over and over again." Similar sentiments were expressed in a recent EPA report.[6]

In theory, the EPA's official policy is to set the size of the fine equal to the economic benefit gained from noncompliance. However, by and large, the states have not adopted the EPA's philosophy, and fines are typically much lower. State inspectors, more sensitive to local economic and political issues and needing to maintain a working relationship with the industries they regulate, tend to use penalties only as a last resort. Their goal is to "achieve compliance by working cooperatively with facility owners." Penalties need be large enough only to "get the attention of management." Thus, state officials tend to reject the **deterrent feature of large fines** highlighted by our economic analysis of crime and punishment, though the federal EPA does sometimes win large, attention-grabbing settlements against companies.[7]

When financial penalties are limited by either statute, fear of bankruptcy, or political realities, or when their impact is blunted by the ability of firms to shift the burden either to insurance companies, taxpayers, or consumers, a role for more costly jail terms emerges.[8] However, because of the high cost of jail terms, the difficulty in

---

[4]While market fundamentals may have underlain the increase in prices, the accident provided an opportunity for a swift, substantial, and profitable increase. See "Bad Times for Exxon" (1989).

[5]Nationwide, in 1988 and 1989, the probability of being fined if caught for a significant air quality violation nationwide was 46%. (U.S. Government Accounting Office 1990).

[6]Testimony of John C. Martin, EPA Inspector General, before Senator John Glenn in "Serious Management Problems in the U.S. Government," Senate Government Affairs Committee, September 28, 1989; See also "The EPA" (1998).

[7]This paragraph and the quotes are drawn from U.S. Government Accounting Office (1990, 33–37). Gray and Deily (1991) present evidence that in countries with high unemployment rates, enforcement officials reduced the number of inspections for plants in the steel industry with a high probability of closing. U.S. EPA (1999) details the federal fines and settlements, some quite large, from fiscal year 1998.

[8]Segerson and Tietenberg (1992) discuss the issues of inefficiency (over-deterrence) and fairness (jail terms for nonnegligent offenders) in criminal prosecution when fines are limited. They conclude that negligence-based prosecutions will generally be efficient; if reputational costs are large, a strict liability rule can also induce efficient levels of compliance.

establishing guilt (as well as the fact that corporate officials donate a lot of money to the political system?), criminal prosecutions for environmental crimes remain an infrequently used option, about 1% to 2% of the total.[9] Most of the executives who do go to jail are from small companies. Cohen (1992) examined a sample of 116 cases representing more than 75% of all firms sentenced for environmental crimes in federal court from 1984 to 1990. The results are provided in Figure 15.2.

Considering just the raw numbers, 93 out of the 116 successful cases (80%) were brought against small firms—those with sales of less than $1 million or fewer than 50 employees. Of these, individuals were sentenced to prison in 23 cases, while fines were levied in the remainder. Compare this with 2 jail terms of the 23 total cases brought against large firms. On the face of it, not only were small firms prosecuted more often, but the likelihood of jail time once convicted appears to be much higher.

However, Cohen notes that small firms were more likely to be involved in additional criminal behavior beyond violating pollution laws (perjury, grand jury tampering, bribery, or conspiracy), while larger firms were more likely to be brought up on charges involving accidental discharge or activity by employees that occurred in clear violation of company policy. Disregarding these observations, Cohen finds that individuals from large and small firms face roughly the same probability of jail time once convicted.

Yet even when contrasting "comparable" cases, it still remained true that 13 out of 15 individuals in Cohen's sample who served time for environmental crimes over the period were from small companies. This imbalance resulted from the prosecutorial focus on small firms. Only 15% to 20% of federal criminal prosecutions for environmental crimes involved firms with annual sales greater than $1 million (Cohen 1992).

Several possible reasons exist for the disproportionate criminal focus on smaller firms. First, of course, there are more small firms than large firms. Second, it may be the case that small firms, with thinner profit margins, are less able to comply with the relevant laws or alternatively don't command the legal and/or political resources necessary to avoid criminal prosecution. Third, it is easier for prosecutors to pinpoint responsibility in small firms. Moreover, small firms are less able to pay large fines, so in some instances, jail time may be all that the prosecutor can get. Or perhaps, as an EPA official told the *Wall Street Journal:* " 'judges don't feel as comfortable' sending a *Fortune* 500 executive to prison" ("Few Big Firms" 1991).

The last two sections have focused on the economic theory of crime and punishment. To some extent, the EPA's official enforcement strategy follows the guidelines

	Small Firms[a]	Large Firms
Number of cases	93	23
Sentences with jail terms	23	2
Simple incarceration rate	25%	9%

FIGURE 15.2 Jail Terms by Firm Size
[a]Less than $1 million in sales or fewer than 50 employees.
Source: Data from Cohen (1992, 1092, footnote 124).

[9]Segerson and Tietenberg (1992) make this point.

laid out here. The agency in fact does look at compliance history in targeting its enforcement efforts, although it falls short of sentencing firms to extensive future audits. In principle, the EPA endorses the greater use of continuous emissions monitoring. The agency also provides publicity about settled cases to insure that negative reputation effects are maximized. Finally, the EPA has officially adopted a policy of tying fine size to the economic benefit of noncompliance, but many states have not accepted this approach.

Yet, as suggested by the data on the imposition of fines and the ability of firms to bargain over them, as well as the skewed distribution of criminal prosecutions, the agency can fail in insuring swift, evenhanded, and certain punishment when violations are detected. Given this background, we now turn to the record of industry compliance.

15.3 The Compliance Record

With technology-based regulation, there are two types of compliance to consider: **initial compliance** and **continuous compliance.** Initial compliance simply requires the installation of the required pollution control technology (BAT, BACT, etc.) and is easy to confirm. Continuous compliance, more difficult to insure, can be checked in two ways. First, inspectors can examine the control technology and determine if it has been maintained and operated properly. Most inspections follow this route.[10] An alternate approach, generally more difficult and expensive, involves sampling emissions to see if they meet the standards specified on a firm's operating permit, if one has been issued.

Some laws, notably the Clean Water Act, the 1990 Clean Air Act amendments, and the enabling legislation for the Toxics Release Inventory, require firms to monitor and self-report their emissions. Falsifying such reports is usually prosecuted as a criminal case. While the EPA has in the past been reluctant to use self-reported emissions as the basis for a violation, private groups have used this information in so-called "citizen suits" discussed in Section 15.5.

While initial compliance performance has been reasonably good, the more important environmental issue is continuous compliance: How well do firms meet the emission standards that are written into their operating permits? Given the vast resources devoted to pollution control efforts in the United States over the last thirty years, it is surprising how little we know about the continuous compliance record of U.S. industrial and municipal pollution sources. There are simply no comprehensive estimates of the degree to which firms and cities comply with relevant environmental laws.

Some data are available. In 1998, of the major facilities inspected by the EPA and the states, 91% were in compliance with the Clean Air Act requirements, 83% were in compliance with RCRA, and only 70% were found to have no significant violations of the Clean Water Act. Yet, these figures almost surely overstate the true rate of continuous compliance with air pollution regulations. Studies from the late 1970s, when the EPA was also reporting 90% compliance rates based on on-site inspections, found actual rates of

---

[10]Russel (1990) reports that in 1979, only 3% of sources deemed to be out of compliance were so-judged on the basis of emissions tests.

continuous compliance to be much lower, around 45%. And a review of RCRA enforcement actions from 1984 to 1988 revealed that in 80% of the cases, no clear evidence of compliance with enforcement orders was available.[11] Why the disparity?

The EPA most commonly relies on announced, on-site inspections, thus giving firms a chance to tune-up and repair their equipment. Major sources are inspected on average only once a year, and the inspection process, characterized by the EPA as "hit-or-miss," lasts only 2 to 4 hours. Inspectors focus attention on insuring that equipment is working properly; actual emissions are rarely tested. Finally, inspections are often hampered by cumbersome or unreliable testing equipment. In one case, for example, although "visible emissions from a major stationary source appeared to be about 60–80 percent opacity—well in excess of the 20% limit," the inspector could not perform his test because of the angle of the sun, and no violation was recorded. Given these limitations, the EPA itself has characterized its on-site inspection process as indicating only "whether a source is capable of being in compliance, rather than whether it is in compliance in its day-to-day operations."[12]

Some comfort can be taken from the fact that of the several thousand Clean Air Act violations uncovered by the inspection process each year, the EPA considers only about 500 to represent **significant noncompliance.** Significant noncompliance includes violations of state implementation plans in nonattainment areas and Class I (prevention of significant deterioration) areas, violations of toxic air pollutant standards, and failure to meet initial compliance requirements for new sources. At the beginning of fiscal year 1990, for example, the EPA and the states had identified 459 facilities in significant noncompliance. By the end of the year, an additional 537 were added to this list, while 584 of the total were either brought into compliance, placed on a compliance schedule, or had become the subject of an enforcement action. But again, this data may not be reliable. A 1998 EPA report found that state enforcement officials were underreporting significant violations of air and water standards (U.S. Environmental Protection Agency 1991b, 6-1; "EPA and States" 1998).

One acknowledged problem for the EPA has been enforcing regulations at government facilities. The federal government manages more than 10,000 facilities subject to environmental regulation. In 1998, the EPA and the states conducted about 1,350 inspections at federal facilities, finding compliance rates for air and hazardous waste regulations to be comparable to the private sector; federal facilities, water pollution performance was poorer than the private sector (U.S. Environmental Protection Agency 2000).

This section has reviewed the compliance record of the private and public sectors in the United States. On the surface, the figures for air and water pollution look encouraging. However, when one digs a bit deeper, it seems probable that official compliance rates overstate the actual degree of continuous compliance in these areas, probably by a substantial margin. In short, and consistent with the economic model developed in the

---

[11]The 1998 data is from the U.S. EPA (2000). Russel (1990) summarizes the continuous compliance studies. RCRA data are from the testimony of John C. Martin, EPA Inspector General, before Senator John Glenn in "Serious Management Problems in the U.S. Government," Senate Government Affairs Committee, 9/28/89.

[12]This paragraph, as well as quotes from the EPA's *1984 Compliance Monitoring Strategy for Major Stationary Sources,* is drawn primarily from the U.S. Government Accounting Office (1990).

first section of this chapter, compliance with environmental regulations cannot be taken for granted. Indeed, in many areas, violations appear to be fairly widespread.

15.4 The Political Economy of Enforcement

The states have the primary responsibility for enforcing most environmental laws.[13] The EPA's role, as characterized by former agency administrator William Ruckelshaus, is to be the "gorilla in the closet," available to back up state efforts.[14] The gorilla's efforts, however, have waxed and waned with the political winds. As indicated in Figure 15.3, criminal enforcement efforts rose from low levels at the end of the Reagan era into the first Bush Administration—from about 150 criminal referrals by the EPA to the Department of Justice to close to 300. Criminal referrals dropped a bit prior to the 1992 election (a pattern seen as well in 1999 to 2000), and then climbed steadily during the Clinton Administration, reaching a peak of almost 600 in 1998. Following the election of President Bush in 2000, enforcement declined substantially, with criminal referrals falling below 350. In 2002, the EPA's Director of Regulatory Enforcement resigned, charging that he had been "fighting a White House determined to weaken the laws we are trying to enforce" ("EPA Official Quits" 2001).

Figure 15.3 clearly illustrates the sensitivity of enforcement efforts to the political climate and **budget pressures.** Because the bulk of enforcement occurs at the state level, variations in enforcement activity across state lines can be substantial. Political struggles between industry and environmental advocates over the size of the environmental agency budget are an annual event in states across the country.

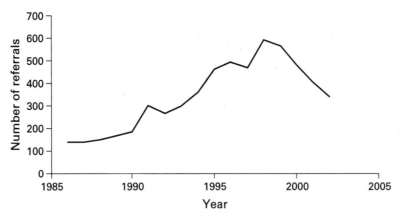

FIGURE 15.3 Trends in Federal Enforcement, 1986–2002 (EPA's Criminal Referrals)

Source: Syracuse University's Transactional Records Access Clearinghouse (TRAC), www.trac.syr.edu; accessed via the Web site of Public Employees for Environmental Responsibility (www.peer.org).

---

[13]For example, state officials conducted 91% of the 37,716 inspections of stationary air pollution sources in 1988. (U.S. Government Accounting Office 1990).

[14]"Testimony of Martin, before Senator John Glenn in "Serious Management Problems in the U.S. Government," Senate Government Affairs Committee, September 28, 1989.

When the EPA gorilla does swing into action, it can impose punishment at three levels. The agency can take an **administrative action** and impose fines directly. These can then be appealed through a quasi-judicial process within the EPA known as administrative review. This approach is by far the most common and accounts for about 90% of the penalties imposed. In 1998, the agency took 3,381 such administrative actions, while the states initiated an additional 11,200 (U.S. Environmental Protection Agency 1999). The EPA can also refer cases to the Department of Justice for prosecution as either a **civil case,** where fines can be levied, or a **criminal case,** where a combination of monetary sanctions and incarceration can be obtained. As one moves up the chain, both the standards of proof required for conviction and the available penalties become higher.

Even at the administrative level of punishment, however, the EPA inspectors are not empowered to impose fines as if they were parking tickets. Typically, a complex process of reporting, documentation, and review will be put in place prior to any penalty being assessed; once assessed, penalties are typically reduced on appeal or in a bargaining process. Figure 15.4 illustrates the steps in the **enforcement procedure** necessary to impose a penalty once an inspector has uncovered a RCRA violation at a hazardous waste facility.

From inspection (at the top), the most common enforcement path (administrative action) proceeds down the left side of the chart. After several steps, one arrives at a box labeled "Compliance agreement final order, establish compliance schedule." At this point, a monetary penalty may be assessed, although the final order might just as easily include only a timetable for compliance. Yet the ballgame is still not over, since the alleged violator can make an appeal to the EPA administrator and, failing that, to civil court. In the event of further noncompliance, the agency might refer the case to the Department of Justice (DOJ) for prosecution as a civil or criminal case.

Part of the haggling over penalties arises from the fact that regulations are not always written so that violations are clear-cut. A recent EPA report called for field-testing regulations prior to implementation to insure that they could actually be enforced (U.S. Environmental Protection Agency 1991a).

A final political-economic constraint on enforcement is the motivation, training, and experience of the EPA's inspectors. The EPA admits that **turnover** is a serious problem in its regional offices and in state enforcement agencies (U.S. Environmental Protection Agency 1991a). EPA employee and harsh critic William Sanjour provides a particularly blunt assessment of the hazardous waste enforcement program: "The job of inspecting hazardous waste facilities in EPA regions is a dead end job that nobody wants. Turnover is high, training is poor and morale is low. Just as in EPA headquarters, young inspectors soon learn that you don't become a hero by finding major violations in hazardous waste management facilities regulated by EPA. [Due to the revolving door among EPA management and the industry,] It's like the young cop busting the whore house that has been paying off the mayor. As a result, inspectors engage in trivial "bean-counting" exercises while looking for another job" (Sanjour 1992, 11).

Sanjour's characterization of the enforcement process as essentially corrupt is, I believe, an overstatement. Most agency officials work hard under difficult conditions to try to get a tough job done. Nevertheless, on occasion, political favoritism in the enforcement process is exposed to public view. In 1992, two regional chief inspectors for the Office of Surface Mining, Reclamation and Enforcement (a non-EPA regulatory

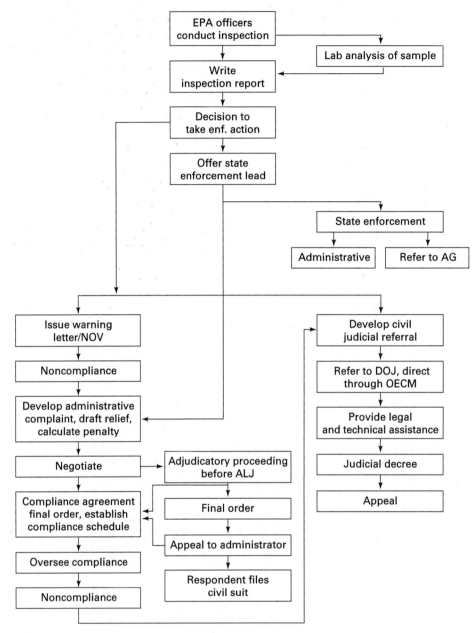

FIGURE 15.4 The RCRA Enforcement Process

Source: Sanjour (1992). Used with permission.

agency) charged that the office director had "ordered them to end investigations, reduce fines, eliminate penalties, divert prosecutions and prevent inspections." In one instance, after a two-year effort to get a strip-mine company to comply with water pollution regulations, a work-stoppage order was rescinded by superiors in Washington after having been in effect for only three days ("U.S. Mine Inspectors" 1992).

Like any other aspect of the regulatory process, enforcement is subject to **political influence.** This can take the form of budgetary restraints, regulations that are either unenforceable or highly cumbersome, or pressures (informal or direct) placed on field workers to take a "nonconfrontational" approach to their work. The point of this section is *not* to suggest that the EPA and state enforcement agencies are corrupt organizations. In fact, the EPA has focused substantial attention over the last few years on more effectively addressing one of its hardest tasks.[15] Rather, the point is merely to recognize the real-world constraints under which the enforcement process operates.

15.5   Citizen Enforcement

When writing most of the major environmental statutes, Congress recognized that public enforcement efforts might well prove inadequate to insure full compliance with the new laws. As a result, a provision in most of the statutes allows private citizens to take violators to court. These **citizen suits** became an increasingly important mechanism for enforcing environmental laws in the 1980s. Only 25 suits were filed in 1979. However, the declining federal enforcement efforts of the early 1980s (noted in Figure 15.3) sparked a growth in private actions increasing the number to 266 in 1986.

Congress limits the enforcement powers of citizens in a variety of ways. Citizens are required to give the alleged violator a sixty-day notice period, providing an opportunity to come into compliance. Any settlements must be reviewed by the EPA and the Justice Department, and citizens cannot sue if public officials are already pursuing a "diligent" enforcement effort.

However, citizen suits do have real teeth. Citizens can sue not only to force firms into compliance but also for damage restoration and often the imposition of penalties. Out-of-court settlements increasingly involve corporate financing of so-called environmentally beneficial expenditures—"donations" to organizations such as the Nature Conservancy, which buy up land for preservation purposes, or the financing of cleanups or environmental studies. Finally, private groups can recover court costs for successful suits.[16]

Given these incentives, why aren't private environmental groups more active in filing suits? The primary problem lies in the difficulty of monitoring emissions and **proving a violation.** The great majority of citizen suits (67%) have been filed under the Clean Water Act, where self-reporting of emissions is required. Environmental groups

---

[15]For a discussion of some of these initiatives, see Wasserman (1992).
[16]This paragraph is based on Mann (1991); see also Naysnerski and Tietenberg (1992).

have been able to obtain these self-reported records (at some expense). Proving a violation has thus been as simple as checking emission records against a firm's permit.

Hazardous waste violations make up most of the remainder (30%) of citizen suits.[17] While violations under RCRA and Superfund are not as easy to prove as Clean Water Act violations, Naysnerski and Tietenberg (1992) point out that the water and hazardous waste statutes are the only ones that allow citizens to sue for the courts to impose **penalties** on violators. Therefore, these are the statutes most likely to attract citizen attention.

Relatively few suits have been brought under the Clean Air Act, since prior to 1990 firms were by-and-large not required to report their emissions or to hold permits specifying legal emissions, and because penalties have not been an available remedy. However, recognizing the importance of citizen suits, the Clean Air Act amendments of 1990 expanded permitting and self-reporting requirements to most stationary air pollution sources. In addition, the act authorized the imposition of penalties for violations established under citizen suits. These steps encouraged citizen enforcement of the Clean Air Act (Buente 1991).

Finally, citizen enforcement can serve a particularly important role in enforcing compliance at government-owned facilities. If EPA or state officials are reluctant to pursue a government polluter for political reasons, citizen suits provide a fallback.

15.6 Cost-Effective Enforcement

Because the states and the EPA will never be provided sufficient resources to insure 100% compliance with all environmental laws, the enforcement agencies must make short-run decisions about how to best allocate their budgeted resources. The EPA's current strategy is to **target areas** for "maximum environmental results," while still maintaining some presence in all areas (U.S. Environmental Protection Agency 1991a, 10). In practice, this may mean paying less attention to hazardous waste enforcement (where health and ecosystem risks are currently thought to be "low"), and more attention to controlling airborne ozone or sulfate pollution, where environmental risks are thought to be higher.

In the long run, however, reducing bureaucratic discretion in the enforcement process appears to provide the best hope for reducing enforcement costs and, thus, increasing compliance rates overall. Three strategies can be recommended. First, require states to establish a penalty formula in which violations will lead to fines with a high probability. Fines need not be large and, indeed, must be low enough to be credibly imposed without bankrupting the violator, but they must be imposed with a high degree of certainty. By recognizing the deterrent value of fines, enforcement officials can get much greater compliance for the enforcement dollar.

Second, write regulations in which violations are clear and easily detected. For example, under the Clean Water Act, violations can be demonstrated merely by

---

[17]The percentages are calculated from data provided in Naysnerski and Tietenberg (1992).

comparing self-reported emissions with allowable emissions of a firm's permit. By contrast, until the 1990 amendments kicked in, proving a violation under the Clean Air Act proved difficult for the EPA and virtually impossible for private citizens.

Finally, rely more heavily on **continuous emissions monitoring,** rather than inspections, for establishing violations. Continuous monitoring greatly increases the probability that a violation will be detected, thus increases the benefits of compliance.

Similar recommendations have been made before. After making his own suggestions for improvement, Russel (1990, 270) speculates that better compliance may in fact not be the real goal of policy. Instead he raises the possibility that "legislation and accompanying regulations are meant to give the *appearance* of strictness while the reality is reflected by a lack of commitment to monitoring and enforcement." While there are obviously powerful political pressures that have shaped the "enforceability" (or lack thereof) of the current regulatory system, the reforms suggested here could help improve the long-run cost-effectiveness of the enforcement process.

15.7 Summary

In the real world, compliance with environmental protection laws is not automatic. To explain noncompliance, economists argue that polluters weigh the marginal benefits of compliance against its marginal costs. If the latter outweigh the former, firms choose to ignore regulations. Given this framework, one way regulators can increase compliance rates is by increasing the marginal benefits of compliance—imposing stiffer fines or prison terms, or more frequent inspection rates for violators.

Alternatively, regulators can in principle lower the marginal costs of compliance by requiring firms to install low marginal cost abatement technology. However, this latter strategy, which provided an argument for command-and-control regulation, has proven less successful than proponents had hoped. In fact, most control technologies lost their effectiveness over time without proper maintenance.

Regulators have two different punishment tools: fines and incarceration. Fines have two advantages: They impose lower social costs (prisons, jailers, and foregone productivity) and require a lower standard of proof. However, the magnitude of fines that can be imposed are limited by bankruptcy constraints as well as political practice. Moreover, firms can shift portions of some types of monetary penalties to insurers, taxpayers, and customers. Neither jail terms nor fines are imposed in a consistent fashion. Most violators receive no fines, fines are often reduced on appeal, and there is wide variation between states. Small companies face the bulk of criminal prosecution for environmental crimes.

The actual compliance record by firms and government agencies is far from perfect. While initial compliance—the installation of required equipment—has been forthcoming, continuous compliance is both harder to monitor and less often achieved. The highest compliance rates are probably achieved by private firms subject to the Clean Water Act, about 75% to 82%, where self-reported emissions monitoring is required.

Turning to political-economic considerations, enforcement activities are hampered by tight budgets, difficult to detect violations, cumbersome inspection procedures, poorly written regulations, complex mechanisms for punishing violators, high turnover among inspectors, and political influence. If legislators and regulators were so motivated, the enforcement process could be made much more effective by recognizing the deterrent value of "certain" punishment, writing enforceable regulations, and relying more heavily on continuous emissions monitoring. The latter two would also encourage private enforcement of regulations through the citizen suits. Recently, there have been initiatives and reforms in these directions, particularly at the national EPA level.

Overall, enforcement is probably the weakest link in the environmental protection chain. This insight will be particularly important in Part IV of this book, where we turn our attention to international issues. If enforcement is difficult in developed countries, it becomes even more challenging in poor countries. In a developing nation, the problems of underpaid and inadequately trained inspectors, combined with very weak governmental authority, can lead quickly to a corrupt and ineffective enforcement process. For these reasons, it is unlikely that a regulatory strategy can be pursued with great effectiveness in many poor countries. This provides a strong rationale for government policy to focus on the development of "clean technology," discussed in Chapters 18 to 20, which reduces the need for regulation in the first place.

A second application of the enforcement lesson relates to international pollution control agreements, the topic of Chapter 23. Such agreements are also only as strong as the underlying enforcement mechanism. If it is difficult for EPA officials to insure compliance with national water quality laws in, say, Ohio or Montana, the problem will be compounded when the agency is forced to consider compliance with carbon dioxide emission limitations in, say, France or Angola. Here the question of credible sanctions emerges. What penalties can be imposed on countries (or firms within countries) that violate an agreement and how will compliance be monitored?

The last four chapters of this book have focused on the question: Is government up to the job? Along the way, we have examined a portrait of the policy process that some might characterize as cynical, others overly optimistic. The main point is that government intervention in the economy to promote environmental goals does not automatically follow any "rational" process, for example cost-minimization or risk reduction. Instead, it is inherently political.

This does not mean that government intervention is necessarily bad, useless, or self-defeating. It simply means that we need to go into it with our eyes wide open. The challenge for environmental economists is to recommend policy reforms that are (1) politically feasible and (2) still effective when implemented in a politically compromised form. The next part of this book will examine two general economic strategies for improving governmental performance in the environmental arena—incentive-based regulation and the promotion of clean technology.

APPLICATION 15.0

Enforcing Auto Emission Limits

Noncompliance with auto emission limits is fairly widespread; as I noted in the text, some 69% of test facilities passed cars that were designed to fail. In a review of the issues faced, Harrington and McConnell (1993) cited faulty testing equipment, exemptions in some states for old (and highly polluting) cars, and poor enforcement. The response of the EPA and Congress to this situation has been to call for improved testing equipment, to restrict exemptions, and to centralize the testing procedure in state-run centers, rather than have the tests done in gas stations. While the last step should improve compliance by testers, it also increases costs to consumers, who will now have to travel farther to get tested.

Figure 15.5 provides Harrington and McConnell's estimates of the marginal costs of reducing volatile organic compounds (VOCs), based on three types of testing equipment the EPA may require. (VOCs are chemical compounds that contribute to ozone pollution or smog.)

The 2500 idle test is the current technology that measures emissions only at the tailpipe; the pressure and purge tests pick up currently unmeasured VOCs that escape from the car's emission recycling system. The IM240 test is a more effective (and expensive) version of the 2500 idle test of tailpipe emissions and has been proposed as a replacement.

1. The horizontal axis measures tons of emission reduction per thousand cars inspected. How much extra per ton does it cost to increase emission reductions from about 2.7 tons (achieved with the 2500 idle test) to about 4.9 tons

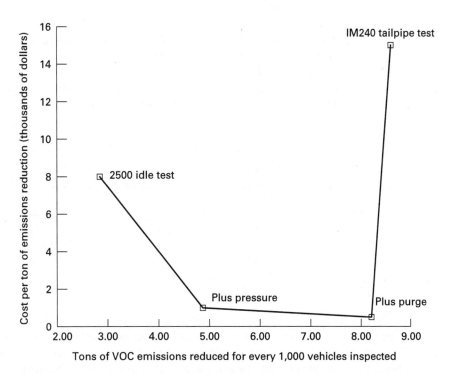

FIGURE 15.5 Marginal Costs of Reducing VOCs Through Improved Enforcement

Source: Harrington and McConnell (1993). Reprinted by permission.

(with a pressure test added)? Does the graph indicate that it is actually cheaper for testing centers to have both a 2500 idle and a pressure test available, rather than just a 2500 idle test?

2. Up to the point where the purge system is installed, the MC of reduction curve slopes downward. Is this the usual shape for an MC of reduction curve? (Refer to Chapter 4.) If not, can you tell a story about technological progress and compliance rates that might explain the downward slope?

3. How much extra does it cost per ton of VOCs reduced to go from an emission reduction of about 8.2 (with the 2500, pressure ,and purge tests) to about 8.7 (with the pressure and purge tests, and the IM240 replacing the 2500)? What does this say about the relative importance of VOC emissions from the tailpipe versus the recycling system? Does this mean that, from an efficiency point of view, the IM240 test is a bad idea?

APPLICATION 15.1

Fun with Graphs

It was stated in this chapter that the EPA officially supports a policy of setting fines to eliminate all monetary gain from noncompliance with regulations. (The states have generally not adopted this policy, opting for smaller fines.)

1. Assume that any violation by a firm will be detected with certainty. In this case, try and figure out what the MB curve of compliance in Figure 15.1 looks like under the EPA's recommended policy. (The MC curve stays the same.) Will the plant manager choose full compliance?

2. In the real world, detection does not occur with certainty. In this case, will the manager choose full compliance under the EPA policy?

KEY IDEAS IN EACH SECTION

15.0 Enforcement is the bottom line in environmental regulation. Without an effective commitment to enforcement, significant and widespread noncompliance will develop.

15.1 In an economic model of environmental crime, economic decision makers weigh the marginal benefits of compliance against the marginal costs. Regulators can **trade-off punishment for detection** to raise the marginal benefits of compliance; detection can be increased via use of **continuous emissions monitors** or a focus on **repeat offenders.** Low marginal compliance costs have been used to justify CAC regulation, but this argument fails if control technology breaks down over time.

15.2 **Fines** are used much more often than **jail terms** because the standard of proof and the cost to the state are lower. However, state enforcement officials tend *not* to impose high enough fines for deterrent purposes. In addition, fines are often **shifted** and reduced through bargaining. Incarceration rates are also not uniform, being much higher for small firm managers.

15.3   There are two types of compliance: **initial compliance,** which has been fairly good, and **continuous compliance.** Data on continuous compliance with environmental laws are not good, but the available evidence suggests **significant noncompliance** in both the private and public sectors. This is due in part to the unreliability and infrequency of on-site inspections.

15.4   Most enforcement is done by the states. The principal political constraint on enforcement is **budgetary pressure.** Enforcement measures take the form of **administrative action** (by far the most common) or can proceed as **civil or criminal cases. Enforcement procedures** are lengthy and complex. There is also high **turnover** among inspectors and some evidence of **political influence** in the enforcement process.

15.5   **Citizen suits** to enforce environmental laws have become increasingly important. Suits are most common where it is easiest to **prove a violation** and where a **penalty** can be imposed on violators.

15.6   One way to improve the cost-effectiveness of enforcement efforts is to **target violations** that pose high levels of risk. In the long run, cost-effective regulation can be achieved by designing regulations that are **easy to enforce, insure punishment** with a high probability, and rely on **continuous emissions monitoring,** rather than inspection, to prove a violation.

REFERENCES

"Bad Times for Exxon, Good Times for the Other Major Oils." 1989. *Fortune,* 8 May.

Buente, David T. 1991. "Citizen Suits and the Clean Air Act Amendments of 1990: Closing the Enforcement Loop." *Environmental Law* 21:2233–2253.

Cohen, Mark A. 1992. "Environmental Crime and Punishment: Legal/Economic Theory and Empirical Evidence on Enforcement of Environmental Statutes." *The Journal of Criminal Law and Criminology* 82, no. 4:1053–1108.

Council on Environmental Quality. 1984. *Environmental Quality.* Washington, DC: U.S. GPO.

"The EPA and States Found to be Lax on Pollution Law." 1998. *The New York Times,* 7 June.

"EPA Official Quits, Chastises White House." 2001. *The Portland Oregonian,* 1 March.

"Few Big Firms Get Jail Time for Polluting." 1991. *Wall Street Journal,* 9 December.

"Gasoline Prices Post a Sharp Rise." 1989. *New York Times,* 13 April.

Goodstein, Eban. 1992. "Saturday Effects in Tanker Oil Spills." *Journal of Environmental Economics and Management* 23:276–288.

Gray, Wayne, and Mary E. Deily. 1991. "Enforcement of Pollution Regulations in a Declining Industry." *Working Paper 89–8.* Worcester, MA: Clark University.

Harrington, Winston, and Virginia D. McConnell. 1993. "Vehicle Emissions Inspection and Maintenance: Where Do We Go from Here?" *Resources* 110, Winter:11–15.

Helland, Eric. 1998. "The Revealed Preference of State EPAs: Stringency, Enforcement and Substitution." *Journal of Environmental Economics and Management,* 35, no. 2:242–261.

Magat, Wesley A., and W. Kip Viscusi. 1990. "Effectiveness of the EPAs Regulatory Enforcement: The Case of Industrial Effluents." *Journal of Law and Economics* 33, no. 2:331–360.

Mann, David S. 1991. "Polluter-Financed Environmentally Beneficial Expenditures: Effective Use or Improper Abuse of Citizen Suits Under the Clean Water Act?" *Environmental Law* 21, no. 175:175–211.

Naysnerski, Wendy, and Tom Tietenberg. 1992. "Private Enforcement of Federal Environmental Law." *Land Economics* 68, no. 1:28–48.

"Penalties Aren't Stopping Land, Water Pollution." 1992. Associated Press Story reported in the Spokane *Spokesman-Review,* 12 December.

Russell, Clifford S. 1990. "Monitoring and Enforcement." In *Public Policies for Environmental Protection,* edited by Paul Portney. Washington, DC: Resources for the Future.

Sanjour, William. 1992. *What EPA Is Like and What Can Be Done About It.* Washington, DC: Environmental Research Foundation.

Segerson, Kathleen, and Tom Tietenberg. 1992. "The Structure of Penalties in Environmental Enforcement: An Economic Analysis." In *Innovation in Environmental Policy,* edited by Tom Tietenberg. Brookfield, VT: Edward Elgar.

Tietenberg, Tom. 1985. *Emissions Trading: An Exercise in Reforming Pollution Policy.* Washington, DC: Resources for the Future.

U.S. Environmental Protection Agency. 1991a. *Enhanced Environmental Enforcement for the 1990s.* Washington, DC: U.S. EPA.

U.S. Environmental Protection Agency. 1991b. *Enforcement Accomplishments Report, FY1990.* Washington, DC: U.S. EPA.

U.S. Environmental Protection Agency. 1999. *1998 Enforcement and Compliance Assurance Accomplishments Report 1998.* Washington, DC: U.S. EPA, Office of Enforcement and Compliance Assurance.

U.S. Environmental Protection Agency. 2000. *The State of Federal Facilities: An Overview of Environmental Compliance at Federal Facilities, FY 1997–1998.* Washington, DC: U.S. EPA, Office of Enforcement and Compliance Assurance.

U.S. Government Accounting Office. 1990. *Air Pollution: Improvements Needed in Detecting and Preventing Violations.* Washington, DC: U.S. GAO.

"U.S. Mine Inspectors Charge Interference by Agency Director." 1992. *New York Times,* 21 December.

Wasserman, Cheryl. 1992. "Federal Enforcement: Theory and Practice." In *Innovation in Environmental Policy,* edited by Tom Tietenberg. Brookfield, VT: Edward Elgar.

PART III

HOW CAN WE DO BETTER?

In Part II of this book, we reviewed the current regulatory picture and discovered that after more than three decades of dedicated national efforts to control pollution and expenditures of hundreds of billions of dollars, our accomplishments are decidedly mixed. With a few exceptions, regulation has essentially held the line against economic and population growth, yet it has failed to achieve its stated objective of substantially reducing many pollutant concentrations to "safe" levels.

We also identified three main obstacles to successful government action to control pollution. First, hampered by imperfect information and motivated by either material gain, peer approval, or ideological commitment, regulators may pursue policies that deviate from their legislative mandate—whether that mandate is safety or efficiency. Second, the current command-and-control (CAC) regulatory structure often discourages cost-effective pollution control in the short run and innovation in new technology in the long run. Finally, the difficult yet vital job of monitoring and enforcing compliance with regulations is often underfunded.

Given this background, Part III will explore the question "How can we do better?" Doing better is defined as achieving a specified pollution goal at lower cost and with greater certainty.

CHAPTER 16

INCENTIVE-BASED REGULATION: THEORY

16.0 Introduction

In the late 1960s, when major new environmental legislation was being contemplated, economists had a bit of advice to offer: Why not harness market incentives to control pollution? The basic idea was twofold. First, make polluting an expensive activity. This would both reduce pollution directly and induce a search for less polluting substitutes. Second, lower the costs of pollution control by leaving decisions about how specifically to reduce pollution up to firms and individuals.

Two schemes were widely discussed. The first was a **pollution tax** (also known as an *effluent* or *emission charge* or *a Pigovian tax*).[1] For example, to reduce the acid rain caused by sulfur dioxide emissions from power plants, one could institute a tax on emissions of, say, $200 per ton of SO_2. Alternatively, one might achieve a rollback through a **marketable permit system** (also known as **tradeable permit** or **cap-and-trade** systems). Here permits would be issued only up to a certain target level of emissions. These permits could then be bought and sold, again putting a price tag on pollution. These two regulatory approaches—pollution taxes and marketable permit systems—are referred to as **incentive-based (IB) regulation,** since they rely on market incentives to both reduce pollution and minimize control costs.

As we saw in Chapter 13, the recommendations of economists were largely ignored in the drafting of the major environmental legislation of the early 1970s. Instead, the nation opted for what we have called the command-and-control (CAC) approach to regulation, requiring uniform emissions across sources and mandating the adoption of particular pollution control technologies. Since that time, economists have maintained a steady drum beat of support for the more flexible incentive-based approach. Twenty-five years later, the mid-1990s saw the first wide-scale test of this type of regulation in air pollution control. Since 1995, sulfur dioxide emission credits

---

[1]After the economist who first proposed pollution taxes, A. C. Pigou.

have been traded among 110 coal-burning electric facilities, mostly in the East and Midwest. At the same time, a tradeable permits system has been introduced in the Los Angeles basin, covering two urban air pollutants: sulfur oxide and nitrogen oxide. And at the international level, permit trading is an important component of the (not-yet-implemented) Kyoto global warming treaty.

From a theoretical perspective, incentive-based systems offer several advantages over a CAC approach. First, IB systems will promote more cost-effective regulation in the short run. (Recall that cost-effectiveness is defined as achieving a given pollution target at the lowest possible cost.) Perhaps more importantly, over the long run IB systems provide incentives for firms to seek out new technologies to lower pollution control costs. Finally, in theory, an IB approach reduces the costly burden of information gathering for regulatory bureaucrats—rather than having to choose which technology is to be deemed BACT or BAT or LAER, regulators need only specify the tax level or the number of permits and then let private incentives take over. Because control over information is a primary means of political influence, as we saw in Chapter 12, IB approaches can reduce such influence in the regulatory process.

However, IB approaches are not without their theoretical drawbacks, including problems of monitoring and enforcement, hot spots (high local concentrations of pollutants), thin markets, and the possible exercise of market power, among others. Overcoming these obstacles to realize the potential of IB regulation is the challenge facing policy makers today.

This chapter examines in some detail the theoretical advantages and disadvantages of IB regulation. Chapter 17 will then take a closer look at the lessons to be learned from our limited practical experience with IB systems and the way that potential problems with the IB approach are being dealt with in the ongoing marketable permit experiments.

16.1 The Cost-Effective Rule

One defining aspect of the stereotypical CAC regulatory approach is its prescription of *uniform standards* for all pollution sources. Economists have widely criticized this requirement, since it essentially blocks any effort to achieve cost-effective pollution control.[2] To see why, we need to understand the

> **Cost-effectiveness rule.** Cost-effectiveness is achieved if and only if the marginal cost of reduction is equal for each pollution source.

It is easy to show that this is true. Consider a town called Grimeville, hosting an oil refinery, A, and a coal plant, B. The Grimeville City Council wants to control total emissions of harmful gunk at 20 tons per day and is considering a uniform standard of 10 tons per day for each plant. Suppose that when refinery A emits 10 tons of gunk, it has marginal reduction costs of $10 per ton, while at an emission level of 10 tons, coal plant B has marginal reduction costs of only $2 per ton. Here's the

---

[2]Uniform standards are also typically inefficient. For example, they mandate the same level of protection for densely and sparsely populated areas. However, uniform standards are easier to defend on safety grounds.

PUZZLE

If the Grimeville City Council imposes a uniform, 10 ton per plant standard, will it be achieving its pollution target cost-effectively?

SOLUTION

No, because there is a less expensive way of keeping pollution at 20 units total in Grimeville. Suppose that plant B decreased its pollution level from 10 tons to 9 tons. This would cost $2. If plant A then increased its pollution from 10 tons to 11 tons, it would save $10. Overall, industry in Grimeville would save $8 and still achieve the desired pollution target.

Whenever the marginal cost of pollution reduction at one source is greater than that at another, overall costs can be reduced *without changing the pollution level* by decreasing pollution at the low-cost site and increasing it at the high-cost site. Thus, cost-effectiveness is achieved *only* when the marginal costs of reduction are equal at all sites.

Let us expand the Grimeville example to illustrate how the city council might identify the cost-effective method of reducing pollution to 20 tons. Table 16.1 lists the complete marginal reduction cost schedules for the two plants.

Table 16.1 reveals that it will cost $1 for plant A to reduce pollution from 20 tons to 19 tons per day, $2 to move from 19 to 18, and so forth. Marginal reduction costs thus rise as pollution falls. Plant B, on the other hand, faces zero marginal reduction costs all the way back to 10 units of gunk. Below 10 units, however, pollution reduction becomes increasingly costly for plant B as well. Of the two, plant B clearly has lower overall emission reduction costs.

The council has a two-part problem to solve: choose pollution levels at the two plants so that (1) total pollution equals 20 tons and (2) marginal reduction costs are (roughly) equal. We already know that cost-effectiveness will require plant A to pollute more than 10 tons, while plant B pollutes less. The simple way to identify the cheapest solution is to try a few combinations.[3] Table 16.2 rearranges the information in Table 16.1 to examine pollutant combinations that add up to a total of 20 tons per day.

We can use the table to find the cost-effective regulatory option. We have already discovered that moving from (10, 10) to (11, 9) lowers total costs by $8. Similarly, moving on to (12, 8) generates savings of $9 at a cost of only $4. Finally, moving to (13, 7) saves an additional $2 ($8 – $6). However, the (14, 6) option increases net costs by $1, since the additional savings ($7) are less than the additional costs ($8). Moving on to (15, 5) is an even worse idea, since the savings are only $6 for an additional expense of $12. Thus, the cheapest regulatory option that achieves total pollution of 20 is plant A: 13, plant B: 7. Note, as our rule predicts, at this point marginal reduction costs are roughly equal.

---

[3]A more general approach is to use algebra. The equations for the marginal reduction costs for plants A and B are, respectively: $MC_a = 20 - x_a$, and $MC_b = 20 - 2x_b$. For cost-effectiveness, these two MC equations should be set equal to each other. We also have the constraint that total pollution must equal 20: $x_a + x_b = 20$. With three equations and two unknowns, we can solve the system to get $x_a = 13.333$ and $x_b = 6.666$.

TABLE 16.1 Marginal Cost of Gunk Reduction in Grimeville

Pollution at Each Plant (tons/day)	MC of Reduction ($/ton) Plant A	MC of Reduction ($/ton) Plant B
20		
	> $ 1	— $ 0
19		
	> 2	— 0
18		
	> 3	— 0
17		
	> 4	— 0
16		
	> 5	— 0
15		
	> 6	— 0
14		
	> 7	— 0
13		
	> 8	— 0
12		
	> 9	— 0
11		
	> 10	— 0
10		
	> 11	— 2
9		
	> 12	— 4
8		
	> 13	— 6
7		
	> 14	— 8
6		
	> 15	— 10
5		
	> 16	— 12
4		
	> 17	— 14
3		
	> 18	— 16
2		
	> 19	— 18
1		
	> 20	— 20
0		

TABLE 16.2 Identifying the Cost-Effective Option

Plant A Pollution (tons of gunk/day)	Plant A Marginal Savings as Pollution Rises	Plant B Pollution (tons of gunk/day)	Plant B Marginal Cost as Pollution Falls
10		10	
	> $10		> $ 2
11		9	
	> $ 9		> $ 4
12		8	
	> $ 8		> $ 6
13		7	
	> $ 7		> $ 8
14		6	
	> $ 6		> $10
15		5	

We can compare total costs at the uniform standard option (10, 10) and the cost-effective option (13, 7) to see how much money we save from the latter choice. Total costs can be calculated as just the sum of all the marginal costs, so total costs at (10, 10) are $1 + 2 + 3 + 4 + 5 + 6 + 7 + 8 + 9 + 10 = 55$. Total costs at (13, 7) are $1 + 2 + 3 + 4 + 5 + 6 + 7 + 2 + 4 + 6 = 40$, for a net savings of $55 - 40 = 15$.

This example illustrates a principal reason why, in general, CAC systems that require uniform standards do not achieve cost-effectiveness. Since both high- and low-cost plants must meet the same standard, in our example of 10 tons per day, opportunities for reducing overall costs are ignored. But why are uniform standards set in the first place? Couldn't the Grimeville City Council achieve a cost-effective solution by going through the above exercise and choosing (13, 7) in the first place?

In general, the answer is no. In the real world, the council might well founder on a lack of information, what economists refer to as **imperfect information.**[4] Only the firms have access to the pollution control cost information in Table 16.1, and they would be unwilling to share this data with the public. Of course, the regulators might still recognize in a qualitative way that refinery A has higher reduction costs than coal plant B, and thus incorporate some concern for cost savings into their regulatory design. As we shall see, some CAC systems do just this.

Yet, such a rough approach would not capture all cost savings. In addition, in the political arena, plant B's owners and residents around plant A might argue against such a move on the grounds of equity or safety. The next section illustrates that, in theory, incentive-based regulation will achieve cost-effectiveness "automatically" through a market mechanism.

16.2 IB Regulation and Cost-Effectiveness

Back in the Grimeville City Council offices, the village economist proposes a tax system for controlling pollution and claims that the tax will deliver cost-effective pollution control. To prove her point, she draws graphs of the two marginal cost of reduction curves, reproduced in Figure 16.1. (Note that she has switched the direction of the horizontal axis—it now shows *increasing* pollution rather than pollution reduction.)[5] She

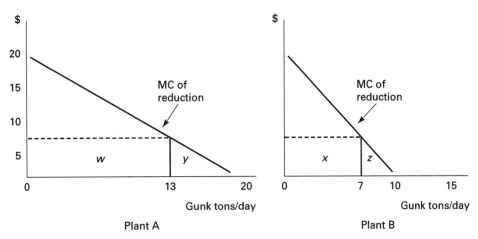

FIGURE 16.1 Pollution Taxes Are Cost-Effective

---

[4]See Appendix 16A for a discussion of regulation under imperfect information.

[5]The reason for this is that it is easier to illustrate cleanup costs and tax revenues when the marginal cost of reduction curve is drawn sloping downward.

then proclaims, "Consider, if you will, the effect of a tax on gunk emissions of $7.50 per ton on the pollution situation in our fair city. Faced with such a tax, plant A will reduce its pollution level from 20 to 13 units. It won't go below 13 tons because for these units it is cheaper for it to pollute and pay the tax than it is to reduce pollution. By a similar logic, plant B will reduce pollution down to 7 tons per day. Because at the final pollution levels (13, 7) the marginal cost of reduction for both firms will be just less than the tax and thus equal to each other, my plan will be cost-effective.

"Moreover," the economist continues, "since pollution now has a 'price,' every day they pollute the firms will pay for the privilege, 20 * $7.50, or $150 in all (areas *w* and *x* in the figure). This will provide them with a tremendous long-run incentive to search out new, less polluting ways of doing business. But best of all, Grimeville will be rich! We'll earn tax revenue from the 20 units of pollution equal to $150 per day!"

For a moment, the audience is awed by the overwhelming clarity and logic of the economist's argument. But only for a moment. "Wait a minute," objects the oil refinery lobbyist. "Grimeville won't earn a dime. Those steep taxes will drive both plants out of business. Not only are you making industry pay to reduce pollution from current levels back to 20 units (areas *y* and *z*), but now you're imposing additional taxes as well!"

"Hmmmm," mumbles the village economist. "We can solve this problem. You'll still have to pay the pollution tax, but we'll give the industry an income tax rebate based on the average pollution tax to make the whole thing 'revenue neutral.' [So much for Grimeville's tax windfall!] As long as the size of the rebate is not connected to your individual firm's efforts to reduce pollution, the pollution tax will still give you an incentive for further reductions."

"But, how will we know where to set the tax?" the village environmentalist demands. "If we set it too low, gunk pollution will be more than 20 tons per day. Then we'll have to adjust the tax upward, and he," pointing at the refinery lobbyist, "is bound to complain about taxes being raised again. Besides, inflation will erode the value of the tax. And even if the tax is inflation-adjusted, pollution levels will keep going up as population and production levels grow."

"Valid points," the economist concedes. "But here's another idea. Suppose, instead of the pollution tax, we institute a marketable permit system."

"A what?" asks the mayor.

"A marketable permit system. Let me explain. We're interested in reducing total pollution to 20 tons per day, correct? Suppose we give each firm 10 one-ton permits allowing them to pollute, but we also allow the firms to buy or sell these permits. What will be the outcome?"

"I'm all ears," says the mayor.

"Plant A, facing high marginal reduction costs, would dearly love to have an eleventh permit. In fact, from Table 16.2 we know it would be willing to pay up to $10 per day to get its hands on one. Plant B, on the other hand, would be willing to sell one permit, reducing to 9, for anything over $2 per day. Thus, a deal will be made. By a similar logic, A would be willing to pay up to $9 for a twelfth permit, and B would sell another for anything over $4. Finally, A would buy the thirteenth for a price of up to $8, while B would part with an additional permit for a price greater than $6. However, the firms would stop there. Plant A would be willing to pay only $7 for the fourteenth permit, while B would have to be paid $8 to reduce down to 6 permits. So, *voila!* Market incentives will generate trade in permits until a cost-effective solution (13, 7) is reached.

"Note that the final price for a permit in this bargaining scenario is between $6 and $8 per day, which is very close to our $7.50 tax. As in the tax case, pollution now has a 'price,' giving firms long-run incentives to develop new, less pollution-intensive techniques so that they can sell their excess permits. Moreover, if new firms enter the area, they can do so only by buying existing permits. Total pollution will be *fixed* at 20 units."

"Wait a minute," objects the environmentalist. "Why should we give away the 'right to pollute'?"

"Well," says the economist, "we do that already whenever we set legal pollution standards. But one alternative would be for the government to sell the permits, instead of giving them away. A price of $7.50 or so would clear the market—since at that price plant A would demand 13, and plant B would demand 7. [Take a minute to check this.] Certain types of auctions would in fact generate such a price. But if you think about it, government sale of permits is really identical to a tax system! Selling permits to pollute one unit at $7.50 per day is the same thing as charging a tax of $7.50 per day for any units of gunk emitted."

"Which is exactly why we oppose permit sales by the government," pipes in the oil refinery lobbyist. "Once again you're asking industry to cough up areas *w* and *x* in taxes, in addition to paying areas *y* and *z* in cleanup costs. But this permit giveaway idea sounds interesting. . . ."

Now the conversation in Grimeville went on well into the night, but at this point I would like to interrupt and summarize the main points. First, both tax systems and marketable permit systems will achieve cost-effective pollution control "automatically," at least on the chalkboard. In either case, *government regulators do not need to know anything about control costs at different sources.* In the case of a tax, regulators merely specify a tax level, observe the market response, and if the induced pollution reduction is too little (or too great), adjust the tax upward (or downward). In the permit case, the government merely specifies the number of permits desired and distributes them by either sale or giveaway.

The discussion also highlights one of the political drawbacks of taxes (and permit sale systems). Polluters, whether firms or consumers, object strenuously to having to pay the government for the right to pollute up to the legal limit, in addition to the cleanup costs they face. For example, if the government were to impose a CAC standard of 13 units for plant A, the firm would have to pay area *y* in Figure 16.1 to clean up from 20 tons back to 13 tons. Under a $7.50 per ton tax (or permit-sale system), the firm would have to pay, in addition to these cleanup costs, $13 \times \$7.50 = \$97.50$, or area *w*. Such additional costs might in fact drive a firm out of business, and thus they impose a **bankruptcy constraint** on the imposition of tax or permit policies.

In principle, pollution taxes or permit sales can be made **revenue neutral** by rebating the revenues back to the affected firms or individuals in the form of income tax cuts. Parties paying the tax would not receive a rebate exactly equal to their pollution tax, since that would negate its effect. Instead, each polluter would receive an average rebate. In this way, average incomes remain the same, but the price of pollution still rises. Such income tax rebates have been widely discussed as a way to reduce both the political opposition to and the regressive impact from any substantial carbon tax imposed to combat global warming.

In addition, substituting pollution tax revenues for a tax on labor (the income tax) would enhance **labor market efficiency,** because in this particular case, people would work harder if they faced lower income taxes. Indeed, recent work on the general equilibrium effects of pollution taxes and marketable permits has shown that if tax or permit sale revenues *are not* recycled, then the short-run costs of the regulation (working through the impact that higher product prices have on labor supply) may become much more significant. For more detail on this point, see Chapter 9.

Finally, because pollution taxes on their own are regressive, any widespread scheme to introduce them should also be part of a package that is at least **non-regressive.** That is, the regressive impact of pollution taxes should be offset by cutting income taxes for poor and working-class people more than for wealthier individuals.

In the case of a cap-and-trade system, rather than permit sales by government, permit giveaways substantially reduce the cost to, and political opposition from, industry. In the example above, where each firm was endowed with ten permits, plant A ultimately had to pay for only three of its thirteen permits, while plant B actually reaped a windfall from the giveaway policy.

The Grimeville discussion of the permit system also demonstrates that, in theory, *the final outcome doesn't depend on whether the permits are sold or distributed free of charge;* in either case a cost-effective solution will be achieved, though who pays how much to whom will vary. This is an important application of the Coase theorem discussed in Chapter 4.

A **Coase theorem corollary** can be stated as follows:

If there is a well-functioning permit market, a cost-effective outcome will be achieved by a marketable permit system *regardless* of the initial ownership of the permits.

Take a minute to convince yourself that even if all 20 permits are initially given to plant A, the cost-effective solution (13, 7) will ultimately result. (Since we have only two firms, market power may be present. You have to assume that plant A isn't interested in driving plant B out of business by refusing to sell any permits!)

Having convinced the Grimeville City Council that, at least in theory, incentive-based systems achieve short-run cost-effectiveness, a final question to the village economist might be, "So what?" How much could we, as a society, really save from a shift to an IB approach? At least a dozen studies have compared the compliance costs of CAC regulation with the costs of a hypothetical cost-effective approach. These studies provide a median CAC cost that is four times as high as the least-cost approach (see Tietenberg 1990). Does this mean that we should expect overall savings of about 300% from a shift to IB regulation?

The answer is no. In practice, IB systems have not performed as well as they do on paper. For a variety of reasons discussed below, real-world pollution tax or tradeable permit approaches do not achieve truly cost-effective regulation. What the studies cited above suggest is that in some markets it is technically feasible to reduce pollution control costs to a quarter of their current level and substantially further in other markets. Thus there is clearly room for doing better. While an IB approach is likely to reduce compliance costs, it will not operate perfectly or capture 100% of the potential cost savings.

Taken as a whole, the studies also suggest that the IB cost advantage diminishes as the pollution standard tightens. At the extreme, Hahn and Noll (1982) estimated that the CAC approach to controlling sulfate pollution in Los Angeles is essentially cost-effective. This is because all sources are already so tightly controlled that there is little flexibility left in the system from which pollution traders can take advantage.[6]

16.3 IB Regulation and Technological Progress

The magnitude of short-run cost savings from incentive-based regulation, while uncertain, is probably substantial. However, potentially more important are the cost savings from long-run technological improvements in pollution control and waste reduction induced by the IB approach.

Taxes and permits generate important incentives for **long-run technological progress** in pollution control. Both systems put a "price" on pollution, so that every unit of pollution emitted represents a cost to the firm or individual. In the tax case, the cost is direct: Less pollution would mean lower taxes. In the permit case, pollution bears an *opportunity cost* since less pollution would free up permits for sale. In both cases, since pollution is now costly to firms, they are provided with the motivation to continuously seek out new ways of reducing pollution.

Figure 16.2 illustrates the benefits of introducing new pollution control technology for a firm under an IB approach. The improved pollution control system lowers the MC of reduction curve to MC', generating savings in two areas. First, the firm pays less for the units it was already cleaning up, area a. Second, the firm also pays less in taxes (or earns money from the sale of permits) by reducing pollution from P_1 down to P_2, area b.

Compare these savings with those achievable under our stereotypical command-and-control system. First, the CAC systems are standard-based. Once the firm has achieved the delegated emission standard (P_1), it gains relatively little by improving pollution control technology. Introducing an improved system gains the firm only area a, since there is no incentive to reduce pollution below P_1.[7]

---

[6]Also, the CAC system in California was designed with some concern for promoting cost-effectiveness. See Tietenberg (1992) and Oates, Portney, and McGartland (1989) for a further discussion.

[7]Maleug (1989) shows that in the marketable permits case, incentives for adopting new technology exist only for firms that are permit sellers. Firms that are permit buyers will actually face lower incentives under an IB than a CAC scheme, because the availability of a permit or tax option gives them a "low-cost" out. For a discussion including diffusion and control agency response to innovation, see Milliman and Prince (1989). The authors conclude that auctioned permits and tax systems are superior to permit giveaways (as well as CAC) in encouraging technological innovation. Under the giveaway system, the innovator will face increased costs if the control agency responds to the innovation by tightening controls.

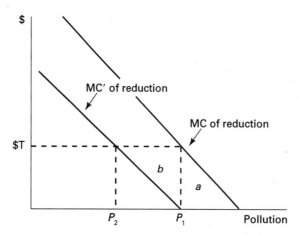

FIGURE 16.2 Incentives for New Technology Under IB and CAC

In addition, because the CAC approach specifies individual technologies as BACT, LAER, and the like, firms face regulatory obstacles in experimenting with new processes. In order to do so, they must convince regulators that the new process will be superior to the industry standard, something the firm may not be able to demonstrate before installing the technology. In addition, firms may be reluctant to raise the industry standard by introducing new technologies that may then become the new BACT. This would force them to adopt the new technology in any new construction.[8]

Finally, the CAC system dampens incentives for innovation due to the new source bias discussed in Chapter 14. By regulating new sources more stringently than old ones, the CAC system encourages firms and individuals to concentrate their energies on making old, high-pollution technologies last longer, rather than developing new, less pollution-intensive substitutes. For example, one study found that the average age of electrical generating capacity in the states with nine of the highest environmental enforcement budgets was 16.5 years to 15 years, compared to 11.5 years for the rest of the states. It is difficult to sort out how much of the age increase was in fact due to higher regulation, because most of the nine were also "rustbelt" states, hit with declining demand for electrical generation in the same period. Yet some of the increase is undoubtedly due to a heightened new source bias.[9]

By putting a price on every unit of pollution, by reducing specific technology requirements, and by leveling the playing field between new and old sources, IB regulation on paper appears to do a better job of promoting long-run investment in new pollution control technologies and waste reduction than does the CAC system. How important are these potential cost savings? This would depend on how fast the pace of technological innovation was accelerated by a switch to IB, a difficult effect to forecast. However, as we saw in Chapter 9, small changes in productivity have large long-run effects on costs, due to the cumulative nature of economic growth. Thus it is safe

---

[8]See Bohm and Russell (1985) for a further discussion.

[9]Maloney and Brady (1988) try to account for demand effects on capacity age in a regression context, but their demand variables both are poor proxies for expected growth and fail to perform well.

to say that heightened incentives for technological progress in pollution control generated by IB regulations are probably more important than the short-run savings available from achieving cost-effectiveness.

16.4 Potential Problems with IB Regulation

There are several potential problems with implementing IB regulation. This section will look at six different issues raised by IB critics. The first two—hot spots and monitoring and enforcement—apply to both tax and permit systems.[10] The last four—thin markets, market power, relocation incentives, and permit life—apply only to marketable permit schemes.

PROBLEMS WITH IB IN GENERAL

Turning our attention first to potential problems associated with both marketable permits and pollution taxes, Grimeville can be used to illustrate the **hot-spot** issue. Hot spots are high local concentrations of pollutants. The IB system would indeed keep total pollution in Grimeville at twenty tons per day. However, residents living near plant A, which would pollute thirteen tons per day under either a tax or a marketable permit scheme, would view the IB system as unacceptable *if* the higher level of emissions translated into a higher health risk.

Different pollutants display a different relationship between the sites at which emissions and damages occur. To illustrate this principle, suppose that Grimeville was divided into two air quality regions, one containing plant A, the other plant B. If gunk were a **uniformly mixed pollutant,** one ton of emissions from either plant would translate into an even concentration of gunk, and its associated health risk, across the two areas. By contrast, if gunk were a **concentrated pollutant,** all the damage done by emissions from plant A would occur in the area adjacent to A. The more general case is that of a **nonuniformly mixed pollutant,** where the bulk of the damage is done locally, but effects do drift into other areas.

IB approaches work best for uniformly mixed pollutants, those evenly dispersed over fairly broad areas. Two examples are chlorofluorocarbons, which deplete the ozone layer, and carbon dioxide, which contributes to global warming. An IB approach would clearly not work for a concentrated pollutant such as nuclear waste, for which uniform safety standards are demanded on equity grounds. To deal with the hot-spot problem in the intermediate case of nonuniformly mixed pollutants, economists have recommended trades (or taxes) based on the contribution of emissions to *ambient* air or water quality. (Recall from Chapter 13 that ambient air quality is the concentration of pollutants actually in the air.)

Implementing such a scheme requires a means of estimating the impact of emissions from specific plants on regional air or water quality. Consider the hypothetical situation in Grimeville illustrated in Figure 16.3. Suppose that due to prevailing wind patterns, one ton of gunk emissions from plant A pollutes 70% in area A and 30% in

---

[10]A final disadvantage of IB systems in real-world applications is that they can result in higher pollution levels. Because CAC systems typically result in *overcontrol* relative to the desired standard, they generate more pollution reduction than do IB schemes. Oates, Portney, and McGartland (1989) illustrate this for the case of total suspended particulates in the Baltimore atmosphere.

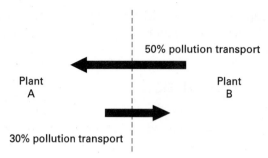

FIGURE 16.3 Nonuniformly Mixed Pollutants in Grimeville

area B. On the other hand, emissions from plant B are split 50/50 between the two areas. At the (13, 7) solution, a hot spot will indeed emerge in area A. In numerical terms, residents in A will face ambient pollution of $13 \times 0.7 + 7 \times 0.5 = 12.6$ tons, while residents in area B will face ambient pollution of $13 \times 0.3 + 7 = 7.4$ tons.

In this case, the Grimeville authorities would need to impose an ambient air quality standard (like the NAAQS discussed in Chapter 13) of 10 tons for each region, and then control emissions in the two regions to meet the ambient standards. To do so using a tax approach would require higher pollution taxes in area A than in area B. Alternatively, if marketable permits were to be used, a given permit would allow lower emissions in area A than in area B.

Carrying this idea beyond Grimeville, taxes would also have to be higher (or the emissions value of a permit lower) in already polluted areas where new sources are more likely to result in a violation of ambient standards. The exact tax levels, or terms of trade for permits between areas, can be determined as long as the relationship between emissions and ambient standards is known (see Tietenberg 1992).

As we will see in Chapter 17, trades of this type do occur under the EPA's "bubble" policy for air pollution control. However, if hot-spot problems proliferate, tax or permit systems can quickly become quite complex and, thus, lose their primary advantage to regulators—simplicity. In addition, the transactions costs for firms are raised if they need to employ complicated air quality models to demonstrate that emission trades will not violate ambient standards (see Atkinson and Tietenberg 1991).

Beyond hot spots, the next and potentially quite serious problem with IB regulation arises in the area of **monitoring and compliance.** As we saw in Chapter 15, one of the primary monitoring techniques used under the CAC system is simply to insure that firms have actually installed the required abatement technology. For example, in about twenty states, cars are required to have catalytic converters yet are not required to pass emissions tests. This monitoring system is clearly imperfect since the control equipment may break down and actual emissions are not checked. It does however provide regulators with a relatively straightforward tool for insuring at least initial compliance.

Unlike the CAC case, however, IB regulation does not specify particular pollution control technologies with known abatement impacts. Thus regulators must rely even more heavily on (currently inadequate) monitoring of emissions to insure compliance with permits or to collect taxes. As was illustrated in Chapter 15, monitoring budgets are a soft political target for regulated industries. Thus, for an IB system of regulation to achieve its potential of reducing pollution at lower cost, a commitment to strict monitoring and stiff enforcement that is insulated from the budgetary axe must be made. Los Angeles is attempting to deal with this problem via technology: "individual smoke-stack monitors that relay emissions information to [regulator's] computers and super-market-style computer bar codes to track the movement of cans of vapor-emitting solutions . . ." such as oils, paints, and solvents (see "New Rules" 1992; "Monitoring Pollution" 1992).

From the enforcement perspective, taxes have an advantage over permit systems because they generate a revenue stream for the government based on emissions. Thus, regulators have an economic incentive to monitor emissions closely to insure maximum government revenues. Brown and Johnson (1984) report that the introduction of taxes on water pollutants in Germany has led government to require better monitoring technologies and to become more aggressive in enforcement.

PROBLEMS WITH PERMIT SYSTEMS

Both cap-and-trade and pollution tax systems share problems of hot spots and a need for strict enforcement. The major problem unique to the marketable permits approach is that many proposed users face **thin markets**—markets with only a few buyers and sellers. The thin market problem is essentially this: Why go to the trouble of "going to the market" when due to the small number of traders there is a low probability of getting a good deal? In the Grimeville case, in order to trade permits, plants A and B would have to go to considerable trouble and expense to calculate with some precision their respective marginal cost of reduction curves, then employ brokers to engage in a face-to-face bargaining process. Is it worth the bother if there is only one other plant in town, which may well not have anything to offer?

As the Grimeville case illustrated, CAC regulation is seldom cost-effective since regulators do not have access to the control cost information necessary to impose least-cost regulation. In thin markets where trades are infrequent and prices not easily defined, IB systems are also hampered by **imperfect information.** Under such conditions, private firms know little about potential permit trades and face large transactions costs in completing such deals. As we shall see in the next chapter, many of the small-scale experiments with permit systems in the United States have foundered on the thin market problem. By contrast, acid rain pollution permits are traded on the futures markets in Chicago. Plant managers can read in the newspaper the going price for an SO_2 credit, greatly reducing informational barriers to trade.

A second problem with permits is the potential for the development of **market power.** Concerns here typically focus on access to permits as a barrier to entry. What if existing firms refuse to sell to new entrants in the market as a way to limit competition? Misiolek and Elder (1989) suggest that this may be a problem when both of the following circumstances hold: (1) New firms are forced to buy permits from direct competitors, and (2) a single dominant firm faces new entrants with higher pollution control costs.

Condition (1) does not generally hold. Under the acid rain program, for example, SO_2 trades are nationwide; thus a utility in Massachusetts would have a hard time blocking the entry of a new power producer that could purchase credits from a non-competitor in Ohio. Why is condition (2) necessary? If there are several existing large firms in the industry, the benefits of excluding new rivals to any given firm are lower. Moreover, the existing firms must maintain an informal agreement not to sell. As the price new entrants are willing to pay of permits rises, each firm will have an incentive to cheat on this agreement.

Economists disagree on how significant this market power problem is (see Misiolek and Elder 1989 and Teitenberg 1985).[11] However, few would argue that the problem is big enough to seriously undermine the appeal of IB regulation. Indeed, the CAC approach has its own entry barriers associated with high cost of compliance for new sources. Nevertheless, concern should be focused on designing IB systems to minimize these problems. In particular, permit giveaways that endow large firms with a substantial share of the permits should be avoided.

A third potential problem with permit systems has been raised in the Los Angeles basin case. The basin plan involves a permit giveaway. By endowing firms with wealth in the form of pollution rights, the permit systems will provide an extra incentive for firms to "sell out" and relocate to a region with less stringent regulation, in this case, Mexico. But supporters of the program have countered that the extra investment resulting from lowered compliance costs would balance any job loss effect from this **relocation effect.**[12]

A fourth possible problem with permits relates to **permit life.** Suppose that the Grimeville City Council issued twenty permits but in five years decided that pollution levels needed to be reduced to ten tons per day. Would the council then have to buy back ten permits from the firms? Here it is important to keep a distinction between "pollution rights," granted forever, and "pollution permits," which can be issued with a limited life.

However, permits with lives that are too short quickly lose their value and are not worth trading. Moreover, to gain the most from permit markets, firms must be allowed to **bank** their permits—that is, if a reduction is made in one year, the permit can be saved, or banked, for trade in a later year. If permits have a limited life, firms will take a use-it-or-lose-it attitude to reducing pollution and banking their permits. Thus, a potential need for further reduction in pollution must be balanced against the negative impact that limited permit lives introduce into permit markets. A different solution to this problem is being pursued in the Los Angeles basin, where permits shrink over time—8% annually for nitrogen oxides (see "Trying a Market Approach" 1992).

A related objection has been raised by many environmentalists: Granting pollution permits "legalizes" pollution and thus takes the social stigma away from pollution as an activity. (An analogy here could be made to the legalization of recreational drugs.) This, it is argued, will lead to a long-run increase in pollution as individual moral codes against polluting weaken. One might counter that existing regulations

---

[11]The latter source also offers a discussion of another form of market power—attempts to manipulate the permit price itself in order to minimize control costs.

[12]The relocation incentive emerges under a marketable permit system relative to CAC regulation. The roughly equivalent effect for a pollution tax is the bankruptcy constraint discussed in Section 16.2.

already mandate some level of pollution as acceptable. Perhaps more importantly, the formal legal status of pollution is probably not one of the primary determinants of social attitudes toward pollution.

To conclude this section, it is useful to point out that although economic theory is very useful in thinking through environmental problems, the real world is always messier than our theory. Indeed, CAC and IB systems are seldom found in their pure forms, and their advantages and disadvantages must be weighed in the context of each specific situation. For example, in a close look at CAC regulation of particulate air pollution in Baltimore, Oates, Portney, and McGartland (1989) discovered that the CAC approach is often not as clumsy as it is made out to be by the economist's stereotype.

In Baltimore, regulators specified different uniform standards for different categories of sources—"industrial coal-fired boilers, grain shipping facilities, etc."—so that all areas in the city achieved a standard of at least 100 ppm. Thus, while CAC regulators did impose uniform standards across categories of sources and mandated the use of specific abatement technologies, they also cast "at least one eye on cost savings." This was reflected in their decision to regulate low-cost categories of sources more stringently than high-cost source categories.

This attention to cost greatly reduced any possible benefits from moving away from CAC and toward an IB system. Oates, Portney, and McGartland (1989, 1240) conclude: "a carefully designed and implemented CAC system may stack up reasonably well relative to a feasible IB counterpart."

In our thirty-year struggle to influence the pollution control debate, economists originally concentrated on singing the praises of a chalkboard form of IB regulation, as against an equally theoretical enemy characterized as CAC. In the process, we have somewhat oversold our product. This section has focused on problems that real-world IB regulation either has faced or is likely to face in its implementation.

The existence of these problems, however, does not mean that the shift to IB regulation is a bad idea. On the contrary, pollution taxes and marketable permit systems have an important role to play in reducing short-run compliance costs, and especially in encouraging long-run innovation in pollution control and waste reduction. The policy challenge is to capture this potential in the face of real-world constraints.

16.5 Summary

As a partial answer to the question "How can we do better?", this chapter has focused on the theoretical arguments in favor of shifting to an IB system of pollution regulation. The economic advantages are twofold: (1) a reduction in the short-run costs of complying with regulations, and (2) greater incentives for long-run cost savings and pollution reduction through technological progress. There is also a political-economic argument to be made in favor of IB schemes. By reducing the information necessary for regulators to make intelligent decisions, IB approaches reduce the influence that political actors can wield in the process.

Incentive-based approaches work by putting a price on every unit of pollution produced by a firm. Short-run cost-effectiveness (equality of marginal reduction costs across all sources) is then achieved "automatically," as firms cut back (or increase) pollution levels until marginal reduction costs are just less than the tax or price of a permit. Because all firms do this, marginal costs of reduction equalize across the economy. Moreover, since any level of pollution costs the firm money, the pollution price also generates a long-run incentive for further pollution reduction through technological innovation.

Although taxes and tradeable permit systems are quite similar in many respects, there are also important differences, summarized in Table 16.3.[13] When permit systems are initiated through permit giveaways, they are much less costly than pollution taxes for the affected firms. Permits also generate a much more certain level of pollution control than taxes and do not need to be adjusted for inflation or population increases and economic growth. However, permit systems have the drawbacks associated with market power, thin markets, the determination of permit life, and relocation incentives. In addition, taxes generate strong incentives for monitoring and enforcement, and if used to replace income taxes, can increase labor market efficiency. Of course, revenues from government permit sales could serve these same two functions.

Other potential problems with both types of IB systems include the generation of hot spots and greater reliance on direct performance monitoring to insure compliance. In spite of these potential problems, IB approaches deserve and are receiving broader attention as mechanisms for reducing pollution control costs and pollution at the same time. The next chapter reviews the record on IB systems to date and discusses some of the challenges in implementation faced in the ongoing acid rain and Los Angeles Basin experiments.

APPLICATION 16.0

Cost-Effective Gunk Control

Two plants are emitting a uniformly mixed pollutant called gunk into the beautiful sky over Tourist-Town. The city government decides it can tolerate total emissions of no more than 100 kgs of gunk per day. Plant G has marginal reduction costs of $100 - 4x$ and is currently polluting at a level of 25, while plant K has marginal reduction costs of $150 - y$ and currently pollutes at a level of 150 (x and y are the level of emissions at each plant).

1. What is the cost-effective pollution level for each plant if total pollution must equal 100? Suppose the city government knows marginal reduction costs at

TABLE 16.3 Taxes and Marketable Permits Compared

Advantages of Permits	Advantages of Taxes
If permits are given away, lower cost to firms	If revenues are used to cut income taxes, labor market efficiency will be improved
More certain pollutant level	If revenues are partially retained by enforcement agencies, enforcement incentives are strengthened
No need for adjustment to account for economic growth or inflation	Issues of thin markets, market power, relocation incentives, and permit life are avoided

---

[13]Taxes and permits also differ in their effects when there is cost or benefit uncertainty. This discussion is deferred to Appendix 16A.

the two plants. In this case could the city obtain cost-effective pollution reduction using a CAC approach? If so, how?

2. In reality, why might the city have a hard time getting this information? What are the two "incentive-based" policies that could be used to get a cost-effective reduction of pollution to 100 units, without knowing the MC of the two firms? Be specific. Discuss two advantages each method has over the other.

3. Suppose the authorities are considering a tradeable emission permit system, in which they give half the permits to each firm, or a tax system. If both systems work perfectly, how much will the firms have to pay, in total, for pollution reduction under the two schemes? (Assume permits are bought and sold by firms at a price equal to the tax.) Could this explain why Tourist-Town would be more likely to adopt a permit giveaway system?

4. Several theoretical studies have shown that incentive-based policies might generate huge cost savings, with the IB approach being as much as twenty-two times cheaper as a CAC approach. Discuss at least three reasons why Tourist-Town might not get such substantial savings in moving from CAC regulation to a marketable permit system.

5. Would a CAC system in Tourist-Town generate benefits in the form of a reduction in hot spots, relative to an incentive-based approach?

6. **(Review of Efficiency)** Suppose the marginal benefits of pollution reduction in Tourist-Town are constant and equal to $64. (Each unit of pollution reduction brings in one more tourist, who spends $64.) Is 100 units of pollution, obtained cost-effectively, an efficient level? If not, will efficiency be achieved through more or less pollution? Why?

KEY IDEAS IN EACH SECTION

16.0 Economists have argued that **incentive-based (IB) regulation** can both lower the short-run costs of pollution control and provide better incentives for long-run technological improvements than the current CAC approach. The two types of IB regulation are **pollution taxes** and **marketable permit systems.**

16.1 This section illustrates that **cost-effective pollution control** can only be achieved when the marginal costs of reduction at each source are equal. Due to **imperfect information,** regulators have a hard time mandating cost-effectiveness.

16.2 The Grimeville City Council meeting is used to illustrate how IB regulation can help achieve cost-effective pollution control "automatically." Three additional points are stressed. (1) Pollution taxes, if used to replace taxes on labor, would increase **labor market efficiency.** (2) Although pollution taxes can be made **revenue neutral** (and **non-regressive**) in theory, in practice they seldom are, so firms prefer permit giveaways. (3) The **Coase theorem corollary** indicates that, in a well-functioning market, cost-effective pollution control can be achieved regardless of the initial distribution of permits.

16.3 More important than short-run cost-effectiveness, IB regulation provides better incentives than CAC does for **long-run technological progress** in pollution control.

16.4   This section discusses some of the disadvantages of IB regulation. Disadvantages of both systems include **hot spots** for the case of **nonuniformly mixed** and **concentrated pollutants,** and **monitoring** and **compliance** problems. Disadvantages specific to permits include **thin markets, market power, relocation incentives,** and **permit life.** Disadvantages specific to taxes include **bankruptcy constraints.**

REFERENCES

Atkinson, Scott, and T. H. Tietenberg. 1991. "Market Failure in Incentive-Based Regulation: The Case of Emission Trading." *Journal of Environmental Economics* 21: 17–31.

Barnes, Peter. 1999. "The Pollution Dividend", *The American Prospect,* 44, May–June.

Bohm, Peter, and Clifford Russell. 1985. "Comparative Analysis of Alternative Policy Instruments." In *Handbook of Natural Resource and Energy Economics,* vol. 1, edited by Allan V. Kneese and James L. Sweeney, 395–460. Amsterdam: North Holland.

Brown, Gardener W., Jr., and Ralph W. Johnson. 1984. "Pollution Control by Effluent Charges: It Works in the Federal Republic of Germany, Why Not in the U.S.?" *Natural Resources Journal* 24: 929–966.

Hahn, R., and R. Noll. 1982. "Designing a Market for Tradeable Emissions Permits." In *Reform of Environmental Regulation,* edited by W. Megat. Cambridge: Ballinger.

Maleug, David A. 1989. "Emission Trading and the Incentive to Adopt New Pollution Abatement Technology." *Journal of Environmental Economics and Management* 16: 52–57.

Maloney, Michael T., and Gordon L. Brady. 1988. "Capital Turnover and Marketable Pollution Rights." *Journal of Law and Economics* 31 no. 1: 203–226.

Mason, Keith. 1991. "The Economic Impact." *The EPA Journal,* January/February.

Milliman, S. R., and R. Prince. 1989. "Firm Incentives to Promote Technological Change in   Pollution Control."

Journal of Environmental Economics and Management, vol. 17, 247–265.

Misiolek, W. S., and H. W. Elder. 1989. "Exclusionary Manipulation of Markets for Pollution Rights." *Journal of Environmental Economics and Management* 16: 156–166.

"Monitoring Pollution at Its Source." 1992. *New York Times,* 8 April.

"New Rules Harness Power of Free Markets to Curb Air Pollution." 1992. *Wall Street Journal,* 14 April.

Oates, Wallace E., Paul R. Portney, and Albert M. McGartland. 1989. "The Net Benefits of Environmental Regulation." *American Economic Review* 79, no. 5: 1233–1242.

Tietenberg, T. H. 1985. *Emissions Trading: An Exercise in Reforming Pollution Policy.* Washington, DC: Resources for the Future.

Tietenberg, T. H. 1990. "Economic Instruments for Environmental Regulation." *Oxford Review of Economic Policy,* vol. 6.

Tietenberg, T. H. 1992. *Environmental and Natural Resource Economics.* New York: Harper Collins.

"Trying a Market Approach to Smog." 1992. *New York Times,* 25 March.

APPENDIX 16A

Imperfect Regulation in an Uncertain World

The discussion in the previous chapter, comparing permits and taxes, was based on the assumption of **perfect information:** that is, regulators were assumed to know *everything* about both the benefits and cost of pollution control. However, we know from our discussion of the real world practice of regulation in Chapter 12 that this assumption is far from the truth. In this appendix, we introduce uncertainty into the analysis. This will highlight an important difference between taxes and permits, based on the costs of regulatory mistakes. Mistakes on the cost side may loom large in controlling greenhouse gas emissions. For that reason, some economists have recommended a hybrid tax/permit system as an alternative to the international cap-and-trade approach negotiated under the Kyoto Protocol.

16A.0   Minimizing the Costs of Being Wrong

We noted above that permits have the advantage of providing a more certain level of pollution control than do emission taxes. This is because taxes have to be adjusted if regulators find pollutant levels resulting from a given tax are lower or higher than expected. Let us explore this issue a bit more fully, with the aid of Figure 16A.1.

Figure 16A.1 illustrates the marginal costs and marginal benefits of pollution reduction for two particular cases. This diagram differs from the ones used previously in the book because the horizontal axis is flipped around. Instead of measuring pollution reduction (cleanup) as we have done before, it now measures pollution emitted. As a result, the MC of reduction curve now slopes downward, reflecting the fact that, at high pollution levels, per-unit cleanup is cheaper. Similarly, the MB of reduction curve now slopes upwards: at high pollution levels, the per-unit benefits of cleanup are also high.

The first panel, with a steep marginal benefit curve, illustrates a pollutant with a **safety threshold.** Cleanup need not be pursued above C', even on safety grounds, since the additional benefits are low. But for cleanup levels below C', damages from additional pollution begin to mount steeply. An example of a pollutant with a safety threshold is the ozone-depleting chlorofluorocarbon (CFC) discussed in Chapter 23. Because the ozone layer has already been saturated with long-lived CFCs released in the past, any *additional* CFC production generates high marginal damages in the form of skin cancers and eye disease.

The second panel of Figure 16A.1, by contrast, illustrates a situation where *costs* are quite sensitive to the level of the cleanup. Pollution reduction to a level of C'' can be pursued relatively cheaply, but beyond C'', costs begin to mount rapidly.

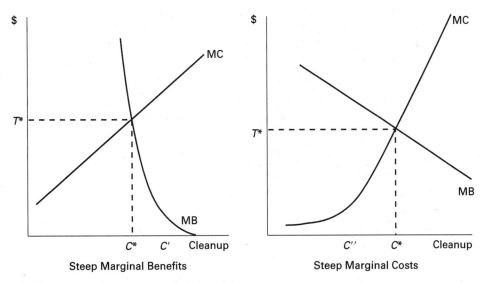

FIGURE 16A.1 IB Regulation, Two Special Cases

Global warming probably fits this picture: Carbon dioxide emissions can be reduced at fairly low cost by pursuing energy efficiency and switching to natural gas, but once these opportunities are exhausted, more expensive options will have to be exercised.

If regulators knew with certainty the location of the curves in Figure 16A.1, then they could achieve efficient pollution reduction to C^* using *either* form of incentive-based regulation. They might issue just enough marketable permits to achieve the desired cleanup or, alternatively, charge a pollution tax of T^*. However, in the real world, regulators seldom if ever have such perfect information. The point of this appendix is to determine, following Weitzman (1974), the approach regulators should use when they are uncertain about the location of the curves *and* are pursuing efficiency as their goal. We will see that when the marginal benefit curve is steep, regulators should use a marketable permit system. By contrast, when the marginal cost curve is steep, a pollution tax system is preferred.

When the marginal benefit curve is steep, regulators will want to keep tight control over the actual quantity of pollutant released into the environment to ensure that the threshold is not far exceeded. Under these circumstances, a marketable permit system is preferred to a pollution tax because of the costs of being wrong. We can see this graphically in Figure 16A.2.

In Figure 16A.2, the efficient level of cleanup is C^*. However, suppose that regulators miss the mark and issue 20% more permits than they should, so that firms clean up only to $\hat{c}$. Then the monetary loss to society is represented by the gray area—the difference between the foregone benefits and increased costs of cleaning up to C^*. By contrast, suppose regulators opted for a pollution tax. Efficiency requires a tax of T^*, but if the regulators are

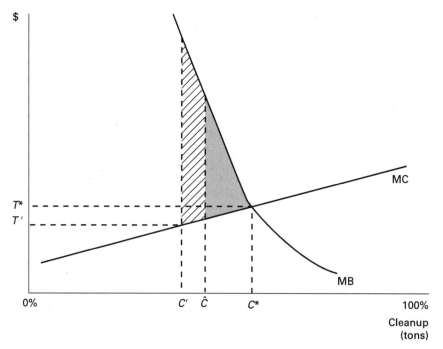

FIGURE 16A.2 Case 1: Permits Preferred

too low by 20%, we get a tax of T'. Facing this tax, firms clean up only to C', and society loses net benefits equal to the gray area *plus* the hatched area as a result. The basic idea here is that a permit approach, because it allows for greater control over actual cleanup levels, keeps pollution relatively close to the safety threshold.

By contrast, when the social costs of being wrong arise more from increased compliance costs and less from the benefits of reduction, a tax policy will be preferred. We can see this in Figure 16A.3.

If regulators undershoot the efficient tax by 20% and set it at T', firms will only decrease cleanup a little, to C'. Because the marginal cost of reduction curve is so steep, firm behavior will not be very responsive to the lower tax. As a result, monetary losses to society will be restricted to the grey area—the difference between lower control costs and higher foregone benefits from cleanup to only C'. By contrast, if regulators mandate a cleanup level that is 20% too low, then firms are forced to make bigger changes in their behavior, reducing pollution to $\hat{c}$.

In this case, overall monetary losses to society become the gray area *plus* the hatched area. The intuition here is that, with a steep marginal cost curve, firms will not change their pollution behavior much with decreased (or increased) pollution taxes. As a result, losses to society from either underregulation or overregulation using taxes will be minimized.

What if both the marginal benefit and marginal cost curves are steep? Then a clear-cut advantage for either method, based on the costs of being wrong, disappears.

16A.1 An Application to Greenhouse Gas Emissions

As we discussed in Chapter 1, in 1997 the industrial nations of the world signed the Kyoto global warming treaty. The treaty would require developed nations to reduce

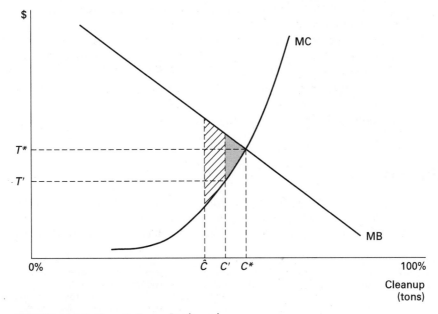

FIGURE 16A.3 Case 2: Taxes Preferred

emissions of global warming gasses; for the United States the target is 7% below 1990 levels by about 2010. The agreement also would allow international trading of carbon credits. Countries who beat their targets can sell to those who cannot achieve them. The treaty is not yet in effect. Japan and most European countries have ratified. The U.S. has not.

In the event that Kyoto is not implemented, McKibbin and Wilcoxen (1997) think they have a better idea.[1] Arguing that cost uncertainty looms quite large for controlling greenhouse gases, they offer a hybrid scheme: On the national level, each country should issue annual permits to greenhouse gas polluters that are *tradeable within the country* up to, say, Kyoto level emissions. Each government should then sell additional annual permits for, say, $25 per ton.

We saw in the previous chapter that permit sales are in fact equivalent to pollution taxes. So the McKibben and Wilcoxen (1997) approach can be thought of as a hybrid system, with a cap-and-trade base and pollution taxes on the top. The advantage of the government permit sales program is to put a ceiling on permit prices of $25, since no one would buy permits at a higher price from their neighbors if they are available from the government for $25.

In defending their proposal, McKibben and Wilcoxen argue: "There is tremendous uncertainty about what the price of an international carbon permit would be, but $100 per ton is well within the range of estimates and some studies have projected prices of $200 or more" (1997). (Other credible studies put project carbon permit prices to meet the Kyoto targets as low as $25 per ton.) Figure 16A.4 illustrates this situation.

Under the hybrid proposal, permit give-aways would allow firms to pollute up to the Kyoto target, 7% below 1990 levels. If the marginal costs of reduction are low, then permit prices would settle in at $25 per ton, and the Kyoto target would in fact be achieved. If, on the other hand, marginal costs turn out to be high, firms would turn to the government to buy excess allowances. In this hypothetical diagram, the $25 per ton sale program leads to more greenhouse gas pollution than allowed under Kyoto: a stabilization of carbon emissions at 10% above 1990 levels.

Why go with the hybrid approach? If the cost optimists are correct, then the Kyoto targets will be achieved. If, on the other hand, the pessimists are right, and marginal reduction costs are high, the economy avoids an expensive crash reduction in greenhouse gas emissions. Avoiding this kind of socially disruptive outcome will be politically important if a second round of deeper cuts needs to be achieved in the future.

16A.2 Summary

This appendix has considered an important distinction between marketable permits and pollution taxes when regulators are uncertain about the precise location of the marginal benefit and cost of pollution reduction curves. (Virtually always!) In such a

---

[1]McKibben and Wilcoxen argue for a permit sufficient to achieve 1990 emission levels and a $10 per ton tax. Variations on this proposal have also been advocated by economists at Resources for the Future, as well as a nonprofit organization, which has dubbed it "SkyTrust," and proposes returning permit sale revenue on a per capita basis to the public, following the model of the Alaska Permanent Fund. See Barnes (1999).

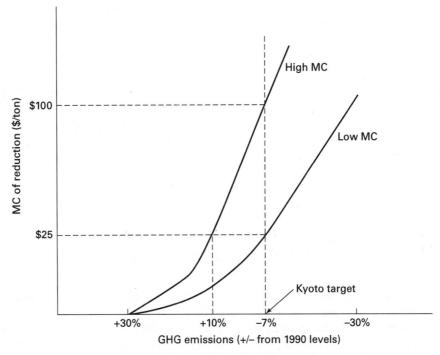

FIGURE 16A.4 Cost Uncertainty and the Hybrid Proposal

case, regulators will not be able to correctly specify either the efficient tax or number of permits. If efficiency is the regulatory goal, then regulators should be concerned about minimizing the costs of any mistakes.

When the marginal benefit curve for cleanup is steep, regulators should opt for a tradeable permit system to keep the actual quantity of pollution close to the threshold. When the marginal cost of reduction curve is steep, a tax system is preferred since a firm's pollution behavior will not be particularly responsive to a tax set too high or too low. If these rules are followed, the efficiency costs arising from imperfect regulation in an uncertain world will be minimized.

APPLICATION 16A.0

Still More on Efficient Gunk Control

Suppose that gunk has marginal benefits of reduction equal to $20 - 2x$, and marginal costs of reduction equal to $5 + x/2$, where x is the tons of gunk reduced.

1. Graph the MB and MC curves to find the efficient level of gunk reduction.
2. As a result of imperfect information, regulators are considering two inefficient policies: a tax 10% below the efficient tax level, and a marketable permit system, with the number of permits to be issued 10% below the efficient reduction level. Use your graph to show the monetary loss to society as a whole of the different policies. Which is more efficient?

3. Suppose regulators did not know exactly where the MB curve lay, but did know that gunk was a threshold pollutant. Should they use a tax or permit system if they are interested in efficient regulation? Why?

REFERENCES

Barnes, Peter. 2001. *Who Owns the Sky?* Washington, DC: Island Press.

McKibben, Warwick, and Peter Wilcoxen. 1997. "A Better Way to Slow Global Climate Change." *Brookings Policy Brief,* 17. Washington, DC: Brookings Institution.

Weitzman, M. L. 1974. "Prices Versus Quantities." *Review of Economic Studies* 41: 447–491.

APPENDIX 16B

Incentive-Compatible Regulation

In Chapter 12, we identified imperfect information as one of the primary obstacles to effective government regulation of the environment. We noted that, due to budget limitations, the Environmental Protection Agency gathers or generates less than full information about most problems before acting. In particular, the agency can sponsor only limited research of its own; as a result, it must often turn to industry for data about the expected compliance costs of regulation. Yet, asking for information about costs from the very industry one is regulating has elements of asking the fox to guard the henhouse. The incentives for cheating are rather high.

In Chapter 12, we also discussed two potential solutions to this problem. One was to build up the institutional capability of the EPA so as to increase its ability to detect inaccurate reports of compliance costs. The second was to design regulatory policy so as to minimize any gains from lying. So-called **incentive-compatible regulation** ensures that the *incentives* faced by the regulated parties are *compatible* with the goal of the regulator. This appendix illustrates how incentive-compatible regulation can work.

16B.0 Incentives to Lie

To motivate the problem, consider the EPA's recent efforts to regulate sulfur dioxide (SO_2) emissions from power plants. Suppose the agency seeks to regulate SO_2 at the efficient level, where the marginal benefits of reduction just equal marginal costs. *If* the EPA knew the costs and benefits, it might then achieve the efficient pollution level in one of two ways. First, it could issue or auction off marketable permits up to the SO_2 target. Or, it could set an emission tax to achieve the same goal. However, as we will show next, if firms are expecting a marketable permit system, they have an incentive to overstate compliance costs. By the same token, if they expect a tax, an incentive exists to understate compliance costs.

Figure 16B.1 illustrates a marginal cost–marginal benefit diagram for analyzing pollution control. The true marginal benefits and costs of SO_2 reduction are reflected by the curves labeled MB and MC. If the EPA had access to this information, efficiency would

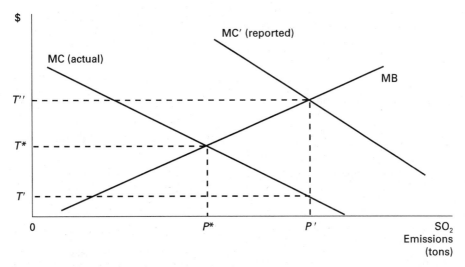

FIGURE 16B.1 Imperfect Information and Permits

require a pollution level of P^*. This, in turn, could be achieved either by auctioning off P^* marketable permits (at a market-clearing price of T^*) or setting a pollution tax at T^*.

However, suppose the EPA must rely on power companies for information about how much it will cost firms to switch over to less-polluting production methods. If faced with a marketable permit system, industry has a clear incentive to lie and *overstate* the cost (MC'). If the industry does so and the EPA uses the industry estimates, the agency will increase the number of permits it sells to P'. This will drive down the price of permits to T' and allow an inefficiently high level of pollution, reducing the firm's cleanup costs.

By contrast, suppose the agency is planning to use a pollution tax to control SO_2 emissions and firms know this. Then, as illustrated in Figure 16B.2, companies have the incentive to *understate* their costs, for example, claiming MC''. The EPA will then consider the efficient pollution level to be P'' and set what it *thinks* is the appropriate tax at T''. By doing this, the emission tax will be reduced (from T^*). However, with a low tax of T'', *actual* pollution will rise to P'''. Again, pollution levels will be inefficiently high and a firm's cleanup costs will be reduced.

Now, after the fact, regulators will be able to tell they have been lied to. How? In the marketable permits case, permit prices will be only T', reflecting real control costs, when the agency expects them to rise to T''. In the tax case, the pollution level will be P''' again, reflecting real control costs, when the agency expects it to be P''. Thus, one approach to solving the problem of imperfect information would be to adjust either the number of permits or the tax level based on the observed outcomes. For example, if the observed pollution level is higher than the regulator predicted, he can raise the pollution tax.

Through such a process, called **iteration,** the regulator might be able to arrive at the efficient tax level or number of permits. However, in practice, it is not easy to adjust either the number of permits or the tax level once they have been established. As was detailed in Chapter 12, setting regulatory policy is a cumbersome and politically charged

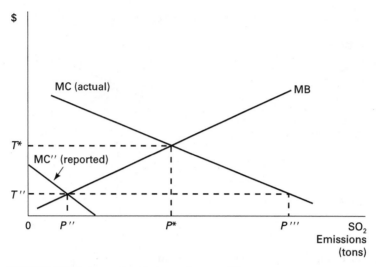

FIGURE 16B.2 Imperfect Information and Taxes

process not amenable to trial and error. Are we then stuck with a recognition that firms will tend to overstate costs if facing a marketable permit system and understate them if facing pollution taxes? Fortunately, no.

16B.1 Incentives to Tell the Truth

An incentive-compatible approach developed by Kwerel (1977) can be used to encourage truthful behavior.[1] This approach mixes a marketable permit system with a tax system to precisely balance the different incentives firms have to lie about compliance costs. It works in the following way. Regulators tell firms that they will combine an auction of marketable permits with a subsidy payment for any pollution reduced over and above the number of permits the firm holds (an **excess emission reduction subsidy**). To see this clearly, we need to use a little mathematical notation. So, let:

p = industry pollution level
L = number of permits made available
z = price of permits
e = subsidy level for emission reductions

The industry's total pollution control costs are thus:

cleanup costs + permit costs − excess emission reduction subsidy
(area under $z * L$ $e * (L − p)$
MC curve)

---

[1]Gruenspecht and Lave (1989) provide a more general review of the literature on environmental regulation under imperfect information.

The trick here is that regulators set the subsidy level, *e,* at the intersection of the MB curve and the *reported* MC curve. Thus, by the costs that they report, firms directly affect not only the number of permits that are issued, but also the subsidy they will receive for any excess emission reductions.

With this setup, we can see how the incentive-compatible mechanism works to encourage truth-telling. First, let us consider what happens if firms overstate their costs. At first glance, this seems like a good strategy. Figure 16B.3 illustrates the situation. By overstating their costs, the firms know that regulators will provide a large number of permits ($\bar{L}$) and set a high emission reduction subsidy at $\bar{e}$. Both of these seem favorable. The catch is that, unlike the case of a straight marketable permit system, the large supply of permits will not cause their price to fall. Instead, the high emission subsidy will cause the permit price that firms have to pay to be driven *up*. As long as *e* is greater than the price of permits, *z,* each firm would do better buying another permit, holding emissions constant and collecting the subsidy for the extra "reduction." But this high demand for permits will cause permit prices to get bid up to $\bar{e}$.

As a result, in equilibrium, the permit price *z* must just equal $\bar{e}$. Because the price of an additional permit just equals the emission subsidy, firms will not come out ahead financially from the subsidy policy and, thus, do not benefit from a high $\bar{e}$. However, as long as the true MC of reduction is less than the subsidy, firms would lose money if they did not reduce pollution and receive the subsidy. As a result, they *will* cut back pollution to $\bar{P}$ even though they hold $\bar{L}$ permits.

Thus, the final equilibrium will look like this: *L*-permits auctioned off at a price just equal to the emission subsidy $\bar{e}$, with firms polluting at a level of $\bar{P}$. But $\bar{P}$ is a lower level of pollution and one more costly to achieve than *P**. Thus, overstating compliance costs will lead firms to bear higher pollution reduction costs than they would if they told the truth.

Is there an incentive to understate costs? Figure 16B.4 illustrates this possibility. If firms underreport costs, then $\hat{L}$ permits will be available, and firms will receive a

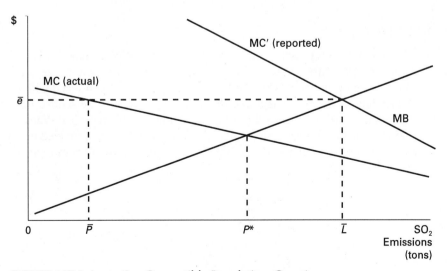

FIGURE 16B.3 Incentive-Compatible Regulation, Case 1

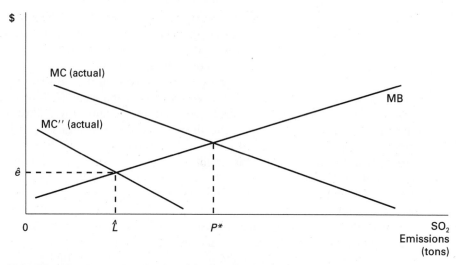

FIGURE 16B.4 Incentive-Compatible Regulation, Case 2

subsidy for emission reductions below $\hat{L}$ of $\hat{e}$. However, since the true marginal costs of reduction exceed the subsidy for excess emission reductions, firms will pollute up to the limit of $\hat{L}$ and not take any subsidies. But, again, this is a stricter and more costly standard than they would have faced if they had told the truth. Understating costs is clearly not a good strategy for firms.

We have just demonstrated that both overstating and understating compliance costs ultimately lead to higher costs for firms than telling the truth. Thus, under this hybrid regulatory mechanism, firms have no incentive to lie. In a nutshell, the advantages to inflating costs that accrue under a straight marketable permit system are here negated by the emission reduction subsidy, which forces up permit prices.

16B.2 Summary

This appendix has provided an introduction to incentive-compatible regulation. We first established that firms have an incentive to overstate compliance costs when faced with marketable permit regulation and to understate costs when faced with pollution taxes. A mechanism was then suggested that precisely balanced these offsetting tendencies by combining a tax-based subsidy policy with a marketable permit system. This hybrid regulatory structure is incentive compatible, because firms are provided an incentive to tell the truth, which is compatible with the regulatory goal of efficient regulation.

APPLICATION 16B.0

CAC and Incentives for Truth-Telling

In 1987, the EPA estimated that the costs of controlling hazardous air pollutant emissions from Coke ovens in the steel industry would be about $4 billion; by 1991 that estimate had fallen to between $250 and $400 million. In the late 1970s, projections for benzene emission control were on the order of $350,000 per plant; in actuality, chemical companies found they were able to use substitutes, which "virtually eliminated control costs" (Mason 1991).

We showed in this appendix that industry has an incentive to overstate costs if faced with marketable permit regulation. Does the same incentive hold for command-and-control regulation, which was used in Applications 16.0 and 16A.0?

1. Assume (1) that the EPA's initial cost estimates above were based on industry sources, and (2) that the EPA sought to regulate these pollutants at the efficient level.[2] Use a diagram to provide a possible explanation for why the cost estimates were so high. (Show that under command-and-control regulation, where a uniform emission standard is set, that industry has an incentive to overstate true costs.)

REFERENCES

Gruenspecht, A., and L. Lave. 1989. "The Economics of Health, Safety and Environmental Regulation." In *Handbook of Industrial Organization, Volume II,* edited by R. Schmalansee and R. Willig. New York: North Holland.

Kwerel, Evan. 1977. "To Tell the Truth: Imperfect Information and Optimal Pollution Control." *Review of Economic Studies* 44 no. 3: 595–601.

[2]In fact, these air pollutants are typically regulated under a safety standard. However, control costs still enter agency decisions as to the stringency of regulation.

INCENTIVE-BASED
REGULATION: PRACTICE

17.0 Introduction

We now have a couple of decades of experience with incentive-based regulation in the United States, primarily with marketable permit systems. Cap-and-trade programs have clearly helped reduce the costs of national efforts designed to phase out both leaded gasoline and the production of ozone-destroying CFCs. But victory has been less clear-cut in the two programs aimed at reducing urban air pollution, from the early EPA Emission Trading Program to the more recent and ambitious RECLAIM (Regional Clean Air Incentives Market) trading system in the Los Angeles basin. Finally, the national sulfur dioxide (acid rain) cap-and-trade program has been underway since 1995, and the initial results have been quite favorable.

Classic pollution taxes, or charges tied to emissions, are used very little in the United States, the exceptions being fees levied on wastewater (sewage) and solid and hazardous waste (pay by the bag garbage fees, tipping fees at landfills). There is, however, a grab bag of different incentive-mechanisms in place that affect environmental quality, ranging from the bottle deposits and mining bonds discussed in Chapter 6, to user fees on federal lands, to insurance and liability requirements for hazardous materials handlers, to subsidies for new technologies.

By contrast, several European countries have had broader experience with emission taxes, though as we will see, none relies on them as an exclusive means of pollution control. European nations historically also have had much higher taxes on energy—electricity, oil, and gasoline. Although energy taxes are not pollution taxes because they do not tax emissions directly, they reduce many important pollutants indirectly.

This chapter will review the record of IB regulation, with an eye toward uncovering the obstacles to its successful implementation. With policy makers developing large-scale plans for carbon taxes or tradeable permits to control global warming, it is doubly important that we learn all we can from the existing track record.

17.1 Lead and Chlorofluorocarbons

As was discussed in Chapter 10, lead is a particularly nasty pollutant, generating developmental problems in children and heart disease and stroke in adults. Lead in gasoline becomes airborne when the fuel is burned in an automobile engine. Unleaded gas is required for most new cars, because lead also damages the catalytic converters used to control other auto pollutants. However, in the mid-1980s, leaded gas was still widely used in older vehicles. Early in 1985, the EPA initiated a phase-in of lower lead standards for leaded gasoline, from an existing 1.1 grams per gallon standard, to 0.5 grams per gallon by July 1985, to 0.1 grams per gallon by January 1986. To ease the $3.5 billion compliance costs associated with such a rapid changeover, the EPA instituted its lead banking program.

Under this program, gasoline refiners that reduced the lead content in their gasoline by more than the applicable standard for a given quarter of the year were allowed to bank the difference in the form of lead credits. These credits could then be used or sold in any subsequent quarter. In addition, the lead credits had a limited life, because the program ended on schedule at the end of 1987, with all refiners required to meet the new standard.

In spite of its short life, the program proved quite successful. More than 50% of refiners participated in trading, 15% of all credits were traded, and about 35% were banked for future trading or use (Hahn 1989, 102). Hahn suggests that cost savings from the program may well have been in excess of $228 million, the EPA's estimate of potential cost savings from a less ambitious program. If this estimate is correct, lead trading reduced costs by less than 10% over a CAC approach. While important, such cost savings from even a successful trading program are substantially below the 400% predicted by some theoretical studies of other markets discussed in the previous chapter.

Lead trading encouraged low-cost firms to accelerate their compliance with the new regulations in order to obtain lead credits for sale. At the same time, firms that had greater problems retrofitting their equipment could pay for an extension by buying lead credits in the market. In this way, the program helped achieve the more stringent lead standards cost-effectively. However, because of the short life of the program, it is unlikely that it had much relative impact on improving pollution control technology in the industry.

What factors underlay the success of lead trading? First, because all refiners were granted permits based on their performance, market power did not emerge as an issue. (In addition, new entrant access was not a problem in this declining market.) Markets were not thin, since trading was nationwide, and firms were already required to develop considerable information about the lead content of their product. Because the permits were shrinking, the issue of permit life did not emerge, and hot spots, although they might have developed on a temporary basis, could not persist. Finally, monitoring and enforcement did not suffer, since the lead content in gasoline was already reported by refiners on a regular basis. In one instance the agency fined a company $40 million for spiking 800 gallons of gas with excess lead ("Trades to Remember" 1992). Thus, none of the theoretical bugaboos identified in Chapter 16 were present in the lead trading market.

In 1988, the EPA introduced a scheme similar to the lead trading program for chlorofluorocarbons (CFCs), which contribute both to depletion of the earth's protective ozone shield and to global warming. Like lead in gasoline, CFCs are being phased out, this time globally, as is discussed further in Chapter 23. The market appears to have functioned relatively well.

Congress also imposed a tax on all ozone-depleting chemicals used or sold by producers or commercial users of these chemicals. The tax rate was set at $1.37 per pound in 1990, rising to $4.90 per pound by the end of the decade. By increasing the price of the final product, the tax has also encouraged consumers to switch to substitute products (see "Congress Rests" 1989).

17.2 Trading Urban Air Pollutants

In contrast to the successes of lead and CFC trading, both national programs, attempts to implement tradeable permit systems at the local level for criteria air pollutants have a mixed record. The nation's first marketable permit experiment, the EPA's Emissions Trading Program, foundered because of thin markets and concerns about hot spots. And hot spots have emerged as a potential problem with the L.A. basin's RECLAIM and mobile emissions trading programs, which has also suffered from dramatic price instability.

The Emissions Trading Program, initiated in 1976, allows limited trading of **emission reduction credits** for five of the criteria air pollutants: VOCs, carbon monoxide, sulfur dioxide, particulates, and nitrogen oxides. Credits can be earned whenever a source controls emissions to a degree higher than legally required. Regulators certify which credits can then be used in one of the program's three trading schemes or banked for later use. The degree of banking allowed varies from state to state.

The three trading programs are the offset, bubble, and netting policies. **Offsets** are designed to accommodate the siting of new pollution sources in non-attainment areas. Under the offset policy, new sources may locate in such regions if, depending upon the severity of existing pollution, they buy between 1.1 and 1.5 pollution credits from existing sources for each unit they anticipate emitting. For example, in the early 1990s, the March Air Force Base near Los Angeles absorbed the staff and equipment of another base that was closing. The March Base anticipated doubling its pollution emissions from power and heat generation, and aircraft operation and maintenance.

> March recruited pollution-credit brokers that acted as middlemen in trades between polluters. Officers also scoured local newspapers and hunted for potential sellers among public documents of previous pollution-credit trades. They made cold calls to refineries and utilities. . . . Eventually, March managed to buy the credits it needed from five sellers, for a total of $1.2 million. They even found a bargain or two, including the right to emit 24 pounds of nitrogen oxide and six pounds of carbon monoxide a day for the rock-bottom

price of $975 a pound—from a machinery company that got the credits by closing down a plant. "This company didn't know what it had," says Air Force Lt. Col. Bruce Knapp ("New Rules Harness Power" 1992).

The offset policy was designed to accommodate the conflict between economic growth and pollution control, not to achieve cost-effectiveness. Over almost twenty years, thousands of offset trades have occurred, but as suggested by the above example, the markets still do not function smoothly. High transactions costs remain a serious obstacle to new firms seeking offsets to locate in a non-attainment area. This is reflected in the fact that, at least in the program's early years, about 90% of offset transactions involved trades within a single firm.

The **netting policy** also focuses on accommodating economic growth and has had a significant impact on compliance costs. This program allows old sources that are expanding their plant or modifying equipment to avoid the technological requirements for pollution control (the new source performance standards discussed in Chapter 13) if any increase in pollution above the standard is offset by emission reduction credits from within the plant. Tens of thousands of netting trades have taken place, saving billions of dollars in reduced permitting costs and abatement investment, while having little if any negative effect on the environment. The netting program has been the most successful of the three, primarily because it has involved only internal trades.

In contrast to the offset and netting trades, the **bubble policy** was designed primarily to generate cost savings and, of the three programs, is most similar to the theoretical marketable permits model discussed in Chapter 16. "Bubbles" are localized air quality regions with several emission sources; a bubble may include only a single plant or may be extended to include several sources within a broader region. Under the bubble policy, emission reduction credits can be traded within the bubble. In its simplest form, a firm may violate air quality emission standards at one smokestack, provided it makes up the difference at another. Of course, trades between plants within a regional bubble can occur as well.

Bubbles were introduced in 1979, three years after offsets, with high expectations of cost savings. One study, for example, predicted that the cost of nitrogen dioxide control in Baltimore might fall by 96%. However, by the early 1980s, only 129 bubble trades had actually occurred, with estimated cumulative savings of less than $0.5 billion. Only two of these trades were estimated to have involved external transactions (see Krupnick 1986 and Hahn 1989).[1] Atkinson and Tietenberg (1991) stress the role of imperfect information and thin markets to explain the relative failure of the EPA's bubble policy. Because of the difficulty in locating potential deals, most firms simply did not participate. Also, each individual trade between firms must satisfy the constraint of no increase in pollution. This results in much less activity than traditional

---

[1]Hahn also describes another disappointing application of marketable permits for water pollutants in Wisconsin. This program appeared to founder on the thin markets problem, as well as limitations on permit life.

models of IB regulation, which unrealistically assume that the constant pollution constraint is met as all feasible deals are consummated simultaneously.

Finally, Atkinson and Tietenberg argue that the lack of inter-firm trading can be explained in part by the non-uniformly mixed nature of the pollutants. Since the NAAQ standards relate to ambient air quality, not emissions, trades of such emission permits require firms to demonstrate through (costly) air quality modeling that ambient standards will not be violated by the trade.

In short, many economists underestimated real-world complications associated with designing permit markets when they generated rosy predictions for bubbles and offsets. Of the theoretical issues discussed in Chapter 16, the problem of thin markets greatly reduced the effectiveness of emissions trading. In addition, the hot-spot problem with non-uniformly mixed pollutants has been vexing. The technical complications involved in demonstrating that emissions trades will not affect ambient air quality substantially raised the transactions costs for firms engaged in external trades under the bubble program.

Hot spots are largely ignored in southern California's two trading programs—a "clunker" purchase program, and the **RECLAIM** (Regional Clean Air Incentives Market) cap-and-trade system. Under the mobile source trading (or clunker) program, stationary sources such as refineries and chemical factories, working through licensed dealers, can purchase and then scrap highly polluting old vehicles (clunkers), and use the pollution credits to avoid clean-air upgrades at their plants. Similar to the EPA's offset program, the system saves companies money, but can lead to hot spots. As one critic notes, the program "effectively takes pollution formerly distributed throughout the region by automobiles and concentrates that pollution in the communities surrounding stationary sources." And in the L.A. case, these communities are often disproportionately Latino or African American.

The mobile source trading program has been criticized from a monitoring and enforcement perspective as well. The program assumes that clunkers purchased would otherwise be on the road, and driven 4,000 miles, for three years. However, there is an obvious incentive for people to turn in cars that were driving on their last gasp, and would have been scrapped soon anyway. Licensed dealers are supposed to prevent this kind of fraud, but the program has nevertheless been hobbled by these kinds of problems (Drury et al. 1999).[2]

In contrast to the clunker program, RECLAIM is a textbook cap-and-trade system. In operation since 1993, the program requires about 330 stationary sources to hold (tradeable) permits for each ton of sulfur dioxide (SO_2) and nitrogen oxide (NOx) emitted. Figure 17.1 illustrates both the number of allowances issued, and the actual emissions by RECLAIM companies. Note that the total number of allowances granted to firms shrinks every year up until 2003. The initial allocation of allowances was quite generous—well above historical pollution levels. It was not until 1998 and 1999 that actual reductions below pre-RECLAIM levels were required for SO_2 and

---

[2]The clunker program has also had some incidences of outright fraud, as well as another type of hot spot problem: the VOC composition from cars varies from that released by stationary sources, such as marine oil terminals. Critics argue that the latter are substantially more toxic than the former. For a general economic analysis of clunker programs see Alberini, Harrington, and McConnell (1993).

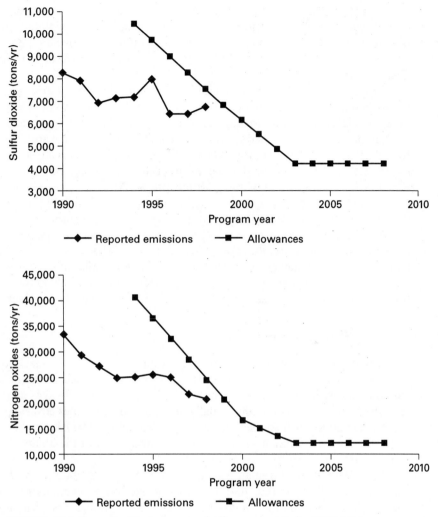

FIGURE 17.1 Reported Emissions and Allowances Under RECLAIM

Source: Luong, Tsai, and Sakar (2000).

NOx, respectively. Indeed SO_2 emissions actually rose during the first two years of the program, and by 1998 they had declined only slightly below 1993 levels, though NOx emissions were down 17%. (The high initial allowances were apparently a political concession to promote industry buy-in.)

The tremendous excess supply of permits led to a slow start for the permit market: in 1994 and 1995 many could not be sold even at a zero price. Moreover, though RECLAIM required continuous emissions monitoring and electronic reporting, it took a couple of years for monitors to be installed and certified at some firms. However, by the end of the decade, the monitoring bugs were mostly worked out, and the allowance constraints were beginning to bind. In fact in 1998, 27 firms violated the regulations, polluting more than their permitted levels. As supply diminished, permit prices rose while trading accelerated; in 1999, 541 trades occurred, valued at $24 million (Luong, Tsai, and Sakar 2000).

RECLAIM was severely tested during the California energy crisis of 2000–2001. At the same time that the number of allowances were shrinking, energy prices went through the roof, and existing California power plants began operating on overtime schedules. As a result, demand for NOx permits in particular shot up, and prices rose almost tenfold—from $4,300 per ton in 1999 to around $39,000 per ton in 2000. As a result, California regulators fell back to command-and-control strategies, pulling power plants out of the RECLAIM program to stabilize emission prices. After a three-year hiatus, in which power producers were required to install technologies capable of reducing emissions by 90%, in 2004 the plants are expected to rejoin the trading program.[3]

As with the clunker program, RECLAIM ignores hot spot issues. This may pose little problem if NOx and SO_2 are regionally mixed. However, critics have argued that toxic co-pollutants may be associated with the criteria pollutants, so SO_2 and NOx hot spots may in fact also generate toxic hot spots. It is not currently known if RECLAIM trading patterns have increased exposure around particular plants (Drury et al. 1999).

17.3 Marketable Permits and Acid Rain

In the mid-1960s, freshwater fishermen in Sweden, Norway, Canada, and the Adirondack Mountains of New York State began to notice a decline in the fishery stocks of mountain lakes. By the late 1980s, Sweden was reporting 14,000 lakes unable to support sensitive aquatic life, with 2,200 virtually dead. In Norway, lakes covering 13,000 square kilometers had lost fish species. In Canada, more than 14,000 lakes were strongly acidified, while in the Adirondacks more than 180 lakes had lost the ability to support most native fish (French 1990).

In the late 1970s, German foresters noted a rapid decline in the health of their resource; by 1985, more than half the forests in the country were damaged in what was termed simply *waldsterben* or forest death. Similar though less dramatic reports of retarded forest growth came from North America, with particular concern about sugar maples and high-elevation red spruce in Canada and the Northeast, and pines in the Southeast and California (French 1990).

Acid rain was the suspected culprit in the damage to both water and forest resources. **Acid rain** is formed when sulfur dioxide, primarily released when coal is burned, and nitrogen oxide, emitted from any kind of fossil fuel combustion, are transformed while in the atmosphere into sulfuric and nitric acids. These acids return to the earth attached to raindrops or in some cases dry dust particles. Researchers have established that acid rain is guilty of acidification of lakes and streams. In the case of forest death, no widespread link has yet been established. However, ground-level ozone

---

[3]"AQMD to Develop Proposal to Restore Power Plants to RECLAIM," June 11, 2003, and "Board Adopts Plan to Reduce Emission Credit Prices," January 19, 2001, South Coast Air Quality Management District, www.aqmd.gov.

(produced by the transformation of nitrogen oxides), possibly in combination with acid rain, has been shown to reduce forest and agricultural productivity.

Acid deposition harms fish and plant life directly and also can cause indirect damage by leaching and mobilizing harmful metals like aluminum and lead out of soil. The impact of acid rain on ecosystem health varies from region to region, depending upon the base rocks underlying the area. Naturally occurring limestone or other alkaline rocks can neutralize much of the direct impact of the acid. Such rocks are not found in the primarily igneous terrain of the Adirondack Mountains in New York State, southeastern Canada, or northern Europe. (This has led some economists, concerned primarily about lost fishing opportunities, to recommend liming lakes sterilized by acid rain as a relatively inexpensive way to deal with the problem.)[4]

In addition to damaging water and forest resources, the acids also erode buildings, bridges, and statues. Suspended sulfate particles can also dramatically reduce visibility. Finally, they contribute to sickness and premature death in humans.[5]

Pollution from sulfur dioxide was at one time concentrated around power plants and metal refineries. The area around Copper Hill, Tennessee, for example, is so denuded of vegetation from now-closed copper-smelting operations that the underlying red clay soil of the region is clearly visible from outer space. In an attempt to deal with these local problems, and with the encouragement of the ambient standards mandated by the Clean Air Act of 1970, smokestacks were built higher. And yet, dilution proved not to be a pollution solution. Sulfur and nitric oxides were picked up by the wind and transported hundreds of miles only to be redeposited as acid rain. The acid rain problem in the northeastern United States and Canada can, thus, be blamed on regional polluters—coal-fired utilities and nitrogen oxide emitters ranging from the Midwest to the Eastern seaboard. Similarly, Germany's forest death and acidified lakes in Sweden and Norway require a Europe-wide solution.

The fact that polluters and victims are in different parts of the country, or even different countries, has made resolving regional pollution problems difficult. For example, the Helsinki Protocol, signed in 1985, committed twenty-one European nations to a sulfur dioxide emissions target of 70% of 1980 levels by 1993. Thirteen European countries, including Spain and the UK, did not sign the protocol. Prevailing westerly winds mean that these countries export around 70% of their SO_2 emissions, while importing relatively little. Subsequently, the UK has reduced sulfur and nitrogen oxide emissions as a requirement of membership in the European Community (World Bank 1992, 155; French 1990).

In the United States, progress on acid rain legislation through the late 1980s was stymied both by opposition from conservative President Reagan and by the fact that

---

[4]On the economics of liming, see Mullen and Menz (1985). Olem (1991) provides a review of the scientific literature. Since the passage of the Clean Air Act of 1990, some environmentalists have supported liming as a complementary strategy to emissions reduction; see, for example, Lechner (1991).

[5]One frequently cited government study maintained that up to 50,000 premature deaths per year might be attributed to sulfate pollution in the United States (Office of Technology Assessment 1984; 47). Even using much more conservative estimates, however, the health effects are significant (Burtraw et al. 1998). Technically, the offending pollutants are suspended acidic aereosols of several types. Acidic sulfates appear to dominate these aerosol mixes. See NAPAP (1991, 132).

[6]See also the description in Firor (1989).

several thousand high-sulfur coal jobs were likely to be lost in Pennsylvania, Indiana, Ohio, and Illinois, as utilities switched to lower-sulfur coal mined in other regions. Of course, many new jobs would be created by the legislation as well, some in the mining of low-sulfur coal, others in the manufacture of scrubbers to remove sulfur prior to its emission, still others in the development of new "cleaner" coal technologies. One study predicted that, on net, the legislation would lead to an overall increase in employment (Wendling and Bezdek 1989). The environmental benefits of the legislation, meanwhile, were expected to be reaped in New York, Vermont, New Hampshire, Maine, and Canada.

Canadian benefits, of course, count little in U.S. politics but, in addition, a major ten-year government study released in 1990 suggested that the impact of acid rain on domestic ecosystems, though serious, was not as widespread as had been feared. Although some of the findings remain controversial, the report drew conclusions in the following areas (see NAPAP 1991, especially Table 6-1).[7]

1. *Water quality.* Fourteen percent of lakes in the Adirondack Mountains (180) were so acidified as to be unable to support many fish species. Although 23% of lakes in Florida were also highly acidic, local fish species were more acid-tolerant. A third area of concern for lakes was found in the Upper Peninsula of Michigan. In addition, some 21% of mountain streams in the eastern highlands were acidified. In the rest of the eastern United States, less than 5% of lakes were seriously acidified. However, about three times as many lakes in the region experienced acid pulses associated with rainstorms or snow melt.

    Continued deposition at 1980 levels was predicted to increase serious acidification by roughly one third. About 75% of acidification in lakes and 50% in streams is accounted for by acid rain. The remainder results from acid mine drainage (especially for streams) and natural sources.

2. *Forest health.* Although the majority of American forests show no damage, acid rain could affect the soil chemistry with an unknown impact in the lower midwestern and southeastern United States over the next 50 to 100 years. Acid rain, in combination with ozone, is currently exacerbating natural stress (disease, insects) faced by red spruce and possibly other trees in high altitude areas of the eastern United States.

3. *Agricultural productivity.* No impact was found on agricultural productivity.

4. *Visibility.* Sulfates are the dominant source of light extinction in the eastern United States. A decrease in ambient sulfate levels of 40% would improve visibility by about 30%. Several contingent valuation studies suggest that people value visibility substantially, particularly in national parks, forests, and recreational areas.

5. *Human-made structures.* Acid rain has increased the rate of deterioration of galvanized steel, bronze, marble, and limestone structures and statues and carbonate-based paints.

---

[7]In contrast to conclusion 2, many Canadian researchers also believe that acid rain is responsible for the sugar maple population's decline in their country. See "Acid Test" (1990). For an interesting discussion of the politics of NAPAP, see "Learning from an Acid Rain Program" (1990).

These environmental concerns, along with the large health risks from sulfate pollution discussed above, finally led to action on acid rain in the 1990 Clean Air Act. The legislation required a 10-million-ton reduction of sulfur dioxide emissions from 1980 levels, down to an annual average of 8.95 million tons per year, and a 2.5-million-ton reduction of nitrogen oxide emissions by the year 2000.[8]

The first stage of the SO_2 rollback was achieved in 1995 by issuing a first round of marketable permits to 110 of the nation's largest coal-burning utilities, mostly in the East and Midwest; the second stage, begun in 2000, imposed tighter restrictions and included another 2,400 sources owned by 1,000 other power companies in the country. To reduce the financial burden on, and political opposition from, utilities and rate payers, most of the permits are not sold by the government. Instead, utilities are simply given permits based on their emission levels in 1986. Each utility receives permits equivalent to 30% to 50% of its 1986 pollution.[9]

Trading is nationwide, although state legislators and utility regulators do have the authority to restrict permit sales. Given such a broad market, a utility in, say, Ohio will have little power to prevent a competitor from setting up shop in the neighborhood merely by refusing to sell permits. Such a firm could simply go shopping in Texas. And finally, to safeguard against potential market power problems arising if new entrants are forced to buy permits from incumbent competitors, the government distributes 2.8% of the permits by auction and sale.

Because sulfur dioxide and nitrogen oxides emitted from the tall stacks of power plants are more or less uniformly mixed on a regional basis (and because midwestern plants are likely to be net sellers), major geographical hot spots are not likely to emerge from the acid rain program (see NAPAP 1991, 447; and Bohi et al. 1990).[10]

The program creates an 8.9-million-ton cap on SO_2 emissions from power plants after the year 2000. However, Congress has the authority to reduce the number of permits even further without buying them back from the firms. The states' authority to impose tighter regulations has also not been affected. Thus, the permits confer no tangible property rights, although firms can certainly expect at least a decade's trading before the emission cap is reconsidered.

On the enforcement front, the acid rain program mandates the installation of continuous monitoring equipment, which is required to be operative 90% of the time and to be accurate to within 10% to 15% of a benchmark technology. The EPA certifies the monitors at each plant; thus, the monitoring process itself retains a CAC flavor. Once a plant's monitoring units are certified, the EPA records all trades and then checks allowances against emissions on an annual basis to insure compliance. One key

---

[8]NOx control will be by means of technology-based uniform emission standards, that is, a CAC approach.

[9]A good discussion of the mechanics of the program can be found in Claussen (1991).

[10]Kriz (1993) reports some opposition to trading from local environmental groups concerned about potential hot spots from specific trades. Kriz also discusses the early trades.

In addition, the possibility of a *temporal* hot spot exists. Because firms are allowed to bank their permits, the 8.9-million-ton sulfur dioxide limit might easily be exceeded in a given year, if many firms should choose to use their banked permits simultaneously. However, if as Bohi et al. (1990) argue, permit prices are not likely to rise substantially, there will be little incentive to bank, and thus this problem will be minimal.

to the success of the program will be the ultimate long-run accuracy and performance of the monitoring technology (Claussen 1991).[11]

Violators face a $2,000-per-ton fine for excess emissions and must offset those emissions the following year. The fine level was set substantially above the expected market price and yet not so high as to be unenforceable. Thus, it represents a very credible threat to firms. In addition, once a violation is established, the fine is nondiscretionary. These factors should lead to more certain enforcement and better compliance. In fact, we have seen 100% compliance through 2000.

As a last note, the acid rain legislation contained measures to compensate high-sulfur coal miners and others who lost their jobs. Funding for support while in job retraining programs was authorized at a level of up to $50 million for five years. Job loss estimates through the late 1990s were on the order of 7,000 in total, almost all of them eastern coal miners (Goodstein 1999).

Before the program was introduced, economists were optimistic that the legislated acid rain trading program, expected to cost about $4 billion annually, would result in savings of between 15% and 25% over a stereotypical CAC option (NAPAP 1991, 510). This optimism arose because the theoretical objections to an IB approach raised in the last chapter, some of which contributed to the disappointing performance of bubbles, did not appear likely to emerge in this case.

To begin with, the existence of a national market with hundreds of participants (including the Chicago Board of Trade) minimizes transactions costs and the thin market problem. Because of the approximately uniformly mixed nature of the pollutants, major hot spots were unlikely to emerge. The potential exercise of market power and speculative behavior was mitigated by the set-aside and auction of a limited number of permits. The issue of permit life has been settled by providing firms with an indefinite guarantee—a cap of 8.9 million tons in 2000 with Congress holding the authority to restrict emissions further. And finally, an up-front commitment to better monitoring technology and streamlined enforcement has been made.

From an economic point of view, the acid rain program was one of the best-laid regulatory plans. Nevertheless, to paraphrase Shakespeare, reality often reveals more complications than are dreamt of in our philosophy. This experiment has been worth monitoring closely as it unfolds; to date, the results have been quite positive.

First, both SO_2 and NOx emissions from the power plants participating in the program have fallen sharply since 1995. Ambient (airborne) levels of sulfur dioxide have declined as well. This decline has been linked to both improvements in visibility in national parks, and significant health benefits—reductions in both sickness and premature death. Based largely on these health benefits, the acid rain program easily passes an efficiency test; Burtraw et al. (1998) have shown that the measurable benefits of the acid rain program far exceed the costs.

On the downside, the reduction in NOx from power plants has been countered by increases elsewhere, mostly from automobiles. Some lakes in New England are showing reductions in acidification, but the Adirondack lakes are displaying little sign of recovery—in part because NOx emissions have failed to decline. Some scientists

---

[11]Details on monitoring specifications were obtained from David Hawkins of the NRDC.

believe that a second round of cuts will be needed to restore the health of the Adiron-dack aquatic systems (U.S. EPA 1999).

The big positive surprise from the program has been the dramatic cost savings: utilities are set to achieve the cutbacks spending less than one quarter of what the cap-and-trade system was originally predicted to cost, which in turn was well below the forecast costs for a traditional command-and-control system. Before the program went into effect, the EPA estimated that compliance costs for the cap-and-trade system would be $4 billion annually; that estimate has now fallen to less than $1 billion. Most analysts thought that marginal con-trol costs (and thus permit prices) for SO_2 would settle in at between $750 and $1,500 per ton. Instead, permits are selling for between $100 and $150 per ton (U.S. EPA 1999).[12]

During the first two years of the program, relatively few trades between different firms actually occurred; in 1995, less than 5% of the permits in circulation traded hands. Both the phenomena of dramatically lower costs and fewer-than-expected trades can be explained in retrospect by the increased flexibility that firms were given under the acid rain program. Rather than install expensive scrubbers (or buy extra permits), most firms met their early SO_2 targets by switching to low sulfur coal or developing new fuel blending techniques. Railroad deregulation led to an unexpected decline in low sulfur coal prices. And with the increased competition from coal, scrub-ber prices fell by half from 1990 to 1995.

Recall that a stereotypical CAC regulation has two features that raise costs: uni-form standards (which block short run cost-reducing trades) and technology-based regulations (which discourage long-run cost savings by restricting firm-level compli-ance options). In the acid rain case, almost all of the initial cost savings came from increased flexibility *within* the individual firm. This included the ability to engage in intra-firm trading (so that any single firm's different plants don't face uniform stan-dards), as well as the ability to use a mix of control technologies.

However, as Figure 17.2 illustrates, inter-firm trading has picked up dramatically in the last few years. Bohi and Burtraw (1997) argue that environmental managers at utilities took a while to exhaust internal cost savings from trade, and then began to look outward.[13] Thus, we can look forward to even greater cost savings as inter-firm trading accelerates. All in all, the acid rain program is beginning to look like a case where economic theory has done a very good job guiding government policy. Emis-sions have been reduced at low cost, and with a high degree of certainty.

17.4 Pollution Taxes in the United States and Europe

As was noted in the introduction to this chapter, the primary American experience with pollution taxes has been in the area of waste disposal. Homeowners typically pay by the gallon for sewage disposal, and waste haulers pay by the ton to dispose of hazardous

---

[12]Not all of these price differences reflect "real" cost savings: Permit prices are lower than anticipated because early bonus allowances added to the near-term supply, thus driving down prices (Bohi and Burtraw 1997). Real cost savings have been on the order of four to eight times greater than predicted, not four to fifteen.

[13]The last three paragraphs are drawn from Burtraw (1996).

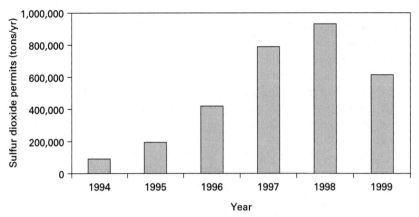

FIGURE 17.2 Inter-Firm Permit Trade Under the Acid Rain Program

Source: The U.S. EPA Acid Rain Program, *www.epa.gov/docs/acidrain.ats/qlyupd.html.*

and solid waste. These closely resemble textbook pollution fees, which in theory should result in conservation measures as disposal costs rise.

However, at least in the case of solid waste, this has not been the general result because the incentives for waste reduction are not passed on to consumers. Much residential, commercial, and industrial municipal solid waste disposal is financed through a lump sum fee. Thus, residential consumers may pay say $10 per week for garbage service regardless of how much garbage they produce. In some communities, city government handles waste disposal, and the fee is included in property taxes; in others, private firms charge for disposal on a weekly or monthly basis.

This presents us with a curious

PUZZLE

Why don't private garbage haulers provide their customers with a unit pricing option? **Unit pricing** refers to paying for garbage disposal by the bag rather than in a lump sum. The lump sum pricing system in effect generates a subsidy from small to large garbage producers. A "smart" garbage firm could offer a unit pricing scheme to small garbage producers. By getting rid of (dumping?) its large garbage customers, the firm could service more customers per trip to the landfill and generate a higher profit margin.

SOLUTION

Sorry, I'm not a garbage hauler, so I don't know the answer to this one. However, it might have to do with the higher transactions costs associated with unit pricing. To implement this approach, a garbage firm might face a considerable challenge marketing its idea, then would have to sell bags to its customers and finally keep track of the number of bags used per customer per week. Perhaps these added costs are enough to offset the extra profit opportunity that a unit-pricing scheme offers. Some evidence to support this view comes from Morris and Byrd (1990), who find that in fifteen of seventeen communities with unit pricing collection was organized as a municipal monopoly, and in one of the exceptional cases unit pricing was legally mandated. At any rate, this example again reminds us that markets that emerge on a chalkboard sometimes have a harder time in the real world.

In the past, solid waste disposal fees have been relatively low. However, as landfills around the country close and political resistance to new construction has arisen, solid waste disposal costs have been rising rapidly. This has led an increasing number of municipalities to experiment with unit pricing, often in combination with curbside recycling programs, as a way to reduce waste flows.[14]

In a study of unit pricing in suburban Perkasie, Pennsylvania, semi-rural Ilion, New York, and urban Seattle, Washington, Morris and Byrd (1990) found that the introduction of unit pricing in the first two communities reduced waste actually generated by 10% or more, while the flow to the landfill was reduced by more than 30%. In addition, these two communities reduced their waste management costs by 10% or more, with the savings passed on to households through reduced fees. At the same time unit pricing was adopted, both of these communities also introduced or expanded curbside recycling.

By contrast, Morris and Byrd also looked at Seattle's program from 1985 to 1987, *prior* to the introduction of curbside recycling in the late 1980s. Seattle had a unit-pricing system in place since 1961 but raised the rates per can substantially over the three years of the study. The response among Seattle residents to the rising rates was to increase trash compaction (locals call it the "Seattle Stomp"), slightly increase recycling rates, and, ultimately, to slightly reduce overall waste generated. The study suggests that in the absence of a good substitute (curbside recycling), waste disposal is fairly insensitive to price increases; that is, it is price inelastic.

Of course, a pollution tax will always drive people to look for unintended substitutes. In the Perkasie case, the shift to unit pricing led to an increase in trash burning, which was subsequently banned, and to an increase in out-of-town disposal. However, the town found no increase in sewage disposal of waste. Seattle reported some increase in illegal dumping. Comparable results have been reported by Fullerton and Kinnaman (1996).

POLLUTION TAXES IN EUROPE

In contrast to the United States' limited experience with pollution taxes, Germany, France, and the Netherlands have all instituted effluent charges for water pollutants.[15]While the taxes are highest in the Netherlands, in no case are they the sole instrument used to control water quality. Rather, effluent systems are grafted on to CAC systems, which mandate standards and control technologies.

---

[14]See the EPA's "Pay as You Throw" Web site at *www.epa.gov/epaoswer*.
[15]This discussion is drawn from Hahn (1989); see also Morgenstern (1996) and Hoerner and Bosquet (1999).

What lessons can be learned from the European experience? First, in all cases, taxes were introduced at low levels and then slowly raised. The real value of taxes has thus *not* been eroded by inflation. However, a tax high enough to be a primary determinant of pollution levels appears to be politically unfeasible in most cases. This point is quite relevant to proposals to employ carbon taxes as a means of controlling global warming. Although theoretically appealing, many analysts have questioned whether a tax that significantly increases the price of gasoline—even if accompanied by an offsetting income tax cut—is politically feasible.

Interestingly, as an apparent means of increasing the political acceptability of pollution taxes, the European countries typically direct the funds raised from the pollution taxes into government-financed investments in improved water quality. Thus, the taxes tend to serve a dual environmental purpose, both encouraging reduction by polluters and subsidizing cleanup efforts by third parties. In practice, it seems, taxes often function like the environmental bond systems discussed in Chapter 6. Finally, as noted in the previous chapter, the German tax system seems to have generated greater monitoring and enforcement efforts by regulators.

17.5 Indirect Pollution Taxes: The Case of Energy

Two weeks before writing this section, I returned from a trip to Denmark where I was visiting my cousins. They had borrowed a friend's house for us to stay in, and when we departed, my cousins left a little envelope with some money in it "to pay for the electricity," they said. This was a little surprising to me, since in America we are used to thinking of electricity as a virtually free good. But due to high taxes on energy, Danes pay about twice as much as we do for electricity. As a result, they think about their energy use more carefully than we do.

The production of energy, via the burning of carbon-based fuels or the fissioning of radioactive material, is a highly polluting process. Most of the criteria air pollutants are generated through the former activity, while nuclear waste results from the latter. As Table 17.1 illustrates, for uncontrolled pollutants such as carbon dioxide, the relationship between energy use and pollution is fairly clear-cut. The United States, with high per capita energy use, also has the highest per capita carbon dioxide emissions. The table also illustrates a strong negative relationship between energy prices and energy consumption. High prices promote low consumption and vice versa. Thus, one strategy to reduce pollution is to *tax it indirectly* by taxing energy use.

However, indirect pollution taxes can generate counterproductive results. Suppose, for example, a gasoline tax were instituted to reduce the emission of greenhouse

TABLE 17.1   Energy Consumption, Prices, and CO_2 Emissions

Country	Energy Consumption per Capita (kg of oil equiv.)	CO_2 Emissions per Capita (tons)	Gasoline Price ($/gallon)
United States	7,905	20.8	$1.24
Japan	3,964	9.0	$4.14
Germany	4,156	10.2	$3.34

Source: The World Development Report by the World Bank (1999) and *Statistical Abstract of the United States* (1996). Energy consumption CO_2 emissions are from 1995; gasoline prices are from 1994, in 1994 dollars.

gases. This might provide an impetus for electric-powered cars. However, to the extent that batteries were charged from electricity produced by coal-fired power plants, CO_2 emissions would rise. Thus, by taxing the fuel instead of its pollution content, one could wind up promoting another, perhaps dirtier, fuel.

The potential for unintended "perverse effects" means that a direct pollution tax is clearly preferred to an indirect energy tax, since the former taxes all sources based on their pollution contribution and promotes a search for all types of cleaner energy sources. Nevertheless, energy taxes do have the advantage of being administratively simpler, particularly if there is no easy formula for assigning pollutant emissions to energy sources.

In 1993, President Clinton proposed a U.S. energy tax based on the energy content (BTU) of different fuels. The main purpose of the tax was deficit reduction, but it was also recognized to have significant environmental advantages. However, the energy tax, expected to raise about $23 billion per year, was strongly opposed by a coalition of energy-intensive industries. As a result, the proposal was dumped in favor of a modest 4.3-cent-per-gallon increase in the gasoline tax. Such a small increase in gas prices had little impact on gasoline use.

Although the gas tax was expected to raise only $5 billion per year, it met fierce opposition in Congress, passing the House of Representatives by two votes and the Senate by one, before the President signed it into law in 1993. And still the issue wouldn't die, returning as a political football in the 1996 and 2000 presidential elections. The point: Pollution taxes, whether direct or indirect, may be theoretically appealing but are politically quite difficult to enact.

17.6 Other Incentive-Based Approaches

Energy taxes are one form of an indirect pollution tax. A variety of other fee-based approaches, while also not classic pollution taxes, are in use in the United States.

USER FEES FOR PUBLIC LANDS

Hikers, recreational fishers, hunters, logging companies, and ranchers must all pay the federal government permit fees for the use of public resources. Many have argued that some or all of these fees are much too low to discourage overexploitation. Nevertheless, they represent a mechanism by which common property resources are priced, and by which marginal damages can, at least in theory, be controlled.

What external costs do hikers impose? Too many hikers can damage trails, and of course, hikers generate congestion externalities—the last hiker crowding the trail reduces the value of the day's hike for all the previous users. Economists have recommended fees as an important component of a land manager's toolbox for rationing access to scarce trails. Similarly, congestion pricing on highways is an economically efficient—though seldom used—way out of urban traffic jams.

ENVIRONMENTAL BONDS

As discussed in Chapter 6, deposit requirements for beverage containers and automobile batteries and bonds posted by strip mines or landfill owners are ways to internalize the social cost of "irresponsible" disposal or development.

INSURANCE AND LIABILITY REQUIREMENTS

Under the Oil Pollution Act of 1990, oil tankers entering U.S. waters must show proof of insurance amounting to $1,200 per gross ton of cargo. An insurance requirement of this type is similar to an environmental bond, and if insurers charge higher rates for tanker operators with riskier histories, insurance markets act to help internalize the social costs of risky behavior. (In the tanker insurance market, in fact, insurance rates do go up for carriers who have more oil spills, but probably not at a rate sufficient to fully internalize the environmental damage costs [Goodstein and Jones 1997].)

Damage insurance is critical to internalize the environmental costs for businesses likely to suffer low probability but high impact accidents. In this regard, the nuclear power industry has long held onto a critical, but hidden governmental subsidy. Because nuclear plants would otherwise be unable to obtain private insurance, the Price-Anderson Act limits liability for nuclear accidents. From 1959 to 1988, the limit was set at $560 million; in 1988 it was raised to $7 billion. Dubin and Rothwell (1990) estimate the value of this subsidy to have been $60 million per reactor per year prior to 1988, and $22 million per reactor per year after 1988.

ELECTRIC POWER: ENVIRONMENTAL ADDERS AND PRODUCTION SUBSIDIES

One interesting attempt to introduce something like a pollution tax in the electricity industry has recently gained momentum in the United States. These "taxes," called **adders,** are only used in the project selection phase and are never actually collected. Adders reflect the external social costs associated with different types of power production and are "added" on to private cost estimates when firms bid to supply electricity to a utility's distribution grid. Thus, cleaner power sources are provided an advantage at the bidding stage. State utility regulators in at least twenty-nine states are either using adders or considering this option.[16]

To achieve efficiency, the adders should reflect the marginal social cost of adopting the technology. Under the most common form of regulation, command and control, this question can be rephrased: How much additional environmental damage will one kWh of, for example, coal electricity inflict on the environment? The efficient approach is to determine pollutant levels per kWh of coal-power and then estimate, using the techniques of risk analysis and benefit-estimation discussed in Chapter 8, the marginal damage from each pollutant.[17] Table 17.2 shows the actual adders used

---

[16]For an overview, see Energy Information Administration (1995).

[17]Adders equal to marginal damages will lead to more efficient pollution control under CAC regulation only. Under a well-functioning marketable permit system, adders are not necessary to achieve efficiency. Why? First, any new source will have to purchase permits from existing firms. Thus, there is no net increase in pollution from a new source and no overall increase in environmental damage. Further, built into a firm's electricity bid will be the price of the permits it has to purchase, which include in turn the additional pollution control costs undertaken by the firm that sold the permits. Thus, all additional social costs of the technology will *already* be reflected in the bid, meaning the appropriate adder is zero. Of course, if a hot spot is expected to emerge at the new source, an adder could be justified on safety (and possibly efficiency) grounds. See Burtraw et al. (1992).

The authors also show that in the case of emissions taxes, an efficient adder will reflect the difference between marginal damage and the tax level. This means that in the case of a tax that results in inefficiently stringent pollution controls, the efficient adder will actually be negative. However, as our review of pollution taxes suggest, this situation is quite rare in practice.

TABLE 17.2   **Electricity Adders in New York State**
(based on cost-of-control estimates)

Externality	Cents/kWh
Sulfur oxides	0.25
Nitrogen oxides	0.55
Carbon dioxide	0.10
Particulates	0.10
Water discharges	0.10
Land use impacts	0.40
Total externality costs	1.40

Source: Ottinger et al. (1990).

in New York State in the mid-1990s. A clean source could gain at most a 1.4 cents/kWh advantage over a dirty competitor in the bidding process.[18]

Under the adder system, some unusual players have been attracted to the electrical generation business. In fact, the school where I used to teach, Skidmore College, put in a bid in conjunction with a private firm to build a natural gas plant. The plan was for Skidmore to use the heat generated by the relatively clean, new gas plant; the plant would thus **cogenerate** heat and electricity. This would allow us to shut down our own oil-based heating system which, in spite of meeting environmental standards, remained relatively dirty (and expensive). The project scored very well on the environmental front. Unfortunately, high production costs for such a small-scale operation meant that our project bid still was not low enough to win.

During the same bidding round, however, analysts working in a New York State Energy office did enter a winning bid. This group is now "producing" power through increased energy efficiency in several state prisons and college campuses. They offered the utility 1.8 MW of peak summer power and 12,000 GWh of overall energy reduction at a competitive price, with dramatic environmental benefits (Barnes, Decotis, and Platt 1992).

Of course, a more straightforward way to promote clean energy is just to subsidize it directly—for example, wind power receives a 1.5 cents/kWh federal production subsidy. Alternatively, subsidies could be eliminated for "dirty" fuels. We will look much more closely at the subsidy issue in the next few chapters.

17.7 Summary

This chapter has reviewed our experience with incentive-based regulation. The primary lesson from the existing marketable permit systems is that a permit market can

---

[18]These numbers are not based on the theoretical ideal sketched in the previous paragraph. Rather than considering the marginal damage done by the additional pollutants (equivalently, the marginal benefit of cleanup), regulators used adder values equal to the additional *cost* of controlling those pollutants. A look at our standard pollution reduction diagram (Figure 4.5) reveals that the two will be equal only under the unlikely case when pollution is controlled at the efficient level. Recognizing this possibility, New York developed a method for calculating the marginal damages caused by the pollutants on a site-specific basis; these adders in fact turned out to be much smaller than the cost of control values. For a harsh criticism of the New York damages study, see Ottinger (1985); Hohnmeyer, Ottinger, and Rennings (1995) provide a good collection of papers on adders. See also Joskow (1992).[16]For an overview, see Energy Information Administration (1995).

be a delicate thing. The fact that markets initially have few players can easily discourage potential traders from participating, thus prolonging the thin market problem. Market designers should strive to minimize transactions costs by providing clear, simple trading rules. Banking provisions should also be clarified at the outset.

Because of hot-spot problems, permit systems in practice work best for uniformly mixed pollutants. For non-uniformly mixed pollutants, permit designers face a trade-off between insuring uniform pollution exposure and achieving a workable permit system. In practice, some compromise of safety seems necessary if a permit system is to be successfully implemented for these types of pollutants. Otherwise, transactions costs will rise and choke off trades.

The main lesson to be learned from our experience with pollution taxes is that they are very hard, if not impossible, to implement at levels high enough to function as a sole means of pollution control. This was clearly illustrated by the fierce opposition to President Clinton's modest gasoline tax proposal of 1993. Thus, taxes and other fee-based mechanisms should be viewed as a complement to, not a substitute for, conventional command-and-control regulation. One example of this is the environmental adder used to influence technology choice in the electricity field.

In practice, pollution taxes often tend to provide a source of revenues for improved pollution control technology. Finally, indirect pollution taxes such as gasoline or energy taxes are often a compromise solution when direct pollution taxes prove politically unfeasible or are too hard to administer. In Europe and Japan, high energy taxes originally imposed as energy security measures, have also functioned to reduce pollution in those countries.

Any type of regulation requires a strong commitment to enforcement to be effective. This is especially true of IB regulation, where no special technology is mandated. In the U.S. context, the two most recent marketable permit initiatives (acid rain and the Los Angeles basin) have featured an up-front commitment to better monitoring technology.

APPLICATION 17.0

Taxing Hazardous Wastes

In 1989, thirty states had instituted taxes on the disposal of hazardous wastes, either at landfills, incinerators, or both. At the same time, federal legislation (RCRA) discussed in Chapter 12 was making land disposal of hazardous waste much more difficult for firms. Sigman (1992) conducted an interesting study in which she looked at the variation in tax rates across the states to address two questions:

1. What impact did the taxes have on the quantity of waste generated?
2. What impact did the taxes have on the choice of disposal method by firms?

Sigman looked at a class of compounds called chlorinated solvents, used primarily for cleaning metals. Some of the data provided in her study are reproduced in Tables 17.3 and 17.4.

1. Based on the data in Table 17.3, do you think the taxes would be more likely to discourage incineration or land disposal?

TABLE 17.3   Data on Chlorinated Solvent Wastes

Selected States	Tax Rate on Land Disposal (1989 $/ton)	Tax Rate on Incineration (1989 $/ton)
California	$170.69	$ 0.00
Connecticut	15.00	15.00
Idaho	21.00	1.00
Tennessee	5.00	2.50
Wisconsin	0.50	0.00
Vermont	112.00	56.00
Average (30 States)	26.95	10.73
Percent of waste disposed (1987–1988)	2%	25%

Source: Sigman (1992: Table 1). Tax rates are for waste generated in-state. Used with permission.

TABLE 17.4   Disposal Costs for Selected Hazardous Wastes (1987, $/ton)

Land Disposal	$ 97–166
Incineration	320–700
Treatment	625–285
Recovery	95–237

Source: Sigman (1992, Table 3 and p. 14). Used with permission.

2. Suppose it was found that overall chlorinated solvent waste production was, on average, lower at plants in Vermont than in Tennessee. Could we simply conclude that the higher taxes were responsible? If not, what other factors would you want to control for to find out the true effect of taxes on waste production?

3. Sigman's most optimistic estimate was that the hazardous waste taxes in place in 1988 reduced overall waste generation by about 10%. (This was presumably made possible by an increase in recycling and/or a reduction in chemical use.) Based on the data in the tables, is such a relatively small effect surprising?

4. Suppose that the tax rates in Table 17.3 were tripled or quadrupled. If government monitoring and enforcement capabilities were inadequate, is it possible that such a move might generate worse hazardous waste pollution problems than we currently have? How?

KEY IDEAS IN EACH SECTION

17.0 This chapter discusses several real-world applications of incentive-based regulation: marketable permits and direct and indirect pollution taxes.

17.1 Perhaps the most successful example of a marketable permit system has been the **lead banking** program, because none of the obstacles identified in the last chapter proved to be significant. A similar trading scheme is now underway for ozone-depleting CFCs.

17.2   In contrast to the lead case, the **Emissions Trading Program** has been disappointing relative to initial expectations. **Emission reduction credits** for criteria air pollutants are traded in the **offset, netting,** and **bubble** programs. Bubbles, in particular, have performed poorly due to imperfect information, thin markets, high transactions costs for non-uniformly mixed pollutants, and unclear permit banking rules. Hot spots have largely been ignored in California's **RECLAIM** and mobile-source ("clunker") trading programs. RECLAIM broke down temporarily under the pressure of the California energy crisis.

17.3   A major ongoing experiment in marketable permits can be found in current efforts to control sulfur dioxide emissions, which cause **acid rain.** This section discusses acid rain's environmental impact, as well as potential obstacles to successfully controlling SO_2 emissions from power plants via trading. From a theoretical perspective, things look pretty good; initial results show higher cost savings than expected.

17.4   Pollution taxes are not widely used in the United States. Major examples are fees for the disposal of solid and liquid waste, both hazardous and nonhazardous. Although disposal costs have risen sharply in recent years, **unit pricing** for disposal is not always employed, and thus, incentives for waste reduction have been diluted. In the absence of recycling or some other substitute for waste disposal, demand is inelastic. Finally, effluent fees are more common in Europe but are still typically used in conjunction with CAC regulation.

17.5   When direct pollution taxes are not feasible, indirect pollution taxes such as energy or gasoline taxes can also help to reduce pollution. The theoretical problem with an indirect tax is that it may have an unintended and counterproductive effect on other behavior. The U.S. gasoline tax hike of 1993 was too small to generate significant environmental benefits.

17.6   While textbook emissions fees are not often found in the United States, there are a variety of other pricing measures in operation, ranging from fees for use of public resources, to environmental bonds, to insurance and liability requirements, to environmental **adders** in the electric utility sector.

REFERENCES

"Acid Test." 1990. *Scientific American* 262, no. 4– 4:18.

Alberini, Anna, Winston Harrington, and Virginia McConnell. 1993. "Determinants of Participation in Accelerated Vehicle Retirement Programs." *Discussion Paper: 93-18.* Washington, DC: Resources for the Future.

Atkinson, Scott, and Tom Tietenberg. 1991. "Market Failure in Incentive-Based Regulation: The Case of Emission Trading." *Journal of Environmental Economics and Management* 21, no. 1:17–31.

Barnes, Patricia, Paul A. Decotis, and Brian Platt. 1992. "A State Government Bidder's Experience and Perspective." In *DSM Bidding: Status and Results.* Bala Cynwyd, PA: Synergic Resources Corporation.

Bohi, Douglas R., and Dallas Burtraw. 1991. "Avoiding Regulatory Gridlock in the Acid Rain Program." *Journal of Policy Analysis and Management* 10, no. 4:676–684.

Bohi, Douglas R., Dallas Burtraw, Alan J. Krupnick, and Charles G. Stalon. 1990. "Emissions Trading in the Electric Utility Industry." *Discussion Paper QE90-15.* Washington, DC: Resources for the Future.

Burtraw, Dallas. 1996. "Trading Emissions to Clean the Air: Exchanges Few but Savings Many." *Resources* 122 (Winter): 3–6.

Burtraw, Dallas, Alan Krupnick, Erin Mansur, David Austin, and Dierdre Farrell. 1998. "Reducing Air Pollution and Acid Rain." *Contemporary Economic Policy* 16, no. 4:379–400.

Burtraw, Dallas, and Karen Palmer. 2003. "The Paparazzi Take a Look at a Living Legend: The SO2 Cap-and-Trade Program for Power Plants in the United States," Discussion Paper 03-15. Washington, DC: Resources for the Future.

Claussen, Eileen. 1991. "Acid Rain: The Strategy." *EPA Journal* 17, no. 1:21–23.

"Congress Rests; Taxpayers Won't." 1989. *Chemical Week* 145 no. 23: 6.

Drury, Richard, Michael Belliveau, J. Kuhn, and Shipra Bansal. 1999. "Pollution Trading and Environmental Injustice: Los Angeles Failed Experiment in Air Quality Policy." *Duke Environmental Law and Policy Forum* 9, no. 2:231–290.

Dubin, Jeffrey A., and Geoffrey S. Rothwell. 1990. "Subsidy to Nuclear Power Through Price-Anderson Liability Limit." *Contemporary Policy Issues* 8:73–78.

Dudek, D. J., and J. Palmisano. 1988. "Emissions Trading: Why Is This Thoroughbred Hobbled?" *Columbia Journal of Environmental Law* 13:217–256.

Energy Information Administration. 1995. *Electricity Generation and Environmental Externalities, DOE/EIA-0598.* Washington, DC: U.S. Department of Energy.

Firor, John. 1989. *The Changing Atmosphere.* New Haven, CT: Yale University Press.

French, Hillary. 1990. "Clearing the Air." In *State of the World 1990,* edited by Lester R. Brown. New York: Norton.

Fullerton, Don and Thomas Kinnaman. 1996. "Household Response to Pricing Garbage by the Bag." *American Economic Review* 86, no. 4: 971–984.

Goodstein, Eban, and Robert Jones. 1997. "Testing the Market for Environment Safety: The Case of Oil Tankers." *Lewis and Clark College Working Paper.* Portland, OR: Lewis and Clark College.

Goodstein, Eban. 1999. *The Trade-off Myth: Fact and Fiction about Jobs and the Environment.* Washington, DC: Island Press.

Hahn, Robert W. 1989. "Economic Prescriptions for Environmental Problems: How the Patient Followed the Doctor's Orders." *Journal of Economic Perspectives* 3, no. 2:95–114.

Hoerner, Andrew, and Benoit Bosquet. 1999. "Environmental Tax Reform: The European Experience," *Working Paper.* Washington, DC: Center for a Sustainable Economy.

Hohnmeyer, O., R. L. Ottinger, and K. Rennings. 1995. *Social Costs and Sustainability: Valuation and Implementation in the Energy and Transport Sectors.* Berlin: Springer-Verlag.

Joskow, Paul. 1992. "Weighing Environmental Externalities: Let's Do It Right." *The Electricity Journal,* May.

Kriz, Margaret. 1993. "Emission Control." *National Journal,* 3 July, 1696–1701.

Krupnick, Alan J. 1986. "Costs of Alternative Policies for the Control of Nitrogen Dioxide in Baltimore." *Journal of Environmental Economics and Management* 13, no. 2:185–197.

"Learning from an Acid Rain Program." 1990. *Science* 251, no. 4999: 1302–1304.

Lechner, Sheryl. 1991. "Liming Acid Lakes: Industry and Environmentalists Have Switched Sides." *Audubon* 94, no. 3:26.

Luong, Danny, Susan Tsai, and Dipankar Sakar. 2000. *Annual Reclaim Audit Report for the 1998 Compliance Year.* Los Angeles: South Coast Air Quality Management District.

Morgenstern, Richard. 1996. "Is There a Double-Dividend?" *Environment* 38, no. 2:16–34.

Morris, Glenn E., and Denise G. Byrd. 1990. "Charging Households for Waste Collection and Disposal." *EPA 530-SW-90-047.* Washington, DC: U.S. EPA.

Mullen, John K., and Frederic C. Menz. 1985. "The Effect of Acidification Damages on the Economic Value of the Adirondack Fishery to New York Anglers." *American Journal of Agricultural Economics* 67:112–119.

NAPAP. 1991. *National Acid Precipitation Program, 1990 Integrated Assessment Report.* Washington, DC: National Acid Precipitation Program.

"New Rules Harness Power of Free Markets to Curb Air Pollution." 1992. *Wall Street Journal* 14 April.Office of Technology Assessment. 1984. *Acid Rain and Transported Air Pollutants: Implications for Public Policy.* Washington, DC: U.S. GPO.

Olem, Harvey. 1991. "Liming Acidic Surface Waters." In *Acidic Deposition: State of Science and Technology,* edited by Patricia Irving. Washington, DC: National Acid Precipitation Program.

Ottinger, Richard L. 1995. "Have Recent Studies Rendered Environmental Externality Valuation Irrelevant?" In *Social Costs and Sustainability: Valuation and Implementation in the Energy and Transport Sectors,* edited by O. Hohnmeyer, R. L. Ottinger, and K. Rennings. Berlin: Springer-Verlag.

Ottinger, Richard L., et al. 1990. *Environmental Costs of Electricity.* New York: Oceana Publications.

Sigman, Hillary. 1992. "The Effects of Hazardous Waste Taxes on Generation and Disposal of Chlorinated Solvent Waste." Paper presented at the American Economic Association Meetings, January 1993.

"Trades to Remember: The Lead Phasedown." 1992. EPA Journal, 18, no. 2.U.S. EPA. 1999. *Progress Report on the EPA Acid Rain Program.* Washington, DC: U.S. EPA Office of Air and Radiation.

Wendling, R. M., and R. H. Bezdek. 1989. "Acid Rain Abatement Legislation—Costs and Benefits." *OMEGA International Journal of Management Science* 17, no. 3:251–261.

World Bank. 1992. *World Development Report 1992.* Washington, DC: World Bank.

C H A P T E R

PROMOTING CLEAN TECHNOLOGY: THEORY

18.0 Introduction

As we have seen in the last two chapters, many environmental economists spent the last couple of decades preparing a theoretical case for and advocating the adoption of incentive-based regulation. Their response to the question "How can we do better?" was to say, "We can achieve the same pollution reduction at less cost."

While IB advocates prescribe better regulatory design for our environmental problems, a more fundamental criticism is increasingly being leveled at *any* regulatory approach to pollution control, including *both* CAC and IB. As was discussed at the end of Chapter 14, regulation faces three generic problems: (1) rapid economic growth, (2) rising marginal costs of control (the "easy" point and stationary sources are already controlled), and (3) the piecemeal problem (pollution regulated in one medium squeezing out elsewhere). As a result, regulation alone, even when incentive-based, may not be sufficient to achieve environmental goals.

Moreover, regulation is highly susceptible to political influence due to its information-intensive nature. Thus, industry spends tens of millions of dollars to influence and defuse the process, and yet still finds itself saddled with burdensome and seemingly irrational regulatory requirements mandated by a frustrated Congress. At the same time, environmentalists charge that the actual regulations have no teeth and are enforced only erratically. As one observer put it, "the classical sense of law is lost in sliding scales of targets and goals, accepted tolerances and negotiated exceptions, discretionary enforcement and discretionary compliance" (Greider 1992, 109).

As indicated in Chapter 14, the regulatory approach taken over the last thirty years *has* made a difference. Pollution levels are well below what they would have been in the absence of regulation, although relative to the initial goal of a "clean and safe" environment, the results have been disappointing. Nevertheless, the widespread perception is that the effectiveness of the regulatory approach is limited by the complexity of the issues at stake and the related opportunities available for political influence. In addition, there is no doubt that the regulatory approach, with its associated need for detailed bureaucratic decision making, has been costly.

Recent interest has focused on the development of clean technologies as a complementary strategy to regulation. Rather than rely solely on controlling pollutants at the "end of the pipe," advocates of this approach argue that government should promote the use of technologies that *reduce polluting inputs and processes in the first place.*

Waste reduction in manufacturing, recycling of wastes, low-input agriculture, energy and water efficiency, renewable resource use, and renewable energy production are often cited as candidates for governmental promotion on environmental grounds. Collectively they may be referred to as **clean technologies (CTs).**

However, this simple formulation begs at least three questions: (1) How can we identify a clean technology? (2) If the technology is so clearly superior, why isn't the market adopting it in the first place? (3) If the market is failing to develop the CT rapidly, how can the government successfully "pick winners" and promote certain types of technologies over others? This chapter explores in more detail the theory of clean technology, focusing on these three questions. Chapter 19 will then consider recent efforts to promote three types of alternative technology: waste reduction in manufacturing, less chemical intensive alternative agriculture, and solid waste recycling. Chapter 20 concludes the CT discussion with a comprehensive look at energy policy.

18.1 Path Dependence and Clean Technology

An early and influential book arguing for the clean technology approach appeared in 1977. *Soft Energy Paths: Towards a Durable Peace,* was written by American physicist Amory Lovins.[1] Lovins viewed the United States as being at a crossroads from which two paths diverged. The first was the road then being followed—a society based on the promotion and production of cheap electricity, via an increased reliance on coal, oil, and nuclear power. Lovins labeled this the "hard" path. By contrast, the "soft" path involved a conscious governmental effort to redirect the economy toward efficient use of energy and the promotion of renewable energy technologies, especially solar power.

Because the soft path depends on decentralized power production and greater reliance on locally available resources, it promised many social benefits: "A soft path simultaneously offers jobs for the unemployed, capital for businesspeople, environmental protection for conservationists, enhanced national security for the military, opportunities for small business to innovate and for big business to recycle itself . . ." (Lovins 1977, 23). But best of all, according to Lovins, it was cheaper.

From a theoretical point of view, government efforts to influence the direction of technological progress can be justified by what economists call **path dependence.**[2]

---

[1]Lovins acknowledges his debt to another author, E. F. Schumacher, whose equally influential book, *Small Is Beautiful: Economics As If People Mattered,* appeared in 1973. Lovins, however, redirected the debate away from a philosophical commitment to issues of scale and toward questions of economic transition.

[2]For an accessible introduction to path dependence theory, see Arthur (1991).

This theory maintains that current production technologies—for example, U.S. reliance on private automobiles for urban transportation—represent only one possible path of development. A potentially cost-competitive alternative in this case might be mass transit, dominant in many European and Japanese cities.

The path a society chooses depends on a variety of factors, including the relative political strength of the conflicting interests, chance historical circumstance, and of course consumer preferences and relative production costs. In the auto example, the U.S. government's decision to construct the interstate highway system beginning after World War II, which in turn promoted suburban development, provided the decisive advantage to private transport.

However, once a path has been chosen, other paths are closed off; this happens for three reasons. First, infrastructure and R&D investments are increasingly directed toward supporting the chosen technology and diverted from the competing path. Second, the chosen technology is able to exploit economies of scale to consolidate its cost advantage. Third, complementary technologies develop that are tailored to the chosen path, further disadvantaging the competing path. In the transportation example, this would include the sprawling retail and housing patterns of U.S. cities, which now virtually require a private vehicle for access.

Path dependence theory suggests that once a path is chosen, there is no easy way to switch tracks. However, in retrospect, we can see that technological choices have social consequences—the adoption of private transport, for example, has borne a substantial environmental cost. Thus, the role of government is to try and influence the current market-driven process of technological development toward a path consistent with a sustainable future. Note that this theory assumes that governments in modern capitalist societies already necessarily play a major role in shaping technological change through infrastructure decisions and subsidy policies; the key here is to insure that role is a positive one.

18.2 Clean Technology Defined

For the purposes of this book, clean technology has four characteristics:

1. It is not speculative.
2. It generates services of similar quality to existing technologies.
3. It has minimum long-run *private* marginal costs comparable to existing technologies.
4. It is environmentally less destructive than existing technologies.

1. *CTs are not speculative.* Point one requires commercial development and application of the technology to be within a few years' reach. Although there certainly is a role for "pure" government sponsored research, if clean technology is intended as a method of environmental improvement, it must be readily available.

2. *CTs provide comparable quality services.* Judging quality can be a difficult task. For example, in sunny climates a cost-saving and convenient way to preheat water for a dishwasher is to install a fifty-gallon drum painted black on the roof. However, early attempts to market such a simple and cost-effective technology foundered on consumer resistance—the barrels looked ugly to most people. On the other hand, some consumers were proud to have an energy saving barrel on their roof.[3] Judgments about "similar quality" are necessarily subjective. Nevertheless, a governmental decision to promote one certain technology over another requires some judgment about the relative quality of service. Bad choices will ultimately be rejected by consumers, leading to failure of the CT policy.

3. *CTs are cost-competitive on a market basis.* Cost comparisons between technologies should be made on the basis of long-run private marginal costs, including taxes and regulatory costs. Why not include external social costs in the comparison? A comparison of private plus social costs does indeed provide the true measure of which technology is theoretically "efficient." However, *if CTs cannot compete on the basis of private costs,* then they will not be adopted, regardless of government efforts to promote them.

For example, consider photovoltaic or solar electricity. In the 1990s, photovoltaic (PV) electricity production cost about $.25 per kilowatt hour (kWh). The cost of *peak power* (on a hot summer day when all the air conditioners are running) in New England was as high as $.20 per kWh, because utilities have to operate oil-fired generators for only short periods of time to satisfy this demand. However, if one includes all the subsidies and externality costs associated with conventional power, it is possible to make a case that PVs were already the "cheaper" technology. Table 18.1 reproduces one such effort.

The information in the table suggests that PVs may *already be* the socially preferred technology for peaking power. Yet if PV prices cannot be brought down to levels competitive in the private market within a few years' time (and many believe they can), their use will not spread rapidly, regardless of governmental efforts to promote them. Clean technologies must be competitive in the marketplace to succeed.

What is meant by **long-run marginal costs?** Simply the cost of producing an additional unit once the technology is mature. CTs can be divided into two categories, based on whether or not they require high-volume production to achieve their long-run minimum marginal cost. **Small-scale CTs** are cost-competitive with existing technologies at low-volume production. Examples would include the installation of housing insulation or low-flow showerheads, the on-farm adoption of less chemical-intensive pest control, or "housekeeping" measures by manufacturing firms to reduce

TABLE 18.1   Social and Private Costs of Peak Power

	Photovoltaics	Fuel Oil
Private costs	$0.25	$0.20
Externality costs	0.00–0.02	0.08
Total costs	0.25–0.27	0.28

Sources: Externality costs are from Ottinger, et al. (1990. 31). Private cost estimates are from Zweibel (1990).

---

[3]Thanks to Dallas Burtraw for this example.

the generation of hazardous waste. While small-scale CTs are by definition currently cost-competitive, they may still experience economies of scale through marketing.

Large-scale CTs, by contrast, require high-production volumes to achieve minimum long-run costs. Examples would include newspaper recycling, photovoltaic or solar thermal electricity production, and the manufacture of energy-efficient consumer durables, such as cars, refrigerators, lights, and air conditioners.

Figure 18.1 illustrates an estimated long-run average cost curve for electricity produced by wind power. Wind electricity costs started out at more than $0.25/kWh in the early 1980s. By 2002, with global wind capacity at 31,000 megawatts, the price had fallen to less than $0.05/kWh. Costs are predicted to fall to $0.03/kWh—competitive with new natural gas plants—when the installed worldwide capacity increases to 80,000 megawatts.

Per unit costs fall for three reasons. First, as the firms invest in research and development (R&D) and gain experience, they generate new and lower-cost methods of organization and production. Second, as the market size increases, firms can take advantage of **economies of scale:** lower-cost production arising from the ability to use specialized machinery and personnel at high volumes. Third, as complementary industries and markets develop, input costs fall.[4]

As drawn, the average cost curve eventually flattens out as opportunities for technological advancement and specialization are exhausted. This portion of the curve is the minimum long-run average cost, and since the average is constant, marginal cost as well. This long-run cost, to the degree it can be estimated, should be the baseline for a comparison between two technologies, for example, wind and oil-powered electricity.

The history of cost forecasting is replete with major disasters, such as the famous prediction that nuclear power would one day be "too cheap to meter." Thus credible

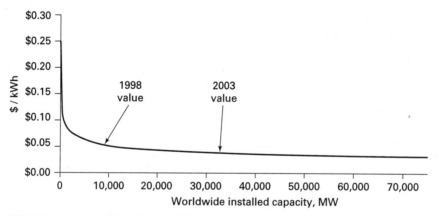

FIGURE 18.1 Long-Run Costs of Wind Power (Estimated $1998)
Source: Goodstein (2000); assumes an 85% progress ratio.

---

[4]You may recall from an earlier course that short-run average costs also fall as firms spread out their fixed costs. Initial investments in plant and equipment, advertising, and service and sales networks do mean that for a given plant size, costs per unit are high at low output levels. However, in the long run, average fixed costs need not fall as an industry grows, since overhead expenses may grow proportionately. In addition, decreasing returns to scale, resulting from managerial breakdown, may set in at some point, causing long-run average costs to actually rise.

forecasts stay as far as possible from scenarios relying on unproven or speculative technologies, and depend instead on the expected costs of implementing known production methods within a relatively short time frame.

4. *CTs are environmentally superior.* Point four in the definition of clean technology insures that it is indeed clean, which is in fact more difficult to establish than it appears. First, it is necessary to account, at least in a rough way, for all of the major environmental impacts of a technology: in manufacturing, use, and disposal. This kind of cradle-to-grave approach is known as **life-cycle analysis.** A second problem arises because different technologies have various types of environmental impacts. This leads to an **adding-up problem,** in which the superiority of one technology over the other may not be clear-cut.

The "diaper wars" debate illustrates both the life-cycle and adding-up problems. Each year, American babies use about 17 billion disposable diapers made of paper and plastic. These diapers account for between 1% and 2% of material entering the solid waste stream, ultimately winding up in landfills or incinerators. In the early 1990s, many argued that cloth diapers, provided through diaper services, offered a clean alternative—comparable in quality of service (including convenience) and price, and better for the environment. With consumer demand spurred by this "green" marketing claim, the diaper service business was booming.

However, as a counter to the solid waste concern, Procter & Gamble (maker of Pampers and Luvs) sponsored a study and related PR campaign, which maintained that reusable cloth diapers generate substantially more water pollution in the washing process than throwaways do in manufacturing. In response, the National Association of Diaper Services sponsored its own research, which undertook a life-cycle analysis of the environmental impact of the two products. The authors of this study found that, in general, liquid effluent from the manufacturing process was less harmful for cotton than disposable diapers, and that the overall water pollution advantage of disposables did not hold for cotton diapers laundered commercially.

At this point, it appears that cotton diapers have an edge in areas with solid waste problems, and overall in terms of manufacturing effluents, although disposables may be preferable in areas where municipal water treatment facilities are overloaded or inadequate. However, the scientific details have not mattered much in the marketplace. Thanks in some large measure to P&G's ad campaign, cloth diaper services have lost their environmental luster and were virtually eliminated as a competitive threat by 1997. In the New York City area, for example, there were no cloth diaper services; the National Association of Diaper Services had less than half the members it had in 1991. (See "In the Diaper Wars" 1997; A. D. Little 1990; Hershkowitz 1990; Lehrburger, Mullen, and Jones 1991).

Life-cycle accounting of environmental impacts is an emerging science that, in certain cases, is capable of identifying the relative pollution impact of different technologies with more or less precision. However, as the diaper case illustrates, a given technology need not dominate another in all pollution areas, and depending upon how the life-cycle boundaries are drawn, conflicting results may arise.[5] At this point, a policy

---

[5]For another example, comparing paper and plastic cups, see Hocking (1991). A theoretical problem with life-cycle accounting emerges when indirect effects (see Chapter 19) are taken into account. Because indirect pollution may be bigger than direct pollution, a technology that appears clean in a life-cycle framework may in fact have lots of dirty processes lurking in the input-output matrix. At this point, indirect effects must be assumed to cancel each other out. This point is explored further in Appendix 19A.

commitment to support one technology over another often must rely on "common-sense" judgments. This in turn means that "close calls," like cloth diapers, should *not* be considered candidates for governmental promotion as clean technologies.

A natural way to solve the adding-up problem and compare two technologies is to monetize and total the expected life-cycle environmental damages from each source. Such a value could be used to compare the social costs of the two technologies, as is done in Table 18.1 for electricity generation from fuel oil and solar power. Note that the clean technology, photovoltaics, does impose some externality costs on society. However, the pollution generated in the manufacture of PVs does substantially less damage than that arising from the burning of oil. By monetizing damages in this way, a CT's environmental superiority can be judged. However, as discussed in point three, adding environmental damages should not be part of an assessment of a CT's *cost*-competitiveness.

This section has provided a working definition of clean technology. We have found that both small- and large-scale technologies can qualify; there is no up-front bias toward "small is beautiful." However, all of the clean technology candidates discussed in this chapter and the next—photovoltaics and other renewable energy technologies, energy efficiency, diaper services (in some areas), recycling, waste reduction and alternative agriculture—achieve their environmental advantage by being relatively labor-intensive and/or relying to a greater extent on locally produced resources. As a result, they often tend to favor smaller-scale technologies, which can also generate higher *local* employment levels.

18.3 If You're So Smart, Why Aren't You Rich?

The first objection raised to the clean technology approach is this: If these technologies are close to commercial development, generate a quality of service and have long-run production costs comparable to existing technologies, *and* are environmentally superior, why aren't private entrepreneurs developing them in the first place? In other words, if CT advocates are so smart, why aren't they rich?

The first response is that, in some cases, they are. For example, ten of thousands of American farmers have adopted various forms of low-input farming; recycling has emerged as an economic form of waste disposal in many communities; service corporations that identify cost-effective energy savings for firms and households are growing rapidly. Thus, market forces do provide some support for clean technologies. Yet, the market share for each of these CTs, while growing, remains tiny.

A variety of obstacles can discourage the market deployment of environmentally superior, cost-effective technologies. Table 18.2 provides a summary. The principal market obstacle is the **lack of a substantial profit advantage** for CTs. There is little incentive for private firms to undertake the marketing efforts necessary to overcome marketplace barriers to rapid diffusion: poor information, thin resale markets, poor access to capital, and high discount rates.[6]

A second substantial barrier arises from current governmental policy: subsidies tilted in favor of existing competitor technologies. These subsidies range from R&D

---

[6]Sullivan (1991) points out that, with the exception of imperfect information, these are not market "failures" in the classic sense. For a discussion of the diffusion literature, see Jaffe and Stavins (1991).

TABLE 18.2   Obstacles to the Rapid Diffusion of CTs

Market Obstacles	Government Obstacles
Lack of profit advantage to overcome: • Poor information • Thin resale markets • Limited access to capital • High discount rates	Subsidy policies favoring dirty technologies Failure of regulation to internalize all externalities

funding, to price supports, to tax credits, to efforts on behalf of industry by state and federal agency personnel. Finally, of course, market prices for the competitor technology fail to reflect externality costs.

MARKET OBSTACLES FACING CTS

Simply because CTs are potentially cost-competitive does not mean they are *more* profitable than existing technologies. Entrepreneurs tend to introduce products to fill a "market niche" and provide at least temporary monopoly profits. Clean technologies, by contrast, generally are not offering a new product; rather they go head-to-head with an existing, well-established technology in a mature industry. Thus, they must enter an already competitive field, where only normal profits can be expected. The only clearcut advantage CTs have is in their environmental impact. While this may provide some marketing leverage, it generally will not guarantee high profitability.

Under normal market circumstances, new technologies often take substantial time to develop a widespread following. This is due to consumers' lack of knowledge (again, imperfect information) about the advantages of the new technology, as well as differences in consumer needs. The transition to any new technology requires a *marketing commitment* to overcome this lack of information. Marketing expenses are **sunk costs,** those that cannot be recovered if an investment fails. The higher the sunk costs associated with an investment, the riskier it becomes.[7]

Clean technologies face particularly high sunk costs (and thus high risk) because they do not "market themselves" by offering a service consumers do not already have. Instead, CTs need to woo consumers from the use of the existing technology. While CTs offer comparable services, they also tend to require users to learn new consumption habits. This requires a big investment in marketing, which cannot be recovered if the business fails.

Moreover, existing firms do not take inroads into their markets lightly. Witness, for example, Procter & Gamble's massive public relations effort to convince consumers that the disposable diaper is not environmentally inferior to cotton. This type of counter-marketing campaign from powerful incumbent firms can make large-scale entry into a CT market even more risky or deter it entirely.

As we saw in the case of marketable permits, imperfect information also generates a **thin market problem.** For example, a homeowner may be reluctant to shoulder

---

[7]From the finance theory point of view, marketing costs tend to be systematic risks; that is, risks that cannot be diversified away. They require a higher rate of return. Sullivan (1991) points out that the risk associated with actually installing energy-efficient equipment tends to be unsystematic, in principle requiring no profit premium. However, consumers and small businesses generally face imperfect capital markets and must absorb much of this risk personally.

the high up-front costs of outfitting her home with energy- and money-saving compact fluorescent lightbulbs because most prospective home buyers know little about them. Thus, she would probably not be able to recoup her initial investment if she decided to sell the house within a few years. Thin markets for durable technologies (those with resale value) tend to dampen the rate of adoption.

Access to capital is a problem for both small- and large-scale technologies. Small-scale CTs often entail an initial-up-front investment, which is compensated for by lower operating costs. Returning to our homeowner, a bank might extend her a home-improvement loan to purchase energy-efficient lightbulbs, although such loans are certainly not common; however, the interest rate charged would be much higher than a utility faces when it borrows several hundred million dollars to build a new power plant. The bank would justify its differential lending practices on the basis of increased transactions costs associated with small loans and, perhaps, increased risk.

At the other extreme, clean technologies with major scale economies, for example, solar electric power, require large amounts of capital for research and development, production, marketing, and service efforts. They also need a pool of specialized human capital—management and technical expertise familiar with the market. In the solar field, the "natural" organizations with access to this kind of capital and expertise are the large corporations in the energy and utility fields. Why, by and large, do these companies ignore clean technologies?

As we learned in Chapter 6, private discount rates are often higher than socially appropriate for environmental investments. **High discount rates** mean that profits made in the future are less valuable than profits earned today. And, as was stressed above, because CTs compete with mature, conventional technologies, a major investment in CTs is not likely to be a profit center in the near term—say a decade or more. Yet, a 20% before-tax rate of return, a common requirement in many U.S. industries, implies roughly a five-year payback on any investment.[8]

This central fact has kept interest in solar, wind, and renewables on the back burner for most large energy and utility corporations; few have interest in R&D investments with long-term payoffs. In addition, these tend to be the very firms with a strong vested interest in the status quo. Why develop products that will compete with already profitable electricity and fuel sales? European and Japanese businesses, facing higher conventional fuel prices, are naturally more interested in energy CTs.[9]

In the absence of commitments to technologies such as solar electricity by large firms, small firms enter to serve niche markets. However, neither substantial R&D nor economies of scale in production can be achieved by these firms. Thus, costs remain high, and the market widens only slowly.

---

[8]Scherer (1988) found median after-tax hurdle rates to be around 15%. He also discusses the argument that during the 1980s fear of takeovers induced managers in large corporations to reduce overhead costs, including substantial cutbacks in research and developmental funding.

[9]Through the late 1980s, the biggest U.S. solar company and the world leader in photovoltaic sales was owned by the oil company ARCO. ARCO purchased the solar company in the late 1970s as a hedge against rising oil prices; in 1986, with oil prices flat, ARCO decided to sell its solar unit. The solar company was purchased by a German electronics firm, Siemens, in 1989, the year it turned its first profit. See also Zweibel (1990), Scherer (1988), and the review article by Porter (1992).

Finally, consumers also appear to require high rates of return for investments in durable CTs. As discussed in Chapter 6, observed discount rates of 50% to 100% are not uncommon for the purchase of energy-efficient air conditioners, refrigerators, or lightbulbs. This unwillingness to commit funds to highly profitable investments reflects a combination of poor information, restricted access to capital, risk aversion, and thin resale markets.

GOVERNMENT OBSTACLES TO CTS

In addition to market barriers, CTs are often disadvantaged by government action in the form of **direct or indirect subsidies** to highly polluting competitors. Consider agriculture, for example. As you may have learned in an introductory economics course, due to the high variability in agricultural prices, the government has historically provided farmers with a guaranteed price floor. If the market price falls below the price floor, say $2.80 per bushel for corn, the government makes up the difference. However, as illustrated in Figure 18.2, the price floor also guarantees an excess supply of corn (q_d to q_s) that the government must stockpile.

One consequence of the surplus production is of course greater pesticide use. The Conservation Foundation estimates that the *surplus* wheat and corn grown in a single year in the U.S. required the application of 7.3 billion pounds of fertilizer and 110 million pounds of pesticides.

In addition to promoting excess pesticide use, however, subsidy programs can directly penalize cleaner agricultural practices. Until recently, price supports were primarily available for a limited number of crops, and these crops (coincidentally?) were very high users of chemical fertilizers and pesticides. Moreover, the subsidy payments for a given year were based on past yields of the crop in question, effectively tying farmers to the production of subsidy crops. A farmer desiring to adopt a CT based on diversification into less chemical-intensive crops and crop rotation as a method of

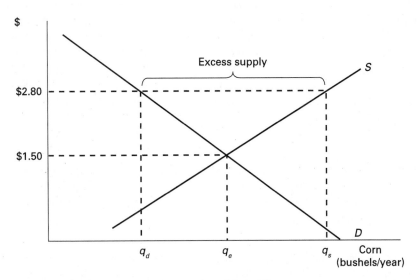

FIGURE 18.2 The Impact of Agricultural Subsidies

fertilization and weed, pest, and erosion control might find herself, thus, doubly damned. Not only would she lose her subsidy this year, but subsidies for any future program crops she grew would also be reduced (Crosswhite and Sandretto 1991; Curtis 1991 cites the Conservation Foundation study).

While farm subsidies provide a very visible example, most CTs face competitor technologies that receive important governmental aid, direct or indirect. As we discussed in the last chapter, for example, solid waste disposal is often paid for through lump sum tax payments, not by unit pricing. This provides a subsidy for large garbage producers, disadvantaging recycling. Recycling is also placed at some disadvantage through a variety of subsidies to raw materials producers. (Office of Technology Assessment 1989). Chapter 20 will focus on subsidies for polluting technologies in the energy field.

This section has provided a look at both market and government obstacles to clean technology adoptions. We now turn to consider how government policy makers can in fact select and promote CTs in the most cost-effective manner.

18.4 Picking the Winning Path

While I was driving to my in-laws' house yesterday, a prominent forest service critic was on the radio. He made the argument that many of the environmental problems in the western United States could be traced directly to bad government decisions reflecting industry's influence: subsidies for ranchers leading to overgrazing; subsidies for timber companies leading to clear-cuts; subsidies for mining companies leading to water contamination and the destruction of wilderness areas; and radiation leaks and releases from government-owned, -leased or -subsidized nuclear facilities.[11]

There are two responses to these governmental efforts at industrial promotion. One is to despair of government's ability to intervene rationally in economic affairs. Traditional conservatives would adopt this position and argue that, in spite of possible market obstacles to the rapid adoption of clean technology, the only thing government should do is to level the playing field by eliminating all subsidies.

Progressives adopt an alternative response. While acknowledging government failures, they also point to environmental success stories, such as weatherization and soil conservation programs, improvements in automobile fuel efficiency, and the creation of wilderness areas. They argue that a blanket call for the elimination of subsidies is naive. The challenge is to recognize the limitations of government intervention and, taking this into account, implement policies to promote CTs.

How can bureaucratic errors and political influence be minimized in this process? A three-step procedure should be followed.

1. *Level the playing field.* To the extent possible, subsidies for dirty technologies should be eliminated, and their external costs should be internalized, preferably through IB regulation. (As we saw in Chapter 16, IB regulation is superior to a command-and-control approach for promoting technological change

---

[10]The OTA suggests that such subsidies are probably not a major barrier to increased recycling in general. Nestor (1991) draws a similar conclusion for newspapers.

[11]For a scholarly analysis along these lines, see Stavins and Jaffe (1990).

within a regulated industry.)[12] "Leveling the playing field" by reducing subsidies and internalizing social costs may provide clean technologies with the edge needed to succeed.[13]

2.   *Promote only clear environmental winners.* Given the uncertainty associated with assessing the actual environmental impacts of different technologies, only CTs with a clear environmental advantage should be considered for promotion.

3.   *Tie subsidies to least-cost performance.* When the government does decide to promote a technology actively, subsidies should be directed only to projects that either are *already* cost-effective, or promise to deliver cost-effective services within a relatively short period of time, say a decade or less. Subsidies to the latter category should be conditioned on observable cost reductions. In sum, government planners should focus attention on **least-cost** technology options, subject to an environmental screen.

This least-cost approach is consistent with path dependence theory; the government is looking for environmentally friendly "infant" industries that need only time-limited support to attain a sufficiently large scale to be self-supporting. The rationale for government subsidies under path dependence theory is to jump-start an industry for its environmental benefit, not provide indefinite promotion efforts.[14]

Least-cost planning of this type achieves two goals. First, government's objective is to speed up, not replace, the market process of adoption of CTs. Market forces will naturally spread technologies with a greater profit advantage faster. The faster the technology spreads, the greater the environmental benefits society reaps.

Second, by using a least-cost approach, bureaucrats can avoid making expensive commitments to technological white elephants. A good example of such a poor choice is nuclear fusion. Fusion is an approach to energy production based on fusing two atomic nuclei together. By contrast, commercial reactors today generate power through fission, the splitting apart of particles. The government commitment to fusion research began in 1952 and continued rising steadily until 1984 when it peaked at about $440 million per year. Today, after at least six decades of federal funding, even fusion optimists concede that commercial power generation would require comparable R&D subsidies for at least another fifty years.[15]

How can we explain the continued flow of substantial funds to this ill-fated project? The allure of fusion has always been its promise of an energy source with limitless

---

[12]CAC regulation does promote substitution *away* from the products or services produced by the regulated industry. As we shall see in the next chapter, by raising the production costs for products such as pesticides and landfill disposal, CAC regulation has led to the development and adoption of cleaner technologies *outside* of the regulated industry.

In addition, under a CT strategy, pollution taxes (or permits) are not viewed primarily as a means to achieve a pollution standard. Rather, they play the role of encouraging the adoption of CTs. Thus, the precise tax level is not as critical in the CT strategy as it is under IB regulation; any level of pollution tax will provide for accelerated diffusion of the CT, with higher taxes leading to faster diffusion.

[13]Larson and Knudson (1991) make this point forcefully for agricultural technologies.

[14]Development economists call this the "infant industry" argument for subsidies; here, however, the government motivation is for the environmental benefit provided by the new technology.

[15]See Hafele (1991) for example.

fuel and, relative to fission, low-waste production. The initial commitment to fusion was made during the Cold War, with the fear that the Russians would gain a competitive edge. The steady flow of dollars then generated a "fusion community"—physicists and engineers at university and federal laboratories, and Department of Energy bureaucrats—dependent for their livelihood on federal subsidies. This fusion community maintained and developed allies in Congress and the White House; fusion funding remained high through the 1970s because of energy security concerns. Finally, within the fusion community, until 1983 there was a tacit agreement to avoid public debate of the economic viability of the technology.[16]

In contrast to the open-ended support of fusion, path dependence theory suggests that a CT program can and should focus on technologies with a clear environmental advantage that will stand on their own relatively quickly. Government can then make only time-limited or performance-based commitments to the technology, and thus avoid the development of vested political interests attached to a particular technology. Fusion would neither have passed an environmental screen nor survived subsidies conditioned on rapid cost reductions.

Following a least-cost strategy insures that policy concentrates on "picking the low-hanging fruit." Doing this gets more environmental protection for a lower investment, with less risk and a lowered probability of prolonged government involvement.

18.5 Promoting Small-Scale CTs

It is useful to divide clean technologies into small- and large-scale groupings, since the market obstacles they face are somewhat different. Small-scale technologies, by definition, do not require large markets to reach their minimum long-run production costs; thus, they are already cost-competitive with existing technologies. The barriers these technologies face to rapid diffusion are related to imperfect information and higher capital costs. Large-scale technologies, by contrast, require assistance in achieving high-volume production before they can be cost-competitive with existing technologies.

Consumer and business resistance to small-scale CTs reflects a natural inclination to stick with "what works," rather than adopt an unknown and possibly risky alternative. As we have seen, the relatively low profit advantage of many CTs discourages private-sector marketing initiatives to overcome this resistance. Government policy should thus be directed at providing information to consumers and reducing perceived risks of adoption. Informational barriers can be dealt with through (1) product labeling requirements, (2) flexible design standards, (3) the reorientation of utility regulation, and (4) technical assistance programs. A program of (5) subsidies for consumers also can attack the information problem, as well as compensate for higher capital costs.

PRODUCT LABELING

The simplest policy step is to require product labeling. For example, the EPA has developed a standard method for testing the miles per gallon that automobiles can achieve and requires firms to publicly report this information. Similar energy-efficiency reporting is required for consumer durables such as refrigerators and air conditioners, and most

---

[16]For a sympathetic look at the fusion community, see Herman (1990).

recently computers, under the EPA's "energy star" program. This list could be expanded to lamps, motors, and other durables. Product labeling requirements provide consumers with ready access to information on the environmental consequences of their purchases.

Poll results indicate that many people are willing to pay a small premium for environmentally friendly products, and during the 1990s, niche markets for recycled paper, organic agricultural products, and even "green" electric power began to develop. To speed up the process, the U.S. government issued regulations governing the use of marketing terms such as "recyclable" and "organic."

In Germany and Canada, the government went further and issued "environmentally friendly" certifications for whole products. In the United States, by contrast, the trend has been for nongovernmental third-party organizations to act as product certifiers. For example, Green Seal is the major nonprofit organization working to develop this kind of private labeling scheme. In spite of being in existence since 1990, the program has taken a while to get underway because of the complexity of identifying "clean" products in a life-cycle framework. Green Seal's approach has been to identify the "major" environmental impacts of a given product, then publish a draft standard for review and comment by affected industries. As of 2000, Green Seal had developed certification standards for several dozen products, including tissue and writing paper, re-refined engine oil, compact fluorescent lighting, and water efficient fixtures. (*Question:* Have you ever seen the Green Seal on a product you bought? If not, why do you think you haven't?)

Another important private labeling initiative is run by a nongovernmental, international organization called the Forest Stewardship Council (FSC). The FSC develops different certification standards for each region and country of the world, and then certifies lumber products as meeting certain minimum environmental standards. The FSC achieved a major victory in 1999, when Home Depot became the first major U.S. hardware chain to agree to sell only certified lumber.[17]

MINIMUM DESIGN STANDARDS

Product labeling programs leave some choice in consumer hands. However, in markets where complex purchases are made infrequently, consumers have a hard time judging the relative merits of available technologies. Here *flexible* design standards, requiring a minimum level of environmental performance, can be introduced. The most well-known example of a design standard is a building code; many local governments have established energy-efficiency requirements for new homes.

The purchase price for an energy-efficient house is typically more than for a leaky alternative. Because consumers are reluctant to absorb larger loans and because banks are hesitant to make them, people naturally opt for the energy-inefficient choice. However, the savings in monthly heating bills from energy efficiency will quickly cover the initial up-front expense, and homeowners will save money in the long run. Thus, from an economic point of view, banks should provide and consumers should shoulder larger loans for an energy-efficient house.

However, neither banks nor consumers are particularly well-equipped to evaluate energy cost-saving opportunities on a case-by-case basis. By mandating minimum

---

[17]See the Green Seal Web site at *www.greenseal.org*. The FSC is at *www.fscoax.org*.

design standards, government closes off the option of the leaky alternative. The risk to all parties of opting for the CT is thus reduced. Banks will soon learn that, due to lower utility bills, they can offer higher loans on new houses, and all parties, including the environment, are better off in the long run.

Energy-efficiency requirements are included in many local building codes. In addition, federal law now requires banks to offer lower-rate, energy-efficiency mortgages, though this regulation is not well-known. Several cities and counties in the United States, including San Francisco and Ithaca, New York, now have retrofit energy standards that must be met for old buildings whenever they are sold, leased, or renovated. The increased cost is passed on to the buyer, who can then qualify for an energy-efficient mortgage (Geller et al. 1991).

Design standards have also been required for lighting, appliances, and electric motors, as a way to promote adoption of these CTs. Design standards provide a "free lunch" when the product's quality is quite generally perceived to be comparable to the conventional technology and its long-run private cost is less. In this case, government is simply mandating the choice that the majority of people would make on their own if given the information. However, design standards become more costly if individual opinion differs substantially as to the CT's quality, or if its cost rises above that of the conventional technology. Nevertheless, even in this case, design standards may still be justifiable as a cost-effective way to control pollution.

UTILITY MARKETING

Another approach to the marketing problem facing small-scale CTs is to have the technologies marketed by large firms, with lower-cost access to both financial and human capital. In the energy field, many states have restructured their regulation of utilities so that the firms can earn a profit on energy conservation. Until recently, utilities had no incentive to promote efficiency—every kilowatt saved was a reduction in their revenue. However, the new regulations recognize that energy saved is also energy freed up for other uses. Thus, investments in energy efficiency are increasingly treated like investments in new generating plants, on which firms are allowed to make a normal profit.

The last few years have seen an increasing level of utility marketing for energy-efficiency efforts. For example, my local utility retrofitted our house's water heater, gave us a low-flow showerhead and some pipe and outlet insulation, and conducted an energy audit, all free upon request. Utilities have also been involved in rebate programs for lightbulbs and appliances, and "refrigerator roundups" where the utility buys up and then junks ancient energy-hog refrigerators. These services are paid for through higher electricity bills. From both an economic and environmental point of view, these are all good investments, because by freeing up electricity, they allow the utility to avoid having to build expensive, polluting power plants.

TECHNICAL ASSISTANCE PROGRAMS

A fourth approach to marketing small-scale CTs is a direct one. Here, government technicians provide advice to firms interested in undertaking CT investments. As we shall see in the next chapter, this direct approach is advocated to promote waste-reducing, clean technologies in manufacturing. It also is the logical way to promote CTs in agriculture, since the government already has a technical assistance program—the state agricultural schools and extension services—in place.

CONSUMER SUBSIDIES

Efforts to provide consumers with information through labeling, standards, utility marketing, and technical assistance can be supplemented by subsidies for CTs. The presence of subsidies provides consumers with an incentive to educate themselves about the product; they also can overcome obstacles to rapid diffusion associated with higher capital costs. For example, the New York State government, using a pool of funds obtained in a court settlement with oil companies overcharging, provides matching grants to public and nonprofit institutions interested in energy-efficiency projects. The projects must have paycheck periods of no more than ten to fifteen years (New York State Energy Office 1992).

Subsidies can take several forms: **tax credits, low-interest loans,** or **grants.** To encourage small-scale CTs, loans and grants are preferable because they are easier to target. Loan applications and grants require groups to justify their investment, discouraging non-serious applicants, and they also provide government officials a means to allocate funds on a least-cost basis.

In addition, a problem with any subsidy program is that it may provide "windfalls" for people planning to adopt the technology anyway (free riders). A study of a tax credit for residential energy savings found that only 8% of the 15 million claimants would definitely or probably not have undertaken the investment without the credit. To deal with this problem, loans and grants can be targeted to working- and middle-class individuals, small businesses, and nonprofit corporations (Hirst et al. 1982).[18] These groups, being resource-constrained, are least likely to adopt the CTs in the first place. Finally, tax credits are typically used by wealthier individuals and corporations and, thus, skew the benefits of the policy in a regressive direction. If tax credits are used, one way to avoid promoting windfalls and tax cuts for the wealthy is to put an income limit on the claim.

18.6   Promoting Large-Scale CTs

In contrast to small-scale technologies, the primary barrier facing large-scale CTs is achieving high-volume production. As illustrated in Figure 18.1, this lowers per unit costs through R&D, learning-by-doing, and scale economies. The key policy issue is to provide some incentive for existing or new firms to enter these markets. This section discusses four policies to encourage such interest: (1) research and development funding, (2) producer subsidies, (3) technology-forcing standards, and (4) infrastructure investment.

RESEARCH AND DEVELOPMENT FUNDING

Figure 18.3 provides some idea of the scale and direction of government funding for R&D into energy technologies. Funding was quite high during the last years of the Carter administration—more than $5 billion in total—reflecting both the liberal perspective of the administration, and widespread public concern about dependence on foreign oil following the OPEC oil embargo of 1974.

---

[18]The tax credit program was also criticized for promoting expensive, rather than effective, energy-efficiency measures. To solve this problem, tax credits could be offered based on energy saved, rather than capital invested.

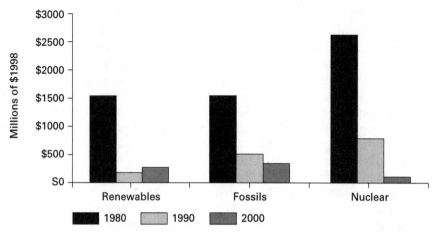

FIGURE 18.3 Department of Energy R&D Expenditures (1980, 1990, 2000)
Source: Department of Energy, Office of the Secretary, and *DOE Energy Resources Portfolio: FY 1999–2001.* Washington, DC: U.S. Department of Energy. Available at *www.osti.gov/portfolio.*

Overall funding fell steeply over the next decade. Conservative Presidents Reagan and Bush (senior) were philosophically opposed to government involvement in economic affairs, including commercial R&D. But renewables and energy efficiency research were particularly hard hit. During the last year of the Carter administration, renewables and conservation received a share of R&D funding comparable to fossil fuels. By 1990, fossil fuels received two-and-one-half times as much support as renewables, while the nuclear research budget was more than three times as large.

With Clinton's election, the renewables budget increased a bit, while R&D support for both fossil fuel and nuclear continued to decline. At the beginning of the century, the R&D shares of renewables and fossil fuels were again roughly comparable, but in absolute dollar terms, well below the levels observed twenty years earlier. The U.S. government R&D budget for renewable energy in 2000 was about $280 million, less than the cost of two F-22 fighter planes.

PRODUCER SUBSIDIES

Another approach to encouraging commercial development is to provide subsidies to producers—tax credits, loans, grants, or purchase guarantees. One form of purchase guarantee is a **price preference.** Many state governments will pay a premium of up to 5% or 10% for recycled products. Government **procurement contracts** are another way of providing infant CT industries with guaranteed markets. We will look more closely at subsidy issues in our discussion of energy policy in Chapter 20.

TECHNOLOGY-FORCING STANDARDS

Beyond the carrots of R&D funding and producer subsidies, government policy markers can also employ sticks. The primary tool here is to make access to the market subject to meeting a **technology-forcing standard.** In contrast to the building energy codes of lighting efficiency standards discussed above for small-scale CTs, technology-forcing standards set a deadline for firms to deliver technology that is *not yet* marketed.

Perhaps the best-known technology-forcing standards are the Corporate Average Fuel Economy, or **CAFE,** standards. In 1975, Congress mandated that car companies had to achieve an average of 18 miles per gallon by the 1978 model year, and 27.5 miles per gallon by the model year 1985. Stiff fines were to be levied on corporations that failed to comply, although a one-year "carryover" was permitted. Firms that exceeded the standard in one year could credit the excess MPG savings for the next year.[19]

From the point of view of increasing vehicle mileage, the CAFE has been a success—average fleet mileage did increase to around 28 miles per gallon, with little additional progress after 1987. The first round of CAFE appears to have been much more important than increasing gas prices (from 1974 to 1982) in achieving these mileage improvements. The CAFE standards may have had an unintended consequence: encouraging car companies to shift production to SUVs. SUVs—considered in 1975 to be light trucks, not cars—were exempt from CAFE mileage standards, and remain so through the writing of this edition (Greene 1990).[20]

A second example of technology forcing regulation is appliance energy standards, which were pioneered in California for refrigerators beginning in the 1970s. The California standard tightened from about 1,500 to 1,000 kWh per year between 1978 and 1988; access to California's market was important enough to manufacturers to spur significant progress. The average new refrigerator cost $64 less per year to run in 1990 than it did in 1970. The federal government adopted appliance standards in 1988; by 1995 average energy use for refrigerators dropped to no more than 700 kWh per year (Fickett, Gellings, and Lovins 1990).

From a theoretical perspective, sufficiently high pollution taxes can always achieve the same result as technology-forcing standards, with any inefficiencies reduced due to greater consumer and manufacturer flexibility (Bold 1987). However, as in many other cases, technology-forcing standards appear to be easier to legislate than do high taxes.

INFRASTRUCTURE INVESTMENT

The final tool available to government to influence the adoption of CTs is perhaps the most powerful. As we noted in the introduction to this chapter, the overwhelming dominance of the automobile in American life has much to do with the government-funded interstate highway system. Infrastructure investment, whether roads, pipelines, dams, or electric lines, have major long-run impacts on both local economic development and environmental quality.

Table 18.3 provides a summary of policy tools that government can use to promote CTs and suggest CTs for which their use may be appropriate. Of course, all these tools can be abused; a successful CT program will require that government policy focus on promoting only cost-effective, environmentally superior technologies. In particular, as was argued in Section 18.3, government subsidies should support only (1) cost-effective small scale technologies and/or (2) large-scale technologies that demonstrate substantial progress toward competitive pricing.

---

[19]One-year "carrybacks" were allowed as well.

[20]An earlier study, Crandall et al. (1986) arrived at the opposite conclusion. However, three years later, Crandall had apparently changed his mind (Crandall and Graham 1989) because he attributed increased highway deaths from car downsizing to the CAFE. For more on the safety issue, see Chapter 20.

TABLE 18.3 Policy Tools for Promoting CTs

Small-scale CTs	
Policy	**CTs**
Product labeling	Energy and water efficiency, recycling, alternative agriculture
Design standards	Energy and water efficiency
Utility marketing	Energy efficiency
Technical assistance	Waste reduction in manufacturing, alternative agriculture, passive solar, wind power
Consumer subsidies: grants, loans, tax credits	Energy and water efficiency, recycling, passive solar
Large-scale CTs	
Policy	**CTs**
R&D	Solar electric, wind power, fuel cell vehicles, biomass fuels, hydrogen fuels, alternative agriculture, waste reduction in manufacturing
Producer subsidies: price preferences, procurement contracts	Solar electric, hybrid electric vehicles, alternative agriculture, waste reduction in manufacturing
Technology-forcing standards	Energy efficiency, hybrid electric vehicles, fuel cell vehicles, recycling
Infrastructure investment	Mass transit, recycling

18.7 Summary

This chapter identifies government promotion of CTs as a potentially attractive alternative to regulation for controlling pollution. At a basic level, the two strategies are complements, not substitutes. By internalizing social costs, regulation provides a more level playing field on which clean technologies can compete. Yet, with the easy "point and stationary source" regulatory gains already achieved, and in the face of pressures from population and economic growth, rapid development and diffusion of CTs will become an increasingly important means of improving environmental quality.

Regulating waste once it is produced exacerbates short-run conflicts between economic growth and environmental quality. While in the long-run, environmental regulation spawns new technologies and creates new industries and jobs, "in the long run," as the economist John Maynard Keynes once said, "we are all dead." As a supplement to the stick of pollution taxes (or other IB regulation), the CT approach offers a carrot of government-promoted, substitute technology. Thus, the short-run trade-off between material well-being and the environment becomes much less stark.

Moreover, path dependence theory suggests that a continued exclusive government focus on end-of-the-pipe regulation of pollutants will lead to technological progress in end-of-the-pipe waste management, rather than in waste-reducing CTs. Concerned primarily with regulatory compliance, and provided with the funding to do so, environmental managers in industry and government will continue to develop expertise in emissions monitoring and enforcement, risk analysis, and benefit–cost analysis; engineers will focus on cheaper ways of scrubbing and filtering emissions, and safer ways of incinerating or burying wastes. While these skills and technologies are important for making regulation work better, they are not primarily the skills and techniques needed for a transition to CTs.

Finally, in practice, we have seen that regulation is an adversarial process in which environmentalists and industry compete in an information-intensive conflict over the drafting and enforcing of standards. A regulatory approach in one sense sets government up to fail, since the affected parties have many opportunities, and much to gain, from influencing the process. The political economy of a CT approach promises to reduce both the day-to-day conflict between regulators and firms, and limit the opportunities for political influence.

Promoting CTs, of course, is certain to have its own bureaucratic problems associated with implementation. Conservative critics would charge that the "light-handed" planning process described here, while nice in theory, would dissolve as soon as a CT agency were established. Once provided a budget, CT promotion would devolve into "heavy-handed" restrictions on industries arbitrarily judged to be "dirty" by environmentally motivated bureaucrats, coupled with expensive crash programs to develop completely ludicrous technologies, located in the districts of powerful members of Congress.

Yet, a political-economic case can also be made that a CT strategy would be an effective complement to regulation, reducing both costs and regulatory conflict with industry. Because CT development would not involve rule making at the level of individual pollutants, or extensive monitoring and enforcement, informational requirements would be diminished. As the need for information falls, so do opportunities for political influence, delay, and indecision. Once funded, technology subsidies are a "win-win" situation; firms are rewarded for reducing pollution, rather than punished for not doing so.[21] Thus, CTs can transform an adversarial relationship into a partnership. Finally, path dependence theory suggests that government subsidy commitments can and should be time-limited and/or performance-based, thus reducing the probability of both picking losers and the development of vested interests.

APPLICATION 18.0

Path Dependence and QWERTY[22]

One of the best examples illustrating path dependent technological development is the arrangement of the letters on the computer keyboard. Next time you sit down to write a paper, notice that the top six keys on the left-hand side spell QWERTY. The standard keyboard, widely used in English-speaking countries, is thus called QWERTY. How did QWERTY develop?

Not on the basis of efficiency. Other keyboard arrangements lead to much faster typing. Instead, QWERTY was designed in the 1870s as a way to prevent typewriter keys from clashing and sticking together on the upstroke.

---

[21]You may recall that in Chapter 4, it was claimed that subsidies for emission reductions were a bad idea, because in the long run this would simply draw other polluters into the business. By contrast, CT subsidies are for better technologies, not for reductions in emissions.

[22]This application is based on David (1985).

1. Use the theory of path dependence to explain why the inefficient QWERTY design still has a monopoly on the market for computer keyboards today.

2. A U.S. Navy study done in the 1940s indicated that the increased efficiency due to a switch from QWERTY to a keyboard with a superior key arrangement would pay for the retraining of a group of typists in ten days. If this is true, why do you think firms do not retrain their typists to use superior keyboards?

3. Suppose, for the sake of argument, that a new keyboard arrangement called BETTER, equally efficient as QWERTY, allowed computer makers to reduce energy use by 20%. BETTER would thus qualify as a clean technology. Should the government be involved in promoting a transition from QWERTY to BETTER? If it did, what steps might you recommend?

APPLICATION 18.1

Designing Subsidies

Governor Blabla has decided that, rather than build a new nuclear power plant to service power needs, the state should save an equivalent amount of energy. As one component of an efficiency plan, he has turned to you, his top aide, to design a policy to encourage adoption of compact fluorescent (CF) lightbulbs. Recall from Chapter 6 that although CFs save a tremendous amount of money (and energy) over their lifetime, they are quite expensive initially ($15 or so per bulb in 2000). In addition, they give off a slightly bluer light than normal bulbs, are generally somewhat larger, and cannot be used with dimmer switches. You've thought up three possibilities:

Utility Rebates   Have publicly regulated electric companies provide "rebates" of 75% of the purchase price to consumers who install CF bulbs. Allow utilities to cover the cost of the program through higher electricity rates.

Government Procurement Contract   Have the state government agree to purchase, using general tax revenues, a large quantity of bulbs from an in-state supplier (at competitive rates). The bulbs would be used to retrofit government buildings.

R&D Subsidies   Provide funds from general tax revenues to in-state firms to develop CF bulbs that can be sold at lower cost and/or are more comparable to standard incandescent bulbs. Continued receipt of such subsidies should be conditional on cost reductions or performance enhancements.

1. For each of the three plans, answer the following questions:
   a. How expensive will the policy be for the state (i.e., taxpayers)?
   b. What obstacles to successful implementation might arise?
   c. If you had to pick one policy to push for, which would it be? Why?

KEY IDEAS IN EACH SECTION

18.1   This chapter focuses on government efforts to promote so-called clean technology as an alternative to regulation. Government intervention in the early stages of technology development and promotion may be justified to achieve environmental goals under a theory known as **path dependence.**

18.2   **Clean technology (CT)** is defined as having four components. (1) CTs are not speculative. CTs must (2) deliver services of a comparable quality and (3) do so with **long-run marginal costs** comparable to existing dirty technologies. (**Large-scale CTs** must achieve **economies of scale** before low-price production can be achieved.) Finally, CTs must (4) be environmentally superior to existing options. Determining this requires considering all major **life-cycle** impacts and addressing the **adding-up problem.**

18.3   Two general obstacles to rapid diffusion of CTs are (1) a **lack of substantial profit advantage** in the marketplace and (2) government **direct or indirect subsidies to competitors.** The lack of high profits means there is little private pull to overcome barriers such as high **sunk costs** (R&D and marketing), **thin markets, access to capital,** and **high discount rates.**

18.4   Government can help pick winners if it (1) levels the playing field. This entails removing subsidies for competitor technologies and internalizing social costs, preferably through IB regulation. It must also (2) focus on environmentally superior options only, and (3) engage in **least-cost planning.** Under a least-cost approach, all subsidies are either time-limited or conditioned on cost-reducing performance.

18.5   This section discusses tools for promoting small-scale CTs. These include (1) product labeling, (2) flexible design standards, (3) utility marketing of energy efficiency, (4) technical assistance programs, and (5) consumer subsidies. Subsidy programs must be carefully designed to avoid **free riders.**

18.6   Large-scale CTs can be promoted by (1) R&D funding, (2) producer subsidies such as **price preferences** and **procurement contracts,** (3) **technology-forcing standards** like the **CAFE,** and (4) infrastructure investment.

REFERENCES

A. D. Little, Inc. 1990. *Disposable Versus Reusable Diapers: Health, Environmental and Economic Comparisons.* Washington, DC: A. D. Little.

Arthur, Brian W. 1991. "Positive Feedbacks in the Economy." *Scientific American,* February, 92–99.

Bold, Frederick. 1987. "Responses to Energy Efficiency Regulations." *Energy Journal* 8, no. 2:111–123.

Crandall, R., and John D. Graham. 1989. "The Effects of Fuel Economy Standards on Automobile Safety." *Journal of Law and Economics* 32, no. 1:97–118.

Crandall, R., H. K. Greunsprecht, T. E. Keeler, and L. B. Lave. 1986. *Regulating the Automobile.* Washington, DC: Brookings.

Crosswhite, William M., and Carmen L. Sandretto. 1991. "Trends in Resource Protection Policies in Agriculture." *Agricultural Resources: Cropland, Water and Conservation Situation and Outlook AR-23.* September. Washington, DC: U.S. Department of Agriculture.

Curtis, Jennifer. 1991. *Harvest of Hope: The Potential of Alternative Agriculture to Reduce Pesticide Use.* San Francisco: Natural Resources Defense Council.

David, Paul. 1985. "Clio and the Economics of QWERTY." *American Economic Review* 75, no. 2:332–337.

Fickett, Arnold P., Clark W. Gellings, and Amory B. Lovins. 1990. "Efficient Use of Electricity." In *Readings From Scientific American.* New York: W. H. Freeman.

Geller, Howard, Daniel Lashoff, Alden Meyer, and Mary Beth Zimmerman, eds. 1991. *America's Energy Choices: Investing in a Strong Economy and a Clean Environment.* Cambridge: Union of Concerned Scientists.

Goodstein, Eban. 2000. "Prices or Policy? The Low Cost Path to Clean Technology." In *Advances in the Economics of Environmental Resources,* edited by Darwin Hall. New York: Elsevier.

Greene, David. 1990. "CAFE or Price?" *The Energy Journal* 11, no. 3:37–57.

Greider, William. 1992. *Who Will Tell the People?* New York: Simon and Schuster.

Hafele, Wolf. 1991. "Energy from Nuclear Power." In *Energy for Planet Earth.* New York: W. H. Freeman.

Herman, Robin. 1990. *Fusion: The Search for Endless Energy.* Cambridge: Cambridge University Press.

Hershkowitz, Allen. 1990. "NRDC Diaper Letter." New York: Natural Resources Defense Council.

Hirst, Eric, et al. 1982. "Household Retrofit Expenditures and the Federal Residential Energy Conservative Credit." *ORNL/ CON-95.* Oak Ridge, TN: Oak Ridge National Laboratories.

Hocking, Martin B. 1991. "Paper versus Polystyrene: A Complex Choice." *Science,* 251: 504–505.

Holdren, John P. 1991. "Energy in Transition." *Energy for Planet Earth.* New York: W. H. Freeman.

Jaffe, Adam B., and Robert N. Stavins. 1991. "The Energy Paradox and the Diffusion of Conservation Technology." Paper presented at NBER Conference on Economics of the Environment.

Koomey, Jonathan, Alan H. Sanstad, and Leslie J. Shown. 1996. "Energy-Efficient Lighting: Market Data, Market Imperfections, and Policy Success." *Contemporary Economic Policy* XIV, no. 3:98–111.

Koplow, Douglas. 1993. *Federal Energy Subsidies: Energy, Environmental and Fiscal Impacts.* Washington, DC: Alliance to Save Energy.

Larson, Bruce A., and Mary K. Knudson. 1991. "Whose Price Wins: Institutional and Technical Change in Agriculture." *Land Economics* 67, no. 2:213–224.

Lehrburger, Carl, Jocelyn Mullen, and C. V. Jones. 1991. *Diapers: Environmental Impacts and Lifecycle Analysis.* Philadelphia: National Association of Diaper Services.

Lotker, M. 1991. "Barriers to Commercialization of Large-Scale Solar Electricity: Lessons Learned from the LUZ Experience." Washington, DC: National Technical Information Service. Sandia National Laboratory.

Lovins, Amory. 1977. *Soft Energy Paths: Towards a Durable Peace.* New York: Harper-Collins.

Lucke, Robert, and Eric Toder. 1987. "Assessing the U.S. Federal Tax Burden on Oil and Gas Extraction." *The Energy Journal* 8, no:4, 51–65.

Nestor, Deborah V. 1991. "Partial Static Equilibrium Model of Newsprint Recycling." *Applied Economics,* 24: 411–417.

New York State Energy Office. 1992. *Hydro-Quebec Economic Study, Draft Report.* Albany: NYSEO.

New York State Energy Office. 1991. *Draft New York State Energy Plan, 1991 Biennial Update.* Albany: NYSEO.

Office of Technology Assessment. 1991. *Beneath the Bottom Line: Agricultural Approaches to Reduce Groundwater Contamination.* Washington, DC: U.S. GPO.

Office of Technology Assessment. 1989. *Facing America's Trash: What's Next for Municipal Solid Waste?* Washington, DC: U.S. GPO.

Ottinger, Richard, et al. 1990. *Environmental Costs of Electricity.* New York: Oceana.

Porter, Michael. 1992. "Capital Disadvantage: America's Failing Capital Investment System." *Harvard Business Reviews,* September–October, 65–82.

Scherer, F. M. 1988. "Corporate Takeovers: The Efficiency Arguments." *The Journal of Economic Perspectives* 2, no. 1:69–82.

Stavins, Robert N., and Adam B. Jaffe. 1990. "Unintended Impacts of Public Investments on Private Decisions: The Depletion of Forested Wetlands." *American Economic Review,* 80: 337–352.

Sullivan, Ronald J. 1991. "Market Barriers to Energy Efficiency Investments." *The Energy Journal* 12, no. 3:15–34.

Zweibel, Ken. 1990. *Harnessing Solar Power: The Photovoltaics Challenge.* New York: Plenum Press.

CHAPTER

19

PROMOTING CLEAN TECHNOLOGY: PRACTICE

19.0 Introduction

In the previous chapter, we defined what was meant by clean technologies and looked in a general way at both the obstacles to and opportunities for their rapid diffusion. This chapter takes a detailed look at three clean technologies: waste reduction in manufacturing; less chemical-intensive, alternative agriculture; and solid waste recycling. The discussion will follow the theoretical outline in the last chapter, considering the following questions: Are these technologies really CTs? What, if any, are the market barriers to diffusion? Has government successfully promoted these technologies? Finally, have the resources devoted to promotion been adequate or excessive?

Before plunging in, however, we need to address a general point about the environmental benefits of potential CTs. The advantages of reducing waste or minimizing the use of toxic inputs can be divided into two categories: direct and indirect. For example, if a farmer finds she can cut pesticide use by 10% through more careful timing of application, the **direct environmental benefit** is less pesticide contamination of surface or ground water. The **indirect benefits** encompass all of the "upstream" effects of a reduction in pesticide production: less pollution and environmental damage at the factory, in the extraction of the petroleum needed to produce the pesticide, in the production of equipment and fuel necessary to manufacture and transport the pesticides, and so forth. Any one direct polluting activity has lurking behind it a whole web of indirect polluting activities.

Indirect pollution is quite significant, probably accounting for more than 50% of the total pollution generated in consumption (Bingham, Anderson, and Cooley 1987). Much of the recent interest behind recycling and pollution prevention technologies has been driven by a desire to capture these "global," indirect environmental benefits from local action.

Indirect environmental benefits are largest for technologies that strictly *reduce* input use. Most potential clean technologies, however, involve substituting one technology for another. The substitute resources employed have their own direct and indirect environmental costs. For example, solid waste recycling requires the purchase and use of (polluting) trucks for collection and transport of materials to recycling mills, as well as (polluting) capital equipment needed to process and remanufacture the recyclables. (Economists have developed tools to keep track of the chain of indirect effects; for more on this, see Appendix 19A.)

As a result of these greater indirect environmental costs, a **recycling** technology will generally be more polluting than a technology involving **reuse,** and a reuse technology will generally be more polluting than one that strictly **reduces** input use. For example, recycling grocery store paper bags is preferable to throwing them away, reusing them is preferable to recycling them, and not using them at all (for small loads) is preferred to both. Clean technology candidates are, thus, ranked in a general order to environmental preference by the **three R's:** *reduce, reuse, recycle.*

19.1 Pollution Prevention in Manufacturing

Pollution prevention refers to cutting the generation of waste at the source, to avoid its handling, treatment, or disposal. Pollution prevention does not include technologies such as recycling and incineration, which reduce the volume of waste after it is produced. Waste reduction often provides a cost advantage to firms because it involves directly reducing the use of inputs.

The acknowledged leader in waste reduction is 3M Company. Beginning in the 1970s, 3M began a corporate campaign to reduce waste in its production processes as a way to cut costs and improve its environmental performance. Between 1977 and 1987, the company achieved a 50% reduction in its generation of hazardous waste, and continued a plan of aggressive reduction during the 1990s. The company has saved more than $1 billion in the process (Office of Technology Assessment 1987; rter 1991).[1]

However, few major manufacturing or chemical firms followed 3M's lead, until 1986. That year Congress created the annual Toxics Release Inventory, in which firms were required to publicly report their air, land and waterborne emissions of 450 chemicals. In the face of public relations pressures generated by the TRI list, many big chemical firms adopted pollution prevention programs. Several companies announced numerical reduction targets on the order of 10% to 40%. By 1992, roughly 70% of the members of the Chemical Manufacturers Association had made at least a token commitment to pollution prevention.

Also in the early 1990s the EPA launched an ambitious pollution prevention effort called the 33/50 program. The EPA attempted to focus industry attention on waste reduction by seeking voluntary reductions of emissions of 17 priority chemicals from the 1988 TRI baseline emissions of 1.46 billion pounds. The program goal was a 33% reduction by 1992 and a 50% reduction by 1995, which explains the program title. EPA provided technical assistance and recognition to program participants.

By 1994 the 50% goal had in fact been met, with program participants reducing about 19% more than those not in the program. Given the voluntary nature of the program, the size and speed of the reduction suggests that chemical emissions reduction

---

[1]For other examples of waste reduction in the private sector, visit the Web site of the National Pollution Prevention Roundtable at http://www.p2.org/.

has indeed been relatively cheap. However, most of the reduction did not come from source reduction, but rather from end-of-the-pipe and other more conventional means. Yet, program participants did reduce their production related waste slightly, while nonprogram participants increased their waste by 9%—indicating the program had some impact on waste reduction (Davies and Mazurek 1997).

Is pollution prevention a CT? From an environmental perspective, if inputs are simply reduced, then by definition, waste reduction has an edge over its competitors. If a process change generates a greater reliance, for example, on paper, then environmental gains from reduced plastic use must be balanced against externalities associated with paper production and use.

On the cost front, private sector waste-reduction initiatives to date have been cost-effective, and the chemical industry response to TRI suggests that substantial industrial waste reduction is economically feasible. Overall, the government's Office of Technology Assessment (1987) has argued that a 10% per year reduction in hazardous waste is an achievable goal for many industries.

In addition, dozens of case studies suggest that a lot of "low hanging fruit" exists. In an EPA-funded pilot project operating out of Colorado State and the University of Tennessee, engineering faculty and graduate students from the two institutions conducted waste minimization assessments of twelve medium-sized manufacturing plants. Overall, the teams recommended waste-reducing measures expected to generate cost savings of $1.28 million per year. Table 19.1 provides a breakdown of the measures for two plants, the first a paint factory and the second a factory producing oil coolers for heavy equipment.

The engineering teams' recommendations ranged from simple "housekeeping" measures, such as putting a lid on a degreasing tank, to more complex process innovations, such as switching from a solvent-based to a vacuum cleaning method. For the two plants, waste reduction ranged from 4% to 99%, while the average

TABLE 19.1   Waste Reduction in Two Manufacturing Plants

Plant	Problem	Recommendation	Annual Waste Reduced	Annual Savings ($1,000/yr)	Payback Period (yrs)
1	Pipe rinse water	Use foam plugs for dry wipe	1,780 gal/yr	11	0.2
1	Solvent disposal	Recycling	3,300 gal/yr	5	0.9
1	Mercury in bactericide	Use organic substitute	3,100 gal/yr	6	0.0
2	Vapors from degreaser	Install cover or	50%	17	0.0
		use ultrasonic cleaning	99%	20	2.4
2	Recycling contaminants	Reduce lubricants	20%	1	0.3
2	Sludge from salt baths	Use mechanical method or	4%	20	2.1
		use vacuum method	80%	203	3.5
2	Paint-contaminated cardboard	Reduce paint loss with air jets	22%	4	0.6
2	Paint-contaminated filters	Electrostatic spray control	36%	11	1.2

Source: Kirsch and Looby (1990, Tables 2 and 3).

payback period was well under one year. The biggest waste reducers also generate the largest annual savings—for example, using ultrasonic degreasing in plant 2. And in spite of the fact that such measures have the longest payback periods, they are probably the most profitable investments due to the large cost savings. The evident cost-effectiveness of these pilot projects in Colorado and Tennessee have been supported by other case studies.[3]

Having established that pollution prevention is indeed a CT, are market forces sufficient to drive major private-sector initiatives in waste reduction? Judging from the limited data available, the answer is probably not. While companies have indeed aggressively reduced emissions found on the Toxics Release Inventory, most of these reductions have come through end-of-the-pipe treatment, recycling or energy recovery, rather than pollution prevention (Davies and Mazurek 1997). During the late 1990s, fewer than 5% of firms in Oregon and Washington were engaged in notable, voluntary measures to reduce their inputs of energy, water, or toxic materials (Goodstein, Sable, and Doppelt 2000).

Why the slow private sector response? Pollution prevention, as is common with CTs, simply does not have enough of a cost advantage over its competitors to redirect corporate thinking away from traditional, proven approaches, with known risks.

Within the pollution prevention field, one can identify both large and small-scale technologies. Small-scale approaches include: "reducing wastewater from cleaning operations involving toxic chemicals, covering vessels containing volatile chemicals, improving inventory controls to eliminate outdated chemicals that become hazardous waste, reusing off-specification products, and replacing water or solvent cleaning of equipment with other methods" (Hirschorn 1990, 37). Exploiting these "housekeeping" or common-sense opportunities nevertheless requires technical expertise.

On the other hand, adoption of a large-scale waste reduction strategy requires a substantial upfront expense, including a commitment to hiring a waste auditing firm, and researching and implementing subsequent changes in production processes. For example, a jewelry company in North Providence Rhode Island hired a consulting firm to design and install an untested water recycling system to prevent the discharge of heavy metals into Narragansett Bay. The risk of recycling lay in the possibility of contamination problems, leading to a poor product quality. In this case, the problems did not materialize, and the firm saved money through reduced water use, water quality monitoring, and regulatory expense (Uva 1989).

While experiences like those at the jewelry firm suggest that waste reduction investments can be profitable, such an undertaking is risky. And particularly for small businesses, pollution prevention must compete for capital with more traditional investments in plant and equipment, product development, and sales. The market has thus been slow to adopt waste reduction for the reasons identified in the last chapter: lack of a profit advantage large enough to overcome the barriers of poor information and limited capital resources. In addition, in the past, corporate environmental managers

---

[2]See, for example, Richardson (1990) and Bridges (1990). For details on industry programs at twenty-nine chemical plants, see Dorfman, Miller, and Muir (1991).

have had limited flexibility to experiment with waste reduction and still remain in compliance with existing regulations.[3]

Given the slow rate of market adoption, what is the role for government in promoting this CT? The first step is to internalize the external costs of toxic pollution: this has been the goal of Superfund, RCRA, and air toxics legislation. Waste disposal costs are also rising due to citizen protests over the citing of waste facilities, the NIMBY phenomenon discussed in Chapter 5. Lois Gibbs, a former resident of Love Canal (the community hit by the chemical dumping incident discussed in Chapter 12), has in fact expressed increasing the cost of disposal as a primary goal of the grassroots environmental movement: "Our overall strategy is to plug up the toilet. If we can stop unsafe facilities from being built, the waste will back up on the corporation's own property, the few remaining waste dumps will charge an arm and a leg, and since all they know is profit and loss, they'll stop producing wastes or reclaim them."[4]

Yet the piecemeal problem associated with regulation implies that not all the toilets can be easily stopped up. Rather than waste reduction, a more likely private sector response to rising off-site disposal costs will be on-site incineration, noncompliance, or illegal dumping. What clean technology-promoting steps should be taken to complement regulatory approaches?

Hirschorn (1990) suggests many of the policy options discussed in the last chapter, including information collection and distribution, on-site technical assistance, tax credits and small business loans, support for R&D, and technology-forcing standards.

Of these options, information distribution and technical assistance is the route that the federal government has pursued to date. The EPA helps support an information clearinghouse, describing waste reduction technologies introduced by firms across the country (http://www.p2.org/). The EPA, through the TRI, also distributes information about toxic releases from manufacturing plants across the country. (To find out what is in the neighborhood air you breathe, visit www.epa.gov/tri.)

Finally, the agency disperses millions of dollars in matching grants to state governments for technical assistance to help firms reduce waste. In my region of the country, the cities of Portland and Seattle, the states of both Washington and Oregon, and the EPA's Region X all operate outreach divisions that provide assistance to firms engaged in pollution prevention measures.

Beyond the carrot of technical assistance and voluntary initiatives to encourage pollution prevention, many states have been using a stick of mandatory waste reduction plans. The intent of such legislation is presumably to focus industry's attention on economically attractive investments in waste reduction. However, the measures may do little to confront the underlying problems of poor information, risk, and access to capital. As Levin (1991) puts it: "mandatory waste management plans turn on companies good-faith execution of waste management audits, could promote risky substitutes because they cover only a small segment of the hazardous waste universe, and seem likely to generate a flood of paperwork seldom reviewed." The EPA also has begun requiring environmental audits as part of its enforcement and compliance efforts (U.S. EPA 1991). This kind of targeted effort seems likely to have a higher payoff.

---

[3]See Hirschorn (1990) for a more detailed discussion.
[4]"Earth Image 1990," *In These Times,* 4/18/90.

To summarize this section: Pollution prevention shows substantial promise as a clean technology, but many efforts are only just getting underway. Why the slow private-sector response? Such efforts do not provide much of a marketing edge. The anecdotal evidence of waste reduction efforts available suggest that the handful of industrial companies with a serious commitment to pollution prevention, such as 3M, also appear to be exceptions that prove the rule.

19.2 Alternative Agriculture and Pesticides

Each year, American farmworkers, landscapers, and homeowners apply about 1 billion pounds of pesticides to crops, fields, lawns, and gardens. Specifically designed to be toxic to insects and other pests, these chemicals unfortunately affect the broader environment as well. Pesticides show up as residue in foods, harm wildlife, contaminate groundwater, and are a significant nonpoint source of surface water pollution in the United States today.

Pesticides and pesticide exposure are regulated under a variety of laws, but still pose significant environmental hazards to farmworkers and farmers, consumers, and wildlife. In the face of these problems, farmers have increasingly been experimenting with CTs in agriculture, stressing biological methods of promoting soil fertility and reducing pests and disease. These include crop rotation to disrupt pest cycles, biological and mechanical weed control and fertilization, reducing pesticide use through scouting, use of resistant species, use of natural predators, and control over planting time. While building on traditional methods, the techniques are thoroughly modern, often computer assisted, and in fact, management intensive. These techniques are collectively known as "low-input," "sustainable," or simply **alternative agriculture.** They all share a reduced reliance on chemical fertilizers and pesticides.[5]

Farming interest in clean technology has arisen in response to the heavy reliance of modern agriculture on petrochemical pesticides, herbicides, and fertilizers, as well as production methods that promote soil erosion. Beginning in the 1940s, American agriculture experienced a technological revolution, based on mechanization, petrochemical inputs, and high-yielding seed varieties. These new technologies yielded impressive productivity gains: Between 1950 and 1980 U.S. crop production doubled, while cultivated land increased only 5% and the number of farmworkers fell by 63%. The success of these new technologies led to the abandonment of traditional methods of weed and pest control, and husbanding of soil fertility, as farmers boosted yields by planting the same crop "fence-row to fence-row," year after year.

However, these productivity gains have leveled off over the last decade, and have left some farmers in an increasingly difficult position. On the economic front, dependence on off-farm resources has increased dramatically, requiring farmers to resort more heavily to credit. This has placed smaller farms, with higher cost access to capital, at a disadvantage. In addition, loss of soil fertility and increasing pesticide resistance sometimes require larger and larger doses of fertilizer and pesticide to maintain yields.

In the environmental arena, farm communities themselves are the most vulnerable to environmental hazards—nitrate pollution from fertilizer in groundwater, and pesticide

[5]For a further discussion, see National Research Council (1989).

exposure in water supplies or on the farm. A National Cancer Institute Study report found that farm cancer rates were substantially above the national average. Although no official explanation for the results was given, one of the authors speculated that pesticide use was primarily responsible ("Farmers May" 1992). Curtis (1992), for example, provides an estimate that 130,000 rural Iowa residents drink well water that exceeds the EPA's legal standard for nitrates, while 5,400 residents in rural Iowa are consuming drinking water with pesticide levels above the EPA's advisory standards. An additional 90,000 are estimated to be exposed to pesticides at levels below the EPA threshold. A review of current pesticide regulation will suggest why promoting alternative agriculture is viewed by some as an attractive supplement to regulation.

PESTICIDES: WORKERS, FOOD, WILDLIFE, GROUNDWATER

As was discussed in Chapter 13, worker exposure to pesticides is currently regulated under the Federal Insecticide, Fungicide and Rodenticide Act (FIFRA). In theory, food is further protected by a safety standard; the EPA is directed to establish "tolerances" for pesticide residues on food designed to eliminate significant health risks.[7] The Food and Drug Administration (FDA) has the responsibility for testing and enforcing these tolerances for fruits, grains, vegetables, and animal feed.[8]

Prior to 1996, critics charged that the EPA's tolerances often reflect outdated or inadequate scientific information on health risks, were based on outdated consumption habits (Americans have been eating more fresh fruit and vegetables lately), and did not adequately protect children, who consume proportionately more food than adults. On the other hand, industry scientists have criticized the tolerances set for raw crops as being unrealistically strict, since pesticide residues are often, but not always, reduced during processing, food preparation, and cooking. Some of these concerns were addressed by Congress in the 1996 Food Quality Protection Act (see Mott and Snyder 1987, Whyatt and Nicholson 1991, and McCarthy 1991).

Finally, pesticide levels in groundwater are subject either to legally binding maximum standards under the Safe Drinking Water Act, or advisory standards under the Federal Insecticide, Fungicide and Rodenticide Act. However, these statutes provide little additional protection. The EPA has yet to set standards for many pesticides under the Drinking Water Act; in addition, violations typically require public notification, not remediation. Under FIFRA, the EPA has handled violations on a case-by-case basis as they have been uncovered. However, groundwater monitoring for pesticide contamination is quite limited. Thus, those exposed to pesticide contamination from drinking water are generally not aware of it.

---

[6]The potential of alternative agriculture to reduce nitrate pollution is unclear, since nitrates also occur in manure. See Crosson and Ekey (1988), and Curtis (1992).

[7]The standards are based on animal studies. Prior to 1996, the EPA commonly used a one in 1 million standard for carcinogens, and a "no observable effects" standard for neurotoxicity and reproductive effects. However, according to Hathaway (1991) the one in a million standard was sometimes waived. In 1996, the Congress passed the Food Quality Protection Act, which mandated a single, minimum standard. However, it also allowed pesticide benefits to be considered when setting tolerance levels for carcinogenic effects.

[8]The USDA enforces tolerances for meat, poultry, and eggs.

What are the risks from pesticide exposure? About 300 different pesticides are used on food in the United States. Of these, about 60 are classified by the EPA as probable or possible human carcinogens. Others are known to be reproductive toxins. Still others are suspected to have a negative impact on human and animal immune systems. In addition, another 200 or so pesticides are widely used in other parts of the world. Developing countries still employ pesticides, such as DDT, which were banned for use in this country in the early 1970s; lack of clean water and sanitation compounds the impact of pesticide exposure abroad.[9]

In 1987 the EPA estimated, with substantial uncertainty, the number of U.S. cancer deaths from pesticide food residue at about 3,000 per year, with an additional 250 arising from pesticide application and other exposure. In addition, occasional news reports of acute pesticide poisonings make food safety one of the public's primary environmental concerns.[10]

One should not conclude from this information that eating fresh fruits and vegetable is, on balance, bad for you. Even while recognizing the risk from pesticide residues in food, a report by the National Academy of Sciences study urged greater consumption of these products. In fact, health risks from other dietary sources—primarily fat and cholesterol—are much greater than the risks from pesticide residue in food. This however does not mean that fruits and vegetables should not necessarily be made safer.

As suggested by the EPA's 1987 ranking, the regulatory process for pesticides is not working as planned. One possible reason relates to the tolerance levels, tightened up in 1996. In addition, FDA's monitoring and enforcement efforts have been criticized as inadequate. FDA necessarily monitors only a small fraction of the nation's food supply, and seldom penalizes growers who ship food with excessive pesticide residue. Moreover, testing for hundreds of pesticides that could potentially be used on food poses real challenges.[11] Again, in response to these problems, enforcement penalties were beefed up by Congress in 1996.

OBSTACLES TO REGULATING PESTICIDES

The pesticide issue reflects many of the problems of "end-of-the-pipe" regulation that have led to increasing frustration with the regulatory system. First, the informational requirements are daunting. Registering a new pesticide is an expensive process, costing

---

[9]Repetto and Baliga (1996) detail the health risks from pesticides, and focus on the problem in developing countries. U.S. industries produce pesticides for export that are banned in the United States.

[10]Cancer cases are from U.S. EPA (1987). See also U.S. EPA (1990).

[11]In 1989, less than 1% of the food sampled had pesticide residues in excess of legal limits; 61% had no detectable pesticides. However, due to slow processing of test results, food with illegal residues is often consumed before the FDA can seize it. A government review of the program found that in 60% of the cases in which domestic food contained illegal residues, the sale of food was not prevented. In no case were penalties levied by the FDA against growers. Thus, it appears that the FDA does not compensate for its low monitoring rate with certain and harsh penalties. The monitoring–penalty trade-off discussed in chapter 15 is not being used here. Perhaps more significantly, as of the late 1980s, the methods that the FDA used to screen food could detect only 41% of the 496 pesticides that could potentially be used on food. Of the 81 pesticides identified by the FDA as requiring high priority monitoring, 33 could not be identified by routine surveillance methods. See Carnevale et al. (1991), U.S. GAO (1986), and Taylor (1988).

from \$5 to \$7 million and taking from one to five years (Shapiro 1990). Outside of pharmaceutical drugs, pesticide registration imposes the most comprehensive scientific reporting requirements on manufacturers of any new product.

Second, in spite of these efforts, setting a safety standard remains difficult because of remaining substantial data gaps. These in turn arise from the potential multiple avenues of toxicity represented by each new pesticide. An efficiency standard, theoretically required in the registration process, introduces the further complications of monetizing improvements in health and environmental quality, as well as pesticide benefits, of uncertain magnitude. In part because the informational requirements are so burdensome, and in spite of a clear legislative mandate requiring a risk–benefit balancing for initial registration, this process is seldom completed in a satisfactory manner; political factors weigh in as heavily as does the benefit–cost analysis.

Finally, once the standards have been set, enforcement is impeded by the inability to adequately monitor pesticide levels in a timely fashion. Technical obstacles arise in tracking pesticide residues on food, and widespread groundwater monitoring is prohibitively expensive. In addition, as we have seen elsewhere, regulators have evidenced a reluctance to punish violators.

Given the multiple uncertainties, environmentalists and industry are locked into a never-ending and costly battle over the evaluation of risks and exposure, the registration of new pesticides and the re-registration of old ones, and the degree to which pesticide laws will in fact be enforced. The National Agricultural Chemicals Association, for example, has a \$7 million annual budget, while the Agricultural Council of America launched a \$50 million effort to "restore public confidence in the safety of the food supply" (Shistar, Cooper, and Feldman 1992). Citizens, and many farmers and farmworkers, meanwhile, continue to feel that the protection of food and water is inadequate. In response, Congress passed new legislation in 1996.[12]

However, even if the reforms succeed, pesticides will remain difficult to regulate for two primary reasons. First, in spite of increased toxicological information, risk assessments will remain poor due to highly **imperfect information.** Second, the **nonpoint source** nature of the pollutant imposes a costly burden on regulators seeking to monitor and enforce regulations.

THE CLEAN TECHNOLOGY APPROACH

The first step in the clean technology approach to the pesticide problem, and related problems of chemical fertilizer pollution and soil erosion, is to ask, are there cost-effective alternatives? The answer appears to be yes. Decades of documented field experience suggests that farmers can successfully reduce pesticide use and still remain profitable. While adoption of alternative agricultural methods may reduce yields

---

[12]For a pre-1996 discussion, see Malloy et al. (1991) and Shapiro (1990). Gianessi, Kopp, and Puffer (1989) find that limited bans of pesticides in areas where groundwater contamination is likely or pollution taxes are preferable from a cost point of view to the EPA's general policy of a total ban. The law is described in "Highlights of the Food Quality Act of 1996," on the Web at www//epa.gov/.

(though it need not), it also reduces costs. The cost reduction is generally sufficient to offset any lost production.[13]

Indeed, Cowan and Gunby (1996) specifically invoke the theory of path dependence to explain how different areas in the Southwest and Israel chose between chemical-intensive agriculture and cost-competitive alternative methods beginning in the 1940s. They argue that alternative agriculture has several sources of increasing returns, or positive feedback mechanisms: Biological pest control has high fixed costs associated with machinery and predator rearing; farmers experience substantial "learning-by-doing"; and farmers also depend on "network externalities"—information gained from fellow farmers and extension agents. Finally, if neighboring farmers are spraying pesticides, this will also kill off natural predators.

These factors make it hard for individual farmers to adopt alternative technologies if their neighbors are not also doing so, while chemical pesticide use faces no such hurdles. However, the Israeli citrus industry was one region that stuck with, and thrived on, biological pest controls. And in Texas, growers successfully shifted back to alternative pest control methods after cotton developed insecticide resistance in the late 1960s. In both cases, government infrastructure and legislative support were critical. The Mexican cotton industry, with no comparable support to that in Texas, simply died out after chemical controls failed.

In addition to being cost-competitive in the long run, alternative farming is generally a CT; that is, it is environmentally superior to conventional agriculture. Critics have pointed out, however, that some of the practices that fall under the alternative heading may, on occasion, lead to greater environmental hazards. For example, Gianessi (1991) notes that scouting for pests on peanut crops in Alabama led to increased fungicide use, as previously undiscovered problems were found. In addition, organic growers use large quantities of sulfur, a naturally occurring compound, to control diseases on grapes. Yet, little is known about the potential impact of exposure to sulfur residues. Thus, some care must be taken in promoting alternative agriculture as a cure to the pesticide problem.

What degree of environmental protection do CTs offer? A study by the Natural Resources Defense Council examined twelve crops grown in California and Iowa. Based on techniques currently being employed in alternative agriculture, the NRDC estimated that potential pesticide reductions for these crops ranged from 25% to 80% (Curtis 1992).

Having argued that alternative agriculture is a CT based on our definition in the previous chapter, what obstacles stand in the way of its widespread adoption? The primary barrier is a low-profit advantage coupled with substantial **adjustment costs.**

A successful transition from conventional chemical-intensive farming is a complex and risky undertaking for an individual farmer. To begin with, farmers need to invest

---

[13]For an annotated bibliography on this issue, see Morris and Canzoneri (1992). See also National Research Council (1989). Crosson and Ekey (1988) conclude that "organic" agriculture, a subset of alternative agriculture, is not as profitable as conventional agriculture, primarily because crop rotation requires keeping considerable acreage in low-value crops. However, the authors still conclude that environmental benefits from alternative agriculture deserve its promotion by the USDA.

substantial resources in learning new techniques. In addition, successful techniques are highly region-specific. Finally, a period of two or three years may be necessary to convert a field worked with conventional methods into a productive alternative field (Reganald, Paperclick, and Parr 1990; Cowan and Gunby 1996). These factors mean that a substantial up-front investment is necessary to redirect a farm onto an alternate path. And while such a farm may experience comparable profitability to a chemical-intensive one, in the highly competitive agricultural field, it is unlikely to be substantially more profitable.

The "organic" label lends only a small marketing advantage. The industry has recently moved beyond specialty health-food stores into major supermarkets. However, this "green marketing" movement is as yet minor, possibly due to consumer distrust of the retailers' claims. Perhaps more significantly, the *Wall Street Journal* reports that the large food-processing firms that control most supermarket shelf space are not yet interested in organic products. "Big Foods fear [is] that launching a no-chemical brand would prompt consumers to look askance at their conventional brands, whose ingredients are grown with everything from synthetic fertilizer to antibiotics" ("Major Companies" 1992).

Alternative agriculture illustrates perfectly the CT dilemma. On the one hand, we appear to have available a technology capable of holding its own in the market, once adjustment costs have been overcome, with clear environmental benefit. On the other, adoption of the technology is slow due primarily to lack of a profit advantage sufficient to overcome costs associated with a transition. What is to be done?

Following our outline in the last chapter, the first step is to identify the agricultural CTs with clear environmental benefits and those with the greatest cost advantage. On the environmental front, this suggests a focus on reducing chemical pesticide use overall through a switch to biological and mechanical methods, and argues against an approach relying principally on substituting pesticides currently thought to be less dangerous for those currently thought to be more dangerous. On the cost front, given the complexity of the transition, it suggests a go slow approach: Avoid a crash program urging farmers to go 100% organic.

The second part of a CT strategy is to attack inappropriate subsidies and begin to internalize environmental costs, preferably through IB regulation. As was discussed in the last chapter, price supports for chemical-intensive crops have been an important obstacle to the spread of CTs. Access to water subsidies also has encouraged pollution-intensive agriculture, since agricultural chemicals and water tend to be complements in production. The farm sector also has traditionally been subject to very light environmental regulation of the CAC variety (see Larson and Knudson 1991).

The third component is to promote CTs directly. Here, agriculture is unique among American businesses in that the government already is deeply involved in the pace and direction of technological change in the industry. Because farming is highly competitive and, thus, a low-profit industry, government has traditionally financed much of the research and development in the field. In addition to this R&D function, the government has also taken a leading role in disseminating information about new techniques through the state-funded agricultural colleges and agricultural extension services.

However, the agrichemical industries have become increasingly important players in the research and development field, as well as in technical assistance. For obvious reasons, these companies tend not to fund research into less chemical-intensive farming. At the same time, academic agricultural researchers must be sensitive to corporate needs since the probability of getting federal funding for any given project is quite low. (Cropper et al. [1991] conclude that academic researchers who comment during special reviews of pesticides tend to support the industry position.)

In addition to agrichemical influence in research, in recent years the government's extension service has focused less and less on on-farm assistance, and more on laboratory research and teaching. Many farmers receive the bulk of their information about farming techniques from fertilizer and pesticide dealers (Curtis 1992; Office of Technology Assessment 1991). Hence, a sensible CT strategy would be first to increase government R&D funding for region-specific strategies to reduce pesticide use. The second step would be to increase the budget for technical assistance, to promote the diffusion of these technologies. Increases in these funds could be financed either through reductions in research on conventional farming techniques, which the private sector now covers adequately, or by modest taxes on agricultural chemicals.

Because of the diverse nature of the possible CT options, direct subsidy programs, such as tax credits or loans to encourage a transition, would be hard to implement without facing a large windfall problem, or actual fraud. However, grants could be channeled to private farmers' groups seeking to do their own CT extension work. In the absence of significant government effort, such groups now provide a primary information source for farmers seeking to reduce chemical inputs. In addition, the relative profitability of CTs can be boosted by revising subsidy policies. Crop rotation and natural fertilization methods should not be penalized, and water subsidies should be reduced.[14]

Recent federal legislation includes some movement on all the fronts just identified. However, the government has by no means adopted a CT approach wholeheartedly. R&D funding for on-farm research into alternative agriculture remains a small percentage of the Department of Agriculture's research and development budget, and extension services in alternative agriculture have not been expanded. Subsidy policies are changing slowly—one interesting reform has been to condition crop subsidies on the adoption of so-called conservation tillage measures (see Application 19.0). Finally, the EPA's primary focus remains on pesticide regulation rather than promotion of alternative agriculture. Overall, the percentage of acreage treated with herbicides and insecticides showed little, if any, downward movement in the 1990s.[15]

---

[14]Office of Technology Assessment (1991) and Curtis (1992) provide a more comprehensive discussion of policies to promote alternative agriculture. Both focus additional attention on Federal Agricultural Marketing Boards, which enforce cosmetic grading standards for fruits and vegetables destined for "fresh markets." Economists have long been critical of these standards as barriers to entry. See, for example, Salant and Goodstein (1990).

[15]See Curtis (1992) for a review of farm policy. According to O'Conell (1991), $11 million was devoted to whole-farm research in alternative agriculture, while an additional $83 million was spent on research related to components of alternative agriculture. Given the systems nature of alternative approaches, the National Research Council (1989) stresses that the former have much greater utility for promoting a transition to CTs. Overall herbicide use was essentially unchanged over the period 1981–1997. See the Council on Environmental Quality Web site, at www.ceq.eh.doe.gov/nepa/reports.

Given the lack of federal pesticide protection for groundwater resources noted above, state governments have been attempting to fill in the gap. Two contrasting experiments are worth noting. California has opted for a regulatory strategy, passing the Pesticide Contamination Prevention Act in 1985. The act requires a state agency to identify pesticides liable to leach into groundwater and to monitor for their presence. Critics have charged that the act, while tough on paper, has been difficult to implement effectively, for the reasons discussed above. By the mid-1990s, the state was monitoring for only a few pesticides (Curtis 1992).

On the other hand, Iowa has been most aggressive in implementing a CT approach to protect groundwater. Rather than opt for further regulation, since 1987 the state has funded public research and education centers through taxes levied on commercial fertilizers, pesticides, hazardous household materials, and landfills. The Office of Technology Assessment (1991) provides the following description of one aspect of Iowa's program:

> The Butler County Integrated Crop Management Project . . . provides cost-share assistance to 50 farmer-cooperators for implementing agrichemical related [reforms]. . . . In the first year, farmers are provided with services free-of-charge by six field scouts trained by the Cooperative Extension Service. The farmer-cooperators are expected to pay $1.50 and $3.00 per acre for scout services in the second and third years, respectively, and then take over full payment for scout services when the project is over. In 1989, the total cost of the services was estimated at $4.50 per acre, with farmers saving about $20 per acre in agrichemical costs. That year, the 50 cooperators reduced nitrogen applications by about 26,000 pounds and improved their net income by a total of $500,000. One farmer-cooperator reported avoiding a loss of $42,000 due to timely treatment of cutworms, while another saved $15,000 in additional fertilizer costs when soil tests showed that he did not have to add phosphorus and potassium. (215)

This kind of cost-effective technical assistance should form the heart of a governmental effort to promote CTs in agriculture.

19.3 Recycling Solid Waste

In contrast to pollution prevention in manufacturing and alternative agriculture, the CT of recycling solid waste has recently received widespread governmental promotion. The number of curbside collection programs grew from 600 in 1989 to over 9,000 in 1999, serving more than 40% of U.S. households ("As Recycling Surges" 1992; "The State of Garbage" 1996).[16] The EPA set an official goal of 35% recycling of solid

---

[16]Long-run average costs per ton for recycling fall as the volume of waste processed increases. One of the sources of scale economies in recycling is in collection—denser collection routes mean that per ton collection costs fall. This is one of the reasons that cost-effective curbside recycling programs are often mandatory and at the least require marketing efforts to insure high-participation rates. However, incineration can be as "mandatory" as recycling—communities with incinerators often have flow control ordinances to insure that the incinerators receive enough waste to operate at close to capacity.

waste by 2005; and the 1990 Federal Pollution Prevention Act declares that recycling is to have precedence over waste disposal as a matter of national policy.

Americans generate more than 232 million tons of garbage each year. Depending upon your perspective, that is (1) enough garbage to fill a fleet of trucks stretching half of the way to the moon, or alternatively (2) garbage that can be landfilled in a space equivalent to less than .00001% of the continental United States (but preferably not in my backyard). On a per person basis, it works out to about three quarters of a ton, twice as much per capita as many European countries. The per capita rate also rose sharply through 1990, but the growth rate has since flattened.[17]

Figure 19.1 illustrates the pre-recycling composition of the nation's garbage. Newspapers and telephone books are the biggest items in the household garbage bag. Plastics pose more of a relative disposal problem than suggested by the table, since they take up 20% by volume of the nation's landfill space.

In 2002, U.S. citizens recycled or composted about 31% of their household waste, up from about 5% to 7% in 1970. Incineration accounted for an additional 10% to 15%, while the remaining garbage was landfilled. Recycling's rapid growth occurred as landfill and incineration costs rose under increasingly tight regulation, and as citizen opposition to the siting of new facilities escalated. Tipping fees at landfills have risen from about $5 per ton in the early 1970s to anywhere from $30 to well over $100 per ton today. Prices rose dramatically in the 1980s due to a perceived "landfill shortage." The dramatic rise leveled off in the early 1990s under the impact of increased recycling and the opening of several large new landfills ("Economics of Trash" 1992). In response to these rising costs, as well as citizen concern over resource waste, local governments across the country have been adopting recycling programs.

Solid waste recycling yields two types of environmental benefits. The most obvious is a **direct benefit:** cleaner waste disposal. Since recycled products are not sent to landfills

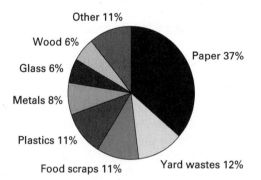

FIGURE 19.1 Composition of Municipal Solid Waste by Weight, 2000 (Prior to Recycling)
Source: "Basic Facts: Municipal Solid Waste." U.S. EPA, Office of Solid Waste, www.epa.gov/epaoswer /non-hw/muncpl/index.htm.

---

[17]Data are from the EPA's Office of Solid Waste Web site, www.epa.gov/epaoswer. Both the "alarmist" and "don't worry" characterizations of the solid waste problem appeared in *The EPA Journal.* See "A Strategy to Control the Garbage Glut," and "Will the U.S. Recycling Approach Work?" July–August 1992.

or incinerators, they do not pose environmental problems in the disposal process. Recall that environmental hazards from state-of-the-art landfills are not as great as from many other pollution sources, primarily because the only significant exposure route is local, via groundwater. Nevertheless, hazards from leachate do exist.

New incinerators, although generally complying with most air pollution regulations, still generate residual hazards from regulated pollutants, as well as some that are still unregulated.[18] Incinerator ash must be disposed of. If this is done via landfilling, the ash also presents a leachate problem.

Indirect benefits constitute the second type of environmental benefit. Table 19.2 compares the production cycle for products made from recycled and virgin materials. The recycling process is of course not pollution-free. In all production stages, recycling generates significant pollution. Unique recycling waste, for example de-inking sludge from paper recycling, also poses serious disposal problems (Office of Technology Assessment 1991). However, relative to production from virgin material, recycling often yields two important indirect environmental benefits: **energy savings** and **upstream pollution** avoided.

Because secondary materials are already "pre-processed," it generally takes much less energy to convert them into finished products. Energy savings in turn often translate into significant environmental benefits. Figure 19.2 shows the energy requirements needed to produce a variety of products from both virgin and recycled materials. Particularly for plastics, the energy savings are impressive, with recycled plastic requiring only about one-fourth the energy of plastic made from virgin material.

In addition to energy savings, the collection and processing of recycled materials can be less environmentally damaging than the production and transport of raw materials from virgin sources. In a life-cycle analysis of five products that monetized environmental costs, Schall (1992) found overall that virgin materials inflicted damages that ranged from 104% (steel) to 618% (aluminum) of damages from using recycled materials. Schall also found that *all* of the advantage accruing to recyclables took the form of indirect benefits.[19]

TABLE 19.2 Production from Recycled and Virgin Materials

Virgin	Recycling
1. Raw material production	**1.** Collection/processing
2. Transport	**2.** Transport
3. Manufacturing	**3.** Manufacturing
4. Distribution	**4.** Distribution

---

[18]Office of Technology Assessment (1989) and Ottinger et al. (1990) discuss the health impacts of both landfilling and incineration. In addition to conventional pollutants, incinerators emit dioxins and heavy metals. Concern about dioxin has recently focused on contamination of milk in cows; see also the discussion of dioxin in Chapter 10.

[19]Schall used marginal abatement cost estimates to monetize damages. As discussed in Chapter 17, a preferred, though generally unavailable, measure would be marginal damage estimates. If regulation is inefficiently strict, Schall's absolute dollar estimates would overstate true damages. However, the ratio figures reported here are less subject to bias.

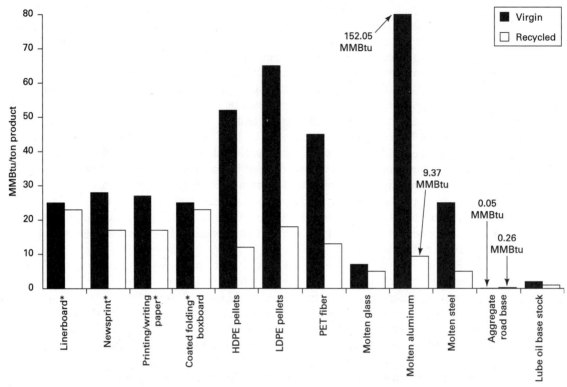

FIGURE 19.2 Energy Consumption in Manufacturing: Virgin versus Recycled Raw Materials

*Using recycled feedstock in paper production while reducing total energy use can actually increase use of purchased (generally nonrenewable) energy, since production from virgin materials uses waste wood to produce energy.

Source: New York State Energy Authority (1994, Figure 3-5). For similar results, see Morris and Canzoneri (1992).

Such indirect benefits from recycling programs are more likely to be reaped when: (1) recycled goods replace products made from nonrenewable resources, for example, old-growth forest or petroleum; (2) goods can be recycled repeatedly; (3) the collection of recycled materials displaces garbage collection, producing little additional pollution; and (4) recycled materials are available closer to manufacturing centers, making transport of recycled materials substantially less pollution-intensive than the transport of raw materials.

Some critics have argued that recycling of old newspapers fit few of these criteria. First, much pulpwood used in the United States is grown on tree plantations, not in old-growth forest. Second, newspaper cannot be repeatedly recycled. Third, recycling systems cannot displace garbage collection completely, and they thus add to urban air pollution. Finally, much of the new recycled mill capacity is being built as expansions to existing mills, close to forests and away from cities, which are the source of the raw materials.[20]

---

[20]Wiseman (1990) makes many of these arguments; for a more polemical view, see Tierney (1996). Pulp plantations are common in the Southeast and on private lands in the Northwest. However, timber from the rain forests in southeast Alaska has been used to manufacture paper diapers.

Defenders of the indirect benefits of newspaper recycling respond that growing and clear-cutting pulp plantations is itself a polluting process, that even limited recycling of newspapers is desirable since it uses less energy in manufacturing than does virgin fiber, and that transport of materials is in fact being reduced.[21] In his life-cycle analysis, Schall (1992) argues that newspaper production from virgin materials results in damages between 143% and 200% of those for production from recycled material.

Whatever the final resolution to this debate, it illustrates the general point made in the introduction—input-reducing technologies have larger indirect benefits than input-substituting technologies (such as recycling). Using recycled products cannot eliminate all indirect pollution, since the recycling process itself requires resources. However, to the extent that recycling satisfies the four criteria outlined above, it does have the potential to yield large indirect benefits by reducing upstream economic activity. Reduced upstream activity in turn lowers overall demands on the planet's resource base: habitat, energy, and the stock of clean air and water.

Recycling can thus have local (direct waste management) and global (indirect) benefits. From an environmental point of view, global benefits have often been thought to dwarf the local benefits. As a result, the latter attribute has motivated popular enthusiasm for recycling. "Think globally, act locally" was the slogan adopted by community groups who first promoted recycling in the 1960s. In its early days, recycling was urged as an environmental duty, and even today most of its political impetus derives from broad support for a cleaner environment. In addition, some of its cost advantage lies in voluntary citizen efforts to sort and/or collect recyclable material. However, recycling did not take off until the local advantages of recycling as a *cost-competitive* waste management strategy became apparent in the late 1980s.

Is recycling cost competitive? Yes, up to a point. Communities developing a waste management plan have to decide on a mix of disposal options, including recycling (and composting), incineration, and landfilling. Thus, a community needs to choose a recycling target, and an incinerator or landfill of the appropriate size to minimize disposal costs. Committing to an incinerator or landfill with large-volume requirements can discourage otherwise cost-effective recycling. Careful analysis is necessary before deciding on the appropriate mix.

Denison and Ruston (1990), working for the Environmental Defense Fund have published a guide to determining cost-effective investment in the different options, based on the present discounted value method laid out in Chapter 6 of this book. When discounting is used, the high up-front cost, and relatively slow startup times for incineration and landfilling, favor recycling. Because much of the expenditure for recycling is for ongoing operations, it occurs in the future and thus has a lower present discounted value.

---

[21]Denison and Ruston (1990) argue that when old newspapers are shipped to mills, they displace otherwise "empty backhauls." Regarding displacement, they report that an efficient recycling system displaces one garbage collection trip for every two recycling trips.

Consider this

PUZZLE

Suppose that a new recycling program is expected to cost GarbageTown $50 per ton, but GarbageTown's existing landfill covers its costs charging only $30 per ton. Could introducing the recycling program actually save the town money?

SOLUTION

Maybe. By extending the life of the existing landfill, a recycling program would forestall expensive new landfill construction in the future. Whether this factor would justify a recycling program could be answered for a specific case using the present discounted value framework. What this puzzle illustrates is that comparing simple per ton disposal costs on a year-to-year basis does not tell us which option is to be preferred.

Per ton disposal costs for each method will in fact vary from site to site and over time as regulations change and the prices for recycled goods fluctuate. The latter can have an important impact on the viability of a recycling program. Figure 19.3 illustrates that both the supply of old newspapers (measured by the number of curbside recycling programs) and the demand for the capacity of recycling mills to process the paper grew steadily over the 1990s.

Used newspapers were fetching good prices through 1987, but these dropped sharply in 1988 as supply increased and export demand dropped. Prices remained low as supply surged in the early 1990s, but then recovered in 1993 as paper companies began completing the construction of new processing mills. Prices spiked dramatically in 1995 as enthusiasm for recycling surged, and a speculative wave swept the industry, only to collapse again in 1996. Since then, prices have been more stable, which suggests a maturing industry.

The uncertainty associated with the prices for recycled goods appears to favor other disposal options; however, if prices rise for recyclables, then incinerators or landfills may find themselves coming up short on waste, leading to higher tipping fees to make up for lost volume. The explosive growth in recycling in the 1990s has generally kept prices down, as new supplies have outstripped the growth in end-use markets ("As Recycling Surges" 1992). Volatile prices in end-use markets mean that recycling programs will "pay" some years and require operating subsidies in others. Ackerman (1996) calculates that the typical recycling program raised disposal costs by $21 per household in 1993 (when prices were low) and saved $5 per household in 1995 (when prices were high).

Of course, city managers' decisions to adopt waste management options are motivated as much by political as economic concerns. The recent rush to recycling has been driven by politics, though boosted by economics. In addition, economic studies forecasting the relative cost-effectiveness of different disposal options are merely educated guesses. A given community planning to adopt a curbside recycling scheme in 1989

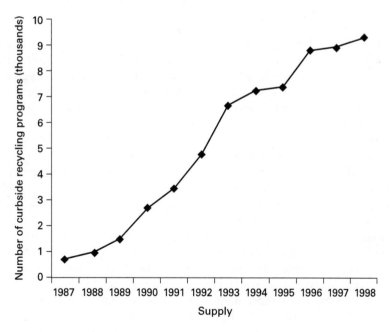

FIGURE 19.3 Supply, Demand, and Price for Old Newsprint

Source: Supply is from Marcia Berss, "No One Wants to Shoot Snow White." 1991. *Forbes,* 14 October, p. 42, and *Biocycle,* various issues. Demand is "Total Use of ONP" from American Forest and Paper Association Web site at http://www.afandpa.org/recycling/graph12.html. Producer Price Index of wastepaper is from the BLS Web site.

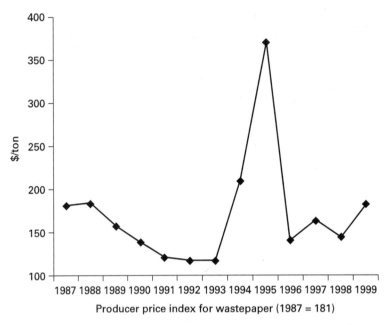

FIGURE 19.3 Supply, Demand, and Price for Old Newsprint (continued)

could hardly have foreseen a 700% growth in supply of recyclables over the next three years and the subsequent collapse of prices in the secondary market. Thus, recycling economics were unfavorable in 1992 in the Minneapolis area, where haulers were dumping or burning recyclables they could not dispose of. At the same time, few would have foreseen the relatively rapid growth in end-user applications and markets leading to a dramatic price spike in the mid-1990s. At this point, it is difficult to assess whether states and communities in general are overinvesting in recycling on purely economic grounds.

The key to the long-term success of recycling has been and will be the development of end-user markets. Of course, the mere existence of cheap sources of junk will inspire entrepreneurs to dream up things to do with it. In recent years, old newspapers have been shredded and turned into animal bedding, while glass has been ground up to use for "glassphalt" road bed.

Here, state and local government actions have been very effective at technology-forcing. For example, the U.S. government purchases large quantities of recycled paper for use in copy machines. The increase in mandatory recycling, recycled content laws, and government purchase programs have all dramatically boosted investment in recycled mill capacity.[22] Chemical manufacturers, responding in part to actual and threatened local bans on plastics, have been working hard to develop recyclable products and

---

[22]For more on purchase programs see Macauley and Walls (2000). Jacques and Ince (1992) maintain that between 15% and 20% of the increase in recycled capacity resulted from state-level recycled content legislation, with the rest resulting from lower prices driven by the surge in local collection programs. The authors strangely refer to the latter phenomenon as a "free-market" phenomenon. The authors also argue that recycled content legislation has led to an inefficient regional distribution of de-inking plants.

create end-user markets. Technology-forcing has worked well here because of the wide diversity of location of these initiatives. Under such circumstances, industry was better off meeting the technology challenge than fighting it.

Recent popular enthusiasm has thus pushed recycling to become a dominant, long-term waste management option. According to William Ruckelshaus, former head of the EPA and now chairman of Browning-Ferris, a major garbage disposal firm, "If the infrastructure gets put into place, with collection systems, processing centers and end-user markets, then it will not matter if the current 'feel good' attitude subsides. Economics will take over and the system will be self-sustaining" ("In Solid Waste" 1991).

Recycling is an example of a successfully promoted CT. As federal regulation (of the command-and-control variety) internalized the environmental costs associated with landfills and incineration, these options became more expensive, and recycling became cost-competitive. At the same time, popular support for recycling at the local level was sufficient to overcome a natural tendency on the part of municipal officials to stick with proven technologies. In addition, carrots in the form of market guarantees, as well as sticks in the form of product bans and content laws, both emerging simultaneously in dozens of locales, have generated substantial investment by the private sector in developing end-use markets for recycled products.

19.4 Summary

This chapter has reviewed the current state of three clean technologies: waste reduction in manufacturing, alternative agriculture, and recycling of municipal solid waste. In all three cases, the first task was to establish that the technologies were in fact CTs: cleaner (in general) than the conventional technologies, and potentially at least as profitable.

The obstacle to rapid diffusion of all the technologies could be boiled down to this: lack of sufficient profit advantage to overcome poor information and risk associated with the CT. Consider for example the paint factory in Table 19.1. State advisers were able to recommend savings of $23,000 per year—nothing to sneeze at, certainly, but probably insufficient to justify hiring a waste assessment firm, of unknown reliability, which might ultimately have come up with nothing. And because of thin markets, waste assessment firms are few and far between, meaning that the paint firm probably did not have an easy opportunity to hire one in the first place.

For farmers, the risk associated with CTs is even higher. Rather than purchasing a new piece of equipment, farmers must sink investments in new management skills and face adjustment costs as alternative methods are introduced. In this case, because some of the environmental costs of conventional farming are borne by farmers directly, they do have a natural interest in switching. Finally, in the recycling case, the profit advantage alone is insufficient to overcome one of the chief attractions of incineration and landfilling for municipal authorities—their relative management simplicity.

Has government successfully promoted these technologies? On the waste reduction front, the most successful government action to date has been a product-labeling effort, the Toxic Release Inventory. The TRI and the EPA's 33/50 program have focused public and industry attention on toxic releases on a plant-by-plant basis and have motivated some companies to begin serious waste reduction efforts. A second strong incentive for waste reduction (as well as on-site incineration and illegal dumping) has been the increase in hazardous waste disposal costs brought on by regulation. Technical assistance programs, though promising, are currently funded at a low level. Mandatory waste reduction plans, less promising, have also been introduced by some states.

In agriculture, rising pesticide costs due to regulation (and decisions by companies not to reregister some old pesticides) may have induced some movement in the direction of CTs. However, because of the difficulty associated with such a transition and the availability of other chemical alternatives, the stick of rising costs may have only limited effect in encouraging movement toward CTs. Organic labeling has helped the industry move forward. But government technical assistance and R&D, though increasing, remain at low levels, while subsidy policies continue to discourage alternative agriculture.

In the recycling case, a combination of regulation-induced rising costs for alternatives and aggressive local promotion has led to tremendous growth in this CT over the last decade. Particularly important has been the development of the recycling infrastructure—processing technologies and end-use markets necessary to support the industry.

The final issue: Are we spending too much promoting these CTs? The evidence suggests that technical assistance programs in industry and agriculture can be quite cost-effective; once established they should be able to recover their own operating costs through fees. This will be increasingly true if costs for hazardous waste disposal and pesticides continue to rise. In addition, a further shift in agricultural R&D funding from conventional to alternative agriculture makes sense, given the presence of private-sector R&D in the former field, financed by agrochemical companies. Finally, with the tremendous flux in markets for recycled goods, it is difficult to tell "on average" whether state and local governments' actions to promote recycling make sense on purely economic grounds.

The tremendous growth in the recycling industry in the early 1990s is quite consistent with the theory of path dependence sketched out in the beginning of the previous chapter. Without aggressive government action, recycling would have remained a limited waste management option, as waste managers stuck with conventional disposal technologies. However, due to public pressure, both public and private infrastructure investment has been undertaken, economies of scale have been realized, and complementary industries developed. Eventually, in Ruckelshaus's words, "Economics takes over," and the nation locks in on a recycling path.

In the long run, nothing is more important to a sustainable economic future than the development of clean technologies. With the earth's combined population and consumption impact expected to triple over the next 50 years, less environmentally destructive means of satisfying human needs must be found and pursued. The delicate task facing government is to channel creative market forces in a clean direction, without unintentionally stifling the very progress it seeks.

APPLICATION 19.0

The Conservation Tillage Program

In 1985, the U.S. Congress changed the rules governing the crop subsidy program. Farmers operating on highly erodible land were required to implement a soil conservation plan (developed in consultation with the extension service of the Department of Agriculture) by 1995 or risk losing their subsidies. Erosion not only lowers the long-run productivity of the farm but also is a major source of surface water pollution. As Chapter 13 pointed out, agricultural runoff of herbicides, insecticides, and fertilizers is the primary source of water pollution nationwide.

A key feature of most soil conservation efforts are so-called *conservation tillage* systems. Conventional tillage systems leave bare dirt fields after the harvest in order to minimize the growth of weeds; by contrast, conservation tillage leaves a minimum of 30% of the soil surface covered with crop residue. The increased residue reduces soil erosion.

Farmers can control weeds in a conservation-tilled field by tilling the surface clear just prior to planting. However, weed problems may still be more severe under conservation tillage, requiring greater use of herbicides. Conservation plans require scrutiny of chemical use and encourage crop rotations to reduce pesticide use.

On the economic front, savings in labor, machinery, and fuel costs from reduced tilling must be balanced against a need for more careful timing of tillage for maximum weed control. Timing of chemical use must also be improved if pesticide and herbicide use is not to grow. By 1993, about 100 million acres, or 36% of U.S. cropland, was planted under some type of conservation tillage system. In 1989, the comparable figure was 25% (Midwest Plan Service 1992; U.S. Department of Agriculture 1993).

1. Can you tell if conservation tillage is a clean technology, as defined in Chapter 18? Why or why not?
2. What tools is the government using to promote conservation tillage?

KEY IDEAS IN EACH SECTION

19.0 This chapter looks at efforts to promote clean technology. Clean technologies yield both **direct** and **indirect environmental benefits.** Indirect benefits from input-reducing technologies are larger than those from input-substituting technologies. As a result CTs are listed in a general order of preference by the **three R's: reduce, reuse, recycle.**

19.1 **Pollution prevention** involves reducing the generation of pollution at the source. Because it often reduces the use of inputs as well, pollution prevention efforts can be profitable and thus qualify as a CT. This section reviews private-sector efforts at pollution prevention, motivated in the chemical industry case by the **Toxics Release Inventory.** The most promising governmental promotion efforts focus on technical assistance programs.

19.2 **Alternative agriculture** includes a variety of practices designed to reduce the use of chemical pesticides and fertilizers. This section emphasizes the difficulties regulators face due to (1) **imperfect information** and (2) the **non-point source** nature of farm pollutants in regulating pesticide residues on food and in groundwater. Major obstacles to alternative agriculture include **high adjustment costs** for individual farmers. Government efforts should focus on reforming subsidy policy and expanding alternative R&D and technical assistance programs.

19.3 Recycling of solid waste yields primarily indirect, rather than **direct, environmental benefits,** because it yields **energy savings** relative to manufacturing from virgin materials and can reduce **upstream pollution.** Recycling has been discouraged by subsidies for incineration and the lack of **unit pricing** for garbage. Recycling economics are less favorable when a high discount rate is used. Recycling can only spread as fast as end-use markets for secondary materials are developed. Finally, the recent success of government efforts to promote recycling illustrates the theory of path dependence in technological development.

REFERENCES

Ackerman, Frank. 1996. *Why Recycle? Markets, Values and Public Policy.* Covela, CA: Island Press.

"As Recycling Surges, Market for Materials is Slow to Develop." 1992. *Wall Street Journal,* 17 January.

Bingham, Taylor H., Donald W. Anderson, and Phillip C. Cooley. 1987. "Distribution of the Generation of Air Pollution." *Journal of Environmental Economics and Management,* 14:30–40.

Bridges, James S. 1990. "Waste Minimization Assessments at Selected DOD Facilities." In *The Environmental Challenge of the 1990s: Proceedings of the International Conference on Pollution Prevention.* Washington, DC: U.S. EPA.

Carnevale, Richard A., Wesley A. Johnson, Craig A. Reed, and Alan Post. 1991. "Agricultural Chemical Residues in Food: Evaluating the Risks." In *Agriculture and the Environment: The 1991 Yearbook of Agriculture.* Washington, DC: USDA.

Cowan, Robin, and Philip Gunby. 1996. "Sprayed to Death: Path Dependence and Lock-in and Pest Control Strategies." *The Economic Journal* 106:521–542.

Cropper, Maureen L., William N. Evans, Stephen J. Berardi, Maria M. Ducla-Soares, and Paul R. Portney. 1991. "The Determinants of Pesticide Regulation: A Statistical Analysis of EPA Decisionmaking." *Discussion Paper CRM 91-01.* Washington, DC: Resources for the Future.

Crosson, Pierre, and Janet Ekey. 1988. "Alternative Agriculture: A Review and Assessment of the Literature." *Discussion Paper ENR88-01.* Washington, DC: Resources for the Future.

Curtis, Jennifer. 1992. *Harvest of Hope: The Potential of Alternative Agriculture to Reduce Pesticide Use.* San Francisco: Natural Resources Defense Council.

Davies, Terry, and Jan Mazurek. 1997. *Industry Incentives for Environmental Improvement: Evaluation of U.S. Federal Initiatives.* Washington, DC: Global Environmental Management Initiative.

Denison, Richard, and John Ruston. 1990. *Recycling and Incineration.* Washington, DC: Island Press.

Dorfman M., C. G. Miller, and W. M. Muir. 1991. *Cutting Chemical Wastes—Update.* New York: INFORM.

"Economics of Trash Shift as Cities Learn Dumps Aren't so Full." 1992. *Wall Street Journal,* 2 June.

"Farmers May be Getting Cancer From Pesticides." 1992. Associated Press story reported in Spokane *Spokesman-Review,* 23 September.

Gianessi, Leonard P. 1991. "Use of Pesticides in the United States." In *Pesticide Residues and Food Safety: A Harvest of Viewpoints,* edited by B. G. Tweedy et al. Washington, DC: American Chemical Society.

Gianessi, Leonard P., Raymond J. Kopp, and Cynthia A. Puffer. 1989. "Regulating Pesticide Use: Social Costs, Policy Targeting and Economic Incentives." *Discussion Paper QE89–21.* Washington, DC: Resources for the Future.

Goodstein, Eban, Karin Sable, and Robert Doppelt. 2000. *Saving Salmon, Saving Money: Innovative Business Leadership in the Pacific Northwest.* Portland, OR: Center for Watershed and Community Health, Portland State University.

Hathaway, Janet S. 1991. "Why Isn't the EPA Reducing Pesticide Risks?" In *Pesticide Residues and Food Safety: A Harvest of Viewpoints,* edited by B. G. Tweedy et al. Washington, DC: American Chemical Society.

Hirschorn, Joel S. 1990. "Preventing Industry Waste." *The EPA Journal,* January–February, 36–39.

"In Solid Waste, It's the Breakdown That Counts." 1991. *New York Times,* 31 March.

Jacques, Romain, and Peter Ince. 1992. "The Economic Impact of State Legislation on Mandatory Recycled Fibre Content: An Application of the North American Pulp and Paper Model." Paper presented at the IUFRO conference, Berlin.

Kirsch, William F., and Gwen P. Looby. 1990. "Waste Minimization Assessment Centers." In *The Environmental Challenge of the 1990s: Proceedings of the International Conference on Pollution Prevention.* Washington, DC: U.S. EPA.

Larson, Bruce A., and Mary K. Knudson. 1991. "Whose Price Wins: Institutional and Technical Change in Agriculture." *Land Economics* 67, no. 2:213–224.

Levin, Michael H. 1991. "Implementing Incentives: Experience and Expectations." In *The Environmental Challenge of the 1990s: Proceedings of the International Conference on Pollution Prevention.* Washington, DC: U.S. EPA.

Macauley, Molly, and Margaret Walls. 2000. "Solid Waste Policy. In *Public Policies for Environmental Protection,* edited by Paul Portney and Robert Stavins. Washington, DC: Resources for the Future.

"Major Companies in the Food Industry Have Little Taste for Organic Products." 1992. *Wall Street Journal,* 10 January.

Malloy, Edward, et al. 1991. "A Harvest of Questions: Chemical in the Food Chain." In *Pesticide Residues and Food Safety: A Harvest of Viewpoints,* edited by B. G. Tweedy et al. Washington, DC: American Chemical Society.

McCarthy, John F. 1991. "Average Residues versus Tolerances." In *Pesticide Residues and Food Safety: A Harvest of Viewpoints,* edited by B. G. Tweedy et al. Washington, DC: American Chemical Society.

Midwest Plan Service. 1992. *Conservation Tillage Systems and Management.* Ames, IA: Iowa State University.

Morris, Jeffrey, and Diana Canzoneri. 1992. "Comparative Lifecycle Energy Analysis: Theory and Practice." *Resource Recycling,* November, 25–31.

Mott, Laurie, and Karen Snyder. 1987. *Pesticide Alert: A Guide to Pesticides in Fruits and Vegetables.* San Francisco: Sierra Club Books.

National Research Council. 1989. *Alternative Agriculture.* Washington, DC: National Academy Press.

New York State Energy Authority. 1994. *Energy Implications of Integrated Solid Waste Management Systems.* Albany, NY: NYSERDA.

O'Conell, Paul F. 1991. "Sustainable Agriculture." In *Agriculture and the Environment: The 1991 Yearbook of Agriculture.* Washington, DC: U.S. GPO.

Office of Technology Assessment. 1987. *From Pollution to Prevention: A Progress Report on Waste Reduction.* Washington, DC: U.S. GPO.

Office of Technology Assessment. 1989. *Facing America's Trash: What Next for Municipal Solid Waste?* Washington, DC: U.S. GPO.

Office of Technology Assessment. 1991. *Beneath the Bottom Line: Agricultural Approaches to Reduce Groundwater Contamination.* Washington, DC: U.S. GPO.

Ottinger, Richard L., et al. 1990. *Environmental Costs of Electricity.* New York: Oceana Publications.

Porter, Michael E. 1991. "America's Green Strategy." *Scientific American,* April, 168.

Reganald, John P., Robert I. Paperclick, and James F. Parr. 1990. "Sustainable Agriculture." *Scientific American,* June, 112–120.

Repetto, Robert, and Sanjay Baliga. 1996. *Pesticides and the Immune System: The Public Health Risks.* Washington, DC: World Resources Institute.

Richardson, Stephanie. 1990. "Pollution Prevention in Textile Wet Processing: An Approach and Case Studies." In *The Environmental Challenge of the 1990s: Proceedings of the International Conference on Pollution Prevention.* Washington, DC: U.S. EPA.

Salant, Stephen, and Eban Goodstein. 1990. "Predicting Committee Behavior in Majority-rule Experiments." *The Rand Journal of Economics* 21, no. 2:293–313.

Schall, John. 1992. "Does the Solid Waste Hierarchy Make Sense?" *Program on Solid Waste Policy, Working Paper 1.* New Haven: Yale University Press.

Shapiro, Michael. 1990. "Toxic Substances Policy." In *Public Policies for Environmental Protection,* edited by Paul Portney. Washington, DC: Resources for the Future.

Shistar, Terry, Susan Cooper, and Jay Feldman. 1992. *Unnecessary Risks: The Benefit Side of the Pesticide Risk-Benefit Equation.* Washington, DC: National Coalition Against the Misuse of Pesticides.

"The State of Garbage in America." 1996. *Biocycle,* April–May.

Taylor, Sarah. 1988. "Developing Pesticide Analytical Methods for Food: Considerations for Federal Policy Formulation." In *Pesticide Residues in Food.* Washington, DC: Office of Technology Assessment.

Tierney, John. 1996. "Recycling Is Garbage." *New York Times Magazine,* June 30.

U.S. Department of Agriculture. 1993. "Farmers Expand Use of Crop Residue Management." *Agricultural Resources: Cropland, Water and Conservation Situation and Outlook,* AR-30, May.

U.S. Department of Agriculture. 1991a. *1990 Fact Book of Agriculture.* Washington, DC: USDA.

U.S. Environmental Protection Agency. 1987. *Unfinished Business: A Comparative Assessment of Environmental Problems.* Washington, DC: U.S. GPO.

U.S. Environmental Protection Agency. 1990. *Reducing Risk: Setting Priorities and Strategies for Environmental Protection.* Washington, DC: U.S. EPA.

U.S. Government Accounting Office. 1986. *Pesticides: Need to Enhance FDA's Ability to Protect the Public From Illegal Residues.* Washington, DC: U.S. GPO.

Uva, Thomas. 1989. "Eliminating Those Regulatory Headaches." *EPA Journal,* November–December.

Whyatt, Robin M., and William J. Nicholson. 1991. "Conducting Risk Assessments for Preschooler's Dietary Exposure." In *Pesticide Residues and Food Safety: A Harvest of Viewpoints,* edited by B. G. Tweedy et al. Washington, DC: American Chemical Society.

Wiseman, A. Clark. 1990. "U.S. Wastepaper Recycling Policies: Issues and Effects." *Discussion Paper ENR 90-14.* Washington, DC: Resources for the Future.

APPENDIX 19A

Input-Output Models and Life-Cycle Analysis

In our definition of clean technology (CT) in Chapter 18, we said that, among other things, a CT had to be "environmentally superior" to conventional technology. We suggested that a measure of environmental superiority might be based on a so-called **life-cycle** approach, which identifies the major environmental impacts of a product from cradle-to-grave. One problem with doing life-cycle analysis is deciding at what stage a product is actually born. Consider a rubber tire. We might go all the way back to the production of petroleum necessary to create synthetic rubber. But why stop there? Why not include as well the manufacture of the drilling equipment necessary to produce the petroleum? Or the manufacture of the machine tools needed to produce the equipment to manufacture the drilling rigs?

This point came up again in our Chapter 19 discussion of waste reduction in manufacturing and agriculture and recycling. Any time total resource use in the economy falls, both direct and indirect benefits are obtained. The **direct environmental benefits** of, for example, improved waste-water recycling in a jewelry factory are reduced emissions of heavy metals. However, **indirect environmental benefits** arise when metals recovered from the recycling process are reused. These indirect benefits include the pollution prevented by: (1) lower levels of mining, smelting, and transporting the metals; (2) lower levels of production and transport of mining equipment; (3) lower levels of production of machinery necessary to make mining equipment; and so on and so forth as we move further "upstream" in the production process.

This appendix illustrates a method that economists have developed to capture all of the complex environmental interactions in an economic system. Using what is called **input-output (I-O) analysis,** it is possible to completely describe all of the direct and indirect pollution created by a particular technology. I-O analysis allows us, at least in theory to do a thorough life-cycle analysis of a product or production technique.[1]

In practice, however, I-O analysis is very data intensive, requiring information about many technical relationships between inputs, outputs, and pollutants in an economy. For this reason, and in spite of its theoretical appeal, I-O is not now widely used for life-cycle analyses of any detail, for example, comparing paper with plastic bags. Instead, most detailed life-cycle analyses done today are of a partial nature, in which analysts try to identify the "major" indirect environmental effects of a production technique or product. Because of cost and data limitations, life-cycle analysts have to *assume* that most of the indirect effects of different technologies are comparable.

This appendix will develop a simple I-O model to make two general points about life-cycle impacts: (1) technologies that reduce overall input use **(input-reducing technologies)** are always clean technologies; (2) technologies that substitute one "clean" input for another "dirty" one **(input-substituting technologies)** may or may not be clean technologies. In such a case, a detailed I-O study would have to be done to establish with certainty whether a proposed CT was really clean.

---

[1]Input-output analysis can also be used to calculate the direct and indirect *employment* effects of different technologies. One such I-O study looking at waste management options for New York City was discussed in Chapter 9.

Unfortunately, case (2) is the one that almost always holds in the real world. For example, suppose I use a more efficient compact fluorescent light bulb and thus save a lot of energy. It might be *possible* (but in fact isn't likely) that switching to the product would generate a big increase in the emission of a deadly hazardous waste in a distant, upstream production process. Given this possibility of large and distant indirect environmental effects of a new technology and the difficulty in identifying *all* these effects by way of a detailed I-O study, can any technology really be called "clean" with certainty?

While recognizing that there are few real-world examples of pure input-reducing technologies, clean technology proponents argue that processes that are *more* input-reducing are *more* likely to be clean technologies.[2] Defining what is meant by "more input-reducing" is itself not easy and can only be done on a case-by-case basis. For example, as we discussed in this chapter, recycling products that would otherwise be made from virgin timber or minerals is likely to substantially reduce net indirect pollution (including any unsustainable drawdown of natural capital) in the extraction and transport phases of production.

Of course, without an I-O study of sufficient detail, no one can say for certain that this is true. But in the real world, as we have seen quite often, policy decisions must always be made with less than perfect information. Under these circumstances, rules of thumb can be helpful. The ordering of the **three R's** discussed in this chapter—(1) **reduce,** (2) **reuse,** (3) **recycle**—provides such a guide, which emphasizes input-reducing technologies over input-substituting technologies.

To summarize: Most technological change involves substituting one input for another. Under these circumstances, establishing whether the new technology is truly cleaner requires an I-O analysis to trace all the direct and indirect environmental effects of the new technology. In practice, this can seldom be done. However, this does not mean we need to abandon the search for clean technology. Instead, technologies with apparent environmental benefits should be subject to partial life-cycle analyses. These can identify any big indirect impacts that might disqualify a potential clean-technology candidate.

The rest of this appendix is organized as follows. The first section develops a simple I-O model and shows that input-reducing technological change is always clean. The next section illustrates how the indirect effects of an input-substituting technology may offset positive direct environmental benefits. The appendix ends with a discussion of how I-O models are used in practice to address macro-level questions about the direct and indirect pollution effects of different technological choices.

19A.0   Input-Reducing Technology

Input-output analysis earns its name because it traces all of the complex relationships between the inputs and outputs of an economic system. I-O models allow us to account for the fact that many outputs are also inputs into other outputs! The first step in doing an input-output analysis is to develop an **I-O table** for the economy

---

[2]Clean technology proponents are not alone in relying on approximations to input-reducing technological change. Economists who study productivity changes in industry often assume that pure input-reducing (Hicks-Neutral) technological change occurs.

being studied. Table 19A.1 shows an I-O amalysis for a very simple economy with only two "products," corn and enriched soil, and one pollutant, dirty water.[3]

Corn is grown in high-quality soil and, as a result of erosion and nutrient uptake, the farming process uses up some of the soil. Enriched soil is also "produced" by feeding corn to animals who then generate manure for fertilizer. Table 19A.1 illustrates these "input-output" relationships in the following way. If we read down the first column, we find that in the production of 1 ton of corn, 0.4 tons of corn (as seed) and 0.2 ton of soil are used up. In addition, as a result of erosion in the corn-farming process, 200 gallons of stream water are polluted with sediment.

Reading down the second column we find that to produce each ton of manure-enriched soil, we require 0.1 ton of corn as animal feed and no enriched soil. Through the run-off of nitrates in the fertilizer, 100 gallons of stream water are polluted for each ton of soil "produced."

The trick behind input-output analysis is to recognize a simple accounting fact: The total output of the economy (corn and enriched soil) must equal the intermediate consumption of these products by producers plus their final consumption by consumers. In other words, the supply of each product has to equal demand. Now, of course, consumers don't eat soil. But consumers do decide how much to invest in preserving natural capital. As explained next, consumers may decide to either build up or run down the stock of soil in the economy. So we now have two relationships that must hold true:

total corn produced = corn used to produce corn + corn used to produce soil + corn eaten by people

total soil "produced" = soil used to produce corn + soil used to produce soil + net increase (or decrease) in the stock of soil

Let us now employ some simple algebra to see how input-output analysis works. If we let x^c and x^s equal the total output of corn and soil each year and y^c and y^s equal the final consumer "demand" for these products on an annual basis, then our two verbal equations above become

$$\text{Supply} = \text{Demand}$$
$$\text{Corn: } x^c = 0.4x^c + 0.1x^s + y^c$$
$$\text{Soil: } x^s = 0.2x^c + 0.0 + y^s$$

TABLE 19A.1   I-O Table for a Corn-Soil Economy

		OUTPUTS	
		Corn	**Enriched Soil**
I N P U T S	Corn (tons)	0.4	0.1
	Enriched soil (tons)	0.2	0.0
	Dirty water (1,000 gallons)	0.2	0.1

---

[3]This model was inspired by a slightly more complex one in Duchin (1990), who also lays out the general theoretical framework for expanding a conventional I-O model to include pollutants.

Here are two equations and four unknowns. To solve the system, we need to specify a level of final demand. Suppose consumers would like to eat 10 tons of corn and want to keep the stock of natural capital (enriched soil) constant. If they do this, the economy will be sustainable, assuming zero population growth. Given this final demand for corn and soil, $y^c = 10$ and $y^s = 0$.

If we substitute these values in, and do a little algebra, we obtain a solution: $x^c = 17.3$ and $x^s = 3.5$. In other words, the economic goal is to satisfy a final demand for corn of 10 tons and yet maintain the stock of enriched soil. To do this, total corn production must be 17.3 tons and total production of enriched soil to replace that used up must be 3.5 tons. Total water pollution in the economy is thus 17.3 * 200 + 3.5 * 100 = 3,810 gallons.

So far, we have illustrated that the final demand for corn and soil preservation will determine how much of these products is also demanded in the intermediate production stages. Let us now use this little model to evaluate whether a proposed new technology is indeed clean. Suppose that farmers figure out a way to reduce soil erosion so that, under the new method, only 0.1 ton of soil is required to produce a ton of corn. With less erosion, water pollution drops to 100 gallons per ton of corn produced. What are the environmental benefits of this proposed CT?

We might look just at the direct benefits: The original economy is producing 17.3 tons of corn at 200 gallons of pollution per ton. Reducing pollution to 100 gallons per ton should cause a direct fall in total pollution from 3,810 to 2,080 gallons. But recall that some of this corn was in fact going to feed animals to produce manure to replenish the soil, which itself caused pollution. Because erosion has been reduced by the new approach (an *input-reducing technology*), the economy can now devote fewer resources to replenishing the soil. This will mean that both the manure and corn sectors can "shrink," yielding even greater indirect environmental benefits. Yet the economy will still produce the same final consumption levels as before.

To see this, we can rewrite our two I-O equations using the new farming technology (replacing the coefficient on x^c in the second equation with 0.1):

$$\text{Supply} = \text{Demand}$$
$$\text{Corn: } x^c = 0.4x^c + 0.1x^s + y^c$$
$$\text{Soil: } x^s = 0.1x^c + 0.0 + y^s$$

Consumers are still interested in eating 10 tons of corn and maintaining the natural stock of soil quality. So, substituting in $y^c = 10$ and $y^s = 0$ as before and solving, we now get: $x^c = 16.9$ and $x^s = 1.7$. With the more efficient farming method, total corn production falls to 16.9 tons, while enriched soil production falls to 1.7 tons. As a result, total water pollution actually falls to 16.9 * 100 + 1.7 * 100 = 1,860 gallons. Thus, including the indirect benefits of lowered corn and manure output leads to a pollution reduction of 220 gallons beyond the direct effect.

This example illustrates a general point: whenever a technology simply reduces input use, it will also reduce pollution in the connected sectors of the economy. Thus, an input-reducing technology will always be a clean technology. Moreover, the combined indirect and direct environmental benefits will be bigger than the simple direct effect.[4]

---

[4]Proofs of these propositions for a general linear model can be found in Axtell (1991). If one moves to a system that allows input substitution in other sectors, this claim holds only as a local approximation.

19A.1 Input-Substituting Technology

Unfortunately, very few technological innovations involve simple reductions in input use. More often, one type of resource is substituted for another. Under these circumstances, direct and indirect environmental effects may offset one another. Let us return to our original I-O model to illustrate this point. Suppose that farmers have been using cow manure to enrich their soil. However, it is discovered that pig manure, in terms of direct effects, is more environmentally sound. For each ton of soil enriched, only 50 rather than 100 gallons of stream water are polluted. The catch: Pigs eat twice as much corn as cows. Is pig manure a clean (!!) technology?

Our input-output table now looks like Table 19A.2. With the pig technology, 0.2 tons of corn are required for every ton of soil enriched, but soil enrichment generates only 50 gallons of pollution per ton. If we write down our I-O equations that specify that total output must equal intermediate consumption plus final consumption, we now get

$$\text{Supply} = \text{Demand}$$
$$\text{Corn: } x^c = 0.4x^c + 0.2x^s + y^c$$
$$\text{Soil: } x^s = 0.2x^c + 0.0 + y^s$$

Consumers are still interested in eating 10 tons of corn and maintaining the stock of soil quality. So substituting in $y^c = 10$ and $y^s = 0$ as before and solving, we now get: $x^c = 17.9$ and $x^s = 3.6$. Relative to the original case we evaluated above, both corn and manure production have to rise to accommodate the pigs' larger appetites and still replace all of the natural capital (soil) that is exhausted.

What happens to water pollution? Table 19A.3 provides a comparison. Manure production has to rise (from 3.5 to 3.6 tons) to satisfy the increased demand for corn. However, nitrate pollution from the manure still falls thanks to the inherent cleanliness of pigs. By contrast, sediment pollution from corn farming rises substantially. However, on a *total* gallons polluted basis, pig manure has to rate as a clean technology since pollution falls from 3,810 to 3,760. Yet, its advantage is much smaller than one might have thought based on a 50% reduction in pollution per ton. Here the indirect pollution from increased production of the substitute resource (corn) offsets the direct gains.

Yet, can we really characterize the pig technology as "clean"? Note that nitrate pollution falls when the pig technology is adopted, but sediment pollution increases. If

TABLE 19A.2   I-O Table for an Input-Output Technology

		OUTPUTS	
		Corn	**Enriched Soil**
I	Corn(tons)	0.4	0.2
N			
P			
U	Enriched soil (tons)	0.2	0.0
T			
S	Dirty water (1000 gallons)	0.2	0.05

TABLE 19A.3   Is Pig Manure a Clean Technology?

Pollution (gallons)	Cow Manure	Pig Manure
Nitrate from manure	3.5 * 100 = 350	3.6 * 50 = 180
Sediment from farming	17.3 * 200 = 3,460	17.9 * 200 = 3,580
Total	3,810	3,760

we add them together, the net result is a decrease in pollution. But what if sediment pollution has more serious ecological or health effects than nitrate pollution? While life-cycle analysis in an I-O framework can (on paper) identify both the direct and indirect pollution generated by a technology, it provides no guidance as to how to weigh their disparate impacts.

One way to do this is to estimate marginal dollar damages associated with each pollutant, then add up the damages and see which technology is "cleaner." Chapter 8 discussed techniques for estimating damage values, and Chapter 17 described how such an approach is being used in the electric utility industry to influence the choice of generating technology. However, uncertainty in these benefit estimates places one more obstacle in the way of completing reliable life-cycle analyses.

The last two sections have discussed a very simple I-O model that illustrates two general points: (1) input reducing technologies are always CTs; and (2) technologies that involve substituting one "clean" input for another "dirty" one may or may not be CTs. While, in principal, the true answer can only be determined via I-O analysis, such analyses are seldom carried out for specific technologies because the data are too poor. Instead, CT proponents argue from a theoretical perspective that technologies that are "more" input-reducing are more likely to be clean. A less complete form of life-cycle analysis than I-O can then be used to identify major indirect effects that might disqualify a potential CT candidate.

19A.2   I-O in the Real World

The little model explored above has only illustrative value. However, economists have developed much more elaborate I-O models that contain economies with dozens of economic sectors and several major pollutants. Linear (matrix) algebra techniques are used to solve these models and calculate the direct and indirect pollution content of different sets of technologies in a fashion conceptually similar to the approach taken above.

While an economy with dozens of sectors is more realistic than one with only two, applied I-O analyses are still not useful for answering detailed questions, such as, "Are cloth diapers cleaner than disposable ones?" Instead, real-world applications of I-O focus on broader questions. Two of these are discussed next.

Bingham, Anderson, and Cooley (1987) examined the general balance between direct and indirect air pollution attributable to the final demand of consumers. Table 19A.4 illustrates their results. For air pollutants, overall the authors found that the direct contribution from consumption is a little more than 50% of the total, ranging to a low of 10% for particulates. The direct contribution of consumption to other negative externalities—water pollution, habitat destruction, scenic impacts—would certainly be less than 50%, since consumers produce substantial direct air pollution via

TABLE 19A.4   Air Pollutant Discharges Due to Consumption

	Distribution of Pollutant Generation Due to Consumption (10^6 mg/yr)		
	Direct	**Indirect**	**Percent of Total Indirect**
Particulates	0.7	6.3	90
Sulfur oxides	1.0	14.7	93
Nitrogen oxides	4.7	9.7	67
Hydrocarbons	10.4	8.4	44
Carbon monoxide	52.7	26.5	33
Total pollutants	69.5	65.6	48

Source: Bingham, Anderson, and Cooley (1987). Used with permission.

the automobile, home heating, and electricity. As a result, indirect pollution probably accounts for well over 50% of the total pollution generated in final consumption.

Bingham et al. also found that total pollution rose roughly on a one-to-one basis with increased consumption. Thus, the wealthiest 10% of American families generated 4 to 6 times as much air pollution as did the poorest 10%. At the same time, as we discussed in Chapter 5, poorer families are more likely to suffer from air pollution exposure.

A second I-O study was conducted by Duchin and Lange (1992) for the United Nations. The authors were asked to explore the environmental outcomes associated with the vision of "sustainable development" outlined in the Bruntland Commission report to be discussed in Chapter 21. Briefly, the Bruntland Commission called for accelerated transfer of clean technology from rich to poor countries. This would allow these nations to grow in a relatively clean way. Along with increased incomes would come a decline in population growth rates. If the process worked according to plan, then within 30 to 40 years, poverty and population growth in poor countries would be dramatically reduced, unsustainable pressures on natural capital would be scaled back, and all this would come at a fairly low pollution cost.

Duchin and Lange used a 44-sector model of the world economy divided into 17 regions. They included three air pollutants: (1) carbon dioxide (global warming); (2) sulfur oxides (acid rain and sulfate air pollution); and (3) nitrogen oxides (global warming, acid rain and smog). They then made a series of relatively optimistic, but still feasible, assumptions about both economic growth in poor countries and the rate of technology transfer from rich to poor countries.

Worldwide, the authors project GDP to grow 150% from 1990 to 2020. On the technology side, over the same period, the authors assume improvements in the efficiency of input use on the order of 20% to 50% in sectors such as transportation, electricity, and construction. Most of this technological change is input-reducing and thus clean, but input-substitution does occur in some sectors. For example, chemical use in the paper industry is assumed to increase with increased recycling.

In the *absence* of rapid and widespread technological improvements (their baseline scenario), Duchin and Lange estimate that air pollutant emissions in all three categories will increase by more than 250% worldwide between 1990 and 2020. Yet, even under the optimistic scenario, emissions are also projected to rise, with carbon dioxide emissions up 73%, sulfur oxide emissions up 26%, and nitrogen oxide emissions up

74%. Nevertheless, taking into account all direct and indirect environmental effects, accelerated transfer of (mostly) input-reducing technology can clearly have a major impact on air pollution levels around the world.

One may debate whether the environmental cost of economic growth under the optimistic scenario is still unsustainably high. Duchin and Lange believe that it is. They conclude that input-reducing efficiency improvements in known technologies are unlikely to allow for sustainable development as defined by the Bruntland Commission. They argue that, rather than relying solely on efficiency improvements in existing technologies, completely new clean technologies will have to be created to accommodate growth in a sustainable fashion. Two such technologies they discuss are mass transit and solar (photovoltaic) electricity.

19A.3 Summary

This appendix illustrates how, in theory, one can trace all of the direct and indirect environmental effects of a new technology using input-output analysis. In practice, I-O analysis is too data intensive to be helpful in microlevel decisions. However, at a theoretical level, I-O models support that, in general, technologies that are more input-reducing are more likely to be clean. Defining what is meant by "more input-reducing" has to be done on a case-by-case basis. I-O models are also helpful in gaining insight into macrolevel questions. The two examples mentioned here involved estimates of the general magnitude of indirect air pollution effects and the degree to which the rapid diffusion of more efficient technologies can promote sustainable development.

APPLICATION 19A.0

Doing Input-Output

Consider the following I-O table, slightly modified from the one in the text:

		OUTPUTS	
		Corn	Enriched Soil
I **N** **P** **U** **T** **S**	Corn(tons)	0.5	0.1
	Enriched soil (tons)	0.3	0.0
	Dirty water (1,000 gallons)	0.3	0.2

1. What does the number "0.1" in the table mean? What does the number "0.3" (the one on the top) mean?
2. Suppose that, as in the text, consumers wish to consume 10 tons of corn and maintain the current stock of enriched soil. What do the two I-O equations look like?
3. Solve the two equations to get the total output of corn and soil needed to satisfy both intermediate and final consumer demand.

4. Now suppose that to accommodate population growth and still maintain a sustainable agricultural base, consumers decide to increase the stock of enriched soil by 1 ton. (They still want to consume 10 tons of corn.) What happens to total corn and soil output?

5. What happens to water pollution in part 4 relative to part 3? Is the decision to boost the stock of enriched soil, in fact, sustainable? If not, can you think of a sustainable way to accommodate population growth?

REFERENCES

Axtell, Robert. 1991. "Cascading Market Inefficiency Through Indirect Effects in the Joint Production of Goods and Externalities." Paper presented at the Eastern Economic Association Meetings. Pittsburgh, PA, March 1991.

Bingham, Taylor H., Donald W. Anderson, and Phillip C. Cooley. 1987. "Distribution of the Generation of Air Pollution." *Journal of Environmental Economics and Management,* vol. 14, 30–40.

Duchin, Faye. 1990. "The Conversion of Biological Materials and Wastes to Useful Products," *Structural Change and Economic Dynamics* 1, no. 2:243–261.

Duchin, Faye, and Glenn-Marie Lange. 1992. *Strategies for Environmentally Sound Economic Development.* New York: Institute for Economic Analysis.

ENERGY POLICY
AND THE
ENVIRONMENT

20.0 Introduction

Of all economic activities, energy production and use present the biggest challenge to the quality of the environment. This book began with an extended discussion of the problem of global warming, due to the release of carbon dioxide from the combustion of fossil fuels. But beyond global warming, energy production and use also yield as by-products acid rain and sulfate pollution, urban air pollution and traffic jams, oil spills, oil drilling and strip mining in sensitive habitats, acid mine drainage, hazardous mine tailings and oil drilling muds, occupational diseases such as black lung, and exposure to radioactivity in the mining, transport, and disposal of nuclear fuel and waste. Our three main energy sources—oil, coal, and nuclear—each have their own environmental drawbacks.

Yet reliable access to reasonably priced energy is the lifeblood of any economic system, and the American economy relies more heavily on it than most. This chapter presents an overview of the current energy picture and then considers the prospects for a cleaner energy path, one based on a combination of renewable energy (solar, wind, and biomass electricity), energy efficiency, and hydrogen fuel cell vehicles. The basic message is that the future is up for grabs. Depending upon the interaction of technology, economics, and government policy, the energy system could follow the current fossil fuels path or switch to either a renewable/efficiency path or, less likely, a high nuclear path.

How costly is a clean energy future likely to be? As was suggested in the introductory chapter on global warming, there is substantial disagreement among economists about the economic impacts of the different options. Some argue that combating global warming by adopting clean energy options will be quite expensive, while others have maintained that, through aggressive energy-efficiency measures, we might actually be able to reduce global warming at a profit. This chapter will look more closely at these arguments.

20.1 The Current Energy Picture

Each year, Americans consume the equivalent of 6.5 gallons of oil per day for each man, woman, and child in the country. Figure 20.1 shows an index of per capita energy consumption in the United States from 1973 to 1999, with 1973 consumption set equal to 1.

Energy use has varied widely over time, depending both on economic conditions and oil prices. In 1974, and again in 1978, the **Organization of Petroleum Exporting Countries (OPEC)** quadrupled the price of oil. Over the period, prices rose from about $3 to $40 per barrel. Both of these oil shocks contributed to subsequent recessions, a short one from 1974 to 1975, and a much deeper one from 1980 to 1983. Figure 20.1 reveals that in the face of the 1974 oil price hike and recession, energy use declined rapidly. However, as the economy recovered in the mid-1970s, energy use began rising again. During this period, American industry and consumers were still dependent on highly energy-inefficient technology.

Energy use plunged again after the second oil price shock, causing the deep recession of the early 1980s. By this time, under the long-term pressure of higher prices and government-mandated efficiency measures, the technological base in the country had become much more energy-efficient. Because energy use stayed flat while the economy continued to grow, the ratio of economic output to energy use also grew. Between 1973 and 1985, *energy use per dollar of GNP produced fell by more than one quarter.*

However, after 1983, oil prices collapsed to less than $20 per barrel, and the U.S. economy experienced steady, if unspectacular, growth through 1989. Figure 20.1 shows that, beginning in 1983, under the influence of low energy prices, a reduced governmental commitment to energy efficiency, and steady economic growth, per capita energy use began to climb again. This growth finally leveled out in the face of the recession of the early 1990s, but resumed after 1991 and continued through the decade. In 1999, Americans were consuming on a per person basis about the same amount of energy that they had twenty years before.

How do Americans stack up against the rest of the world in energy use? Unfortunately, as Figure 20.2 illustrates, we are close to the top of the heap among wealthy countries. What explains the wide variation in international demand for energy illustrated in the figure? National income, of course, but climate, population density, energy prices, transportation infrastructure, and government conservation policy are all also important factors. Canada loses on all fronts—cold climate, low population density, low energy prices, a transport system geared to the automobile, and a government with a relatively laissez-faire attitude, by international standards, toward energy conservation. Electric power in Norway is also cheap, due to abundant hydropower.

Germany and Japan, each of which uses about half as much energy per capita as we do in the United States, have comparable climates. However, both are much more densely populated and have urban and interurban transport systems designed heavily around mass transit. Of the two, Japan has pursued energy efficiency most aggressively. Before the first oil shock in 1974, Japan already had one of the most

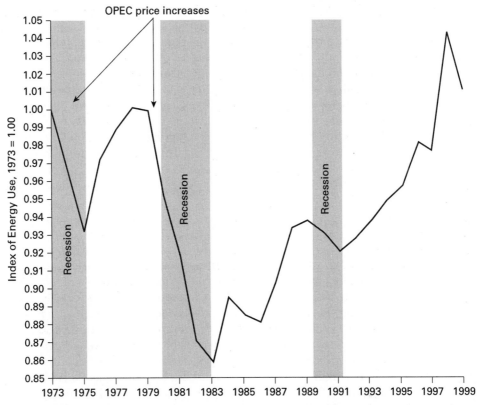

FIGURE 20.1 United States Energy Consumption per Capita, 1973–1998

Source: The Statistical Abstract of the United States, 1999, Tables 2 and 955. Reported energy use after 1991 is adjusted downward by 2.5 quads, to maintain consistency with earlier data.

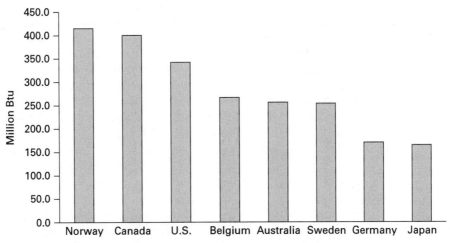

FIGURE 20.2 Energy Consumption per Capita, International Comparisons

Source: U.S. DOE.

energy-efficient economies; since then, the nation has improved its efficiency by one third, compared to a 25% improvement in other industrial countries.

The *Wall Street Journal* cities two successful government policies: (1) Japanese factories are required to have at least one energy conservation engineer on site who must pass a rigorous national test. (2) Japanese companies are allowed to keep energy prices high, provided they channel profits into R&D into energy research. These governmental measures have led to dramatic improvements in Japan's energy efficiency ("How Japan Became" 1990).

This section has provided a brief overview of the U.S. energy picture. The three primary uses of energy are for electricity, heat, and transportation. The next few sections will provide a more detailed look at the major energy technologies available in these sectors and will discuss policies designed to promote a cleaner energy future.

20.2 Technology Options: Electricity and Heat

Options for attacking energy needs for electricity and heat exist on both the demand and supply sides. **Demand-side management (DSM)** involves promoting technologies that use energy more efficiently. Note that many conservation measures, such as turning down the thermostat from 68 to 65 degrees or driving 55 mph on the highway, are not efficiency measures since they involve some sacrifice in consumption. By energy efficiency we mean technologies that generate a comparable quality of service using less energy. Such DSM measures "produce" energy by freeing up supply.

In earlier chapters, we have discussed many DSM options: compact fluorescent lighting (Chapter 6), energy-efficient building codes, and standards for refrigeration and lighting (Chapter 18). Other DSM measures include using waste energy from electricity production to heat buildings (cogeneration), as well as adoption of energy-efficient industrial motors and cooling and cleaning appliances.

The potential for cost-effective DSM is substantial. Figure 20.3 shows two estimates of the potential for reduced electricity consumption. The Electric Research Power Institute maintains that electricity use could be reduced about 25% at a cost of less than $0.04 per kWh (roughly the cost of power from a new coal plant). More optimistically, the Rocky Mountain Institute argues that, at that price, we could reduce consumption by 70%. Both estimates suggest that many DSM measures qualify as clean technologies by being cost competitive and environmentally superior.

Moving on to the supply side of the market, half a dozen major options exist for producing heat and electricity. Coal is currently the primary fuel source for producing electric power in the United States (52%), with nuclear second (20%), natural gas third (16%), hydroelectric power fourth (9%), petroleum fifth (3%), and other renewables last (2%). Natural gas, oil, and passive solar technologies are also used to generate heat. Each option has its own environmental and/or economic problems; each also has promising technologies that supporters maintain are capable of addressing those problems.

The dominance of coal in electric power generation to date has been due to one primary factor—a reliable, low-priced fuel source. The technology for producing electricity

FIGURE 20.3 Potential for Electricity Savings through DSM

Source: "Efficient Use of Electricity," in *Readings From Scientific American,* Arnold P. Fickett, Clark W. Gellings, and Amory B. Lovins. Copyright © 1990 by Scientific American, Inc. All rights reserved. Used with permission.

from coal is well-developed, and because domestic coal resources are abundant, the supply of fuel is not subject to the disruption and price fluctuations associated with oil.

On the other hand, coal's environmental and social problems are well known. In addition to problems of acid rain and criteria air pollutants discussed in Chapter 13, underground mining for coal is quite dangerous, while strip mining disturbs natural ecosystems. Both can generate acid drainage problems. Coal transport also has a major impact on the nation's roads.

Looking to the future, coal-burning power plants have recently faced tighter regulation of their sulfur dioxide and nitrogen oxide emissions in order to control acid rain. Coal's long-run outlook hinges mostly on the progress of effort to stop global warming. Electric power contributes about 33% of America's carbon dioxide emissions, mostly from coal. Any serious effort to control the greenhouse effect will require that coal-burning power production be restricted, if not ultimately eliminated.

Nuclear power faces both economic and environmental challenges. There are currently about 110 plants operating in the United States, though no new plants have been ordered since the mid-1970s. Due to mounting costs resulting from increased regulation and construction costs, nuclear electric power from new U.S. plants would currently be cost-competitive only if siting and permitting procedures were dramatically streamlined. Given the historical record of construction delays, a new nuclear facility would probably deliver power at about $0.12 to $0.16 per kilowatt hour, more than twice the cost of power from coal.[1] The nuclear slowdown has been worldwide. Even in countries more nuclear-dependent than the United States, such as France and Japan, new facility orders have dropped dramatically.

A primary factor leading to rising costs has been construction delays from opposition to the siting and permitting of production and waste disposal facilities. There has been much debate about the safety of nuclear facilities, with most concern focused on a Chernobyl-type core failure, or meltdown. In 1985, the Nuclear Regulatory Commission estimated the probability of a severe core meltdown at one of 109 U.S. reactors at 45% by 2005 (Ottinger et al. 1990). Estimates of cancer-induced fatalities from meltdowns have ranged from zero (Three Mile Island) to as high as 500,000 for Chernobyl, though most fatality estimates for Chernobyl are much lower. A Nuclear Regulatory Commission study predicted that a worst-case disaster in a populous area of the United States might generate about 100,000 deaths. Based on these figures, nuclear

---

[1]The cost of power from a new nuclear unit is very difficult to estimate because none have been ordered in the United States since the 1970s. Much of the uncertainty in costs is due to political factors: A good portion of nuclear's expense has resulted from construction delays and unanticipated retrofits required to meet new regulatory requirements (Cantor and Hewlett 1988). Reducing costs in the nuclear industry would thus require a dramatic streamlining of the permitting and siting process. However, in the face of intense public concern about safety, such an outcome seems highly unlikely.

Flavin (1987) provides a 1985 cost estimate, based on industry sources of $0.12 per kWh. Hall (1990) puts private costs at between $0.14 and $0.16 per kWh. These estimates seem reasonable, given the fact that the political opposition to any new plant is likely to be substantial.

Nuclear optimists see the technology as cost-competitive. Westinghouse, for example, maintains that its new modular reactors could generate power for as low as $0.042 per kWh, given timely permitting and construction. (It is not clear whether this estimate assumes scale economies from mass-producing the modular units.) Manne and Richels (1990) and the New York State Energy Office (1991) also view new nuclear plants as a relatively low-cost option.

power presents something of a social gamble: the possibility of accidents generating either a small or very large number of fatalities.

Recall that in Chapter 17 we learned that sulfate pollution from coal-fired power plants may be responsible for as many as 50,000 premature deaths *each year*. Comparing worst cases on a risk-assessment basis, nuclear power production currently stacks up favorably compared to coal. Bear in mind, though, that improved coal technologies as well as the 1990 Clean Air Act are expected to cut sulfate emissions substantially. In addition, risks to those living close to a nuclear power plant will be higher, perhaps explaining intense local opposition to siting.

Moreover, a risk assessment looks only at the relative probability of death, without assessing the magnitude of the potential disaster—whole communities destroyed overnight. As we noted in Chapter 8, people will buy insurance to avoid very risky situations that occur with low probability. Stronger opposition to nuclear power facilities may, thus, reflect simple risk aversion.

Finally, public distrust of scientific risk assessment in the nuclear field—whether by government or industry officials—is very high. (Witness *The Simpsons!*) In part, this is due to the widespread perception that the Nuclear Regulatory Commission (NRC), which enforces safety standards for nuclear power, has been captured by the industry.[2] In part, it is due to uncertainty in the science. Official estimates of "safe" exposure to radiation have been repeatedly lowered (Ottinger et al. 1990, 370).

The other major environmental issue facing the nuclear industry is waste disposal.[3] Nuclear waste is divided into two categories: high-level and low-level waste. **High-level waste** consists of spent fuel rods and waste from weapons production; it remains toxic for hundreds of thousands of years. **Low-level waste** includes contaminated clothing and equipment from nuclear power plants and defense establishments, and wastes from medical and pharmaceutical facilities. Nuclear power accounts for about 80% of the radioactivity found in low-level civilian waste. The radioactive elements in most low-level waste decay to levels the NRC considers harmless within one hundred years, although about 3% of this waste needs to be isolated for longer periods (Office of Technology Assessment).

Currently, there are no operating permanent waste storage facilities for high-level waste in the United States, although a facility for defense waste is being built in Carlsbad, New Mexico, and one is planned for civilian waste at Yucca Mountain in Nevada. However, public opinion polls in Nevada put opposition to the plant at 4 to 1. The Bush administration and Congress endorsed the site in 2002. After the DOE files for a construction permit, which is not expected before December 2004, the Nuclear Regulatory Commission (NRC) will have four years to rule on the repository's future. With the NRC's sanction, the DOE can begin construction (Nadis 2003).

There are currently three commercial waste facilities for low-level waste, although these sites are increasingly reluctant to accept out-of-state waste. In 1985

---

[2]Flavin (1987, 44) quotes "dissident" NRC commissioner James Asseltine as saying, "This commission believes its job is to protect the industry and not the public. . . . There's a misplaced sense of optimism, even to the point of ignoring the messages we're getting from the operating experiences of the plants."

[3]Other issues include worker safety, both for uranium miners and plant operators, as well as problems associated with decommissioning old plants. See Ottinger et al. (1990).

Congress directed each state to come up with a site for disposing of its low-level waste. However, the law was ruled unconstitutional by the Supreme Court in 1992, putting the ball back into the hands of the federal government and electric utilities ("High Court" 1992). As a result of the unresolved storage question, both high- and low-level waste have been piling up in temporary facilities at commercial power plants and government installations. Regardless of the future of nuclear power, solving the waste disposal problem should be a major environmental priority.

The main waste disposal options are burial in geologically stable formations or above-ground storage. Given the extraordinarily long-term nature of the waste's toxicity, the scientific community is divided on the safety of various permanent waste disposal options.[4] Regardless of the technical issues at stake, however, political opposition to the siting of waste facilities has essentially put a brake on nuclear power. Solving the disposal problems—technical and political—for existing waste is essential before we move on to produce more of it.

Unlike most other energy sources, production of nuclear power inherently requires ongoing government involvement. First, the possibility of nuclear terrorism has meant that government must closely monitor shipments of fuel and waste. Some nuclear supporters even envision the need for an international solution to the waste problem to avoid nuclear terrorism (Hafele 1990). Second, the need for intense regulation of reactor safety has led to extensive bureaucratic involvement in reactor design, operation, and maintenance. Finally, public opposition to siting, as well as the long-lived nature of waste, has meant that government has taken over the responsibility for trying to solve the disposal problem.

Nuclear power is a significant player in the energy field today as a result of ongoing government support. As we will see in our discussion of subsidy policy, nuclear power in the United States has been aggressively supported by government funds. In France, the country with the world's biggest commitment to nuclear power, the industry is state-owned and heavily subsidized (Flavin 1987).

Yet this remains nuclear power's principal advantage—thanks to the substantial investment of public funds it is today a proven source of large-scale electricity production, albeit somewhat expensive. Nuclear's best hope in the United States is that global warming quickly proves itself to be a serious environmental threat, requiring an immediate reduction in coal-fired power production. Only then will intense local opposition to facility siting, leading to construction delays and high costs, have a significant chance of being overcome.

Natural gas, composed primarily of methane, is the cleanest of fossil fuels: It has a low-sulfur content and yields about 70% more energy for each unit of CO_2 emitted than does coal. As a result, it is likely to increase its share of the electric power and heating markets over the next few years. However, from an economic point of view, natural gas has two primary drawbacks—a supply that is relatively small and unevenly distributed geographically. If natural gas were to be substituted for coal in all applications, the world's supply of known and estimated undiscovered reserves might be

---

[4]Carter (1987) argues that from a technical point of view, waste management is probably the least risky aspect of nuclear power. He provides an overview of the debate.

exhausted in as little as fifty-five years. Any major shift to natural gas in the United States would also increase dependence on foreign suppliers. Both of these factors mean that the price of natural gas is likely both to be volatile and to rise over time (Fulkerson, Judkins, and Sanghvi 1990).

In addition, methane itself is a greenhouse gas. Thus, if a switch from coal to natural gas is undertaken to avoid global warming, careful controls must be implemented to prevent the release of methane into the atmosphere during production or transport. This, too, will raise the price of energy generated by natural gas.

The final major energy category is renewables: primarily hydroelectric, solar, and wind energy.[5] **Hydroelectric power** currently contributes about 10% of the nation's electricity. About half of the nation's potential hydro sites have been developed. Although, from a pollution perspective, hydroelectric energy is relatively clean, dam projects can have significant environmental impacts, ranging from the flooding of ecologically valuable lands to negative impacts on aquatic life, such as salmon.

Solar energy is divided into two categories: **active solar,** which produces electric power (and heat as a by-product), and **passive solar,** which produces heat. The major use of passive solar is for heating water for direct use, but it can also be used to heat and cool homes.

The two principal active solar technologies are **photovoltaic** power, produced directly from solar cells, and **solar thermal** power, produced by focusing the sun's energy to heat a fluid, which is then used to create electricity. Although commercial solar thermal plants in California today deliver power at less than $0.10 per kWh, solar thermal is limited to sunny climates. However, for such areas, including much of the developing world, solar thermal has substantial potential.

Photovoltaic cells (PVs) potentially face no such geographic limitations. In fact, one of the first widespread applications of PVs is expected to be in the Northeast, where it costs utilities about $0.20 per kWh to service peak summertime demand. Commercial applications of PVs are currently concentrated in remote areas where hookup to conventional power systems is expensive. Although PV costs in the early 2000s were high, at about $0.20 per kWh, a history of very rapid technological progress provides optimism that PVs will be cost-competitive as a major baseload technology within the next ten to twenty years.

Today's new PV plants produce 25 MW of solar cells per year. One recent analysis suggests that the construction of larger plants will bring significant economies of scale: In a 500 MW plant, costs could fall by 70% or more, making solar a competitive option for household electricity generation in European markets.[6]

Photovoltaic systems are very low-risk projects: Fuel sources are assured at a constant (zero) price, and there is no danger of increased environmental regulation in the future. For this reason, Lotker (1991) argues that utilities should require a lower rate of return from solar projects than others. The discount rate used to evaluate a PV project matters, because PV systems have very high up-front investment costs and very low operating and maintenance costs.

---

[5]Other renewable sources of energy with less near-term economic potential include geothermal, tidal, and wood.

[6]The study was done by the international consulting firm KPMG for GreenPeace, Netherlands (KPMG 2000).

PVs hold out the lure of clean, low-cost power. (Most of the negative environmental effects of PVs can be traced to the manufacture of silicon chips.)[7] PV supporters envision a decentralized power system, with PV roofing tiles producing independent power for each household. Low-cost PVs would certainly be one important link in the technological chain necessary to promote sustainable development in poor countries.

The most promising renewable electric technology is **wind power.** In 2002, global installed capacity was about 31,000 MW, equivalent roughly to twenty-one nuclear power plants. One of the world's largest wind farms opened in 1999 in Lake Benton, Minnesota; it was producing power for $0.045 per kWh.[8]

The major economic obstacle to wind energy is site evaluation; customized wind analysis must be performed prior to locating a wind farm. The major environmental impact is noise and aesthetics, though the former problem has been reduced in modern designs. (In spite of a common belief that wind farms are dangerous to birds, avian mortality has been quite low at most sites.) Twelve states, mostly in the Midwest, contain 90% of the nation's wind potential (Weinberg and Williams 1990).

While in theory, wind production could satisfy all U.S. electricity needs, in practice, there is one major obstacle: storage and transport. Both wind and active solar technologies produce power on an intermittent basis when the wind blows or the sun shines. Thus, effective long-run development of these resources will require **storage.** The current solution is to use the electricity grid; PV and wind power now supply electricity to the existing system for distribution. However, because electricity is lost in the transmission process, grid storage and transport are limited. A variety of technologies are being explored, primarily improved batteries. Other options include using electricity to pump water behind a dam, compress air, or create hydrogen, all to be used for future power production.[9]

20.3 Policy Options: Electricity and Heat

Given these different energy technologies, how should we as a nation proceed? Chapter 16 provided a three-part approach for evaluating decisions like this:

1. Pick the clean, low-cost technology.
2. Increase CT profitability by eliminating subsidies and/or internalizing social costs for competitor technologies, preferably through IB regulation.
3. Promote the technology directly.

STEP 1—PICKING WINNERS

On the environmental scale, efficiency comes in first, wind power second, solar power third, natural gas fourth, with nuclear power and coal vying for last place. Ranked in terms of current costs, efficiency measures appear cheapest, with natural gas second, wind power third, new coal plants fourth, nuclear fifth, and solar last. However,

---

[7]See Ottinger et al. (1990) for a discussion of the environmental impact of photovoltaics.

[8]"1999 Is Best Year Ever for Global Wind Energy Industry," American Wind Energy Web site, www.awea.org. Power from Lake Benton was actually sold at $0.03 per kWh, since it benefits from the federal tax credit of 1.5 cents per kWh.

[9]See Zweibel (1990) for a further discussion. Storage technologies will reduce the cost of fossil electric power as well, since inexpensive power could be produced at night and sold during times of peak demand. Thus, storage R&D is likely to proceed independent of renewable development.

ranked in terms of feasible, long-run average costs, photovoltaics have a reasonable shot at being competitive with coal.

The low-hanging fruit in this case are clearly efficiency and wind power; photovoltaics, though risky, present a good bet.[10] Is there a case for aggressive promotion of nuclear? Probably not at this point. While nuclear plants can undoubtedly be made safer, few feel that nuclear costs in the United States can be substantially reduced below their current range of more than $0.12 per kWh and still provide a politically acceptable margin of safety.[11] Efficiency, wind, and photovoltaics offer a more feasible, cleaner, and cheaper option to fossil fuels than nuclear.

STEP 2—LEVEL THE PLAYING FIELD

The current U.S. energy market is far from the ideal of a free market; government intervention is widespread through both regulation and subsidy. For 1989, the latest year for which comprehensive estimates have been made, Koplow (1993) calculated that federal subsidies ranged from a high of $36 billion to a low of $21 billion.[12] The author identified two main categories of subsidies: tax breaks and expenditures supporting industry by federal agencies.

To provide a feel for the type of expenditure undertaken by government agencies, Table 20.1 details the agencies involved in supporting just the exploration phase of oil production. One of the biggest agency subsidies to the oil industry, not quantified in the Koplow report, is spending by the military to protect Persian Gulf oil fields. Hall (1992) estimated that annual defense spending to protect oil imports was $14.8 billion. Hall's estimate did not include the costs of the two Gulf wars.

Who wins and who loses from the federal subsidies? Table 20.2 and Figure 20.4 break down the subsidies between the major energy sources. Efficiency and non-hydro renewables, the two clean technologies identified above, receive only 5.4% of the total. The major beneficiaries of subsidy policies are clearly the conventional fuel sources—nuclear and fossil fuels received 88.5% of all energy subsidies.

The fact that coal, oil, and fission (nuclear) technologies receive the bulk of subsidies is not surprising; they also supply the bulk of the country's power (and have important political constituencies). In addition, if global warming proves to be less serious than currently thought, coal will likely remain our major electric fuel. Thus, R&D to support reducing conventional pollutants from coal plants is certainly reasonable. However, even on an energy-adjusted basis, coal and nuclear fission received the highest subsidies calculable, with efficiency coming in last (Koplow 1993, Table 11).

This discussion of subsidy policy highlights two points. First, energy markets are not free markets; government intervention to promote technologies has been and continues

---

[10]Hydro and solar thermal electricity are also attractive technologies on economic and environmental grounds. However, they have somewhat limited long-run potential in the United States.

[11]Regarding costs, see footnote 5. On the safety issue, see "A Comeback for Nuclear Power?" *National Geographic,* August 1991, as well as Office of Technology Assessment (1990).

[12]The high-end estimate measures the value of the subsidy to industry; the low end measures the accounting cost to government. To illustrate why the two may vary, suppose a government agency provides $1,000 in free services to a company. A company paying a 30% corporate income tax would have to earn $1,300 to purchase equivalent services in the marketplace. Of course, the opportunity cost to government is in fact $1,300, since it loses the $300 in tax revenue by subsidizing the company's activity. High- and low-end estimates also incorporate other uncertainties. See Koplow (1993) for further elaboration.

to be substantial. Thus, our current energy mix, in which coal dominates, is not a "natural" outcome of market forces. Coal has received tremendous federal subsidies, including large R&D expenditures, to develop cleaner coal technologies, which have allowed the industry to expand. Second, federal policy currently tilts the playing field heavily

TABLE 20.1   Federal Agency Subsidies for Oil Exploration

Support Activity	Agency Involvement
Procurement	U.S. Geological Survey, National Oceanic and Atmospheric Administration, and Bureau of Indian Affairs all provide survey, mapping, and development support.
Technological development	Department of Energy finances R&D on oil extraction.
Industry infrastructure	Bureau of Land Management provides low-cost access to leases.
Risk reduction	Fish and Wildlife Service conducts environmental impact assessment of Arctic drilling.

Source: Koplow. *Federal Energy Subsidies: Energy, Environmental and Fiscal Impacts.* Washington, DC: Alliance to Save Energy, 1993, p. 46, Appendix A-2. Used with permission.

TABLE 20.2   Federal Energy Subsidies by Sector, 1989[a]

Energy Source	Subsidy Level (1989 $Million)	Percent of Total Subsidy
Fossil	17,125	59.8
Coal	6,800	23.7
Oil	7,114	24.8
Natural gas	3,212	11.2
Mixed oil and gas	0	0.0
Nuclear	8,223	28.7
Fission	7,809	27.3
Fusion	414	1.4
Hydroelectric	500	1.7
Emerging renewables	769	2.7
Nonethanol biomass	321	1.1
Solar	167	0.6
Wind	51	0.2
Geothermal	206	0.7
Other	24	0.1
Other supply sources	1,260	4.4
Ethanol	707	2.5
Waste to energy	339	1.2
Mixed supply	46	0.2
Supply efficiency	169	0.6
Demand-side efficiency	775	2.7
Total	28,652	100.0

[a]These are the mid-range estimates calculated from Koplow (1993, Table 6). See footnote 12 for a more detailed discussion of Koplow's "high" and "low" estimation methodology.

Source: Koplow. *Federal Energy Subsidies: Energy, Environmental and Fiscal Impacts.* Washington, DC: Alliance to Save Energy, 1993, p. 16. Used with permission.

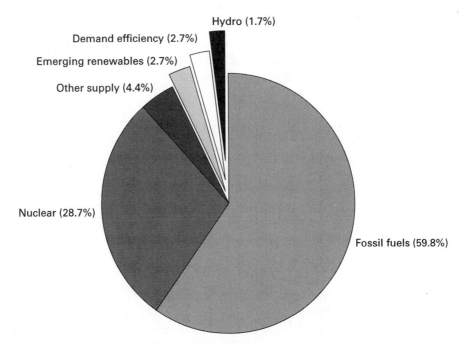

FIGURE 20.4 Federal Energy Subsidies by Sector, 1989

Source: Data taken from Koplow. *Federal Energy Subsidies: Energy, Environmental and Fiscal Impacts.*
Washington, DC: Alliance to Save Energy, 1993, p. 16.

against renewables and energy efficiency. The government's substantial support of conventional technology works against market penetration of inherently clean alternatives.

Reducing the subsidies for conventional options, or at least leveling the playing field by boosting subsidies for clean technologies, is necessary for their promotion. What about internalizing externalities associated with conventional fuels? The major externalities associated with fossil fuels used for heat and electricity are urban air pollution, acid rain, and global warming. Regulations covering the first two have recently been tightened under the Clean Air Act of 1990.

A tax on the carbon content of fuels has been widely discussed as a means of combating global warming. A carbon tax of between $50 and $100 per ton is thought to be sufficient to reduce emissions to below 1990 levels; such a tax would raise the price of oil and coal between 45% and 90% and natural gas between 25% and 50% (Pearce 1991). While such a tax is unlikely in the near term, it would certainly hasten the development of clean alternatives.

Nuclear advocates often maintain that, on safety grounds, the industry is over-regulated, which explains its cost disadvantage. Yet given public opposition to facility siting, regulation may well need to tighten if new nuclear facilities are built. Realistic assessments of waste disposal costs and decommissioning expenses (no one has yet disposed of an abandoned nuclear facility) should also be built into cost per kWh estimates for any new facilities.

STEP 3—DIRECT PROMOTION OF CTS

Here we will proceed by example, considering government policy to directly promote small-scale (energy efficiency) and large-scale (solar) technologies. The basic message is that, to avoid waste and counterproductive incentives as well as to insure equity, subsidies should be carefully targeted. Begin with a

PUZZLE

Suppose that Octopus Power is considering providing a weatherization service to about a quarter of its customers "free of charge." Why? Because, by reducing energy demand, it will be able to avoid building a new power plant. However, since there is no such thing as a free lunch, the utility will pay for the weatherization by charging higher electricity rates for all its customers. Is the weatherization subsidy a good idea?

SOLUTION

Probably not. The problems with the plan highlight a variety of pitfalls facing all efforts to promote energy efficiency: These include equity issues, strategic behavior, free riding, and rebound effects.

Here is the **equity issue.** By providing the weatherization service free of charge, Octopus would provide dramatic benefits to a quarter of its clients at the expense of the rest. While the company and ratepayers will save money in total, most of Octopus's clients will be worse off than if the power plant were built.

Another possible problem is **strategic behavior;** by subsidizing one portion of the population, Octopus may inadvertently discourage others from weatherizing on their own. This group may hold back until more subsidies become available. Octopus may also be paying more than it needs to for conservation due to the potential for **free riding;** some who would have otherwise weatherized on their own may take advantage of the subsidy.

Finally, there is the problem of **rebound effects.** Because electric bills for weatherized homes are now lower, residents will spend some of their increased income on keeping their house warmer or buying new appliances, which uses more electricity. The size of the rebound effect in the electricity field is the subject of current debate.[13]

An alternative plan helps resolve all these issues: Have the residents whose buildings are weatherized pay the bill. Consider a house with pre-weatherization electricity use of 12,000 kWh per year; weatherization reduces it to 10,000 kWh. The residents could thus afford a substantial rate increase (from $0.05 up to $0.06 per kWh for example) and still come out with the same overall electricity bill ($0.06 per kWh * 10,000 kWh = $600; $0.05 per kWh * 12,000 kWh = $600).

If energy-efficiency measures are truly cost-effective, then in theory it will always be possible to design a financing mechanism by which *the recipient ultimately pays* for

[13]Hobbs (1991) develops a "most-value" test, which incorporates all these factors for determining when DSM measures are efficient. He also discusses the rebound issue. On this point, see also Geller et al. (1992).

a substantial portion of the service *and still comes out ahead.* That is, cost-effective efficiency investments can be designed to generate something close to a Pareto improving situation.

In practice, the government or utility ratepayers at large may still need to absorb the risk and marketing costs necessary to overcome poor information and access to capital on the part of its clientele. For example, one utility found that requiring participants to pay for insulation to cover hot-water heaters, *even though the clients would save money at zero risk,* reduced program participation substantially. Lowered participation, in turn, increased the cost per kWh saved by 350% due to scale economies in operating the program.[14]

Yet, *minimizing* the subsidy level by requiring recipients to pay at least a portion of the cost will reduce problems of inequity, strategic behavior, free riding, and rebound effects. This general rule will be true for any subsidy policy designed to encourage small-scale CTs.

Efforts to promote large-scale solar power through subsidies should be crafted with a similar eye toward the potential for waste. In the photovoltaic field, the challenge is to reduce PV costs. As discussed in Chapter 18, there are essentially two ways to do this: (1) Develop better technology through R&D and (2) capture cost savings through economies of scale and learning by doing. In the early 1980s, government policy makers prematurely took the latter route, funding flashy but uneconomic solar demonstration projects at the expense of basic R&D. At the same time, tax credits for the purchase of solar units were instituted to encourage the purchase of PVs; however, because PV was still not a competitive technology, when the credits expired in 1986, the PV market collapsed (see Walton and Hall 1990 and Zweibel 1990).

By the late 1990s, the United States government began to promote cost reductions by stimulating PV markets. President Clinton proposed a seven-year, $193 million dollar package, in which purchasers could credit the first 15% of rooftop PV array, with a cap of $2000. Such programs have been successful in the past in encouraging the adoption of solar technology. However, they are relatively expensive (since they are not targeted) and run the danger of subsidizing obsolete technology.[15] In an analysis of the tax credit proposal, Hoerner and Gilbert (1999) argue that while it passes a benefit–cost test, the credit package alone would not be sufficient to drive cost reductions big enough to allow PV to achieve mass market penetration.

Photovoltaic power is so attractive that, in the long run, it is likely to be developed by private industry regardless of U.S. government policy. The question really is when and by whom? Path dependence theory tells us that, if PV arrives later rather than sooner, in the interim, we will continue to invest in long-lived infrastructure to support our fossil fuel economy. Thus, attempts to capture environmental benefits through a transition to PV will become more difficult. The "who" question is also important from an economic point of view. Our European and Asian competitors are

[14]This example is cited in Hobbs (1991). One way to boost participation rates would be to penalize nonparticipants by charging them extra for the energy they refused to save. See Katz (1989).
[15]Durham et al. (1988) find that state tax credits significantly increased the rate of adoption of solar water heaters.

currently showing the most interest in photovoltaics—not surprising, given their higher energy costs. This is in spite of the fact that most of the important basic PV research has been done in America.

To summarize this subsection: CT-promoting subsidies need to be carefully tailored. Consumer subsidies need to minimize pitfalls such as equity problems, strategic behavior, rebound effects, and free riding. Subsidies targeted at large-scale technologies should strike an appropriate balance between research and development and market building.

20.4 Technology Options: Transport

Our transportation system relies almost exclusively on oil and accounts for the bulk of petroleum use. The United States currently consumes about 17 million barrels of oil (about 3 gallons per person) per day, about 45% imported. Close to 26% of U.S. imports come from the Persian Gulf, a figure likely to rise in coming years. The Organization of Petroleum Exporting Countries (OPEC), whose members are primarily Middle Eastern nations, control three quarters of the world's proven oil reserves.

The social costs of oil use fall into three categories: (1) taxpayer subsidies (discussed in Section 20.3), (2) environmental externalities, and (3) energy security. In developed countries, motor vehicles are a major source of urban air pollution, accounting for half of the nitrogen oxide (NOx) and volatile organic compound (VOC) emissions, and nearly two thirds of the carbon monoxide (CO) emissions. (Recall from Chapter 13 that nitrogen oxide causes airborne acid pollution and, in combination with VOCs, ground-level ozone. CO reduces the oxygen content of the blood.) While autos contribute to local pollution problems, they are also a major source of carbon dioxide, the principal greenhouse gas. Worldwide transportation accounts for 14% of CO_2 emissions from fossil fuels, and this figure rises to 35% in the United States (MacKenzie and Walsh 1992; Hoerner and Gilbert 1999).

The **energy security** issue arises from the impact that dramatic oil price swings have had on the U.S. economy over the last twenty years. Oil price shocks, the latest from the Persian Gulf War, have been associated with and have deepened our last three economic recessions. In addition, such price shocks substantially boost inflation. Estimates of the economic costs of dependence on oil have ranged from $1 to $20 a barrel (Greene and Duleep 1992).

Related to the energy security issue is the fact that high U.S. demand (about 25% of world consumption) for oil props up the price. As a result of our major presence in the market, we have what economists call **monopsony power** over the price; a unilateral cut in U.S. demand would lower oil prices around the world. Greene and Duleep (1992) estimate that a decline in U.S. demand of 1 million barrels per day would translate into a price drop of between $0.45 and $0.80 per barrel of oil.

Unlike the case for electricity and heat, few clean technologies as defined in Chapter 18 appear in the transport field. All options that offer environmental improvements over oil come at some price, either in private costs or convenience. However, because of the social costs associated with petroleum use, an economic case can certainly be made for promoting alternative technologies.

The major technology options can be divided into two categories. The first includes those options compatible with continued reliance on private auto transportation: increased fuel efficiency and switching to cleaner fuels. The second involves a switch to alternative transportation modes: urban mass transit, intercity and long-haul rail, car pooling, and even bicycling and walking.

FUEL EFFICIENCY

Of all the options, increased fuel efficiency comes closest to being a simple Clean Technology as defined in Chapter 18. In the late 1990s, Japanese automakers began to introduce so-called **hybrid vehicles.** Hybrids run on batteries in the city, and on gasoline engines on the highway. The batteries recharge while the vehicles are running on gas, so there is no need to plug the car in at night. These vehicles get between 40 and 70 mpg, twice the fuel efficiency of conventional vehicles. Do they save the consumer money? In 2000, a four-door Toyota Prius sedan could be purchased for about $2,000 more than a comparable conventional vehicle. The Prius also has about a 20 mpg advantage. With gas at $1.50 per gallon, the average consumer would save about $250 per year—an eight-year payback period. Ford and GM are expected to release hybrid models in 2004.

More radical efficiency gains are imaginable; Amory Lovins (1995) of the Rocky Mountain Institute has been an advocate of ultralight, aerodynamic vehicles he calls "hypercars." He argues that complete redesign and re-engineering—rather than the marginal modifications now pursued by automakers—could boost fuel efficiency by a factor of 10, with no compromise in safety or performance.

Safety and performance have indeed been the major concerns raised about fuel-efficient cars. One way to achieve better fuel performance is through "downsizing"—building smaller, lighter cars. However, in the past, lighter cars have proven less safe in a collision with a heavier vehicle. Based on these factors, a National Academy of Sciences panel concluded (with some dissent) that the fleet downsizing between 1975 and 1990 led to an increase of perhaps 2,000 traffic fatalities per year in the early 1990s.

Critics have charged that this is a substantial overestimate, since it fails to take into account that smaller cars pose less danger to others, as well as the fact that the disparities between car sizes—another factor in accidents—shrank as the fleet downsized through 1990. (Of course, disparities grew dramatically again in the 1990s with the SUV fad; and SUVs themselves face safety concerns relating to rollovers.) Moreover, small cars have become safer in recent years, as engineers have focused increasing attention on crash problems, and new, high-strength, lightweight materials have been developed. The true impact on safety of increased fuel performance could, in fact, be zero. Nevertheless, to the extent that fuel efficiency is achieved through downsizing, there is likely to be some safety impact (Office of Technology Assessment 1991; Greene and Duleep 1992; National Academy of Sciences 2002). In addition, American consumers have a taste for many energy-intensive features: large size, four-wheel drive, rapid acceleration. Increased fuel efficiency may require giving some of this back.

In addition to safety and performance concerns associated with improved fuel economy, increased fuel efficiency in the long run can be swamped by other factors. The first is increased driving. Total **vehicle miles travelled** increased at a rapid rate of 3.3% per year between 1970 and 1988; by the late 1990s they were still growing at a rate of 1.6%. Over the 1970 to 1988 period, miles per vehicle traveled rose from 10,000 to more than 11,500; total miles rose even faster as the number of cars per family increased.

There is also the possibility of a rebound effect—better fuel efficiency will lead to savings, some of which will be spent on increased driving. Estimates of the rebound effect in auto transport are in the 10% range. Finally, American drivers have been shifting from cars to light trucks and SUVs, which get much poorer mileage. As a result of all these factors, during the period in which the fuel efficiency of the *auto* fleet increased by about one-third—1970 to 1988—total U.S. fuel consumption by cars, trucks, and busses still grew by 40% (MacKenzie and Walsh 1992; Office of Technology Assessment 1991; Greene and Duleep 1992; Hoerner and Gilbert 1999).

FUEL SWITCHING

The second transport option is fuel switching. Because of concerns about global warming, most observers of the auto industry see a medium term transition away from an internal combustion engine to **fuel cells.** You may remember from a high school physics experiment that if you run electricity through water, it splits the molecules into hydrogen and oxygen. Fuel cells do the reverse. They combine hydrogen and oxygen in the presence of a catalyst to produce electricity; the only immediate by-product is water vapor!

In the short term, fuel cell vehicles will be powered either by liquid fuels (gasoline or ethanol derived from biomass) or by natural gas. These fuels will be converted on-board into hydrogen. In the longer run, car tanks are likely to get filled up directly with hydrogen gas. This may sound dangerous, but because hydrogen vents quickly, in the event of a crash, hydrogen vehicles will be less likely to explode than gasoline powered ones. If the hydrogen gas were to be produced using renewable energy (electric current from wind, solar or biomass run through water) *fossil fuel combustion and pollution would be eliminated completely* from the transport sector.

Fuel cells are used in a few metropolitan bus systems; they are currently too expensive for private vehicles. However, all the major auto companies are pursuing fuel cell research. Limited commercial release of fuel cell vehicles by Honda and DaimlerChrysler is slated to begin in 2004, but the vehicles remain quite expensive (see www.fueleconomy.gov).

A final fuel switching option is to use electricity from battery-powered cars. A precondition for **electric vehicles** to make global environmental sense is the development of clean electricity. Otherwise, use of electric vehicles will result in little overall reduction in pollutants. Moreover, there is concern that the use of lead-based batteries will generate significant environmental problems.

However, because they have essentially zero on-site emissions, cars powered by batteries charged from coal, oil-fired, or nuclear plants could be used to improve urban air quality. In effect, the air pollution could be exported from the city to the vicinity of the electric generating facility.

Estimates of the potential cost-competitiveness of battery-powered cars range widely. Electric cars will cost more than conventional vehicles but have lower maintenance and fuel costs and last longer. The biggest concern is performance. Electric vehicles produced to date have relatively short cruising ranges, although this problem has been side-stepped via the use of hybrid engines discussed in the last section. Given their short range, non-hybrid electric vehicles will see their first widespread use as urban commuting vehicles, provided that improvements in battery technology are forthcoming.

MODE SWITCHING

Urban mass transit—rail or bus—has considerable environmental advantages over private transport. First, because these options are more energy-efficient, they reduce both local and global air pollution problems. For example, a busload of 40 commuters on a 10-mile trip to work emit 1,140 pounds less of carbon dioxide than if they had driven their cars to work (MacKenzie and Walsh 1992).

In addition to increased efficiency for a given passenger-mile-traveled, mass transit helps slow the growth in total miles traveled. Holtzclaw (1991) estimates that cities with well-developed mass transit systems experience substantially lower rates of miles traveled per person. In a comparison of two San Francisco suburbs with similar histories, households living in the neighborhood served by transit since 1975 traveled only two-thirds as many miles by car in 1988; one mile on the transit system appeared to reduce total vehicle miles traveled by four. In other words, even when people used their cars, they traveled shorter distances, because the greater residential and retail densities that developed along with the mass transit system reduced the need for auto travel.

America's high reliance on private auto transport clearly illustrates the importance of **path dependence** in technological development, discussed in Chapter 18. Why do some cities depend heavily on cars while others have well-developed transit systems? Adler (1991) describes a twenty-year political battle over transport options beginning in Los Angeles in the late 1920s. Downtown business interests favored an electric rail system to funnel shoppers into the central city; outlying business interests argued for freeways. Ultimately, the latter group triumphed and, in the late 1940s, the state and federal government began a massive spending program to construct the highway system that has subsequently shaped southern California. Without *comparable* governmental support, the mass transit system in the area collapsed.

By contrast, Toronto has North America's best public transportation system. Here, central city interests triumphed in municipal government; a key victory involved the defeat of a major freeway project in 1971. The Toronto city government has also kept mass transit a viable long-run option through zoning laws. These encourage relatively dense residential neighborhoods, as well as business development, in the area of mass transit stations (Friskin 1991).

However, the dominance of private auto transport is not based solely on accidents of history. Cars clearly have an edge in convenience and greater mobility. Thus, as incomes have risen in developed countries, people have tended to opt for auto travel. The decline of mass transit has occurred in spite of the fact that in the United States private transport—including vehicle purchase, finance charges, insurance, and fuel—costs the average commuter about twice as much as using public transport (Friskin 1991; Lowe 1991).

The suburban sprawl that now characterizes most American cities means that private transport is a virtual necessity for shopping, getting to work and school, and for recreation. In addition, many residents of developed countries have shown an evident preference for auto travel. Thus, any rapid switch to mass transit will be difficult. Nevertheless, given the potential environmental benefits from mass transit—greater efficiency and reduced passenger-miles traveled—a gradual transition to this mode could be promoted where economically feasible.

A more attractive short-run form of mode switching may involve inter-urban travel; roughly one third of air travel involves trips of fewer than 600 miles. **High-speed rail** is a potentially attractive alternative for this market in terms of convenience and cost. From an environmental perspective, rail can use as little as one-third the energy that air travel uses (Geller et al. 1992).

20.5 Policy Options: Transport

What is the case against petroleum-based automobile transport? The primary concerns are urban air pollution, global warming, and energy security. To this list, we should add congestion, oil spills, and oil drilling in sensitive habitat. What kind of a technology promotion response do these externalities justify?

POLICY OPTIONS FOR FUEL EFFICIENCY AND FUEL SWITCHING

Fuel efficiency appears to be closest to a CT. In fact, under a variety of scenarios, achieving greater fuel efficiency standards through technology-forcing regulation passes a benefit–cost test. In 2002, the National Academy of Sciences (2002) concluded that, using known technologies, fuel economy could be raised substantially over the next decade at no net cost to consumers. SUV mileage, for example, could be improved by 25% to 40%, with the increased vehicle costs more than offset by the (discounted) fuel savings. Moreover, the Academy agreed that these improvements could be achieved with no compromise in safety or performance. Taking into account the external benefits from both reduced greenhouse gas emissions and increased oil security, the committe recommended that "the federal goverment [take action] to ensure fuel economy levels beyond those expected to result from market forces alone" (5).

Having argued that tighter CAFE standards could probably be justified on efficiency grounds, is there a better way to achieve fuel efficiency? Several types of emission-related fees might be considered: gas taxes, "feebates," emission taxes, and the adoption of pay-by-the mile auto insurance. **Gas taxes** have the advantage of simultaneously forcing fuel-efficiency improvements and attacking the growth in vehicle miles. CAFE standards, by contrast, probably increase the growth in vehicle miles through the rebound effect.

The problem with gas taxes is that they would have to be very high to force efficiency improvements on the order of 10 mpg, a 30% to 35% increase over the current level of 28 mpg. As casual evidence, European cars are about as efficient as American cars of a similar size though gas prices are at least double and in some cases are four times as high. Greene (1990) estimates a maximum price elasticity of mpg of 0.21, meaning that a 1% increase in price leads to a 0.21% increase in fuel economy. This suggests that prices would have to rise from $1.36 per gallon to $2.15 per gallon to achieve only a 10% increase in mpg.[16]

Several other fee-based approaches to encourage fuel efficiency and switching have been proposed. One interesting possibility is an **auto emissions tax.** When cars go in for their annual inspection, owners could be required to pay a tax based on their total emissions: the product of emissions per mile and yearly mileage. This would have the effect both of encouraging cleaner fuels (based on market criteria) and reducing miles driven.[17] The tax could be tailored to suit regional needs.

Another widely discussed possibility has earned the nickname **feebates.** Feebates combine a fee on gas-guzzling cars with a rebate on fuel-efficient cars. A feebate policy would thus be revenue-neutral in an obvious way, have the politically attractive feature of punishing evildoers and rewarding the good, and probably not be regressive, since poor folks would opt for the subsidy. Davis (1991) estimated that a feebate proposal in California, DRIVE+, would achieve about a 10% reduction in both emissions and fuel use. The United States currently does have a gas-guzzler tax on vehicles achieving less than 22.5 mpg, though no rebates (MacKenzie and Walsh 1992).

Feebates appear to be a better alternative to high gas taxes for encouraging a market-driven shift to fuel efficiency. However, by lowering the cost of fuel-efficient automobiles, feebates might increase the growth in vehicle miles. In addition, setting the right feebate schedule to get precisely a 10 mpg increase in fuel efficiency would require some experimentation.

A final suggestion has been reforming auto insurance so as to provide a **pay-by-the-mile** option. Auto insurance is quite expensive, but is currently paid in a lump sum. Yet this unfairly penalizes drivers who are on the road less frequently. If accident rates correlate with miles driven, then people who drive less should have lower payments. Billing could be based on odometer checks or electronic monitoring of miles driven. Converting an annual insurance bill to a per mile basis works out to an equivalent charge of about $1.50 per gallon of gas—certainly a big enough charge to affect people's driving habits! Baker and Barret (2000) estimate that this would reduce miles traveled by 10% to 20%, and suggest that a very small tax credit of $100 per year would be sufficient to start a stampede in the direction of pay-by-the-mile insurance on the part of low-mileage drivers.

All of these policies—tougher CAFE standards, higher gas taxes, feebates, emission taxes, pay-by-the-mile insurance—would also help promote a switch to cleaner cars: hybrid, electric, and fuel cell vehicles. However none of these policies are currently in effect. In their absence, however, another approach has been quite effective at generating auto industry interest in alternate fueled cars: California's Zero Emission Vehicle **(ZEV)** regulation. To deal with smog problems in southern California, in

---

[16]Greene (1990) also finds that even during the period of rapidly escalating gas prices, the CAFE standards were much more important than gas prices in driving fuel efficiency up.

[17]Collinge and Stevens (1990) discuss such an approach.

the mid-1990s the state instituted a requirement that 10% of all vehicles sold in 2003 must have "zero" (later modified to include "ultra-low") emissions. This means that a car company selling in California must not only produce a qualifying vehicle, but must also price it low enough to satisfy the 10% requirement. Massachusetts and New York have introduced similar policies.

The California requirement, combined with concerns about global warming, has sparked a research race among car companies. The first commercial fruits of this effort have been the Japanese hybrids. To support a competitive American ZEV, the U.S. government created a research program in the mid-1990s called the Partnership for a New Generation of Vehicles. In 1999, the government contributed $250 million in research dollars, matched by $980 million from Ford, GM, and Daimler-Chrysler. And in 2000, Ford produced a prototype hybrid sedan as part of the program. Compared with the Japanese success at getting hybrids to market, the lack of results arising from the partnership have been disappointing (Buntin 2000). In 2001, President Bush cancelled the PNGV program; GM and Ford nevertheless indicated that they would be selling a hybrid vehicle in 2004.

POLICY OPTIONS FOR MODE SWITCHING

Mass transit is often viewed as a highly subsidized, noncompetitive option vis à vis private transport. Indeed, transit does receive substantial government subsidies. The systems in Toronto and New York, for example, cover about two-thirds of their costs through fees, while fares in Seattle recover only 30% of costs (Friskin 1991). Less often recognized is that private auto transport also receives public subsidies that can rival those of transit systems. Table 20.3 provides estimates of some of these subsidies on a per vehicle basis.

The table does not contain estimates of hard-to-measure benefits related to defending Persian Gulf Oil supplies or the external costs of congestion, which would add significantly to the total. Nor does the table include the urban air pollution and greenhouse costs of auto travel. Nevertheless, even omitting these items, private vehicle owners directly cover only about 72% of the measurable costs associated with vehicle use. The rest of the bill is footed by taxpayers or nonauto insurance premiums.

In addition, the marginal cost of constructing new highways can be quite high. Goldstein (1991) compares the capital expenses of the BART system in San Francisco with the costs of a comparable freeway system (including vehicles) and finds that BART was a good buy. Transit systems can win out in terms of the cost-effective delivery of new transport.

As noted above, the primary advantage of transit is the way that it "naturally" reshapes urban and suburban densities. With denser living patterns, transit does much more than simply replace auto trips in and out of the city. It also substantially reduces vehicle transport for shopping and entertainment. At the same time, cities dominated by urban and suburban sprawl have a hard time providing competitive mass transit. Thus, zoning laws are needed to lay the groundwork for a successful transit system.

Most economists have focused on promoting mode switching by removing subsidies for private transport (for example, tax-free, employer-provided parking) and internalizing externalities, particularly those associated with congestion. Congestion

TABLE 20.3   Selected Subsidies for Private Auto Transport

Source of Social Cost	Annual Cost Not Borne by Drivers ($ per car)
Roadway construction	69
Roadway maintenance	42
Highway services (ambulance, fire, police)	360
Parking	589
Accidents (pedestrians, cyclists)	291
Total subsidy per car	1,352
Total private cost per car (fuel, taxes, depreciation, insurance, and so on)	3,820
Subsidy/total cost	0.26

Source: MacKenzie, Dower, and Chen (1992) provide gross subsidy levels. I convert them to a per vehicle basis using figures of 144 million cars (parking) and 188 million total vehicles (other costs) found in *The Statistical Abstract of the United States,* 1991. The figure for private costs, based on 10,000 miles per year, is also obtained from this source.

generates a variety of problems: wasted commuting time, increases in vehicle operating costs, pollution and accident rates, lowered productivity through worker fatigue and stress, and slowed delivery of products. While most of these costs are borne by vehicle travelers as a group, the commuting decision is a classic open access problem (discussed in Chapter 3).

The individual commuter may recognize that, by taking her car to work, she will slow down average traffic by fifteen seconds. This is a small amount of time to her and a cost she is willing to bear. But fifteen seconds times several thousand commuters quickly adds up to large social costs. With each commuter viewing the problem in the same way, the result is a "Tragedy of the Commons" quite similar to an overfished ocean.

With the highways being common property, some kind of rationing system is necessary. One rationing system is price: Many economists have advocated toll systems to internalize congestion externalities. These systems can be quite sophisticated, with sensors in the road bed monitoring passing traffic equipped with electronic identification, and generating monthly bills. One way to attack congestion is **congestion or peak-load pricing:** charging higher tolls for travel during congested hours. However, this may have the effect of shifting work habits and commuting times without reducing overall vehicle use. While this may be useful for reducing certain urban air pollutants, it would not have much impact on greenhouse gases. Congestion pricing would tend also to be regressive unless the funds raised were used to compensate for this problem.

A non-price rationing scheme involves **dedicated traffic lanes.** These lanes are reserved for (or dedicated to) buses and multi-occupant vehicles and effectively lower the price of car pooling or bus travel. Dedicated lanes offer a carrot to those interested in mode switching, which could be combined with the stick of congestion pricing and higher parking fees. In addition, since poorer people tend to take the bus, the overall income impact of dedicated lanes would be progressive.

20.6 Slowing Global Warming at a Profit?

Having provided a review of energy technology choices and policy options, we can now return to an important question posed in the introduction to this book: How much will it cost to slow down and eventually halt global warming? Recall that estimates ranged from a high of tens of billions of dollars per year in costs to possible net profits for the economy from increased efficiency.

Optimists see the government moving in a rational manner to implement cost-effective demand-side measures, while funding R&D in renewable energy sources to bring their costs down to a level competitive with coal and gasoline by early in the twenty-first century. Optimists are not overly concerned about government failure because of the existence of very obvious "low-hanging fruit," especially in the heat and electricity field and possibly in hybrid-electric vehicles for transport. Because they see these governmental demand and supply-side efforts as ultimately delivering energy services at lower cost than the technologies in use today, global warming can actually be reduced while yielding a net economic benefit.

Pessimists, on the other hand, do not believe that government efforts to promote energy efficiency will be very successful. First, they fear that technology-forcing standards (like the CAFE) will generate self-defeating problems such as new source bias, that poorly thought out design standards will retard rather than promote technological change, or that money will simply be wasted by bureaucrats promoting cost-ineffective measures. Second, government must bear the real marketing costs necessary to speed up the slow diffusion of energy-efficient technologies, reducing the net savings. Third, they argue that easy efficiency measures will soon be exhausted, meaning that even a successful, short-term government effort to promote efficiency cannot be sustained. Finally, pessimists tend to feel that renewable energy options do not have the dramatic economic promise that optimists claim.

In spite of their disagreements, however, both optimists and pessimists agree on the general direction that government policy should take to reduce the costs of slowing global warming. First, there should be an increased commitment of government R&D funds to non–carbon-based and renewable energy sources. The earlier that cost-competitive technology alternatives become available, the lower will be the cost of reducing greenhouse gases. As we noted in Chapter 9, early cost savings become especially important over time, because they free up capital for investment, which raises future productivity.[18]

Beyond R&D funding, there is disagreement over whether government should make efforts to promote clean energy sources. However, most economists feel that if it does so, to the extent possible such efforts should rely on an incentive-based approach. Thus, government should not try to sort out whether photovoltaic-powered electric vehicles or biomass-based ethanol fuels will be a cheaper, greenhouse-friendly transportation option and then develop and implement a promotional strategy; the better approach is simply to impose a non-regressive carbon tax on all energy sources and then let the issue be decided in the market. However, as I have stated repeatedly, taxes (or tradeable permit systems) are not always politically feasible or easy to implement;

---

[18]Hogan (1990) also argues that expensive energy may retard the rate of technological progress in the non-energy sector, because such progress in the past has been energy-intensive.

thus, a role will remain for direct promotion of clean technologies in attacking the global warming problem.

20.7 Summary

This chapter ends with a story suggesting two things. First, a more-or-less optimistic outcome to the global warming problem is potentially achievable. Second, major pitfalls need to be avoided along the way.

During the mid-1970s, in the face of the OPEC oil price hikes, the U.S. Congress became concerned about energy security. It took three principal measures: (1) funding substantial R&D in renewable technologies, (2) instituting a 15% tax credit for energy investments, and (3) requiring public utilities to purchase any power produced by qualifying independent facilities at the utility's "avoided" or marginal cost of production.

The state of California took the most aggressive stance toward developing alternative energy sources, instituting its own 25% energy investment tax credit and a property tax exemption for solar facilities, and requiring utilities to provide ten-year, avoided-cost contracts to independent power producers. These contracts were based on the high energy prices of the early 1980s. At the time, they appeared to shield ratepayers from further fuel increases; in retrospect, they protected alternative energy producers from the dramatic decline in oil prices.

This attractive environment fueled a rush of investors, many looking only for lucrative tax shelters. In fact, at the height of California's efforts to promote alternative energy, investors were guaranteed a return on their investment *through the tax benefits alone.* The federal credit required only that the project be in service (even limited service) for five years, while the California tax credits could not be recovered by the government if the project failed to generate any power after its first year.

Into this environment, a variety of technology and design options were introduced, most of dubious value and most failed. Many of the better ideas, however, were based on work that had been begun under the federal R&D programs. Eventually, two success stories emerged: wind and solar thermal electricity. Figure 20.5 illustrates the dramatic progress made in reducing costs for these two technologies over a fifteen year period. Solar-thermal is now close to competitive; wind power is even closer to this goal, selling at an unsubsidized price of less than $0.05 per kWh.

There is little doubt that, without aggressive governmental action in the early 1980s, wind and solar thermal electricity today would not be commercial options for producing power. As evidenced, both industries were highly concentrated in California. As noted, virtually all of the world's solar thermal power is produced in the state, while California led the world in wind technology, in 1990 producing about 80% of the world's wind power. Denmark, with strong governmental support, has since captured that leadership role. Nevertheless, California today still has enough wind capacity to meet the needs of the city of San Francisco.

The optimistic moral of this story is that government policy can be effective in promoting clean technology. The pessimistic moral is that it can spend much more money than necessary to do so. The research and development and tax credit policies of the mid-to-late 1970s were untargeted and poorly designed. Spurred on by fears of $40-a-barrel oil, as well as unrealistic promises from the supporters of renewable

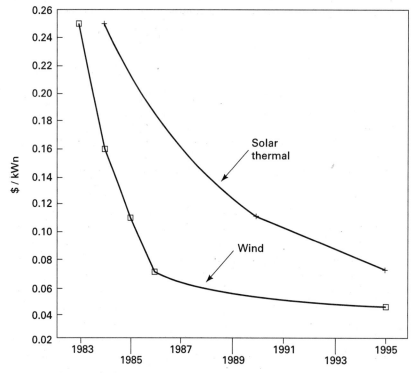

FIGURE 20.5 Costs of Wind and Solar-Thermal

Source: Data for this figure are mid-range estimates in Williams. 1990. "Low-Cost Strategies for Coping with CO_2 Emission Limits." *The Energy Journal* 11, no. 2:51–74. Wind figures for 1995 are estimated. The solar thermal estimated for 1995 is from SEG X, which has now been canceled, and the 1995 estimate includes a portion of natural gas-fired power. See "A Bright Light Goes Out," *Nature,* December 5, 1990, p. 345.

energy, the programs set out to secure new sources of energy soon at any price. As a result, a lot of money went for uneconomic demonstration projects and into the hands of tax farmers rather than wind farmers.

In addition, governmental efforts in the 1970s were motivated primarily by energy security, not environmental concerns. Yet, as a result of these programs, in the 1990s we now have two competitive, clean technologies on the shelf to address pollution control. To put a last optimistic spin on the story: If a shotgun approach to technology promotion like that applied in the 1970s nevertheless yielded competitive, clean options within a decade, a more focused approach can probably achieve similar results at lower cost.

There is some evidence that government policy makers learned the lessons of the 1970s. The magazine *Nature* reports that today "conversations among the National Renewable Energy Laboratory researchers all tend toward the same course: five minutes of science and an hour of policy. No more going for the environmental soft spot; now they argue that renewables make good business sense" ("The Future" 1991). By keeping government attention focused on clean technologies, we have the best chance of combating global warming at a low cost and maybe even at a profit.

The last five chapters have examined the question "How can we do better?" in protecting the quality of our environment, where doing better has been defined as achieving a given level of pollution reduction at lower cost and with greater certainty. We have explored two ideas: incentive-based regulation and clean technology promotion. We have argued first that IB regulation, where technically and politically feasible, provides more cost-effective pollution control and better incentives for technological change than does the dominant command-and-control system.

However, we have also seen that the regulatory process itself—whether CAC or IB—is costly and conflict-ridden. As a result, recent economic attention has been focused on policies designed to promote technologies that reduce pollution in the first place. The path dependence theory suggests that government can and should use selective subsidies tied to cost reductions as a cost-effective complement to regulation; by tying subsidies to performance, a means is provided to avoid government failure in promoting clean technology.

The next section of the book turns to global problems. An optimistic view of the world sees rapid economic development in poor countries based on clean technologies, leading to a stabilization in the world population as living standards rise and birth rates fall. But even under this scenario, the global population will almost double to 10 billion people before it stabilizes. Can the global ecosystem survive this impact? Clearly, the rapid development of clean technology is a prerequisite to a sustainable future. My own view is that without cheap, readily available solar and wind energy, it will be difficult for poor countries to achieve rapid enough economic growth to stabilize population growth without poisoning the global environment in the process. In my mind, *the most important task* for environmental economists is to help design and implement policies to speed up the diffusion of clean technologies.

APPLICATION 20.0

Promoting Electricity Conservation[19]

Suppose that you are in charge of the demand side management program at Megabucks Power and your state public utility commission has just decided that you can now count energy-efficiency measures as equivalent to investments in new generating capacity. This means you can recover efficiency investment costs plus a normal profit through higher electric rates for your customers.

You have the following information at your fingertips: Megabucks currently produces 1 billion kWh and anticipates needing another 100 million next year to service new residences. You are currently charging $0.05 per kWh; new generating capacity (a coal plant) would come in at $0.06 per kWh. Buying the coal plant would mean Megabucks could sell 1.1 billion kWh for an average price of $0.0509 per kWh [$0.0509 per kWh = (1 b kWh * $0.05 per kWh + 0.1 b kWh * $0.06 per kWh) / 1.1 b kWh)].

Fortunately, there is a CT at hand. It is possible to *reduce demand* by 100 million kWh through a program that weatherizes one quarter of the (identical) houses in your service area. Best of all, weatherization can be obtained at a cost of only $0.03 per kWh or an overall investment of $3 million [$3 m = 0.1 b kWh * 0.03 per kWh].

---

[19]This application is adopted from Katz (1989).

Your challenge: Which of your customers pays for the $3 million program? Your assistant, Mr. Offthecuff, has a plan. "Let's select one quarter of the houses at random and provide the weatherization service for free. We can recover the costs by raising electricity rates for everybody. Overall, our customers will be better off since collectively they will save $3 million" [($0.06 – $0.03) per kWh * 0.1 b kWh].

Good idea?

KEY IDEAS IN EACH SECTION

20.0 This chapter looks at technology options and government energy policy in the areas of electric generation and transport. The energy path that the United States follows over the next few decades will depend on the interaction of technology, economics, and government policy.

20.1 U.S. energy use per capita fluctuates based on the price of oil, government-mandated efficiency measures, and economic growth. **OPEC** oil shocks have had an important effect on energy use over the last twenty years. Americans today use about as much energy per capita as they did in 1974, but still about twice as much as several European countries and Japan.

20.2 Technology options for electricity (and heat) break down into six main categories. (1) **Demand-side management (DSM)** (energy efficiency) has substantial cost-effective savings potential. (2) New **clean coal technologies** may soon reduce conventional pollutants from coal plants but not greenhouse gas emissions. (3) **Nuclear power** faces unresolved **high- and low-level waste** storage issues, as well as widespread political opposition. (4) **Natural gas** is the most greenhouse-friendly fossil fuel but has a somewhat limited supply. (5) **Hydroelectric** supply can be expanded but at a cost to flooded ecosystems. (6) **Solar power** can be divided into **passive** and **active** categories, with the latter including **photovoltaics** and **solar thermal.** (7) **Wind** is a very attractive candidate, especially in the Midwest. Wind and solar will require improved means of **electricity storage.**

20.3 Based on environmental advantage and cost-effectiveness, CT candidates for electric power generation include efficiency, wind power, and solar power. Two steps to promote these CTs are (1) level the playing field by reducing subsidies for "dirty" technologies and/or internalizing externalities through IB regulation, and (2) invest in the new technologies directly. Here, however, **equity issues, strategic behavior, free riding, rebound effects,** and the right mix between R&D and market development all need to be considered.

20.4 Technology Options for transport break down into three categories. (1) On net, **fuel efficiency** appears to be relatively cheap. In particular, **hybrid vehicles** hold great promise for cost-effective improvements. Economic benefits include increased **energy security** and lower oil prices through the **monopsony effect.** Costs include possibly **reduced performance** and **safety.** (2) **Fuel switching** options include hydrogen **fuel cells** and **electric vehicles.** In the medium term, fuel cells will be powered by gasoline or biomass derived ethanol, or natural gas. Electric vehicles remain limited by range. (3) **Mode switching,** from autos to mass transit, yields as a significant benefit an

increase in residential density, reducing the **growth in vehicle-miles-travelled. High-speed rail** is a CT alternative to short-haul air travel.

20.5   Fuel efficiency appears to be a CT under our definition. Tools to promote efficiency include the **CAFE** standards, **gas taxes, feebates, emissions fees,** and insurance reforms promoting **pay-by-the-mile,** each of which has advantages and disadvantages. In the area of fuel switching, **R&D partnerships** and California's **technology-forcing** regulation for **ZEVs** has pushed developments of hybrids, fuel cells, and electric vehicles. Finally, in the area of mode switching, when subsidies to auto transport are considered, transit systems may be considered CTs. To encourage mode switching, tools such as **congestion (peak-load) pricing** and **dedicated traffic lanes** can be used.

20.6   Economists are divided in their evaluation of the costs of slowing global warming. **Optimists** and **pessimists** differ both on the existence of clean energy technology and the extent to which government can effectively promote it. At a minimum, however, an increased government commitment to R&D in non-carbon fuels, a reduction in subsidies for fossil fuels, and more effective IB regulation are agreed on.

20.7   The development of solar thermal and wind power in California supports an optimistic view regarding a government energy policy but also illustrates the potential for government to waste available funds.

REFERENCE

Adler, Sy. 1991. "The Transformation of The Pacific Electric Railway." *Urban Affairs Quarterly* 27, no. 1:36–50.

Baker, Dean, and James Barret 2000. "Energy Insurance," *The American Prospect* 11, no. 17:18–19.

Buntin, James. 2000. "Breakdown Lane," *The American Prospect* 11, no. 17:16–18.

Cantor, Robin, and James Hewlett 1988. "The Economics of Nuclear Power." *Resources and Energy* 10:315–335.

Carter, Luther. 1987. *Nuclear Imperatives and Public Trust: Dealing with Nuclear Waste.* Washington, DC: Resources for the Future.

Collinge, Robert A., and Anne Stevens. 1990. "Targeting Methanol or Other Alternative Fuels: How Intrusive Should Public Policy Be?" *Contemporary Policy Issues* 8:54–61.

Davis, William B. 1991. "Economic Incentives to Improve Vehicle Fuel Use and Emissions." NRDC/Sierra Club Testimony Before the California Energy Resources and Development Commission. San Francisco, CA: NRDC.

Durham, Catherine A., Bonnie G. Colby, and Molly Longstreth. 1988. "The Impact of State Tax Credits and Energy Prices on Adoption of Solar Energy Systems." *Land Economics* 64, no. 4:347–355.

Fickett, Arnold P., Clark W. Gellings, and Amory B. Lovins. 1990. "Efficient Use of Electricity." In *Readings From Scientific American.* New York: W. H. Freeman.

Flavin, Christopher. 1987. *Reassessing Nuclear Power: The Fallout from Chernobyl.* Washington, DC: Worldwatch.

Friskin, Francis. 1991. "The Contributions of Metropolitan Government to the Success of Toronto's Public Transit System." *Urban Affairs Quarterly* 27, no. 2:227–248.

Fulkerson, William, Roddie R. Judkins, and Manoi K. Sanghvi. 1990. "Energy from Fossil Fuels." In *Readings From Scientific American.* New York: W. H. Freeman.

Geller, Howard, Daniel Lashoff, Alden Meyer, and Mary Beth Zimmerman. (eds.). 1992. *America's Energy Choices.* Cambridge, MA: Union of Concerned Scientists.

Goldstein, David B. 1991. "Energy and Capital Cost Savings from New Rail Transit Systems: An Illustration of Least-Cost Methods for the Transportation Sector." NRDC/Sierra Club Testimony Before the California Energy Resources and Development Commission. San Francisco, CA: NRDC.

Greene, David L. 1990. "CAFE or Price?" *The Energy Journal* 11, no. 3:37–57.

Greene, David L., and K. G. Duleep. 1992. "Costs and Benefits of Automotive Fuel Economy Improvement: A Partial Analysis." *ORNL-6704.* Oak Ridge, TN: Oak Ridge National Laboratory.

Hafele, Wolf. 1990. "Energy from Nuclear Power." In *Readings From Scientific American.* New York: W. H. Freeman.

Hall, Darwin C. 1992. "Oil and National Security." *Energy Policy* 20, no. 11:1089–1096.

Hall, Darwin C. 1990. "Preliminary Estimates of Cumulative Private and External Costs of Energy." *Contemporary Policy Issues* 8:283–308.

"High Court Eases State Obligation Over Toxic Waste." 1992. *New York Times,* 20 June.

Hobbs, Benjamin F. 1991. "The 'Most-Value' Test: Economic Evaluation of Electricity Demand-Side Management Considering Customer Value." *The Energy Journal* 12, no. 2:67–91.

Hoerner, Andrew, and Avery Gilbert 1999. "Assessing Tax Incentives for Clean Energy Technologies," *Working Paper 3.* Washington, DC: Center for a Sustainable Economy.

Hogan, William W. 1990. "Comments on Manne and Richels: 'CO$_2$ Emission Limits.'" *The Energy Journal* 11, no. 2:51–74.

Holtzclaw, John W. 1991. "Explaining Urban Density and Transit Impacts on Auto Use." NRDC/Sierra Club Testimony Before the California Energy Resources and Development Commission. San Francisco, CA: NRDC.

"How Japan Became So Energy Efficient: It Leaned on Industry." 1990. *Wall Street Journal,* 10 September.

Katz, Myron B. 1989. "Utility Conservation Incentives: Everyone Wins." *The Electricity Journal,* October, 26–35.

Koplow, Douglas. 1993. *Federal Energy Subsidies: Energy, Environmental and Fiscal Impacts.* Washington, DC: Alliance to Save Energy.

KPMG. 2000. "Solar Energy: From Perennial Promise to Competitive Alternative." Amsterdam: Greenpeace. On the Web at http://www.greenpeace.org/~climate/ renewables/reports/kpmg8.pdf.

Lotker, M. 1991. "Barriers to Commercialization of Large-Scale Solar Electricity: Lessons Learned From the LUZ Experience." Washington, DC: Sandia National Laboratory, NTIS.

Lovins, Amory. 1995. "Hypercars: The Next Industrial Revolution." In *Transportation and Energy: Strategies for a Sustainable Transportation System,* eds. Daniel Sperling and Susan Shaheen. Washington, DC: American Council for an Energy Efficient Economy.

Lowe, Marcia. 1991. "Rethinking Urban Transport." In *State of the World, 1992.* Washington, DC: Worldwatch.

MacKenzie, James J., and Michael P. Walsh. 1992. *Driving Forces.* Washington, DC: World Resources Institute.

MacKenzie, James, J., Roger C. Dower, and Donald D. T. Chen. 1992. *The Going Rate: What It Really Costs to Drive.* Washington, DC: World Resources Institute.

Manne, Alan S., and Richard G. Richels. 1990. "CO$_2$ Emission Limits: An Economic Cost Analysis for the U.S.A." *The Energy Journal* 11, no:2:51–74.

Nadis, Steve. 2003. "Man Against a Mountain." *Scientific American,* March.

National Academy of Sciences. 2002. *Effectiveness and Impact of Corporate Average Fuel Economy (CAFE) Standards.* National Academy Press: Washington, DC.

New York State Energy Office. 1991. *Draft New York State Energy Plan, 1991 Biennial Update.* Albany, NY: NYSEO.

Office of Technology Assessment. 1990. *Replacing Gasoline: Alternative Fuels for Light Duty Vehicles.* Washington, DC: U.S. GPO.

Office of Technology Assessment. 1991. *Improving Automobile Fuel Economy.* Washington, DC: U.S. GPO.

Ottinger, Richard L., et al. 1990. *Environmental Costs of Electricity.* New York: Oceana Publications.

Pearce, David. 1991. "The Role of Carbon Taxes in Adjusting to Global Warming." *The Economic Journal* 101, no. 407:938–948.

"Solar Power." *Contemporary Policy Issues* 8:283–308.

"The Future Is Now (Again)." 1991. *Nature,* 5 December.Walton, A. L. and Darwin C. Hall (1990).

Weinberg, Carl J., and Robert H. Williams. 1990. "Energy from the Sun." In *Readings From Scientific American.* New York: W. H. Freeman.

Zweibel, Ken. 1990. *Harnessing Solar Power: The Photovoltaics Challenge.* New York: Plenum Press.

PART

IV

CAN WE RESOLVE GLOBAL ISSUES?

To this point, this book has focused primarily on environmental quality within a single wealthy country, the United States. We have explored the normative debate over the "right" level of pollution; considered political-economic realities that can constrain the effectiveness of government action to achieve these goals; and in the last five chapters, analyzed two broad approaches to "doing better"—incentive-based regulation and clean technology promotion. In this final part of the book, we will extend the lessons learned to resolving issues of global environmental concern: ozone depletion, global warming, loss of species diversity, and management of the global commons—the ocean and Antarctica.

As one steps outside the national border of a developed country, two things are immediately apparent. First, we are an awesomely wealthy people. A personal example brought this home to me. When I was in Africa, my driver was admiring my work boots, and wanted to know what they cost. I admitted that the salary he earned in three months, and on which he supported his entire family, would barely be enough to buy them.

The second fact: As significant as our environmental problems are, they pale in comparison to those faced by people in poor countries. Hardship and suffering from water and air pollution, soil erosion and degradation, and deforestation and flooding are serious, dramatic, and widespread in the less developed world.

This part of the book will explore the complex links between widespread poverty in poor countries (working in part through high population growth rates), high levels of consumption in rich countries, and environmental degradation at both the global level and in the less developed world. We will also consider a variety of policies that governments in both rich and poor countries can take to reverse this environmental decline. Finally, we end with a look at the economics of global environmental agreements.

The stakes are high. By the year 2100, our grandchildren may be living on a planet supporting a stable population of 10 billion people, in an environmentally sustainable fashion. On the other hand, our grandchildren may be sharing the globe with a population of 13 billion people (and rising), in a world where environmental life support systems will surely be stressed beyond recovery. The ultimate outcome depends in large measure on the actions of those of us who have sometimes contemplated buying boots at $100 a pair.

CHAPTER 21

POVERTY, POPULATION, AND THE ENVIRONMENT

21.0 Introduction

In John Steinbeck's famous book *The Grapes of Wrath,* the main character Tom Joad returns to the family farm in Oklahoma during the dustbowl of the early 1930s to find his family evicted by the local land company, and their house abandoned. He asks this now-crazy neighbor, Muley, "What's the idear of kickin' folks off?" Muley replies:

> You know what kinda years we been havin'. Dust coming up and spoilin'
> ever'thing so a man didn't get enough crop to plug up an ant's ass. An' the
> folks that owns the lan' says, 'We can't afford to keep no tenants.' An' they
> says, 'The share a tenant gets is just the margin a profit we can't afford to
> lose.' An' they says, 'If we put all our land in one piece we can jus' hardly
> maker her pay.' So they tractored all the tenants off the lan'.[1]

Joad's family hits the road for California, the promised land, only to arrive midwinter with thousands of others, finding "no kinda work for three months," misery, and starvation. In the final scene of the book, one of the women, whose baby has just been born dead from malnourishment, breast-feeds a starving fifty-year-old man.

Joad's story illustrates the process of economic development in a nutshell. In the United States the 1930s, 1940s, and 1950s saw a transition from small-scale, labor-intensive farming to highly mechanized, chemical-intensive, large-scale agriculture. In the process, particularly during the depression, tens of thousands of farmers were pushed off the land through evictions, as large landowners consolidated small plots of land into larger, technically more efficient units. From 1950 to 1990, the number of farm residents in the United States dropped from 23 million to 4.5 million. Many of these farmers were African Americans from the South, who subsequently migrated to industrial cities in the North and Midwest.

---

[1]John Steinbeck, *The Grapes of Wrath* (New York: Viking Press, 1939), p. 64.

This **agrarian transition** away from an economy based on traditional small farming to one based on large-scale, market oriented agriculture has to date been a universal feature of market-driven economic development. The **traditional economic development** challenge is to productively absorb the millions of workers—holding now-useless farming skills, often illiterate or semiliterate—who are "freed up" from agriculture. In the traditional model, increases in agricultural productivity keep food prices low, benefiting urban consumers. At the same time, surplus labor from the agricultural sector fuels growth in other areas, leading to a rise in general living standards and "successful development."

The worldwide depression of the 1930s, the backdrop for *The Grapes of Wrath,* made this a difficult task. In the United States, we have been rather fortunate. For a period of about thirty years after the depression ended, much of the displaced, unskilled agricultural labor was absorbed by the booming manufacturing economy of the 1950s and 1960s. However, even in the United States, the process is not yet complete. As our economy began to "deindustrialize" in the late 1970s and 1980s (see Chapter 9), high-paying, unskilled jobs began to dry up. Since then, absorbing the low-skilled sons and daughters of low-skilled agricultural migrants, many of them from minority groups, has again emerged as a development challenge.

The tragic experience of Joad's family is unfortunately a common one in many developing countries. On the one hand, traditional agriculture has become less and less viable, in part because of government policies such as subsidized credit favoring large-scale agriculture. On the other hand, many (but not all) poor countries have been stuck in a virtual depression for the last fifteen to twenty years. Over the last few decades, large-scale, capital-intensive agriculture has displaced tens of millions of Third World farmers. These workers then either migrated onto less suitable, ecologically sensitive land, became landless agricultural laborers (often able to find "no kinda work" for many months), or else moved to urban shanty towns in search of jobs in the stagnant industrial or state sectors.

The central point of this chapter is that "solving" the economic development problem—providing productive work and income for displaced farmers and their children—is in fact part and parcel of addressing local and global environmental concerns. **Sustainability,** defined in Chapter 6 as *preventing the deterioration* of average living standards for future generations, cannot be achieved unless poverty is directly addressed, because poverty and environmental degradation go hand in hand. Yet, the environmental consequences of economic growth can no longer be ignored; overall living standards do not rise automatically with economic growth as conventionally defined.

The specter of rapid population growth hanging over this entire picture is intimately connected with desperately high rates of poverty. As we will discuss below, poor people have very rational economic reasons for preferring large families. A basic lesson is thus that providing cheap birth control—throwing condoms at the problem—is only one part of a successful strategy for reducing birth rates in developing countries. Providing health, education, and employment opportunities for the poor majority, especially for young women, and then coupling this with comprehensive family planning services must be part of an effective package for reducing population growth rates.

Beyond poverty and population, the environmental damage people do depends not only on our absolute numbers but also on the natural capital depleted and waste products generated by each person. The average person born in the United States, Europe, or Japan has a dramatically larger impact on the global environment than does a child from a poor country. Yesterday—spent driving my daughter to school, writing this book at my computer (with occasional trips to the refrigerator), taking the family out for a burger at dinnertime, and watching TV in my nice warm house—I arguably contributed more to global warming, ozone depletion, *and* tropical deforestation than a typical Brazilian would in a month or two. As an upper-middle-class American, I consume more than *100 times the resources* used by the average individual from a poor country.

This of course is just another way of restating the IPAT equation from Chapter 7. Total environmental damage can be decomposed into three parts: the number of people, consumption per capita, and the damage done by each unit of consumption. The "population" problem is indeed concentrated in poor countries; 90% of world population growth in the next century will occur in the developing world. However, through legal and illegal immigration, poor country population pressure spills over into affluent countries. For example, largely as a result of legal immigration, the U.S. population is expected to increase by 50% (to 393 million) by the year 2050.[2]

By contrast, the "consumption" problem is currently centered in the rich countries. This too will begin to change as a growing number of poor country residents aspire to the consumption levels found in rich countries. The point here is not to make you or me feel guilty about our affluent lifestyle. Rather, we need to recognize that one needs to focus as much attention on reducing the environmental impact of high consumption in rich countries as reducing population growth in poor countries.

This chapter will provide an overview of these complex and interrelated topics: poverty, rapid population growth in the South, overconsumption in the North, environmental degradation, and sustainable economic development.

21.1 Poverty and the Environment

In rich countries, it is commonly assumed that environmental quality can only be improved by sacrificing material consumption. Indeed, this is the whole premise behind benefit–cost analysis laid out in the first part of the book. In poor countries, by contrast, a broadbased growth in income will, in many respects, tend to improve the quality of the environment. This section discusses four of the close connections between poverty and the environment.

1. For poor people, many environmental problems are problems of poverty. The biggest environmental health threat facing most people in poor countries is **unsafe drinking water,** compounded by **inadequate sewage** facilities. About 1 billion people are without access to safe water, and more than 1.7 billion are without adequate sanitation. Billions of illnesses each year and millions of deaths are attributed to water pollution (World Bank 1992).

Exposure to **indoor air pollution** (smoke) from cooking and heating sources ranks close to urban air pollution as a concern. Some 400 million people worldwide are

---

[2]March 1996 U.S. Census Estimates, Middle Series, at http://www.census.gov/population/projections/nation/npaltsrs.txt.

exposed to unsafe levels of indoor smoke, as opposed to 700 million for outdoor air pollutants, but exposure to indoor pollution is typically more intense. Smoke inhalation contributes to about 4 million deaths per year among infants and children.[4] Figure 21.1 illustrates how these basic environmental conditions improve with increases in income (World Bank 1992).

2. Poor people cannot afford to conserve resources. Out of economic necessity, poor people often put an unsustainable burden on the natural capital in their immediate environment. Urban residents scour the immediate countryside for fuel—firewood or animal dung—leading to deforestation or the elimination of fertilizer sources. Landless

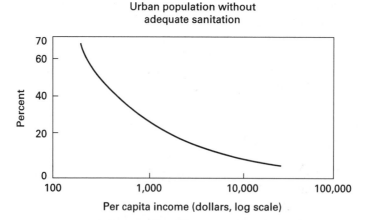

FIGURE 21.1 Safe Water and Sanitation by Income

Source: From *World Development Report 1992* by The World Bank. Copyright © 1992 by The International Bank for Reconstruction and Development/The World Bank. Reprinted by permission of Oxford University Press, Inc.

farmers are pushed into overfarming small plots, farming on steep mountain slopes that soon wash out, or farming in clear-cut rain forests incapable of sustaining agriculture.

While poor people in search of subsistence often stress their immediate environment beyond easy repair, the much higher consumption levels of rich country residents have a substantially larger global impact. For example, commercial ranching for beef exports to European markets has had a bigger impact on Brazilian deforestation than small farmers (Browder 1988, 251). Similarly, the dust-bowl, which helped drive Joad's family out of Oklahoma, resulted in part from improper farming practices driven by a rising urban demand for wheat. We will address the impact of rich country consumption on environmental degradation below. But subsistence needs also play an important role.

3. Richer people "demand" more pollution control. As per capita income rises in a country, people begin to express a more effective demand for pollution control. Figure 21.2 illustrates cross-country data gathered from market-oriented countries for four types of pollutants—ambient concentrations of particulate matter and sulfur dioxide, and per capita production of municipal waste and carbon dioxide. The two regulated air pollutants first rise as per capita income grows, but then begin to fall. By contrast, unregulated or lightly regulated pollutants such as carbon dioxide and municipal waste grow along with per capita income.

The inverted U-shape displayed by the heavily regulated air pollutants reflects what has been called the **Environmental Kuznets Curve** hypothesis. This hypothesis states that as economic growth proceeds, certain types of pollution problems first get worse and then get better. (The original Kuznets curve hypothesized a similar relationship between the *inequality of income and wealth* and economic growth.) What might explain an environmental Kuznets curve? Partly **education.** As income rises, so do levels of awareness regarding environmental threats. Partly, it could be explained by expanding democracy. As income rises, political participation tends to increase. As a result, people are provided the opportunity to express a **political demand for pollution control.** (When data from the former communist regimes are included, the inverted U-shape disappears.) Partly, it has to do with a **shift in industrial composition**—wealthier countries rely more on services and other relatively "clean" industries, while less-developed countries have more basic manufacturing and mining. (Indeed, some of the improvement in air quality in developed countries may simply reflect a shift of dirty manufacturing industries to poor countries.) Finally, the relationship can be explained by **relative risk considerations:** when life spans are short due to inadequate nutrition or access to basic health care, concerns about respiratory, neurological, and reproductive diseases, or cancer from pollution, are dampened.

As this discussion indicates, per capita income in Figure 21.2 is in fact "standing in" for a variety of political and economic social changes that accompany economic development. For this reason, the simplistic environmental Kuznets curve hypothesis—that growth alone leads to pollution reductions—has not held up to scrutiny, but it has sparked much further research.[3] In addition, Figure 21.2 clearly reveals that

---

[3]Special issues of both *Ecological Economics* (Vol. 25, No. 2, May 1998) and *Environment and Development Economics* (Vol. 2, No. 4, October 1997) have been devoted to this topic. Cavlovic et al. (2000) provide a meta-analysis. For conflicting views on the export of pollution to developing countries see Suri and Chapman (1998), as well as the survey in Goodstein (1999).

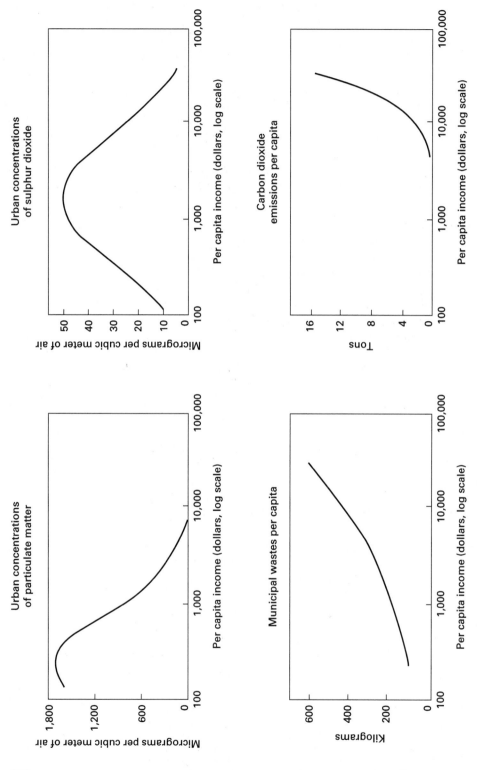

FIGURE 21.2 Regulated and Unregulated Pollutants by Income (Per Capita)

Source: From *World Development Report 1992* by The World Bank. Copyright © 1992 by The International Bank for Reconstruction and Development/The World Bank. Reprinted by permission of Oxford University Press, Inc.

lightly regulated or unregulated pollutants such as solid waste and carbon dioxide increase in tandem with income and production levels. (We should recall, in addition, that at least some of the "reduced" sulfur dioxide and particulate emissions documented in Figure 21.2 have in fact re-emerged as hazardous solid waste in the form of ash and sulfur sludges.) Hazardous waste production is also probably highly correlated with per capita income. As regulations on these pollutants become more stringent, will their per capita generation also begin to decline in wealthier countries? The graphs in Figure 21.2 cannot predict this.

4. Population growth slows with increased income. The final link between poverty and the environment lies in income growth as a means of population control. As we will see in the next section, as societies grow wealthier, families almost universally have fewer children.

These four interconnections between poverty and the environment reveal that, in poor countries, one need not "trade off" rising material living standards for improved environmental quality. In fact, the *only* effective way to improve environmental conditions is to alleviate the tremendous poverty faced by many of the people in these nations.

21.2 The Population Picture in Perspective

When my grandparents were born at the turn of the twentieth century, there were about 1.6 billion people alive on the planet. When my parents were born, around 1930, that number had risen to 2 billion. On my own birthday in 1960, I joined some 3 billion inhabitants. When my first daughter turned two in 1990, global population had climbed to 5.3 billion. If she has a child, her daughter or son will be born in a world with about 7.5 billion other people. And if my grandchild lives to be 80, she will likely die, at the end of the twenty-first century, on a planet supporting somewhere between 9 and 15 billion people.

Figure 21.3 provides a graphical representation of world population growth spanning these five generations, 200 years. Under the United Nation's "medium" scenario, effective population control is achieved over the next few decades, with growth rates falling to less than $\frac{1}{2}$ of 1% by 2040. Given these assumptions, global population will stabilize at around 10 billion people. This is a bit less than twice the number alive today.

Note that "medium" doesn't mean this prediction will come true without serious changes—in particular, it requires fairly rapid, widespread adoption of birth control. By contrast, a world in which fertility rates fall, but only slowly, leads to a 2050 population of 10.7 billion and still rising. On the other hand, one could imagine a highly optimistic scenario. If we achieve global zero population growth by 2040, this gets us down to 7.4 billion in 2050. The point here is that relatively small changes in fertility over the next two decades will have big impacts on global population by midcentury.[4]

The "pessimistic" population growth line is drawn from a 1992 publication by the World Bank, and is there for illustrative purposes—if fertility rates fail to decline at

---

[4]"The World at Six Billion" 1998, United Nations Population Division (NY: Department for Economic and Social Information and Policy Analysis) and "World Population Prospects: The 1998 Revision," 1998, United Nations Population Division (NY: Department for Economic and Social Information and Policy Analysis), both on the Web at http://www.un.org/esa/population/.

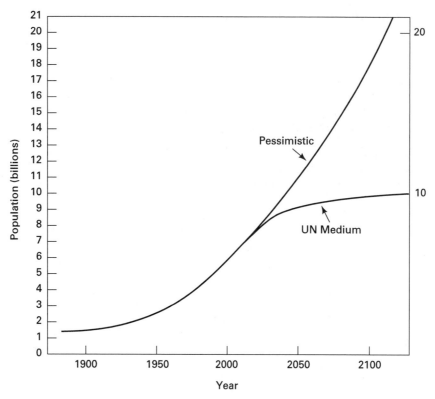

FIGURE 21.3 World Population, 1900–2100

all, then global population will continue to rise, at the extreme, to 20 billion by the year 2100.[5] The actual number is highly uncertain; at some point, growth would be forcibly checked by large-scale famine, disease, war, or ecological disaster. In an interesting recent book called *How Many People Can the Earth Support?*, the author culled results from some sixty studies (dating back to 1679!) and found answers that tended to range from 4 to 16 billion (Cohen 1995).

Given the magnitude of the environmental problems we face today, it is almost inconceivable to imagine the impact that 10 billion of us will have on the planetary ecosystem, let alone 15 to 20 billion. Population pressure must clearly be counted as a major global environmental threat in the medium- and long-term. At the more local level, population growth is increasingly overwhelming the ability of poor country governments to provide educational, health, and sanitary services. As poverty deepens in these countries, environmental stresses multiply for the reasons discussed in the previous section.

In Chapter 7 we discussed the **Malthusian** perspective on population growth—named after the famous eighteenth-century economist Thomas Malthus. Reviewing

---

[5]A 1% growth rate after the year 2000 would generate a year 2100 population of 16 billion; at 1.5%, "projected" population rises to 26 billion. The World Bank (1992, Figure 1.1) provides the pessimistic projection reproduced in Figure 21.3.

briefly, Malthus predicted that a population growing at a geometric rate would soon outstrip the (slower) growth of food supply, leading to a catastrophic "natural check" on population—war, famine, or disease. Yet Malthus's gloomy prediction has yet to come true on a global scale; as we saw above, population growth continues even in the face of substantial poverty worldwide. To date, we have avoided a Malthusian fate because of impressive technological developments in the field of agriculture—the so-called "Green Revolution" also discussed in Chapter 7.

Moreover, Malthus's basic assumption, that population growth grows geometrically, also does not always hold. Not including immigration, wealthy countries have very low population growth rates, often *below* zero. The availability of effective birth control, not foreseen by Malthus, has meant that families are able to control their "natural" reproductive tendencies if they so desire. In general, the motivation to control family size appears to be greater for wealthier families.

The complex link between rising incomes and lower population growth is discussed below. But its presence has lead some observers to argue that poor countries are merely passing through a high-population growth phase. This phase resulted from a decline in death rates due in turn to the introduction of modern medicine in the 1940s and 1950s. As average incomes rise in these countries, it is argued, birth rates will fall and a "natural" **demographic transition** to low population growth will occur.

Indeed, population growth rates worldwide were low, less than 1% from 1900 to 1950. As modern health care practices spread in the 1950s however, growth rates in the developing world exploded to well over 2%. After cresting in the late 1960s, population growth rates have fallen in many places including China and India, the middle income countries, and the developed countries: Globally the rate of population growth fell to 1.3% from 1995 to 2000. The population problem has "taken care of itself" to a remarkable extent in countries like Korea, which experienced rapid and widely shared economic growth. Population growth rates in that country fell from 2.4% in 1960 and 1970 to 0.9% in 1990.[6]

The 1990s saw generally good news on the population front. The medium population projections for 2050 presented in Figure 21.3 are *more than 2 billion people lower* than those I presented in the first edition of the book written only ten years ago. Why? The decade between 1985 and 1995 saw large, unexpected fertility declines in South Central Asia and Africa. During the two-year period from 1994 to 1996 alone, the United Nations lowered its global estimate of the number of children per woman from 3.10 to 2.96. Again, these small changes add up to a big drop in projected numbers over a half century. Nafis Sadik, director of the U.N. Population fund, credits the fertility decline to the fact that many countries began lifting family planning restrictions in the early 1980s.[7]

At the same time, tragically, over the next decade population growth in Africa and Southeast Asia will be slowed by the devastating impact of the AIDS virus. In Southern Africa, several countries have seen life expectancy more than cut in half, and population growth rates are expected to drop from highs of 2% to 3% in the late

---

[6]Wattenberg (1990) expresses the anti-Malthusian view.
[7]Hanley, Charles. "UN Summit—Population," AP Wire story, June 1997.

1980s to become slightly negative by 2003. Economic and political decline in Eastern Europe is also reducing life expectancy in that region.

Because more and more couples worldwide are adopting birth control—and because of the devastating impact of AIDS in Africa—Malthusian predictions of runaway global population growth seem significantly less likely than they did ten years ago. Yet in many poor countries, rapid population growth continues to pose an ecological and economic development problem. The United Nations predicts that by 2050, some sixty-seven developing countries will have twice their current population. Some have argued that in these regions, a **vicious cycle** is developing: poverty generating high rates of population growth generating more poverty which then leads to higher levels of population growth, and so on. For such countries, economic growth alone may not break this cycle; without aggressive measures to control population growth, the demographic transition to low population growth rates experienced by other countries may be delayed for some time.[8]

21.3 An Economic Approach to Family Size

At several points in this chapter, I have asserted that higher incomes tend to be associated with lower population growth rates. As a general rule this is true, both across countries and within countries. In Colombia, Malaysia, and Brazil, for example, the poorest 20% of households support, on average, 30% of the nation's children. By contrast, the wealthiest 20% of households have only 9% of the children (Birdsall and Griffin 1988). Yet the relationship is not a hard and fast one. For example, the high-income oil-exporting countries tend to have high fertility rates, while low-income countries such as Sri Lanka and China have reduced their population growth rates to low levels. In the United States, poor families (including welfare families) are *not* larger than average.

Many factors determine family size—religious and cultural norms obviously play a prominent role. Yet the strength of the **poverty-fertility relationship** suggests that *economic* factors are quite important as well. Evidently, people choose to vary their family size depending upon their income level. So, this suggests the following

PUZZLE

Suppose you are a farm worker, recently married, living in Pakistan. In a good year, you might make $200. Infant mortality rates are high—your children will have a one in ten chance of dying during their first year. The likelihood of your children attending more than a couple of years of school is also very small. Nationwide, only 38% of boys and 27% of girls attend primary school, and you are

---

[8]Population doubling projections are from "The World at Six Billion," 1998, United Nations Population Division (NY: Department for Economic and Social Information and Policy Analysis), on the Web at http://www.un.org/esa/population/. For a contemporary Malthusian view, see Daly (1990) or Musambachime (1990).

[9]These results hold when household poverty is measured on a per capita basis. Families with more children tend to be "richer" in absolute terms.

among the least likely to have access to such services. Systems of public welfare, "social security" retirement pensions, and public health care are very limited.

1. What are the economic benefits and costs to you, the parent, of having children?
2. On strictly economic terms, would you prefer to have two babies or five?

SOLUTION

Economic benefits.   In poor countries such as Pakistan, families are the primary social safety net. If you should become too sick or old to work, your children will be your basic source of support. Thus an important motive for having children is for **economic insurance.** A second reason is that children's labor, controlled by the parent, can help provide a direct **income supplement** for the family. Children as young as six or seven can be (and are) employed in agriculture and manufacturing, sometimes to the (meager) economic benefit of their parents.

Economic costs.   Raising children is a costly endeavor, both in terms of money and time. In economic terms, parents' child-rearing efforts, and the monetary resources they devote to this endeavor, can be thought of as an investment in the future productivity of their children.

Given this economic calculus, the answer for our farmworker is probably five children rather than two.

Let us look a little more closely at the issue of desired family size. The fact that children provide economic insurance and an income supplement does not *necessarily* mean that a big family is advantageous. Given limited resources, a family could potentially obtain comparable economic benefits following one of two approaches: a **high-investment strategy** with one or two children, or a **low-investment strategy** with many children.

The high-investment strategy would involve focusing all available resources on one or two children—insuring they survived infancy, were provided with a healthy diet, and went on to attend school. Such a child might well land a good job and increase family income substantially. In contrast, the low-investment strategy would be to have many children, recognizing that one or more would likely die young, but that the remainder would survive to contribute a small amount to the family income and insurance network. In short, the low-investment strategy is to substitute quantity for quality.[10]

While in principle, both strategies are open to all, for our farm laborer with his limited resources and restricted access to public services, the high-investment strategy is very difficult to pursue. Moreover, it is tremendously risky. Suppose, that after five years of intensive investment, a single child dies. Thus, he generally prefers five children to two. Yet, as income rises, the high-investment strategy begins to be more attractive. Resources for the long-term (fifteen- to eighteen-year) investment are

---

[10]This basic model was originally proposed by Becker and Lewis (1973). For a more current perspective, see Dasgupta (1995).

more readily available, and access to better health care means that the chances of premature death decline.

The analysis of the poverty-fertility link in this section suggests an effective route to population control: Changing parents' economic family plan from a low- to high-investment strategy, where the focus is on the "quality" rather than the "quantity"of children.

21.4 Controlling Population Growth

The benefit–cost model of family size is a very crude one, omitting as it does very important issues of culture, kinship, religion, love, and affection. Yet it does a good job explaining the strong relationship between poverty and fertility observed in many places around the world. In particular, because there are *good economic reasons* for poor people to have large families, simple provision of low-cost birth control is unlikely to solve the population problem (though it would certainly help). Can we use this benefit–cost model to suggest other effective policies for controlling population growth?

1. BALANCED GROWTH AND REDISTRIBUTION

The poverty–fertility relationship seems to provide a straightforward way to control population: Eliminate poverty! Unfortunately, if this were easy to do, nations would have done so already. It does remain true, however, that balanced and rapid economic development that raises the material welfare of the poor majority is one of the most effective population control measures available. Korea's precipitous drop in population growth, noted above, can be attributed primarily to the country's dramatic economic success in the 1960s and 1970s. The gains from economic growth, based on labor intensive manufacturing, were widely shared (Repetto 1985).[11]

In addition to balanced growth, another way to reduce poverty and thus population growth rates is through **redistribution of wealth** from the rich to the poor. Redistribution often takes the form of publicly provided social services: education, health care, public pension plans. Another possibility is **land reform**—the breaking up of huge, underutilized estates into smaller units, made accessible to landless farmers. Land reform has long been urged in Latin America and other parts of the developing world. This form of redistribution can help to stabilize rural-to-urban migration, increase food production, decrease poverty, reduce population growth rates, and reduce environmental pressure on marginal agricultural lands.[12]

Redistribution can occur between poor and rich classes within countries, or between poor and rich countries. For example, land reform is sometimes financed (involuntarily) by the wealthy landowning class, when their land is taken by the government at below market prices; land reform can also be financed by the developing nation's taxpayers in general, when the landowners are fully compensated by the government; or it can be financed by international development organizations, with money from rich countries.

---

[11]Women also entered the workforce at a rapid rate, which as discussed is an important factor in reducing population growth rates.

[12]Moene (1992) argues in a general equilibrium context that these beneficial effects are most likely to occur in land-poor countries when land is redistributed to landless farmers, rather than small farmers.

Forster (1992) has suggested an innovative way for the international community to promote land reform. She advocates **debt-for-farmland swaps,** in which poor countries are forgiven some of their debt to rich countries in exchange for land reform financing. Landless farmers who are pressuring environmentally sensitive areas, such as rain forests or steep terrains, could be resettled with these funds onto productive arable land.

Debt-for-farmland swaps (and their kin, debt-for-nature swaps discussed in detail in the next chapter) in some sense involve a redistribution of wealth from rich country residents (bank shareholders and taxpayers) to poor countries. Yet they can also be viewed as an investment in a sustainable future. Forster (1992) estimates that debt-for-farmland swaps could preserve tropical rain forests for an investment of $11 per hectare, as opposed to reforestation costs of $750 to $1,100 per hectare.

At the broad, macro level, rapid and balanced economic development combined with redistributionist policies is clearly the best "contraceptive." Yet both growth and redistribution have been hard to achieve in many parts of the world. Fortunately, it is possible for even poor countries to substantially reduce population growth rates through more targeted policies in the areas of health, education, and family planning.

2. REDUCED INFANT AND CHILDHOOD MORTALITY

Improved public health is an important factor in reducing long-run population growth rates. Our benefit–cost approach to family size suggested that improved health care would help slow population growth for one principal reason: The risk associated with investing in a child's health and education would be reduced, encouraging families to substitute quality for quantity.[13]

In the short run, however, reducing childhood and infant mortality accelerates population growth, as parents take some time to adjust their desired number of babies to the new conditions. As noted above, during the 1950s and 1960s population growth rates in poor countries exploded, often doubling, as common diseases were brought under control by modern medicine, but fertility rates remained high.[14] Since then, fertility and thus population growth rates have fallen around the world, though they still remain a severe problem in most poor countries. Part of the demographic transition, described in Section 21.2 is reflected in this adjustment on the part of parents to lower childhood mortality rates.

Childhood and infant mortality can be attacked at relatively low cost by providing public health and education services. For example, one of the most common causes of infant death in poor countries is dehydration from diarrhea. This disease can be treated using a simple prescription: clean water with a little sugar.

3. EDUCATION

Our economic model of family size tells us that population growth will slow when parents follow a strategy of "high investment" in their children. A key element making

---

[13]In addition, in high mortality areas, only when mortality rates drop do parents have to concern themselves at all with birth control. Falling infant mortality rates thus initiate behavioral changes, which make fertility control more likely (Birdsall and Griffin 1988).

[14]The adjustment process is compounded because, as Birdsall and Griffin (1988) report, parents don't replace dead children on a less than one-to-one basis and typically don't fully "insure" against infant mortality by having larger families.

such a strategy possible is **access to education.** This is true for three reasons. First, the availability of education directly lowers the cost of pursuing a high-investment strategy to all parents, educated and uneducated alike. Second, as parents become educated themselves, a strategy of substituting quality for quantity also becomes easier, since the parents can provide guidance to the children.

Finally, as parents become educated, their wages tend to rise. This increases the **opportunity cost of parents' time,** making a low-investment strategy less attractive. This is true because a low-investment, "quantity" strategy requires a bigger commitment of time devoted to child rearing than does a high investment, "quality" strategy. Another way to look at this is that, as the parents' wages rise, family income and economic insurance are better served by parents working than by raising more children.

For this reason, education is particularly important for women, since they do most of the child rearing. One of the best ways to control fertility is to have women participating in the *modern sector* of the economy. All poor women work. However, employment in agricultural or household labor does not appear to reduce fertility (Birdsall and Griffin 1988). As the opportunity cost of the woman's time rises, a quantity strategy becomes less and less attractive for the family as a unit.

Education for women appears to have a strong impact on fertility control for other reasons as well. To this point, we have treated the "family" as a homogeneous unit, yet men and women play different roles in the family and may have different ideas about the desirability of limiting family size. In the developing world, as in rich countries, the responsibility for taking birth control measures—whether abstinence, prolonged breast-feeding, or a technological approach—generally falls on the woman. Thus, the direct consumers of birth control devices and fertility control information are generally women, providing another argument for improved female education.

More importantly, however, most of the world's societies are male-dominated, **patriarchal cultures.** In such societies, women often must obtain approval from their husbands in order to control their fertility. This distinction is important, because holding all things equal, it is probably true that women prefer to have fewer children than men do. This is likely for a number of reasons: Women do the vast majority of the hard work involved in child rearing; child rearing interferes with women's other economic activities; and childbirth represents a significant health risk for many women. Thus, policies that strengthen women's status and bargaining position within the family itself, for example, better education or access to paid employment, are likely to have important effects on fertility decisions, independent of their impact on *overall* family income and economic insurance.

4. FAMILY PLANNING

Having argued above that poor people may have good reasons for having large families, it is also true that a big obstacle to pursuing a high-investment strategy is lack of access to family planning services. There remains a large unsatisfied demand for birth control worldwide. Outside of subSaharan Africa, close to 50% of women in poor countries desire no more children, and about two thirds of those who want a larger family would prefer to postpone bearing their next child. At the same time, one source estimates that in three quarters of the world's poor countries, birth control is not affordable for the average individual.[15]

In general, better-educated, wealthier, urban women are better able to actually achieve fertility control. But, effective outreach programs have been able to reduce and, in some cases, almost eliminate urban/rural gaps. Programs that rely on well-trained workers, provide follow-up and support to clients, provide a variety of contraceptive methods, and imbed family planning in a more comprehensive system of public health services have proven quite effective in lowering fertility rates. In one well-studied case in Bangladesh, such a program increased contraceptive use from 10% to 31% in two years, reducing the number of births by about 25% (Birdsall and Griffin 1988).

A comprehensive program of public health, education (especially targeted at women), and family planning can be an effective way to reduce population growth, even in the absence of rapid, balanced growth, and/or explicitly redistributionist policies. Poor countries that have been able to successfully pursue some combination of these policies include Costa Rica, Cuba, Mexico, Colombia, Sri Lanka, Indonesia, China, Zimbabwe, and the southern Indian state of Kerala. Family planning programs, along with economic growth, have been credited with dramatic fertility declines in Taiwan and Thailand (World Bank 1992; Rand 1998).

Current funding for population control in poor countries is about $10 billion, with developed countries contributing only about 25% of the total. The World Bank (1992, 174) has estimated that an expenditure of an additional $7 billion per year might reduce long-run global population by 2.5 billion people! For comparison, this is about a third of what Americans spend in barbershops, beauty shops, baths, and health clubs each year. Given this, *investment in family planning is one of the most cost-effective measures available for addressing global environmental problems ranging from global warming to loss of biodiversity.*

5. COERCIVE POLICIES

The policies described above all function by encouraging parents to *voluntarily* control family size. Some nations, notably China and India, have used coercive birth control methods. China, a country a little larger than the United States but with less good-quality agricultural land, is home to 1.3 billion people, more than four times as many as live in the United States. Even if the Chinese achieve zero population growth today, because of the country's age distribution, the number of people in the country is likely to increase to 1.9 billion before stabilizing.

Prior to 1980, China's Communist government had achieved impressive reductions in fertility primarily by pursuing the noncoercive strategies discussed above: raising the status of the poor through growth and redistribution, and providing education, health care, family planning services, and retirement benefits. The number of children per family fell from more than 5.0 in 1970, to 2.7 in 1979.

In 1980, in order to head off a surge in population as the Chinese baby boom reached child-bearing age, the government instituted its so-called **One-Child Policy.**

---

[15]See Birdsall and Griffin (1988) and "Cost Said to Rule Out Birth Control for Many," *New York Times,* July 2, 1991. The study was done by the Population Crisis Committee and defines a supply of affordable birth control as requiring less than 1% of annual income.

Urban dwellers were legally limited to a single child, while rural families were allowed to have two or more children. The policy was enforced with a mixture of subsidies, fines, peer pressure, and on occasion physical coercion. Families who had only one child were provided monthly stipends, given access to better schools, and taxed at a lower rate. Economically coercive fines, which might amount to more than a year's salary, were imposed for a child over the legal limit. Pregnant women were harassed by neighborhood committees, and forced abortions, while not widespread, apparently did occur.

By 1990, the average number of children per family had fallen to 2.5. In 1992, after a two-year campaign to boost sterilizations, the number had reportedly dropped to 1.9—zero population growth. The *New York Times* reported in the mid-1990s that the average Chinese viewed the policy as unpleasant but needed, something like income taxes. Public acceptance of the policy has always been much higher in urban than rural areas; and as China's economic and political system began to open up in the 1990s, the policy became increasingly difficult to enforce in the countryside.

One ugly by-product of the One-Child Policy has been a rise in sex selection of male infants through abortions of female fetuses, and probably an increase in female infanticide. Chinese census figures from the late 1980s indicate about half a million anticipated female births are failing to show up on the records each year. However, most of these "missing" girls are probably given up for adoption, or raised in secret. In China, sons are especially important from the point of view of economic insurance, since daughters traditionally "marry out" of the family.

China's One-Child Policy—relying on voluntary measures, severe economic and social pressure, and occasional physical coercion—has worked, though sometimes at a tragic human cost. Noncompliance, although evident, was not widespread enough to undermine the policy. Because China is such a huge country, the overall impact of China's family planning and birth control program has been tremendous. If the birth rates evident in 1970 had persisted, over the period from 1970 to 1990 an additional 240 million Chinese—a number roughly equivalent to the population of the United States—would have been born.[16]

The physically coercive aspects of the Chinese program, while never dominant, have been "accepted" for two mutually enforcing reasons: The Chinese government exercises effective authoritarian political control over the population, *and* the goal of the policy appears to be generally supported. Many Chinese people appear to have accepted a sustainability argument that sacrifice on the part of current generations is necessary to preserve a decent quality of life for the future.

By contrast, in the 1970s the democratically elected Indian government initiated an aggressive birth control policy that included financial incentives for sterilization. Charges of economic coercion and evidence of forced sterilization brought the program to a halt and have since generated considerable public suspicion of all government birth control programs (Jacobson 1987).

---

[16]The information on the One-Child Policy presented here is drawn from "China, With Ever More Mouths to Feed, Pushes Anew for Small Families"; "A Mystery From China's Census: Where Have Young Girls Gone?"; "China's Crackdown on Births: A Stunning and Harsh Success"; "Births Punished by Fine, Beating or Ruined Home"; and "Rural Flouting of One Child Policy Undercuts China's Census," *The New York Times,* 6/16/91, 6/17/91, 4/25/93, 4/25/93, 4/14/2000.

It is unlikely that, outside of China, coercive population control methods are likely to be applied. In many parts of the world, they are morally unacceptable. In addition, except under unusual circumstances of an effective, authoritarian regime, and widespread if grudging popular support, such policies are unlikely to be effective. Indeed they are likely to be counterproductive. Luckily, they are also not necessary to stabilize the global population at a sustainable level. Noncoercive, relatively cheap, and in many cases cost-effective measures exist to nudge parents into voluntarily pursuing a high-investment family strategy.

The good news is thus that we need not wait around to see if the near future holds a "natural" demographic transition to a sustainable world population or a vicious neomalthusian cycle of population growth and misery. Neither do we need to follow a coercive path. Instead, policies that raise the material welfare of poor people by promoting balanced growth and redistribution, as well as targeted policies in the areas of health care, education, and family planning, should be sufficient to reach the goal of stabilizing the planetary population at a sustainable level.

21.5 Consumption and the Global Environment

Population control advocates (like me) are sometimes accused by people in poor countries of racism or even genocide. Why, they ask, do you recommend aggressive, if noncoercive, steps to limit the numbers of (mostly) black or brown people in poor countries, when, in fact, the vast majority of global ecological damage can be traced directly or indirectly to the affluent lifestyles of the (mostly) white people in rich countries?

There are two elements to the **consumption-pollution link.** The first is straightforward. Because inhabitants of rich countries are responsible for over two-thirds of global economic activity, at least two-thirds of global pollution can be laid at our doorstep. The western European countries, the United States, and Japan comprise about 15% of the world's population but consume 71% of the world's output (World Bank 1992, Table A.2). As a result, rich country consumption has to date been responsible for most of the global atmospheric pollution—global warming, ozone depletion, acid rain, and radioactive contamination. Rich countries have had by far the biggest impact on polluting and overfishing the oceans. And rich country inhabitants have generated mountains of toxic wastes that are now, on occasion, finding their way to poor countries for disposal.

In addition to generating global pollution problems, there is a second element to the consumption-pollution link. High levels of consumption demand in rich countries have been responsible for an unsustainable drawdown in environmental quality and the stock of natural capital in many poor countries. We will see an example of this when we trace the so-called "hamburger connection" to rain-forest depletion later in this chapter. The expansion of beef ranching in Costa Rica has led to a destruction of the nation's rain-forest resource without sufficient compensating investment in created capital.

Many poor countries rely on the export of primary resources or agricultural commodities to earn money for imported fuel, food, consumer goods, and weapons. In principle, this trade is environmentally sustainable. However, sustainability requires that any drawdown in the stock of natural capital—whether oil or mineral reserves, rain-forest resources, topsoil, or air and water quality—be compensated for by investment in created capital. As we discussed in Chapters 6 and 7, if a nation's natural capital is depleted faster than new capital is created, then unsustainable development occurs.

The overwhelming demand for resources in rich countries—ranging from gasoline, to steel, to bananas, to beef—has in many cases depleted the natural capital stock in poor countries, *without* commensurate investment in created capital. Why has this occurred? Historically, colonial governments tended to drain resource-generated wealth from their colonies, investing little in human capital or infrastructure. In the postcolonial period, falling relative prices for primary resources, low taxes on politically powerful resource-based industries, and high levels of spending on military and imported consumption goods by ruling elites have constrained investment in created capital. Finally, as we will see in the next section, the burden of debt repayment has led to a flow of created wealth *from* poor to rich countries over the last fifteen years.

The point here is not to assign blame to rich countries or ruling elites for the poverty in the former colonies. Rather, the point is simply to recognize that high levels of rich country demand can have as much to do with environmental damage in poor countries as do high population growth rates. Thus growing, transporting, and cooking a year's worth of my favorite breakfast—a banana (Ecuador), a cup of coffee (Guatemala), and a chocolate donut (cocoa, Ghana; sugar, Honduras) uses up about $400 of market resources. This process contributes much more to environmental degradation in those countries—pesticide contamination of water, loss of topsoil, deforestation, and global warming—than does providing breakfast for a person whose *entire yearly income* is $400 or less.

This is also not to say that trade in agricultural commodities or any other goods are, on balance, bad for the environment. We will take up the issue of trade policy in the next chapter. Rather, to insure sustainability, the gains from trade must be invested in created capital sufficient to offset the drawdown in natural capital. *If they are not,* then rich country consumption leads to unsustainable development in poor countries as surely as does rapid population growth.

This section has discussed the two ways in which high levels of consumption in rich countries and environmental problems, both global and those in poor countries, are linked. At the global level, an obvious and direct correspondence exists between consumption and pollution. In addition, high levels of demand in rich countries have indirectly promoted a drawdown of the stock of natural capital and environmental quality in poor countries. If natural capital depleted through resource or pollution-intensive exports is not being replaced by investment in created capital, high-consumption levels in rich countries can fuel unsustainable resource depletion in poor countries. Many argue that this kind of unsustainable development has in fact been occurring. Given these links, are the critics of population control right? Are neomalthusians, perhaps motivated by unconscious racism, focusing on the wrong problem?

I argue instead that *both* overpopulation and overconsumption represent serious threats to the global environment and sustainable development in poor countries. There is mounting evidence that rapid population growth is dramatically compounding the problem of economic development, thereby putting tremendous pressure on local environments. Moreover, as the poor both grow in number and aspire to living standards found in the developed world, their impact on global environmental problems will become more and more significant. By the year 2025, for example, poor countries are expected to surpass the rich countries as the main contributor to global warming.

Yet we are indeed being shortsighted, at best, if we insist solely on blaming the reproductive behavior of poor people in poor countries both for their own environmental problems and for the global ones to which they contribute. High levels of consumption in affluent countries are primarily responsible for the global environmental crisis and have indirectly promoted an unsustainable drawdown of natural capital in many poor countries.

Earlier in the book (Chapter 11) we discussed a variety of tools for addressing the overconsumption problem in wealthier countries. So far in this chapter, we have examined theoretical links between poverty, population growth, northern consumption patterns, and the prospect for sustainable development. We now turn to a concrete example.

21.6 Sustainable Development in Costa Rica?

Costa Rica (see location in Figure 21.4) is a country of about 4 million people. It is considered to be a "lower-middle" income country, with per capita income of $2,640 per year. We focus on Costa Rica here, because in many respects it is a developmental "success story." Table 21.1 provides some statistics that summarize Costa Rica's recent economic and demographic history.

We begin with the crude, often inaccurate, yet commonly employed measure of development: Gross Domestic Product (GDP) per person. GDP was defined in Chapter 6 as the sum total of all market income generated in an economy in a given year. GDP does not include nonmarket production (child rearing and housework, for example), or negative environmental externalities. It also does not account for a drawdown in the stock of natural capital.

Nevertheless, a comparison of GDP growth with population growth from 1990 to 1997 paints an initially optimistic portrait: Aggregate GDP growth averaging 3.7% per year outstripped population growth of 2.5% per year. This meant that by the end of the decade, economic output and material wealth *per person* was significantly higher than at the beginning. As we shall see next, this does not necessarily mean that the average Costa Rican was "better off"—GDP *does not* include environmental costs, and the wealth gains may have been unevenly distributed—but the larger slice of pie per person at least made it *possible* for average material living standards to rise.

TABLE 21.1   Development Data for Costa Rica

Per capita income, 1997	$2,640
Debt per capita, 1997	$ 965
ANNUAL GROWTH RATES	
GDP (1990–1997)	3.7%
Population (1975–1980)	3.0%
Population (1995–2000)	2.5%
Forest (1990–1995)	−3.1%
Pasture (1982–1994)	6.9%

Source: World Resources Institute, various tables. *Earth Trends* (www.wri.org).

FIGURE 21.4 Central America

In addition, while the country still had a fairly high population growth rate of 2.5% in the 1990s, this figure has been falling steadily. Many observers credit Costa Rica's development successes partially to its democratic political culture. Due to the absence of native Indians to serve as slaves, Costa Rica—like the states of the Northern United States—originally developed a system of agriculture based on small farmers who owned their own land. While the rise of banana and coffee plantations in the late 1800s, and more recently cattle exports, has greatly increased land concentration, Costa Rica's small-farmer history shaped a relatively egalitarian culture.[17]

By contrast, much of Latin America developed along the lines of the Southern United States, with a plantation-style agriculture. Small farmers under this system were originally enslaved Indians, later tenants or sharecroppers, with little political or economic power. This social structure generated massive concentrations of land and economic power in the hands of a relatively small elite, deep racial divides, and in the twentieth century, a dominant military presence in government required to maintain these unequal economic and political relationships.

Costa Rica's egalitarian historical legacy has left it with several advantages for sustainable development: a relatively effective governmental bureaucracy; few military expenses (the army was actually banned in 1949); a commitment to education, especially of women; and an advanced welfare system that focuses on basic health care delivery to poor citizens. These latter two aspects of Costa Rican policy have been very important in reducing population growth rates.

Yet even in Costa Rica, it is uncertain whether recent economic progress can be considered sustainable.[18] First, the agrarian transition discussed above is well under way in

---

[17]This explanation of Costa Rican exceptionalism is widely accepted. See, for example, Bieszaz, Bieszaz, and Bieszaz (1982).

[18]For a contrary view see Pearce and Atkinson (1993), who find that national savings have exceeded the depreciation of man-made and natural capital in recent years in Costa Rica.

Costa Rica. Capital and chemical intensive farming has been displacing traditional small-scale agriculture, leading to a growth in landlessness and urban migrants. From 1970 to 1983, the percentage of the Costa Rican labor force in agriculture declined from 42.2% to 33% (Leonard 1987). In spite of the spread of capital-intensive agriculture, however, food production per capita actually fell during the 1980s, at about 1% per year, and total food production fell further throughout the 1990s. How can we explain this?

Part of the explanation lies in the **hamburger connection.**[19] Increasing beef consumption in the developed world, along with major subsidy programs for ranching financed by international lending agencies and governments, has fueled the growth of the export beef industry in Latin America.[20] As Table 21.1 reveals, pasture land in Costa Rica grew at an astounding 6.9% per year over the 1980s through the mid-1990s.[21] Much of this came at the expense of rain forest (down 3.4% per year over the decade) or marginal hillside lands, but ranching also has expanded significantly into prime agricultural land. Cattle ranching has extended to include well over half of Central America's good agricultural land.[22] Ranching requires very little labor: Carriere (1991, 192) reports that pasture requires only six days of labor per hectare annually, compared, for example, to 37 for beans or 137 for coffee.

This kind of economic growth is potentially unsustainable for a variety of reasons. First, ranching in the rain forest leads to rapid destruction of natural capital. Deforested areas in Costa Rica can often maintain pasture for only six years or so before the resource is degraded (Carriere 1991). Recall that depleting the stock of natural capital is not necessarily unsustainable. However, sustainability does require that any drawdown of natural capital be compensated for by an increase in created capital, an issue we will consider below.

Ranching in prime agricultural lands also exacerbates problems of unemployment and hunger. Low employment levels in ranching mean that few workers displaced from prime land will be reemployed in the agricultural sector, and the displaced who formerly grew some or all of their own food are now likely to face hunger as either urban migrants or farmers pushed on to ecologically sensitive land, further depleting the nation's natural capital. In addition, greater poverty leads to higher population growth rates, exacerbating sustainability problems.

Finally, little of the beef is destined for local markets, so most Costa Ricans do not benefit from lower beef prices. In fact, due to crowding out from the beef industry, we have seen that domestic food production per capita has actually *dropped*. In addition, to the extent that expensive beef does replace inexpensive beans as a primary protein source in the culturally preferred local diet, the poor are likely to suffer from greater protein deficiencies.

---

[19]Pearce and Myers (1990) use this term.

[20]Leonard (1987, 88) reports that in the early 1970s half of all agricultural credit in Costa Rica was going to support the livestock industry, and that aid agencies, at least until recently, strongly advocated cattle production. This is in spite of the fact that on a per acre basis, livestock generate low export earnings. Leonard also suggests that ranching has succeeded on prime farm land in part because of the absence of infrastructure necessary to develop higher value-added crops. Pearce and Myers (1990) discuss the importance of subsidies for livestock development in Brazil.

[21]By contrast, land devoted to agriculture grew at only 0.4% per year.

[22]Carriere (1991) provides data for Costa Rica; see also Leonard (1987).

Could the country benefit at all from the growth of this industry? Yes. Some beef processing and shipping centers will provide urban employment. More importantly, profits earned from the export beef industry might be reinvested in Costa Rica—developing jobs, education, and infrastructure. In other words, Costa Rica *could* use the profits from the ranching industry to finance its agrarian transition, effectively replacing its depleted natural capital with created capital.

Unfortunately, investment levels have been low in all of Latin America, including Costa Rica, since the late 1970s. A variety of reasons explain this, but significant among these has been the tremendous burden of debt that Latin American countries owe to American, Japanese, and European banks.

During the 1970s, First World banks loaned tremendous sums of money to government agencies and private companies in poor countries around the world. Latin America's external debt rose from $7.2 billion in 1960 to $315.3 billion in 1982. It is not fully clear what motivated this irresponsible lending binge; however, little of the money was productively invested. Much of it financed imports of consumer goods from First World countries or else disappeared into private bank accounts. As a result by 1982, most countries were struggling just to make interest payments on the debt.[23]

During the 1980s, a series of rescheduling and compromises were worked out, but over the decade capital continued to flow out of the poor countries. In 1990, for example, Latin American countries paid out over $8 billion in interest payments and $15 billion in principal to First World banks (World Bank 1992, Table 22).

Costa Rica has one of the highest per capita external debts in the world. On average, each individual (via the government) owes First World banks about $960, more than one-third of the average yearly income in the country. Costa Rica pays out about 10% of the total value of its exports as payment on this debt (World Bank 1992). This eats up most of the profits from its cattle ranching and other export industries, meaning that little was left over to help finance the agrarian transition. Thus, natural capital stocks were being depleted by the ranchers without compensation in the form of created capital.

To summarize: At the beginning of this section I noted that the rising GDP per capital observed in Costa Rica during the 1990s need not have translated into sustainable development in the longer run. A closer look at the economic growth pattern based on cattle ranching revealed why.[24] First, the expansion of the export beef sector involved a direct drawdown on a segment of the nation's natural capital—the rain forest. Second, by creating more unemployed, land-hungry farmers, the growth in ranching both put an additional stress on forest resources and exacerbated population growth pressures. Finally, due to the debt burden, the depletion of natural capital was not compensated for by an increase in created capital. Instead, a substantial portion of the export profits flowed abroad to First World banks.

The growth of the export beef industry in Costa Rica into the 1990s was, by most measures, unsustainable development. Yet the situation in Costa Rica is brighter than most developing countries. In Costa Rica, one can at least identify a primary obstacle to sustainable development as the debt owed to banks in wealthy countries. Absent

---

[23]O'Brien (1991) provides the figures on the debt growth.

[24]For a more formal discussion of the conditions in which trade leads to unsustainable development, see Pezzey (1993). In one case, he finds that trade, relative to autarky, reduces sustainability in an "impatient" country.

that burden, the country has the underlying political resources necessary to manage its agrarian transition through investment in people and capital. And the Costa Rican state has reduced subsidy programs that have helped fuel unsustainable ranching practices. Finally, Costa Rica has a well-developed welfare state capable of delivering the health-care and education services needed to slow population growth rates.

For many other less developed countries, debt has also had a devastating impact on capital creation. As such, it has served as a major drag on sustainable development.[25] Yet, the sustainability challenge in most developing countries is *primarily a political one.* Highly unequal concentrations of wealth and political power in poor countries mean that government actions—for example, to promote cattle ranching—often are not taken with the welfare of the majority in mind. Yet, as we have seen, the well-being of the poor majority is a prerequisite for sustainability.

21.7 Envisioning a Sustainable Future

When one surveys the often overwhelming and interrelated problems of environmental degradation, poverty, population growth, overconsumption, and political powerlessness in poor countries, hopes for a future brighter than the present seem dim. Yet, what promise does exist comes from an increasing ecological recognition that the earth is genuinely a single spaceship. In just the last decade, citizens in rich countries have started to become aware that the life-support systems of our own affluent lifestyles, and those of our children, are critically affected by the economic security of poor children in São Paolo, Brazil, in the Ghanaian countryside, and indeed throughout the world. Global environmental threats such as greenhouse warming, ozone depletion, and biodiversity loss due to deforestation, as well as increasing legal and illegal immigration by the poor, remind us that we ignore our less fortunate sisters and brothers at our own peril.

This recognition is indeed quite recent and has just begun to take hold. The term "sustainable development" itself gained widespread currency only in 1987 with the publication of a book by the United Nations called, suitably, *Our Common Future.* Also known as the **Bruntland Commission Report,** after the commission's chair Gro Bruntland, the report sought to serve warning—a brighter future can be imagined, but it will not come without hard and conscious work upon our part.

The report called for urgent national and international action on four key **sustainability steps** described below (World Commission on Environment and Development 1987, Overview).[26] Underlying all the policy discussion is one common thread: Rich countries will have to bear much of the investment cost of achieving a sustainable future.

---

[25]From 1980 to 1990, Mexico's rate of gross domestic investment was −3.5%, for Honduras, −0.7% (World Bank 1992). For empirical confirmation of the debt overhang effect on investment, see Borensztein (1991), and Cohen (1993). For a general discussion of the debt problem, see the Symposia in the *Journal of Economic Perspectives,* Winter, 1990.

[26]I take some liberties with the commission's format. The authors place the urban challenge on par with population growth. I subsume the former under the latter. They also subdivide technology needs into energy and clean manufacturing.

For a discussion of the feasibility of the Bruntland Commission strategy for sustainable development in an input-output framework, see the Appendix to Chapter 19.

1. POPULATION AND HUMAN RESOURCES

Rapid population growth clearly undercuts sustainable development efforts. The Bruntland Commission predicted that between 1985 and the year 2000, cities in Third World countries would grow by about 60%, nearly three quarters of a billion people. Thus, just to maintain current, and in many cases desperately inadequate infrastructure, shelter, and educational facilities, poor countries would have to increase investment in these areas by more than one half in the short term. Fortunately, we are learning how to effectively control population growth. But the process itself—focusing on reducing infant deaths, providing education services, and effective family planning—is not cheap.

2. FOOD SECURITY

Joad's story in *The Grapes of Wrath* illustrates the agrarian transition underlying the traditional model of economic development: low-productivity, labor-intensive small farmers driven off the land by high-productivity, capital-intensive agriculture. And, to the extent that industrial jobs are available in the urban centers to absorb displaced farmworkers, the process "works," in spite of tremendous hardships suffered by families like Joad's.

Unfortunately, such industrial jobs are not emerging in many poor countries. Instead, the cities are teeming with unemployed and underemployed workers. As a result, there is little rationale for governments to actively promote capital-intensive agriculture in poor countries to displace even more farmworkers; instead, policy should focus on improving the productivity of small farmers. In addition, much of the "modern" farm sector has focused on the production of export crops, rather than food production for domestic consumption. Poor countries need to boost domestic food production to improve food security and basic nutrition.

One of the best ways to both encourage small farmers and increase food output is to reduce subsidies that keep urban food prices artificially low. (Higher food prices are necessary to keep farmers in business.) Yet, this can only be achieved politically if money is available to cushion the blow to poor urban residents of food price hikes. Such a policy again will require resources that poor countries do not have.

3. IMPROVED TECHNOLOGY

The Bruntland Commission's third focus was on the need for cleaner technology. Under the UN's medium assumptions, world population is liable to grow to 10 billion people before stabilizing in the mid–twenty-first century. Consumption per capita could easily triple. Thus, our children will grow into middle age on a planet supporting a much larger population, each consuming two or three times as many goods and services. Now imagine tripling or quadrupling the world's stock of conventional automobiles, coal-fired power plants, hazardous and nuclear waste, or land devoted to housing and agriculture. Under this kind of scenario, sustainability is simply impossible.

Thus, the development of clean energy and manufacturing technologies (as discussed in Chapters 19 and 20) is a fundamental prerequisite for a sustainable future. This is true because population growth cannot be stabilized without improving the material welfare of poor people in poor countries. Cheap energy and cheap basic manufactured goods are essential to achieve a sustainable global population. Yet, unless this material production can be achieved with substantially less environmental impact than it generates today, ecological degradation will undermine sustainability directly.

In essence, poor countries will have to "leapfrog" the dirty, resource-intensive development pattern successfully pursued by the rich countries, to both raise incomes and stabilize population growth. They can only do so, however, if new, clean technologies are developed and made available by those in rich countries with the resources to do so.

4. RESOURCE CONSERVATION

Because of open access to common property and high market discount rates, natural resources are often depleted at an unsustainable rate. Thus, there is a need for action to preserve much of the stock of natural capital remaining in poor countries, for the benefits of future generations. However, given massive poverty in these countries, even when national preserves are set aside, few resources are available for preventing their immediate, if technically illegal, exploitation. Poor countries will be able to do little to conserve natural resources on their own.

In summary, the Bruntland Commission Report yields two lessons. First, through the vision it provides of a sustainable planetary future, it suggests a framework for analyzing national and international environmental policy. In the next few chapters, we will look at a variety of tools available for coping with the worldwide environmental crisis. We now have four questions we will want to ask of such policies: What are the impacts on population growth? On improving food security? On promoting the development and diffusion of clean technology? On resource conservation? The answers, of course, will be complex, and often contradictory, but these sustainability steps are the four fronts on which simultaneous progress must be made.

The second lesson of *Our Common Future* is that it truly is our common future. Whether the planet will ultimately accommodate 10 billion people in a sustainable fashion, or 15 billion or 20 billion in a downward spiral of environmental degradation, conflict, and impoverishment, is a decision entirely in our hands. And by our hands, I mean the people who are reading this book. We are the beneficiaries of four hundred years of "dirty" development; we are also the richest people ever to walk the face of the earth. As such, we are the ones with the ability to design policies to channel global resources into resolving these four problems, and we are the ones who will determine whether our favored historical position is ultimately sustainable or not.

Where are the resources to come from? One attractive source is military spending. In 1995, the world was spending close to $900 billion a year on arms, in many cases with poor countries buying from rich ones. Table 21.2 illustrates that for twenty-three days of global military expenditure, substantial progress could be made addressing problems of population growth and resource conservation.

The political challenge involved in diverting resources from military to environmental spending is formidable. Even more difficult will be policies that curtail

TABLE 21.2   Military Expenditures and Development

Policy	Cost (Billions $1995)	Days of Military Expenditure
Action plan for tropical forests	$1.9	0.8
Action plan for desertification	6.5	2.8
Worldwide clean water project	43.0	18.4
Contraceptives to all who desire them worldwide	1.5	0.6
Total	36.8	22.5

Source: Program cost data from the World Commission on Environment and Development (1987), *Our Common Future* (New York: University Press); military spending information from Arias Oscar, Jordana Friedman, and Caleb Rossiter, "Less Spending, More Security," Year 2000 Campaign to Redirect World Military Spending to Human Development, http://www.connix.com/~clouette/cpa/arias.html.

consumption in rich countries (for example, through debt relief) to invest in sustainable development in poor countries. And yet, I personally am more optimistic that the challenge can be met today than I was twenty years ago, when as a student I first confronted the relentless mathematics of population growth, and its intimate relationship with the desperate poverty found worldwide.

In the 1970s and 1980s, a belief often prevailed that the rich could grow richer while the poor grew poorer; that we in the wealthy countries could in some sense wall-off the poverty and population problems of the Third World.[27] Today, worldwide environmental threats—global warming, ozone depletion, and loss of biological diversity—have made this a less and less tenable position. For the first time in history, rich countries now have a direct and increasingly important economic stake in helping poor countries to stabilize their population growth rates. Because this can be done most effectively by improving the lives of the poorest on the planet, achieving a sustainable future is a real possibility.

21.8 Summary

This chapter has outlined the fundamental connections between poverty, population growth, overconsumption, and sustainable development. The first step was to characterize the general challenge of economic development as productively absorbing labor freed up in the agrarian transition from small-scale, labor-intensive farming to large-scale, capital-intensive agriculture. It is important to note that, while the agrarian transition has to date been a universal feature of development, the speed at which it occurs is greatly affected by government policies, such as subsidized credit for large farmers, or subsidies that depress food prices and thus discourage food production by small farmers.

Due to an increasing awareness of the importance both of natural capital as an input into economic growth, and of negative environmental externalities as an outcome of economic growth, interest has shifted away from traditional development

---

[27]See, for example, Lucas (1976).

models to those focusing on sustainable development. Because sustainability is defined in terms of the welfare of the average individual over time, and the average individual in less developed countries is quite poor, sustainable development must concentrate attention on the status of the poor.

Sustainable development will tend to increase environmental quality for four reasons. First, exposure to two of the most pressing environmental problems in poor countries—polluted water and indoor air pollution (smoke)—are a direct result of poverty. Second, poor people cannot afford to conserve resources, and so they often put unsustainable pressure on their local environment. Third, as incomes rise, for a variety of reasons, certain regulated pollutant concentrations decline. Finally, income growth is one of the most effective population control measures available.

There is a debate over the extent of the population problem. On one side are those who foresee a "natural" demographic transition to a stable global population as economic progress proceeds in poor countries. By contrast, neomalthusians have argued that a vicious cycle is developing, in which poverty leads to high population growth rates that engender more poverty. Such a cycle, they argue, has already begun to overwhelm the beneficial effects of economic growth in many places. As a result, they are worried that the demographic transition is stalling out, and that global population will rise far above the 10 billion figure before being checked by physical or social limits.

The debate between neomalthusians and proponents of a natural demographic transition is about whether the global population will rise in the next 100 years to 9 to 11 billion, or 14 to 20 billion. From a policy point of view, however, there is little disagreement. Both sides agree that effective, noncoercive population control methods can speed up the demographic transition, and should be implemented.

Controlling population growth is not as simple as dispensing low-cost birth control devices, though this certainly helps. Poor people often have good economic reasons for having large families. Parents around the world depend on children for economic insurance and income supplements. Because of limited opportunities, and risk, poor families tend to pursue a low-investment, "quantity" strategy when choosing family size. Encouraging families to adopt a high-investment, "quality" strategy is the crux of an effective population control program.

Balanced economic growth and/or general economic redistribution are the most effective ways to alleviate poverty, and thus make a high-investment strategy feasible for many families. However, such outcomes, desirable for many reasons, have often been difficult to achieve. Yet, even poor countries have had success in achieving lower birth rates by pursuing a mixture of three policies: (1) reducing infant and childhood mortality, (2) improving access to education, especially for women, and (3) providing comprehensive family planning services. (Of course, these policies are also a form of redistribution of income and can help promote balanced growth.) Finally, coercive measures, both economic and physical, have been employed by China and India to control population growth. Aside from important moral issues, outside of China such programs may be counterproductive.

The pressure that people place on their environment depends not only on absolute numbers but also on the number of goods they consume and the damage that each good does. While in poor countries, overpopulation is the primary threat to both local and global environmental quality, in rich countries, consumption behavior is the problem. The consumption-pollution link arises from both the disproportionate share of global consumption engaged in by rich countries and the *potential* for an unsustainable drawdown of natural capital and environmental resources fueled by rich country consumption.

Cost Rica illustrates both the potential for and the obstacles to achieving sustainable development. While the country made substantial progress in reducing population growth rates in the 1980s, the increasing importance of its export beef industry threatens to counteract these sustainability gains. First, the industry has drawn down Costa Rica's rain forest stock directly. At the same time, profits from this industry have been siphoned off to repay the tremendous debt accumulated in the 1970s and have not been fully reinvested in created capital within the country. Moreover, cattle ranching has displaced many small farmers, who have increased pressure both on rain-forest lands and urban environments. Increased poverty among the landless farmers, as well as reduced production of food per capita, may also lead to higher birth rates, reducing progress made in reducing population growth.

Is a sustainable future possible? The Bruntland Commission provided an outline of the steps necessary to get us from here to there. They include controlling population growth, creating food security, improving technology, and conserving natural capital. All these options will be expensive and ultimately must be funded primarily by rich countries. The increasing recognition that rich country welfare depends on sustainable progress in poor countries makes this program at least potentially feasible from a political perspective. One possible pool of resources to finance the sustainable development program can be found in current world expenditures on military hardware and personnel.

APPLICATION 21.0

High Income Counties and Hazardous Waste

Some recent evidence (Bohara et al. 1996) shows that hazardous waste sites in the United States display an inverted U-shape relationship with county income. That is, as income in a county rises, the number of hazardous waste sites at first increases and then decreases, with a turning point of between $17,000 and $21,000 per capita. (The authors also find evidence of "environmental racism" [Chapter 5]. Controlling for income, a higher white population saw a significant drop in the number of hazardous waste sites.)

Do you take the evidence on income to mean that richer counties ultimately generate less hazardous waste? Why or why not?

APPLICATION 21.1

Childhood Mortality and Population Growth

Reducing the rate of infant and childhood mortality in poor countries clearly leads to a short-run increase in population growth. Use the economic model of family size developed in this chapter to explain why population growth experts nevertheless advocate improved public health measures as an important component of a population control strategy.

KEY IDEAS IN EACH SECTION

21.0   In large measure, successful **traditional economic development** means productively absorbing the labor freed up in the **agrarian transition.** Because poverty and environmental degradation go hand in hand, economic development is required for **sustainability;** however, sustainable development must also recognize the environmental costs of economic growth.

21.1   There are four connections between poverty and environmental quality. (1) Poor people suffer from **unsafe drinking water, inadequate sewage,** and **indoor air pollution.** (2) Poor people degrade local resources because they cannot afford not to. (3) Some regulated pollutants display an inverted U-shape as a function of income. This relationship has generated the **Environmental Kuznets Curve** hypothesis, and may be due to **education, relative risk considerations, political demand for pollution control,** and a **shift in industrial composition.** (4) Wealthier people tend to have lower rates of **population growth.**

21.2   Median and "highly pessimistic" **population growth scenarios** are laid out in this section. Under the former, world population will stabilize at 10 billion people; under the latter, it will quadruple over the next century to 20 billion. Growth predictions change rapidly with small changes in fertility rates. To date the **Malthusian** population trap, resulting from an arithmetic growth in food supply and a geometric growth in population, has been avoided. This is due in part to the Green Revolution and in part to the **demographic transition** to low birth rates in rich countries. However, a **vicious cycle,** in which population growth leads to poverty that sustains high population growth, is supported by recent trends in global food production per capita.

21.3   The **poverty-fertility relationship** is explained by an economic model in which all parents seek **economic insurance** and an **income supplement** from children. Due to lack of resources and risk, poor parents choose a **low-investment (quantity) strategy,** rather than a **high-investment (quality) strategy.**

21.4   Based on the model, population growth can be controlled in the following ways: (1) balanced economic growth and/or **redistribution of income** (perhaps via **land reform,** or a **debt-for-farmland swap**); (2) reduced **infant and childhood mortality;** (3) **access to education** (educated parents have a **higher opportunity cost of time;** education can also enhance women's status and decision-making ability in a **patriarchal culture**); and (4) comprehensive **family planning.** These measures, designed to change parental behavior by increasing opportunity, have proven successful. In addition to such measures, China has employed more **coercive** forms of population control in its **One-Child Policy.**

21.5   There are two elements to the **consumption-pollution link.** (1) Because rich countries consume most of the world's resources, we are responsible for most of the world's global pollution problems. (2) Rich country demand can lead to an unsustainable drawdown in natural capital in poor countries.

21.6 The **hamburger connection** between Costa Rican producers and rich country consumers is used to illustrate how export agriculture in a debt-burdened context might lead to unsustainable development. Although the country's gross domestic product (GDP) grew faster than its population in the 1990s, economic expansion based on cattle ranching has degraded rain-forest resources and increased the number of landless farmers. To the extent that compensating investment in created capital has not occurred, growth in the beef industry has lowered net national welfare.

21.7 The **Bruntland Commission Report** for the United Nations identified four **sustainability steps** necessary to achieve sustainable development. (1) Slow **population growth;** (2) boost **food security** by improving the productivity of small farmers; (3) develop and diffuse **clean technology;** and (4) engage in effective **resource conservation.** Each of these steps will cost money, much of which will have to come from rich countries. One source of funding would be to divert funds from global military spending.

REFERENCES

Becker, Gary S., and H.G. Lewis. 1973. "Interaction Between Quality and Quantity of Children." *Journal of Political Economy* 81:279–288.

Bieszaz, Richard, Karen Bieszaz, and Mavis Bieszaz. 1982. *The Costa Ricans.* Englewood Cliffs, NJ: Prentice Hall.

Birdsall, Nancy M., and Charles C. Griffin. 1988. "Fertility and Poverty in Developing Countries." *Journal of Policy Modeling* 10, no. 1:29–55.

Bohara, Alok, Kishore Gawande, Robert Berrens, and Pingo Wang. 1996. "Environmental Kuznets Curves for U.S. Hazardous Waste Sites." *Working Paper.* Albuquerque: University of New Mexico.

Borensztein, Eduardo. 1991. "Will Debt Reduction Increase Investment?" *Finance and Development* 28, no. 1:25–27.

Browder, John O. 1988. "Public Policy and Deforestation in the Brazilian Amazon." In *Public Policies and the Misuse of Forest Resources,* edited by Robert Repetto and Malcolm Gillis. Cambridge: Cambridge University Press.

Carriere, Jean. 1991. "The Crisis in Costa Rica: An Ecological Perspective." In *Environment and Development in Latin America,* edited by David Goodman and Michael Redclift. New York: Manchester University Press.

Cohen, Daniel. 1993. "Low Investment and Large LDC Debt in the 1980s." *American Economic Review* 83, no. 3:437–449.

Cohen, Joel. 1995. *How Many People Can the Earth Support?* London: W. W. Norton.

Daly, Herman. 1990. "How Big Is the Population Factor?" *EPA Journal,* July/August, 31.

Dasgupta, Partha. 1995. "Population, Poverty and the Local Environment," *Scientific American* 272, no. 2:40–46.

Forster, Nancy R.. 1992. "Protecting Fragile Lands: New Reasons to Tackle Old Problems." *World Development* 20, no. 4:371–382.

Jacobson, Jodi L. 1987. *Planning the Global Family.* Washington, DC: Worldwatch.

Leonard, H. Jeffrey. 1987. *Natural Resources and Economic Development in Central America.* Oxford: Transaction Books.

Lucas, George (ed.). 1976. *Lifeboat Ethics.* New York: Harper and Row.

Moene, Karl Ove. 1992. "Poverty and Land Ownership." *American Economic Review* 82, no. 1:52–64.

Musambachime, Mwelma. 1990. "The Impact of Rapid Population Growth on Economic Decline: The Case of Zambia." *Review of African Political Economy* 448, no. 2:81–91.

O'Brien, Phillip J. 1991. "Debt and Sustainable Development in Latin America." In *Environment and Development in Latin America,* edited by David Goodman and Michael Redclift. New York: Manchester University Press.

Pearce, David, and Giles D. Atkinson. 1993. "Capital Theory and the Measurement of Sustainable Development: An Indicator of 'Weak' Sustainability." *Ecological Economics* 8, no. 2:103–108.

Pearce, David, and Norman Myers. 1990. "Economic Values and the Environment of Amazonia." In *The Future of Amazonia: Destruction or Sustainable Development?* edited by David Goodman and Anthony Hall. New York: St. Martins Press.

Pezzey, John. 1993. "Sustainability Policies in Models of Trade with Exhaustible Resources." Paper presented at the American Economic Association Meetings, Anaheim, CA.

Rand. 1998. "International Family Planning." *Population Policy Briefing.*

Repetto, Robert. 1985. "Population, Resource Pressures, and Poverty." In *The Global Possible: Resources, Development and the New Century,* edited by Robert Repetto. New Haven, CT: Yale University Press.

Wattenberg, Ben J. 1990. "How Big is the Population Factor?" *EPA Journal,* July/August, 30.

World Bank. 1992. *World Development Report 1992: Development and the Environment.* New York: Oxford University Press.

World Commission on Environment and Development. 1987. *Our Common Future.* New York: Oxford University Press.

ENVIRONMENTAL POLICY IN POOR COUNTRIES

22.0 Introduction

At the end of Chapter 21, we identified four interrelated **sustainability steps** that need to be pursued in poor countries if the ultimate vision of a sustainable future for human beings is to be realized. These four policy goals are (1) stabilizing population growth, (2) achieving food security, (3) promoting the development and adoption of clean technology, and (4) conserving natural capital. This chapter moves on to consider a variety of other steps that poor and rich countries can take to promote the four policy goals.

As in our discussion of environmental policy in the United States, we need to be fully aware of the constraints that government policy makers in poor countries face. Because the potential for government failure in poor countries is large, due in part to much stronger business influence over policy, the first half of this chapter analyzes measures designed to harness the profit motive in pursuit of sustainable development. First, poor country governments should eliminate environmentally destructive subsidy policies. Second, by strengthening property rights, governments can reinforce profit-based motives for conservation.

While government can do a lot by selectively disengaging itself from market transactions, and improving private incentives for conservation, government ultimately must be counted on to take an effective, proactive role in promoting sustainable development. This chapter thus goes on to examine the role that regulatory and clean technology strategies must play.

Finally, we end with a trio of related topics: resource conservation, debt relief, and international trade. The basic message of the chapter is that achieving the four sustainability steps is not cheap; without substantial financial flaws from wealthy countries, it is doubtful whether sustainable development in poor countries can be achieved.

22.1 The Political Economy of Sustainable Development

Before jumping into specifics, we need to pause to consider the constraints under which government policy operates. Part II of this book focused considerable attention on the obstacles to effective government action in the United States, raised both by imperfect information and the opportunity for political influence.

The United States is a wealthy country, with a fairly efficient marketplace and government. By contrast, the average person in a less developed country is a very poor person, and this poverty undermines the efficiency of both markets and governments. Per capita annual income in low-income countries is about $600, or about $1.75 per person per day. But even these abysmal figures disguise the true extent of poverty, since there is considerable wealth inequality *within* countries.

In general, most countries have a small **political-economic elite** who control a disproportionate share of national income and wield disproportionate influence over political events. Even in a developed country like the United States, the top 20% of the population owns more than 70% of the nation's wealth and takes in 44.3% of the annual income.[1] The income distribution in poor countries is typically much more uneven. For example, the top 20% of the population in four central American countries—El Salvador, Guatemala, Nicaragua, and Honduras—receive between 54% and 66% of the national income (Leonard 1987, 51).

This kind of tremendous economic and political disparity often has a historical basis in the period of colonial rule. For example, throughout Latin America, the current, dramatic concentration of landownership in the hands of a small percentage of the population can be traced to the *hacienda* system established by the Spanish colonists. Or consider another example. Britain granted Zambia independence in 1964 after exploiting that nation's rich copper deposits for 40 of its 70 years of colonial rule. At independence, only 100 Africans out of a population of 3.5 million had received a college education, and fewer than 1,000 were high school graduates (Musambachime 1990).

At the risk of very gross oversimplification, the typical class structure in a developing country can be represented by the pyramid in Figure 22.1.[2] At the top are a small group of wealthy landholders, industrialists, and military officers, often educated in western universities. Businessmen in this group include both local capitalists and local managers of multinational corporations. Below them come the urban middle class: teachers, professionals, state employees, factory workers, miners, and soldiers. The vast majority of the population are the poor: urban shanty-town dwellers subsisting on part-time work, rural small farmers, and landless laborers.

Sustainable development—increasing NNW for the average individual—by definition requires focusing on the lower class, since they are the average individuals. Moreover, it is this group, who out of brute necessity, often run down the local stock of natural capital in a nonsustainable fashion. As we begin to evaluate development and environmental policy in poor countries, the question we thus need to ask is, "Does the policy improve or exacerbate the position of the poor?"

---

[1]*Statistical Abstract of the United States,* 1992. Washington, DC: U.S. Dept. of Commerce.
[2]For a succinct review article on Third World politics, see Weaver, Holmquist, and Ford (1990).

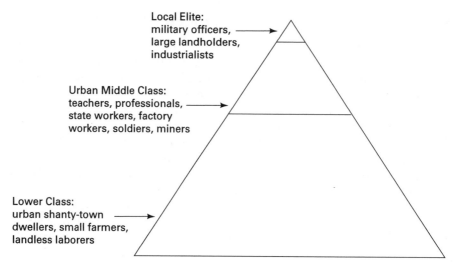

FIGURE 22.1 Class Structure in Poor Countries (Generalized)

Unfortunately, because the lower class generally has little political power in developing countries, this question is seldom central to policy design. Elite-dominated governments, often maintaining their power through military force, rarely provide democratic avenues for those adversely impacted by government policy to register their protests. Yet, for environmental progress, the ability to protest is vital.

As was argued in Chapter 12, the primary environmental lesson from the Communist experience is that a lack of democracy will stifle the recognition of environmental problems. Absent substantial pressure from those affected, government will have neither the power nor the inclination to force economic decision makers—whether state bureaucrats, managers of private corporations, or ordinary citizens—to recognize and internalize the external environmental costs generated by their actions. Perhaps for this reason, increasing landlessness among small farmers, leading to severe pressure on marginal rural lands and massive urban migration, has not, until recently, been viewed as the major environmental problem that it indeed has become.

In addition to nonrecognition of important problems, when government leaders are not democratically accountable, opportunities for corruption multiply. This is especially true when even top government officials in poor countries fail to achieve a standard of living common to the middle class in western countries. Not surprisingly, given their very low pay and level of training, corruption among low-level bureaucrats in poor countries is not uncommon. Thus, as a general rule, government bureaucracies in poor countries are not particularly efficient. (The few developing countries for which this is not true tend to be economically quite successful.)[3] As a result, even when development/environmental problems are in fact recognized, and policies are set up to attack them, progress may be quite slow.

---

[3]Though not necessarily in a sustainable fashion. Examples include Taiwan, Korea, China, Singapore, Botswana, and Costa Rica.

Partly in response to government failures in poor countries, so-called nongovernmental organizations (NGOs) have emerged to deal with issues of rural development, small-farmers rights, urban service provision, and natural resource protection. NGOs include international development and human rights groups, the international arms of environmental and conservation groups, local environmental groups, peasant and rural workers unions, and urban activist groups.

To summarize: For a variety of reasons including colonial history, small political-economic elites, undemocratic governmental structures, and poorly trained and paid bureaucrats, factors leading to government failure are compounded in poor countries. Given this potential, policies that depend on sophisticated analytical capabilities, or aggressive monitoring and enforcement are not likely to succeed in many parts of the developing world.

Unlike in wealthy countries, the "environmental movement" is very small in poor countries. Thus progress toward sustainable development must spring from either environmental concern on the part of ruling elites or a nonenvironmental interest on their part in population control, food security, technological innovation, or resource conservation. No strong groundswell drives the political process in a sustainable direction.

The lack of popular environmental counterpressure also means that business interests have a much freer hand in affecting environmental policy in poor countries. Both **domestic** and **multinational businesses** operate in the developing world. Domestic firms are owned and operated by residents of the poor country; multinational firms operate in many countries around the globe and are typically headquartered in a developed country.

Multinational companies have a particularly strong presence in resource-based industries in less developed countries. Between 80% and 90% of world trade in tea, coffee, cocoa, cotton, forest products, tobacco, jute, copper, iron ore, and bauxite is under the control of three to six such companies. However, multinationals have also invested heavily in manufacturing in poor countries, especially in chemicals (World Commission on Environment and Development 1987, 85).

The influence of business, whether domestic or multinational, on environmental policy goals can be positive. For example, businesses can create jobs leading to balanced growth and a subsequent reduction in population growth rates. Or they can import or develop new clean technology. However, the influence can also be negative. Businesspeople may bribe officials to obtain subsidized access to timber or other resources, and understate profits to avoid taxation.[4] Or businesses might promote subsidized credit programs, allowing them to import capital-intensive agricultural technologies that displace farmworkers, on net, leading to an increase in unemployment and poverty. Or business might use its resources to discourage the passage and/or enforcement of environmental or resource protection legislation.

---

[4]In Papua, New Guinea, for example, Thompson (1992) reports that prior to 1986, no logging company had ever declared a profit or paid income tax. Estimates of losses from transfer pricing in the country ranged from $42 million to $55 million per year.

The point here is to neither condemn nor praise business as an agent of environmental change in poor countries.[5] Rather, the point is simply to remember that business managers, whether multinational or domestic, are generally not interested in sustainable development. They are interested in profit. To the extent that profit opportunities promote sustainable development, business will do so as well. However, businesses will just as eagerly pursue profit-driven options that are ultimately unsustainable.

Likewise, the point is not to condemn governments in poor countries as hopelessly corrupt or inefficient. There are many examples of government success as well as failure in the developing world. Ultimately, we *must* rely on poor country governments to undertake effective action if we seek to achieve a sustainable future. There is simply no other choice.

22.2 Ending Environmentally Damaging Subsidies

Both rich and poor countries around the world maintain a broad array of **subsidies** for particular industries with the purported intent of promoting economic development. Some of the forms these subsidies take include special tax breaks, privileged access to imported parts and materials, protection from international competition, low-cost access to natural resources, the provision of subsidized or interest-free loans, and investment in infrastructure.

Unfortunately, many of these subsidy policies have had the effect of undermining the four steps to sustainability discussed above. This section will look closely at the forest industry, where government policy has often worked to promote a rapid and unsustainable exhaustion of the resource. To begin with, governments often sell public timber to logging companies at prices that are "too low." By this I mean that governments **fail to capture all the resource rent** associated with the timber. As discussed in Chapter 6, for timber harvesting to be sustainable, *all* of the resource rent must be retained in the host country and invested in created capital.

In the recent past, the governments of Ghana, Indonesia, and the Philippines have received less than 38% of the total rents from timber production in the form of sales revenue and taxes (see Repetto 1988a).[6] By failing to capture all the rents, governments make logging artificially profitable, and this speeds up the depletion of the resource. In addition, once timber sales have been consummated and roads built, it has proven very difficult for governments to enforce environmental contract terms in remote areas, or to monitor illegal cutting and smuggling of timber.[7]

Many governments also engage in **infrastructure development** to support forestry—building roads and ports, and surveying and grading timber. In the extreme,

---

[5]There is substantial debate over the role that multinational corporations in particular play in promoting or hindering sustainable development. In my own research (Goodstein 1989), I found that absentee ownership of coal resources hindered development in Appalachia, vis à vis the rest of the southern United States. I argue that the most important impact of absentee ownership was the restriction in the growth of a local business class interested in promoting manufacturing development.

[6]The figures for Indonesia and the Philippines are from 1979 to 1982, and for Ghana, 1971 to 1974.

[7]Thompson (1992) details how difficult this process can be for the case of Papua, New Guinea.

taxpayers actually pay firms to harvest timber. This has occurred in the United States, where the Forest Service sells timber at prices that do not cover its administrative and road-building expenses. In 1995, this direct subsidy from the Forest Service was close to $230 million (see Wall Street Journal, 19 February 1997, and Repetto 1988b).

Poor countries have also **subsidized "downstream" industries,** which process raw timber into lumber and other finished wood and paper products. Subsidies include substantial tax breaks and subsidized credit, as well as placing bans on the export of unfinished logs. Many of these policies have not been successful, however, due to high tariffs in rich countries designed to protect *their* wood processing industries. Moreover, due to a lack of domestic competition, wood processing industries in poor countries tend to be very inefficient and require continuous subsidies. In addition, their existence puts further pressure on the government to artificially lower timber prices to maintain employment.[8]

Governments have also sponsored **colonization projects** to resettle landless farmers in rain-forest areas. Such conversion efforts have been judged a sustainable success in peninsular Malaysia, where about 12% of the country's forest has been converted to permanent tree crops such as rubber and palm oil since 1950 (Gillis 1988). However, efforts in Brazil and Indonesia have failed, with the land being abandoned after deforestation. In part, this failure has resulted from poor soil quality. In addition, the policies have been hampered by inadequate, though still substantial, government efforts to develop distribution and marketing channels for small farmers in remote areas. Subsidies for these programs, from the government and the World Bank, ranged as high as $10,000 per household in Indonesia, a country with a GNP per capita of $560 (Repetto 1988a).

Finally, as was discussed in the Costa Rica case in Chapter 21, governments have been quite active in promoting the spread of **cattle ranching** in forested areas. This process has advanced furthest in the Brazilian Amazon, where cattle ranching has caused more than 70% of total deforestation (Browder 1988). Under the theory that ranching would serve as a spur to the general economic development of the Amazon, and concerned about securing its national borders through settlement, the Brazilian government pumped more than $730 million into the beef industry between 1966 and 1983. However, Browder (1988) shows that by 1985, few of the government-supported Amazon ranches could have survived without continuing subsidies.

To summarize: With the ostensible goal of supporting resource-based economic development (and influenced by factors as diverse as national defense and personal gain), policy makers in poor countries have established an array of subsidies for logging companies, forest product industries, small farmers, and large ranchers. With a few exceptions, such policies have failed to generate stand-alone industries and have continually drained capital from other sectors. With limited economic progress, population growth has not declined. Because of the policy emphasis on ranching instead of basic foodstuffs, and the failure of small farm programs to take root, food security has not improved. And little clean technology has been developed or introduced.

---

[8]Deacon (1992) points out, however, that export bans on raw logs may still on balance reduce the rate of deforestation.

At the same time, subsidy policies have led to unsustainable declines in natural capital—the forest resource. In addition, they have generated environmental damage ranging from siltation and flooding, to forest fires, to a tremendous loss of biodiversity. Finally, native inhabitants of the forests have lost access to their means of subsistence, and their cultural survival is threatened.

This section has explored in detail some of the subsidy policies that promote rapid deforestation around the world, for little if any net economic benefit to poor countries. Subsidies for other products that aggravate environmental damage include energy, pesticides and fertilizer, and irrigation water. In Egypt, India, Brazil, China, and Mexico, for example, electric power has been sold at less than 60% of production cost, with the government making up the difference through tax revenues (World Bank 1992, 68–69). The increased demand for power sparked by lower prices has brought with it associated environmental change from hydroelectric, coal, and nuclear power plants.

Environmentally damaging subsidies are not unique to poor countries, as our discussions of the U.S. Forest Service and of energy and agricultural subsidies in Chapters 19 and 20 make clear. And just as subsidy elimination is difficult in rich countries, so it will be in poor countries. Subsidies can seldom be eliminated without some form of **compensation** for the losers.

In addition, compensation is often required on the grounds of basic **fairness** when subsidies benefit the poor. For example, a major obstacle to food security arises when governments hold prices for basic foods, for example bread or cooking oil, below their market-clearing price. Low prices drive farmers into bankruptcy. Recognizing this effect, and interested in boosting agricultural output, the former USSR decontrolled bread prices in December 1991. Figure 22.2 illustrates what happened. Prices were initially controlled at about 0.2 cents per pound, leading to a restriction in the available supply, the development of shortages and long lines, and black markets. (Average monthly income in Russia was about $20.)

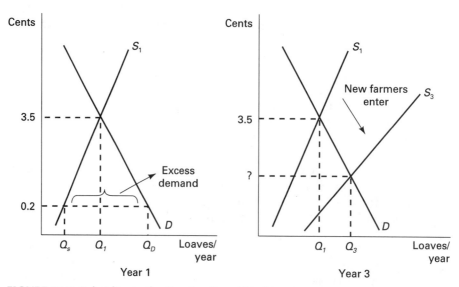

FIGURE 22.2 Subsidies in the Russian Bread Market

By June 1992, prices had jumped to 3.5 cents per pound, more than a sixteenfold increase. In the long run (two years or so), more farmers would be expected to enter the wheat market, shifting the supply curve out and driving bread prices down to some intermediate level. Yet, the sudden decontrol meant at least several years of suffering for Russians, particularly those unable to work.

To cushion the blow of increased prices, the government provided income supplements. One family interviewed by the *New York Times* was receiving child-support payments for food, clothing, and day care from the government totaling $4.40 per month. But political pressures in early 1993 still led to at least symbolic action to restore price controls on basic goods ("In Choppy Russian Economy" 1992; "Russia Says Curbs" 1993).

Russia is a relatively wealthy country, yet removing food subsidies there has led to considerable hardship. In poor countries, eliminating food price controls without increasing the income of the poor can lead to starvation. During the 1980s, at least a dozen food riots shook poor countries as governments, under the prodding of the International Monetary Fund, lifted price controls without taking adequate measures to boost poor people's income (Tibesar and White 1990).

On political and sometimes, equity grounds, removing environmentally damaging subsidies requires resources to compensate people who lose out. Nevertheless, eliminating such subsidies presents a cheap way to improve environmental quality in poor countries. Removing subsidies requires no ongoing governmental expense, and sustainability can be enhanced through the productive use of the resources freed up.

22.3 Establishing and Enforcing Property Rights

Way back in Chapter 3, we identified one of the primary causes of pollution and resource degradation—open access to common property. Recall that the **open access problem** arose when individuals considered only the private benefit and costs from exploiting a shared resource—air, land, or water—without taking into account the external social costs imposed on others. Recall also that traditional societies managed common property problems through informal social controls and moral sanctions.

However, as traditional control mechanisms have broken down, and both population and consumption pressures have risen, the free access problem has emerged as a major underlying source of environmental degradation worldwide. When the **property rights** or titles to resources such as land or fisheries are not clearly defined, the people who exploit the resource have little incentive to engage in **profit-based conservation** or invest in long-lived environmental protection measures such as erosion control. To improve this situation, government has three options.

1. COMMUNAL OWNERSHIP

Where an existing community is managing the property sustainably, government policy can protect and enforce the existing communal property right. Often this will mean restricting access to outsiders and may require imposing limitations on the use of sophisticated technology. For example, in one case, cooperative fishing agreements in southern Brazil broke down when nylon fishing nets were adopted by some members of the group, giving them an "unfair" advantage. In addition, under Brazilian law, the group could not exclude outsiders, who also used such nets. The primary advantage of communal ownership patterns, when they can be supported by cohesive communities, is that they tend to be quite sustainable.[9]

2. STATE OWNERSHIP

Government can declare the land a national forest, reserve, or park, or regulate an ocean fishery. However, a simple declaration is inadequate. Government must also devote the necessary resources to protecting the boundaries of the reserve in order to prevent unauthorized uses. This kind of enforcement task can be extremely difficult for most poor countries. Even in a country with a relatively efficient bureaucracy such as Costa Rica, one source estimated that landless farmers had cleared one quarter of the total forest reserves that the government had set aside for protection.[10] (See Chapter 23 for an analysis of efforts to improve this situation.)

A recent effort by Chile to manage its ocean fisheries involves an overall quota system, controls on boats and fishing gear, and a licensing scheme. In this case, assistance to strengthen enforcement and monitoring capabilities will be provided by Nordic countries and the World Bank (World Bank 1992, 84).

3. PRIVATE OWNERSHIP

The final option is to assign property rights to private individuals. However, this process also is more difficult than it seems on the surface. First, it is not free, since government resources must be put to work delineating and enforcing private property rights. More importantly, privatization can easily contribute to increased poverty.

Privatizing commonly held property will often hurt those who previously had access under traditional law. For example, privatization of rural land in Kenya led to married sons and wives losing their traditional land rights, since they were not represented in the process. And in many instances, privatization schemes provide an advantage to wealthy and/or educated individuals to increase their wealth at the expense of the poor (Barrows and Roth 1990). This type of privatization is counterproductive from a sustainability point of view, since it tends to increase poverty and downgrade women's social status, thus increasing population growth rates while reducing food security. Privatization efforts designed to boost profit-based conservation must therefore be conducted carefully so as to increase rather than decrease both the social status of women and general employment opportunities.

Privatizing forested land can also have ambiguous environmental impacts. For example, as a way to clearly establish ownership uses, many poor countries require that settlers clear the land in order to take title (as was the practice on the U.S. frontier). This process of course encourages deforestation. Yet without actual occupation and use of the land, settlers and government officials would have a hard time validating whose claim to a piece of land is legitimate. Even where clearance is not required, establishing legal title to land in many poor countries can take years. As a result, farmers tend to clear the land anyway in order to establish *de facto* control.

---

[9]The Brazilian example is from the World Bank (1992, 70). Katz (2000) emphasizes the role of "social capital" in resource management. For good surveys, see Bromley (1991) or Hanna and Munasinghe (1995).

[10]The estimate is from Fundacion Neotropica, an environmental organization in Costa Rica, cited in Carriere (1991).

Yet, because they risk losing their land, farmers who have not attained legal title tend to underinvest in profit-based conservation measures (see Chapter 6) like erosion control, as well as investments that increase farm output.[11] To encourage such measures, governments can speed up the titling process; for example, by employing more surveyors and land clerks and by providing better law enforcement to prevent illegal evictions. This will increase the security of farmers' private property rights and should encourage them to invest more in their land.

Clarifying and strengthening property rights is a way to directly reduce environmental damage by "internalizing externalities." When property rights are clearly defined, then the owner—a community, the government, or an individual—bears a larger part of the social costs of environmental resource degradation or depletion. Individual and community ownership schemes have an advantage in this respect over government ownership, since people at the local level are directly affected by resource degradation. As a result, they have a greater incentive than do government managers to maintain the productivity of the piece of the environment they "own."

Ownership at the individual or community level will thus tend to promote profit-based conservation, while conservation under state ownership depends on the strength of environmental concern within the governing elite. As we have argued above, such concern may be quite weak, and even where strong, the enforcement capabilities of poor country governments can make resource conservation and environmental protection difficult.

Yet privatization alone is no panacea. In a study of East African farmers, Barrows and Roth (1990) concluded that due to a lack of credit, marketing infrastructure, technical assistance, and in some cases *increased* uncertainty under the new legal structure, the displacement of traditional communal land holdings by private farms has had little impact on agricultural investment. They conclude that privatization is most useful when it serves as a safeguard against the taking of small-farmer land by politically powerful individuals.

The first two sections of this chapter have focused on ways in which poor country governments can improve environmental quality either by selectively reducing environmentally damaging subsidies, or by strengthening communal and private property rights in order to promote profit-based conservation. We now move on to a consideration of more proactive government policy: regulation and clean technology promotion.

22.4 Regulatory Approaches

Environmental regulation is a new phenomenon in the developed world, with most of the major laws having been passed within the last twenty-five years. Regulation is even more recent in poor countries: Mexico, for example, passed its comprehensive federal environmental law only in 1988.

Chapters 16 and 17 have already provided an in-depth look at the theory of regulation. It was argued there that in general, an **incentive-based** system (pollution taxes or marketable permits) is both more cost-effective in the short run, and better at

---

[11]Southgate formalizes this argument (1990).

encouraging technological advancement in the long run, than a so-called **command-and-control** approach to pollution control. Recall that a stereotypical command-and-control system features (1) uniform emission standards for all sources and (2) the installation of government-mandated pollution control technologies. The inflexibility in the approach means that cost-saving opportunities that can be captured by incentive-based systems are not exploited, and that incentives for improved technology are limited. This lesson holds for poor countries as well, with a couple of *caveats*.

First, as we learned in Chapter 15, monitoring and enforcement is the weakest link in the regulatory process in rich countries. This observation holds even stronger in poor countries. Mexico, for example, has been trying to beef up its enforcement efforts, partly in response to the North American Free Trade Agreement, discussed later in this chapter. Yet, in spite of some highly publicized efforts, including plant shutdowns, enforcement remains quite weak by U.S. standards. One spot survey of six U.S. companies operating along the border found that none of them held required environmental permits (U.S. General Accounting Office 1992). Thus, the primary focus of regulatory policy in the developing world must be **enforceability.**

Pollution taxes can improve enforcement, because government benefits materially from enforcing the law. This is especially true if the enforcement agency is allowed to keep some portion of the fines. Command-and-control systems also have some enforceability advantages, when regulators can force firms to install low marginal cost ("automatic") pollution control technologies. However, recall that even such automatic technologies, like catalytic converters or power plant scrubbers, break down and require maintenance.

In poor countries with efficient court systems, one way to improve enforcement would be to encourage the use of citizen suits against polluters, discussed in Chapter 17. Another recommendation has been to allow foreign nongovernmental organizations to sue U.S.-based multinational corporations in U.S. courts for violations of poor country environmental laws.[12]

The second rule that poor country governments must heed in selecting regulatory instruments is to seek **administrative simplicity.** For example, during the mid-1980s severe particulate pollution from state-owned and multinational chemical plants, steel mills, and other industrial and power facilities in Cubatao, Brazil, led to the evacuation of many residents to a nearby soccer stadium. While in principle, a marketable permit or particulate tax system might have been introduced to control the pollution, instead the authorities directed the firms to install scrubbers and switch to low-sulfur oil—classic command-and-control tactics (World Bank 1992, 131). It is doubtful that local authorities had either the technological capabilities or the staff to develop, monitor, and enforce a sophisticated incentive-based system. This is particularly true since extensive field testing of tradeable permit or pollution tax systems in rich countries has not yet occurred.

In practice, avoiding administrative complexity and insuring enforceability means that pure incentive-based systems (pollution taxes or marketable permit systems) may

---

[12]Naysnerski and Tietenberg (1992) make the first suggestion. Harvard Law Review (1990) argues a more ambitious variant of the second.

not be feasible. However, the use of **indirect pollution taxes** will often be a good approach. In contrast to direct pollution taxes, which tax the emission of pollutants directly, indirect pollution taxes impose fees on inputs to, or outputs from, a polluting process. Examples include energy or fuel taxes (discussed in Chapter 20), or taxes on timber production.

The example of taxes on timber sold to mills (called **royalties**) is an interesting one, since it illustrates some of the problems raised by indirect taxation of pollution. The idea is that by taxing rain-forest timber production, logging will become less profitable, leading to a reduction in this activity. This in turn may be desirable because logging contributes to environmental damage ranging from siltation and flooding, to loss of biodiversity, to an aggravation of global warming. The situation is illustrated in Figure 22.3.

In a classic supply-and-demand analysis, increased royalties raise costs to firms, causing some to drop out of the market. This shifts the supply curve up to S', and the timber brought to market drops to T'. This appears to be the desired result of the policy. However, an offsetting effect may in fact lead to a much smaller reduction in the actual area logged. As royalties are raised, fewer tree species become profitable to harvest. Yet to get the remaining profitable species, firms may still need to clear-cut the same acreage. Firms then remove the profitable species, leaving much of the timber that would formerly have been brought to market behind, a process called *high grading*. Thus, although increased royalties will have a big effect on the timber brought to market, they may have a smaller impact on the acreage logged.

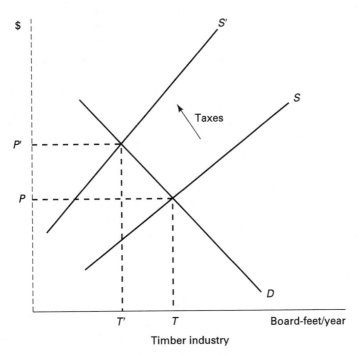

FIGURE 22.3 Increased Royalties and Logging Activity

To solve this problem, one might suggest a more direct pollution tax—a royalty based on the acreage logged. Such a tax would get at the problem in an up-front way. But monitoring logging activity is much harder than slapping a tax on logs as they come to the mill, so the indirect tax wins out on enforceability grounds. Another alternative would be to vary royalties by species, with higher taxes on high-value trees, as is done in the Malaysian state of Sarawak. This reduces high grading and thus can have a bigger impact on acreage reduction.[13] In summary, the lesson from the timber royalty case is that indirect pollution taxes *are not* direct pollution taxes, and their ultimate effect on pollution or resource degradation cannot be taken for granted. The impact of indirect taxes on the environmental problem at hand must be carefully considered.

This is not to say, however, that indirect pollution taxes are a bad idea. Well-designed indirect taxes can have a substantial impact on environmental problems. In addition to such measures, cost-saving flexibility can be built into command-and-control regulatory structures wherever possible. To see how the use of an indirect tax combined with flexibility in a command-and-control regulatory approach can reduce the costs of pollution control, we turn to the case of air pollution control in Mexico City.

Mexico City is home to both 20 million people and more than half of Mexico's non-oil manufacturing output. Air pollution in the city is among the worst in the world. One study suggested that simply breathing the air had a health effect comparable to smoking forty cigarettes per day.[14] During the winter of 1991 the pollution problem was at an all-time high: Athletes were warned not to train outside, birds dropped dead out of the trees, and vendors began selling oxygen on the street. The government began to take steps to control the problem, including the shutdown of some major private and public-owned industrial facilities, and incentive-based measures such as increased parking fees in the central city. By the year 2000, significant improvements had been achieved.[15]

In a World Bank study, Eskeland constructed a marginal cost of reduction curve for air pollution from motor vehicles in the city, reproduced in Figure 22.4. The curve starts out at the left with measures that actually save money: retrofitting some high-use public vehicles to natural gas and recovering refueling vapors. However, the options for further improvement—first emission standards, then strengthened inspection, and then improvements in fuel—become increasingly costly. Eskeland estimated that using these command-and-control measures alone, pollution could be reduced by 1.2 million tons per year, at a cost of about $1,800 per ton for the last unit removed.

However, as indicated by the dotted line, if the measures were coupled with a relatively low **gasoline tax** (of about $0.05 per liter), the same pollution reduction could be achieved at lower cost. As you can see in the graph, Eskeland estimated marginal savings of about $300 per ton of air pollution for the last ton reduced. The reason: The gas tax would reduce overall driving, and forestall the need for more

---

[13]Though it need not. In fact, which system reduces overall logged acreage more will depend on which system reduces logging profitability more. Repetto (1988a) provides the information on the royalty structure in Sarawak.

[14]The study was done by the U.S. Embassy and is cited in Lepkowski (1987).

[15]"Smog City," and "Pay to Breathe," *The Economist,* May 18, 1991, and February 16, 1991, and "Terrific News in Mexico City," *New York Times,* January 5, 2001, p. A1.

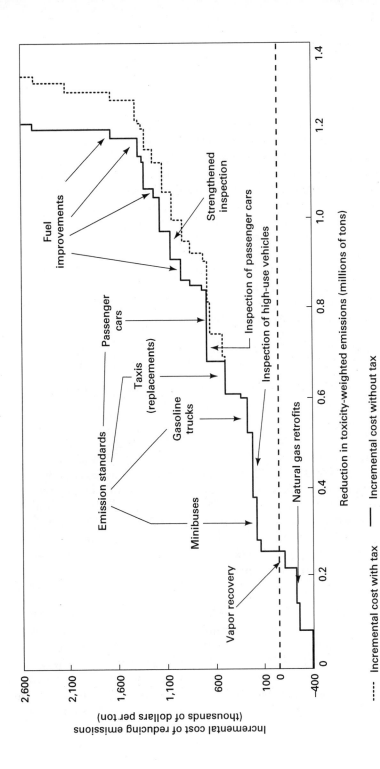

FIGURE 22.4 Air Pollution Control in Mexico City, Marginal Costs from Vehicles

Source: From *World Development Report 1992* by The World Bank. Copyright © 1992 by The International Bank for Reconstruction and Development/The World Bank. Reprinted by permission of Oxford University Press, Inc.

expensive command-and-control measures to achieve a given reduction in pollution. In fact, the government has since raised gasoline taxes by a substantially higher margin than the study recommended.

However, because a gasoline tax is not a direct emission tax, it is not fully cost-effective. For example, both dirty and clean cars are taxed at the same rate. The equal marginal cost of reduction principle necessary for cost-effectiveness (Chapter 16), is thus not satisfied. As a result, Eskeland (1991) recommended that cleaner cars receive a rebate of some of their gas tax when they are inspected, thus encouraging their purchase. In another move toward cost-effectiveness, the Mexican government has required taxi drivers to buy new, cleaner vehicles every three years. This measure generates a large environmental bang for the buck because taxis are driven ten times as far per year as are private cars.

The government has also pursued one symbolic but highly cost-ineffective regulatory policy: the Day Without a Car program. Under this program, travel by car, depending on the license plate number, is banned on a specified workday. This brief description provides a good opportunity to present a

PUZZLE

Will the Day Without a Car program necessarily cause families to reduce overall driving?

SOLUTION

By now, you have probably figured out that the answer to these puzzles always seems to be no. First, car travel is unlikely to fall by one fifth, because people will simply drive more on other days of the week to accomplish their shopping and recreational tasks. This substitution effect will cause the overall decline in driving to be small. Moreover, some families, for whom compliance with the regulation is very costly, will likely buy a second car. Access to a second vehicle would actually *increase* driving for such a family.[16] Of course, the program may yield other benefits, in particular, raising public awareness.

This section has argued that for reasons of enforceability and ease of administration, poor countries will most often rely on command-and-control regulatory methods, combined with indirect pollution taxes. Often, the two measures can complement one another. In addition, careful analysis will often reveal fairly simple ways to increase the cost-effectiveness of both indirect pollution taxes and command-and-control regulatory systems. Examples from Mexico City include gas tax rebates for clean cars at inspection time, and tight regulation of highly polluting sources like taxi cabs.

---

[16]Eskeland (1991) makes these points.

22.5 Sustainable Technology: Development and Transfer

In addition to regulation, promoting the adoption of more sustainable technology is the other proactive tool that poor country governments have to improve environmental quality. Chapters 18 through 20 provide a general discussion of **clean technology.** There we defined a clean technology as one capable of delivering comparable services at comparable long-run private costs to existing technology, *and* doing so in an environmentally superior fashion. In poor countries, we need to tack on an additional condition. In the interests of controlling population growth by reducing poverty, technologies that the government promotes should also (1) increase employment and/or (2) improve the economic position of the poor, especially women. So-called **sustainable technologies** are clean technologies that also help reduce poverty.[17]

This section addresses three questions about promoting sustainable technology. First, how can sustainable technologies be identified? Second, how are they developed? Third, what steps can be taken to promote their diffusion?

Technologies can be judged sustainable only after field testing and may only be sustainable under certain conditions. For example, Ton and Jong (1991) take a detailed look at the introduction of irrigation pumps and a new type of rice into a drought-stricken region of northern Mali. The new technology increased yields dramatically *and* increased employment. Overall food security thus rose. The increased yields also made it possible for the communities to afford the imported capital necessary for production, at least in principle. (Outside support from the United Nations had not yet been withdrawn.) However, the greater centralization of production fostered by the pumps concentrated economic power in the hands of males of a wealthier ethnic group, thus increasing both gender and income inequality.

Is this technology sustainable? At this point, it is hard to tell. Over time, one would need to answer the following two questions. First, in the absence of outside aid, can the villagers afford to operate and maintain their more capital-intensive production method? In other words, is the technology really profitable and thus self-sustaining? Second, do the income and food security benefits of higher yields outweigh the increase in inequality? In other words, are women and the ethnic minority group on balance better off after the introduction of the new technology? If the answer to both of these questions is yes, then we would judge the technology sustainable.

Bhalla and James (1991) report that three very modern technologies—photovoltaic electricity (discussed in Chapter 20), electronic load controllers for small-scale hydropower, and laser-guided leveling of irrigated fields—have proven to be clean technologies when applied under the right circumstances in poor countries. That is, they are both cost-effective and clear environmental winners. (Level fields conserve irrigation water.) In addition, photovoltaics and load controllers appear to have had no direct negative impact on employment, thus qualifying as sustainable technologies. Laser-guided leveling on the other hand reduces the number of workers needed in the

---

[17]Sustainable technologies differ from appropriate or intermediate technologies in that they need not be small-scale or locally produced. Sustainable technologies can *include* traditional, intermediate, conventional, or emerging technologies, or any blend.

irrigation process. However, *if* the water freed up from improved irrigation is used to grow more crops, overall employment will expand.

This example reflects a more general point: Calculating the overall employment impact of a new technology is a difficult, though not impossible, task. Even if a technology leads to direct job loss, the increased efficiency *may* free up resources that can be invested elsewhere in the poor country economy, creating more jobs.[18] Nevertheless, *assuming* this kind of effect is not good policy. Governments should stay away from promoting cost-effective technologies that substantially reduce employment.

Sustainable technologies need not be sophisticated. Examples include erosion control methods such as building rock or clay dikes or planting trees, and efficient cooking stoves, which reduce charcoal use by several hundred percent. These technologies can dramatically improve environmental quality while boosting the material well-being of people in poor countries (Wardman and Salas 1991; Tibesar and White 1990). The short-term cost-effectiveness of these technologies is essential. Poor people cannot afford to adopt new techniques unless their advantages are clear-cut and substantial.

How are sustainable technologies developed? In Chapter 21, it was stressed that rich countries must bear much of the cost of research and development of technically sophisticated clean technologies—photovoltaic cells being a good example. However, external aid is often needed to establish and promote simple sustainable technologies as well. A **nongovernmental organization (NGO)** called Plan International financed a project in the African country of Burkina Faso, which serves as a good example. The NGO found that reintroducing traditional erosion control techniques, using mostly locally crafted implements, boosted yields of peanuts and grains by over 100% over the period 1985 to 1987. After this period, outside agronomical assistance was gradually withdrawn, and the project became self-sustaining. The Burkina Faso government, while supportive of the project, simply had no money to invest in it (Wardman and Salas 1991).[19]

While potentially beneficial technologies will often have to be developed with assistance from the rich countries, the actual users of the technology must be closely involved in the design process. This is true first because poor country residents, particularly farmers, often have the greatest knowledge of potential solutions to a given problem. Second, if the technologies do not suit the needs of the users, they will never be adopted, no matter how "sustainable" they are in theory.

Poor country governments, sometimes in combination with international development agencies and NGOs, can employ a wide range of tools to promote sustainable technologies, ranging from design standards for technology, to technical assistance programs, to consumer and producer subsidies, to research and development grants.

---

[18]Moreover, there are indirect effects on employment as well. For example, a shift to photovoltaics might reduce the number of workers not only in the coal-powered electricity industry but also in upstream production in firms that manufacture power plants or in coal mines. Similarly, it would boost employment in the semiconductor industry. Economists use a technique called input-output analysis to examine the direct and indirect employment effects of new technologies. See Appendix 19A.

[19]Yield increases were measured vis à vis the surrounding countryside. Yields were also improved by importing a superior variety of sorghum. In addition, the project included agro-forestry and husbandry components.

The advantages and disadvantages of these options, summarized in Table 22.1, were discussed in detail in Chapter 16 and will not be further reviewed here.

While government efforts to promote technologies are important, the private sector and **multinational corporations** in particular will typically play the dominant role in diffusing new techniques of production and consumption. Sometimes these technologies are sustainable, sometimes not. One beneficial influence of direct foreign investment by multinational corporations in manufacturing is that they may bring with them cleaner production technologies. For example, Wheeler and Martin (1993) found that multinational investment has promoted the diffusion of relatively clean technology in the paper and pulp industries.

On average, multinationals, with higher profits, higher visibility, and easier access to technology, probably have somewhat better environmental and safety records than do domestic firms in poor countries. Nevertheless, and not surprisingly, multinational operations in the developing world are generally much dirtier and dangerous than are their similar facilities in rich countries.[20]

The most well-known example of this so-called double standard was illustrated in the wake of a 1984 chemical explosion in Bhopal, India, at a plant owned by a subsidiary of Union Carbide. More than 2,000 people were killed and up to 200,000 injured, many severely, by a toxic gas cloud. While the Bhopal plant was technologically similar to a sister plant in West Virginia, safety systems in Bhopal were very poorly maintained (Lepkowski 1987). In another particularly egregious example of a corporate double standard, the drug company Ciba-Geigy subjected six Egyptian boys to a pesticide spray to test exposure levels ("How a Drug Company" 1984).

Multinationals do not automatically transfer clean technology. In a study of pesticide use in Mexico, Goodman (1987) argues that multinationals *could* help solve the problems by promoting safer techniques developed in the United States, *and* that such efforts are in the long-run interests of such firms if they seek to avoid expensive regulation in Mexico. However, the companies do not see it this way.

TABLE 22.1 Policies for Sustainable Technology

Policy	Small-scale Sustainable Technologies
Design standards	Energy and water efficiency
Technical assistance	Waste reduction in manufacturing, alternative and agroforestry, passive solar, wind power, energy and water efficiency
Small grants/loans/tax credits	Energy and water efficiency, active solar, passive solar, agriculture and agroforestry, wind power, energy and water efficiency
Policy	**Large-scale Sustainable Technologies**
R&D	Agriculture and agroforestry
Infrastructure investment	Mass transit, agriculture and agroforestry, active solar, wind power, telecommunications

[20]These points are developed respectively by Pearson (1987) and Castleman (1987).

Instead, multinational pesticide firms to date have preferred a low profile and have done little to modernize Mexican pesticide practices.

Multinationals have also promoted highly unsustainable technologies in poor countries. For many years, for example, Nestlé Corporation heavily advertised bottle feeding of babies in poor countries, as a "modern" alternative to breast-feeding. This was a disastrous and often deadly practice for poor infants, whose families are without access to clean water or funds to purchase adequate amounts of formula. Nestlé reduced its aggressive advertising only after a prolonged boycott effort by consumers in rich countries ("Nestlé" 1991).

More generally, manufacturing and agricultural production methods imported from rich countries by multinationals tend to be fairly capital-intensive. A chemical plant in Mexico is very much like a chemical plant in Ohio. If taxes on these firms are low and/or their profits are not reinvested locally, the use of this capital-intensive technology may lead to little net increase in employment or reduction in poverty, while at the same time aggravating environmental problems.

How can poor countries nudge the technologies introduced by the private sector in the direction of sustainability? First, improved environmental regulation and enforcement would help insure that technology choices are "clean" relative to current practice. In addition, shareholders and consumers in rich countries can exert pressure on multinationals to adopt more sustainable policies and technologies.

Regulating technologies for their employment impact on sustainability, however, is quite difficult. (Again, imperfect information rears its ugly head.) As a result, widespread command-and-control regulation of the actual production techniques employed by multinational or domestic firms in order to boost employment is likely to be ineffective and may even be counterproductive. For example, Bhopal's chemical plant did not have a computerized safety monitor standard in developed countries, in part because Indian law required firms to choose labor-intensive over capital-intensive production techniques where possible.[21] Poor countries should instead focus on extracting reasonable tax, technology licensing, or reinvestment concessions from multinational firms to promote sustainable development efforts elsewhere in the economy.

This section has defined a sustainable technology as a clean technology, which also helps reduce poverty. The rapid diffusion of such technologies in poor countries is crucial if they hope to outrun a neomalthusian cycle in which increased poverty leads to high rates of population growth, generating more poverty, and so on. Such technologies must also alleviate poverty in a clean way, because environmental degradation in many poor countries is already quite severe. With global population set to increase substantially over the next fifty years, dramatically exacerbating environmental decline, poor countries must "leapfrog" the path of dirty development followed by their rich neighbors. Sustainable technology may deliver the means to do so.

However, developing, identifying, and diffusing sustainable technologies are expensive tasks, which will not be accomplished without a major and ongoing commitment of resources from rich countries. At the same time, the recipient countries must be a full partner in the process. On my desk I have a beautiful picture of a modern

---

[21]And, in part, because it was more expensive. See Lepkowski (1987). Stewart (1990) provides a somewhat more favorable interpretation of the overall Indian experience in technology regulation.

windmill on a hilltop in eastern Zimbabwe, built there by a Danish aid group to electrify a remote village. Unfortunately, the windmill had been inoperative for over a year when I took the picture. The village was unable to raise the money to buy spare parts, which had to be imported from Denmark. The lesson: A successful sustainable technology depends much more on the social needs, capabilities, and organizations of the people it is intended to serve than it does on the provision of hardware.

22.6 Resource Conservation and Debt Relief

Several times over the last few chapters I have remarked that it has proved difficult for poor countries to successfully conserve natural resources—forests, wetlands, range lands, and fisheries—by simply setting aside reserves and parks. Problems are faced both in establishing such protected areas and in managing the regions once they have been created.

Over the last few years, we have seen fierce battles in the United States over wilderness set-asides to protect the habitat of the spotted owl in the Pacific Northwest, to reduce logging in the Tongass National Forest in Alaska, and to prohibit oil development in the Arctic National Wildlife Refuge. Similar **development-environmental struggles** are played out in poor countries, but the stakes there are more dramatic. Both desperately poor people and wealthy development companies desire access to the resource, and together they can form a potent anti-conservation political force.

Even when a protected area has been established, the government faces the often overwhelming **enforcement** task of preventing game poaching, illegal logging, and the invasion of landless farmers. Thus, there has been an increasing recognition among environmentalists that protecting natural resources in poor countries requires directly addressing the economic needs of the poor people who depend on, and threaten, those resources. This section will explore two related policy options for strengthening the link between resource protection and economic opportunity—sustained yield resource development and debt-for-nature swaps.

Sustained yield resource development means using available renewable natural capital in an ecologically sustainable way. Under a sustained yield rule, harvests cannot exceed the regenerative capacity of the land or fishery (see Chapter 7). To illustrate this concept, let us consider the economics of deforestation in the Amazon rainforest in Brazil.

As illustrated in Figure 22.5, three primary forms of activity exist in the Amazon, which sometimes follow in sequence. First, the jungle is clear-cut, by either logging companies, small farmers, or commercial ranchers. The latter two groups tend to simply burn the fallen timber. Small farmers, sometimes following roads built by loggers, grow crops for a few years. However, these early migrants often move on, either abandoning their land or selling out to cattle farmers. This technology is known as shifting cultivation or slash-and-burn agriculture.

There is ongoing debate as to the motivation for land abandonment by both small farmers and cattle ranchers: Some argue that the poor-quality tropical soils make rain-forest farming unsustainable; others maintain that poor and politically powerless pioneers are unable to hold on to the property that they farm as a second wave of wealthier migrants move in. Finally, reductions in subsidies have led to some abandonment by ranchers (see Schneider 1993 and Carriere 1991).

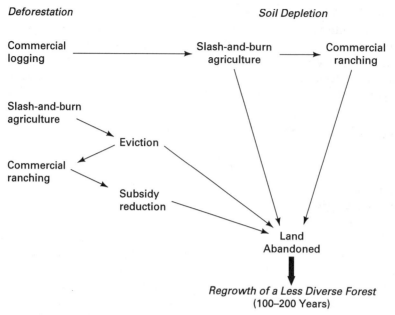

Deforestation

Soil Depletion

FIGURE 22.5 The Deforestation Process

When populations and farm plots are small, slash-and-burn agriculture can generate a sustained yield, since the jungle is given time to recover. However, as population pressure has increased, and ranchers have moved in to follow the farmers, the system has in some cases become ecologically untenable.

How could sustained yield resource development proceed in the Amazon? As we will see, the rain forest *does* have substantial economic value that might be exploited in an ecologically sustainable fashion. Doing so will require applying a successful mix of the policies described above: eliminating unsustainable subsidies, clarifying property rights, and promoting sustainable technologies via measures such as technical assistance programs, infrastructure development, and subsidized credit programs. The problem is compounded, however, by the fact that much of the benefit of sustained yield development accrues to people outside of the rain forest, particularly to those in rich countries. Getting us to pay "our share" for the public good of rain-forest protection becomes an added policy challenge.

What sustained yield values does the rain forest hold? First, experience has shown that there are profitable, **sustained yield farming and ranching methods** suitable for tropical forest soils, which do not require shifting cultivation (Barrows and Roth 1990). Governments can encourage farmers to adopt these sustainable technologies both by promoting them directly through technical assistance programs and targeted credit subsidies, and by eliminating subsidies for unsustainable practices. Deforestation will be slowed if farmers and ranchers can eliminate their voracious need for more and more land.

More generally, the *standing* forest is increasingly viewed as a resource with substantial economic value. From a commercial perspective, Pearce and Myers (1990) report that the **harvesting of wild products,** such as meat and fish, and primates (for medical research), could generate an annual income of $200 per hectare, more than is earned either by one-time clear-cutting or by unsustainable cattle ranching.[22] Developing this potential would require both nurturing a marketing and transportation infrastructure, and clarifying property rights within the rain forest. Some kind of communal or private ownership would be necessary to avoid the overharvesting of profitable wild resources such as nuts, meat, or vegetable oils on commonly held property.

The rain forest holds two other important commercial products: **medicine** and a **gene pool for agriculture.** Tropical forest species form the basis for pharmaceutical products whose annual sales are valued at well over $12 billion (Pearce and Myers 1990). The forest undoubtedly contains many more valuable species, thousands of which may be lost each year. However, the medical value of the rain forest lies not only in its biodiversity; the native Amazon people also have a medical knowledge base that is also being threatened by deforestation. Finally, the huge gene pool represented by the forest is economically important for breeding disease-resistant and high-yield agricultural crops.

In addition to these commercial benefits, the forest yields a variety of utilitarian environmental services. One of these is a **carbon sink;** a substantial portion of the world's carbon dioxide is tied up in the rain-forest biomass. When the forests are burned, the CO_2 is released into the atmosphere, contributing to global warming. In addition, the rain forest serves as a **rainfall regulator,** by recycling much of its own moisture. As deforestation proceeds, the Amazon basin may well likely dry out, affecting rainfall patterns throughout Brazil.

Finally, many people have expressed considerable moral interest in protecting the rain forest, its natural species, and its human cultures. From an economic point of view, this concern represents an **existence value** for the rain forest (see Chapter 8). Especially in rich countries, people have expressed a willingness to pay for rain forest preservation independent of the material economic services that the tropical forest might provide.

The benefits from medical, agricultural, environmental, and existence value services provided by the rain forest accrue primarily to those living outside of the Amazon, and indeed, Brazil. Thus rain-forest protection is a classic **public good,** as described in Chapter 3. Many of us have been solicited by environmental groups to contribute money to efforts to "save the rain forest." While each of us has a material stake in such a project, we also have an incentive to **free ride** on the efforts of others to provide the public good. As a result, economic theory predicts that rain-forest protection groups will raise less than the amount of money we as a society are really willing to pay for such efforts.

This in turn means that private-sector efforts to promote sustained yield development in the Amazon will be inefficiently low on a simple benefit–cost basis. Traditionally, economists have argued that government needs to step in and use its power to

---

[22]Pearce and Myers (1990) report that commercial logging returns about $150/hectare, while Browder (1988) finds ranching income to average $112.50/hectare. See also the special issue of *Environmental Development Economics* 4, no. 2, May 1999.

tax in order to provide an efficient quantity of public goods—whether a national park, clean air, or national defense. In an international context, this implies that in order to protect the narrow economic interests of their citizens, rich country governments will have to raise aid money for rain-forest protection. Of course, such aid might also be justified on the grounds of economic sustainability and fairness to future generations.

In summary, in poor and densely populated countries, the only feasible way to conserve natural resources is often to link conservation with enhanced economic opportunity. Governments can do this by using the variety of tools discussed in this chapter. Around the world, dozens of such efforts have been launched in recent years, including a successful effort to both cultivate tourism and reduce its environmental impact in the Nepalese Himalayas, and a less successful attempt to protect the wintering grounds of the monarch butterfly in Mexico (Brandon and Wells 1992). However, such efforts are currently underfunded. Because rich countries are often major beneficiaries of resource preservation, an efficient level of conservation will only be achieved if a mechanism is established by which rich country residents pay for the benefits they receive.

One example of such an approach lies in debt relief. As was discussed in Chapter 21, during the 1970s and early 1980s, the developing countries accumulated a huge quantity of debt owed to private banks in rich countries. Merely paying the interest on this debt remains a tremendous burden on poor countries today. For example, we saw that Costa Rica has paid out as much as 10% of its export earnings each year in debt service. The debt burden poses a major obstacle to sustainable development, since it reduces investment in the created capital that poor countries desperately need.

One way to relieve the debt burden and simultaneously invest in resource conservation is through a **debt-for-nature swap.** Under a debt-for-nature swap, a rich country group (government, nongovernmental organization, or bank) will pay off a portion of the loan, typically at a deep discount. Banks are willing to sell this debt at a paper loss, since they suspect they will not be repaid in full anyway. In exchange, poor country governments must agree to invest a certain amount of money into a resource conservation program at home. These programs tend to focus on beefing up enforcement and supporting sustained yield resource development at existing preserves. The actual ownership of the natural resource does not change hands (Deacon and Murphy 1992).

The developing country benefits in several ways. First, the debt is reduced.[23] Second, it can undertake needed conservation measures at home. Finally, the conservation program can be financed using local money, not scarce foreign currency (dollars, yen, or deutschemark). It is thus "cheaper" from the poor country's perspective. Figure 22.6 provides the details of a swap between the Brazilian government and the U.S.-based NGO, the Nature Conservancy.

Debt-for-nature swaps are one way in which residents of rich countries can express their demand for resource preservation in poor countries. However, their use has been fairly limited. Consummated deals through 1997 had reduced total debt in poor countries by around $1.5 billion, about 1% of total Third World debt. About one quarter of

---

[23]Sachs (1990) and Bulow and Rogoff (1990) both point out that the actual debt burden may not fall by the full value of the swap. Since the swap strengthens the position of the creditor nation (and suggests the likelihood of further swaps), the value of the debt on secondary markets may rise. Issuing bonds to pay for the swaps in local currency is also inflationary.

1. The Nature Conservancy buys $2.2 million in Brazilian debt owed to a private bank. The bank agrees to a price of $850,000 for the debt, $0.38 to the dollar.

2. The Nature Conservancy donates the debt to FUNUTURA, a Brazilian conservation NGO. FUNUTURA, in turn, uses it to buy $2.2 million in long-term Brazilian government bonds, paying 6% interest, or $132,000 per year.

3. These funds accrue to a partnership between the Nature Conservancy, FUNUTARA, and IBAMA (the Brazilian EPA). Their goal is to manage the Grande Serpao Veredas National Park, in the interior highland of the country. Endangered mammals who have taken refuge in the park include the jaguar, the pampas deer, the manned wolf, the giant anteater, and the harpie eagle.

4. The management strategy includes purchasing "buffer zone" lands around the park, hiring park rangers, and promoting sustained yield resource development. Early priorities include such basic measures as the purchase of a motor boat and a four-wheel drive vehicle, and the construction of a park headquarters.

FIGURE 22.6 A Debt-for-Nature Swap in Brazil

Source: Fundaçao Pró-Natureza and The Nature Conservancy (1991).

these swaps have been financed by private parties, primarily conservation NGOs. The rest of the efforts have been paid for by rich country governments (Deacon and Murphy 1997).

The limited use of the option reflects in part resistance on the part of poor country governments, who are concerned that environmentalists from rich countries will "lock up" their resource base. Probably more significant is the fact that NGOs in rich countries have been able to raise only limited funds for such purposes. Due to the free-rider problem, discussed above, such an outcome is predicted for private groups that seek to provide public goods. At the same time, government efforts have been limited for lack of political support.

Some economists have recommended a major expansion of the debt-for-nature concept, in which debtor nations would pay most of their debt in local currency into an international environment fund. This fund would finance sustainable development and family planning measures. Under one scheme, rich country governments would compensate banks for unpaid debt at 50% of its current market value, through a tax on gasoline (Bigman 1990).[24] If debt-for-nature schemes are in fact effective in conserving resources in poor countries, and the record is too recent to fully judge, a significant expansion could well be justified on benefit–cost grounds.

22.7 Trade and the Environment

In 1999, tear gas wafted through the streets of Seattle, following protests by environmentalists and union members at a meeting of the World Trade Organization, or WTO. The WTO is an international body that oversees trade and investment agreements negotiated between member states; the mission of the WTO is to promote

---

[24]Bigman (1990); Bulow and Rogoff (1990) present a similar, if less ambitious proposal, to reduce public debt. They also argue that the potential for government relief of private debt makes both banks and poor countries reluctant to settle the matter. Sachs (1990), by contrast, makes the case for relief of both private and public debt, through a negotiated reduction in interest rates.

increased global trade and investment. The protestors' message was that the WTO, through its promotion of free-trade, was exacerbating global environmental problems and undercutting workers rights. Earlier in the decade, similar concerns created headlines during the debate over the **North American Free Trade Agreement (NAFTA).** NAFTA, a 1993 agreement between Canada, Mexico and the United States was designed to reduce tariff and subsidy trade barriers and eliminate restrictions on foreign investment and capital mobility. Passage of NAFTA in the U.S. was hotly contested, in part because of fears it would exacerbate environmental decline in all three countries.

There are essentially three environmental arguments against free-er trade, and one environmental argument in favor, all well illustrated by the NAFTA debate. The argument for the free-trade act was that, by stimulating investment and economic growth in Mexico, poverty will be reduced and cleaner technologies will be imported and adopted (Grossman and Krueger 1991; Reppelin-Hill 1999).[25] As we learned in Chapter 20, **poverty reduction** in poor countries can have important environmental benefits, as water and air quality improve, pressures on non-renewable resources decline, more resources are available for investment in health-care, education, and family planning, and parents are provided with the option of pursing a quality rather than a quantity strategy for family size. In the case of NAFTA in particular, Pastor (1992) argued that the agreement process strengthened both democratic and environmental political movements within Mexico.

Environmental critics of the treaty lodged three principal objections.[26] First, they argued that, in fact, it would not reduce poverty. For example, NAFTA requires the Mexican government to significantly reduce subsidies for corn farmers. It was feared that hundreds of thousands of small farmers might lose their livelihoods, as cheap northern grain enters the market. (Canada and the U.S. have built up tremendously productive farm-sectors through their own subsidy policies.) While urban dwellers in Mexico might benefit from lower corn prices, they would also suffer from substantially increased migration to the cities, and downward pressure on wages. As a result, it was possible that they too would be worse off. With greater poverty would come higher birth rates, and more pressure on local resources (Robinson et al. 1992; Levy and Van Wijnbergen 1992, 16; Koechlin and Larudee 1992).

Levy and van Wijnbergen (1992) argued that this problem could have been dealt with by increasing public investment in rural roads and irrigation projects for small farmers. By increasing productivity and land values, small farmers would be able to survive with lower corn prices. The authors concluded that such a program would actually have cost less than the current corn subsidy program, which benefits wealthy commercial farmers as well as poor subsistence farmers. However, if such a program was not undertaken in conjunction with NAFTA, environmental gains from poverty reduction were less likely to materialize.

By the late 1990s, it was clear that the adjustment and assistance programs for small farmers in Mexico were in fact quite minimal. In addition, U.S. grain exports to Mexico grew rapidly, though urban consumers appeared not to benefit substantially

---

[25]For supportive views of the impact of trade on the environment, see Dean (1992) and Bhagwati (1993).
[26]For an overview of environmental objections to free trade, see Daly (1993).

from lower prices due to monopoly pricing. And finally, somewhat surprisingly, Mexican maize production in subsistence areas appears to have stayed relatively constant. U.S. producers grabbed all of the growth in the market, but rural farmers continued to produce for their own subsistence. The bottom line: U.S., not Mexican farmers profited from the growing internal market, and U.S. and Mexican wholesalers, not Mexican consumers, appear to have gotten the largest share of the increased surplus (Nadal 1999; Ackerman et al. 2003). Thus, poverty has neither increased nor decreased much as a result of the trade impacts working through the corn sector.

The second charge against the treaty was that Mexico, with its **weak environmental enforcement** apparatus, would face dramatic and escalating pollution problems as a result of increased investment in manufacturing and vegetable production. There is evidence, for example, that pesticide pollution would increase in Mexico (but decrease in Florida) following a trade agreement. The following judgment was thus made: Environmental improvements that accompany reductions in poverty and the import of technology will not compensate for the direct increase in pollution. On balance, it was argued, free-er trade will lead to deteriorating environmental conditions in poor countries. Ironically, in the maize case, it appears that the reverse is true: as U.S. corn production increased by close to 1% to serve the Mexican market, agricultural pollution shifted from Mexico to the United States (Abler and Pick 1993; Ackerman et al. 2003).

Again, the response from supporters of trade was, strengthen enforcement activities, don't restrict trade. NAFTA does contain a "side-agreement" on environmental issues which in principal gives parties the ability to prod businesses that "persistently" violate environmental laws to comply. However, the process is so complex and restrictive that it is unlikely to see much use; to date the commission set up to oversee complaints has accomplished little.[27]

The final environmental charge against a free trade agreement is that environmental regulations in rich countries will be weakened as (1) **business mobility increases,** and (2) foreign governments and companies issue **trade-based challenges to environmental laws.** This process is known as a **downward leveling** of regulatory standards. In Chapter 9 we learned that differences in the stringency of environmental regulation in fact appear to have little influence on business location decisions. Much more important are wage differences and access to markets. Given this, U.S. lawmakers appear to have little to lose by maintaining strong environmental standards. Indeed, Mexico could begin stringently enforcing its laws without sacrificing investment from the United States.

Unfortunately, it is not always reality but perception that matters in regulatory decisions. Much of the public and many policy-makers appear to believe that strong environmental standards discourage investment. Evidence from the few industries in which environmental regulation *has* discouraged investment can be used as a stick by industry to weaken standards.

---

[27]See "Some Questions and Answers on NAFTA." 1993. *The Wall Street Journal,* 17 November; the body set up by NAFTA, the North American Commission for Environmental Cooperation, has its Web site at www.cec.org.

Free trade agreements can also lead to downward leveling since they give foreign governments and corporations the ability to challenge certain regulations as trade barriers. Table 22.2 provides a list of several recent challenges. One of the most widely cited has been a case in which the U.S. government imposed a ban on the import of Latin American tuna. The embargo was enacted because these countries were not using fishing techniques required by U.S. law to reduce the incidental killing of dolphins and other marine animals. Mexico challenged the embargo under the terms of the General Agreement on Tariffs and Trade, a predecessor to the WTO. The trade court ruled in Mexico's favor, arguing that member nations were not allowed to dictate production methods beyond their borders. The United States was forced to rescind the ban or face international trade sanctions.

An unanticipated feature of NAFTA that has raised major concern relates not to restrictions on trade, but rather on investment. A clause in the treaty, known as "Chapter 11," prohibits countries from expropriating the property of investors without compensation. Under this clause, companies have started to sue governments who impose environmental regulations, arguing that these regulations are in effect, expropriations of profit. For example, Methanex, a Canadian company, sued the state of California for nearly $1 billion when they banned a gasoline additive suspected of causing cancer called MBTE that was produced in a California plant by Methanex. In effect, Chapter 11 may flip the established property rights regime over,

TABLE 22.2 Trade Challenges to Environmental Regulation

Measure	Trade Agreement	Challenger	Decision
U.S. ban on Latin American tuna imports	GATT	Mexican govt.	Ban declared illegal
Danish requirement that drinks be sold in reusable deposit containers	Treaty of Rome	U.K. govt., European beer manufacturers	Deposit requirement upheld, reuse weakened
U.S. ban on asbestos	U.S.-Canada FTA	Quebec govt.	Ban overturned on other grounds; trade issue referred to GATT
Canadian requirement that fish must be sampled prior to export, to promote conservation	U.S.-Canada FTA	—	Requirement declared illegal
Canadian review of natural gas export license	U.S.-Canada FTA	U.S. energy companies	Review dropped
U.S. standards for reformulated gasoline	WTO	Venezuelan government	Standards revised
Japanese efficiency standards for auto engines	WTO	U.S. govt., auto manufacturers	Under WTO review
California ban on MBTE	WTO	Methanex Corp.	Review dropped on a technicality

Sources: Based on data from Shrybman (1992); "U.S. Defeated in Its Appeal of Trade Case," *New York Times,* May 30, 1996, p. D1; and Wallach and Sforza (1999).

giving companies the right to pollute, rather than states the right to prevent pollution. If Methanex wins their case, California will be under intense pressure from the Federal government to either change their law, or pay off the company. In 2002, a three-member WTO dispute panel, deliberating in secret, ruled against Methanex on a technicality, but the company has the right to rebring the case.

As Table 22.2 illustrates, by prohibiting import and export bans, regulations, and tariffs, free-trade agreements can tie environmental agency hands. In effect, environmental decisions made by democratically elected bodies (congresses and parliaments) can be overruled by a very closed international legal process, of which the primary treaty charge is to promote free trade for the sake of efficiency gains. Moreover, as we will discuss further in the next chapter, international trade agreements administered by the WTO may weaken international environmental agreements such as the one designed to protect the ozone layer. Trade agreements may have to be amended if such environmental treaties are to use trade sanctions as enforcement tools (French 1993).[28]

This section has provided a look at the debate over the environmental impact of free trade agreements. Clearly, trade can be a vital component of any strategy to promote sustainable development. When trade works to reduce poverty, it can provide environmental benefits in the form of greater investment in air and water quality, reduced pressure on the local environment, and lowered population growth rates.

However, the economic growth that accompanies free trade agreements need not reduce poverty. In the Mexican case, the "losers" from NAFTA are likely to be the large class of small corn farmers. As a result, the treaty may well lead to a net increase in Mexican unemployment, more rural to urban migration, and a reduction in urban wages.

More generally, we saw in Chapter 21 that trade in natural resource–based industries can foster unsustainable development. This occurs when the *full* resource rent is not reinvested in created capital in the developing country. In a world in which poor country governments are both debt-burdened and have difficulty collecting and productively investing tax revenues from resource-based industries, such an outcome is not unlikely.[29]

Critics have also charged that, in spite of the environmental benefits that accompany growth, the direct increase in pollution will lead to a decline in environmental quality in poor countries. Finally, they charge that environmental regulations in rich countries will be weakened as business mobility increases and legal challenges are lodged by international competitors.

Is free trade good or bad for the environment? Freer trade is generally championed by economists because it tends to increase efficiency, and as we know from Chapter 4, more efficient production means a bigger overall economic pie. The environmental challenge is to channel the efficiency gains from trade into investment in a sustainable future. From this perspective, freer trade should be viewed as a means to an end—stabilizing population growth, enhancing food security, transferring sustainable technology, and conserving resources—not as an end in itself. Yet at this point, trade agreements have only just begun to acknowledge environmental and sustainability concerns (French 1993).

---

[28]For an analysis of the potential impact of NAFTA on U.S. standards see Center for International Environmental Law (1993). NAFTA's Chapter 11 and the Methanex case are described in detail in a 2002 Bill Moyers PBS video entitled Trading Democracy.

[29]Pezzey (1993) develops a formal model of the impact of trade on sustainability.

22.8 Summary

Environmental policy in poor countries cannot be narrowly viewed as "controlling pollution." The complex and conflicting problems of poverty, population growth, and environmental and resource degradation require a broader focus: promoting sustainable development. This task in turn can be broken down into four subareas: controlling population growth, insuring food security, promoting clean and sustainable technology, and conserving natural resources.

This chapter has considered several general steps that governments can take in these directions. These include reducing environmentally damaging subsidies; working to clarify and enforce communal or private property rights; regulating pollution in as cost-effective a manner as possible; promoting the development and transfer of sustainable technology; conserving natural capital by encouraging sustained yield resource development; and insuring that the gains from trade are funneled into measures promoting sustainable development.

One recurring theme in this chapter has been the question of who will pay for these programs. Until recently, many poor countries have questioned the wisdom of environmental or natural resource protection, reasoning that they could not afford to engage in such measures. There is an increasing recognition, however, that improving environmental quality is often a good economic investment. The financial reality remains unchanged, however. Poor countries still cannot afford to make many of these investments.

As an example, the people of Burkina Faso would benefit greatly if the erosion control measures discussed in Section 22.5 were widely disseminated, boosting agricultural productivity and incomes, and slowing down population growth rates and rural to urban migration. Yet the country is desperately poor. As a result, such programs are proceeding at a snail's pace, funded through private donations by people in affluent countries.

Ultimately, sustainable development in poor countries is unlikely to occur without a substantial commitment of resources by those of us in rich countries. This commitment can take a variety of forms: research and development in clean and sustainable technologies ranging from solar and wind power to biotechnology to improved refrigerators and stoves; funding of family planning efforts; debt relief in the form of debt-for-nature or debt-for-farmland swaps; international aid for rural development projects; financial and technical assistance in the implementation of environmental regulatory programs; the removal of trade barriers to poor country products; and adjustment aid to help poor countries reduce their own environmentally damaging subsidies.

In some instances, this kind of resource commitment is justified on the basis of narrow self-interest. Global pollution problems such as the accelerated greenhouse effect and ozone depletion *will not* be adequately addressed without such efforts. Natural resources that we in rich countries value—medical products, agricultural gene pools, wild animal species, wilderness—*will be* rapidly exhausted if we do not pay our share for their protection. Beyond narrow self-interest, however, resources must be committed by those of us in rich countries if we want to insure a high quality of life for our children and grandchildren.

The environmental impact of continuing population and consumption growth may be simply to intensify the problems of local air and water pollution, disposal of solid and hazardous waste, exposure to toxic chemicals, and the disappearance of green spaces and wild creatures. On the other hand, such trends may lead to new and unimagined changes in the global environment. Within the last decade, two such threats have emerged: global warming and ozone depletion. The final chapter of the book turns to the increasingly critical issue of global environmental regulation.

APPLICATION 22.0

Subsidy Removal: Environmental and Social Impact[30]

Some have argued that removing government controls that keep food prices down is a necessary step to insure food security. In addition, some maintain, the subsequent increase in price will also reduce soil erosion by giving farmers stronger incentives (and access to capital) to invest in long-term erosion control measures.

1. It seems counterintuitive to argue that increasing the price that consumers face for food will, in many cases, actually improve access to food. How can you explain this line of reasoning?
2. In the short run, who would suffer most from lifting price controls on food? How can this problem be addressed?
3. Can you think of a reason why rising food prices might actually increase soil erosion?

APPLICATION 22.1

Environmental Regulation and Nontariff Barriers

In 1989, the United States imposed a ban on the export of unprocessed logs from public lands in the Pacific Northwest, with the purported intent of slowing down deforestation of the spotted owl ecosystem. Japan objected to the ban, arguing that it is a "thinly disguised nontariff barrier" to trade. "The ban does not meet the environmental objective, since it does not apply to processed wood products. [Rather] it will raise the price of unprocessed wood to Japan (the U.S. is the largest timber supplier to Japan) and encourage ailing U.S. wood processing industries."[31]

From the U.S. perspective, of course, aiding our wood-processing industries might seem like a good idea, particularly if the burden of higher prices is borne by a principal competitor. The danger, of course, is that this kind of action might prompt retaliation by the Japanese in the form of trade restrictions on U.S. products.

To sort out whether environmentally motivated regulations or product standards are genuine, or are instead thinly disguised trade barriers, Dean (1992: 16) makes the following suggestion: Standards or regulations must not only meet the environmental objective but also do so in a *least-cost* way.

---

[30]This problem draws in part on an unpublished paper by S. Barret (1990) called "Macroeconomic Policy Reforms and the Third World Soil Conservation," summarized in Dean (1992).
[31]This summary of the Japanese objection is found in Dean (1992).

1. Do you think the Japanese objection, as stated, is correct?
2. Do you think the ban is an environmental measure or a trade barrier?
3. Dean argues that if a regulation or product standard does not meet the environmental objective in a least-cost way, then we may be justified in assuming it to be a trade barrier. Do you agree?

KEY IDEAS IN EACH SECTION

22.0 This chapter considers sustainability policy in poor countries. The basic message is that none of these policies is cheap; in many cases, success will require investment aid from wealthy countries.

22.1 We begin with a brief consideration of the possibility of government failure due to imperfect information and political influence, both compounded by a lack of resources and small **political-economic elites.** Both **multinational** and **domestic business** can have substantial political influence in poor countries.

22.2 Removing **environmentally damaging subsidies** in industries such as timber, energy, and agriculture is the first policy considered. For example, tropical deforestation is promoted by (1) **failure to capture resource rents** ("low" timber prices); (2) **infrastructure development;** (3) **subsidized "downstream" industries;** (4) **colonization projects;** and (5) **subsidized cattle ranching.** When subsidies are removed, **compensation** is often required both on political and **fairness** grounds.

22.3 Reducing **open access to common property** is a second policy. This can be achieved by strengthening **property rights,** whether **communal, state,** or **private.** When ownership rights are strengthened, owners are more likely to engage in **profit-based conservation.** Private and communal owners in poor countries often have greater incentives, and more resources, than do state managers for good management. Yet privatization can penalize the poor and is itself a difficult task for poor country governments to manage well.

22.4 The general points made in Chapters 16 and 17 about **incentive-based** versus **command-and-control** regulation hold true in poor countries. However, special attention must be paid to **enforceability** and **administrative simplicity. Indirect pollution taxes,** such as **timber royalties** or **gasoline taxes,** are thus appealing, but because they don't tax pollution directly, their environmental effect must be carefully considered. Flexible or targeted CAC measures are also good regulatory strategies.

22.5 A **sustainable technology** is a **clean technology** that also improves the economic position of the poor majority. Government can promote the development and diffusion of sustainable technology using tools such as **subsidies** and **infrastructure investment.** Major sources of technology transfer are **nongovernmental organizations** (NGOs) and **multinational corporations.** Poor countries can encourage the transfer of clean technology by instituting environmental regulation and by obtaining adequate tax concessions from multinationals for reinvestment elsewhere in the economy.

22.6   Two obstacles to resource conservation in poor countries are the intensity of the **development-environment conflict** and the difficulty of **enforcement.** One way to address these problems is through **sustained yield resource development.** Examples from the rain forest include **sustained yield farming and ranching; harvesting of wild products;** prospecting for **pharmaceuticals** and **agricultural genes;** and tourism. However, the forest also delivers nonmarketable **(public)** goods, such as a **carbon sink, rainfall regulator,** and **existence value.** The **free-rider problem** means that, without some collective mechanism for rich countries to pay for preservation, inefficiently low levels of preservation will occur. One such mechanism is a **debt-for-nature swap.**

22.7   If the **North American Free Trade Agreement (NAFTA)** in fact leads to **poverty reduction** in Mexico as its supporters maintain, it may improve environmental quality. However, as **corn subsidies** are eliminated as a result of the treaty, poverty may in fact deepen. In addition, through **weak environmental enforcement** and a **downward leveling** of regulatory standards (in turn arising from **increased business mobility** and **trade-based regulatory challenges**), NAFTA may undermine environmental quality in all three countries.

REFERENCES

Abler, David G., and Daniel Pick. 1993. "NAFTA, Agriculture and the Environment in Mexico." *American Journal of Agricultural Economics* 75.

Abler, David, Adrian Rodriquez, and James Shortle. 1999. "Trade Liberalization and the Environment in Costa Rica." *Environment and Development Economics* 4, no. 3:359–376.

Ackerman, Frank, Timothy Wise, Kevin Gallagher, Luke Ney, and Regina Flores. 2003. "Environmental Impacts of the Changes in US-Mexico Corn Trade Under NAFTA." NACEC. Global Development and Environment Institute, working paper no. 03-06. Medford, MA: Tufts University.

Barrows, Richard, and Michael Roth. 1990. "Land Tenure and Investment in African Agriculture: Theory and Evidence." *The Journal of Modern African Studies* 28, no. 2:265–298.

Bhagwati, Jagdish. 1993. "The Case for Free Trade." *Scientific American,* November, 41–49.

Bhalla, Ajit S., and Dilmus D. James. 1991. "Integrating New Technologies with Traditional Economic Activities in Developing Countries: An Evaluative Look at 'Technology Blending.'" *The Journal of Developing Areas* 25:477–496.

Bigman, David. 1990. "A Plan to End LDC Debt and Save the Environment Too." *Challenge* 33, no. 4:33–37.

Brandon, Katrina Eadie, and Michael Wells. 1992. "Planning for People and Parks: Design Dilemmas." *World Development* 20, no. 4:557–570.

Bromley, Daniel. 1991. *Environment and Economy: Property Rights and Public Policy.* Cambridge, MA: Blackwell.

Browder, John O. 1988. "Public Policy and Deforestation in the Brazilian Amazon." In *Public Policies and the Misuse of Forest Resources,* edited by Robert Repetto and Malcolm Gillis. Cambridge: Cambridge University Press.

Bulow, Jeremy, and Kenneth Rogoff. 1990. "Cleaning Up Third World Debt Without Getting Taken to the Cleaners." *Journal of Economic Perspectives* 4, no. 1:31–42.

Carriere, Jean. 1991. "The Crisis in Costa Rica: An Ecological Perspective." In *Environment and Development in Latin America,* edited by David Goodman and Michael Redclift. New York: Manchester University Press.

Castleman, Barry. 1987. "Workplace Health Standards and Multinational Corporations in Developing Countries." In *Multinational Corporations, Environment and the Third World,* edited by Charles S. Pearson. Chapel Hill, NC: Duke University Press.

Center for International Environmental Law. 1993. "Integrating Labor and Environmental Concerns into the North American Free Trade Agreement." Washington, DC: CIEL.

Daly, Herman. 1993. "The Perils of Free Trade." *Scientific American,* November, 50–57.

Deacon, Robert T. 1992. "Controlling Tropical Deforestation: An Analysis of Alternative Policies." *Working Paper in Economics 4–92.* Santa Barbara, CA: UC, Santa Barbara.

Deacon, Robert, and Paul Murphy. 1997. "The Structure of an Environmental Transaction: The Debt for Nature Swap." *Land Economics* 73, no. 1:1–24.

Deacon, Robert T., and Paul Murphy. 1992. "The Structure of an Environmental Transaction: The Debt-for-Nature Swap." Paper presented at the American Economic Association Meetings, Anaheim, CA, January 1993.

Dean, Judith. 1992. "Trade and the Environment: A Survey of the Literature." *Policy Research Working Paper WPS966.* Washington, DC: World Bank.

Eskeland, Gunnar S. 1991. "Demand Management in Environmental Protection: Fuel Taxes and Air Pollution in Mexico City." Paper presented at the American Economic Association Meetings, January 1992.

French, Hillary. 1993. "Reconciling Trade and the Environment." In *State of the World, 1993,* edited by Lester Brown. New York: W. W. Norton.

Fundaçao Pró-Natureza, and The Nature Conservancy. 1991. *Grande Sertao Veredas National Park Debt Conversion Proposal, Revised Draft.* Washington, DC: Nature Conservancy.

Gillis, Malcolm. 1988. "Malaysia: Public Policies and the Tropical Forest." In *Public Policies and the Misuse of Forest Resources,* edited by Robert Repetto and Malcolm Gillis. Cambridge: Cambridge University Press.

Goodman, Louis W. 1987. "Foreign Toxins: Multinational Corporations and Pesticides in Mexican Agriculture." In *Multinational Corporations, Environment and the Third World,* edited by Charles S. Pearson. Chapel Hill, NC: Duke University Press.

Goodstein, Eban. 1989. "Land Ownership, Development and Poverty in Southern Appalachia." *The Journal of Developing Areas,* 23 no. 4:519–534.

Grossman, Gene M., and Alan B. Krueger. 1991. "Environmental Impacts of a North American Free Trade Agreement." *Economics Discussion Paper 158.* Princeton, NJ: Woodrow Wilson School.

Hanna, Susan, and Mohan Munasinghe. 1995. *Property Rights and the Environment: Social and Ecological Issues.* Washington, DC: The World Bank.

Harvard Law Review. 1990. "Developments—International Environmental Law: Extraterritorial Environmental Regulation." *Harvard Law Review* 104, no. 7:1609–1638.

"How a Drug Company Deals With Disputes Over Its Medicines." 1984. *Wall Street Journal,* 1 June.

"In Choppy Russian Economy, A Family Jury Rigs a Budget." 1992. *New York Times,* 20 January.

Katz, Elizabeth. 2000. "Natural Resource Management in Guatemala." *Land Economics* 76, no. 1:114–132.

Koechlin, Timothy, and Mehrene Larudee. 1992. "The High Cost of NAFTA." *Challenge,* 35-5:19–26.

Leonard, H. Jeffrey. 1987. *Natural Resources and Economic Development in Central America.* Oxford: Transaction Books.

Lepkowski, Wil. 1987. "The Disaster at Bhopal—Chemical Safety in the Third World." In *Multinational Corporations, Environment and the Third World,* edited by Charles S. Pearson. Chapel Hill, NC: Duke University Press.

Levy, Santiago, and Sweder van Wijnbergen. 1992. "Transition Problems in Economic Reform: Agriculture in the U.S. Mexico Free-Trade Agreement." In *Economy-Wide Modeling of the Economic Implications of a FTA with Mexico and a NAFTA with Canada and Mexico.* Washington, DC: U.S. International Trade Commission.

Musambachime, Mwelma. 1990. "The Impact of Rapid Population Growth on Economic Decline: The Case of Zambia." *Review of African Political Economy,* 448, no. 2, 81–91.

Nadal, Alejandro. 1999. *Assessing Environmental Effects of the North American Free Trade Agreement (NAFTA): An Analytic Framework (Phase II) and Issue Studies.* Montreal: North American Commission for Environmental Cooperation.

Naysnerski, Wendy, and Tom Tietenberg. 1992. "Private Enforcement of Federal Environmental Law." *Land Economics* 68, no. 1:28–48.

"Nestlé: Battling the Boycotts." 1991. *New York Times,* 28 July.

Pastor, Robert A. 1992. "NAFTA as the Center of an Integration Process: The Non-trade Issues." In *North American Free Trade: Assessing the Impact,* edited by Nora Lustig, Barry Bosworth, and Robert Z. Lawrence. Washington, DC: Brookings.

Pearce, David, and Norman Myers. 1990. "Economic Values and the Environment of Amazonia." In *The Future of Amazonia: Destruction or Sustainable Development?* edited by David Goodman and Anthony Hall. New York: St. Martin Press.

Pearson, Charles S. 1987. "Introduction." In *Multinational Corporations, Environment and the Third World,* edited by Charles S. Pearson. Chapel Hill, NC: Duke University Press.

Pezzey, John. 1993. "Sustainability Policies in Models of Trade with Exhaustible Resources." Paper presented at the American Economic Association Meetings, Anaheim, CA.

Repetto, Robert. 1988a. "Overview." In *Public Policies and the Misuse of Forest Resources,* edited by Robert Repetto and Malcolm Gillis. Cambridge: Cambridge University Press.

Repetto, Robert. 1988b. "Subsidized Timber Sales from National Forest Lands in the United States." In *Public Policies and the Misuse of Forest Resources,* eds. Robert Repetto and Malcolm Gillis. Cambridge: Cambridge University Press.

Reppelin-Hill, Valerie. 1999. "Trade and the Environment: An Empirical Analysis of the Technology Effect in the Steel Industry." *Journal of Environmental Economics and Management* 38, no. 4:283–301.

Robinson, Sherman, Mary E. Burfisher, Raul Hinojosa-Ojeda, and Karen E. Thierfelder. 1992. "Agricultural Policies and Migration in a U.S.-Mexico Free Trade Area: A Computable General Equilibrium Analysis." In *Economy-Wide Modeling of the Economic Implications of a FTA with Mexico and a NAFTA with Canada and Mexico.* Washington, DC: U.S. International Trade Commission.

"Russia Says Curbs on Profit Are Not a Change in Policy." 1993. *New York Times,* 7 January.

Sachs, Jeffrey. 1990. "A Strategy for Efficient Debt Reduction." *The Journal of Economic Perspectives* 4, no. 1:19–29.

Schneider, Robert. 1993. "Land Abandonment, Property Rights, and Agricultural Sustainability in the Amazon." *LATEN Dissemination Note #3.* Washington, DC: World Bank, Latin America Technical Department.

Shrybman, Steven. 1992. "Trading Away the Environment." *World Policy Journal* Winter, 93–110.

Southgate, Douglas. 1990. "The Causes of Land Degradation Along 'Spontaneously' Expanding Agricultural Frontiers in the Third World." *Land Economics* 66, no. 1:93–101.

Stewart, Frances. 1990. "Technology Transfer for Development." In *Science and Technology: Lessons for Development Policy,* edited by Robert E. Evanson and Gustav Ranis. Boulder, CO: Westview Press.

Thompson, Herbert. 1992. "The Forestry-Timber-Logging Industry in Papau New Guinea." *Capitalism, Nature, Socialism* 3, no. 3:49–70.

Tibesar, Arthur, and Rodney White. 1990. "Pricing Policy and Household Energy Use in Dakar, Senegal." *The Journal of Developing Areas* 24, no. 1:33–48.

Ton, Kees, and Kees de Jong. 1991. "Irrigation Technology and Social Change: An Analysis of Social Variables of Technology." *Journal of Developing Areas* 25:197–206.

U.S. General Accounting Office. 1992. *U.S. Mexico Trade: Assessment of Mexico's Environmental Controls for New Companies.* Washington, DC: U.S. GAO.

Wallach, Lori, and Michelle Sforza. 1999. *Whose Trade Organization? Corporate Globalization and the Erosion of Democracy.* Washington, DC: Public Citizen.

Wardman, Anna, and Luci G. Salas. 1991. "The Implementation of Anti-Erosion Techniques in the Sahel: A Case Study From Kaya, Burkina Faso." *The Journal of Developing Areas* 26, no. 1:65–80.

Weaver, Frederick S., Frank W. Holmquist, and Michael D. Ford. 1990. "Third World Politics: Three Textbook Versions." *The Journal of Developing Areas* 25, no. 1:107–116.

Wheeler, David, and John Martin. 1993. "Prices, Policies and the International Diffusion of Clean Technology: The Case of Wood Pulp Production." Paper presented at the American Economic Association Meetings, Anaheim, CA.

World Bank. 1992. *World Development Report 1992: Development and the Environment.* New York: Oxford University Press.

World Commission on Environment and Development. 1987. *Our Common Future.* New York: Oxford University Press.

CHAPTER 23

THE ECONOMICS OF GLOBAL AGREEMENTS

23.0 Introduction

This book began with a discussion of a looming environmental problem with world-wide repercussions: global warming. Due to the buildup of carbon dioxide and other industrial gases in the atmosphere, most scientists agree that the planet will grow measurably warmer over the next hundred years. How much warmer remains in question, but the distinct possibility exists that global warming may cause catastrophic changes. This possibility makes global warming one of the biggest environmental challenges that humans will face in the twenty-first century.

Since our early introduction to the greenhouse effect, we have explored four difficult, but general, environmental economic questions. The answers to these questions can help us address the global warming problem. First, how much pollution—in this case, global warming—is too much? We considered three broad answers to this normative question: efficiency, safety, and ecological sustainability. Efficiency advocates would have us carefully balance the very real costs of slowing global warming against the obvious benefits. Both safety and ecological proponents find benefit–cost analysis too narrow a basis for choice, and advocate a freeze if not a rollback of carbon dioxide emissions, in spite of the cost.

The second issue: What are some of the obstacles to effective government action in achieving our goals? Suppose we set a target to stabilize carbon dioxide emissions at 1990 levels. Are we in fact likely to get there? Government policy makers are hampered by imperfect information. In addition, the possibility of political influence over environmental policy emerges when regulators must make discretionary choices. Our thirty-year experience with environmental regulation indicates that ambitious pollution reduction goals have proven difficult to achieve. Enforcement in particular has proven a weak link in the regulatory chain.

Our third question was, Can we do better? The book suggested two possible answers: (1) smarter regulation and (2) a shift in government focus to the promotion of clean technology. Incentive-based regulation carries the promise of reducing pollution in a more cost-effective and technologically dynamic fashion than the current reliance on command-and-control methods. In the greenhouse case, this means carbon taxes or marketable permit systems can help us achieve our goals at lower cost than mandating particular types of carbon dioxide emission reduction technology.

In addition to better regulation, the government can initiate a proactive policy promoting the rapid development and diffusion of clean technology. To qualify as clean, a technology must be found cost-competitive, either immediately or after only a short period of subsidy. If the government follows this selection rule, the policy of promoting clean technology will also be cost-effective. Clean technologies with substantial power to reduce carbon dioxide emissions include energy efficiency, solar electric, and wind power.

The fourth and final question: Is an effort to combat global warming consistent with the need for sustainable development in poor countries? On the one hand, boosting the incomes of the poor majority of the planet in order to increase food security and ultimately reduce population growth rates will work against this goal in the short term. Yet, the consumption of the poorest half of the planet's inhabitants is not currently the main greenhouse problem. Moreover, reduced population growth is a vital step in any program to control global warming. At the same time, promotion and diffusion of sustainable technology, and greater efforts to conserve forest resources will directly reduce carbon dioxide emissions.

This chapter of the book considers one last and formidable obstacle toward progress on global environmental issues such as slowing the greenhouse effect: the need for coordinated international action. International action, in turn, will result only from *effective* international agreements. Such agreements are unfortunately hard to achieve, and once reached, can prove difficult to enforce.

We begin by analyzing the incentives that a nation has first to join an international pollution control agreement, and second to comply with the terms of that agreement once it is signed. We then turn to a discussion of the tools available for enforcing such treaties. The chapter then moves on to analyze two international agreements on ozone depletion and biodiversity. We end by coming full circle with a consideration of the prospects for an effective treaty to halt global warming.

23.1 Agreements as Public Goods

Effective international agreements are hard to develop. The basic problem is that agreement on burden-sharing is difficult to achieve. In principle, each country might contribute its **true willingness to pay** for a treaty.[1] This willingness to pay in turn would depend on both the benefits received and the ability to pay, which might vary widely between nations. For example, low-lying Bangladesh and Egypt have a tremendous stake in slowing global warming and preventing a sea-level rise. Yet both countries are poor and would have a difficult time financing strong measures to

---

[1]For a further discussion of willingness to pay, see Chapter 8.

reduce CO_2 emissions. On the other hand, a landlocked, wealthy country like Switzerland has a high ability to pay but may have fewer immediate interests at stake.

A poor country's willingness to pay to join an agreement will typically be much smaller than a rich country's, simply because it has a much lower national income. Yet poor country participation will often be vital. For example, if China were to industrialize further, using its vast coal reserves, global warming would accelerate considerably. Given China's low willingness to pay for a reduction in global warming (as a result of its low income), a **compensation fund** would have to be established for China to sign a greenhouse treaty. Those with a high willingness to pay (typically rich countries) would have to pay for China to adopt less polluting and expensive energy sources. Otherwise, it would not be in China's interests to sign the treaty.

If each nation did contribute its true willingness to pay, then the agreement process would generate an efficient level of global pollution control. However, a country's underlying willingness to pay for an agreement is not well-defined in the first place and is certainly not transparent to negotiators from other nations. Therefore, each nation's bargainers will have an incentive to *understate* their true interest in a treaty in the hopes that others will shoulder more of the burden. In the extreme, a country might not sign a global warming or other environmental treaty at all *but still benefit* from the efforts of other nations.

This is just another form of the **free-rider problem** we have encountered several times in the book, beginning in Chapter 3. From an economic point of view, an international pollution control agreement is a **public good,** which has to be provided *voluntarily* by the private nations of the world. Reducing global warming is a public good, because there is no way to exclude free riders from enjoying the benefits provided by the treaty.

The public good nature of environmental treaties has two implications. First, treaties will tend to be **too weak** from a benefit–cost point of view, since signatory nations are reluctant to reveal and commit their true willingness to pay in the bargaining process. Second, once signed, nations will have a strong **incentive to cheat** on the agreement. Unilateral cheating is another way to free ride on the pollution control efforts of others. Of course, if everyone cheats, the agreement will collapse.

While the theory of public goods predicts that international environmental treaties will be both weak and susceptible to enforcement problems, agreements nevertheless do get signed and efforts are made to insure compliance. Table 23.1 lists some of the most significant environmental treaties now in effect.[2]

23.2 Monitoring and Enforcement

In Chapter 3, we noted two ways to overcome the free rider problem: government provision of the public good and social pressure. Within a single country, government typically supplies the public good of environmental protection, using its ability to tax, fine, and jail to prevent free riding (pollution) by private individuals and corporations. In the United States, for example, environmental laws are passed by Congress, and the regulatory details are then worked out and enforced by the Environmental Protection Agency and the Justice Department.

---

[2]For a good general discussion of these issues, see Sand (1990).

TABLE 23.1   Global Environmental Agreements

Formal Name (Common Name)	Year Signed	Prominent Nonmembers, 2000
The Antarctic Treaty System	1959	Self-limited membership
Nuclear Test Ban Treaty	1963	France, China
The Convention on International Trade in Endangered Species of Wild Flora and Fauna (CITES Treaty)[a]	1973	
New Management Procedure of International Whaling Commission (Whaling Moratoria)	1974	
Law of the Sea (not currently in force)	1982	United States, United Kingdom, West Germany
Montreal Protocol on Substances that Deplete the Ozone Layer (Montreal Protocol)	1987	
The Basel Convention on Transboundary Movement of Hazardous Wastes and Their Disposal (Basel Convention)[b]	1989	African nations
Kyoto Global Warming Treaty	1997	United States, Australia
Rio Convention on Biodiversity[c]	1992	United States

Treaty Web sites:

[a]www.wcmc.org.uk/CITES

[b]www.ban.org

[c]www.biodiv.org

At the international level, the treaty is the equivalent of an environmental law. However, *no* international government exists that coerces nations into undertaking the broadly agreed-upon steps, nor is there likely to be one soon. The United Nations has no authority over its member nations in the environmental arena.[3]

Nevertheless, each treaty does set up its own **inter-governmental organization (IGO),** which is charged with overseeing the agreement. Countries seldom agree to give IGOs the authority to actually enforce treaty agreements; this would be giving away too much sovereignty. However, IGOs can be still be given substantive powers. One of these is to set **non-binding standards** that states are "expected" but not required to meet. The second is to **monitor** compliance with agreements.

For example, in a 1991 revision of the Antarctic treaty, an environmental committee has been appointed to which each nation must submit information on its management procedures. Environmental Impact Statements (see Chapter 7) are also now required for new activities, including tourism, sponsored by a member nation. Social pressure can then be brought to bear on states that either fail to achieve the standards or are out of compliance with the broader terms of the treaty. The environmental group Greenpeace has effectively "shamed" countries with particularly poor environmental records on the continent.[4]

---

[3]For a further discussion, see French (1992).

[4]See "Mining Banned," and "Antarctic: Exploration or Exploitation?" *The New Scientist,* October 12, 1991, and June 22, 1991.

Such **social pressure** is the second way in which free riding has traditionally been controlled. However, a well-orchestrated public relations campaign encouraging the United States to join with the "community of nations" was insufficient to get it to sign a biodiversity treaty in 1992 in Rio de Janeiro. Such moral pressures are even less likely to be effective in insuring compliance once treaties have been signed. Nevertheless, bad publicity and community pressure, as in the Antarctic case mentioned above, remain among the important tools of international negotiation.

Given the lack of an international pollution control agency, and the limited effectiveness of social pressure, the burden of enforcement will fall on measures written into the treaty itself. Treaty members must agree in advance on the sanctions to be levied against noncomplying members or nonmembers. In the absence of such sanctions, compliance is liable to be very poor. For example, the CITES treaty regulating trade in endangered species relies primarily on national enforcement efforts. According to the World Wildlife Federation, an environmental group that voluntarily monitors CITES, about one third of the member nations have never filed the required biennial progress report. Most nations that do report have done so in a very tardy manner. The basic problem is a lack of committed resources. Even in a rich country such as the United States, a lack of trained customs officials means that up to 60,000 parrots have entered the country illegally in a single year (Heppes and McFadden 1987).

There are two basic enforcement tools: restricting access to a compensation fund and imposing trade sanctions. The simplest mechanism is to establish a **compensation fund** to act as a carrot for both joining a treaty and complying with its terms. Such compensation funds, however, can only induce compliance by poor countries.

Trade sanctions are the most powerful tool available. As we shall see below, their mere existence played an important part in the success of the agreement to control depletion of the ozone layer. Sanctions tend to be restricted to goods related to the treaty. This is useful, since it minimizes the possibility that the imposition of sanctions for enforcement purposes will degenerate into a trade war. For example, under the CITES treaty, a ban on trade in wildlife products from Thailand was imposed in 1991 to encourage that country to crack down on illegal exports. At least nineteen international environmental agreements authorize some form of trade sanction (French 1992).

23.3 The Ozone Layer and Biodiversity

This section will examine two environmental treaties: the 1987 Montreal Protocol to control the depletion of the ozone layer, and the 1992 Rio Earth Summit agreement on biodiversity. We will focus on the factors that promoted agreement and the enforcement mechanisms built in. In the ozone case, we also have a compliance record to examine.

OZONE DEPLETION

The earth's upper atmosphere is surrounded by a thin shield of a naturally occurring chemical known as ozone. Ozone at ground level is better known as smog and is quite harmful. By contrast, the **ozone layer** surrounding the earth serves a beneficial role by screening out the sun's harmful ultraviolet rays. Exposure to ultraviolet rays causes skin cancer and eye disease, reduces the productivity of agriculture, and can kill small terrestrial and marine organisms at the base of the food chain. Over the last twenty years, it has become apparent that the ozone layer is threatened by the buildup of human-made chemicals in the upper atmosphere.

These chemicals, known as chlorofluorocarbons (CFCs), were invented in the 1940s.[5] They have since served as aerosol propellants, coolants in refrigerators and air conditioners, foam-blowing agents, and gaseous cleansers for medical and computer equipment. They are also very long-lived stock pollutants. CFCs released into the atmosphere from discarded refrigerators today will continue to break down the ozone layer for up to a hundred years.

The potential for significant ozone depletion by CFCs was first established in 1974. In spite of the serious health and ecological effects of ozone depletion, uncertainty about the scientific link between depletion and CFCs slowed international regulatory action. Although the United States unilaterally banned CFCs as aerosol propellants in 1977, few other countries followed suit. In 1982, a benefit–cost analysis published in the prestigious *American Economic Review,* while acknowledging substantial uncertainty, argued *against* regulating CFC use on efficiency grounds (Bailey 1992). This position was also advanced by CFC manufacturers.

Nevertheless international concern over the problem was mounting, fueled by a 1985 British study documenting a huge, seasonal **ozone hole** over Antarctica. Less severe, but measurable depletion was occurring throughout the middle latitudes. In 1987, building on six years of United Nations efforts, twenty-four countries signed the **Montreal Protocol** to Protect Against Atmospheric Ozone Reduction. Just *after* the protocol was signed, a conclusive scientific link between ozone depletion and CFCs was at last established.

The treaty called for a ten-year, 50% reduction in CFC production by each country from a 1986 baseline. The treaty made some concessions to poor countries, which would otherwise be locked into current levels of low consumption, and which were hardly responsible for the global problem in the first place. Developing countries were given a ten-year grace period before cutbacks would have to be made. In addition, rich countries were urged, but not required, to set up an assistance fund to ease the transition (Somerset 1989).

These incentives were insufficient to attract India and China, both of whom viewed the benefits of cheap refrigeration from CFCs as too high to forego. As a result, a 1990 revision of the Protocol required rich countries to establish a fund of $260 million to finance the adjustment to CFC replacements in poor countries, with $60 million contributed by the primary CFC producer, the United States. This fund provided a sufficient inducement for most of the remaining nonmember countries to join, including India and China.

As a way to discourage free riding by nonmembers, the treaty mandated trade restrictions on CFCs. Parties to the treaty were required to ban imports and exports of

---

[5]Halons, used in fire extinguishers, are also human-made ozone-depleting gases. Much of this discussion applies to halons as well as CFCs.

CFCs, many products containing CFCs, products produced with CFCs, and technologies for producing CFCs to nonmember countries. These trade sanctions limited the gains from nonmembership and thus reduced free riding. However, these restrictions could conceivably be challenged under the General Agreement on Tariffs and Trade (GATT) as an obstacle to free trade (French 1993).[6]

The half-dozen companies that produce the great bulk of CFCs worldwide ultimately supported the 1987 Montreal Protocol, although they viewed the goal of a 50% reduction as greater than necessary. But by 1988, faced with mounting evidence of ozone depletion, the major producer DuPont announced its intentions to phase out CFCs altogether by the year 2000. In 1990, the Protocol nations also revised the treaty to call for a complete ban by the year 2000. In 1992, after a finding that an accelerated phaseout might save an additional million lives through reduced skin cancer, the treaty nations agreed to eliminate CFC production by 1996. The compensation fund was also boosted to $500 million.[7]

Compliance with the early terms of the treaty by the rich countries was quite good; the accelerated phaseout adopted in 1992 was possible because several nations were already ahead of schedule. As discussed in Chapter 17, the United States adopted an incentive-based regulatory approach—tradeable permits combined with indirect pollution taxes—to meet its treaty obligations. Because of the ten-year grace period provided to developing countries, it is difficult to evaluate global compliance. We do know that CFC smuggling (in the form of freon) is a growing problem. And some press reports suggest that India and China will face a difficult time meeting their present deadlines over the next few years. China apparently *increased* production of some CFCs during the late 1990s (see "India" 2000, "The China Syndrome" 1999, and Munasinghe and King 1992).

The first two sections of this chapter suggested, on theoretical grounds, that the prospects for obtaining enforceable international agreements on the environment were not good. In many ways, the Montreal Protocol contradicts such a gloomy picture. In spite of scientific uncertainty, initial international agreement was obtained. The threat of trade sanctions helped overcome the free-rider problem. A sufficient compensation fund was eventually established to bring poor countries on board. The pollution control target was dramatically tightened as scientific knowledge advanced, and compliance has been remarkably good in the developed countries.

Several factors help explain the success of the Protocol. The dramatic discovery of the ozone hole over the Antarctic provided an initial boost to the treaty process, as did findings of a comparable Arctic hole in 1992. Once the agreement had been signed, however, two additional factors worked in its favor. First, because there were only six main corporations involved in the production of CFCs, monitoring the progress of the CFC phaseout has been relatively easy. Second, clean technological

---

[6]French (1993). A nonsignatory to the Protocol could challenge the Protocol under GATT.

[7]The treaty contains at least one loophole: Production can be continued to service existing equipment and for "essential uses." See "Ozone Protection Treaty Strengthened," *Science News,* December 12, 1992; and "The Resistible Rise of Skin Cancer," *New Scientist,* May 16, 1992.

substitutes for CFCs have developed quickly as a result of the imminent ban. Early predictions of prohibitively high compliance costs proved faulty.

What are these substitutes? One estimate is that about 29% of the CFC market is served by conservation and recycling, and 32% by a switch to organic compounds and water (for cleaning and foam blowing). The environmental impact of these techniques is much more benign than the CFCs they replace. The remaining 39% of the market, primarily in refrigeration, required the development of new synthetic chemicals (Manzer 1990). The industry has developed hydrofluorocarbon (HFC) and hydrochlorofluorocarbon (HCFC) substitutes. HFCs are "ozone friendly" but not as efficient a coolant. Unfortunately, HCFCs also deplete the ozone layer, though at a rate well below CFCs. HCFC production was frozen at 1991 levels under the 1992 update of the Montreal Protocol and is slated to be phased out in 2030.[8]

To sum up: The Montreal Protocol has proven to be a stunningly successful environmental treaty. Beginning with initial meetings in 1980, through the 50% cuts agreed to in 1987, and the accelerated phaseout decided on in 1992, it took "only" sixteen years to effectively ban the production of CFCs. The dark side is that this was not fast enough. Because CFCs are so long-lived (and because of HCFCs and other ozone depleters), the ozone problem will get worse before it gets better. Under a year 2000 CFC ban, scientists estimated that the concentration of ozone-depleting chemicals would triple over 1989 levels by the year 2010; the Antarctic ozone hole is continuing to grow into the twenty-first century ("Substitute CFCs" 1989). Given the dramatic elevation in skin cancers likely to emerge even given the 1996 phaseout, CFCs have already earned their place in the history books as one of the most destructive pollutants released into the environment.

BIODIVERSITY

Protecting **biodiversity** means protecting endangered species—not only cuddly mammals but also the entire ecosystems in which they live. As we discussed in the last chapter on deforestation, preserving the stock of genetic material found in natural ecosystems is important not only for its **existence value** but also for two utilitarian reasons: **pharmaceuticals and agricultural breeding.** As an example, a strain of Mexican maize, discovered in 1977, had a natural immunity to two serious viral diseases. Hybrid corn seeds based on the genetic material in the maize are now available from U.S.-based seed companies.

The fact that Mexico will receive no compensation for this profitable innovation helps explain why the valuable resource of biodiversity is threatened (Sedjo 1992). Historically, genetic material has been viewed as an **open access** common property

[8]HCFCs deplete the ozone at 2% to 10% the rate of CFCs. This information and the HFC quote are from "Atmosphere of Uncertainty: Businesses Dependent on CFCs Cooperate, Innovate and Wait," *Scientific American,* April 1990. HFCs have also been found to cause benign cancers in rats at very high doses. The EPA has judged them "safe." See "EPA Sees No Problem with CFC Substitutes," *Chemical and Engineering News,* September 28, 1992. On phaseout of HCFCs, see "Ozone Protection Treaty Strengthened," *Science News,* December 12, 1992.

resource. Seed and drug companies based in rich countries would send prospectors to tropical countries that are host to the vast majority of the world's species. (A single tree in an Amazon rain forest contained forty-three species of ants, more than in the entire British Isles!) They would return with samples to be analyzed for prospective commercial uses. If a plant or animal then generated a profitable return, the country from which it originated would receive no benefit. Host country residents, not being able to realize any of the commercial value of biodiversity, have thus been little interested in conservation.

This situation has begun to change a bit, thanks in large part to improvements in technologies that have made large-scale screening and cataloging of species economically attractive. Costa Rica has recently struck several deals with a U.S.-based drug company, Merck, as well as several U.S. foundations and universities to develop a "forest prospecting industry." The long-run goal is to train a Costa Rican workforce capable of regulating biological prospectors. Costa Rica will then grant access to its forests conditional on receiving a share of profits from any agricultural or pharmaceutical innovations ("Prospectors" 1991). Building a strong institutional base for this industry is important so that Costa Rica can prevent illegal prospecting, as well as forestall efforts by corporations to synthesize a new drug based on a botanical finding, and then fail to report it.

Essentially what Costa Rica is doing is shifting an open access common property resource into a state-owned resource, by beefing up its technical **enforcement capabilities.** This in turn greatly strengthens the incentive for profit-based conservation (see Chapter 22). Costa Rica is well-placed to do this on its own, because, as we noted in Chapter 21, it has a relatively efficient bureaucracy, has a highly literate population, already has an extensive national park network, and has strong links with U.S.-based conservation groups.

Global efforts to protect biodiversity have taken the form of a treaty signed at the Earth Summit in Rio De Janeiro in 1992. The initiative has three central features. First, nations are required to inventory and monitor their biological assets. Second, conservation efforts centered around sustained yield resource development (see Chapter 22) are to be pursued, conditional on financial support from wealthy countries. Finally, the treaty specified that a product developed from the genetic resources of a country remained the intellectual property of the host nation, unless a company had agreed to a profit-sharing mechanism in advance (Hathaway 1992). In other words, under the treaty a country like Mexico would have a legal right to block the sale of hybrid corn seeds developed from Mexican maize unless it was guaranteed a share of the profits. How such a provision will be enforced remains an open question.

At the Rio Summit, developing nations tried to get the rich countries to agree to commit 0.7% of their annual GDP to sustainable development projects, up from 0.4% (from $55 billion to $98 billion annually). However, no such firm commitment was forthcoming. An additional $5 billion in annual aid over the next five years was pledged at the summit, with 80% coming from Japan, 16% from the European Community, and 4% from the United States. Some of this aid helped finance the conservation programs under the biodiversity treaty.

The Rio agreement was weakened by developing countries that objected to initial attempts to list particular species and habitats as endangered (the approach taken in the 1973 CITES treaty on wildlife trade). Ultimately, the agreement was signed by 158 nations, with one significant holdout: the United States. The United States had several objections, but primary was the provision that assigned property rights to genetic resources to host countries.

Under the agreement, these rights must be purchased by foreign and domestic firms. As we noted in Chapter 22, whenever common property resources are privatized, those who previously had free access will lose out. In this case, multinational seed and pharmaceutical companies, many of them U.S.-based, were the losers. A U.S. biotech industry spokesperson put it this way: "It seems to us highway robbery that a Third World country should have the right to a protected invention simply because it supplied a bug, or a plant or animal in the first place. It's been weighted in favor of developing nations." While Japan and Britain shared some of the U.S. reservations, these two nations ultimately signed on under pressure from domestic environmental groups. In 1993, newly elected President Clinton reversed the U.S. stand taken at the conference and announced we would sign the treaty;[9] however, the U.S. Senate still has refused to ratify.

The Rio agreement is important from a symbolic point of view, in that the rich countries formally acknowledged the need for a transfer of resources in order to protect biodiversity. Few are optimistic, however, that the treaty as currently framed will do more than slow down the massive acceleration in species extinction we are currently witnessing.

First, the treaty itself contains no requirement that rich countries contribute to the conservation fund. While significant monies were committed at Rio, no ongoing financial mechanism was established. Second, while the Rio treaty formally assigns to each country the property rights to its genetic resources, no enforcement mechanism is set up. What if biotech companies ignore or circumvent the international law? Without the kind of technical enforcement capability that Costa Rica is building up, the property rights provision of the treaty is liable to be fairly hollow.

The prospects for strengthening the Rio biodiversity treaty are not good for two related reasons. First, it is very hard to assess compliance with and progress toward an agreement the goal of which is to "protect biodiversity." As the treaty acknowledges, the problem of species extinction is a diverse and deeply rooted one, ultimately driven by rapid population growth and desperate poverty in poor countries. In short, effectively preserving biodiversity means *achieving sustainable development* throughout the less developed world. As discussed in Chapter 22, this will require a substantial increase in the transfer of technology and other resources from wealthy countries to poor ones.

The second obstacle to an effective international agreement is closely related. The loss of biodiversity is unlikely to galvanize the massive aid efforts from the developed world essential to such an effort. The daily extinctions of dozens of species of

---

[9]The United States was also concerned about efforts to regulate international trade in genetically engineered products on safety grounds, and the control over the conservation fund set up by the treaty. See "U.S. to Oppose Treaty on Protection of Resources," *New York Times,* May 30, 1992. The quote is from "Biodiversity Convention a 'Lousy Deal' Says US," *New Scientist,* July 4, 1992. Clinton's decision is reported in "Not Just Hot Air," *Time,* May 3, 1993. For an update on the treaty, visit the treaty Web site at www.biodiv.org.

plants, insects, and animals in the tropical rain forest may deprive my children of important medicines and agricultural products. However, this threat is a negative and distant one: The loss of biodiversity may reduce well-being, but it does not immediately threaten many human lives. By contrast, action to ban CFCs in the ozone case was forthcoming because of the potential for direct and positive harm: massive increases in skin cancer and blindness.

To sum up: The framework laid at Rio for protecting biodiversity was certainly helpful, but success on the scale of the Montreal Protocol is unlikely to be duplicated. Instead, follow-up meetings are likely to focus, unproductively, on rich country funding levels. As a result, nongovernmental conservation organizations, multinational drug and agricultural companies, and host country governments will now have to take the lead in protecting biodiversity for its own sake. As the next section discusses, however, protecting tropical forests might be an important side-benefit of a global warming agreement.

23.4 Stopping Global Warming: Theory

The prospects for progress on an effective international agreement to control global warming fall midway between the examples of the Montreal Protocol and Rio biodiversity treaty. Like ozone depletion, and unlike the loss of biodiversity, global warming represents a distinct, positive threat to a wide range of nations. Also like ozone depletion, the greenhouse threat arises from several well-defined atmospheric pollutants—primarily carbon dioxide (CO_2) and methane. Thus a treaty can be structured around the concrete goal of controlling these pollutants, instead of an ill-defined target of "preserving ecosystems." These two features—the prospect of **positive harm** to our children, and the existence of a **well-defined problem**—both improve the prospects for an effective agreement.

However, a global warming treaty shares many of the problems faced in the biodiversity case. Foremost among these is the vastly **decentralized** nature of the problem. Unlike the case of CFCs, there are millions of producers of carbon dioxide and methane. Virtually no sector of a modern economy operates without producing CO_2, and methane pollution arises from sources as diverse as natural gas pipelines, rice paddies, and cattle ranches. The CO_2 problem seems a bit less daunting when it is reduced to its two main contributors—coal-fired power plants and gasoline-powered transport. Nevertheless, before clean energy alternatives to these technologies (discussed in Chapter 20) are fully cost competitive, enforcement looms as a major obstacle to an effective treaty.

In addition, as in the loss of biodiversity, both **deforestation** and **population growth** in poor countries are important sources of the greenhouse effect. Although the majority of greenhouse gas emissions are currently generated by the rich countries, sometime over the next two decades, emissions from poor countries will dominate. This means that "solving" global warming is also tied up with the momentous task of achieving sustainable development in the less-developed world.

Under a business-as-usual scenario, over the next century CO_2 levels in the atmosphere will rise to double their preindustrial level—560 parts per million—leading to a global temperature increase of between 1.5 and 11 degrees Fahrenheit. Figure 23.1 outlines a different future. Here, concerted efforts to reduce greenhouse gas emissions—beginning now—lead to a stabilization of CO_2 concentrations in the atmosphere at 450 ppm. Such an effort would not stop further warming—it is too late for that. However,

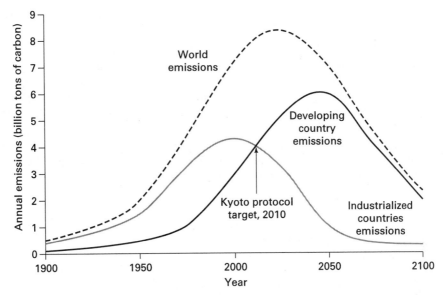

FIGURE 23.1 Stabilizing CO_2 Concentrations at 450 ppm

Source: Bernow et al. (1999). Used with permission.

taking action now would reduce and eventually stop global temperature increases, as well as prevent insurance against the likelihood of a greenhouse disaster if the high-end temperature forecasts are borne out. Figure 23.1 also shows clearly that developing countries in the South will meet and soon far outstrip CO_2 emissions coming from the industrialized North. This will be true even if emissions in the North do not start falling.

Achieving the CO_2 emission reductions in Figure 23.1—on the order of 90% over the next hundred years in the rich countries—may seem like an impossible task. However, the diagram simply reflects an assumed phase-out of fossil fuels and a transition to a cheap, clean energy future: with electricity provided by wind, solar, and biomass, and transportation powered by hydrogen fuel cells. These are not pipe-dream technologies. The uncertain questions, however, are how quickly can their costs drop to competitive levels, and how rapidly can these technologies be transferred to the South, where emissions are growing the fastest?

It is apparent that, unlike the Montreal Protocol, an effective treaty to slow down global warming cannot focus primarily on regulatory control of industries (and consumers) in the rich countries. Instead, it must eventually confront a broad range of interrelated and difficult development issues: poverty, population growth, and deforestation. Fortunately, the ultimate task still remains the narrow and quantifiable one of reducing carbon and methane emissions.

With this background, the bare bones of a successful treaty must do three things: (1) mandate numerical **emission reduction targets** for carbon dioxide and methane; (2) provide a mechanism by which rich countries effectively **transfer technology and resources** to poor countries to finance sustainable development; and (3) provide strong **enforcement** mechanisms. A good tool for accomplishing these three goals simultaneously would be an international **marketable permits** system.

How would this work? Figure 23.2 illustrates one version of the process. An initial treaty would first put an annual cap on targeted global emissions of a greenhouse pollutant, say CO_2. A share of the annual total would then be allocated to each nation. Some have suggested that carbon permits be allocated based on a nation's population, others have suggested an initial fifty-fifty split between rich and poor countries. At any rate, for the system to work, poor countries would have to emerge from the process with an excess supply of permits, while rich countries would have an excess demand.

The next step in the process would be for rich nations to trade expertise and technology to poor nations in exchange for permits. Trade would only be authorized for measures that lead to demonstrable reductions in greenhouse gas emissions. To lessen the opportunity for corruption, trade in cash would be discouraged. A poor country

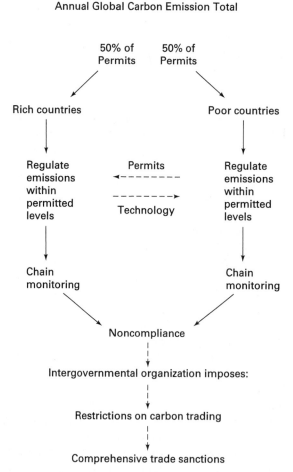

FIGURE 23.2 Model Greenhouse Treaty

thus might trade 1 million tons of CO_2 for a shipment of photovoltaic solar cells, a boatload of condoms, 100 forestry experts, and one environmental economist.[10]

Each country would then be responsible for reducing CO_2 emissions to the level specified by the tradeable permits held. This could be done through an "internal" marketable permit system, carbon taxes, command-and-control regulation, or programs to promote investment in clean technology. An intergovernmental organization (IGO) established by the initial treaty would have to have broad compliance monitoring powers. One possibility is **chain monitoring** in which the countries are ranked by CO_2 emissions, and each nation is monitored by the next biggest emitter (Holley 1991).[11] Presumably, such monitors would have an economic incentive to insure their (larger) competitors were not cheating on an agreement.

Finally, a permit system could be enforced by restricting trade in permits to countries who were either exceeding their permitted emissions, or violating other terms of the agreement. Poor country sales would be restricted, as would rich country purchases. One beauty of the permit system is that it gives countries something that can then be taken away if they refuse to comply. Finally, the treaty would have to authorize more **comprehensive trade sanctions** against a nation that repeatedly or willfully failed to meet its permitted emissions requirements.

The near-term prospects for this kind of comprehensive agreement, including both rich and poor countries, are not good. First, such a treaty might be painted as a large scale foreign aid program. Such initiatives are currently politically unpopular in rich countries. Second, an effective treaty would both require nations to allow foreign or intergovernmental monitoring of compliance, and authorize the imposition of full-scale trade embargoes for willful noncompliance. To date, countries have seldom agreed to give up this much sovereignty. Finally, uncertainty as to the magnitude of the problem provides an excuse for inaction. However, as in the ozone case, greenhouse gasses are very long-lived. Thus, by the time the magnitude of global warming is confirmed, it may be too late to take any effective action.

23.5 Stopping Global Warming: Reality

At the Rio de Janeiro Earth Summit in 1992, the U.S. government did plead uncertainty, and successfully weakened the **framework global warming convention** that was ultimately signed. The European nations were originally pressing for a schedule of timetables and cutbacks aimed at substantially *reducing* global CO_2 emissions. President Bush, the elder, by threatening to boycott the Rio summit altogether, was able instead to achieve a much weaker agreement. Ultimately, the nations made only a nonbinding commitment to "try" and stabilize carbon emissions at 1990 levels by the

---

[10]Economists have traditionally argued that in a world of perfect information, payment in cash is preferable to payment-in-kind of the type discussed here. This is because it is assumed the recipient better knows how to spend his money than the donor. In this case, however, the global agreement specifies expenditures for a certain purpose, and payment in kind is easier to monitor than payment in cash. For a general argument along these lines, see Blackorby and Donaldson (1988).

[11]The biggest emitter, the United States, would in turn monitor several medium sized countries. For a good discussion of greenhouse compliance, see di Primo, Stein, and Wagner (1992).

year 2000. This effort failed—emissions in the United States for example, rose about 11% over the period.[12]

The governments of the world reconvened in Kyoto, Japan in December 1997, and signed a stronger agreement calling for a total reduction in greenhouse gasses to 5% below 1990 levels by about 2010. For the United States, the target is 7% below 1990 levels, for Japan, 6%, and for the European Union, 8%. The **Kyoto Protocol** only imposed emission targets and timetables on the industrialized countries. The rationale here was twofold: First, greenhouse gases are longlived, so although poor countries will soon catch up in terms of annual emissions, the cumulative emissions from developed countries will remain primarily responsible for climate change over the medium term. Second, poor countries don't have the resources to invest in the alternative technologies—fuel cell vehicles, solar and wind-powered electricity—that are needed to address the global warming problem.

Thus, the idea behind the Kyoto agreement—explicitly modeled on the Montreal Protocol—was that rich countries would go first and develop low-cost alternatives to gasoline-powered automobiles and coal-fired power plants. These technologies would then spread from the North to the South, allowing poor countries to "leap-frog" the fossil fuel–based development patterns followed by the rich countries.

The **Clean Development Mechanism** under the current Kyoto accord—in which rich countries gain credit for clean investments in poor countries—is one prototype for technology transfer. If and when Kyoto is expanded to include limits on developing country emissions, a global carbon cap-and-trade system will build on this approach. The trading system should provide excess carbon allowances to poor countries; these could then be "sold" to rich countries in exchange for access to solar power or fuel cell technologies, or for help in protecting standing forests. Kyoto currently does incorporate a more limited marketable permit approach; the **Joint Implementation** procedure would allow for trade in carbon rights between the industrialized countries subject to emission limits.

As I write the fourth edition of this text, the Kyoto accord has been ratified by the European countries, Canada, and Japan. If Russia ratifies, then a sufficient number of countries will have joined for the treaty to bind on member countries. Regardless, the current ratifiers are moving ahead with implementing legislation designed to reduce greenhouse gas emissions in their countries. The UK, for example, has pledged a 60% reduction in emissions by 2050. Australia and the United States are the major industrial countries that have failed to ratify; indeed, in 2001 President Bush withdrew the United States from the Kyoto process. In its place he has advocated a voluntary program on the part of industry to reduce the rate of growth of emissions, but not emissions themselves. (Note this is a far weaker standard than that agreed to by his father in 1992 at the framework convention in Rio.) Conservative opposition to the treaty has centered on two arguments: uncertainty as to the potential damages from climate change, and the argument that poor countries should be parties to the treaty and forced to reduce emissions on the same timetable as rich countries. Otherwise, it is argued, U.S. industry will be at a competitive disadvantage leading to large-scale job

---

[12]"How Bush Achieved Global Warming Pact with Modest Goals," *The Wall Street Journal,* 5/27/92. "Now, With Treaty On Climate Signed, Countries Promise Stricter Measures," *The New York Times,* 6/13/92. President Clinton announced in 1993 that we would meet the Rio target by 2000. See "Not Just Hot Air," *Time,* 5/3/93.

loss. As we saw in Chapter 9, this kind of widespread jobs-environment conflict, while often predicted in the past, has never materialized (Goodstein 1999).

Whether urgent international action on global warming is in fact justified is the subject of an important economic (and ethical) debate, explored in Chapters 1 and 20. The general consensus among economists, however, is that the initial steps to control CO_2 emissions (improved energy efficiency, fuel switching away from coal, and the control of natural gas leaks) will not be particularly costly. Indeed, as noted in Chapter 1, many of the economists working on global warming issues have publicly called for action—ranging from a modest $10 per ton tax to Kyoto compliance—based on efficiency arguments. Given this, the U.S. actions in the 1990s have been unfortunate from a global benefit–cost perspective.

As the Montreal Protocol case illustrates, a treaty process is a long, drawn out affair. The Kyoto Protocol, though much stronger than the Rio Convention of 1992, is a far cry from the effective agreement outlined in Figure 23.2. It deals only with step one, establishing numerical reduction targets, but does not address in a serious way the other two requirements: resources for sustainable development and enforcement. From this perspective, our nation's opposition undercuts the substantial insurance value that would have been provided by an agreement that at least addressed the first of the three necessary steps. The treaty process must be well-advanced in the event that the additional bolder steps are to be seriously contemplated.

Nevertheless, as the biggest greenhouse gas emitter, the U.S. position is illustrative of the general problem of forging agreements outlined in the introduction to this chapter. Relative to its much more energy efficient Japanese and European competitors, the U.S. economy includes more actors likely to lose from a global warming treaty. Thus, the opposition to the process has been strongest from our country.

I stated above that one of the factors favoring a global warming treaty is that the greenhouse effect is liable to inflict positive and significant harm on the citizens of many nations. As an example of a clear and present danger yielding an impressive international response, we can look to the appearance of the ozone hole in 1985 which spurred nations into signing the Montreal Protocol. If the greenhouse effect does in fact lead to a substantial increase in global temperature, we would indeed be lucky if some bad weather materializes sooner rather than later. If instead, we warm only slowly, an effective global warming treaty may come too late.

23.6 Summary

This chapter identifies a basic obstacle to effective international action on global environmental problems: the public good nature of an agreement. Free riding means that agreements are likely to be too weak from an efficiency perspective and to be susceptible to noncompliance. International bodies set up to administer agreements may monitor compliance but have few enforcement powers. One informal tool is community pressure. Formal enforcement mechanisms must be written into a treaty and include restricted access to a compensation fund and targeted trade sanctions.

The Montreal Protocol to protect the ozone layer represents the most successful environmental treaty to date. In a period of sixteen years, nations moved from skepticism about the need to regulate CFCs at all, to banning the bulk of production. The treaty's success can be traced to three factors: (1) the rapidly mounting evidence of a significant health threat; (2) the centralized nature of CFC production, which minimized enforcement problems; and (3) the speedy development of low cost CFC substitutes.

By contrast, the Rio biodiversity agreement has value primarily as a symbol of concern. The treaty formally recognizes two key points: (1) Rich nations must finance sustained yield resource development projects in poor countries if biodiversity is to be preserved, and (2) an important obstacle to profit-based conservation has been open access by multinational firms to genetic resources. However, the treaty is very weak on enforcement mechanisms, and rich nations have little political incentive to pay the necessary price to beef up the treaty.

The prospects for a global warming treaty are enhanced by the positive threat posed and the focus on a handful of pollutants. However, as in the biodiversity case, solving the problem would in fact require achieving sustainable development in poor countries—increasing incomes in a clean fashion while reducing population growth. An effective treaty would mandate emission reductions, provide a means to transfer technology and resources to poor countries, and have a built-in enforcement mechanism. An international tradeable permits system has these three features. In addition, enforcement would have to be guaranteed by the threat of comprehensive trade sanctions.

This book has ended, as it began, with a discussion of global warming. Today, I have compounded this problem by actions as simple as driving to work and turning on my computer. Yet global warming is just one of the pressing environmental problems we will face in the coming years. From the siting of waste facilities at the community level, to regulatory policy at the national level, to sustainable development around the globe, environmental challenges abound. While these problems are formidable, for our children's sake, we have no option but to face them squarely. This book has provided some tools for doing so.

At the risk of repeating myself (again!), let me summarize the three-step approach that we have developed:

Step 1. Set your environmental goal.
   Efficiency, safety, or ecological sustainability?
Step 2. Recognize the constraints on effective government action.
   Imperfect information, political influence, and inadequate enforcement.
Step 3. Look for ways to do better.
   Incentive-based regulation and clean technology promotion.

Now, get to work.

APPLICATION 23.0

After the Warming

In the BBC science-fiction drama, *After the Warming,* a historian looks back from the year 2050 at our efforts to deal with the problem of global warming. It turns out that we do adopt a fairly effective tradeable permit system for greenhouse gases, beginning in the late 1990s. (Unfortunately, due to positive feedback in the form of disrupted ocean currents, year 2050 residents find themselves having to redouble their efforts to keep the planet from overheating.)

Nations that violated the treaty, the historian informs us, lost their carbon-trading rights until they came back into compliance.

1. Would this enforcement mechanism work for developing countries? Developed countries? Why or why not?
2. The show describes the growth of a powerful and rather efficient "Planetary Management Authority" (sort of like "The Federation" on *Star Trek*), which uses advanced technology to monitor compliance and make enforcement decisions. Is it likely that compliance could be effectively monitored by a centralized world agency?

KEY IDEAS IN EACH SECTION

23.0   This chapter discusses the economics of global pollution control agreements.

23.1   Each country has a true **willingness-to-pay** for a pollution control agreement that is a function of both its income and the environmental benefits it is likely to receive. However, because agreements are **public goods,** the **free-rider problem** means they will be both **too weak** from an efficiency (and safety) point of view and provide **incentives for cheating.**

23.2   Monitoring compliance is typically the responsibility of an **intergovernmental organization (IGO)** set up by each treaty. IGOs can also issue **nonbinding standards** and **monitor** compliance. The three main enforcement tools are **social pressure,** restricted access to **compensation funds,** and targeted **trade sanctions.**

23.3   This section describes two agreements. First, the **Montreal Protocol** initiated a global phaseout of **chlorofluorocarbons (CFCs)** to protect the earth's **ozone layer.** The treaty succeeded due to (1) the clear and present danger from the **ozone hole,** (2) a narrowly defined problem, and (3) ease of enforcement due to limited number of producers. Second, the Rio Convention on Biodiversity seeks to protect **biodiversity** (important for **existence value** and as a gene pool) by encouraging member nations to inventory reserves, take conservation measures, and provide host countries with a share in **pharmaceutical and agricultural breeding** profits. The treaty has little more than symbolic value due to (1) a clear but distant danger of negative harm, (2) a broadly defined problem, and (3) inability to take action without funding from rich countries.

23.4   How likely is an effective **global warming treaty?** Pros include the likelihood of **positive harm** and the existence of **well-defined** pollutants. Cons arise from highly **decentralized** producers and the fact that a greenhouse treaty would have to confront sustainability issues ranging from **deforestation** to **population growth.** An effective treaty would have three components: (1) **numerical emission targets;** (2) **technology and resource transfers;** and (3) **good enforcement.** A **marketable permit system,** combined with **chain monitoring** and **comprehensive trade sanctions,** is one model that fits these requirements.

23.5   The UN **Framework Convention on Climate Change** was negotiated in Rio de Janeiro in 1992 and called for voluntary efforts to prevent growth in emissions, which failed. Subsequent meetings led to the signing of the **Kyoto Protocol,** which would require the industrial nations collectively to reduce greenhouse gas emissions 5% below 1990 levels by about 2010. The Protocol does incorporate developing countries into a carbon trading system through the **Clean Development Mechanism,** and also includes a textbook cap-and-trade component for the industrial nations known as **Joint Implementation.** The United States has withdrawn from the Kyoto accord; if Russia ratifies, most other industrial countries will move forward with implementation.

REFERENCES

Bailey, Martin. 1982. "Risks, Costs and Benefits of Fluorocarbon Regulation." *American Economic Review* 72, no. 2:247–250.

Bernow, Stephen, Karlynn Cory, William Dougherty, Max Duckworth, Sivan Kartha, and Michael Ruth. 1999. *America's Global Warming Solutions.* Washington, DC: World Wildlife Fund.

Blackorby, Charles, and David Donaldson. 1988. "Cash Versus Kind, Self Selection and Efficient Transfers." *American Economic Review* 78, no. 4:691–700.

di Primo, Juan C., Gotthard Stein, and Herman F. Wagner. 1992. "Verifying Compliance with an International Convention on Greenhouse Gasses." *Environment* 34, no. 2:4–6.

French, Hillary. 1993. "Reconciling Trade and the Environment." In *State of the World, 1993,* edited by Lester Brown. New York: W. W. Norton.

French, Hillary. 1992. "Strengthening Global Environmental Governance." In *State of the World, 1992,* edited by Lester Browne. New York: W. W. Norton.

Goodstein, Eban. 1999. *The Trade-off Myth: Fact and Fiction about Jobs and the Environment.* Washington, DC: Island Press.

Hathaway, Oona. 1992. "Whither Biodiversity? The Global Debate Over Biological Variety Continues." *Harvard International Review* 15, no. 2:58–60.

Heppes, John B., and Eric J. McFadden. 1987. "The Convention on Trade in Endangered Species: The Prospects for Preserving Our Biological Heritage." *Boston University International Law Journal* 5, no. 2:229–246.

Holley, Susan E. 1991. "Global Warming: Construction and Enforcement of a Global Accord." *Stanford Environmental Law Journal* 10:44.

"India Running Out of Time on the Montreal Protocol." 2000. *The Hindu,* 1 April.

Manzer, L. E. 1990. "The CFC-Ozone Issue: Progress on the Development of Alternatives to CFCs." *Science* 7, no. 6:31–35.

Munasinghe, Mohan, and Kenneth King. 1992. "Accelerating Ozone Layer Protection in Developing Countries." *World Development* 20, no. 4:609–618.

"Prospectors for Tropical Medicines," *New Scientist,* October 19, 1991.

Sand, Peter. 1990. *Lessons Learned in Global Environmental Governance.* Washington, DC: World Resources Institute.

Sedjo, Roger A. 1992. "Property Rights, Genetic Resources and Biotechnological Change." *Journal of Law and Economics* 35, no. 1:199–213.

Somerset, Margaret. 1989. "An Attempt to Stop the Sky from Falling: The Montreal Protocol to Protect Against Atmospheric Ozone Reduction." *Syracuse Journal of International Law and Commerce* 15, no. 39:391–429.

"Substitute CFCs Will Stoke Global Warming." 1989. *New Scientist,* 13 May.

"The China Syndrome." 1999. *The Guardian* (London).

Selected Web Sites for Environmental and Natural Resource Economists

(All of these sites are live from the Resources Link at my site: www.lclark.edu/~eban.)

MY NUMBER-ONE SITE:

Resources for the Future (RFF is the premier environmental economics research organization in the country—this should be your first stop for a research project, with top quality papers on virtually every subject you might want to research): www.rff.org

DATA SOURCES AND ENVIRONMENTAL RESEARCH ORGANIZATIONS:

- Climate Ark (global warming): www.climateark.org
- Environmental Working Group Farm Subsidy Database 1996-2001: www.ewg .org/farm
- The EPA Economy and the Environment: www.epa.gov/economics
- The National Bureau of Economic Research: www.nber.harvard.edu
- Real World Results (emission trading site): www.etei.org
- Resources for Economists on the Internet: www.econwpa.wustl.edu /EconFAQ/EconFAQ.html
- SkyTrust (emissions trading, global warming): www.aecsinc.org/Skytrust /whatis.html
- The Toxics Release Inventory: www.epa.gov/tri

INTERNATIONAL DATA AND RESEARCH ORGANIZATIONS:

- The World Resources Institute: www.wri.org
- The World Bank: New Ideas in Pollution Regulation: www.worldbank .org/nipr
- The World Trade Organization: www.wto.org

ENVIRONMENTAL ECONOMICS ORGANIZATIONS:

- Association for Environmental and Resource Economics (mainstream): www.rff.org
- International Society for Ecological Economics (ecological): www.ecologicaleconomics.org

Author Index

SUBJECT INDEX

536